HUGH JOHNSON'S POCKET WINE BOOK 2027

Hugh Johnson's Pocket Wine Book 2027

First published in Great Britain in 2026 by Mitchell Beazley, an imprint of
Octopus Publishing Group Limited,
Carmelite House, 50 Victoria Embankment,
London EC4Y 0DZ
www.octopusbooks.co.uk

An Hachette UK Company
www.hachette.co.uk

The authorized representative in the EEA is Hachette Ireland,
8 Castlecourt Centre, Dublin 15, D15 XTP3, Ireland (email: info@hbgi.ie)

First edition published 1977

Revised editions published 1978, 1979, 1980, 1981, 1982, 1983, 1984, 1985, 1986, 1987, 1988, 1989, 1990, 1991, 1992, 1993, 1994, 1995, 1996, 1997, 1998, 1999, 2000, 2001, 2002 (twice), 2003, 2004, 2005, 2006 (twice), 2007, 2008, 2009, 2010, 2011, 2012, 2013, 2014, 2015, 2016, 2017, 2018, 2019, 2020, 2021, 2022, 2023, 2024, 2025, 2026

Distributed in the US by Hachette Book Group
1290 Avenue of the Americas, 4th and 5th Floors,
New York, NY 10104

Distributed in Canada by Canadian Manda Group
664 Annette St, Toronto, Ontario, Canada M6S 2C8

A CIP record for this book is available from the British Library.

ISBN: 978-1-78472-874-8

MIX
Paper | Supporting responsible forestry
FSC www.fsc.org FSC® C008047

General Editor **Margaret Rand**
Commissioning Editor **Hilary Lumsden**
Publishing Director **Alison Starling**
Senior Editor **Alex Stetter**
Proofreader **David Tombesi-Walton**
Art Director **Yasia Williams-Leedham**
Designer **Jeremy Tilston**
Picture Research Manager **Jennifer Veall**
Senior Production Manager **Katherine Hockley**

Printed and bound in China

Mitchell Beazley would like to acknowledge and thank the following for supplying photographs for use in this book:

Getty Images: PodhorskyLesek/500px/ 1; **iStock:** THEPALMER 7, **Pexels:** Pixabay 12

Illustrations on pp.353–68 by **Hilary Fitzgerald Campbell**

France

	Red Bordeaux		White Bordeaux		Alsace
Vintage	Médoc/Graves	Pom/St-Ém	Sauternes & sw	Graves & dry	
2025	6–8	6–7	6–7	8–9	7–8
2024	6–7	6–7	6–8	6–8	6–8
2023	7–8	6–8	7–8	7–8	7–8
2022	7–8	7–8	7–9	6–7	6–7
2021	5–7	5–7	7–8	7–9	6–8
2020	7–8	7–9	7–8	7–8	8–9
2019	7–9	6–9	7–8	7–9	6–8
2018	8–9	8–9	7–9	7–8	7–8
2017	6–8	6–7	8–9	7–8	9–10
2016	8–9	8–9	8–10	7–9	7–8
2015	7–9	8–10	8–10	7–9	7–9
2014	7–8	6–8	8–9	8–9	7–8
2013	4–7	4–7	8–9	7–8	8–9
2012	6–8	6–8	5–6	7–9	8–9
2011	7–8	7–8	8–10	7–8	5–7
2010	8–10	7–10	7–8	7–9	8–9
2009	7–10	7–10	8–10	7–9	8–9
2008	6–8	6–9	6–7	7–8	7–8
2007	5–7	6–7	8–9	8–9	6–8

France, continued

	Burgundy			Rhône	
Vintage	Côte d'Or red	Côte d'Or white	Chablis	North	South
2025	7–8	7–8	7–8	8–9	6–7
2024	6–8	6–7	6–8	7–8	7–8
2023	7–9	6–8	7–8	6–8	6–8
2022	7–9	7–9	7–8	7–8	6–8
2021	6–8	7–8	7–8	6–8	6–8
2020	6–8	7–9	6–8	7–8	6–8
2019	7–9	7–10	7–9	8–9	7–9
2018	6–9	7–8	7–9	7–9	6–8
2017	6–9	8–9	8–9	7–9	7–9
2016	7–8	6–8	5–7	7–9	8–9
2015	7–9	6–8	7–8	8–9	8–9
2014	6–8	8–9	7–9	7–8	6–8
2013	5–7	6–7	6–8	7–9	7–8
2012	8–9	7–8	7–8	7–9	7–9

Beaujolais 25 23 22 21 20 19 18 17 15 14, crus will keep. **Mâcon-Villages** white 25 23 22 21 20 19 18 17 15. **Loire** sweet Anjou, Touraine 25 23 22 21 20 19 18 15 10 09 07 05 02 97 96 93 90; Bourgueil, Chinon, Saumur-Champigny 25 23 22 21 20 19 18 17 15 14 10 09 06 05 04; Sancerre, Pouilly-Fumé 25 23 22 21 20 19 18 17 15 14; Muscadet 25 23 22 21 20 19 18 17 16 15 14.

HUGH JOHNSON'S POCKET WINE BOOK 2027

GENERAL EDITOR

MARGARET RAND

Contributors

To demonstrate that no one person can be up to date with the vinous affairs of every wine-producing country in the world, this is the book's team of contributors:

Key: ❶ Facebook; ❷ Instagram; ❸ X (Twitter); ❹ website; ❺ book/press; ❻ blog/other media

Luis Atunes PhD, Portugal, Madeira, Azores: ❷ @czaterxarax; ❺ *The Book of Iberian Wines, Vinho Grandes Escolhas*
Helena Baker DipWSET, Czechia, Slovakia: ❶ helena.baker.73; ❷ @bakerwine837; ❸ @HelenaB62554469; ❹ bakerwine.cz
Kristel Balcaen DipWSET, Belgium: ❶ kristel.balcaen.1; ❷ @kristel_balcaen; ❹ wineandwords.be; ❺ *Wijnboek voor Foodies, Kookboek voor Wijnliefhebbers*
Amanda Barnes MW, S America: ❶ SouthAmericaWineGuide; ❷ @southamericawineguide; ❸ @amanda_tweeter; ❺ *South America Wine Guide*
Raymond Blake, Burgundy: ❷+❸ @blakeonwine; ❹ blakeonwine.com; ❺ Côte d'Or
Samantha Cole-Johnson, Oregon: ❷ @samanthacolejohnson; ❹ jancisrobinson.com
Ian D'Agata, Alsace, Italy, Malta, Asia: ❷ @ian_dagata; ❹ iandagata.com, terroirsense.com/en; ❺ *Italy's Native Wine Grape Terroirs; Native Wine Grapes of Italy*
Sarah Jane Evans MW, Spain: ❶ Sarah Jane Evans MW; ❷+❸ @sjevansmw; ❹ sarahjaneevans.com; ❺ *The Wines of Northern Spain, The Wines of Central and Southern Spain*
Jane Faulkner, Australia: ❶+❷+❸ @winematters; ❺ *Halliday Wine Companion*
Simon Field MW, Champagne: ❻ *The World of Fine Wine*
Caroline Gilby MW, Albania, Bosnia & Herzegovina, Bulgaria, Croatia, Hungary, Kosovo, Montenegro, N Macedonia, Romania, Serbia, Slovenia, Cyprus: ❶ Caroline Gilby MW; ❷ @CarolineGilby; ❺ *The Wines of Bulgaria, Romania and Moldova; Wines of Serbia: A New Chapter*
Susan H Gordon PhD MFA, Georgia, Maryland, New England, New Jersey, New York State, North Carolina, Pennsylvania, Vermont, Virginia: ❷ @drsusanhillaryg; ❺ *ForbesLife, Gastronomica, The Story of Prosecco Superiore*
Michael Karam, Lebanon: ❺ *Wines of Lebanon, Arak and Mezze, Tears of Bacchus, Lebanese Wine: A Complete Guide*; ❻ *Wine and War* (Amazon Prime)
Chris Kissack, Loire ❶ drchriskissack; ❷+❸ @chriswinedoctor; ❹ thewinedoctor.com
James Lawther MW, Bordeaux: ❹ jancisrobinson.com; ❺ *The Finest Wines of Bordeaux, On Bordeaux*
Konstantinos Lazarakis MW, Greece: ❶ Konstantinos Lazarakis II; ❷ @Konstantinos_Lazarakis_MW; ❸ @Lazarakis; ❹ wspc.gr, aioloswines.gr; ❺ *The Wines of Greece*
John Livingstone-Learmonth, Rhône: ❸ @drinkrhone; ❹ drinkrhone.com; ❺ *The Wines of the Northern Rhône*
Michele Longo, Italy: ❷ @michele_nebbiolo; ❹ iandagata.com; ❺ *Italian Wine Terroirs, The Grapes and Wines of Italy, Barolo Terroir, Barolo & Co*
Adam Sebag Montefiore, Israel, Türkiye, N Africa: ❹ adammontefiore.com; ❺ *Jerusalem Post, Wine Route of Israel, Wines of Israel; Domaine du Castel: The Biography; Golan Heights Winery*
Rod Phillips, Canada: ❷ @rodphillipswine; ❹ rodphillipsonwine.com; ❺ *Wines of Canada, French Wine: A History, 9000 Years of Wine, Un curé dans les vignes*
Margaret Rand, General Editor, England: *see* back flap of book
Christina Rasmussen, Scandinavia, Bugey, Jura, Savoie: ❷ @christinarasmussen_; ❸ @Christina_SvR; ❹ littlewine.io, christinarasmussen.co
John Saker, NZ: ❷ @john_saker_wine; ❹ johnsaker.com; ❺ *Pinot Noir: The New Zealand Story, How to Drink a Glass of Wine*; ❻ Te Whenua
Ulrich Sautter, Germany, Switzerland, Luxembourg: ❹ falstaff.com, weinverstand.com
Eleonora Scholes, Black Sea & Caucasus: ❷ @spaziovino; ❹ spaziovino.com
Luzia Schrampf, Austria: ❶+❷ @LuziaSchrampf; ❺ *111 Austrian Wines You Must Not Miss, 111 Sparkling Wines Worldwide You Must Not Miss* (both with D Dejnega)
Matthew Stubbs MW, SW France, Midi, Provence, Corsica: ❷ @vinecole_wine_education; ❹ vinecole.com
Sean P Sullivan, Washington State, Idaho: ❶+❷ @northwestwinereport; ❸ @nwwinereport; ❹ northwestwinereport.com; ❺ *Seattle Metropolitan*
Tim Teichgraeber, California: ❶ TimSkyscraper; ❷ @timskyscraper; ❻ modernwine.blogspot.com
James Tidwell MS, Arizona, Colorado, Michigan, Missouri, Nevada, New Mexico, Ohio, Oklahoma, Texas, Wisconsin, Mexico: ❶ JamesTidwellMS; ❷+❸ @winejames; ❹ texsom.com
Philip van Zyl, S Africa: ❶ Philipvanzyl; ❺ *Platter's by Diners Club South African Wine Guide*

Contents

How to use this book

The top line of most entries consists of the following information:

1. **Aglianico del Vulture** Bas
2. ★★★
3. 17' 18 19 20 21' 22 (23)

1. **Aglianico del Vulture** Bas

Wine name and region. Abbreviations of regions are listed in each section.

2. ★★★

Indication of quality – a necessarily rough-and-ready guide:

★	reliable, everyday quality
★★	very good quality
★★★	excellent
★★★★	outstanding, compelling
★ etc.	Stars are coloured for any wine that, in our experience, is usually especially good within its price range. There are good everyday wines, as well as good luxury wines. This system helps you find them.

We try to be objective, but no wine rating can ever be wholly objective.

3. 17' 18 19 20 21' 22 (23)

Vintage information: those recent vintages that are outstanding, and of these, which are ready to drink this year and which will probably improve with keeping. Your choice for current drinking should be one of the vintage years printed in **bold** type. Buy light-type years for further maturing.

22 etc.	recommended years that may be currently available
21' etc.	vintage regarded as particularly successful for the property in question
18 etc.	years in bold should be ready for drinking (those not in bold will benefit from keeping)
20 etc.	vintages in colour are those recommended as first choice for drinking in 2027 (*see also* Bordeaux introduction, p.106)
(23) etc.	provisional rating

The German vintages work on a different principle again: *see* p.177.

Abbreviations

Style references appear in brackets where required:

r	red
w	white
dr	dry
sw	sweet
s/sw	semi-sweet
sp	sparkling

DYA	drink the youngest available
NV	Non Vintage; in Champagne this means a blend of several vintages for continuity
CHABLIS	properties, areas or terms cross-referenced within the section; all grapes cross-ref to Grape Varieties chapter on pp.12–22
Foradori	entries styled this way indicate wine especially enjoyed by Margaret Rand and/or the author of that section (mid-2025–26)

For help in sourcing wines in this book we recommend winesearcher.com

If you have any feedback, please contact us on pocketwine@octopusbooks.co.uk

Agenda 2027

In the 50 years this book has been published – every year for 50 years; did I mention that? – the wine world has expanded enormously. We drink wines now from Oregon, Uruguay, Bolivia, Armenia, Croatia, Slovenia... The last two weren't even countries when this book first appeared. We explore grape varieties we'd never heard of a few years ago and probably haven't heard of now either. (Lasin? Grk? Thought not.) We experiment with pét-nat and orange wines, and with a bit of luck we've moved away from the tyranny of critics' scores.

There is good wine to be found everywhere, and perfectly drinkable wine is not expensive. But we want something more than "perfectly drinkable". Good wine, and very good wine, is not cheap. We have seen runaway price inflation at the very top end, driven ultimately by market forces; the more people want to throw their money at Grand Cru burgundy, the more expensive it will get. Will this continue? There are signs of a pause, simply because consumers are digging their heels in. And the good news is that the wines we are buying instead are better now than they have ever been.

Yes, I know you've heard that before. But in the past fortnight I have tasted many super-expensive wines from Burgundy and many astonishingly exciting wines from Greece and Spain at – what? – half the price? Less? They are not the cheapest wines on the market. There is a place for ultra-cheap wines, but you don't need to buy a book on them. This book is about value and excitement, not cheapness per se.

How widespread is the mindset that wine, like food, should be cheap? The extraordinary prices asked for the most expensive wines help to feed the idea that expensive wine is all a trick being played on the gullible. The low prices for industrial wines in supermarkets back it up: cheap wine has never been so good. It may use industrial quantities of herbicides and pesticides, but it tastes clean, fresh and fruity. Not compelling, but drinkable. If you can't tell the difference, it will do.

Wine that is worth thinking about, wine that is worth talking about, is not like this. Ignore the people who say they want to "demystify" wine. Wine that is worth drinking has layers of mystery that are worth penetrating; wine that is worth drinking is worth investigating, worth following to the next level of understanding. It might be viticulture; it might be winemaking; it might be the history of a landscape and the social and economic forces that shaped the vines that were grown and the wines they made. Bordeaux, Port and Sherry were shaped by transport links and export markets. Burgundy wouldn't be burgundy without a rich medieval ducal court that demanded Pinot Noir rather than Gamay. And think of the effect of Prohibition on US wine.

Winemakers come to wine from a million different directions, as we can see from a few of the people in this book. Susana Balbo (Argentina) battled hyperinflation and cars that ran (or didn't) on sugar-cane alcohol; she brought in cash in hard times by sewing. Dermot Sugrue (England) left Limerick, Ireland, for media studies and French in East Anglia, became a financial adviser and then worked a vintage in Pomerol. Ondine de la Feld of Tenuta di Tavignano (Italy) was an architect; she absolutely did not want to take over the estate. When she did, she found that (a) she knew nothing about wine and (b) the staff wanted to get rid of her. She still misses architecture.

You don't come from backgrounds like these in order to do the same old, same old. Fifty years ago (did I mention that we're 50 years old this year?), there was a lot of same old, same old. Now there isn't any – at least in the realm of wine that is worth drinking and worth talking about.

Last year we talked a lot about the price you should pay to get the best price:quality ratio. All of that is still valid, and all through the book you'll find producers, and wines, singled out for particularly good value. But this year we're focusing on climate change – not to preach, but to examine how it is changing flavours. Much of the time, so far, it's producing better wine: riper, less green, readier earlier. Producers have to learn to manage that ripeness, the higher alcohol and lower acidity that go with them. How they're doing it – the questions and the solutions they bring, their experiments and theories – is making wine intensely innovative. It's one of the reasons that there are so many very good wines from regions we'd never heard of 50 years ago.

Many of the names in this edition were also in that first edition. Occasionally we might taste a wine from back then and exclaim over how well it has lasted, how it is still alive. Will some of today's wines last as long? Ask me in 50 years. Are they better now, today? Yes.

Fifty years ago, we were on the edge of a technological revolution in wine. Now it's about sustainability, low-intervention and the re-examination of historical ideas and methods. The questions now are, What is quality? What is correctness? What is eccentricity?

The questions in 50 years will be different again. Ask me then.

Margaret Rand
General Editor

12 wines to try in 2027

In last year's edition, we laid down the criteria for what we consider good value in the modern wine world. Prices have risen since then, not least thanks to tax increases, but all these wines fit into our value sweet spot. They're not all bargain basement, but they all overdeliver.

Red wines

Barba Yannis Xinomavro, Alpha Estate Ecosystem, NW Greece

Pale red, pure and tense, with notes of tar and redcurrant, plus herbs and earth, aromatic and with good structure and elegance. If this sounds not totally unlike Barolo, you wouldn't be wrong: it reminded me of Barolo too. It's not a lookalike, but it is an unusually elegant expression of Xinomavro, which can be quite burly. Alpha Estate is a big go-ahead property in northwest Greece, the heartland of Xinomavro, with vines planted at high altitude. It's visitor-friendly too, should you happen to be in the area.

Mouhtaro, Muses Estate, Central Greece

Now be honest, have you ever heard of the Mouhtaro grape? It was discovered/rediscovered some years ago by Athanasios Zacharias, who owned this estate before passing it on to his children. It grows at the foot of Mount Helicon; it's still rare and comes as a bit of a surprise on first tasting, but by the end of a glass you'll have got the hang of it. Perfumed, with fennel, eucalyptus, mint, citrus, red fruits and good acidity. Very moreish.

Alma de Unx Garnacha, Bodegas San Martín, Navarra, Spain

If you want value right now, young, unoaked Spanish Garnacha or Monastrell is a superb resource. This is Garnacha at a bargain price. It's fresh, lavender-scented and detailed, elegant and at ease, perfumed but with enough concentration at its core to be serious. Bodegas San Martín is the co-op of Alma de Unx (owned by Anecoop), so we're not talking about a tiny, artisan operation; but a well-run co-op is a very useful thing.

Yakut, Kavaklidere, Eastern Anatolia, Türkiye

This is another seriously inexpensive wine – an everyday wine, even. It's not grand or serious, but you notice it for its lovely spicy fruit, good acidity and texture of pure silk. It's unusual and characterful, from a typical Turkish combination of Öküzgözü and Boğazkere. I visited Kavaklidere some years ago and was struck by how go-ahead it was, in a country that gives little support to winemakers. They know what they're doing, and it shows.

Las Gundiñas, Raúl Pérez, Bierzo, Spain

Raúl stands out in a crowd; his hair and beard make him resemble an 18th-century ornamental hermit. So you might expect something unusual from his wines. This red from the Mencía grape is savoury, with layers of complexity and flavour, yet overall bright, enlivening, vigorous, brisk and elegant. It will brighten a dull day and match a thrilling one. If it came from a classic region, it would be twice the price.

Newfound Gravels Grenache, Napa Valley, California, US
Grenache, plus Counoise and Syrah, with the grace of Gredos rather than the concentration of McLaren Vale. Natural yeasts, 100% whole-cluster fermentation, large-format oak, plus concrete, for ageing; the result is beautiful. It sneaks into our definition of good value at the higher end. Lavender, black fruit and wild herbs, elegantly precise and defined.

White wines

Corallian Classic Cuvée, Langham Wine Estate, England
Lovely savoury, salty, stony fizz, very alive, great depth, from chalk and flint country; it's about as far west as the chalk goes. The innovative, even eccentric winemaking evolved from the ad hoc buildings on the farm and was inspired by grower Champagnes rather than the big houses. It's not a big-budget operation, and the wine has huge character.

Altitude White, Novus Winery, Peloponnese, Greece
Remarkably good value, and remarkably good. Delicate, subtle, fresh, combining tension and jasmine, roses and salt. It's aromatic but not cloying, just 12.7% alcohol. This Moschofilero plus Assyrtiko and Malagousia blend is a great example of the sort of original flavours that Greece can offer.

Rays Road Chardonnay, Kumeu River, New Zealand
A beautifully subtle, layered wine that drives forward on the palate with flavours of citrus and ripe stone fruit and ends with perfect poise. It's aged in used oak that had a light, long toast, and it's from a company that has long made some of the most accomplished, delicately handled wines in NZ. The inspiration is clearly burgundian but the price is not: Kumeu River makes more expensive Chardonnays, but this is the bull's-eye for value.

Encruzado, Quinta dos Carvalhais, Dão, Portugal
Indigenous Encruzado manages to be both serious, structured and elegant, and sappy, salty and lively, with flavours of tarragon and almonds. Plus lovely complexity and texture. The high altitudes and granite soils of Dão bring out its structure and freshness, and this quinta is owned by Sogrape, a company of which I have been a fan for many years. Try this with pork.

Lieserer Niederberg-Helden Riesling, Axel Pauly, Mosel, Germany
An outstanding Riesling Kabinett is about as good as you can get in white wine, and this is a beauty. The vines are 80 years old, growing in blue and grey slate on a steep slope; *Helden* means "heroes". Filigree, tense, structured, delicate, steely, aromatic; a bit of residual sugar and 12.5% alcohol. Indigenous yeasts too. It's a wine of lovely purity and precision.

Am Berg Grüner Veltliner, Bernhard Ott, Wagram, Austria
Ott's entry-level wine is amazingly good value for something so graceful and seductive. Think butter, bay leaves, a touch of lemon... delicacy and length wrapped up in subtlety. This is a real bargain. Ott is based in Wagram, with one parcel in Kamptal; also biodynamic, spontaneous fermentation, 100% stems, Stockinger barrels. He took over from his father at the age of 20. And papa? Went off to grow apricots.

Grape varieties

The pendulum has swung, big time. First it was ancient and almost-extinct varieties that caught everybody's imagination: the romance of discovering an unidentified wine in a vineyard, or somebody's garden, and finding that it's a variety last grown widely hundreds of years ago, when the climate was different – and that now that the climate is different again, it might work again. Italy and Portugal have an enormous wealth of old varieties, which will be the vinous solution to a changing climate. And then came PIWI varieties. The name (which is a brand) stands for Pilzwiderstandsfähig. They are crossings, often over several generations, of *Vitis vinifera*, the European wine vine, with American fungus- and disease-resistant *Vitis* species. They require less spraying and make organic and biodynamic viticulture more possible in awkward climates. You might come across Solaris or Souvignier Gris; there are many others. The familiar international grapes are not going away. They have forged superb reputations in many countries, and they give many of the greatest wines in the world. But now they're not the only choice.

All grapes and synonyms are cross-referenced in SMALL CAPITALS throughout every section of this book.

Grapes for red wine

Agiorgitiko Greek; the grape of Nemea, now planted all over Greece. Versatile and delicious, from soft and charming to dense and age-worthy. A must-try.

Aglianico S Italy's best red, the grape of Taurasi; dark, deep and fashionable.

Alfrocheiro Portuguese; A Preto is same grape. Lovely aromas: blackberry, strawberry, plus freshness, dark colour, fine tannins. Can be v.gd, esp in Dão.

Alicante Bouschet Stylish in Alentejo, Chile, Douro (for Vintage Port), esp old vines.

Aragonêz *See* TEMPRANILLO.

Auxerrois *See* MALBEC, if red. White Auxerrois has its own entry in White Grapes.

Băbească Neagră Moldovan trad "black grandmother grape"; light body and ruby-red colour.

Babić Dark grape from Dalmatia, grown in stony seaside vyds around Šibenik. Exceptional quality potential.

Baga Portugal. Bairrada grape. Dark, tannic, fashionable. Needs a gd grower.

Barbera Widely grown in Italy, best in Piedmont: high acidity, low tannin, cherry fruit. Ranges from serious and age-worthy to semi-sweet and frothy. Fashionable in California and Australia; promising in Argentina.

Bastardo Iberian TROUSSEAU.

Blauburger Austrian cross of BLAUER PORTUGIESER, BLAUFRÄNKISCH. Simple wines.

Blauburgunder *See* PINOT N.

Blauer Portugieser Central European, esp Germany (Rheinhessen, Pfalz, mostly for rosé), Austria, Hungary. Light, fruity reds: drink young, slightly chilled.

Blaufränkisch (Kékfrankos, Lemberger, Modra Frankinja) Widely planted in Austria's Mittelburgenland: medium-bodied, peppery acidity, fresh; berry aromas, eucalyptus. Can be top quality: Austria's star red. Often blended with CAB SAUV or ZWEIGELT. Lemberger in Germany (esp Württemberg), Kékfrankos in Hungary, Modra Frankinja in Slovenia.

Bobal Spain. Can be rustic; best at high altitude; gd acidity.

Boğaskere Tannic and Turkish. Produces full-bodied wines.

Bonarda Ambiguous name. In Oltrepò Pavese, an alias for Croatina, soft fresh *frizzante* and still red. In Lombardy and Emilia-Romagna, an alias for Uva Rara. Different in Piedmont. Argentina's Bonarda can be any of these or something else. None is great.

Bouchet St-Émilion alias for CAB FR.

Brunello SANGIOVESE, splendid at Montalcino.

Cabernet Franc [Cab Fr] In Bx: more important than CAB SAUV in St-Émilion. Outperforms Cab Sauv in Loire (Chinon, Saumur-Champigny, rosé), in Hungary (depth and complexity in Villány and Szekszárd) and often in Italy. Much of NE Italy's Cab Fr turned out to be CARMENÈRE. Used in Bx blends of Cab Sauv/MERLOT across the world.

Cabernet Sauvignon [Cab Sauv] Characterful: slow-ripening, spicy, herby, tannic, with blackcurrant aroma. Main grape of the Médoc; also makes some of the best California, S American, E European reds. Vies with SHIRAZ in Australia. Grown almost everywhere, but few places make great varietal Cab Sauv: usually benefits from blending with eg. MERLOT, CAB FR, SYRAH, TEMPRANILLO, SANGIOVESE, etc. Makes aromatic rosé. Top wines need ageing.

Cannonau GRENACHE in its Sardinian manifestation; can be v. fine, potent.

Carignan (Carignane, Carignano, Cariñena) Low-yielding old vines fashionable everywhere from S France to Chile, via S Africa. Lots of depth, vibrancy, but must never be overcropped. Found esp in California, Israel, N Africa, Spain (as Cariñena).

Carignano *See* CARIGNAN.

Carineña *See* CARIGNAN.

Carmenère Old Bx variety now a star (rich, deep) in Chile (where it's pronounced "carmeneary"); being looked at again in Bx.

Castelão *See* PERIQUITA.

Cencibel *See* TEMPRANILLO.

Chiavennasca *See* NEBBIOLO.

Cinsault (Cinsaut) A staple of S France, v.gd if low-yielding, hopeless if not. Makes gd rosé. One of parents of PINOTAGE.

Cornalin du Valais Swiss speciality with high potential, esp in Valais.

Corvina Dark and spicy; one of best grapes in Valpolicella blend. Corvinone, even darker, is a separate variety.

Côt *See* MALBEC.

Dolcetto Source of relatively light red in Piedmont. Now high fashion.

Dornfelder Gives deliciously light reds, straightforward, often rustic, and well coloured in Germany, parts of the US, even England.

Duras Spicy, peppery and structured; Gaillac and parts of Tarn V, SW France.

Fer Servadou Exclusive to SW France, aka Mansois in Marcillac, Braucol in Gaillac and Pinenc in St-Mont. Redolent of red summer fruits and spice.

Fetească Neagră Romania: "black maiden grape" with potential as showpiece variety; can give deep, full-bodied wines with character.

Freisa Old Piedmontese vine, related to NEBBIOLO. Acidic, tannic, strawberry fruit, quite aromatic. Can be sparkling or semi-sparkling; gd, can be acquired taste.

Frühburgunder (Pinot N Précoce) Old German mutation of PINOT N: Ahr but also Franken, Württemberg, where it is aka Clevner. Lower acidity than Pinot N.

Gamay Light, fragrant, best in Beaujolais crus (*see* France): quality can be high, ageable 2–10 yrs. Also Savoie, Switzerland, Canada, Australia, NZ. California's Napa Gamay is Valdiguié.

Gamza *See* KADARKA.

Garnacha (Cannonau, Garnatxa, Grenache) Major pale grape for warm climates, expresses site well. Combines high alc with delicacy, floral notes; lighter now even in Priorat. Important in Châteauneuf-du-Pape. Rosé and *vin doux naturel* in S France, Spain, California. Old-vine versions prized in S Australia. Often blended. Cannonau in Sardinia, Grenache in France.

Garnatxa *See* GARNACHA.

Graciano Spanish; part of Rioja blend. Aroma of violets, tannic, lean structure, a bit like PETIT VERDOT. Difficult to grow but increasingly fashionable.

Grenache *See* GARNACHA. **GSM**: GRENACHE/SHIRAZ/MOURVÈDRE blend.

Grignolino Italy: gd everyday table wine in Piedmont.

Kadarka (Gamza) Spicy, light reds in E Europe. In Hungary revived, esp for Bikavér.

Kalecik Karasi Turkish: sour-cherry fruit, fresh, supple. Bit like GAMAY. Drink young.

Kékfrankos Hungarian BLAUFRÄNKISCH.

Lagrein N Italian, dark, bitter finish, rich, plummy. DOC in Alto Adige (*see* Italy).

Lambrusco Productive grape of lower Po Valley; cheerful, sweet, fizzy, can be v.gd.

Lefkada Cyprus; gd quality. Tannic; usually blended. Vertzami in Greek homeland.

Lemberger *See* BLAUFRÄNKISCH.

Liatiko Crete; aromatic herbs, blackberry fruit, relatively soft, v.gd. Can be sun-dried for sweet.

Limnio Greek; different from LIMNIONA; v. ancient, gd weight, tastes of bay.

Limniona Greek; deep colour, gd weight, acidity, spicy red fruit. Think MENCÍA.

Listán Prieto *See* PAÍS.

Malbec (Auxerrois, Côt) Minor in Bx, major in Cahors (alias Auxerrois) and the star in Argentina. Dark, dense, tannic but fleshy wine capable of real quality. High-altitude versions in Argentina best.

Mandilaria Greek; aka Mandelaria. Characterful, firm tannins, often blended.

Manseng Noir SW Fr Basque origin. Deep colour, tannic; interesting for lowish alc.

Maratheftiko Deep-coloured Cypriot grape with quality potential.

Marselan CAB SAUV X GRENACHE, 1961; gd colour, structure, supple tannins, ages well. A success in China.

Mataro *See* MOURVÈDRE.

Maturana Tinta Spain; Rioja; revived. Deep colour, aromatic, peppery, soft tannins.

Mavro Most planted black grape of Cyprus but only moderate quality. Best for rosé.

Mavrodaphne Greek; means "black laurel". Sweet fortifieds, speciality of Patras, also in Cephalonia. Dry versions too, great promise.

Mavrotragano Greek, almost extinct; now revived; found on Santorini. Top quality.

Mavrud Probably Bulgaria's best. Spicy, dark, plummy late-ripener native to Thrace. Ages well.

Melnik Bulgarian; from region of same name. There are two Melniks: Shiroka (Broadleafed) M and its offspring, Early M. Both have dark colour, nice dense, tart-cherry character and age well.

Mencía Making waves in Bierzo, N Spain. Aromatic, steely tannins, lots of acidity.

Merlot Star of Pomerol and (with CAB FR) St-Émilion; vital in the Médoc. Found almost everywhere; plummy, fragrant; but more often dull than great. Worst is soft, soupy; best transcends grape and expresses terroir. Most is in-between.

Meunier *See* PINOT M.

Mission *See* PAÍS.

Modra Frankinja *See* BLAUFRÄNKISCH.

Modri Pinot *See* PINOT N.

Monastrell *See* MOURVÈDRE.

Mondeuse In Savoie; the skier's red; deep-coloured, gd acidity. Related to SYRAH.

Monica Sardinia; name might cover several varieties. Gentle, earthy, soft.

Montepulciano Deep-coloured, dominant in Italy's Abruzzo and important along Adriatic coast from Marches to S Puglia. Also name of a Tuscan town, unrelated.

Morellino SANGIOVESE in Maremma, S Tuscany; esp Scansano.

Mourvèdre (Mataro, Monastrell) A star of S France (eg. Bandol, growing influence Châteauneuf), Australia (aka Mataro) and Spain (aka Monastrell). Excellent dark, aromatic, tannic; gd for blending. Also S Australia, California, S Africa.

Napa Gamay Identical to Valdiguié (S France). Nothing to get excited about.

Nebbiolo (Chiavennasca, Spanna) One of Italy's best; makes Barolo, Barbaresco, Gattinara and Valtellina. Intense, nobly fruity, perfumed wine; tannins now better managed, still improves for yrs.

Négrette SW France; Fronton. Blends with SYRAH: purply black, fruity, sappy wines.

Negroamaro Puglian "black bitter" red grape with potential for either high quality or high volume.

Nerello Mascalese Sicilian red grape, esp Etna; characterful, best v. elegant, fine.

Nero d'Avola Dark-red grape of Sicily, quality levels from sublime to industrial.

Nielluccio Corsican; plenty of acidity and tannin, gd for rosé.

Öküzgözü Soft, fruity Turkish grape, usually blended with BOĞASKERE, rather as MERLOT in Bx is blended with CAB SAUV.

País (Listán Prieto, Mission) Trendy/trad in Chile, rustic but improving fast. Listán Prieto in Canaries, Mission in CA.

Pamid Bulgarian: light, soft, everyday red.

Periquita (Castelão) Common in Portugal, esp around Setúbal. Firm-flavoured, raspberryish reds develop a figgish, tar-like quality.

Petite Sirah Nothing to do with SYRAH; gives rustic, tannic, dark wine. Brilliant blended with ZIN in California; also found in S America, Mexico, Australia.

Petit Verdot Excellent but awkward Médoc grape, increasingly planted in CAB areas worldwide for extra fragrance. Mostly blends, some gd varietals, esp in Virginia.

Pinotage Singular S African cross (PINOT N X CINSAULT). Had a rocky ride; getting better from top producers. Rosé gd too. "Coffee Pinotage" (sw) aimed at youth.

Pinot Crni *See* PINOT N.

Pinot Meunier (Schwarzriesling) [Pinot M] The 3rd grape of Champagne, aka Meunier, great for blending, occasionally fine in own right. Best on chalky sites (Damery, Leuvigny, Festigny) nr Épernay. Some still red.

Pinot Noir (Blauburgunder, Modri Pinot, Pinot Crni, Spätburgunder) [Pinot N] On a roll; Burgundy no longer has monopoly of great wines. California, Australia, NZ, Germany can be outstanding. PINOTS BL/GR mutations of Pinot N. Important in fizz. Pinot N Précoce: *see* FRÜHBURGUNDER.

PIWI Trademark; hybrids bred for disease resistance, cold climates. Reds incl Cabernet Cortis, Cabertin, Regent, Souvignier Gr.

Plavac Mali (Crljenak) Croatian, and offspring of ZIN, aka PRIMITIVO, Crljenak, Kratosija. Lots of quality potential, can be alcoholic, dull.

Ploussard *See* POULSARD.

Poulsard (Ploussard) Jura; ancient, indigenous. Difficult to grow, make; can be ethereal, elegant, pale.

Primitivo S Italian, originally Croatian; big, dark, rustic, modish because genetically identical to ZIN. Early ripening, hence name. Original name for both: Tribidrag.

Refosco (Refošk) Italy, esp Colli Orientali. Deep, flavoursome, age-worthy, likes warmth. Dark, high acidity. Refošk in Slovenia and points e, genetically different, tastes similar. Illogically, PDO TERAN on limestone karst in Slovenia.

Rubin Bulgarian cross, NEBBIOLO X SYRAH. Peppery, full-bodied.

Sagrantino Italian grape grown in Umbria for powerful, cherry-flavoured wines.

St-Laurent Dark, smooth, full-flavoured Austrian speciality, tricky to grow and make. Can be light and juicy or deep and structured. Also in Pfalz.

Sangiovese (Brunello, Morellino, Sangioveto) Tuscany and central Italy. At best, sublime, long-lasting; richness balances tea-scented astringency. Dominant in Chianti, Vino Nobile, Brunello di Montalcino, Morellino di Scansano, fine IGTs. Also Umbria (eg. Montefalco, Torgiano), Romagna, Marches. Not so clever in warmer, lower-altitude Tuscan coast, nor in other parts of Italy despite nr-ubiquity. Also Argentina, Australia, US.

Sangioveto *See* SANGIOVESE.

Saperavi The main red of Georgia, Ukraine, etc. Blends well with CAB SAUV (eg. in Moldova). Huge potential, some gd winemaking.

Schiava *See* TROLLINGER.

Schioppettino NE Italian, high acidity, high quality. Elegant, refined, can age.

Schwarzriesling PINOT M in Württemberg.

Sciacarello Corsican, herby and peppery. Not v. tannic.

Shiraz *See* SYRAH.

Spanna *See* NEBBIOLO.

Spätburgunder German for PINOT N.

Syrah (Shiraz) The great Rhône red grape: tannic, purple, peppery, matures superbly. Important as Shiraz in Australia. Widely grown and a gd traveller.

Tannat SW France; raspberry-perfumed, highly tannic force behind Madiran, Tursan etc. Also rosé. Star of Uruguay; also other parts of S America.

Tempranillo (Aragonêz, Cencibel, Tinto Fino, Tinta del País, Tinta Roriz, Ull de Llebre) Aromatic, fine Rioja grape; synonyms in (in order above): S Portugal, La Mancha, Rib del D, Castile, Douro, Catalonia. Elsewhere too. Fashionable; elegant in cool climates, beefy in warm. Early ripening, long-maturing.

Teran (Terrano) REFOSCO close cousin. Not grape of Slovenia's PDO Teran, illogically.

Teroldego Rotaliano Trentino's best indigenous variety; serious, full-flavoured, esp on the flat Campo Rotaliano.

Tinta Amarela *See* TRINCADEIRA.

Tinta del País *See* TEMPRANILLO.

Tinta Negra (Negramoll) Used to be Tinta Negra Mole. Madeira's most planted; mainstay of cheaper Madeira. Now too in Colheita wines (*see* Portugal).

Tinta Roriz *See* TEMPRANILLO.

Tinto Fino *See* TEMPRANILLO.

Touriga Nacional [Touriga N] Top Port grape, now widely used in the Douro for floral, stylish table wines. Australian Touriga is usually this; California's Touriga can be either this or Touriga Franca.

Trincadeira (Tinta Amarela) Portuguese; v.gd in Alentejo for spicy wines. Tinta Amarela in the Douro.

Trollinger (Schiava, Vernatsch) Popular pale red in Württemberg; aka Vernatsch and Schiava. Covers group of vines, not necessarily related. In Italy, snappy.

Trousseau (Bastardo) Jura. Robust, age-worthy. Bastardo in Iberia. Also found in California, Oregon.

Ull de Llebre *See* TEMPRANILLO.

Uva di Troia Italy; Puglia and s. Deep colour, aromatic, spicy. Can be rich, opulent.

Vernatsch *See* TROLLINGER.

Vranac W Balkans, old and varied. Related to ZINFANDEL – they're all connected around there. Soft, high tannin, colour, alc, can age.

Xinomavro Greece's answer to NEBBIOLO. "Sharp-black"; some rosé, still or sparkling. Top quality, can age for decades. Being tried in China.

Zinfandel [Zin] California. Blackberry-like, sometimes metallic flavour. Love it or hate it. Can be serious, structured, long-ageing, or simple. Pink too. Same as S Italian PRIMITIVO.

Zweigelt (Blauer Zweigelt) BLAUFRÄNKISCH X ST-LAURENT, popular in Austria for aromatic, dark, supple wines. Underrated. Also in Hungary, Germany.

Grapes for white wine

Airén Bland workhorse of La Mancha, Spain: fresh if made well. Old-vine versions can surprise.

Albariño (Alvarinho) Fashionable, expensive in Spain: apricot-scented, gd acidity. Superb in Rías Baixas; shaping up elsewhere, but not all live up to the hype. Alvarinho in Portugal just as gd: aromatic Vinho Verde, esp in Monção, Melgaço.

Aligoté Burgundy's 2nd white grape, now trendy and often serious. Widely planted in E Europe, Russia.

Alvarinho *See* ALBARIÑO.

Amigne One of Switzerland's speciality grapes, trad in Valais, and esp Vétroz. Full-bodied, tasty; often sweet but also bone-dry.

Ansonica *See* INSOLIA.

Arinto Portuguese, rather gd; mainstay of aromatic, citrus Bucelas; also adds welcome zip to blends, esp in Alentejo.

Arneis Fine, aromatic, appley-peachy, high-priced NW Italian grape, DOCG in Roero, DOC in Langhe, Piedmont.

Arvine Rare but excellent Swiss *spécialité*, from Valais. Also Petite Arvine. Dry or sweet, fresh, long-lasting wines with salty finish.

Assyrtiko Greek, esp Santorini; one of best grapes of Med, balancing power, minerality, extract and high acid. Built to age. Could conquer the world...

Auxerrois Red Auxerrois is a synonym for MALBEC, but white Auxerrois is like a fatter, spicier PINOT BL. Found in Alsace; much used in Crémant; also Germany.

Bacchus German-bred crossing, England's answer to NZ SAUV BL. Can be shrill; makes gd orange.

Beli Pinot *See* PINOT BL.

Blanc Fumé *See* SAUV BL.

Boal *See* BUAL.

Bourboulenc This and the rare Rolle make some of the Midi's best whites.

Bouvier Indigenous aromatic Austrian grape, esp gd for BA, TBA, rarely dry.

Bual (Boal) Makes top-quality sweet Madeira wines, not quite so rich as MALMSEY.

Camaralet Jurançon. Aromatic; adds complexity to GROS MANSENG-led dry wines.

Carricante Superb grape of Etna Bianco; lemon and herbs, acidity, ages 20 yrs.

Catarratto Prolific white grape found all over Sicily, esp in w in DOC Alcamo.

Cerceal *See* SERCIAL.

Chardonnay (Morillon) [Chard] Grape of Burgundy and Champagne, ubiquitous worldwide, easy to grow and vinify. Reflects terroir but also winemaker's intentions: often a fashion victim. Can be steely or fat. Also the name of a Mâcon-Villages commune. Morillon in Styria, Austria.

Chasselas (Fendant, Gutedel) Swiss. Neutral, can be elegant (Geneva); refined, full (Vaud); exotic, racy (Valais). Fendant in Valais. Also in France, esp Savoie. Gutedel in Germany, esp S Baden. Elsewhere usually a table grape.

Chenin Blanc [Chenin Bl] Wonderful white grape of the middle Loire (Vouvray, Layon, etc). Wine can be dry or sweet (or v. sweet), but with plenty of acidity. Superb old-vine versions in S Africa, esp Swartland.

Cirfandl *See* ZIERFANDLER.

Clairette Important Rhône/Midi grape, white and rosé versions, gives freshness, restrained degree, part of many blends, incl Tavel rosé.

Colombard Slightly fruity, nicely sharp grape, makes everyday wine in S Africa, California and SW France. Often blended.

Cortese Italian; grape of Gavi. Fairly neutral, pleasant, fresh.

Dimiat (Dimyat) Perfumed Bulgarian grape, made dry or off-dry, or distilled. Far more synonyms than any grape needs.

Encruzado Portuguese, serious; fresh, versatile, ages well; esp gd in Dão.

Ermitage Swiss for MARSANNE.

Esgana Cão *See* Sercial.

Ezerjó Hungarian, with sharp acidity. Name means "thousand blessings".

Falanghina Ancient grape of Campanian hills (Italy); gd dense, aromatic dry whites.

Fendant *See* CHASSELAS.

Fernão Pires *See* MARIA GOMES.

Feteascǎ Albǎ / Regalǎ (Királyleanyka, Leanyka) Romania has two Feteascǎ grapes, both with slight MUSCAT aroma. F Regalǎ is a cross of F Albǎ and Frâncușǎ; more finesse, gd for late-harvest wines. F NEAGRǍ (unrelated) is dark-skinned.

Fiano High quality, giving peachy, spicy wine in Campania, S Italy.

Folle Blanche (Gros Plant) High acid/little flavour make this ideal for brandy. Gros Plant in Brittany, Picpoul in Armagnac, but unrelated to true PICPOUL. Also respectable in California.

Friulano (Sauvignonasse, Sauvignon Vert) N Italian: fresh, pungent, subtly floral. Best in Collio, Isonzo, Colli Orientali. Found in nearby Slovenia as Sauvignonasse; also in Chile.

Fumé Blanc *See* SAUV BL.

Furmint (Šipon) Superb, characterful. Trademark of Hungary: both principal grape in Tokaji and vivid, vigorous dry wine, mineral, apricot-flavoured. Šipon in Slovenia. Some grown in Rust (Austria) for sweet and dry.

Garganega Best grape in Soave blend; also in Gambellara. Top, esp sweet, age well.

Garnacha Blanca (Grenache Blanc) White version of GARNACHA/Grenache, much used in Spain and S France. Low acidity. Can be innocuous or surprisingly gd.

Gewurztraminer (Traminac, Traminec, Traminer, Tramini) [Gewurz] A v. pungent grape, spicy with aromas of rose petals, face cream, lychees, grapefruit. Often rich and soft, even when fully dry. Best in Alsace; gd elsewhere. Relatively unaromatic if just labelled Traminer (or variants). In Italy, Traminer Aromatico for (dr) "Gewurz" versions. (Note umlaut in German.) SAVAGNIN is non-aromatic.

Glera Uncharismatic new name for Prosecco vine: Prosecco is now wine only in the EU but still a grape name in Australia.

Godello Top quality (intense, mineral) in nw Spain. Called Verdelho in Dão, Portugal, but unrelated to true VERDELHO.

Grasă (Kövérszőlő) Romanian; name means "fat". Prone to botrytis; important in Cotnari, potentially superb sweet wines. Kövérszőlő in Hungary's Tokaj region.

Graševina *See* WELSCHRIESLING.

Grauburgunder *See* PINOT GR.

Grechetto Ancient grape of central/S Italy: vitality, style. Blended or solo in Orvieto.

Greco S Italian: there are various Grecos, probably unrelated, perhaps of Greek origin. Brisk, peachy flavour, most famous as Greco di Tufo. Greco di Bianco is from semi-dried grapes. Greco Nero is a black version.

Grenache Blanc *See* GARNACHA BLANCA.

Grillo Italy: main grape of Marsala. Also v.gd full-bodied dry table wine.

Gros Plant *See* FOLLE BLANCHE.

Grüner Veltliner [Grüner V] Austria's fashionable flagship white; v. diverse – from simple, peppery, everyday, to great complexity, ageing potential. Useful because gd at all levels. Found elsewhere in Central Europe and outside.

Gutedel *See* CHASSELAS.

Hárslevelű Other main grape of Tokaji, but softer, peachier than FURMINT. Name means "linden-leaved"; gd in Somló, Eger as well.

Heida Swiss for SAVAGNIN.

Humagne Swiss speciality, older than CHASSELAS. Fresh, plump, not v. aromatic. Humagne Rouge is not related but increasingly popular: same as Cornalin d'Aosta. Cornalin du Valais is different. (Keep up at the back, there.)

Insolia (Ansonica, Inzolia) Sicilian; Ansonica on Tuscan coast. Fresh, racy wine at best. May be semi-dried for sweet wine.

Irsai Olivér Hungarian cross; aromatic, MUSCAT-like wine for drinking young.

Johannisberg Swiss for SILVANER.

Kéknyelű Low-yielding, flavourful grape giving one of Hungary's best whites. Has the potential for fieriness and spice. To be watched.

Kerner Quite successful German cross. Early ripening; flowery (but often too blatant) wine with gd acidity.

Királyleanyka *See* FETEASCĂ ALBĂ/REGALĂ.

Koshu More or less indigenous Japanese table-turned-wine grape, much hyped. Fresh, tannic. Orange versions gd.

Kövérszőlő *See* GRASĂ.

L'Acadie Blanc Cold-climate Canadian hybrid; some weight, honeyed; gd fizz.

Laški Rizling *See* WELSCHRIESLING.

Leányka *See* FETEASCĂ ALBĂ/REGALĂ.

Len de l'El Gaillac; aka Loin de l'Oeuil. Versatile; usually blended; gd dessert wines.

Listán *See* PALOMINO.

Longyan (Dragon Eye) Chinese original; gd substantial, aromatic wine.

Loureiro Best Vinho Verde grape after ALVARINHO: delicate, floral. Also in Spain.

Macabeo *See* VIURA.

Maccabeu *See* VIURA.

Malagousia Rediscovered Greek grape for gloriously rose-scented wines.

Malmsey *See* MALVASIA. The sweetest style of Madeira.

Malvasia (Malmsey, Malvazija, Malvoisie, Marastina) Italy, France and Iberia. Not a single variety but a whole stable, not necessarily related or even alike. Can be white or red, sparkling or still, strong or mild, sweet or dry, aromatic or neutral. Slovenia's and Croatia's version is Malvazija Istarka, crisp and light, or rich, oak-aged. Sometimes called Marastina in Croatia. Malmsey (as in the sweetest style of Madeira) is a corruption of Malvasia.

Malvoisie *See* MALVASIA. A name used for several varieties in France, incl BOURBOULENC, Torbato, VERMENTINO. Also PINOT GR in Switzerland's Valais.

Manseng, Gros / Petit Exuberantly fruity whites from SW France, esp Jurançon, Pacherenc and Irouléguy. Gros Manseng is picked earlier and tends to be made dry. Petit Manseng is picked later, often sweet.

Maria Gomes (Fernão Pires) Portuguese; aromatic, ripe-flavoured, slightly spicy whites in Barraida and Tejo.

Marsanne (Ermitage Blanc) Principal white grape (with ROUSSANNE) of N Rhône; gd in Australia, California, Valais (Ermitage Bl). Soft, full wines, age v. well.

Maturana Blanca Spain; Rioja; being revived. Acidity, alc, citrus-herbal notes, complex. Maturano is separate Italian (Lazio) grape: high quality, aromatic.

Mauzac SW France. Aromatic, note of apples. Best known for sparkling.

Melon de Bourgogne *See* MUSCADET.

Misket, Red Bulgarian. Pink-skinned, mildly aromatic; the basis of most country whites. There are many other Miskets, all recent crosses and less planted.

Morillon CHARD in parts of Austria.

Moscatel / Moscato *See* MUSCAT.

Moschofilero Pink-skinned, rose-scented, high-quality, high-acid, low-alcohol Greek grape. Makes white, some pink, some sparkling.

Müller-Thurgau [Müller-T] Aromatic wines to drink young. Makes gd sweet wines but usually dull, often coarse, dry ones. In Germany, most common in Pfalz, Rheinhessen, Nahe, Baden, Franken. Has some merit in Italy's Trentino-Alto Adige, Friuli. Sometimes called RIES X SYLVANER (incorrectly) in Switzerland.

Muscadelle Adds aroma to white Bx, esp Sauternes. In Victoria used (with MUSCAT, to which it is unrelated) for Rutherglen Muscat.

Muscadet (Melon de Bourgogne) Light, refreshing, dry wines with seaside tang, plus serious ageable ones. Also found (as Melon) in parts of Burgundy.

Muscat (Moscatel, Moscato, Muskateller) Many varieties; best is M Blanc à Petits Grains (alias Gelber Muskateller, Rumeni Muškat, Sarga Muskotály, Yellow M, Tămâioasă Românească). Widely grown, easily recognized, perfumed, sweet, often fortified (Australia, France's *vin doux naturel*). Most Hungarian Muskotály is M Ottonel except in Tokaj, where Sarga Muskotály adds perfume to blends. Some dry (eg. Alsace, Austria, parts of S Germany). Light Moscato fizz in N Italy.

Muskateller *See* MUSCAT.

Narince Turkish; fresh and fruity wines.

Neuburger Austrian, rather neglected; mainly in the Wachau (elegant, flowery), Thermenregion (mellow, ample-bodied) and n Burgenland (strong, full).

Olaszrizling *See* WELSCHRIESLING.

Païen *See* SAVAGNIN.

Pálava Czech, rather gd. Pink-skinned, rose aromas, gd freshness.

Palomino (Listán) Great grape of Sherry; little intrinsic character, gains all from production method. Now table wine too. As Listán, makes dry white in Canaries.

Pansa Blanca *See* XAREL·LO.

Pecorino Italian: not a cheese but alluring dry white from a revived variety.

Pedro Ximénez [PX] Makes sweet brown Sherry under its own name, and used in Montilla, Málaga. Also in Argentina, Australia, California, Canaries, S Africa.

Petit Courbu SW France. Age-worthy, some distinction.

Picolit NE Italian, used for late-harvest (sw); grapes dried on mats or left on vine, with botrytis or not. Delicate wine, should be v.gd, sometimes is.

Picpoul (Piquepoul) S French, best known in Picpoul de Pinet. Should have high acidity. Picpoul N is black-skinned.

Pinela Local to Slovenia. Subtle, lowish acidity; drink young.

Pinot Bianco *See* PINOT BL.

Pinot Blanc (Beli Pinot, Pinot Bianco, Weissburgunder) [Pinot Bl] Mutation of PINOT N, similar to but milder than CHARD. Light, fresh, fruity, not aromatic, to drink young; gd for Italian *spumante*, and potentially excellent in the ne, esp high sites in Alto Adige. Widely grown, not esp fashionable. Weissburgunder in Germany and best in s: often racier than Chard.

Pinot Gris (Pinot Grigio, Grauburgunder, Ruländer, Sivi Pinot, Szürkebarát) [Pinot Gr] Popular as Pinot Grigio in N Italy, even for rosé, but top, characterful versions can be excellent (Alto Adige, Friuli); trad *ramato* is skin-contact. Cheap versions are just that. Terrific in Alsace for full-bodied, spicy whites. Once important in Champagne. In Germany can be alias Ruländer (sw) or Grauburgunder (dr): best in Baden (esp Kaiserstuhl) and S Pfalz. Szürkebarát in Hungary, Sivi P in Slovenia (characterful, aromatic).

PIWI Trademark; hybrids bred for disease resistance. Useful in cold climates. Whites incl Cab Bl, Muscaris, Sauvignac, Solaris.

Pošip Croatian; mostly on Korčula. Quite characterful and citrus; high-yielding.

Prosecco Old name for grape that makes Prosecco. Now you have to call it GLERA.

Renski Rizling Rhine RIES.

Rèze Super-rare ancestral Valais grape used for *vin de glacier*.

Ribolla Gialla / Rebula Acidic but characterful. In Italy, best in Collio. In Slovenia, trad in Brda. Can be v.gd. Favourite of amphora users.

Rieslaner Rare German cross (SILVANER X RIES); fine Auslesen in Franken and Pfalz.

Riesling (Renski Rizling, Rhine Riesling) [Ries] The greatest, most versatile white grape, diametrically opposite in style to CHARD. From steely to voluptuous, always perfumed, far more ageing potential than Chard. Great in all styles in Germany; forceful, steely in Austria; lime-cordial fruit, toast in S Australia; rich, spicy in Alsace; often v.gd elsewhere.

Riesling Italico *See* WELSCHRIESLING.

Rkatsiteli Found widely in E Europe, Russia, Georgia. Can stand cold winters and has high acidity; protects to a degree from poor winemaking. Also in NE US.

Robola In Greece (Cephalonia) a top-quality, floral grape, unrelated to RIBOLLA GIALLA but related to Rebula.

Roditis Pink grape, all over Greece, usually making whites; gd when yields low.

Roter Veltliner Austrian; unrelated to GRÜNER V. There is also a Frühroter and an (unrelated) Brauner Veltliner.

Rotgipfler Austrian; indigenous to Thermenregion. With ZIERFANDLER, makes lively, lush, aromatic blends.

Roussanne (Bergeron) Rhône grape of real finesse, called Bergeron in Savoie. Now popping up in California and Australia. Can age many yrs.

Ruländer *See* PINOT GR.

Sauvignonasse *See* FRIULANO.

Sauvignon Blanc [Sauv Bl] Distinctive aromatic, grassy to tropical wines. Grassy, pungent NZ style taken over world; trad blackcurrant-leaf Sancerre-style more rewarding. Blended with SÉM in Bx. Sauv Gr is pink-skinned, less aromatic version with untapped potential.

Sauvignon Vert *See* FRIULANO.

Savagnin (Heida, Païen) Jura; ancient. Makes oxidative *vin jaune*; "ouillé" ("regular", topped-up) cuvées v.gd too. Aromatic mutation is GEWURZ. In Switzerland, Heida, Païen, or Traminer. Full-bodied, high acidity. Savagnin Rose (Roter Traminer), pink-skinned; can be outstanding in Alsace.

Savatiano Greek; much used (and improved) for Retsina. Herbal, fresh.

Scheurebe (Sämling) Grapefruit-scented German RIES X SILVANER (possibly), esp successful in Pfalz (Auslese and up). Can be weedy: must be v. ripe to be gd.

Sémillon [Sém] Gives lusciousness to Sauternes, but less important for dry white Bx. Superb in Australia, S Africa, beeswax richness with age.

Sercial (Cerceal, Esgana Cão) Portuguese: makes the driest Madeira. Cerceal, also Portuguese, seems to be this plus any of several others.

Seyval Blanc [Seyval Bl] French hybrid of French and American vines; v. hardy, attractively fruity. Popular and reasonably successful in E US and England.

Silvaner (Johannisberg, Sylvaner) Can be excellent in Germany's Rheinhessen, Pfalz, esp Franken, plant/earth flavours, mineral. As Johannisberg in Valais (Switzerland) v.gd. Lightest of Alsace grapes, but can be concentrated, textured.

Šipon *See* FURMINT.

Sivi Pinot *See* PINOT GR.

Spätrot *See* ZIERFANDLER.

Sylvaner *See* SILVANER.

Tămâioasă Românească *See* MUSCAT.

Timorasso Italy; Piedmont; rare, revived; high quality. Acidity, stone-fruit, honey.

Torrontés Name given to a number of grapes, mostly with an aromatic, floral character, sometimes soapy. A speciality of Argentina; also in Spain. DYA.

Traminac Or Traminec. *See* GEWURZ.

Traminer Or Tramini (Hungary). *See* GEWURZ.

Trebbiano (Ugni Blanc) Principal white grape of Tuscany, but all over Italy in many guises. Rarely rises above plebeian except in Tuscany's Vin Santo. Some gd dry whites under DOCs Romagna or Abruzzo. Trebbiano di Soave, aka VERDICCHIO, only distantly related; T di Lugana now called Turbiana. In S France (Ugni Bl), Cognac (St-Émilion). Mostly thin, bland; needs blending (and better growing).

Ugni Blanc [Ugni Bl] *See* TREBBIANO.

Verdejo The grape of Rueda in Castile, potentially fine and long-lived.

Verdelho Great quality in Australia (pungent, full-bodied); rare but gd (and medium-sweet) in Madeira.

Verdicchio Potentially v.gd, muscular, dry; central-E Italy. Wine of same name.

Vermentino Italian, sprightly with satisfying texture; ageing capacity.

Vernaccia Name given to many unrelated grapes in Italy. Vernaccia di San Gimignano is crisp, lively; Vernaccia di Oristano is Sherry-like.

Vidal French hybrid grown in Canada for Icewine. Also Sweden, US.

Vidiano Crete; powerful, stylish. Lime/apricot, gd acidity; gd fizz too.

Viognier Ultra-fashionable Rhône grape, finest in Condrieu, less fine but still aromatic in the Midi. Often gd to v.gd elsewhere.

Viura (Macabeo, Maccabéo, Maccabeu) Workhorse white grape of N Spain, much in Rioja, Cava country, over border in SW France; gd quality potential.

Weissburgunder PINOT BL in Germany.

Welschriesling (Graševina, Laški Rizling, Olaszrizling, Riesling Italico) Not related to RIES. Light and fresh to sweet and rich in Austria; ubiquitous in Central Europe, where it can be remarkably gd for dry and sweet wines.

Xarel·lo (Pansa Blanca) A trad Catalan grape, for Cava (with Parellada, MACABEO). Tannic, can age, can be superb. Lime cordial in Alella, as Pansa Blanca.

Xynisteri Cyprus's most planted white grape. Can be simple and is usually DYA, but when grown at altitude makes appealing, mineral whites.

Zéta Hungarian; BOUVIER X FURMINT used by some in Tokaji Aszú production.

Zibibbo MUSCAT of Alexandria on Sicily. Dry to v.gd sweet passito from dried grapes.

Zierfandler (Spätrot, Cirfandl) Found in Austria's Thermenregion; often blended with ROTGIPFLER for aromatic, orange-peel-scented, weighty wines.

Wine & food

Does food and wine matching matter less than it did? I would say yes, because food is more varied, and because wine is less demanding of particular foods than it used to be. The absence of harsh tannins in reds now means that most reds will not fight with most food, and many reds will match happily with what one used to think of as white-wine food; the less oaky whites of today are similarly versatile. It becomes more a matter of weight and balance and flavour profile: of fitting wine into the mixture of flavours on the plate. Some things still don't work – red Bordeaux with grilled Dover sole is not going to be ideal. And nor (to the constant surprise of most Brits) will it go with soft cheese. On p.35 you'll find a box of can't-go-wrong favourites with food; the entries below should give more ideas.

Before the meal – apéritifs

Don't be tempted by quantity over quality here. The best value is Fino Sherry, the most expensive is gd fizz – but if you're going for fizz, make sure it's gd. Or how about a magnum of rosé?

First courses

Antipasti / tapas / mezze Aka picky bits: a selection of savoury, salty, meaty, cheesy, fishy, veggie bits and pieces works perfectly with Fino Sherry, XYNISTERI, orange wines. Roasted peppers, aubergines, also charcuterie suit young fruity reds: CAB FR, KADARKA. Top aged fizz if the occasion warrants.

Burrata Richness in excelsis. Often comes with sweetly pickled veg. Worth top Italian white: FIANO or Cusumano's GRILLO. Or mature SÉM or CHENIN BL.

Carpaccio, beef or fish Beef version works well with most wines, incl reds. Tuscan is appropriate, but fine CHARDS are gd. So are pink and Vintage Champagnes or English fizz. Give Amontillado a try. **Salmon** Chard or Champagne. **Tuna** VIOGNIER, California Chard, Sancerre. Or sake.

Charcuterie / prosciutto / salami High-acid, unoaked red works better than white. Simple Beaujolais, BARBERA, Etna, REFOSCO, SCHIOPPETTINO, TEROLDEGO, Valpolicella. If you must have white, it needs acidity. Chorizo makes wines taste metallic. Prosciutto with melon or figs needs full dry or medium white: CHENIN BL, FIANO, MUSCAT, VIOGNIER.

Dim sum Classically, China tea. Alsace PINOT GR or German dry RIES; light PINOT N. For reds, soft tannins and freshness are key. Bardolino, GARNACHA, Rioja; Côtes du Rhône. Also NV Champagne or English fizz.

Eggs *See also* SOUFFLÉS. Not easy: eggs have a way of coating your palate. Omelettes: follow the other ingredients; mushrooms suggest red; Côtes du Rhone is a safe bet. With a truffle omelette, Vintage Champagne, or perhaps Volnay. Florentine, with spinach, is not a winey dish.

gulls' eggs Push the luxury: mature white burgundy or Vintage Champagne.

oeufs en meurette Burgundian genius: eggs in red wine with a glass of the same.

quails' eggs Blanc de Blancs Champagne; VIOGNIER.

Mozzarella with tomatoes, basil Fresh Italian white, eg. Soave, Alto Adige. VERMENTINO from Liguria or Rolle from the Midi. *See also* VEGETABLE/AVOCADO.

Oysters, raw NV Champagne, Chablis, MUSCADET, white Graves, Sancerre, or Guinness. Experiment with Sauternes. Manzanilla is gd.

stewed, grilled or otherwise cooked Puligny-Montrachet or gd NZ CHARD. Champagne is gd with either.

Ozempic No idea. You tell me.

Pasta Red or white according to the sauce:

creamy sauce (incl carbonara) Orvieto, GRECO di Tufo. Young SANGIOVESE.

meat sauce MONTEPULCIANO d'Abruzzo, Salice Salentino, MALBEC.

pesto (basil) sauce BARBERA, VERMENTINO, NZ SAUV BL, Hungarian FURMINT.

seafood sauce (eg. vongole) VERDICCHIO, Lugana, Soave, GRILLO, unoaked CHARD.

tomato sauce Chianti, Barbera, Sicilian red, ZIN, S Australian GRENACHE.

Pâté Chicken liver calls for pungent white (Alsace PINOT GR, or MARSANNE), smooth red, eg. light GARNACHA or PINOT N. More strongly flavoured (duck, venison) needs Chianti Classico, Gigondas, or gd white Graves. Amontillado can be marvellous match, as can young Port.

foie gras Sweet white: Sauternes, Tokaji Aszú 5 Puttonyos, late-harvest RIES or PINOT GR, Vouvray, Jurançon *moelleux*, GEWURZ. Old dry Amontillado. Note hot fresh foie gras (not pâté) needs mature Vintage Champagne.

Risotto Follow the flavour:

funghi porcini Finest mature Barolo or Barbaresco.

nero A rich dry white: VIOGNIER or even Corton-Charlemagne.

seafood A favourite dry white.

vegetables (eg. Primavera) PINOT GR from Friuli, Gavi, youngish SÉM, DOLCETTO or BARBERA d'Alba.

Soufflés As show dishes, these deserve ★★★ wines:

cheese Mature top PINOT N or Bx, CAB SAUV, etc. Or fine mature white burgundy, Hunter SEM or Rioja.

fish (esp smoked haddock with chive cream sauce) Dry white, ★★★ burgundy, Bx, Alsace, CHARD, etc.

spinach (tough on wine) Light non-tannic red or white. Champagne (esp Vintage) can also spark things with the texture of a soufflé.

Fish

Abalone Dry or medium white: SAUV BL, unoaked CHARD. A touch of oak works with soy sauce, oyster sauce, etc. In Hong Kong: Dom Pérignon (at least).

Anchovies Fino, obviously. Or try orange wine.

bocquerones VERDEJO, unoaked SÉM.

salade niçoise Provence rosé.

Bacalão Salt cod needs acidity: young Portuguese or Italian (r/w). Or Italian ditto. Orange can be gd. Creamier recipes indicate richer white.

Bass, sea Fine white, eg. Clare RIES, Chablis, white Châteauneuf, ALBARIÑO, VERMENTINO, WEISSBURGUNDER. Rev up the wine for more seasoning, eg. ginger, spring onions; more powerful Ries, not necessarily dry.

Beurre blanc, fish / scallops with Deserves gd unoaked white with maturity: Hunter SEM, Premier Cru Chablis, CHENIN BL, RIES, Swartland white blend, gd Austrian, Etna CARRICANTE.

Caviar Iced vodka (and) full-bodied Champagne (eg. Bollinger, Krug). Don't (ever) add raw onion.

Ceviche Can be applied to anything now, but here, it's fish. RIES, GRÜNER V, TORRONTÉS, VERDELHO, orange. Manzanilla.

Crab (esp Dungeness) and RIES together are part of the Creator's plan. But He also created Champagne.

Chinese, with ginger & onion German Ries Kabinett or Spätlese Halbtrocken. Rhône white, GEWURZ.

cioppino SAUV BL; but West Coast friends say ZIN. Also trad-method sparkling.

cold, dressed Top Ries (Alsace, Australian, Austrian, Mosel) or ASSYRTIKO, CHENIN BL.

crab cakes Any of the above.

softshell Unoaked CHARD, ALBARIÑO or top-quality German Ries Spätlese.

Cured fish Salmon can have a whisky cure, a beetroot cure; all have sweetness and pungency. With gravadlax, sweet mustard sauce is a complication. SERCIAL Madeira (eg. 10-yr-old Henriques), Amontillado, Tokaji Szamarodni, orange wine. Or NV Champagne.

Curry Vague term for a vast range of flavours. S African CHENIN BL, Alsace PINOT BL, Franciacorta, fruity rosé, not too pale and anodyne; look at other flavours. Prawn and mango need more sweetness, tomato needs acidity. Mild spice is gd with aged sparkling. Fino can handle heat. So can IPA or Pilsner.

Fish pie (with creamy sauce) Can be homely or fancier. ALBARIÑO, Soave Classico, RIES Erstes Gewächs, CHARD, Spanish GODELLO.

Grilled, roast or fried fish Also applies to **fish & chips**, **tempura**, **fritto misto**, **baked**...

cod, **haddock** CHARD, PINOT BL, MALVAZIJA.

Dover sole Perfect with fine wines: white burgundy or equivalent.

halibut, **turbot**, **brill** Best rich, dry white; top Chard, mature RIES Spätlese.

monkfish Meaty but neutral; full-flavoured white or red, according to sauce.

mullet, grey VERDICCHIO, unoaked Chard, rosé.

oily fish like herrings, **mackerel**, **sardines** More acidity, weight: ASSYRTIKO, VERDELHO, FURMINT, orange, rosé.

perch, **zander** Top white burgundy, Mosel, Grand Cru Alsace, mature top fizz.

plaice, **flounder** Light, fresh whites.

red fish like salmon, **red mullet** PINOT N. For salmon, also best Chard, Grand Cru Chablis, top Ries.

skate, **ray** Delicate, but brown butter, capers need oomph: Alsace, ROUSSANNE, CHENIN BL.

swordfish Full-bodied dry white (or why not red?) of the country. Nothing grand.

trout Gd Chard, Furmint, Ries, Malvazija, Pinot N.

tuna Best served rare (or raw) with light red: young Loire CAB FR or Pinot N. Young Rioja is a possibility.

whitebait Crisp dry whites, eg. Furmint, Greek, Touraine SAUV BL, Verdicchio, white Dão, Fino, rosé, orange. Or beer.

Kedgeree Full white, still or sparkling: CHARD, SÉM, GRÜNER V, German Grosses Gewächs or (at breakfast) Champagne.

Lobster with a rich sauce Eg. Thermidor: Vintage Champagne, Cru Classé Graves, ROUSSANNE, mature CARRICANTE, top CHARD. Alternatively, for its inherent sweetness, Sauternes, Pfalz Spätlese, even Auslese.

plain grilled, **or cold with mayonnaise** NV Champagne, Alsace RIES, Premier Cru Chablis, Condrieu, Mosel Spätlese, GRÜNER V, Hunter SEM, white Rioja or local fizz.

Mussels marinière MUSCADET sur lie, unoaked CHARD, ASSYRTIKO. Or try light, brisk English red.

curried Alsace RIES or PINOT BL.

Paella, shellfish Full-bodied white or rosé, unoaked CHARD, ALBARIÑO, or GODELLO. Or local Spanish red.

Prawns, crayfish with garlic Keep the wine light, white, orange, or rosé, and dry. Fino too.

with mayonnaise CHARD or rosé.

with spices Up to and incl chilli, go for a bit more body, but not oak: dry RIES or Italian, eg. FIANO, GRILLO. *See also* CURRY.

Sardines in saor Local neutral, fresh white with acidity.

Sashimi KOSHU comes into its own here, either as orange or white, and can deal with wasabi and soy, within reason. Otherwise, try white with body (Chablis

Premier Cru, Alsace RIES) with white fish, PINOT N with red. Both need acidity. Simple Chablis can be too thin. If soy is involved, then low-tannin red (again, Pinot). Remember sake (or Fino).

Scallops An inherently slightly sweet dish, best with medium-dry whites. Worth pushing the boat out.

in cream sauces German Spätlese, Montrachet, or top CHARD.

grilled or seared Hermitage Bl, GRÜNER V, Pessac-Léognan Bl, Vintage Champagne or PINOT N.

with Asian seasoning CHENIN BL, GEWURZ, GODELLO, Grüner V.

Scandi fish dishes Scandinavian dishes often have flavours of dill, caraway and cardamom and combine sweet and sharp notes. Go for acidity and some weight: FALANGHINA, GODELLO, VERDELHO, Australian, Alsace or Austrian RIES.

Shellfish Dry white with plain boiled shellfish, richer wines with richer sauces. RIES is the grape.

plateaux de fruits de mer Etna white, MUSCADET de Sèvre et Maine, PICPOUL de Pinet, Alto Adige PINOT BL.

Smoked fish All need freshness and some pungency; Fino Sherry works with all.

eel Often with beetroot, crème fraîche: Fino again, or Mosel RIES.

haddock Quality Chablis, MARSANNE, CHENIN BL, GRÜNER V. *See also* SOUFFLÉS.

kippers Try Oloroso Sherry or Speyside malt.

mackerel Not wine-friendly. Try Fino.

salmon Condrieu, Alsace PINOT GR, Grand Cru Chablis, German Ries Spätlese, Vintage Champagne, vodka, schnapps, or akvavit.

trout More delicate: Mosel Ries.

Squid / octopus Fresh white: ALBARIÑO, MUSCADET, Greek, sparkling, esp with salt-and-pepper squid. Squid ink (risotto, pasta) needs Soave.

Sushi Hot wasabi is usually hidden in every piece. KOSHU is 1st choice. Failing that, German Trocken, Greek white, ALVARINHO, GRÜNER V or NV Brut Champagne. Obvious fruit doesn't work. Or, of course, sake or beer.

Tagine N African flavours need substantial whites to balance – Austrian, Rhône – or crisp, neutral whites that won't compete. Go easy on the oak. VIOGNIER or ALBARIÑO can work well. So can Amontillado Sherry.

Taramasalata A Med white with personality, Greek if possible. Fino Sherry works well. Try Rhône MARSANNE.

Teriyaki A way of cooking, and a sauce, used for meat, as well as fish. Germans favour off-dry RIES with weight: Kabinett can be too light.

Meat / poultry / game

Barbecues The local wine: Australian, Argentine, Chilean, S African are right in spirit. Reds need tannin, vigour, freshness; don't have to be grand.

Beef (*see also* Steak), boiled Red: Light Douro, BLAUFRÄNKISCH, PINOT N or SYRAH. Medium-ranking CHARD is gd. In Austria you may be offered skin-fermented TRAMINER. Mustard softens tannic reds, horseradish kills your taste; can be worth the sacrifice.

roast An ideal partner for fine red, esp Pinot N. *See* above for mustard. The silkier the texture of the beef (wagyu, Galician, eg.), the silkier the wine. Wagyu, remember, is about texture; has v. delicate flavour.

stew, daube Sturdy red: Pomerol or St-Émilion, Cornas, Hermitage, Napa CAB SAUV, Ribera del Duero, BARBERA, SHIRAZ, or Douro red.

stroganoff Dramatic red: Amarone, Barolo, Hermitage, Priorat, late-harvest ZIN. Georgian SAPERAVI or Moldovan Negru de Purkar.

Boudin blanc CHENIN BL, esp when served with apples: dry Vouvray, Saumur, Savennières, S African; mature red PINOT N if without.

Boudin noir / morcilla Local SAUV BL or CHENIN BL (esp in Loire). Or Beaujolais cru, esp Morgon. Or light TEMPRANILLO. Or Fino.

Brazilian dishes Pungent flavours that blend several culinary traditions. Rhônish grapes work for red, or white with weight: VERDICCHIO, CHARD. Or orange. Or a Caipirinha (better not have two).

Cajun food Gutsy reds, preferably New World: ZIN, CARMENÈRE, SHIRAZ. Fish or white meat: off-dry RIES, MARSANNE, ROUSSANNE. Or, of course, cold beer.

Cassoulet Fresh red from SW France (Corbières, Fitou, Gaillac, Minervois, or St-Chinian) or BAGA, SHIRAZ, TEMPRANILLO.

Chicken / turkey / guinea fowl, roast Virtually any wine, incl v. best bottles of dry to medium white and finest old reds (esp burgundy). Sauces can make it match almost any fine wine (eg. coq au vin: r or w burgundy, or *vin jaune* for that matter).

chicken Kiev Alsace RIES, Collio, CHARD, Bergerac rouge.

fried Sparkling works well.

Chilli con carne Young red: Beaujolais, TEMPRANILLO, ZIN, Argentine MALBEC, Chilean CARMENÈRE. Or beer.

Chinese dishes Food in China is regional – like Italian, only more confusing. It's easiest to have both white and red; no one wine goes with all. Peking duck is pretty forgiving. Champagne becomes a thirst-quencher. Beer too.

Cantonese Big, slightly sweet flavours work with slightly oaky CHARD, PINOT N, off-dry RIES. GEWURZ is often suggested but rarely works; GRÜNER V is a better bet. You need wine with acidity. Dry sparkling (esp Cava) works with textures.

Shanghai Richer and oilier than Cantonese, not one of wine's natural partners. Shanghai tends to be low on chilli but high on vinegar of various sorts. German and Alsace whites can be a bit sweeter than for Cantonese. For reds, try MERLOT – goes with the salt. Or mature Pinot N, but a bit of a waste.

Sichuan VERDICCHIO, Alsace PINOT BL, or v. cold beer. Mature Pinot N can also work; but *see* above. The Creator intended tea.

Taiwanese LAMBRUSCO works with trad Taiwan dishes if you're tired of beer.

Choucroute garni Alsace PINOT BL, PINOT GR, RIES, or lager.

Cold roast meat Generally better with full-flavoured white than red. German or Austrian RIES, lightish CHARD are v.gd, as is light GARNACHA. Leftover Champagne too.

Confit d'oie / de canard Young, brisk CAB FR, California CAB SAUV or MERLOT, Priorat cuts richness. Alsace PINOT GR or GEWURZ match it.

Coq au vin Red burgundy. Ideal: one bottle of Chambertin in the dish, two on the table. *See also* CHICKEN.

Dirty (Creole) rice Rich, supple red: NZ PINOT N, Bairrada, GARNACHA, MALBEC.

Duck / goose PINOT N is tops. Also other red in the Pinot idiom, like GARNACHA; also BLAUFRÄNKISCH. Or rich white, esp for goose: Pfalz Spätlese or off-dry Grand Cru Alsace. With oranges or peaches, the Sauternais propose drinking Sauternes, others Monbazillac or RIES Auslese. Mature and weighty Vintage Champagne handles accompanying red cabbage surprisingly well. So does decent Chianti.

Peking *See* CHINESE DISHES.

roast breast & confit leg with Puy lentils Madiran (best), St-Émilion, Fronsac, Maremma.

wild duck Worth opening gd Pinot N. Austrian, Tuscan red (easy on oak) also gd.

with olives Top-notch Chianti or other Tuscans.

Filipino dishes Spanish-influenced flavours, lots of garlic, bell peppers, adobo, not always super-spicy. Straightforward unoaked white with acidity (adobo can have a burst of vinegar) or fizz, Côtes de Gascogne, Rueda, RIES, rosé, even light red.

Game birds, young, roast The best red wine you can afford, but not too heavy. Partridge is more delicate than pheasant, which is more delicate than grouse. Up the weight of wine accordingly, starting with youngish PINOT N, BLAUFRÄNKISCH, SYRAH, GARNACHA, and moving up.

cold game Best German RIES or mature Vintage Champagne.

older birds in casseroles Gevrey-Chambertin, Pommard, Châteauneuf, Dão, or Grand Cru Classé St-Émilion, Rhône.

well-hung game Vega Sicilia, great red Rhône or NZ Syrah, Ch Musar.

Game pie, hot Red: Oregon PINOT N, St-Émilion Grand Cru Classé.

cold Quality white burgundy or German Erstes Gewächs, Etna red, Champagne.

Goat (hopefully kid) As for lamb.

Jamaican curry goat *See* INDIAN DISHES. And don't forget Malbec.

Goulash Flavoursome young red: Hungarian Kékoportó, ZIN, Uruguayan TANNAT, Douro, MENCÍA, young Australian SHIRAZ, SAPERAVI; or dry Tokaji Szamarodni.

Haggis Fruity red, eg. young claret, young Portuguese or Spanish red, CAB SAUV, MALBEC or Rhône blend. Or, of course, malt whisky.

Ham, cooked A gift to wine. Softish PINOT N (Côte de Beaune, Martinborough); Loire red or BLAUFRÄNKISCH; sweetish German white (RIES Spätlese); lightish CAB SAUV (eg. Chilean), or New World Pinot N. And don't forget the heaven-made match of ham and Amontillado.

Hare Jugged hare calls for flavourful red: not-too-old burgundy or Bx, Rhône (eg. Gigondas), Bandol, Barbaresco, Ribera del Duero, Rioja Res. The same for saddle or for hare sauce with pappardelle.

Indian dishes Various options: dry Sherry is brilliant. Choose a fairly weighty Fino with fish, and Palo Cortado, Amontillado or Oloroso with meat, according to weight of dish; heat's not a problem. The texture works too. Otherwise, medium-sweet white, v. cold, no oak: Orvieto *abboccato*, S African CHENIN BL, Alsace PINOT BL, TORRONTÉS, Indian sparkling, Cava or NV Champagne. Rosé is gd all-rounder. For tannic impact Barolo or Barbaresco, or deep-flavoured reds, eg. Châteauneuf, Cornas, Australian GRENACHE or MOURVÈDRE, or Valpolicella Amarone – will emphasize the heat. Hot-and-sour flavours need acidity.

Sri Lankan More extreme flavours, coconut. Sherry, rich red, rosé, mild white.

Japanese dishes A different set of senses come into play. Texture and balance are key; flavours are subtle. A gd mature fizz works well, as does mature dry RIES; you need acidity, a bit of body, and complexity. Dry FURMINT can work well. Umami-filled meat dishes favour light, supple, bright reds: Beaujolais perhaps, or mature PINOT N. Full-flavoured yakitori needs lively, fruity, younger versions of the same reds. KOSHU with raw fish – but why not sake? Orange Koshu with wagyu beef. *See also* FISH/SASHIMI, SUSHI, TERIYAKI.

Korean dishes Fruit-forward wines seem to work best with strong, pungent Korean flavours. PINOT N, Beaujolais, Valpolicella can all work: acidity is needed. Non-aromatic whites: GRÜNER V, SILVANER, VERNACCIA. Beer too.

Lamb, roast One of trad and best partners for v.gd red Bx, or equivalents from elsewhere. In Spain, finest old Rioja and Ribera del Duero Res, or Priorat, in Italy ditto SANGIOVESE. Fresh mint is gd, but mint sauce should be banned.

milk-fed A delicate dish that deserves top, delicate GARNACHA, even white Rueda or Rhône.

slow-cooked roast Flatters top reds but needs less tannin than pink lamb. *See also* TAGINES.

Liver, incl venison Young red: Bairrada, BLAUFRÄNKISCH, Breganze CAB SAUV, Italian MERLOT, Médoc, Priorat, St-Joseph, ZIN.

calf's Red Rioja Crianza, Fleurie. Or a big Pfalz RIES Spätlese.

Mexican food Californians favour RIES, esp German. Or beer.

Moussaka Red, rosé: Ajaccio, Corbières, Côtes de Provence, Greek red, young ZIN, SANGIOVESE, TEMPRANILLO.

Mutton A stronger flavour than lamb, and not usually served pink. Needs a strong sauce. Robust red; top-notch, mature CAB SAUV, SYRAH. Sweetness of fruit (eg. Barossa) suits it.

'Nduja Calabria's spicy, fiery spreadable salumi needs a big, juicy red: young Rioja, Valpolicella, CAB FR, AGLIANICO, CARIGNAN, NERELLO MASCALESE.

Osso bucco Low-tannin, supple red such as DOLCETTO d'Alba or PINOT N. Or dry Italian white such as Soave.

Ox cheek, braised Superbly tender and flavoursome, this flatters the best reds: Vega Sicilia, St-Émilion. Best with substantial wines.

Oxtail Rather rich red: St-Émilion, Pomerol, Pommard, Nuits-St-Georges, Barolo, or Rioja Res, Priorat or Ribera del Duero, California or Coonawarra CAB SAUV, Châteauneuf, mid-weight SHIRAZ, Barolo, Amarone.

Paella Young Spanish wines: red, dry white, or rosé: Penedès, Somontano, Navarra, or Rioja.

Pastrami Alsace RIES, young SANGIOVESE, or St-Émilion.

Pigeon or squab PINOT N is perfect; or young Rhône, Argentine MALBEC, young SANGIOVESE. Try Franken SILVANER Spätlese. With luxurious squab, top quite tannic red.

pastilla Depends on sweetness of dish. As above, or if authentically sweet, try RIES Spätlese, Alsace PINOT GR with some sweetness.

Pork A perfect rich background to a fairly light red or rich white.

belly Slow-cooked and meltingly tender, needs red with some tannin or acidity. Italian would be gd: Barolo, DOLCETTO or BARBERA. Or Loire red, or lightish Argentine MALBEC. With Chinese spices, VIOGNIER, CHENIN BL.

Mangalica pork Fashionable, fatty. KÉKFRANKOS or other brisk red.

pulled Often with spicy sauce: juicy New World reds.

roast Deserves ★★★ treatment: Médoc is fine. Portugal's suckling pig is eaten with Bairrada; S America's with CARIGNAN; Chinese is gd with PINOT N.

with prunes or apricots Something sweeter: eg. Vouvray.

Pot au feu, bollito misto, cocido Rustic red wines from region of origin; SANGIOVESE di Romagna, Chusclan, Lirac, Rasteau, Portuguese Alentejo or Spain's Yecla, Jumilla.

Quail Succulent, delicate: try red or white. Rioja Res, mature claret, PINOT N. Or mellow white: Vouvray, Hunter SEM.

Quiche Egg and bacon are not great wine matches, but one must drink something. Alsace RIES or PINOT GR, even GEWURZ, is classical. Beaujolais could be gd too.

Rabbit Lively, medium-bodied young Italian red, eg. AGLIANICO del Vulture, REFOSCO; MALBEC, Chiroubles, Chinon or dark rosé.

as ragu Medium-bodied red with acidity: Aglianico, NEBBIOLO.

with mustard Cahors, Malbec.

with prunes Bigger, richer, fruitier red.

Satay SHIRAZ, Alsace or NZ GEWURZ. Peanut sauce: problem for wine. Orange?

Sauerkraut (German) German RIES, lager or Pils. (But *see also* CHOUCROUTE GARNI.)

Singaporean dishes Part Indian, part Malay and part Chinese, Singaporean food has big, bold flavours that don't match easily with wine – not that that bothers the country's many wine-lovers. Off-dry RIES is as gd as anything. With meat dishes, ripe, supple reds: Valpolicella, PINOT N, DORNFELDER, unoaked MERLOT, or CARMENÈRE.

Steak Rare steak needs brisker, more tannic reds; well done needs juicy, fruity reds, eg. young Argentine MALBEC. Fattier cuts need acidity, tannin.

au poivre A fairly young Rhône red or CAB SAUV. Nothing too sweetly fruity.

fillet Silky red: Pomerol or PINOT N.

fiorentina (bistecca) Chianti Classico Riserva or BRUNELLO.

from older cattle Has deep, rich savouriness. Top Italian, Spanish red.

Korean yuk whe (world's best steak tartare) Sake.

ribeye, tomahawk, tournedos Big, pungent red: Barolo, Malbec, SHIRAZ, Rioja.

sirloin Suits most gd reds. Bx blends, Tuscans.

tartare Vodka or light young red: Loire, Pinot N, BLAUFRÄNKISCH. Aussies drink GAMAY with kangaroo tartare, charred plums, Sichuan pepper.

T-bone Reds of similar bone structure: Barolo, gd Cab Sauv, SYRAH, Ribera del Duero, Douro.

wagyu Delicate, silky red, or orange.

Steak-&-kidney pie or pudding Red Rioja Res or mature Bx. Pudding (with suet) wants vigorous young wine. Madiran with its tannin is gd. Or Greek.

Stews & casseroles Village burgundy or equivalent if fairly simple; otherwise lusty and full-flavoured red, eg. young MENCÍA, Corbières, BARBERA, BLAUFRÄNKISCH, SHIRAZ, ZIN, etc.

Sweetbreads Rich dish, so grand white wine: top RIES or Franken SILVANER Spätlese, Grand Cru Alsace PINOT GR, MARSANNE or Condrieu, depending on sauce.

Tagines Depends on what's under the lid, but fruity young reds are a gd bet: GARNACHA, MERLOT, SANGIOVESE, SHIRAZ, TEMPRANILLO. Amontillado is great, as is aged Tawny Port. Amarone is fashionable.

chicken with preserved lemon, olives VIOGNIER.

Tandoori chicken RIES or SAUV BL, young red Bx or light N Italian red served cool. Also trad-method fizz or, of course, Palo Cortado or Amontillado Sherry.

Thai dishes Ginger and lemongrass call for pungent SAUV BL (Loire, Australia, NZ, S Africa) or RIES (Spätlese or Australian). Most curries suit aromatic whites with a touch of sweetness: GEWURZ also gd.

Tongue Any red or white of abundant character. Alsace GEWURZ or PINOT GR, gd GRÜNER V. Also Loire reds, BLAUFRÄNKISCH, TEMPRANILLO, full, dry rosé/orange.

Veal A friend of fine wine. Rioja Res, CAB blends, PINOT N, NEBBIOLO, German or Austrian RIES, Vouvray, Alsace PINOT GR, Italian GRECO di Tufo.

vitello tonnato Full-bodied whites: CHARD. Light reds (Langhe Nebbiolo, TEMPRANILLO) served cool. Or a southern rosé.

Venison Large-scale reds, incl MOURVÈDRE solo or blended. SYRAH, ZIN, Languedoc, Barolo, Bx, top mature CAB SAUV; or rich white (Pfalz Spätlese, Alsace PINOT GR).

with sweet & sharp berry sauce Try a German Grosses Gewächs RIES, or Chilean CARMENÈRE, or Syrah.

Vietnamese food RIES, dry or up to Spätlese, German, Austrian, NZ, also GRÜNER V, SÉM. For reds, BLAUFRÄNKISCH, CAB FR, PINOT N.

Wild boar Serious red: top Tuscan or Priorat. NZ SYRAH. I've even drunk Port; Amarone would be a compromise.

Vegetable dishes

With few tannins to help or hinder, matching wine to veg is about sweetness, acidity, weight and texture. *See also* FIRST COURSES.

Agrodolce Italian sweet-and-sour, with pine kernels, sultanas, capers, vinegar and perhaps anchovies. Go to fresh white: VERDICCHIO, unoaked CHARD. Etna rosato. Or orange.

Artichokes Not great for wine. Orange or orangish, esp of PIWI or aromatic grapes. Greek (precisely, 4-yr-old MALAGOUSIA, but easy on vinaigrette). Never ever red.

Asparagus Is lightly bitter and needs acidity, if it needs wine at all. Asparagus solo: skip the wine. With other ingredients: go by those.

Aubergine Comes in a multitude of guises, usually strongly flavoured. Sturdy reds with acidity are a gd bet: SHIRAZ, Greek, Lebanese, Bulgarian, Hungarian, Turkish. Structured white, eg. VERDICCHIO, or go further and have orange wine.

Avocado Not a wine natural. Dry to slightly sweet RIES Kabinett will suit the dressing. Otherwise, light and fresh: ALIGOTÉ, TREBBIANO, PINOT GRIGIO.

Beetroot Mimics a flavour found in PINOT N. You could return the compliment. New-wave (ie. light) GARNACHA/Grenache is also gd, as is GAMAY.

Bitter leaves: radicchio etc. Bone-dry, aged Palo Cortado. But easy on the dressing. Fab combo. Or NEBBIOLO, LAGREIN, white VERMENTINO, orange.

roast radicchio, chicory etc. SANGIOVESE, BLAUFRÄNKISCH, Etna red.

Cauliflower roast, etc. Go by the other (usually bold) flavours. Try Austrian GRÜNER V, GARNACHA, NZ PINOT N.

cauliflower cheese Crisp, aromatic white: Sancerre, RIES Spätlese, MUSCAT, ALBARIÑO, GODELLO. CHARD too, and Beaujolais-Villages.

with caviar – yes, really. Vintage Champagne.

Celeriac, slow-roast or purée Won't interfere with rest of dish. Acidity works well, so classic CAB blends, SANGIOVESE, PINOT N, according to dish.

remoulade with smoked ham Needs bright red: DOLCETTO, simple GAMAY, Etna. Or white GRÜNER V.

Chestnuts Earthy, rich red: Tuscan or S Rhône.

Chickpeas Look at the other flavours in the dish. Casserole works with TEMPRANILLO or S French reds.

hummus Any simple red, pink or white, or, of course, Fino.

Chilli Some like it hot, but not with your best bottles. Tannic wines become more tannic; if you like that, go for it. Light, fruity reds and whites are refreshing: TEMPRANILLO, MERLOT, MALBEC, NZ SAUV BL. Same for **harissa**. *See also* MEAT/CHILLI CON CARNE, CHINESE DISHES, INDIAN DISHES.

Couscous with vegetables Young red with a bite: SHIRAZ, Corbières, Minervois; rosé, esp Etna; orange wine; Italian REFOSCO or SCHIOPPETTINO.

Dhal Comes with many variations, but all share aromatic earthiness. Simple, warm-climate reds work best: CARMENÈRE, Dão, S Italian.

Fennel-based dishes SYLVANER, SAUV BL, English white, or young TEMPRANILLO.

deep-flavoured braised fennel Light BLAUFRÄNKISCH, PINOT N.

Fermented foods *See also* CHOUCROUTE GARNI, KOREAN DISHES, SAUERKRAUT. Kimchi and miso are being worked into many dishes. Fruit and acidity are generally needed. If in sweetish veg dishes, try Alsace.

Grilled Mediterranean vegetables Italian whites, or for reds Brouilly, Greek, BARBERA, TEMPRANILLO or SHIRAZ.

Lentil dishes Sturdy reds such as Corbières, ZIN or SHIRAZ. *See also* DHAL.

Mac 'n' cheese As for CAULIFLOWER CHEESE.

Mushrooms (in most contexts) A boon to most reds and some whites. Context matters as much as species. Pomerol, California MERLOT, Rioja Res, top PINOT N, or Vega Sicilia.

button or Paris with cream Fine whites, even Vintage Champagne.

ceps / porcini Ribera del Duero, Barolo, Chianti Rùfina, CAB SAUV/Bx.

on toast Best claret, even Port.

Onion / leek tart / flamiche Fruity, off-dry or dry white: Alsace PINOT GR or GEWURZ is classic; Canadian, Australian or NZ RIES; Jurançon. Or Loire CAB FR.

Peppers, cooked Mid-weight Rhône grapes, CARMENÈRE, Rioja; or ripe SAUV BL (esp with green Hungarian wax peppers).

stuffed Full red, white, orange, or pink: Languedoc, Greek, Spanish, Etna.

Pickled foods & vinegar Vinegar and wine don't match, it's true, but pickled foods are everywhere. Try out Alsace or German RIES with CHOUCROUTE/SAUERKRAUT (*see* MEAT). With pickled veg as part of a dish, just downgrade the wine a bit (no point in opening best bottles) and make sure it has some acidity. (Or have beer.) In dressings, experiment with vinegars: Sherry vinegar can work with Amontillado, etc., big reds; Austrian apricot vinegar is delicate; balsamic can work with rich Italian reds. Wine just has to work harder than it used to.

Pumpkin / squash ravioli or risotto Full-bodied, fruity dry or off-dry white: VIOGNIER or MARSANNE, demi-sec Vouvray, Gavi or S African CHENIN. If you want red, MERLOT, ZIN.

Ratatouille (or piperade) Vigorous young red: Chianti, Languedoc, NZ CAB SAUV, MALBEC, MERLOT, TEMPRANILLO. A gd rosé can be best of all.

Roasted veg Can be root veg or more Mediterranean, but all have plenty of sweetness. Rosé, esp with some weight, or orange wine. Lightish reds with acidity to match the dressing. Pesto will tilt it towards white with weight.

Saffron Found in sweet and savoury dishes, and wine-friendly. Rich white: ROUSSANNE, VIOGNIER, PINOT GR. Orange wines can be gd too. With desserts, Sauternes or Tokaji. *See also* MEAT/TAGINES.

Salsa verde Whatever it's with, it points to more acidity, less lushness in the wine.

Seaweed (nori) Depends on the context. *See also* FISH/SUSHI. Iodine notes go well with Austrian GRÜNER V, RIES.

Sweetcorn fritters Often served with a hot, spicy sauce. Rosé, orange, or neutral white all safe.

Tahini Doesn't really affect wine choice. Go by rest of dish.

Tapenade Manzanilla or Fino Sherry, or any sharpish dry white or rosé. Definitely not Champagne.

Tomatoes Generally call for acidity in wine: think of Italian reds like BARBERA, Etna, NEBBIOLO, etc., for deep-flavoured cooked tomatoes. White with acidity for raw.

Truffles Black truffles are a match for finest Right Bank Bx or Volnay, but even better with mature white Hermitage or Châteauneuf. White truffles call for best Barolo or Barbaresco of their native Piedmont. With buttery pasta, Lugana. Or at breakfast, on fried eggs, BARBERA.

Watercress, raw Makes every wine on earth taste revolting.

Wild garlic leaves, wilted Tricky: a fairly neutral white with acidity will cope best.

Desserts

Apples: Cox's Orange Pippins with Cheddar cheese Vintage Port.
Russets with Caerphilly Old Tawny, or Amontillado.
pie, etc. Sweet Vouvray or similar.

Bread-&-butter pudding Fine 10-yr-old Barsac, Tokaji Aszú, or Australian botrytized SEM.

Cakes *See also* CHOCOLATE, COFFEE, RUM. Bual or Malmsey Madeira, Oloroso or Cream Sherry. Asti, sweet Prosecco.

Cheesecake Sweet white: Vouvray, Anjou, or Vin Santo – nothing too special.

Chocolate Don't try to be too clever. Texture matters. BUAL, California Orange MUSCAT, Tokaji Aszú, Australian Liqueur Muscat, 10-yr-old Tawny or even young Vintage Port; Asti for light, fluffy mousses. Or *vins doux naturels* (VDN) Banyuls, Maury, or Rivesaltes. Some like Médoc with bitter black chocolate, though it's a bit of a waste of both. A trial of SYRAH with bitter chocolate showed that you shouldn't, ever. Armagnac, or a tot of gd rum.

Christmas pudding, mince pies Tawny Port, Cream Sherry or that liquid Christmas pudding itself, PEDRO XIMÉNEZ Sherry. Tokaji Aszú. Asti, or Banyuls.

Coffee desserts Sweet MUSCAT, Australia Liqueur Muscats, or Tokaji Aszú.

Creams, custards, fools, syllabubs *See also* CHOCOLATE, COFFEE, RUM. Sauternes, Loupiac, Ste-Croix-du-Mont or Monbazillac.

Crème brûlée Sauternes or Rhine Beerenauslese, best Madeira, or Tokaji Aszú.

Ice cream & sorbets PX with vanilla, or Australian Liqueur MUSCAT, or none. Sorbets: definitely none.

Lemon flavours For dishes like tarte au citron, try sweet RIES from Germany or Austria or Tokaji Aszú; v. sweet if lemon is v. tart.

Meringues (eg. Eton mess) Recioto di Soave, Asti, mature Vintage Champagne.

Nuts (incl praline) Finest Oloroso Sherry, Madeira, Vintage or Tawny Port (nature's match for walnuts), Tokaji Aszú, Vin Santo, or Setúbal MOSCATEL. Cashews and Champagne. Pistachios with Fino. **Salted nut parfait** Tokaji Aszú, Vin Santo.

Orange flavours Experiment with old Sauternes, Tokaji Aszú, or Orange MUSCAT from California.

Panettone Vin Santo. Jurançon *moelleux*, late-harvest RIES, Barsac, Tokaji Aszú.

Pears in red wine Rivesaltes, Banyuls, or RIES Beerenauslese.

Pecan pie Orange MUSCAT or Liqueur Muscat.

Raspberries (no cream, little sugar) Great with cream and something in the Sauternes spectrum.

Rum flavours (baba, mousses) MUSCAT – from Asti to Australian Liqueur, according to weight of dish.

Strawberries, wild, no cream With red Bx (most exquisitely Margaux) poured over. **with cream** Sauternes or similar sweet Bx, Vouvray *moelleux*, or Vendange Tardive Jurançon.

Summer pudding Fairly young Sauternes of a gd vintage.

Sweet soufflés Sauternes or Vouvray *moelleux*. Sweet (or rich) Champagne.

Tiramisù Vin Santo, young Tawny Port, MUSCAT de Beaumes-de-Venise, Sauternes, or Australian Liqueur Muscat. Better idea: skip the wine. Best idea of all: skip the tiramisù.

Trifle Should be sufficiently vibrant with its internal Sherry (Oloroso for choice).

Zabaglione Light-gold Marsala or Australian botrytized SEM, or Asti.

Wine & cheese

Counterintuitively, white is a safer option than red. Fine reds are slaughtered by strong cheeses. But aged Tawny Port is wonderful with most cheese, and orange wine is a gd standby too. Remember (despite exceptions): the harder the cheese, the more tannin the wine can have; the creamier the cheese, the more acidity is needed in the wine. Cheese is classified by its texture and the nature of its rind, so its appearance is a guide to the type of wine to match it.

Bloomy-rind soft cheeses: Brie, Camembert, Chaource CHARD, white Rhône, Swartland white blend. Not tannic red.

Blue cheeses The extreme saltiness of Roquefort or most blue cheeses needs sweetness: Sauternes, Tokaji, youngish Vintage or Tawny Port, esp with Stilton. Intensely flavoured old Oloroso, Amontillado, Madeira, Marsala and other fortifieds go with most blues. Dry red does not. Trust me.

Cooked cheese dishes: fondue Trendy again. Light, fresh white as below.

frico Cheese baked or fried with potatoes or onions, trad in Friuli; high-acid local REFOSCO (r), or RIBOLLA GIALLA (w).

macaroni or cauliflower cheese *See* VEGETABLE DISHES/CAULIFLOWER.

Mont d'Or Delicious baked, and served with potatoes. Fairly neutral white with freshness: GRÜNER V, Jura Savagnin.

Fresh cream cheese, fromage frais, mozzarella Light crisp white: Portuguese, Jura, Loire; juicy rosé can work too.

Hard cheeses: Gruyère, Manchego, Parmesan, Cantal, Comté, old Gouda, Cheddar Hard to generalize, relatively easy to match. Gouda, Gruyère, some Spanish, and a few English cheeses complement fine claret or CAB SAUV and great SHIRAZ/SYRAH. But strong cheeses need less refined wines, preferably local ones. Granular old Dutch red Mimolette, Comté, or Beaufort gd for finest mature Bx. Also for Tokaji Aszú. But try tasty whites too: Jura, Vin Jaune. And orange.

Natural rind (mostly goats' cheese): St-Marcellin Sancerre, CARICCANTE, Jurançon, Savoie, Soave, CHARD; or young Vintage Port.

Semi-soft cheeses: Livarot, Pont l'Evêque, Reblochon, St-Nectaire, Tomme de Savoie Powerful white Bx, even Sauternes, CHARD, Alsace PINOT GR, dryish RIES, mature Hunter SEM, S Italian and Sicilian whites, aged white Rioja, dry Oloroso Sherry. The strongest of these cheeses kill almost any wines. Try marc or Calvados.

Washed-rind soft cheeses: Carré de l'Est, mature Époisses, Langres, Maroilles, Milleens, Münster Local reds, esp for Burgundian cheeses; vigorous S French, Corsican, S Italian, Sicilian, Bairrada, S African, Australian. Also powerful whites, esp Alsace GEWURZ, MUSCAT. Gewurz with Münster, always.

Food & your finest wines

With v. special bottles, the wine guides the choice of food rather than vice versa. The following is based largely on gastronomic conventions, some bold experiments and much diligent and on-going research.

Red wines

Amarone Classically, in Verona, risotto all'Amarone or pastissada. But if your butcher doesn't run to horse, then shin of beef, slow-cooked in more Amarone.

Barolo, Barbaresco Risotto with white truffles; pasta with game sauce (eg. pappardelle alla lepre); porcini mushrooms; Parmesan.

Great Syrahs: Hermitage, Côte-Rôtie, Grange, Vega Sicilia Beef, venison, or well-hung game; bone marrow on toast; English cheese (Lincolnshire Poacher) but also hard goats'-milk and ewes'-milk cheeses such as England's Lord of the Hundreds. I treat Côte-Rôtie like top red burgundy.

Great Vintage Port or Madeira Walnuts or pecans. A Cox's Orange Pippin and a digestive biscuit is a classic English accompaniment.

Red Bordeaux, v. old, light, delicate wines (eg. pre-82) Leg or rack of young lamb, roast with a hint of herbs (not garlic); entrecôte; simply roasted partridge; roast chicken never fails.

fully mature great vintages (eg. 82 85 89 90 00) Shoulder or saddle of lamb, roast with a touch of garlic; roast ribs or grilled rump of beef.

mature but still vigorous (eg. 05 09 10) Shoulder or saddle of lamb (incl kidneys) with rich sauce. Fillet of beef marchand de vin (with wine and bone marrow). Grouse. Avoid beef Wellington: pastry dulls the palate.

Merlot-based Beef (fillet is richest) or well-hung venison. In St-Émilion, lampreys.

Red burgundy Consider the weight and texture, which grow lighter/more velvety with age. Also the character of the wine: Nuits is earthy, Musigny flowery, great Romanées can be exotic, Pommard relatively sturdy. Roast chicken or (better) capon is a safe standard with red burgundy; guinea fowl for slightly stronger wines, then partridge, grouse, or woodcock for those progressively richer and more pungent. Hare and venison are alternatives.

great old burgundy The Burgundian formula is cheese: Époisses (unfermented); a fine cheese but a terrible waste of fine old wines. *See* above.

vigorous younger burgundy Duck or goose roasted to minimize fat. Or faisinjan (pheasant cooked in pomegranate juice). Coq au vin, or lightly smoked gammon.

Rioja Gran Reserva, top Duero reds Richly flavoured roasts: wild boar, mutton, venison, saddle of hare, whole suckling pig.

White wines

Beerenauslese (BA) / Trockenbeerenauslese (TBA) Biscuits, peaches, greengages. But TBAs don't need or want food.

Condrieu, Ch-Grillet, Hermitage Bl Pasta, v. light, scented with herbs and tiny peas or broad beans. Or v. mild tender ham. Old white Hermitage loves truffles.

Grand Cru Alsace Gewurz Cheese soufflé (Münster cheese).

Pinot Gr Roast or grilled veal. Or truffle sandwich. (Slice a whole truffle, make a sandwich with salted butter and gd country bread – not sourdough or rye – wrap and refrigerate overnight. Then toast it in the oven. Thanks, Dom Weinbach.)

Ries Truite au bleu, smoked salmon, or choucroute garni.

Vendange Tardive Foie gras or tarte tatin.

Old Vintage Champagne (not Blanc de Blancs) As an apéritif, or with cold partridge, grouse, or woodcock. The evolved flavours of old Champagne make it far easier to match with food than the tightness of young wine. Hot foie gras can be sensational. Don't be afraid of garlic or even Indian spices, but omit the chilli.

late-disgorged old wines These have extra freshness plus tertiary flavours. Try with truffles, lobster, scallops, crab, sweetbreads, pork belly, roast veal, chicken. Saffron is flattering to old Champagne.

old Vintage Rosé Pigeon, veal.

Sauternes Simple crisp buttery biscuits (eg. langues de chat), white peaches, nectarines, strawberries (without cream). Not tropical fruit. Pan-seared foie gras. Lobster or chicken with Sauternes sauce; Ch d'Yquem recommends oysters (and indeed lobster). Experiment with blue cheeses. Rocquefort is classic but needs one of the big Sauternes. Savoury food, apart from cheese, seldom works. Cantonese dishes can be gd. A chilled glass as an apéritif can be even better.

Sherry VOS or VORS Just some almonds or walnuts, or gd cheese. And time to appreciate them.

Tokaji Aszú (5–6 Puttonyos) Foie gras recommended. Fruit desserts, cream desserts, even chocolate can be wonderful. Roquefort. It even works with some Chinese, though not with chilli – the spice has to be adjusted to meet the sweetness. Sichuan pepper is gd. Havana cigars are splendid. So is the naked sip.

Top Chablis White fish simply grilled or *meunière*. Dover sole, turbot, halibut are best; brill, drenched in butter, can be excellent. (Sea bass is too delicate; salmon passes but does little for the finest wine.)

Top white burgundy, top Graves, top aged Ries Roast veal, farm chicken stuffed with truffles or herbs under the skin, or sweetbreads; richly sauced white fish (turbot for choice) or scallops, white fish as above. Lobster, wild salmon.

Vouvray moelleux, etc. Buttery biscuits, apples, apple tart.

Fail-safe face-savers

Some wines are more useful than others – more versatile, more forgiving. If you're choosing restaurant wine to please several people or just stocking the cellar with basics, these are the wines: **Red** BARBERA d'Asti/d'Alba, BLAUFRÄNKISCH, Beaujolais, Chianti, GARNACHA/Grenache, young MALBEC (easy on the oak), PINOT N, SYRAH (more versatile than Shiraz). **White** Alsace PINOT BL, ASSYRTIKO, cool-climate CHARD, CHENIN BL, Fino Sherry, GRÜNER V, dry RIES, Sancerre, gd Soave, VERDICCHIO. And the greatest of these is Ries. Make sure to think of **Orange**. Always go for the best producer you can afford, and don't get too hung up on appellations or even vintages, within reason. If you can't afford gd Chablis, buy Assyrtiko, not cheap Chablis.

France

More heavily shaded areas are the wine-growing regions.

Abbreviations used in the text:

Al	Alsace
Beauj	Beaujolais
Burg	Burgundy
Bx	Bordeaux
Cas	Castillon-Côtes de Bordeaux
Chab	Chablis
Champ	Champagne
Cors	Corsica
C d'O	Côte d'Or
Ldoc	Languedoc
Lo	Loire
Mass C	Massif Central
Prov	Provence
N/S Rh	Northern/Southern Rhône
Rouss	Roussillon
Sav	Savoie
SW	Southwest
AC	appellation contrôlée
ch, chx	château(x)
dom, doms	domaine(s)

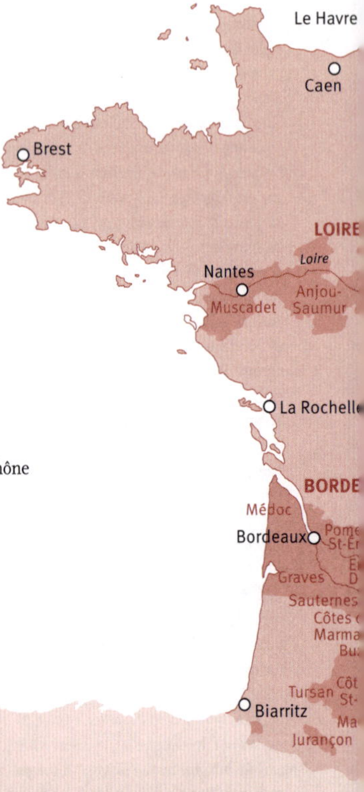

Given that so many of the classic regions of France used to be at the margin, climate-wise, you might expect France to be a beneficiary, so far, of climate change. And so it is: the wines of Bordeaux, Burgundy, Champagne, the Loire and Alsace have never been so good, so ripe, so drinkable, so really delicious – no longer the acquired taste they could sometimes be when this book was launched. For drinkers, the choice is better than ever, mitigated only by rising alcohol levels. Can you get round those? Yes, to some extent. Vintages vary, and so do grape varieties; and producers are gradually adjusting their vineyards to varieties and clones (and to viticulture) that can deal with different conditions. The problem is that you plant a vineyard for the long term, and then conditions change in ways you hadn't expected. If we look at a label and tut at the alcohol, we are forgetting that we're looking at an artisan product, not an industrial one. In the pages that follow, you'll find pointers to freshness, to drinkability, and to value in this most varied of wine countries.

France entries also cross-refer to Châteaux of Bordeaux

Recent vintages of the French classics

Red Bordeaux

Médoc / Red Graves For many wines, bottle-age is optional; for these it is indispensable. Minor chx from light vintages may need only 1 or 2 yrs these days, but even modest wines of gd yrs can improve for 10 or so, and the great chx of these yrs can profit from double that time.

2025 Hot, dry; v. low yields. Powerful Cab Sauv but balanced.
2024 Difficulties ripening Cab Sauv. Variable. Earlier drinking.
2023 Mildew. Powerful but balanced Cab Sauv. Potential to age.
2022 Hot, dry. Cab Sauv dense but supple tannins; gd ageing potential.
2021 Complicated: frost, rain, mildew. Cab Sauv variable but classic. Be choosy.
2020 Cab Sauv rich, dark, expressive. High alc but elegant. Low yields.

2019 Great balance; concentrated, fresh. Much Cab Sauv in blends. Will age.
2018 Pure, aromatic Cab Sauv. Rich, powerful (alc high), balanced. Long term.
2017 Attractive wines: gd balance, fairly early drinking. Volumes often small.
2016 Cab Sauv with colour, depth, structure. Vintage to look forward to.
Earlier fine vintages: 15 10 09 08 06 05 00 98 96 95 90 89 88 86 85 82 75 70 66 62 61 59 55 53 49 48 47 45 29 28.

St-Émilion / Pomerol
2025 Merlot generally gd. Colour, fruit, structure. Low yields.
2024 Mildew, coulure, rot. Low yields. Modest yr.
2023 Merlot hit hardest by mildew. Yields variable; gd in top terroirs.
2022 As Méd. Young vines suffered. Merlot excellent on limestone, clay soils.
2021 Merlot hit by frost, mildew. Low yields, variable quality. Cab Fr did better.
2020 Merlot rich and gourmand. Cabs Fr/Sauv also v.gd. Great potential.
2019 Drought. Merlot excellent on limestone, clay soils. Sandier areas suffered.
2018 Powerful but pure. Best from limestone, clay soils. Mildew affected yields.
2017 Balanced, classic fruit-cake flavours. Will be quite early drinking.
2016 As Méd. Some young vines suffered in drought but overall v.gd.
Earlier fine vintages: 15 10 09 05 01 00 98 95 90 89 88 85 82 71 70 67 66 64 61 59 53 52 49 47 45.

Red burgundy

Côte d'Or Côte de Beaune reds generally mature sooner than grander wines of Côte de Nuits. Earliest drinking dates are for lighter commune wines, eg. Volnay, Beaune; latest for GCs, eg. Chambertin, Richebourg. Red burg, with less tannin, is generally more appealing young than equivalent red Bx. But great red burg is more age-worthy, and rewarding, than is usually supposed.
2025 Growing season gd, challenging harvest, rain delays. Indicators gd to v.gd.
2024 Wet, mildew and more. Côte de Nuits worse hit than Côte de Beaune.
2023 Huge crop, fewer stems used. Careful sorting = quality, quantity.
2022 Approachable now but yrs to go. Balance, delicious length. Nascent classic.
2021 Out of adversity came something approaching triumph; gd early drinkers.
2020 Concentrated: some superb, some too robust. Follow favoured producers.
2019 June/July heat gave lavish wines, many great, gd acid, a few too robust.
2018 Sumptuous reds, gd young or old. Some rather too lush, opulent.
2017 Generally appealing, enjoyable now. Don't overlook for bargains.
2016 Spring frost. Some spectacular reds with great energy, fresh acidity.
2015 Dense, concentrated, as 05 but juiciness of 10. Patience needed.
Earlier fine vintages: (drink or keep) 12 10 09 08 05 02 99 96; (mature) 93 90 89 85 78 76 71 69.

White burgundy

Côte d'Or Whites are now rarely (sadly) made for long ageing, but top wines should still improve for 10 yrs or more. Most Mâconnais and Chalonnais (St-Véran, Mâcon-Villages, Montagny) usually best drunk young (2–5 yrs). Scourge of premox still hangs over wines post-1995 and 5 yrs+ old. Beware.
2025 Warm spring accelerated growth. Harvest started early. Initially looks v.gd.
2024 Challenging: rain, mildew. As reds.
2023 Generous harvest. Variable, some excellent, others lush, less refined.
2022 Summer heat after early rain. Abundant flavours. Some marvellous.
2021 Trounced by frost, but survivors are promising. Will be rare jewels.
2020 Crop gd, unlike reds. Powerful, surprising freshness; v. promising.
2019 Rich after summer heat. Best retained delicious acidity. Some stellar.

2018 Hot season challenged the vignerons. Opulent. Choose carefully.
2017 Triumph. Poised, elegant, lingering. All excellent. Rivals 14.
2016 Small, frosted crop, inconsistent results. Some wonders. Don't ignore.
Earlier fine vintages (ready): 15 14 12 10 09 08 07 05 02 99.

Chablis Meteorogical infamy has been Chablis's lot in recent yrs, yet gd wines continue to be made. Hail and frost the main offenders, allied to biblical rainfall in 2024. GCs of top vintages need at least 5 yrs, can age superbly for 15+; PCs proportionately less, but give them 3 yrs at least. Then serve at cellar temp, cool not iced, and decant. Yes, really.
2025 Promising growing season. Harvest rain an issue. Quality generally gd.
2024 Rain, frost, hail. Extremely challenging, yet quality is promising.
2023 Summer oscillated between heat/rain. Challenging; results generally gd.
2022 Well-balanced wines in gd volumes, despite drought and heat.
2021 Frost calamity. Some remarkably gd survivors.
2020 Hot and dry, but wines have turned out well, esp at higher end.
Earlier fine vintages: 19 18 17 12 10 08 02 00.

Beaujolais

25 Low volume, gd quality. 24 Weather-beaten, esp rain. Small crop.
23 Variable summer, but promising. 22 Early harvest, wines lovely now, best will keep. 21 Dismal yr, some successes. 20 Harvest v. early, drinking well.
19 Hot, dry summer, gorgeously juicy, satisfying wines.

Languedoc-Roussillon

2025 Heat spikes, storms, wildfire; timely rains. Yields down; quality looks v.gd.
2024 Small quantites, drought. Extended ripening, pristine fruit, elegance.
2023 Dry, esp Rouss. Low yields. Intense, fresh reds, esp Carignan, Mourvèdre.
2022 Drought lowered some yields, overall gd quality. Carignan, Grenache top.
2021 Frost, drought, pre-harvest rain in Ldoc, variable. Rouss fared better, v.gd.

SW France

2025 Earliest on record due to heatwave. Hot days, cool nights = exciting wines.
2024 Challenging. Spring frost, storms, hail. Best producers look promising.
2023 Mixed, but generally low yields. Mildew, hail, heat. Pick carefully.
2021 Relentless frost, rain, mildew, more rain. Keep to older vintages for reds.
2022 Crop size reduced by frost, then drought and heat. Quality likely to be gd.
2020 Summer heat, drought. A little uneven but gd, occasionally exceptional.

Northern Rhône

Small hillside plots, often granite, some schist; top reds (Cornas, Côte-Rôtie, Hermitage) can live 30 yrs+. White Hermitage can age as red.
2025 Exceptional reds, small harvest; will age. Compact whites; tiny in Condrieu.
2024 Superior to much of France. Reds pure, inviting. Tasty Cornas. Whites gd, expressive; Condrieu variable.
2023 Variable, tannins mild, can cellar. Côte-Rôtie gd, also n of St-Joseph, Cornas. Condrieu v.gd, whites gd.
2022 Prominent fruit, brio at Côte-Rôtie, Cornas, reds gd, some v.gd. Appealing, rounded, table-friendly whites.
2021 Aromatic reds. Hermitage, Cornas (depth, gd) fuller than aromatic Côte-Rôtie. Not to keep. Beautiful whites, top Condrieu.
2020 Stylish reds. Côte-Rôtie perfumed, outstanding Hermitage (r/w). Top whites, esp if Marsanne-based, v.gd.

2019 Tremendous reds, Côte-Rôtie; like 16 with more stuffing. No hurry. Whites concentrated. Note Hermitage, St-Joseph.

2018 Scaled-up reds, Hermitage, Côte-Rôtie. Whites: depth, surprising freshness; Condrieu, Hermitage, St-Péray.

2017 V.gd, esp Côte-Rôtie. Full reds, more robust than 16, firm tannins, give time. Whites for hearty food, Condrieu variable.

2016 Reds harmonious, classic at Côte-Rôtie, gd to v.gd. Stylish Cornas. Marvellous Hermitage whites, other whites precise.

Southern Rhône

2025 Small harvest, late rains, v. heavy at Châteauneuf, after high heat. Concentrated reds, fair freshness, Châteauneuf uneven. Sturdy whites.

2024 Pleasing low alc, fresh, stylish potential on reds. Elegant Châteauneuf, dynamic, v.gd Gigondas. Clear flow whites.

2023 Grenache handled heat, drought. Gigondas did well, Châteauneuf mixed, purity in top wines. Whites gd, balanced.

2022 Heat; dense reds, forward aromas, some tannin issues, best balanced. Châteauneuf gd. Firm, full whites, for *la table*.

2021 Select with care: v. drinkable, aromatic reds from best names. Whites can be exceptional, best-ever Châteauneuf.

2020 Can be variable at modest price. Top: rich, splendid, gd acidity. Whites tricky from less gd zones, stick to best.

2019 Deep reds. Intense Grenache. Châteauneuf back on form, Gigondas excellent. Top names demand patience. Whites v.gd.

2018 Mixed, can be gd. Early signs of advance in reds already. Note Vinsobres, Lirac, Rasteau. Whites v. full.

2017 Drought, can be variable. Full, bold reds, tannins coming together. Top doms best. Rasteau gd. Full whites.

2016 Excellent for all. Sensuous reds, much life. Sun-filled whites; keep some.

Champagne

2025 Small crop but high quality, ripe fruit.

2024 Frost, hail, mildew, but some promising Chard. Freshness

2023 Large yield, enormous berries. Overall promising, esp Chard.

2022 Relief at big, gd yr; hot in vein of 18, but long growing season.

2021 Cold spring, April frost, mildew = v. low yields. Sad in Marne V.

2020 Miraculous trio: 18 19 20. Beautiful ripe forward yr.

2019 Excellent quality. Pure fruit, tension, better acidity than much-lauded 18.

2018 Best in Pinot GCs of N Montagne. Chard more mixed: heat stress.

2017 Athletic wines of grace, energy. Fresh early drinkers.

Earlier fine vintages: 12 10 09 08 07 06 04 02 00 98 96 95 92 90.

The Loire

2025 Hot, dry, a little rain at harvest. Excellent potential in all styles.

2024 Wet summer, harvest. Muscadet hit hard. Whites light; delicate reds.

2023 Warm summer, pre-harvest rain. Yields gd, quality potentially gd.

2022 Despite heat/drought, v.gd to exceptional: early, perfect fruit; gd yields.

2021 Frost, mildew, hail. Fine autumn. Fresher style than recently.

Alsace

2025 Dry, warm days, cool nights; earliest harvest in memory; promising, esp crystalline Ries.

2024 V. wet. Rain means wines from flatland vyds better than usual.

2023 V.gd Pinot N, Ries. Outstanding Muscat (best since 10). No noble rot, little if any memorable late-harvest.
2022 Gd, lowish acid, clay-limestone soils best; great Sylvaner.
2021 Tumultuous rain, disease. Pinots suffered, but sunny Sept gave fine Ries.
2020 Refined, elegant, scented across board, as growers master climate change.
2019 Hot; top Ries, Pinot Gr, Gewurz can be v.gd. Plains wines could struggle.
Earlier fine vintages: 15 10 08 02 96 95 92 90 89 88.

Abymes Sav On limestone rubble of Mont Granier by APREMONT. DYA. Vin de SAV AOP cru. Jacquère grape. Try ★ 13 Lunes (organic/bio), ★★ A&M QUENARD, ★★ Dom de Chevillard (organic), Crocs Blancs, ★ Giachino (organic), Labbé, P&S Ravier.

Agapé Al ★★→★★★★ Riquewihr winery, est 2007 by Vincent Sipp after split from SIPP-MACK. Five top villages, 12 ha, 25 parcels give v. saline, bone-dry, sustainably organic wines; quite the following. Best: PINOT BL **22**, RIES GC Rosacker 20, SCHOENENBOURG 19'.

Agisson, Jean-Philippe Lo ★★★ Classy oak-aged SANCERRE; also runs cellars at DAGUENEAU. Single-vyd CUVÉES La Purgatoire, Les Chasseignes, top-notch 19 20' 21 **22'** 23 (25); gd POUILLY-FUMÉ La Belle Endormie.

Agrapart Champ ★★★ **17'** 18' 19' 20 21 Precise CHAMP from deep chalk vyds in AVIZE. Impressive quartet: Experience, L'Avizoise 19, Mineral, 20, also ungrafted single parcel ***Venus 20.*** Also Terroirs Extra Brut GC BLANC DE BLANCS GC, Les 7 Crus. Revealingly named Complanted 21.

Ajaccio Cors ★★→★★★ AOP W CORS. Lots of granite. SCIACCARELLU star here, lovely VERMENTINO too.

Alary, Dom S Rh ★★★ Top CAIRANNE, stylish red guided by son Jean-Etienne's Burg schooling. Time-honoured sites, mature vines. Forthright, long-lived Cairanne Jean de Verde (r, gd w), full Brunote (r), stylish CÔTES DU RH (w), gd VDF L'Exclus.

Albert de Conti, Dom SW Fr Branch of C family (TOUR DES GENDRES). Polymorphe MALBEC/CAB SAUV; striking dry MUSCADELLE Conti-ne Périgourdine; pét-nat.

Allemand, Thierry N Rh ★★★★ 01' 05' 06' 07' 08' **09' 10'** 12' 13' 15' **16' 17' 18'** 19' 20' 21' 22' 23' 24' 25' Stirring tale: Thiérry started from scratch, now son Théo. Top CORNAS, organic DOM, low sulphur. Deep, smoky wines. Best: Reynard (mineral, complex, 20 yrs+); Chaillot (racy) drinks sooner.

Alliet, Philippe Lo ★★★★ Leading DOM in CHINON; Philippe with son Pierre. ***Coteau de Noiré, L'Huisserie*** 05' 09' 10' 15' 16 17 18' 19 20 22' 23 (25). VIEILLES VIGNES, white gd.

Aloxe-Corton C d'O ★★→★★★ 10' 12' 15' **17** 18' 19' 20' 21 22' 23 24 The n end of CÔTE DE BEAUNE, famous for GC CORTON, CORTON-CHARLEMAGNE. Others less compelling. Tasty reds improved by recent warm yrs. Reasonable value. Best: Capitain-Gagnerot, Follin-Arbelet, RAPET, Senard, TOLLOT-BEAUT.

Alsace ★★→★★★★ Vosges rain-shadow effect means driest French wine region: aromatic, fruity, full white, increasingly gd PINOT N; some gd SYRAH (strictly VDF). Varietal labelling, so wines easy to grasp. Sec (dr), demi-sec (medium-dr), *moelleux* (medium-sw), *doux* (sw) indicated on back label, or numerical scale, so you know what you're getting (more or less).

Alsace Grand Cru Al ★★★→★★★★ **08' 10' 12 13 14** (esp RIES) **115 17' 18 19'** 20 23' Only 51 GC, incl some of the world's greatest vyds (Brand, HENGST, RANGEN, Sporen). Since 22 vintage, Hengst, Kirchberg de Barr, Vorbourg PINOT N can also be GC-labelled. Huge geological diversity means terroir-lovers' bonanza; but some GCs are too large; PC in gd sites coming v. slowly if at all (bureaucratic roadblocks). Some of world's most age-worthy whites (40 yrs+) **61 67 71 75 83 90 08 10** 19.

Alzipratu Cors ★★★→★★★★ Between sea and mtns; bio: gd-value Fiumeseccu; Iniziu (r), pale herbal NIELLUCCIU; Pumonte (r/w), serious CUVÉES.

Amadieu, Pierre S Rh ★★→★★★ Merchant-vyd owner, gd sites. Altitude at GIGONDAS: Grand Romane, Romane Machotte (50s GRENACHE); gd CLAIRETTE. CAIRANNE DOM Hautes Cances (dashing). VACQUEYRAS merchant range.

Amiot, Guy & Fils C d'O ★★★ CHASSAGNE family originally from Paris; PC Cailleret is winery's "back garden"; *bâtonnage*, long *élevage* yield plump wines at variance with current citrus-infused zeitgeist. Tiny production mouthfilling MONTRACHET.

Amirault, Yannick Lo ★★★★ Leading DOM in BOURGUEIL, ST NICOLAS DE BOURGUEIL. Classy age-worthy Grand Clos, Les Malgagnes, Petite Cave, Quartiers: 05 09 10' 15' 16 17 18' 19 20 22' 23 (25). CHENIN BL Bâtard-Princesse, gd IGP experiment.

Ampeau C d'O ★★★ Step back in time at MEURSAULT DOM: long-aged releases (c.25 yrs old). Properly mature, succulent whites, replete with truffled fruit: reminder of what was lost through premature oxidation. Reds less sumptuous.

Angerville, Marquis d' C d'O ★★★→★★★★ Leading VOLNAY DOM. Great range of PCS topped by CLOS des Ducs (MONOPOLE). Elegant, balanced, harmonious. Racy ALIGOTÉ. Daughter Margot now involved. *See* DOM DU PÉLICAN.

Anjou Lo ★→★★★★ Complex region, exciting dry CHENIN BL in ANJOU BL, SAVENNIÈRES. Sweet COTEAUX DU LAYON, QUARTS DE CHAUME getting rare. Reds more variable, but ANJOU-VILLAGES can be cellar-worthy. Off-dry, trad rosé CABERNET D'ANJOU, Rosé d'Anjou can be fun. Some leading VDF.

What is the most popular Occitan wine name? Médoc.

Anjou Blanc Lo ★→★★★★ 17 19' 20 21 22 23 (25) Most exciting Lo AOP; laser-sharp dry CHENIN BL. Try Bablut, BAUDOUIN, ***Belargus***, Bergerie, Bernadeau (VDF), CADY, Fesles, Juchepie, Le Clos Galerne, OGEREAU, PIERRE-BISE, PIERRE MÉNARD, PLAISANCE, ***Richard Leroy*** (VdF), SANSONNIÈRE (VdF), Terra Vita Vinum. Don't drink too young.

Anjou-Villages Lo ★→★★★ 15' 16 17 18' 19 20 22 23 (25) Cellar-worthy CABS FR/SAUV blends; 100% Cab Sauv from schistose soils can be gd surprise; Bergerie, PIERRE-BISE, ***Ogereau***. Enclave Anjou Brissac (aka Anjou-Villages-Brissac): Bablut, Montgilet, ***Rochelles***.

Antech, Maison Ldoc ★★★→★★★★ Françoise A-Gazeau (7th generation), leading light of LIMOUX fizz: M Le Mauzac simply best BLANQUETTE; CRÉMANT Eugénie delights. Méthode Ancestrale sweetly fruity.

AOP (appellation d'origine protégée) / AC or AOC (appellation contrôlée) Government control of origin and production (but not quality) of most top French wines; around 45% of total. AOP is new term.

Aphillanthes, Dom Les S Rh ★★→★★★ 22' 23 24 25 Authentic organic/bio DOM on baked, stone-laden PLAN DE DIEU. Punchy wines, value: des Galets, VIEILLES VIGNES (50s GRENACHE). CÔTES DU RH (r/w); GIGONDAS Promesse; RASTEAU 1921.

Apremont Sav Largest cru of SAV, thus quality varies. Steely, light Jacquère on limestone rubble. Keep up to 4 yrs. ★: 13 Lunes (organic/bio), Blard, Masson, Perrier, Richel. ★★: Dupraz (organic). ★★→★★★: Chevillard (organic), Apffel (organic/bio), Giachino (organic).

Arbin Sav A SAV cru. Dark, spicy MONDEUSE on steep slopes. Drink to 8 yrs+. ★: A&M QUENARD, Cellier de la Baraterie (organic), F Trosset, Jacquet. ★: Genoux (organic/bio). ★★: Magnin (last yr 22).

Arbois & Arbois-Pupillin Jura wine tourism capital. AOP of N Jura: (w) CHARD and/or SAVAGNIN; (r) PINOT N, POULSARD, TROUSSEAU; VIN JAUNE. Several private growers now organic, many bio. ★: D Petit, Overnoy-Crinquand. ★★: Renardière. ★★: Bottes Rouges, Fumey-Chatelain, Gahier, Grapp'A, La Pinte, Ratte. ★★→★★★: ***Touraize***. ★★→★★★: Adeline Houillon & Renaud Bruyère, Aviet, Cellier Saint

Benoît (contributor personal connection), Dom de la Borde, DOM DU PÉLICAN, Philippe Chatillon. ★★★→★★★★: MAISON OVERNOY, ***Stéphane Tissot***, ***St-Pierre***, Tournelle. For extra value look to Fruitière Vinicole d'Arbois (co-op).

Ardèche S Rh ★→★★ 23 24 IGP Granite terraces, often more flexible rules VDF (DOM des Accoles). Also HQ for Rhône Vin Nature, all VdF (A Calek, Les Deux Terres, Mazel). Quality rising, often gd value. Direct reds; MARSANNE, VIOGNIER (CHAPOUTIER). Best: SYRAH, also GAMAY (often old vyds). Restrained Ardèche CHARD by LOUIS LATOUR (Grand Ardèche much oak). Also CH de la Selve; Doms de Vigier, du Grangeon, JF Jacouton; Mas d'Intras (organic).

Ardoisières, Dom des Sav IGP Vin des Allobroges; organic/bio; vyds outside AOP. Superb, eclectic ★★★: Améthyste (r), Quartz Altesse, Erythrite MONDEUSE, Schist (w). ★★: Argile (r/w). ★★: Silice NÉGOCE CUVÉES (r/w) excellent value.

Arlaud C d'O ★★★→★★★★ Leading MOREY-ST-DENIS estate energized by Cyprien A. Assured flavours from exceptional BOURGOGNE Roncevie up to GCS. Fine Morey PCS. Magnificent vaulted tasting room. Watch.

AR Lenoble Champ ★★★ Siblings in Damery; Chouilly CHARD elegance underwrites focus on res wines aged under cork in magnum. Archetypal BLANC DE BLANCS GC 13' 15 17' 18; BLANC DE NOIRS PC PINOT N Bisseuil perfect antidote 12 13. MV Prestige Les Aventures, single-plot Chouilly.

Arlot, Dom de l' C d'O ★★→★★★ AXA-owned estate; stylish, fragrant across range from HAUTES-CÔTES to GC ROMANÉE-ST-VIVANT. Star: NUITS CLOS des Forêts St-Georges. Reds fully destemmed since 2021. Interesting whites too.

Armand, Comte C d'O ★★★→★★★★ MONOPOLE CLOS des Epeneaux may be POMMARD's most graceful, GC quality. AUXEY, VOLNAY gd value. Stylish ALIGOTÉ.

Arnoux-Lachaux C d'O ★★★★ VOSNE superstar. All change under Charles Lachaux: no-till, high-trellised, unhedged vines, v. light-hand vinification, whole bunches, *élevage* in ceramic "barrels", no oak. Sublime. Breathtaking prices. PCS Grand Suchots, Reignots; GC ROMANÉE-ST-VIVANT.

Arretxea, Dom SW Fr ★★★→★★★★ Pioneering bio estate in remote Basque AOP IROULÉGUY. All styles, but whites (Hegoxuri, Schistes) standout.

Astrelles, Les C d'O ★★→★★★ New GEVREY on block; 12 ha + 6 bought-in yield c.48 wines. All destemmed. Minute production of PC Lavaux St-Jacques, GC MAZIS-CHAMBERTIN. Spanking-new winery 2024.

Aube Champ (aka Côte des Bar) CHAMP's southerly vyds; v.gd PINOT N by great Reims houses (KRUG, VEUVE CLICQUOT). Often different climate from core of Champ; temperamentally Burgundian. Rain, heat 21; promising 22'; capacious 23; low-yield 24 25.

Aubuisières, Dom des Lo ★★→★★★ Leading VOUVRAY dom. Historically a source of fine sweets 89' 90' 96 97 02' 03 08 09 10 14 18 20 22. Focus today on SEC and fizz 20 22 23 (25). Le Bouchet, Le Marigny, Le Petit CLOS superior.

Audoin, Cyril C d'O ★★→★★★ Cyril A crafts MARSANNAY (r); style, conviction, vibrant, lasting flavours: Au Champ Salomon. Varying use of whole bunches, seeks stem ripeness. Also rosé: "white version of PINOT N".

Aupilhac, Dom d' Ldoc ★★★ Excellent bio estate led by MONTPEYROUX champion Sylvan Fadat. Old vines. Les Cocalières (r/w) lightly oaked. La Boda (r/w), v. smart blends. Fabulous 100% CARIGNAN VDF.

Auxey-Duresses C d'O ★★→★★★ (r) 15' 16 17 18' 19' 20' 21 22' 23 24 (w) 14' 15 17' 18 19' 20' 21 22' 23 24 MEURSAULT neighbour. Reds enjoying climate change. Whites, "junior Meursault", can be v.gd: Les Hautés vyd. Best: (r) COCHE-DURY, COMTE ARMAND, d'Auvenay (Boutonniers), Gras, Jessiaume, Paquet, Prunier; (w) Diconne, Lafouge, LEROUX, Paquet, VINCENT J-M, VINCENT P. Source of value.

Avize Champ ★★★★ Côte des Blancs GC CHARD of focus, purity: AGRAPART, Bonville, SELOSSE, DE SOUSA, Thienot. Large co-op provides base wines to biggest houses.

Aÿ Champ ★★★→★★★★ Revered PINOT N village, home of BOLLINGER, DEUTZ. Mix of merchants and growers, more oak than elsewhere (Giraud). Aÿ Rouge (AOP COTEAUX CHAMPENOIS) now excellent in riper yrs 18' 19' 20 22.

Ayala Champ ★★★ 13 14 19' 20' Revitalized AŸ house, owned by BOLLINGER. Try BLANC DE BLANCS 16, BRUT NATURE, BRUT MAJEUR and No. 7 13, ***La Perle 14'***, Collection No. 16.

Ayze (Ayse) Sav ★★ Cru closest to Mont Blanc. Rare Gringet grape: mineral fizz; dry, age-worthy whites. Belluard's iconic winery now re-baptized ★★★ DOM du Gringet (organic), new owner. Exquisite fizz: Dom Béléma (organic), Le Coteau du Môle (dr only), Michel Bufflier, Montessuit, Vallier (dr only).

Bachelet Burg ★★★→★★★★ Long-est CÔTE DE BEAUNE family traces origins to 1648. ***B-Monnot*** for superb village wines and BÂTARD-M, Bernard B (MARANGES), Jean-Claude B for similar quality in CHASSAGNE (PC Boudriotte), ST-AUBIN. No relation to Denis B (great GEVREY-CHAMBERTIN).

Balthazar, Franck N Rh ★★★ **18** 19 **20' 21** 22' 23' 24' 25' Organic, wonderful small DOM at CORNAS. Chaillot (incl 1914 SYRAH), frisky zero-added-sulphur version. Pretty 100% ROUSSANNE ST-PÉRAY (w).

Bandol Prov ★★★→★★★★ Regarded as best red wine of PROV, but rosé still dominates sales. MOURVÈDRE shines at this AOP overlooking Med, supported by GRENACHE, CINSAULT. Rosés vary from Prov-style to darker, gastronomic that can age. Underrated white (5%): CLAIRETTE, UGNI BL, occasionally SAUV BL. Top: DOMS de la Bégude, de la Ribotte, des Trois Filles, du Gros'Noré, Dupuy de Lôme, Guilhem Tournier, La Bastide Blanche, Lafran Veyrolles, La Suffrène, Le Galantin, Mas de la Rouvière, Pibarnon, Pradeaux, RAY-JANE, Roche Redonne, TEMPIER, Terrebrune, Val d'Arenc, Vannières.

Banyuls Rouss ★★★→★★★★ Undervalued, often brilliant VDN from steep, terraced vyds, overlooking Med, nr Spanish border. COLLIOURE same area. From GRENACHE of all colours. Young, fresh style is *rimage*, but stars are RANCIOS, long-aged, pungent, intense. Wood-aged GC, 30 mths min. Divine with dark chocolate. Best: DOMS de la Rectorie, du Mas Blanc, la Tour Vieille, MADELOC, Piétri Géraud, Vial Magnères; Bila-Haut, CLOS Saint Sebastien, COUME DEL MAS, Les Clos de Paulilles. Co-op gd too. *See also* MAURY.

Bardi d'Alquier, Dom Ldoc ★★★→★★★★ Owners Sophie and Thibaut Bardi's FAUGÈRES bio DOM continues to impress. Premières (r), perfumed; Les Grandes Bastides, brooding, truffley SYRAH. Don't ignore Les Vignes du Puits (w).

Barmes-Buècher, Dom Al ★★→★★★ Wettolsheim 18-ha estate, bio (1998), gd CRÉMANT, SGN. Best: lieu-dit CLOS Sand RIES 19' 24', SYLVANER Rosenberg **22'**, GC Steingrubler GEWURZ.

Barrique 225-litre oak barrel. Now more subtle use, or none. Cost: €850+/barrel.

Barsac Saut ★★→★★★★ 14 15' 16' 18 **19 20 22** 23 24 (25) Neighbour of SAUT, similar botrytized wines from lower-lying limestone; fresher, less powerful; 25 potential quality. Top: ***Climens***, COUTET, DOISY-DAËNE, ***Doisy-Védrines***. Value: Cantegril, Closiot, La Clotte Cazalis, Liot.

Barthod, Ghislaine C d'O ★★★→★★★★ Quintessence of CHAMBOLLE-MUSIGNY. Son Clément further refining style. Grace and harmony abound, delicacy yet depth. Wonderful range of 11 different PCS, incl Baudes, Beaux Bruns, Cras, Fuées = Chambolle masterclass. BOURGOGNE Rouge can age 10 yrs, gd value.

Bâtard-Montrachet C d'O ★★★★ 08' 09' 10 12 14' 15 17' 18 19' 20' 21 22' 23 24 Most opulent of MONTRACHET GCS, 12 ha (between 40+ owners), downslope from Le Montrachet. More power than neighbours Bienvenues-B-M (more elegant) and CRIOTS B-M. Seek out: BACHELET-Monnot, BOILLOT (both H and J-M), FAIVELEY, GAGNARD, LATOUR, LEFLAIVE, LEROUX, MOREY, O LEFLAIVE, PERNOT, RAMONET, SAUZET, VOUGERAIE. Also J-C BACHELET, J CARILLON for Bienvenues version.

Baudouin, Patrick Lo ★★→★★★ Figurehead in ANJOU. Top dry single-vyd CUVÉES: CLOS de Bruandières, Le Cornillard, Zersiles 16 18 19 20 23 (25). Also COTEAUX DU LAYONS 1896, Les Bruandières. Fine QUARTS DE CHAUME.

Baudry, Dom Bernard Lo ★★★→★★★★ No. 1 in CHINON? Probably. Now run by son Matthieu. Cellar uber-classy La Croix Boissée (limestone), Le Clos Guillot (clay, limestone), Les Grézeaux (gravel) 05' 09 10' 15' 16 17 18' 19 20 21 22' 23 (25). New Les Mollières (limestone) decent. Drink Les Granges (sand), white, rosé young.

Baumard, Dom des Lo ★★ Renowned ANJOU DOM run by Florent Baumard. Cellar bone-dry SAVENNIÈRES CLOS du Papillon 02' 05 08 10' 14 18 19 20 (22) (23) (25). COTEAUX DU LAYON, QUARTS DE CHAUME 03 05 07' 09 10 16 18 19 (20) (22) (25), serve as fresh, linear gateway wines.

Baux-de-Provence, Les Prov ★★★ Beautiful, touristy village, AOP. Almost all organic. Mostly red: CAB SAUV, GRENACHE, SYRAH. White: CLAIRETTE, GRENACHE BL, Rolle, ROUSSANNE. TRÉVALLON best, prefers IGP Alpilles. Also gd: CH ROMANIN, Dalmeran, d'Estoublon, DOM HAUVETTE, Lauzieres, Mas de Carita, Mas de Gourgonnier, Mas de la Dame, Mas Ste Berthe, Terres Blanches, Valdition; atypical Milan.

Béarn SW Fr ★→★★ AOP DYA Reds from ★ JURANÇON co-op, DOMS Guilhémas, Lapeyre. Same grapes as MADIRAN, Jurançon.

Beaucastel, Ch de S Rh ★★★★ 05' 06' 07' 09' 10' 12' 13' 15' 16' 17' 18' 19' 20 21 22' 23 24 Organic CHÂTEAUNEUF estate, large galet-stone soils: old MOURVÈDRE, core of exceptional Hommage à Jacques Perrin (r, 30 yrs+), 100-yr-old ROUSSANNE VIEILLES VIGNES (w, 5–25 yrs). Only 30% GRENACHE, dark-fruited, easy red (less grand now). Complex CÔTES DU RH Coudoulet de Beaucastel (r, 10 yrs+). Famille Perrin GIGONDAS, RASTEAU, VINSOBRES (top) all authentic. Organic Perrin Nature Côtes du Rh (r/w). La Vieille Ferme (r/w/rosé) v. gd value. Maison Les Alexandrins, N Rh merchant-vyds venture. Eco cellars (no concrete), also gin, grape-scented oils, Miraval PROV rosé, shops, restaurant. (*See also* Tablas Creek, US.)

Beaujolais Beauj ★→★★★ Now resurgent name. Time to rediscover insistent fruit flavours; more structure from hillside vyds. Avoid industrial examples. Also sold as COTEAUX BOURGUIGNONS. Can be simple yet serious. Serve cool.

Beaujolais Primeur / Nouveau Beauj Raised image, destroyed reputation: BEAUJ of new vintage, released on 3rd Wed in Nov. Dead end, not a slip road to greater delight. Enjoy juicy fruit, then move on. Still casts a baleful shadow.

Beaujolais-Villages Beauj ★★→★★★ 19' 20' 21 22' 23 24 Widespread appellation: 38 communes, usually hillside. May specify best village, eg. Lantigné. Try CH de Basty, Ch des Vergers, F Berne, F Forest, J-M BURGAUD, N Chemarin. Wines of quality, value.

Beaumes-de-Venise S Rh ★★ (r) 19' 20' 22' 23 24' Village nr GIGONDAS, mix of Triassic high zones, plain vyds. Emphatic reds: CH Redortier; DOMS de Fenouillet, Durban, LA BOUÏSSIÈRE (character), la Ferme St-Martin (organic), Les Baies Gouts, Martinelle, Mathiflo, Piéblanc (organic), St-Amant (gd w). Leave for 2 yrs. VDN MUSCAT, serve cold, grapey-honeyed, ages too: DOMS Beaumalric, Bernardins (complex), Coyeux, DURBAN (rich, 20 yrs), Fenouillet (brisk), Fontavin (stylish), Perséphone (stylish), Pigeade (v.gd), VIDAL-FLEURY, co-op Rhonéa. Tender CÔTES DU RH whites (dr Muscat, VIOGNIER).

Beaune C d'O ★★→★★★ 10' 12 15' 16 17 18' 19' 20 21 22' 23 24 Wine capital of Burg, more reliable than exciting. Classic merchants: BOUCHARD, CHANSON, DROUHIN, JADOT, LATOUR; more recent contenders Bernstein, Lemoine, LEROUX, Moret D, Pacalet. Top DOMS: Bellène, Besancenot, Croix, DE MONTILLE, Dominique LAFON, Morot, plus iconic HOSPICES DE BEAUNE. Too many red PCS devalue coinage, but try Bressandes, Cras, VIGNES Franches for grace; more power from Grèves. White: ***Clos des Mouches (Drouhin)***, CLOS St-Landry.

Beauregard, Ch de Burg ★★→★★★ Unmissable POUILLY-FUISSÉ: Frédéric Burrier: Les Reisses, Ménétrières, Vers Cras. Fine BEAUJ: FLEURIE, MOULIN-À-VENT.

Beaurenard, Dom de S Rh ★★★ 19' 20 21' 22' 23' 24 Organic/bio CHÂTEAUNEUF, young-generation drive, consistency. Handsome red, stylish white. Boisrenard old-vine, deeper, some oak (r/w). Two gd RASTEAU reds (stately and old-vine Argiles Bleus).

Belargus, Dom Lo ★★★★ ANJOU superstar. New-wave ANJOU BL, dry, mineral, acid-rich (Bonnes Blanches, Quarts, Rouères, ***Treilles***, more). SAVENNIÈRES (Gaudrets, Ruchères) similar 18 19 20 21 22 23 (25). QUARTS DE CHAUME (increasingly rare) worth a try.

Bellivière, Dom de Lo ★★★→ ★★★★ Top DOM in COTEAUX DU LOIR, JASNIÈRES run by Clément Nicolas. Precise, mineral CHENIN BL: Calligramme, VIEILLES VIGNES Éparses (dr/sw) 15' 16' 18' 19 20' 22 23 (25). Drink others younger. Reds (Hommage à Louis Derré, Rouge-Gorge), v.gd Pineau d'Aunis.

Bergerac SW Fr ★→★★★ (w) 20 22 23 24 (25) AOP, been in shadow of BX for too long but now breaking free, showing own identity. Varied landscape, rolling hills, more continental climate. Multitude of appellations, Côtes de Bergerac for sweet white or fuller red from lower yields. Montravel more limestone soils. Huge variations in styles, quality. Best: ALBERT DE CONTI, ★★ CH de la Jaubertie, DOM de l'Ancienne Cure, Malfourat, MOULIN CARESSE (also Montravel AOP), Thénac, Tirecul La Gravière, ★★★ ***Tour des Gendres***, VIGNOBLE des Verdots, reliable co-op Cave de Sigoules. *See* sub-AOPs: MONBAZILLAC, PÉCHARMANT and SAUSSIGNAC.

Bertagna, Dom C d'O ★★★ VOUGEOT-based DOM, impressive roster of GCS, PCS, incl MONOPOLE CLOS de La Perrière, 1 ha VOSNE Beaux Monts. Abundant fruit, gd depth. Also CHAMBOLLE Les Amoureuses, planted on rocky sliver, tiny quantity.

Beyer, Léon Al ★★★★ Since 1580, one of AL's great names. Comtes d'Eguisheim GEWURZ (GC Pfersigberg) one of best; RIES R de Beyer showcases underrated GC Eichberg. Dry, food-friendly, virtually ageless (40 yrs+). Grand SGNS 71', 94', 98'.

Bichot, Maison Albert Burg ★★→★★★★ Major BEAUNE merchant/grower, DOMS in BEAUJ (Rochegrès), CHAB (LONG-DEPAQUIT), MERCUREY (Adélie), NUITS (CLOS Frantin), POMMARD (Pavillon). Impressive, far more reliable than previously. Largest buyer at HOSPICES auction (25% by value, 2025).

Billaud Chab ★★★→★★★★ Difficult CHAB choice between DOM Billaud-Simon back on form under FAIVELEY ownership and Samuel B's sensational wine under own label, incl value BOURGOGNE d'Or. Both brilliant, age-worthy. Proper Chab.

Billecart-Salmon Champ ★★★★ Revered family house, 7th generation. Supremely reliable Rosé; Louis BLANC DE BLANCS 08 12; single-plot CLOS St-Hilaire 02 04' 05' 06 09; NF Billecart 02 08; excellent ***Elisabeth Salmon Rosé*** 02 06' 09 12. Innovative Les Rendez-vous: No. 3 MEUNIER, No. 4 CHARD, No. 5 PINOT N. Chef de CAVE Florent Nys: focus on single vyds, lower dosage. Impeccably run.

Bize, Simon C d'O ★★★ Chisa B makes delicious bio whole-bunch reds, from BOURGOGNE to GC LATRICIÈRES-CHAMBERTIN. Also SAVIGNY Grands Liards, PCS Guettes, Vergelesses; tasty whites. Once dependable, now exemplary. Value.

Blagny C d'O ★★→★★★ 10' 12 15' 16' 17 18' 19' 20' 21 22' 23 24 On hillside above MEURSAULT, PULIGNY. Overlooked until recently. Reliable value. Own AOP for reds, now shedding austere cloak. Whites sold as Meursault-Blagny PC. Evocative vyd names: La Jeunelotte, Pièce Sous le Bois, Sous le Dos d'Ane. Best: (r) Lamy-Pillot, LEROUX, MATROT; (w) de Cherisey, JOBARD, LATOUR, LEFLAIVE.

Blanc de Blancs White from white grapes only, esp CHAMP. Note: describes style, not quality.

Blanc de Noirs White (or slightly pink or "blush", or "gris") wine from red grapes, esp CHAMP: more elegant now, v. modish.

Blanck, Paul & Fils Al ★★★→★★★★ Five GC, four lieu-dits, 35 wines, 80% exported: GEWURZ, PINOT GR, RIES (best, GC SCHLOSSBERG 18' 19' 23), SYLVANER (22' v.gd).

Blanquette de Limoux Ldoc ★★ Lively, appley fizz; 90% MAUZAC, plus CHARD/ CHENIN BL. AOP CRÉMANT DE LO, more classic with Chard, Chenin Bl, PINOT N, less Mauzac. Ancestrale original sweet style. Sieur d'Arques co-op dominates. Try Delmas, La Coume-Lumet, LAURENS, Les Hautes Terres, MAISON ANTECH, Monsieur S, Robert.

Blavia Bx ★→★★ 19 20 22 23 (25) Ex-Blaye AOP (2025). Site-specific parcels within BLAYE-CÔTES DE BX. MALBEC-LED, with CABS SAUV/FR, MERLOT.

Blaye-Côtes de Bordeaux Bx ★→★★ 20 22 23 (25) Mainly (90%) MERLOT-led red AOP on right bank of Gironde. A little dry white (mainly SAUV BL). Best CHX: Bel-Air la Royère, Bourdieu, Cantinot, des Tourtes, Gigault (CUVÉE Viva), Haut-Bertinerie, Haut-Canteloup, Haut-Grelot, Jonqueyres, Monconseil-Gazin, Mondésir-Gazin, Montfollet, Peybonhomme Les Tours, Roland la Garde. Also go-ahead VIGNERONS de Tutiac co-op (r/w).

Boeckel, Dom Al ★★★ Mittelbergheim organic winery; rich but refined, outstanding SYLVANER GC ZOTZENBERG 20' 22'; fine RIES Wibbelsberg 17' 19'; rich CLOS Eugénie 18 19'.

Boillot C d'O Leading Burg family. ★★★ Jean-Marc (POMMARD), esp fine, long-lived (w); ★★★→★★★★ Henri (MEURSAULT), stylish, thrilling (r/w); ★★★ Louis (CHAMBOLLE), great reds, both Côtes; brother Pierre (DOM Lucien B) ★★→★★★ (GEVREY). Marthe Henry B (Meursault), no close relation, interesting post-modern wines. Seek out all, esp Henri B.

Boisset, J-C Burg Ultra-successful merchant-grower. Umbrella group for numerous labels. Boisset label in safe hands of winemaker Gregory Patriat, based in NUITS. Try ***Dom de la Vougeraie***. Recent additions: (Burg) Alex Gambal, VINCENT GIRARDIN. High-end JCB CRÉMANTS labelled as "Brut Burgundy". Also in BEAUJ, Jura, California (Gallo connection), Canada, Chile, Uruguay.

Boizel Champ ★★★ Family-run but part of Lanson Empire value. BLANC DE BLANCS NV, esp on base of 17' 18' 19'. CUVÉE Sous Bois, wood well handled. Prestige Cuvée Joyau de France 08 12 (released on PLACE DE BX), Joyau de France Rosé 12.

Bollinger Champ ★★★★ Great classic house; power, glory; chef de CAVE Denis Bunner. BRUT Special NV sings since 2012, RD 02 04' 05' 07 08, Grande Année 08 12 14 15', Vintage Rosé 12 14 15. Recent releases show new faces of eponymous PINOT N villages, thus far Verzenay (VZ 15 16 19), Tauxières 17 20, AŸ 18. Sublime ***Vieilles Vignes Françaises*** 12 15; La Côte aux Enfants (still) 14 16, new sparkling 13 14' 15. B Cuvée instead of GA for 16.

Bonnaud, Ch Henri Prov ★★★→★★★★ Top DOM in tiny AOP PALETTE, nr Aix. Silky red, elegant rosé. Quintessence (CLAIRETTE) v. fine.

Bonneau du Martray, Dom C d'O (r) ★★★ (w) ★★★→★★★★ CORTON-CHARLEMAGNE (now labelled Charlemagne), owned by Stanley Kroenke (Screaming Eagle, US); 3 ha leased to DRC. Intense, long-ageing, glorious fruit, with underlying minerality. Older vintages not so sure. Some red CORTON. Tiny holding of Bâtard-Montrachet.

Bonnes-Mares C d'O ★★★★ 93 96' 99' 02' 05' 09' 10' 12' 15' 16' 18 19 20 21 22' 23 24 GC between CHAMBOLLE-MUSIGNY and MOREY-ST-DENIS with some of latter's robust, *sauvage* character. Structured, firm. Magnificence comes with age. Best: ARLAUD, d'Auvenay, Bart, BRUNO CLAIR, DE VOGÜÉ, Drouhin-Laroze, DUJAC, GROFFIER, H BOILLOT, JADOT, MORTET, ROUMIER, VOUGERAIE.

Bonnet, Alexandre Champ ★★★ In Les Riceys, nearer to CHAB than Épernay. Beguiling range: CÔTEAUX CHAMPENOIS (w) 18 20, La Fôret Rosé de Saignée 16 18 19, Les Contrées (incl all) Sept CÉPAGES 18 19. Les Vignes Blanches 19. Ambassador for long-undervalued vyds of AUBE.

Bonnezeaux Lo ★★★ 47' 89' 90' 95 96' 97' 09' 10' 11' 14 15 18' 19 20 22 23 (25) Overlooked AOP for sweet CHENIN BL from schist. Best: ***Fesles***, Petit Val, Petite Croix, Terrebrune, Trottières. Find Fesles, René Renou/Terrebrune old vintages.

Bordeaux ★→★★ 20 22 23 (25) Catch-all AOP for generic Bx (c. half production). Most brands (***Dourthe***, MOUTON CADET, ***Sichel***) in this category. Up to 10% new grapes (MARSELAN, TOURIGA N, etc.) now permitted. Try CHX Bauduc, Bel Air Perponcher, BONNET, Reignac, Turcaud.

Bordeaux Supérieur Bx ★→★★ 20 22 23 (25) Higher min alc, lower yield, aged longer than BX. Mainly bottled at property. Consistent CHX: Argadens, Bolaire, Camarsac, de Rolland (Astéries), de Seguin, Grand Village, Landereau, Le Grand Verdus, MÉAUME, ***Parenchère*** (CUVÉE Raphaël), Penin, ***Pey la Tour*** (Rés), Pierrail, Reignac, ***Thieuley***.

Borgeot C d'O ★★★ Remigny-based; excellent BOURGOGNE C D'O CHARD, prepares ground for delicious PULIGNY-MONTRACHET Le Meix. SANTENAY Comme Dessus.

Borie-Manoux Bx Admirable BX shipper. Part of Group BCAP: BATAILLEY, LYNCH-MOUSSAS, TROTTEVIEILLE; NÉGOCIANT Mähler-Besse.

Bott-Geyl Al ★★★→★★★★ In Beblenheim, GEWURZ v.gd (Sonnenglanz 15 16), RIES best (GC Mandelberg 17). Stellar GC, esp SCHOENENBOURG 17' 18 19.

Bouchard Père & Fils Burg ★★→★★★ Owned by Artemis Domaines (CLOS DE TART, EUGÉNIE). Rebranded as CÔTE DE BEAUNE DOM: CÔTE DE NUITS vyds transferred to Eugénie. Whites best in MEURSAULT and GC, esp CHEVALIER-MONTRACHET. Flagship reds: BEAUNE VIGNE de L'Enfant Jésus, CORTON. Recent change continues apace; best vyds now under DOM des Cabottes label. Potential finally about to be realized?

Boudignon, Thibaud Lo ★★★★ Leading SAVENNIÈRES DOM. Replanted historic vyds; precise, mineral: ***Clos de la Hutte***, de Fremine, La VIGNE Cendrée, uber-rare Franc de Pied 16 18' 19 20 21 22 23 (25). ANJOU BL v.gd.

Bouïssière, Dom La S Rh ★★★ Major quality GIGONDAS, robust, age well. Font de Tonin (r, 50s GRENACHE), some oak; VACQUEYRAS (r, 60s Grenache); fine CLAIRETTE; Vin de Table (r).

Boulay, Gérard Lo ★★★★ Leader in SANCERRE. Top single-vyd CLOS de Beaujeu, La Côte, ***Monts Damnés*** 17 19 20 21 22' 23 (25). Drink DOM CUVÉE youngish. Red Oriane gd.

Bouley C d'O ★★★ VOLNAY stars, at van of cutting-edge higher-trained viticulture. Delicious reds, esp Volnay PCS, from cousins Thomas and Pierrick at respective DOMS. Engaging from 1st to last sip, never overbearing.

Bourgeois, Henri Lo ★→★★★ Large but high-quality SANCERRE DOM-NÉGOCIANT. Cellar-worthy ES-56 (was La Bourgeoise), ***d'Antan***, Jadis, La Côte des Monts Damnées 17 18 19 20 22' 23 (25). Single-vyd Le Cotelin, Les Côtes aux Valets, Les Ruchons.

Bourgogne Burg ★→★★★ (r) 15' 17 18' 19' 20' 21 22' 23 24 (w) 14' 17' 18 19' 20' 21 22' 23 24 Basic Burg AOP. Seek brilliant egs from top DOMS. Can state subregion, eg. CÔTE CHALONNAISE, HAUTES-CÔTES, or C D'O. White from CHARD unless B ALIGOTÉ. Red from PINOT N unless declassified BEAUJ crus (sold as B GAMAY) or B Passetoutgrains (Pinot/Gamay, with 30%+ of former); v.gd value.

Bourgueil Lo ★★→★★★ 05' 09' 10' 15' 17 18' 19 20' 21 22' 23 (25) Don't overlook this Lo CAB FR AOP. Gravel terraces, clay-limestone soils can be superb: ***Yannick Amirault***, Bel Air, ***Chevalerie***, La Butte, Lamé Delisle Boucard, L'Oubliée, Minière. Drink wines from sandy soils young.

Bouscassé, Dom SW Fr ★★★ 18 19 20 21 22 23 (24) BRUMONT's other property in MADIRAN. Quite ST-ÉM-like reds. Stars: Les Jardins Philosophiques (w, PETIT COURBU); VIEILLES VIGNES (r, TANNAT).

Bouvet-Ladubay Lo ★★→★★★ Of the large fizz houses, this is one of the better.

SAUMUR, CRÉMANT DE LO, huge range covering all bases. Trésor v. reliable, gd value, Brut Zéro, Instinct. ***Ogmius*** excellent, v. rare.

Bouzereau C d'O ★★→★★★ Extended family, MEURSAULT to core. DOM Michel B is leader (marvellous BOURGOGNE C D'O), but try also Jean-Marie B, Philippe B (CH de Cîteaux), Vincent B or B-Gruère & Filles for gd-value whites; v. reliable.

Bouzeron Burg ★★→★★★ 17' 18 19 20' 21 22' 23 24 Tiny CÔTE CHALONNAISE village, unique AOP for ALIGOTÉ. Stricter rules, greater potential than straight BOURGOGNE Aligoté. Can be wonderful, age-worthy. Chanzy, esp ***de Villaine***, outstanding. Also Bourgogne Côte Chalonnaise CHARD, PINOT N.

Bouzy Rouge Champ ★★★ 15' 18' 19 20 22 Still red of famous PINOT N village. Formerly like v. light burg, now with more intensity (climate change, better viticulture). Best: COLIN, Paul Bara, VEUVE CLICQUOT, LAHAYE, PIERRE PAILLARD.

Boxler, Albert Al ★★★★ Jean B one of greats. Not just GC but GC subzones (Sommerberg's Dudenstein, Eckberg, Vanne; Brand's Kirchberg, Wibtal, exceptional 24). Rare PINOT BL Res 22' (no AUXERROIS). Great buy, hard-to-find SYLVANER 22'. Wondrous SGNS MUSCAT 18', PINOT GR 23 nr perfect.

Brana, Dom SW Fr Driving force in ★★★ IROULÉGUY. Ilori (w) great value from MANSENGS; Herri Mina (w) top CUVÉE owned by Jean-Claude Berrouet (CH PÉTRUS). Bizi Berri (r) rare, from revived Basque varieties.

Briday Burg ★★→★★★ Rully-based (50th anniversary, 2026). Lovely composure, value. Punching above weight: creamy RULLY MONOPOLE CLOS de Remenot (w, 45-yr-old vines). Below radar, seek out.

There are over 50,000 different molecules in wine. Somebody has counted them.

Brin, Dom de SW Fr ★★→★★★ Organic, 14-ha estate in GAILLAC championing all-local varieties. Braucol aka FER SERVADOU, Duras, Prunelart, and some tangy whites from MAUZAC, Loin de l'Oeil. Smart *méthode ancestrale* fizz too.

Brocard, J-M Chab ★★→★★★ Quality, commercial acumen under one roof: CHAB Ste Claire, fine range of PC, GC. Son Julien B: impressive bio range under 7 Lieux label. Dependable, age-worthy, deserves greater recognition.

Brochet, Emmanuel Champ ★★★ Bijou producer from steep Mont Bernard. Extra BRUT pure, exhilarating, organic, in barrel 9 mths. Excelled in sumptuous **18'** 19' 20. ***Haut Chardonnay Extra Brut*** 09 12 14' 15 16. Le Mont Benoît PC excellent too.

Brouilly Beauj ★★ 19' 20' 21 22' 23 24 Largest and most s of ten BEAUJ crus: solid, structured with some depth of flavour, approachable early but can age 3–5 yrs. Top: CHX de la Chaize, des Tours; DOMS Chermette, ***J-C Lapalu***, L&R Dufaitre, Piron. Terre des Brouilly: joint promotion with adjacent CÔTE DE BROUILLY.

Brumont, Alain SW Fr ★★★★ MADIRAN luminary and powerhouse, owner of BOUSCASSÉ, MONTUS. Single-vyd La Tyre terrific. PACHERENCS outstanding, dry, mostly PETIT COURBU, "revolutionary" sweet cuvées 100% PETIT MANSENG.

Brut Champ Term for dry classic wines of CHAMP. Dosage usually less than of yore. Under 6g residual sugar = Extra Brut, increasingly modish.

Brut Ultra / Zéro Bone-dry (no dosage) in CHAMP (aka Brut NATURE). LAURENT PERRIER Ultra Brut one of 1st; increasingly modish; quality better with warmer summers. ***Pol Roger Pure***, ROEDERER Brut Nature Philippe Starck 12' **14'** 15 19, VEUVE FOURNY Nature.

Bugey Small AOP w of SAV. Light, fresh fizz; all colours of still; organic. Crus: Cerdon (pink GAMAY/Poulsard *méthode ancestrale* with touch of sugar, lower alc), Manicle (CHARD, PINOT N), Montagnieu (Altesse, MONDEUSE, sp). White mainly Altesse (Roussette du B AOP), Chard. Red/rosé: GAMAY, Mondeuse, Pinot N. Serve Cerdon from ★★ Raphaël Bartucci, Renardat-Fache. Try Bartschi, ★★ Bonnard (bio), ★ Cortis (bio), ★ Duport (bio), ★ D'Ici Là , ★ Grangeons de l'Albarine, ★★ Pacotille, ★ Peillot or Tissot. Delicious Gamay from ★★ Tailleurs Cueilleurs.

FRANCE

Buisson, H&G C d'O ★★→★★★ Bros Franck and Frédérick form dynamic duo at bio ST-ROMAIN DOM. Peach/citrus-infused Sous le Château. Watch.

Burgaud Beauj ★★★ Jean-Marc B from MORGON, top bottlings of Charmes, Corcelette, Côte du Py, Grands Cras, etc. cry out for ageing. BEAUJ standard-bearer, risen to top from tiny beginnings in 1989. Nephew Alexandre promising too.

Burn, Ernest / Clos Saint-Imer Al ★★→★★★★ Francis B picks late: rich, balanced, often off-dry: AL-best SGN MUSCAT 22' 24'; dry SYLVANER (Al's best?) from MONOPOLE CLOS Saint-Imer in GC GOLDERT 15' 16 17 18 19 21 22' 23'; v.gd GEWURZ, PINOT GR 10 12 15' 18 20'.

Bursin, Agathe Al ★★★→★★★★ 17' 18' 19' 20' Fast becoming AL PINOT N address of note: classy, pure. Whites often slightly off-dry: Bollenberg lieu-dit, GC Zinnkoepflé (GEWURZ 23' with creamy chicken; VT 22' magical). Recognized queen of SYLVANER (outstanding v.old vines Eminence 23', Lutzental 24').

Buxy, Cave de Burg ★→★★ Leading CÔTE CHALONNAISE co-op for decent CHARD, PINOT N. Founded 1931, 100s of members. Easily largest supplier of AOP MONTAGNY. Reliable, gd value. Don't sniff; "co-op" isn't always pejorative.

Buzet SW Fr ★★ 20 22 23 (24) AOP along the Garonne nr Agen, BX style. Dominated by exemplary co-op: 95% of production incl CHX de Guèyze, Padère. Look also for Vigouroux-managed Dom de Tournelles.

Cabardès Ldoc ★★★ Underrated AOP in W LDOC overlooking Carcassonne. Med varieties GRENACHE, SYRAH meet Atlantic CAB SAUV, MERLOT: sleek black fruit with Med herbs. Rosé too. Try CHX DE SALITIS, de Pennautier (LORGERIL), La Bastide Rougepeyre; DOMS Bancalis, DE CABROL; Maison Ventenac.

Cabernet d'Anjou Lo ★→★★ Old-school off-dry rosé AOP featuring CABS FR/SAUV. Historically made to age (70s/80s vintages from ***Bablut*** prove it). Otherwise drink young; Bergerie, Montgilet, OGEREAU.

Cabidos, Ch de SW Fr ★★★ 19 20 22 23 Outstanding CH in BÉARN; similar to JURANÇON (from PETIT MANSENG): ★★ St Clément; ★★★ Gaston Phoebus, luscious and tremendous value. Superb L'Or (only once or twice/decade).

Cabrières Ldoc ★★★ Small, hilly LDOC AOP nr PÉZENAS, famed for rosé incl world's most expensive. Intriguing reds. Top: CAVES D'ESTABEL (co-op), Mas de Valbrune.

Cabrol, Dom de Ldoc ★★★→★★★★ Flagship CABARDÈS estate, outstanding value. SYRAH-based Vent d'Est, fragrant, fiercely Med style. Vent d'Ouest, more CAB SAUV, quieter, herbal. Pique de Nore, floral, saline GRENACHE BL/PETIT MANSENG/CHENIN BL.

Cadillac-Côtes de Bordeaux Bx ★→★★ 20 22 23 (25) Long, narrow, hilly zone on right bank of Garonne. Mainly MERLOT with CABS SAUV/FR. Medium-bodied, fresh reds. Cellar 2–8 yrs. Best: Alios de Ste-Marie, Bel-Air, Biac, ***Carsin***, CH Carignan, CLOS Chaumont, Clos Ste-Anne, de Fontenille, de Haut Coulon, de Lyde, Le Doyenné, Mont-Pérat, Plaisance, Réaut (Carat), ***Reynon***, Suau.

Cady, Dom Lo ★★→★★★ Reliable ANJOU DOM: fine range of COTEAUX DU LAYONS; dry Clos du Moulin Ste Catherine 19' 20' 22 23 (25).

Cahors SW Fr ★★★ 18' 19 20 22 23 24 Historical AOP on River Lot. Red only, nearly all MALBEC, lots of styles. Gentler extraction today, more concrete, amphorae, large vats for ageing. Easy-drinking: ★★ CH de Hauterive, CLOS Coutale. More substance: ★★★ CHX DE CHAMBERT, DU CÈDRE, ★★ Gaudou, Hautes-Serres, La Coustarelle, Lamartine, Les Croisille, Mas La Périé, Mercuès, Ponzac; Clos d'Un Jour, ***Clos Triguedina***, Clos Troteligotte, DOM Cosse-Maisonneuve, de la Bérengeraie, Haut-Monplaisir.

Cailbourdin, Alain and Loïc Lo ★★→★★★ Popular father/son team in POUILLY-FUMÉ. Style tightening up under Loïc. Top: ***Nanogyra*** (was Les Cornets) 19 20 21 22 23 (25). Cellar-worthy oaked Triptyques (Silex from flint, Calcaire from limestone) 16 18 19 20 (22) (23) (25).

Cailhol Gautran, Dom Ldoc ★★★ Thoughtful bio MINERVOIS, 5th generation. No added sulphur. Reds: expressive La Table du Loup, opulent Villa Lucia (rewards ageing). MUSCAT de St Jean gd.

Cailloux, Les S Rh ★★★ 10' 16' 18 19' 20' 21 22' 23 24' Gold-standard CHÂTEAUNEUF DOM, high value. Terroir-truth reds (esp 10 yrs+); fine *garrigue* white. Special Centenaire (oldest GRENACHE 1889) 16' 19'.

Cairanne S Rh ★★→★★★ 20' 22' 23 24' Elegant, suave, dark fruits, herbs, value: CLOS des Mourres (organic), Clos Romane (body); DOMS ALARY (top, organic), Boisson, Brusset (depth), Chemins de Sève, Cros de Romet, des Amadieu (bio), ESCARAVAILLES, Grands Bois (organic), Grosset, Hautes Cances (sleek), Jubain, ***Oratoire St Martin*** (bio), Rabasse-Charavin (punch), RICHAUD (flair), Roche. Table-friendly, stylish white.

Calmel & Joseph Ldoc ★★★ Trailblazing duo seeking out fruit from top terroirs from TERRASSES DE LARZAC to COLLIOURE, plus innovative IGPS. Best PINOT N in LDOC, DOM La Magdelaine, from high vyds in CORBIÈRES.

Camin Larredya SW Fr ★★★★ World-class bio JURANÇON; excellent (dr/sw). Flagship Au Capcéu (sw), low-yield, late-harvest, delicious, from hilltop.

Canard-Duchêne Champ ★★→★★★ House owned by ALAIN THIÉNOT; modernizing. Léonie increasingly gd; impressive-if-young Léonie Rosé 24'. Charles VII BLANC DE BLANCS and NOIRS NV. BRUT Vintage 13' 14' 15 16; AVIZE Gamin 13 17' 19'. Renaissance slow but sure.

Canon-Fronsac Bx ★★→★★★ 18 19' 20' 22 23 (25) Tiny enclave within FRON, otherwise same wines. Clay-limestone soils. Best: rich, full, cellar-worthy. Try Barrabaque, Canon Pécresse, Cassagne Haut-Canon la Truffière, du Gazin, GABY, Grand-Renouil, Lamarche Canon, MOULIN PEY-LABRIE.

Caraguilhes, Ch Ldoc ★★★ Super-reliable large bio CORBIÈRES DOM. Great-value La Font Blanche GRENACHE/ROUSSANNE/VERMENTINO. Impressive Le Trou de l'Hermite (r) from warm-stone Boutenac TERROIR. Flagship Solus (r/w).

Carême, Vincent Lo ★★→★★★★ Top VOUVRAY DOM. Classy single-vyd dry *Le Clos* 16 17 18 19 20 21 22 23 (25), CLOS de la Roche, Le Peu Morier close behind. Fine *moelleux* too. Brut Nature, Plaisir Ancestral (sp) no-brainers.

Carillon C d'O ★★★ PULIGNY bros went separate ways in 2010: Jacques aims for ageability (PC Referts); François favours immediacy in elegant fruit, soft texture (Combettes, Folatières, Cap au Sud VDF CHARD). Delicious village Puligny (both).

Cassiopée, de C d'O ★★ Talloulah and Hugo Mathurin started 2020 with 5 ha of MARANGES hillside. Cramped cellar: amphorae rub shoulders with oak. Try Maranges Les Plantes, strawberry-cherry delight from ancient 100-yr-old+ vines.

Cassis Prov ★★→★★★ Small AOP nr Marseille, known for CLAIRETTE, MARSANNE: CLOS Ste Magdeleine, DOMS de Ferme Blanche, DU PATERNEL, Quatre Vents.

Chablis

A unique iteration of CHARD, replete with notes of "stone and savour". Warmer summers may change that. Best are delicate but intense, some with a lactic note that calls to mind natural yoghurt. Age bestows amplitude. **Best:** BILLAUD, DAUVISSAT (V), FÈVRE (W), Michel (L), MOREAU (C), ***Pinson***, RAVENEAU. **Also gd:** Bessin, BROCARD (J-M), CHABLISIENNE, Collet, Dampt (D), Davenne, ***Defaix*** (B), Defaix (D-E), Droin, DROUHIN-Vaudon, Duplessis, Fèvre (N&G), ***Garnier***, Grossot, LAROCHE, LONG-DEPAQUIT, ***Malandes***, MOREAU-Naudet, ***Moreau*** (L), Pattes Loup, Picq, Piuze, Pommier, Oudin, Tribut, Vocoret (E&E), ***Vrignaud***. **Look for:** Brocard (J), Dauvissat (J & Fils), CH de Béru, d'Henri, de Moor, Gautheron, Goulley, Lavantureux.

Castelnau, De Champ ★★★ Co-op merged with Nicolas Feuillatte. Excellent BLANC DE BLANCS, Vintage 02 08 09. Innovative Prestige Collection Hors d'Age, MEUNIER in spotlight. Impressive Hors Categorie NV CT 2016. Chef de CAVE Carine Bailleul.

Castillon-Côtes de Bordeaux Bx ★★→★★★ 19 20 22 23 (25) Appealing neighbour of ST-ÉM; similar, usually gd value. Independent AOP Cas for red and white in 2026? Top: Alcée, Ampélia, Cap de FAUGÈRES, CLOS Les Lunelles, Clos Louie, ***Clos Puy Arnaud, d'Aiguilhe, de l'A***, de Pitray, Joanin Bécot, l'Aurage, ***l'Hêtre***, La Brande, ***La Clarière, Le Rey***, Montlandrie, Peyrou, Poupille, Veyry.

Cathiard, Dom Sylvain C d'O ★★★★ Sébastien C makes glorious wines at celebrated VOSNE DOM; picks late, destems: Malconsorts, Orveaux, Reignots; plus NUITS Aux Thorey, Murgers. New generic BOURGOGNE range.

Cattier Champ ★★★ Under-the-radar brand now reviving. Beautiful, invigorating.

Cauhapé, Dom SW Fr ★★★ Leading JURANÇON estate, exceptional whites (dr/sw). Dry L'Escapade, unusual blend PETIT MANSENG/Camaralet, great value. Sweet Quintessence, exquisite, raisined, harvested Xmas Eve.

Cave Cellar, or any wine establishment.

Cave coopérative Growers' co-op winery; over half of all French production. Wines often well priced, probably not most exciting. CAVE DE TAIN (N Rh), CHABLISIENNE gd egs. Many co-ops closing down.

Cave d'Irouléguy SW Fr ★★★ Well-run co-op covering half of IROULÉGUY. All styles quality-focused, some organic; excellent tastings. Try Omenaldi (r), Xuri (w).

Cazeneuve, Ch Ldoc ★★★ Consistently gd PIC ST-LOUP. Top: Le Causse (SYRAH), rewards ageing. Cynarah (r) delightfully fruity, herbal; v.gd Les Calcaires (r).

Cazes, Dom Rouss ★★★ Masterful VDNS: RIVESALTES Aimé Cazes (aged in *foudre* 22 yrs), super-value Ambré, Grenat, Tuilé. Impressive dry from largest bio vyd in France. MAURY SEC. Top red Le Crédo CÔTES DU ROUSS-VILLAGES. Also Alter, Ego, Rolle in Stone (w, VERMENTINO), Les CLOS de Paulilles (BANYULS, COLLIOURE).

Cébène, Dom de Ldoc ★★★★ Mesmerizing bio FAUGÈRES DOM run by impassioned Brigitte Chevalier. Flagship Felgaria (MOURVÈDRE-led), elegance, power, ages well. Les Bancels SYRAH et al, earlier drinking, no less fine. Belle Lurette shows what CARIGNAN can do. Vivaciously fruity À la Venvole.

Cèdre, Ch du SW Fr ★★→★★★ 18 19 20 22 23 (24) Organic, min-intervention, excellent, v. approachable CAHORS. Tamed tannins, lower alc, gentle ageing in *foudres*. Delicious everyday ★★ MALBEC IGP. Consultant to CHX Haut Monplaisir, Ponzac (both Cahors).

Single vineyards – the new Champagne

Champagne's reputation has long rested on the creative tension between a marginal climate and the virtues of blending grapes, regions and yrs. Yet its secret is terroir. Now that climate is marginally less marginal, it's becoming more possible for single-vyd wines to stand alone, and more and more houses are releasing them. Dramatically expensive CLOS wines incl KRUG's CLOS DU MESNIL, PHILIPPONNAT's magisterial Clos des Goisses, BILLECART-SALMON's Clos Saint-Hilaire; more modestly priced incl CATTIER's Clos du Moulin or PIERRE PÉTERS's Chétillons. Growers, unsurprisingly, given their less extensive land ownership, have come to excel in this area, incl many labels from Jacques SELOSSE and Cédric Bouchard. There are many many more; three outstanding are Le Petit Clos from Jean Vesselle, Les Perrières from ULYSSE COLLIN, and La Croix d'Aumonier by Penet Chardonnet. Every yr more such wines enter the fray.

Cellier aux Moines Burg ★★★ Leading GIVRY DOM traces origins to 1130; based in eponymous vyd; much investment this century, impressive results under winemaker Guillaume Marko. Interesting CÔTE DE BEAUNE, but star is home vyd.

Cépage Grape variety. *See* pp.12–22.

Cérons Bx ★★ 22 23 (25) Tiny AOP. Sweet wines next to BARSAC (limestone), less intense. Best: CHX de Cérons, du Seuil, Grand Enclos, Haura.

Chablis ★★→★★★ 17' 18' 19' 20 21 22 23 24 Wine world's most traduced name? Pure-fruited yet shot through with stony savour, gd Chab is a beguiling iteration of CHARD. Climate change adds succulence, but some challenging recent yrs. PETIT CHAB, DYA, lighter, value. (*See also* box, p.51.)

Chablis Grand Cru Chab ★★★→★★★★ 10' 12' 14' 15 17' 18' 19' 20 21 22 23 24 Block of seven s-facing vyds, 105 ha, perfectly situated on slope. Grandest CHAB, needs 5–15 yrs to reveal complexity. Try vyds: Blanchots (floral), Bougros (incl Côte Bouguerots), CLOS (most patrician), Grenouilles (spicy), Preuses (finesse), Valmur (structure), Vaudésir (plus brand La Moutonne). Undoubtedly best-value Burg GCS.

Chablisienne, La Chab ★★→★★★ High-achieving co-op responsible for huge slice of CHAB production; v.gd value. Trade up to bio CUVÉES of Chab, PETIT CHAB. Don't miss GC CH Grenouilles: a winner on palate and wallet.

Chablis Premier Cru Chab ★★★ 17' 18' 19' 20 21 22 23 24 Well worth exploring. Hillside sites can deliver great satisfaction, variety. Most benefit 3–5 yrs' age. Racy, pure: Montmains, Vaillons, Vaucoupin. More charming: ***Côte de Léchet***, Fourchaume. Greater opulence: Mont de Milieu, ***Montée de Tonnerre***, Vaulorent.

Chambert, Ch de SW Fr ★★★★ Gorgeous bio property in W CAHORS; v. reliable estate wine; superb yet pricey *parcellaires*. Pound for pound, best value is Grand Vin, from oldest vines. Try restaurant, stunning views over vyds.

Chambertin C d'O ★★★★ 90' 93 96' 99' 02' 05' 09' 10' 12' 14 15' 16 17 18' 19' 20' 21 22' 23' 24 Commanding in youth, compelling with age, masculine burg. Meat and muscle abound, lavish fruit in best. Imperious; more charm recently. Producers who match potential: Bernstein, CHARLOPIN, Damoy, DOM LEROY, DUGAT-Py, DROUHIN, MORTET, REBOURSEAU, ROSSIGNOL-TRAPET, ROUSSEAU, TRAPET. CLOS de Bèze next door, a little more accessible, glorious symphony from nose to finish: Bart, B CLAIR, Damoy, Drouhin, Drouhin-Laroze, DUROCHÉ, FAIVELEY, GROFFIER, JADOT, Prieuré-Roch, Rebourseau, Rousseau.

Chambolle-Musigny C d'O ★★★→★★★★ 99' 02' 05' 09' 10' 12' 15' 16 17 19' 20 21 22' 23 24 Even the name seduces. Silky, velvety, more structure recently. Charmes, Combe d'Orveau for substance; Cras, Fuées, bewitching Amoureuses cleave more to received reputation; GCS BONNES-MARES, MUSIGNY. Stars: BARTHOD, GROFFIER, MUGNIER, ROUMIER, VOGÜÉ. Also gd: Amiot-Servelle, DROUHIN, FELETTIG, HUDELOT-Baillet, POUSSE D'OR, RION, Sigaut.

Champagne Sparkling wines of PINOT N, MEUNIER and CHARD: 33,805 ha, heartland c.145 km e of Paris. Sales 270m+ bottles/yr. Top markets: US then UK. Some PINOT BL further s in AUBE adds freshness. Other sparkling, however gd, cannot be called Champ. Thrives on chalky tension, biscuity development (autolysis). Rise in Prestige lables, some from single vyds. (*See* box, opposite.)

Champagne le Mesnil Champ ★★★ Top co-op in centre of Le Mesnil-sur-Oger; exceptional GC CHARD village. ***Cuvée Sublime*** 13' 15 17' 19 20 from finest site. Majestic CUVÉE Prestige 08 09 12 16. Chef de CAVE Gilles Marguet.

Champagne Marguet Champ ★★★ Unfazed by having KRUG as neighbour in Ambonnay, 5th-generation Benoît transformed estate, bio (2009). Names reveal philosophy: Sapience Rosé 19 20 22; ***Shamen Brut*** 12 14' 15 16 18; Shamen Rosé 20. Top single-vyds: La Grande Ruelle, Le Parc, Les Crayères.

Champalou Lo ★★→★★★ Charming, elegant VOUVRAY from Céline Champalou and husband Kevin (CHARLES JOGUET winemaker). Sweet La Moelleuse, Les Tries 89' 95 96' 97 02' 03 09 15 18 (22). SEC and DEMI-SEC Les Fondraux 18 19 20 22 (25); v. consistent fizz.

Chandon de Briailles, Dom C d'O ★★★ Decade-long improvement; bio, min sulphur, whole bunches, no new oak. Brilliantly pure (r) CORTON-Bressandes, PERNAND-VERGELESSES PC Île de Vergelesses.

Chanson Père & Fils Burg ★★→★★★ Continues to improve (est 1750). Quality whites (CHASSAGNE PC Chenevottes, CLOS DES MOUCHES, CORTON-Vergennes), reduced use of whole bunches in reds. Purchase of 50 ha in CÔTE CHALONNAISE cements transition from merchant to DOM, as does new label design.

Chapelle-Chambertin C d'O ★★★ 99' 02' 05' 09' 10' 12' 15' 16 18' 19' 20' 21 22' 23 24 Lighter neighbour of CHAMBERTIN; thin soil does better in cooler, damper yrs. More elegant, less structured. Slightly below radar. Top: Damoy, DROUHIN-Laroze, JADOT, PONSOT, ROSSIGNOL-TRAPET, TRAPET, TREMBLAY.

Chapoutier N Rh ★★→★★★★ High-profile, ubiquitous grower-merchant, bio vyds. Deep SYRAH: low-yield CÔTE-RÔTIE La Mordorée. HERMITAGE: L'Ermite (intricate r/w), Le Pavillon (granite, forthright r), Cuvée de l'Orée (w, stylish), Le Méal (r/w). ST-JOSEPH Les Granits (r/w). Top: ***Hermitage w***, time for complexity, all old-vine MARSANNE, ***Chante-Alouette***. Also CONDRIEU Chéry, ST-PÉRAY Hongrie. Duché d'Uzès (r/w) value. Deep GRENACHE CHÂTEAUNEUF: Barbe Rac, Croix de Bois. Signargues (r). Hotel, wine bars in Tain. Also CÔTES DU ROUSS-VILLAGES (DOM Bila-Haut), COTEAUX D'AIX-EN-PROV, RIVESALTES; FERRATON (Hermitage), Trenel (BEAUJ), CH des Ferrages (PROV). In AL, Australia.

Charbonnière, Dom de la S Rh ★★★ 16' 19' 20' 22' 23 24' Maret sisters conjure resounding CHÂTEAUNEUF: (r) Estate, VIEILLES VIGNES (best), Mourre des Perdrix, Hautes Brusquières; (w) crystalline, luxe apéritif. Peppery VACQUEYRAS (r).

Charlopin C d'O ★★★ Large DOM, 25 ha. Philippe C makes impressive range of reds. More elegance in recent yrs. Value BOURGOGNE C D'O, MARSANNAY; gd range GCS for top of line. Son Yann C, DOM C-Tissier also worth following.

Charmes-Chambertin C d'O ★★★★ 99' 02' 03 05' 09' 10' 12' 15' 16 17 18' 19' 20' 21

Châteauneuf: leaders at the Papal court

Leading names at this large, multifaceted (soils, blends, styles) appellation: CHX DE BEAUCASTEL, Gardine, Mont-Redon, Mourre du Tendre (depth), Nalys, Nerthe, RAYAS, Sixtine, Vaudieu; DOMS Albin Jacumin (stylish), André Mathieu, Barroche (flair), BEAURENARD (bio, classy), Bois Pointu, Bosquet des Papes (full), Chante Cigale (genuine), Chante Perdrix, CHARBONNIÈRE, CHARVIN, CLOS DES PAPES, CLOS du Caillou (organic), CLOS DU MONT-OLIVET (authentic), Clos St-Jean (scale), Cristia (also max purity Chapelle St Théodoric), de la Biscarelle (fruit), de la Janasse (strength), DE LA MORDORÉE, de la Vieille Julienne (bio, complex), du Banneret (trad), Durieu, Fontavin, Font-de-Michelle, Galet des Papes, Grand Tinel, Grand Veneur (organic), Henri Bonneau (depth), Famille Ferrando (style), LES CAILLOUX (value), MARCOUX (bio, esp VIEILLES VIGNES), Mas du Boislauzon (robust), Pegaü, Pères de l'Église, Pierre André (bio, terroir), Porte Rouge, Famille P Usseglio, R Usseglio (bio, style), Roger Sabon (full), Sénéchaux (polished), Vieux Donjon (classic), VIEUX TÉLÉGRAPHE. Whites: Chx de Beaucastel (mighty ROUSSANNE), Gardine, RAYAS, Vaudieu; Doms Albin Jacumin, Beaurenard, Clos des Papes (long life), Les Cailloux (genuine), Marcoux (stylish), R Usseglio (v.gd Roussanne), Vieux Donjon (authentic, depth), Vieux Télégraphe (deep, terroir).

22' 23 24 GEVREY GC, 31 ha, incl neighbour MAZOYÈRES-CHAMBERTIN. Sumptuous, suave, berry-cherry fruit, fragrant finish. Best: ARLAUD, BACHELET, Castagnier, Coquard-Loison-Fleurot, DUGAT, DUJAC, DUROCHÉ, LEROY, MORTET, Perrot-Minot, REBOURSEAU, Roty, ROUSSEAU, Taupenot-Merme, VOUGERAIE.

Chartogne-Taillet Champ ★★★★ Disciple of SELOSSE, Alexandre C, now celebrated in own right; bio inclinations. BRUT Ste Anne NV, single-vyds ***Couarres Château***, Le Chemin de Reims, Les Alliées and Les Barres both 100% MEUNIER. Superb Hors Serie BLANC DE BLANCS **16'** **18** 19.

Charvin, Dom S Rh ★★★ 09' 10' 12' 15' **16'** **17'** **18'** 19' 20' **21'** 22' 23' 24' One of best CHÂTEAUNEUF, genuine terroir declaration, gd value; 85% (average) 50-yr-old GRENACHE, vat-raised. Only one red: mineral, high-energy, needs time. Recent gd white. Long-lived, v.gd CÔTES DU RH (r).

Chassagne-Montrachet C d'O ★★→★★★★ (w) 08' 09 12' **14'** 15 17' 18 19' 20' 21 22' 23 24 Excitement abounds, style, quality. Great white vyds Blanchot, Cailleret, LA ROMANÉE, Ruchottes and GCS. Thrilling flavours. Try COLIN, GAGNARD, MOREY, PILLOT families; DOMS AMIOT, Dancer, HEITZ, MOREAU, Niellon, RAMONET. Reds can age superbly: Boudriotte, CLOS St-Jean, Morgeot.

Château (Ch) Estate, big or small, gd or indifferent, esp BX (*see* pp.106–25). Literally, castle or great house. In Burg, DOM is usual term.

Château-Chalon Jura ★★★→★★★★ 10' **14** **15** 16 17 **18** Not a CH but AOP and village, summit of VIN JAUNE elegance from SAVAGNIN grape; min 6 yrs' barrel-age under veil of yeast, organic, worth investing. Drink with Comté cheese (or with/in a chicken dish). Ages for decades; old vintages of Henri Maire reliable, excellent value. ★★★ Chevassu-Fassenet. ★★★ Berthet-Bondet, Courbet, Rousset-Martin. ★★★→★★★★ Stéphane TISSOT (bio), ***Macle***.

Château-Grillet N Rh ★★★★ 10' 12' 14' 15' 16' 17' **19** **20'** **21'** 22' 23' 24' 25' Outlier in N Rh, VIOGNIER different from CONDRIEU, France's smallest AOP: 3.7-ha, sand-granite, terraced amphitheatre. Vast price. Owned by F Pinault of CH LATOUR. Tight, fine, intricate, gradual opening, can be great at 20 yrs. Scented, oily VIOGNIER: drink lightly chilled, decanted, with refined dishes. CONDRIEU La Carthery since 2017, vyd nearby; sound CÔTES DU RH (w).

Châteaumeillant Lo ★→★★ 22 23 (25) Small AOP, s of REUILLY. Simple GAMAY and PINOTS N/GR (r/rosé): Lecomte, Roux, Rouzé.

Châteauneuf-du-Pape S Rh ★★★→★★★★ 09' **10'** 12 15 **16'** **17** 19' 20' **21** 22' 23 24 Worldwide renown, 3200 ha, 35% organic/bio. Maze of sand, clay, limestone, stones; up to 13 grapes (r/w), mostly GRENACHE, plus SYRAH, MOURVÈDRE (increasing, important), Counoise; multiple styles; c.60 gd DOMS (other 120 fair to dodgy, not all bottled). Spice, plums, herbs, best wait 8 yrs+; should be pure, caressing. From 90s to mid-10s too many sipping only. Young generation more finesse-freshness aware. Small, trad doms for value. Avoid: new oak, 16% abv, hoisted prices. Cracking whites, sell fast: upfront, fruity, or rich, deep, best can age 15 yrs+ (21 24). (For top names, *see* box, opposite.)

Chave, Dom Jean-Louis N Rh ★★★★ 05' 07' **09'** 10' **11'** **12'** **13'** 15' **16'** 17' 18' 19' 20' 21' 22' 23' 24' 25' Top-class 15-ha family DOM at HERMITAGE, added precious 0.6 ha of Méal (2025). Sensuous SYRAH, incl occasional, v. pricey Cathelin. Complexity in long-lived whites (mainly MARSANNE). ST-JOSEPH (r), smoky, single-vyd CLOS Florentin (since 2015). Merchant range: lively St Joseph Offerus (r), supple CÔTES DU RH Mon Coeur, gd-value Hermitage Farconnet (r), Blanche (w).

Chénas Beauj ★★★ 18' 19' 20' 21 22 23 24 Smallest BEAUJ cru, Chénas village lies outside appellation. Firm, age-worthy, gd value, merits more attention. Reference: ***Thillardon***. Also Janodet, LAPIERRE, Pacalet, Piron, Trichard, co-op.

Chevalier-Montrachet C d'O ★★★★ 08' 09' **10** **12** 14' 15 17' 18 19' 20' 21 22' 23 24 Upslope of MONTRACHET, can rival big brother. Poised, precise. Long-lived but accessible early. LEFLAIVE; special CUVÉES Les Demoiselles from JADOT, LOUIS LATOUR; La Cabotte from DOM des Cabottes (BOUCHARD). Also: Chartron, COLIN P, Dancer, DE MONTILLE, Niellon, RAMONET, VOUGERAIE.

Cheverny Lo ★→★★ 22 23 (25) AOP between Loire and Cher. Simple whites (SAUV BL/CHARD/Menu Pineau), rosé/reds (GAMAY/PINOT N/CAB FR/CÔT). Drink young: Cazin, Huards, Tessier, Veilloux.

Chevillon, R C d'O ★★★ Dark-fruited, muscular but not overtannic PCS: Bousselots, Chaignots, Pruliers accessible; Cailles, Les St-Georges, Vaucrains to age.

Chevrot C d'O ★★→★★★ Appealing, juicy MARANGES: Sur les Chênes, PC Croix Moines. Decent whites: ALIGOTÉ Tilleul, Maranges Fussière. CRÉMANT too.

Chidaine, François Lo ★★★→★★★★ Leading MONTLOUIS-SUR-LOIRE DOM; single-vyd range. Dry CLOS du Breuil, Les Bournais 17 18 19 20 22 23 (25). Varying ageing potential, caution advised. Clos Habert, Les Tuffeaux (both s/sw), Moelleux (sw) v.gd. Vines in ***Clos Baudoin*** (VOUVRAY, VDF label).

Chignin Sav AOP (Jacquère, MONDEUSE); Chignin-Bergeron (ROUSSANNE). Try ★★: Berthollier, J-F Quenard. ★★: A Berlioz, A&M QUENARD. ★★★: Partagé (bio).

Chinon Lo ★★→★★★ 05' 09' 10' 15' 16 17 18' 19 20 22' 23 (25) Top CAB FR AOP, cellar-worthy wines from limestone, clay, gravel. Sandy soils drink younger. Best: ***Alliet***, BAUDRY, CHARLES JOGUET, CLOS des Capucins, Gasnier, Grosbois, J-M Raffault, NOBLAIE, Olga Raffault, Pallus, Pascal Lambert, Saut au Loup, Wilfrid Rousse. DOM de Beauséjour currently rising like a phoenix. Tiny volumes dry CHENIN BL (Baudry, Noblaie best). Also rosé.

Chiroubles Beauj ★★ 15' 18' 19' 20' 21 22' 23 24 Small, vertiginous BEAUJ: bush vines and pink granite, engaging wines. Try Berne, CH de Javernand, Cheysson, LAFARGE-Vial, Métrat, Passot, Raousset, or merchants DUBOEUF, ***Trenel***.

Chorey-lès-Beaune C d'O ★★→★★★ 15' 17 18 19' 20 21 22' 23 24 Village just n of BEAUNE. TOLLOT-BEAUT is standard-bearer for satisfying, fruity wines at reasonable prices. Also Arnoux, DROUHIN, Gay, Guyon, JADOT, RAPET, ROUGET.

Clair, Bruno C d'O ★★★ Understated, never flashy, marked by a lighter weave than some. New generation – Arthur, Edouard, Margaux – beginning to harness full potential. CHAMBERTIN-Clos de Bèze (standout), GEVREY-CHAMBERTIN (CLOS ST-JACQUES, Cazetiers), MARSANNAY (gd value), SAVIGNY La Dominode (old vines). Best whites from CORTON-CHARLEMAGNE, MOREY-ST-DENIS. Watch.

Clairet Bx Between rosé/red. AOP BX Clairet: CHX de Fontenille, Penin, THIEULEY. Now new Claret AOP too: light, inoffensive.

Clairette de Die N Rh ★★ Alps foothills sparkler, esp MUSCAT (s/sw), top apéritif, musky, tasty, value, low alc. Or dry CLAIRETTE, can age 3 yrs. Note Achard-Vincent (organic/bio), Carod, David Bautin (organic), Jaillance (value), J-C Raspail (organic, IGP SYRAH), Poulet & Fils (Chatillon-en-Diois r).

Clape, Dom N Rh ★★★→★★★★ 05' 06' 07' 09' 10' 12' 14' 15' 16' 17' 18' 19' 20' 21' 22' 23' 24' 25' CORNAS as it should be: complex, initially tannic, mineral-glinted hillside SYRAH; be patient. Vintage truth each yr. Ideal gift for a godchild. Need 7 yrs+, live 25+. Younger-vines Renaissance is cool, direct. Superior CÔTES DU RH, ST-PÉRAY (MARSANNE), VDF (r).

Clape, La Ldoc ★★★→★★★★ Driest, sunniest, windiest LDOC AOP. MOURVÈDRE hotspot with SYRAH, GRENACHE for characterful herb-scented red with freshness from sea breezes. Salty, herbal white from BOURBOULENC with dash of ROUSSANNE: underrated, seek out. CHX Anglès, Bouisset, Camplazens, Capitoul, LA NÉGLY, Laquirou, Le Bouïs, l'Hospitalet, Mire l'Etang, Pech-Céleyran, PECH REDON, Ricardelle, ROUQUETTE SUR MER; DOM Sarrat de Goundy; La Combe Saint-Paul.

Climat Burg Individual named vyd (almost interchangeable with lieu-dit).

Clos Distinct (walled) vyd, often in one ownership (esp AL, Burg, CHAMP). Often prestigious. Sometimes rather loosely applied in Burg.

Clos Alivu Cors ★★→★★★ AOP PATRIMONIO. Stylish, fresh wines from talented Eric Poli, also owner of DOM Poli, gd-value AOP CORS (r/w/rosé), IGP Île de Beauté.

Clos Canarelli Cors ★★★ Spectacular bio estate in Figari, s tip of AOP CORS. Reviving indigenous grapes plus more mainstream NIELLUCCIO, SCIACARELLO. Core range gd value: Rosé. Excellent Tarra di Sognu (r/w), rare Tarra d'Orasi (r/w) from ungrafted vines.

Clos Cibonne Prov ★★★ Small estate nr Toulon, making red/rosé from rare local Tibouren as AOP CÔTES DU PROV. Beautiful trad labels, gastronomic, ethereal wines. Tentations range: fruitier, early drinking.

Clos Culombu Cors ★★★ Innovative DOM in Corse-Calvi, blending indigenous varieties with NIELLUCCIO, VERMENTINO. Impressive Storia di range (r/w).

Clos d'Alzeto Cors ★★★ Highest vyd in CORS, 500m (1640ft). AJACCIO (r) from SCIACARELLO, prestige VERMENTINO, floral, fine.

Clos de L'Écotard Lo ★★→★★★ SAUMUR DOM run by Thibaud Chevré, gd whites: Les Pentes 20 21 22 (23) (25). Fine Les Quarts St-Vincent (sp). Red yet to impress, but early days.

Clos de Tart C d'O ★★★★ 05' 08' 10' 13' 14 15' 16' 17 18' 19' 20' 21 22' 23 24 Expensive MOREY-ST-DENIS GC. MONOPOLE of Pinault/Artemis empire (CHX GRILLET, Latour, etc.). Becoming more refined with plot-by-plot vinification while retaining natural intensity. La Forge de T gd value. Best days may still be ahead.

Clos de Vougeot C d'O ★★★→★★★★ 03' 05' 09' 10' 12' 13' 15' 16 17 18' 19' 20' 21 22' 23 24 CÔTE DE NUITS GC, many owners; 50 ha, needs trimming. Shedding ho-hum reputation. Best need 10 yrs+. Gaining composure in recent warm yrs. Keys: philosophy, technique, position in vyd. Top: ARNOUX-LACHAUX, CH de la Tour, EUGÉNIE, ***Faiveley***, GRIVOT, ***Gros (Anne)***, ***Hudelot-Noëllat***, LEROY, ***Liger-Belair*** (both), MÉO-CAMUZET, MORTET, ***Vougeraie***. Also v.gd: Castagnier, Clerget (Y), Coquard-Loison-Fleurot, DROUHIN, Forey, MONTILLE, ***Mugneret-Gibourg***.

Clos del Rey Rouss ★★★ Small family DOM punching above weight, vyds on 300m (984ft) plateau: superb L'Aragone (CARIGNAN), spicy La Noia (old GRENACHE).

Clos de la Roche C d'O ★★★★ 90' 93' 96' 99' 02' 05' 08 09' 10' 15' 16' 17 18' 19' 20' 21 22' 23 24 Overlooked though not underpriced: finest GC of MOREY-ST-DENIS (though LAMBRAYS, TART challenging) grace, gravitas counterpoised. Glorious with time. Reference: ARLAUD, ***Dujac***, H LIGNIER, PONSOT. Also AMIOT, Bernstein, Castagnier, Coquard, LEROY, LIGNIER-Michelot, POUSSE D'OR, Remy, ROUSSEAU.

Clos des Fées Rouss ★★★→★★★★ Legendary estate run by enigmatic Hervé Bizuel. La Petite Siberie (r), exquisite CÔTES DU ROUSS pure GRENACHE; Sorcières (r/w) gd value; Le Chat de Marquis, scented IGP TEMPRANILLO.

Clos des Lambrays C d'O ★★★→★★★★ 09' 10' 15' 16' 18' 19' 20' 21 22' 23 24 All-but-MONOPOLE GC vyd at MOREY-ST-DENIS, LVMH-owned. Big investment, leap in quality. Fruit, sweet spice, lingering finish. Splendid new vat room, sepulchral hush. Also PCS: NUITS La Richemone, PULIGNY CLOS du Cailleret, Les Folatières.

Clos des Mouches C d'O ★★★ (w) 05' 09' 10' 14' 15 17' 18 19' 20' 21 22' 23 24 PC vyd in several Burg AOPS. Mostly reds, but famous for glorious BEAUNE white. *Mouches* = honeybees; see label of DROUHIN's Beaune (ages magnificently). Also BICHOT, CHANSON (Beaune); plus CLAIR, MOREAU, Muzard (SANTENAY); Germain (MEURSAULT).

Clos des Papes S Rh ★★★★ 05' 07' 09' 10' 12' 13' 14' 15' 16' 17' 18' 19' 20' 21' 22' 23' 24' 25 Prime CHÂTEAUNEUF DOM, burg elegance, consistency; handsome, high-interest GRENACHE/MOURVÈDRE (r, drink at 2–3 yrs or from 8+); sophisticated white (demands top cuisine; 2–3 yrs, then 10–20).

Clos du Mesnil Champ ★★★★ KRUG's walled vyd in GC Le Mesnil. Dates from 1698. Richly indulgent CHARD. On-going battle between mature 95 and 96, Cavalier vs Roundhead. Wait a little longer for similar duel between 02 and 08. Also aristocratic 03' 04, overperforming 06'. Look forward to 12 13' and, many yrs hence, 18 19' 20 *et seq.*

Clos du Roi C d'O ★★→★★★ Frequent Burg vyd name, sometimes as CLOS du Roy. Best vyd in GC CORTON (DE MONTILLE, POUSSE D'OR, VOUGERAIE); top PC vyd in MERCUREY, future PC (still waiting) in MARSANNAY. Less classy in BEAUNE.

Clos Naudin, Dom du Lo ★★★★ Arguably appellation leader in VOUVRAY. Philippe Foreau now handed reins to son Vincent. ***Moelleux Rés*** **89' 90' 95 97 02' 03 05 09 10 15 16** 18 19 20 22 23 (25). Also Vouvray's best fizz.

Clos Rougeard Lo ★★★★ **05' 09 10' 14 15' 16 17 18'** 19 20 21 22 (23) (25) Cult SAUMUR-CHAMPIGNY DOM. High quality kept by new winemaker Cyril Chirouze. Huge recent investments, prices to match. SAUMUR Bl Brézé (w) v.gd.

Clos St-Denis C d'O ★★★ **90' 93' 96' 99' 02'** 05' **09' 10'** 12' 15' 16' 17 18' 19' 20' 21 22' 23 24 MOREY-ST-DENIS GC. Sumptuous young, silky with age: DUJAC, PONSOT (Laurent P from 2016). Also: Amiot-Servelle, ARLAUD, BERTAGNA, Castagnier, Coquard-Loison-Fleurot, Heresztyn-Mazzini, JADOT, Jouan, LEROUX.

Clos Ste-Hune Al ★★★★ World's greatest dry RIES single site from Trimbach monopole cru in GC Rosacker; 100th anniversary (2024). Super **61' 67' 71' 75' 13' 15'** 17' 18 **19'** 20' 23 (need 10 yrs); 22' (nr perfection).

Clos St-Jacques C d'O ★★★→★★★★ **93 96' 99' 02'** 05' **09' 10' 12'** 15' 16 **17** 18 19' 20' 21 22' 23 Hillside PC in GEVREY, perfect SE exposure. Shared by CLAIR, ESMONIN, FOURRIER, JADOT, ROUSSEAU. (Each holding runs top to bottom.) Power, poise; in right hands rivals some GCS. Best sublime with age.

Clos Teddi Cors ★★★ AOP PATRIMONIO; beautiful, remote DOM on granite soil of Agriates desert. Intense, powerful Grande Cuvée (r), NIELLUCCIU; rich, polished VERMENTINO, perfect with sea bass.

Clusel-Roch, Dom N Rh ★★★ **09' 10' 11 12' 13' 14** 15' **16' 17'** 18' 19' 20' 21' 22' 23' 24' 25' Organic (tricky on hillsides, rare) CÔTE-RÔTIE, mostly Serine (pre-clone SYRAH). Tight, ferrous reds, can be austere recently: no hurry. Les Schistes (entry point), La Viallière (finesse), Les Cinq Lieux (nuanced), Les Grandes Places (long-lived). Son Guillaume C makes v.gd Coteaux du Lyonnais (GAMAY, w).

Coche, Fabien C d'O ★★★ In shadow of cousin (below), insiders' pick. Signature citrus style, ages well, nutty splendour eventually. Lovely MEURSAULT Rouge.

Coche-Dury C d'O ★★★★ Legendary MEURSAULT DOM led by Raphaël C. Extraordinarily beautiful, profound whites from ALIGOTÉ to CORTON-CHARLEMAGNE; pretty reds too. Bank-breaking prices, hard to justify.

Colin C d'O ★★★→★★★★ Extended family of CHASSAGNE, ST-AUBIN vinous nobility. Superlative whites: pure, poised, persistent. Current generation: Pierre-Yves C-MOREY, DOM MARC C, Joseph C, cousins BRUNO C, Philippe C, Simon C.

Colin-Morey Burg ★★★→★★★★ Pierre-Yves C-M continues to burnish his reputation with vibrant tingling whites, esp ***St-Aubin***, CHASSAGNE PC, with characteristic gunflint aromas. Bland labels give no hint of complex glories within. Exemplary, age-worthy, esp Aligoté for shallower pockets.

Collin, Ulysse Champ ★★★→★★★★ Cerebral grower on Côteaux du Petit Morin, sw of Vertus. Single vyds only, all subtly oaked, low dosage. Les Pierrières, Les Enfers (both BLANC DE BLANCS), Les Maillons Brut (BLANC DE NOIRS) and Rosé de Saignée, Le Jardin d'Ulysse. A CHAMP odyssey, not lacking drama, tension.

Collines Rhodaniennes N Rh ★★ IGP ("Rhodanienne" = "of the Rhône"). Tempo, value, local feel, incl long-life Seyssuel (schist, smoky), granite hills, plateau reds; top names involved. Mostly SYRAH (best), also GAMAY, mini-CONDRIEU VIOGNIER (best). Reds: A Chatagnier, A Paret, A PERRET, Avallet (Seyssuel), Bonnefond, Bott, CLOS de la Bonnette (organic), E Barou (organic), Eymin Tichoux (Seyssuel), ***Jamet***, JASMIN, J-M GÉRIN, L Chèze, Monier-Pérreol (bio), N Champagneux, S Pichat, Rosiers, ROSTAING, Vins de Vienne (Seyssuel),

Y CUILLERON. Whites: Alexandrins, Amphores, A Perret (v.gd), Barou, ***G Vernay***, P-J Villa, X Gérard, Y CUILLERON.

Collioure Rouss ★★★ Dry wines (r/w/rosé), same vyds as BANYULS, mtn and Med styles, among greatest in ROUSS. Mainly GRENACHE of all colours. Top: DOMS Augustin, Bila-Haut, de la Rectorie, du Mas Blanc, du Traginer, La Tour Vieille, MADELOC, Vial-Magnères; COUME DEL MAS, CLOS Saint Sebastien, Les Clos de Paulilles. Co-ops Cellier des Templiers, l'Étoile.

Comte Abbatucci Cors ★★★ Prominent bio DOM in S CORS, saviour of indigenous varieties. Humble but top-quality VDF. CUVÉE Fustine, Valle de Nero (r/rosé). Collection range recalls military connections of ancestor, pal of Napoleon.

Condrieu N Rh ★★★→★★★★ 23' 24 25 Cradle of VIOGNIER, simple town, hillside sand-granite vyds, only c.225 ha. Best lighly scented, or mineral, acacia blossom, pear, apricot. Best: mystical, fragrant; avoid clumsy oak, sweetness, alc. Growers, and vines, adapting to hot yrs, so alc less, fruit clear recently: 24 variable, 25 tiny crop. Top wines live 10 yrs. 80 producers, not all gd. Rare white friendship with asparagus. Best: A Paret, ***A Perret***, Boissonnet, CHAPOUTIER, CLOS de la Bonnette (organic), C Pichon, DELAS, L Faury (esp La Berne), DOM Merlin, F Merlin, F Villard (elegant), GANGLOFF (rich), GUIGAL, ***G Vernay*** (brilliant Coteau de Vernon), M Clerc (trad), MONTEZ, Mouton (profound), Niéro, ROSTAING, ST COSME, Semaska, X Gérard (value), Y CUILLERON (stylish).

Corbières Ldoc ★★→★★★ Rugged large AOP: Wild West of LDOC. *Garrigue*, mtns and sea meet in remote and fascinating region. Brilliant value, real variety and interest. Fabulous reds based on CARIGNAN (Cru Boutenac). Some v.gd whites. Try CHX Aiguilloux, Aussières, Borde-Rouge, CARAGUILHES, de Sérame, Grand Moulin, La Baronne, Lastours, La Voulte-Gasparets, Les Palais, OLLIEUX ROMANIS, Pech-Latt, Vaugelas; DOMS de Fontsainte, de la Cendrillon, de Villemajou, DES DEUX CLÉS, du Grand Crès, du Vieux Parc, PY, Trillol; CLOS de l'Anhel, Clos du Cers, Famille Fabre, Grand Arc, Les Clos Perdus, MAXIME MAGNON, Sainte-Croix, Serres Mazard. Castelmaure co-op.

Cornas N Rh ★★★ 05' 09' **10'** 12' 15' **16' 17'** 18' 19' 20' **21'** 22' 23' 24' 25' Previously obscure, now high-profile ARDÈCHE granite-slope SYRAH, only 165 ha, top names prices shot up. Smouldering, always mineral-iron fused. Some (highest, recent vyds) made for early fruit, really need 5 yrs+. Top: A&E Verset (organic), ***Allemand*** (top two), BALTHAZAR (pure, incl zero sulphur), Chaboud-Cellier, ***Clape*** (benchmark), Colombo (modern), Courbis (modern), DELAS, DOM DU TUNNEL (rich), Dumien Serrette (value), G GILLES (stylish), J&E Durand (dashing fruit), Lemenicier (trad), Lionnet (organic), M Barret (bio), M Bourg, P&V Jaboulet, Tardieu-Laurent (stylish, oak), Voge (oak), V Paris (esp v. fine La Geynale).

Corsica / Corse ★★→★★★ Wild, rugged, breathtaking: not called "Île de Beauté" IGP for nothing. Warm but cooled by altitude; sea breezes give freshness. Over

A changing Cornas

Before 2000, there was just one vintage, 90, that gave a clue to what is now est as a sunny richness in the wines of CORNAS. Subsequently, 03, with an August harvest (more regular these days), gave wines of jam-like concentration, a far cry from the rocky tannic wines of the past. Since the late and hot 2010s, growers are vinifying with a lighter touch and have reverted to incl stems to preserve freshness and to lower alc. The result is wines of charm, tender tannins and a fluent level of drinking, requiring less waiting around. A fine example of this is 24, blessed with tasty, flowing wines, life span 20–25 yrs, less than previously. Out: game dishes. In: braised shoulder of lamb, veal chop with rosemary.

half is rosé. Reds elegant, spicy from SCIACARELLO, structured from NIELLUCCIO aka SANGIOVESE; tangy VERMENTINO whites. VDN sweet MUSCATS. Local varieties championed by top producers CLOS CANARELLI, COMTE ABBATUCCI et al. Nine AOPS incl crus PATRIMONIO in n, AJACCIO to w. AOP Corse plus villages Calvi, Coteaux du Cap Corse, Figari, Porto-Vecchio, Sartène. Top: Antoine Arena, ALZIPRATU, CLOS ALIVU, Clos Canereccia, Clos Calviani, Clos Capitoro, CLOS CULOMBU, CLOS D'ALZETO, Clos Nicrosi, Clos Poggiale, CLOS TEDDI, Clos Venturi; DOMS de Grenajolo, Fiumicicoli, Giacometti, Maestracci, Orsucci, Peraldi, PIERETTI, PINELLI, Poli, Saperale, Torraccia, YVES LECCIA, U STILICCIONU, Vaccelli.

Corton C d'O ★★→★★★★ 05' 09' 10' 12' 15' 17 18 19' 20' 21 22' 23 24 Too much is GC, can be stellar, sometimes dull; improving. Choose carefully. Best vyds: CLOS DU ROI, Bressandes, Renardes, Rognet. Top: BOUCHARD, CHANDON DE BRIAILLES, DRC, Dubreuil-Fontaine, FAIVELEY (CLOS des Cortons), Follin-Arbelet, MÉO-CAMUZET, RAPET, TOLLOT-BEAUT. Can be value: Bichot, Camille Giroud, Capitain-Gagnerot, Clavelier, DOM des Croix, H&G BUISSON, MALLARD, POUSSE D'OR, Terregelesses. Best white from Vergennes vyd: CHANSON, CH DE MEURSAULT, HOSPICES DE BEAUNE.

Corton-Charlemagne C d'O ★★★→★★★★ 05' 09' 10' 14' 15' 17' 18 19' 20' 21 22' 23 24 Potentially scintillating GC, thrilling when on song, should age well; sw- and w-facing limestone slopes, plus band around top of hill. Top: BIZE, BOUCHARD, CLAIR, ***Coche-Dury***, DRC, FAIVELEY, HOSPICES DE BEAUNE, JADOT, Javillier, LATOUR, Mallard, MONTILLE, RAMONET, RAPET, Rollin. Rare sister AOP, Charlemagne, used by BONNEAU DU MARTRAY, ***Dom Vougeraie***.

Pinot Noir and Pineau d'Aunis: so named because clusters resemble pine cones.

Costières de Nîmes S Rh ★→★★ 24 25 Spread out 2540 ha (30% organic), sw of CHÂTEAUNEUF; stony soils, most Med Rh red, maritime freshness nr Camargue; gd with garlic, imposing dishes. Red (GRENACHE, SYRAH) robust, salted, spiced, up to 15 yrs. Best: CHX de Beaubois (organic/bio), de Grande Cassagne, de Montfrin (organic), de Nages (gd w), d'Or et de Gueules (full), La Tour de Beraud (fruit), L'Ermitage, Mourgues-du-Grès (organic), Roubaud (fruit), Vessière (w); DOMS de la Patience (organic), du Vieux Relais, du Petit Romain, Galus, Gassier, M KREYDENWEISS (bio); CHAPOUTIER (organic), CLOS des Boutes (organic/bio), Mas Carlot (organic), Mas des Bressades (organic), Mas Neuf, Terre des Chardons (bio). Up-tempo, table-friendly rosés; best white stylish (esp ROUSSANNE).

Cotat, François Lo ★★→★★★★ Cult SANCERRE VIGNERON in Chavignol. Age-worthy wines demand 10 yrs to show value. Try Les Culs de Beaujeu, ***Les Monts Damnés***.

Coteaux Bourguignons Burg ★ DYA Mostly reds, GAMAY, PINOT N. AOP (est 2011) to replace BOURGOGNE Grand Ordinaire and to sex up basic BEAUJ. Rare whites ALIGOTÉ, CHARD, MELON, PINOTS BL/GR. Also covers rosé.

Coteaux Champenois Champ ★★★ AOP for still wines of CHAMP, eg. BOUZY, AMBONNAY. Vintages as for Champ. Better reds with climate change 12' 18 19 20. Impressive range of CC Grands Blancs based on 17' by CHARLES HEIDSIECK, burgundian by inclination. Also gd: Drappier, Egly Ouriet, SELOSSE, TARLANT. Not to forget BOLLINGER's La Côte aux Enfants 18 19 22.

Coteaux d'Aix-en-Provence Prov ★★ Mostly pale, fruity rosé from AOP centred on Aix: CINSAULT, GRENACHE. Some reds: CAB SAUV in cooler n (Pigoudet, Revelette, VIGNELAURE). In warmer spots, Med grapes often more interesting: CHX Calissanne, de Beaupré, La Realtière, Les Bastides, Les Béates, Paradis; DOM d'Eole (on Alpilles). *See also* LES BAUX-DE-PROV.

Coteaux d'Ancenis Lo ★→★★ 22 23 (25) Minor AOP in MUSCADET country for unfussy (r/w/rosé). Malvoisie (PINOT GR) can be interesting: Galloires, Landron-Chartier.

Coteaux de l'Aubance Lo ★★→★★★ 18' 19 20 22 (23) (25) ANJOU sweet AOP, more nervy, mineral than COTEAUX DU LAYON; gd value, esoteric. Try **Bablut**, Bois Brinçon, Montgilet, Rochelles, Terra Vita Vinum.

Coteaux du Giennois Lo ★→★★ 23 (25) Value alternative to POUILLY-FUMÉ, SANCERRE, just downriver from both. At best lively SAUV BL, decent reds (GAMAY/PINOT N). Drink young. Try Berthier, Langlois, Quintin, **Villargeau**.

Coteaux du Layon Lo ★★→★★★★ 07' 09 10 11' 13 14 15 16 17 18' 19 20 22 (23) (25) Leading AOP for botrytized CHENIN BL, incl six villages and PC Chaume. Best: BAUDOUIN, BELARGUS, Bergerie, CADY, Forges, Juchepie, **Pierre-Bise**, PIERRE MÉNARD & OGEREAU.

Coteaux du Loir Lo ★→★★★ AOP on the Loir (tributary of Loire); taut CHENIN BL 16' 18' 19 20' 22 (23) (25); reds incl fine Pineau d'Aunis. Try wines of enclave JASNIÈRES. Best: **Bellivière**, Maisons Rouges.

Coteaux du Quercy SW Fr DYA AOP between CAHORS and GAILLAC. Hearty country wines based on CAB FR, plus TANNAT or MALBEC. Active co-op challenged by independents: ★★ DOMS du Guillau, Lacoste, Revel.

Coteaux du Vendômois Lo ★→★★ Minor AOP on upper Loir above COTEAUX DU LOIR. Mostly CHENIN BL 22 23 (25). Pineau d'Aunis (r/rosé). Try DOM de Montrieux.

Coteaux Varois-en-Provence Prov ★★ High, cooler AOP, chalk; light, appealing rosé. GRENACHE, CINSAULT, SYRAH, VIOGNIER in cooler n. Tiny-volume red, gd, fruity with lift. Try CHX des Annibals, la Calisse, Carpe Diem, DE L'ESCARELLE, Lafoux, Miraval (Brad Pitt), St Julien, Trians; DOMS des Aspras, du Deffends, du Loou, La Grand'vigne, La Rose des Vents, Les Terres Promises, Routas, St Mitre.

Côte Chalonnaise Burg ★★→★★★ Reliable quality, gaining greater recognition. Lighter, ever-improving BOUZERON for ALIGOTÉ; **Rully** for accessible wines (r/w); **Mercurey** and GIVRY, more structure, can age; MONTAGNY for leaner, often impressive CHARD (hidden treasure in right hands).

Côte d'Or Burg Golden or e-facing slope. Département name applied to central and principal Burg vyds: CÔTE DE BEAUNE, CÔTE DE NUITS.

Côte de Beaune C d'O ★★→★★★★ The s half of C D'O. Also, little-seen, hilltop AOP above BEAUNE (should be renamed Collines de Beaune). DROUHIN's versions (r/w) also incl declassified Beaune PC. Try DOM VOUGERAIE too. Confusingly, C de B-Villages is different – often a blend from lesser villages of s half of C d'O. Read label carefully.

Côte de Brouilly Beauj ★★ 18' 19' 20' 21 22' 23 24 Hard to generalize: varying styles depending on soil, from easy, fruity to firm, structured. Merits premium over BROUILLY: CH THIVIN, Brun, Dufaitre, LAFARGE-Vial, Le Grappin, Martray, Pacalet.

Côte de Nuits C d'O ★★→★★★★ The n half of C D'O. Nearly all red, n to s: MARSANNAY, FIXIN, GEVREY, MOREY, CHAMBOLLE, CLOS DE VOUGEOT, VOSNE, NUITS. Wine doesn't get more patrician, or expensive, than best CdN.

Côte de Nuits-Villages C d'O ★★ 15' 16 17 18' 19' 20' 21 22' 23 24 AOP for extreme n/s of CÔTE DE NUITS; can be bargains. Specialists: Chopin, Gachot-Monot, Jourdan. Top vyds: CLOS du Chapeau (ARLOT), Croix Violette (FOURNIER, Pernot), Faulques (Millot), Leurey (J-J Confuron), Meix Fringuet (TRAPET), Montagne (many), Robignotte (Jourdan), Vaucrains (JADOT). Best (w): Monts de Boncourt.

Côte Roannaise Lo, Mass C ★★→★★★ 18' 19 20' 21 22' 23 (25) Small AOP high on the Loire in Massif Central; granite, basalt perfect for GAMAY. Best: Pothiers, **Sérol**, and can age. Also Giraudon.

Côte-Rôtie N Rh ★★★→★★★★ 09' 10' 12' 15' 16' 17' 18' 19' 20' 21 22' 23' 24' 25' Mainly SYRAH, nibble of VIOGNIER, *en finesse* violets, pretty fruit, style connects with burg. Schist wines dark, granite wines more tender. Allow 5–10 yrs+. Long-lived 10 15 19 25, silken 20, pure 21, pretty fruit 22, expressive 23, flowing 24. Top: **Barge**, B Chambeyron, Billon (drive), Bonnefond (crisp, oak), Bonserine (La Garde), Bott (modern), Burgaud, CHAPOUTIER, **Clusel-Roch** (organic),

Degache (Maisons Blanches), DELAS, DOM de Rosiers, Duclaux, Gaillard (oak), Garon, GUIGAL (long oak), ***Jamet***, Jean-Luc Jamet, JASMIN (pure), J-M GÉRIN, J-M Stéphan (organic), Lafoy (improver), Levet (trad), L Faury, MONTEZ, Parpette (Le Plomb), ***Rostaing*** (fine), Semaska, S OGIER, S Pichat (Grandes Places), VIDAL-FLEURY (La Chatillonne), X Gérard, Y CUILLERON.

Côtes Catalanes Rouss ★★★ Arguably France's most thrilling IGP (r/w/rosé). From fruity gd-value from big Vignerons Catalans co-op, to serious age-worthy wines from some of ROUSS's finest growers. CLOS DES FÉES, DANJOU-BANESSY, Gauby, CH de l'Ou, Lafage, Le Soula, ODYSÉE, Paetzold, among others for top wines. Covers most of ROUSS except BANYULS, COLLIOURE, which are IGP Côte Vermeille.

Côtes d'Auvergne Lo, Mass C ★→★★ 22' 23 (25) Small AOP high on the Allier in Massif Central. Straightforward, light Burg wines from CHARD, GAMAY, PINOT N. Try: Desprat Saint-Verny, Les Chemins de l'Arkose, Miolanne, Sauvat.

Côtes de Bordeaux Bx ★ AOP for reds. For cross-blending CAS, FRANCS, BLAYE, CADILLAC and Ste-Foy. If Cas, Cadillac, etc. comes before Côtes de Bx, expect single terroir, stiffer controls. BLAYE-CÔTES DE BX, FRANCS-CÔTES DE BX, Ste-Foy Côtes de Bx: some dry white too. Try CHX Dudon, Malagar, Pilet.

Côtes de Bourg Bx ★→★★ 20 22 23 (25) Solid, savoury reds, a little white from e bank of Gironde; MALBEC, key element. Top CHX: Brûlesécaille, Bujan, de la Grave (Caractère), ***Falfas***, Fougas-Maldoror, Grand-Maison, Haut-Guiraud, Haut-Macô, Haut-Mondésir, La Grolet (Tête de Cuvée), Le Clos du Notaire, Macay, Puy d'Amour (Grain de Folie), ***Roc de Cambes.***

Côtes de Duras SW Fr ★→★★ 19 20 22 23 24 (25) Quirky, underrated BERGERAC AOP; BX styles with sweet twist: Mauzac, Ondenc grapes. Best known for crisp dry whites: ★★ DOMS de Laulan, Grand Mayne, Mouthes le Bihan; gd co-op, Berticot.

Côtes de Gascogne / Comté Tolosan SW Fr Usually DYA. Two catch-all IGPS covering most of sw. Kaleidoscope of styles, mostly entry level: ★★ Joy, Menard Pellehaut, Plaimont, Tariquet for Gascony; DOM de Ribonnet for Tolosan. Unbeatable value, infinite possibilities, wide selection of grapes.

Côtes de Millau SW Fr ★ Small, Med-influenced AOP in beautiful Gorges du Tarn close to Millau viaduct. Home to a gd co-op. Best independents: DOMS du Vieux Noyer, La Tour-St-Martin, Montrozier.

Côtes de Provence Prov ★→★★★ DYA Huge volumes of fashionably pale rosé; AOP from swathe of vyds, Marseilles to Cannes and inland. Together with COTEAUX D'AIX, COTEAUX VAROIS accounts for 90% of PROV rosé. White (increasingly 100% Rolle) and red (GRENACHE, SYRAH; MOURVÈDRE nearer coast) can be more interesting. Five subzones: La Londe, STE-VICTOIRE best, plus Fréjus, Notre Dame des Anges, Pierrefeu. Top: CHX D'ESCLANS, de l'Îlle, Gasqui (bio), La Gordonne, La Mascaronne, Léoube, Malherbe; CLOS CIBONNE (primarily Tibouren), DOMS ***Gavoty***, Ott (Ch de Selle, Clos Mireille); Estandon, MIRABEAU, Rimauresq.

Côtes du Brulhois SW Fr ★ 19 20 22 23 (24) Small AOP nr Agen, most oceanic of Garonne, Tarn appellations. Softer version of TANNAT (obligatory) and CAB SAUV, MALBEC, MERLOT in support. Local co-op unusually supportive of a few independents. Best for quaffing reds, pinks.

Côtes du Forez Lo, Mass C ★→★★ 21 22 23 Small AOP high on the Loire in Massif Central, above CÔTE ROANNAISE. Delightfully drinkable GAMAY, best drunk young: Bonnefoy, Guillot, Poyet, ***Verdier-Logel.***

Côtes du Jura Jura AOP covering all Jura, but esp around Poligny and s. Organic. White dominates: mineral, salty CHARD, SAVAGNIN of all styles, incl VIN JAUNE. Light, earthy PINOT N, Poulsard, TROUSSEAU. ★★: Chevassu. ★★: Berthet-Bondet, Courbet, Croix & Courbet, Grappe, Macle, Pignier. ★★→★★★: Marnes Blanches. ★★→★★★: Buronfosse, Dolomies, Dom Overnoy, Pieds sur Terre. ★★★: ***Cavarodes***, Maison Maenad, Nicolas Jacob. ★★★→★★★★: ***Ganevat***, ***Labet***, Miroirs.

Côtes du Marmandais SW Fr (r) 18 19 20 22 23 (24) AOP, 300m (984ft) as crow flies from BX, increasingly eccentric thanks to local Abouriou grape and SYRAH. ★★★ Cult winemaker ELIAN DA ROS flagship DOM. ★★ Doms Beyssac, Bonnet, Cavenac, CH Lassolle (blend with usual Bx grapes). Co-ops dominate (95%).

Côtes du Rhône S Rh ★→★★ 24 25 Crisis-hit (28,000 ha, low sales, prices, vyds abandoned), incl v.gd SYRAH of Brézème, St-Julien-en-St-Alban (N Rh). Handful of interesting, gd reds (CHÂTEAUNEUF estates, big value) vs dull, mass produced. Supple, stylish, spice in best. Mainly GRENACHE, also Syrah, often old CARIGNAN. Most best drunk young. Vaucluse best, then Gard (Syrah). Whites on the up (esp 24), best refined, value.

Côtes du Rhône-Villages S Rh ★→★★★ 23 24 25 Full, spiced reds from 8000 ha, incl 21 named S Rh villages, some ghost-like. Best: dark fruit, flair, gd value. Red core: GRENACHE, plus SYRAH, MOURVÈDRE. Improving white, best stylish, often incl ROUSSANNE, VIOGNIER with usual CLAIRETTE, GRENACHE BL, best *à table*. Top three: PLAN DE DIEU (gd range), SÉGURET (quality, choice), VISAN (improving, many organic). *See* MASSIF D'UCHAUX (fresh), SABLET (notable w), VALRÉAS; St-Gervais (DOM Sainte-Anne). (*See* box, below, for best growers.)

Côtes du Roussillon (Villages) Rouss ★→★★★ Generic AOP for ROUSS (r/w/rosé), often gd value. Blends based on GRENACHES N/BL/Gr, with CARIGNAN, SYRAH and MACCABEO for whites. AOP Côtes du Rouss-Villages, red only, smaller, old vines, mostly schist, some v.gd; 32 villages: Caramany, Latour de France, Les Aspres, Lesquerde, Tautavel named on label. Try Boucabeille, CAZES, Charles Perez, CLOS DES FÉES, Clot de l'Oum, des Chênes, Gauby, Les VIGNES de Bila-Haut (CHAPOUTIER), Mas Becha, Mas Crémat, Mas de la Devèze, Modat, Piquemal, Rancy, ROC DES ANGES, Thunevin-Calvet, Venus. Co-ops Brial, Carmany gd. *See also* CÔTES CATALANES.

Coudoulet, Dom Ldoc ★★★ Innovative DOM in MINERVOIS. Fine La Livinière, CH de Cesseras, IGP from 20 different varieties: ASSYRTIKO, PINOT GR, PETIT VERDOT, PETITE SIRAH, PINOT N.

Coulée de Serrant Lo ★ 18 19 20 21 23 Historic CHENIN BL AOP; wonderful 7-ha ANJOU vyd, but troubled by high alc, botrytis, premox. Proprietor Nicolas Joly makes other SAVENNIÈRES, also problem-prone (mousy Les Vieux Clos 22).

Coume del Mas Rouss ★★★→★★★★ Close to Med. Folio (w) barrel-ferment Grenache Gr. Schistes (r) 30-parcel GRENACHE N. Quadratur (r), top COLLIOURE. Outstanding VDNS incl rare BANYULS Bl.

Courcel, Dom de C d'O ★★★ Pommard structure without undue heft, a dextrous combination. Top: age-worthy PCS Épenots, Rugiens. Interesting Croix Noires.

Village allsorts: best of Côtes du Rhône-Villages

21 villages, all sorts, sleepy to dynamic: try Gadagne (full, spiced), MASSIF D'UCHAUX, St-Maurice (rare, stylish, cool r/w), Ste-Cécile (medium weight), Signargues (robust), VISAN; CHX Bois de la Garde, Fontségune, Signac; DOMS Aure, Bastide, Bastide St Dominique (organic), Bois de St Jean (full), Buissonnade (organic), Cabotte (bio, elegance), Coste Chaude (organic), Crève Coeur (bio, character), Echevin (gd w), Espigouette (full), Florane (bio), Grand Veneur, Grands Bois (organic), Gravennes (smooth), Janasse (top class), Jérôme, ***Les Aphillanthes*** (bio), Martin (punchy), Montbayon, Montmartel (organic), Mourchon, Pascal Chalon (bio), Pasquiers (organic), Pique-Basse (gd organic w), ***Rabasse-Charavin***, Reméjeanne (v.gd r/w), Renjarde, Romarins, Saladin (organic), STE-ANNE, Valériane; CAVE de RASTEAU Ortas, Les Vignerons d'Estézargues (GRENACHE range best, incl Doms Génestas, Pierredon).

Cour-Cheverny Lo ★★→★★★ 18 19 20 22 23 (25) Tiny CHEVERNY AOP enclave for rare Romorantin. Firm acidity. Can age, esp *moelleux*. Try ***Cazin***, Huards, Tessier.

Crémant AOP for quality classic-method fizz from AL, BX, BOURGOGNE, Die, Jura, LIMOUX, Lo, Luxembourg, SAV. Many gd egs.

Crémant de Loire Lo ★★→★★★ Large AOP for fizz. Styles vary, elegant CHARD, mineral CHENIN BL, rosé. Big-name SAUMUR houses provide value: BOUVET-LADUBAY, Langlois-Château. Highest quality from smaller DOMS: Fesles, Lambert, ***Plaisance***, Rocheville.

Criots-Bâtard-Montrachet C d'O ★★★ 09 10 12 14' 15 17' 18 19' 21 22' 23 24 Tiny MONTRACHET satellite, 1.57 ha, downslope of BÂTARD-M. D'Auvenay for lottery winners. More accessible from Blain- or Fontaine-GAGNARD, LAMY and Caroline MOREY. Hangs on Montrachet's coat-tails. Doesn't burnish the term GC.

Cros, Dom du SW Fr Philippe Teulier was pioneer of MARCILLAC. Started with 1 ha, today is largest independent producer, 30 ha. Flagship ★★ Le Sang del Paїs (r) from FER SERVADOU, locally known as Mansois.

Cros Parantoux Burg ★★★→★★★★ Cult PC in VOSNE, made famous by Henri Jayer. Now made by MÉO-CAMUZET, ROUGET. (Haunting Jayer magic hard to replicate.)

Crozes-Hermitage N Rh ★★→★★★ 23 24 25' Cited as France's most profitable AOP, but demand slowing after fast expansion. SYRAH from mostly flat vyds: quality gd to variable; dark fruits, licorice, black-olive flavours; most drink 2–5 yrs. Tight, cooler (more intrigue) Syrah from granite-loess hills n of HERMITAGE: dark red-fruited, iron; need time. Simple CUVÉES ideal for celebrations. Oaked, older-vine wines gradually reveal, cost more. Top: ***A Graillot*** (ace La Guiraude), Aléofane (r/w), Belle (organic), Betton (esp w), CHAPOUTIER, ***Dard & Ribo*** (low sulphur, old vines, much character), DELAS (Le CLOS, DOM des Grands Chemins), G Robin, Les Vins de Vienne; DOMS Combier (organic, Clos des Grives r), de Thalabert (JABOULET), de la Ville Rouge (bio), des Entrefaux, des Hauts-Châssis, des Lises (fine), ***du Colombier*** (***Gaby*** r/w), Dumaine (organic), Habrard (organic), ***Laurent Fayolle*** (stylish Clos Cornirets), Les Bruyères (bio, big fruit), Machon, Martinelles (trad), Melody (r/w), Mucyn (fine), Remizières (oak), Rousset (top Picaudières), S Michelas (organic), Vendome (organic), Y Chave. Drink ***white*** (mostly MARSANNE) early, run of v.gd yrs, value.

Cuilleron, Yves N Rh ★★★ Leading CONDRIEU, always elegant, restrained. Large increase in production recently, now organic. Best: Les Chaillets. Also gd: old-vine ST-JOSEPH (r) Les Serines, Essence d'Automne (sw). CÔTE-RÔTIE, oaked (La Viallière). COLLINES RHODANIENNES Ripa Sinistra (SYRAH, Seyssuel). Whites: gd MARSANNE, VIOGNIER.

Cuve close Quicker method of making fizz in tank. Bubbles die away in glass much faster than with *méthode traditionnelle*.

Cuvée Usually indicates a blend. In CHAMP, means 1st and best juice off the press.

Dagueneau, Louis-Benjamin Lo ★★★→★★★★ Iconic POUILLY-FUMÉ DOM; all wines VDF since 2017. Top: Buisson Renard, Le Mont Damné, Pur Sang, ***Silex*** 17 18' 19 20 21 22' 23 (25).

Danjou-Banessy, Dom Rouss ★★★★ Extraordinarily complex, fresh; bio. In Agly V. IGP CÔTES CATALANES; v.gd La Truffière (r/w), Roboul, mostly MOURVÈDRE. Ethereal Estaca 130-yr-old GRENACHE.

Dard & Ribo N Rh ★★★ High-interest wines from talented duo, correctly loved by natural-wine supporters. Consistent; handmade, charm, age well. Old-vine CROZES-HERMITAGE, ST-JOSEPH (Pitrou r/w). White Crozes Les Bâties, ROUSSANNE.

Dauvissat, Vincent Chab ★★★★ Outstanding bio CHAB using old barrels and local 132-litre *feuillettes*. Complex, age-worthy, similar to RAVENEAU relatives. Best: La Forest, Les CLOS, Preuses, Séchet. Try also DOM Jean D & Fils (no relation). Proper Chab.

Deiss, Dom Marcel Al ★★★→★★★★ Famous Bergheim estate favouring field blends: rich, often off-dry Altenberg de Bergheim 22', Engelgarten 18, SCHOENENBOURG 13' 17' 20 (delicious) 22'. Young Mathieu D follows father Jean-Michel, now more precision, purity at all levels: marvellous Burg **22** 23', Grasberg 21'. Now v.gd PINOT N (r).

Delamotte Champ ★★★ Fine, small CHARD house in s. Managed with SALON by LAURENT-PERRIER. BRUT, fascinating Rosé, BLANC DE BLANCS 08 13' 14 15'; 18 19' 20 trilogy promises much; 19 *primus inter pares*.

Delas Frères N Rh ★★★ Owner-merchant, CONDRIEU, CROZES-HERMITAGE, CÔTE-RÔTIE, notably HERMITAGE vyds. ROEDERER-owned. Sleek reds, bit technical, consistent level, high prices. Best: Côte-Rôtie Landonne; Hermitage DOM des Tourettes (r/w), ***Les Bessards*** (r, granite snap, much finesse 15 yrs+), Ligne de Crête (subtle); ST-JOSEPH Ste-Épine (r, complex, time); S Rh Grignan-les-Adhémar (r, value); VACQUEYRAS DOM des Genêts. Whites risk-free, mainstream, lighter recently.

Delaunay, Edouard C d'O ★★★ Old Burg name revived in NUITS and l'Étang-Vergy by dynamic Laurent D; wide range NÉGOCIANT CUVÉES. Gaining widespread plaudits: v.gd-value Septembre BOURGOGNE CHARD, PINOT N. Best yet to come.

Demi-sec Half-dry – in practice more like half-sweet (CHAMP c.45g/l dosage).

Department 66 Rouss ★★★ Napa winemaker Dave Phinney's DOM in MAURY; old vines, smart winery. Smart wines too. Opulent Painted Scars CÔTES CATALANES GRENACHE, SYRAH; Others (r), mineral, approachable.

Derenoncourt, Stéphane Bx International winemaker. Owns ***Dom de l'A***. Vignerons Consultants now run by partners.

White Rhônes, often max 10% production, fly out the door, unlike reds. Tricky.

Deutz Champ ★★★★ ROEDERER-owned. Winemaker Caroline Latrive (ex-AYALA). Supreme CHARD ***Cuvée Amour de Deutz*** 08 13 15' 16; AdD Rosé **12 13** 15 16; CUVÉE William Deutz 08 **12 13 14'** 15; BLANC DE BLANCS 13 **14 16'** 17'. Single-vyd PINOT N: Côte Glacière, Meurtet 18.

Deux Clés, Dom des Ldoc ★★★ Burgundians Gaëlle, Florian Richter bring light touch to terroir-driven wines (r/w) from old vines in deepest CORBIÈRES. IGP Vallée du Paradis terrific CARIGNAN.

Devaux Champ ★★★ Côte des Bars. Reliable CUVÉE D Brut, Rosé; Coeur des Bar pair BLANC DE BLANCS/NOIRS. Organic Coeur de Nature. Also high-profile project with Michel CHAPOUTIER: Sténopé 08 **09 10 11'** 12. So far so v.gd.

Dirler-Cadé, Dom Al ★★★→★★★★ Top old-vines MUSCAT GC Saering 23', Spiegel 22'; SYLVANER VIEILLES VIGNES 17' 18' 19 20 22 23; v.gd Saering and Kitterlé RIES **10 14'** 17' 18 19 20 22. Luscious Bux PINOT GR VT 23. Amazing GEWURZ Spiegel VT **19** 23 (Gewurz Saering VT almost as gd). Now gd CRÉMANTS.

Dom (Domaine) Property, except next entry. *See* under name, eg. TEMPIER, DOM.

Dom Pérignon Champ ★★★★ Vincent Chaperon, chef de CAVE of MOËT & CHANDON's luxury CUVÉE. Plénitude releases: long bottle-age, recent disgorgement, huge price, at 7, 16, 30 yrs+ (P1, P2, P3); superb ***P2*** **02** 04' 06' 08, still-vibrant P3 **70 82** 85 **90 93'**. More PINOT N focus (since 2000) 08 **10** 12 **13'** 15 17'. Superb, ultra-expensive rosé too. Quantity, quality both shrouded in mythology; both v. high. Direct access to 900 ha of vines incl 14 of the 17 GCS.

Dopff au Moulin Al ★★★→★★★★ Pioneer of AL CRÉMANT in pretty Riquewihr; some wines dilute but GEWURZ GCS Brand, Sporen **12** 16 18' 20', RIES SCHOENENBOURG 13 17', SYLVANER de Riquewihr 19' v.gd. Some gd buys, hidden gems.

Dourbie, Dom de la Ldoc ★★★ Smart bio DOM, serious CINSAULT Intemporal. Mala Coste (GRENACHE BL/ROUSSANNE), taut, complex. Fun pét-nat from old LDOC grape Terret. Arty labels.

Dourthe Bx Sizeable merchant-grower; eight properties (incl CHX BELGRAVE, Grand Barrail Lamarzelle Figeac, LA GARDE, PEY LA TOUR) managed by Pénélope Godefroy, ex-Artemis Domaines (LATOUR, CH-GRILLET).

Drappier, Michel Champ ★★★→★★★★ Family-run AUBE house. Fine PINOT N, 60 ha+, bio; Pinot-led NV, BRUT ZÉRO, Brut *sans souffre*, Millésime d'Exception 18 19 20, Prestige CUVÉE Grande Sendrée **12 13 15** 16, plus GS Rosé 08 **09 10'** 12; Cuvée Quatuor (four CÉPAGES). Superb 95' **82** (magnums). Excellent Trop M'en Faut! from rare Fromenteau grape. More use of large oak *foudres*.

DRC (Dom de la Romanée-Conti) C d'O ★★★★ Grandest estate in Burg. MONOPOLES ROMANÉE-CONTI, LA TÂCHE, major parts of ÉCHÉZEAUX, GRANDS-ÉCHÉZEAUX, RICHEBOURG, ROMANÉE-ST-VIVANT, plus 0.68 ha of MONTRACHET. Also CORTON (from 09), superb CORTON-CHARLEMAGNE (since 19). Glorious wines, thunderous prices.

Drouhin, Joseph & Cie Burg ★★★→★★★★ Grower-NÉGOCIANT in BEAUNE; vyds (bio) incl (w) Beaune ***Clos des Mouches***, MONTRACHET (Marquis de LAGUICHE) and large CHAB holdings. Wide range of stylish reds: CHOREY-LÈS-BEAUNE, Beaune, CHAMBOLLE, VOSNE (Petits Monts) and GEVREY. Purchase of Rapet (ST-ROMAIN) and CH de Chasselas (ST-VÉRAN), added 20 ha. Run by four siblings, next generation also involved. Also Dom Drouhin Oregon (US).

Duboeuf, Georges Beauj ★★→★★★ Mixed reputation: saviour of BEAUJ vs too much BEAUJ NOUVEAU. Always major player. Reliable source for Beauj crus that age remarkably well, Mâcon bottlings. Don't let ubiquity obscure many other producers.

Dugat C d'O ★★★→★★★★ Cousins Claude and Bernard (Dugat-Py) made excellent, deep-coloured GEVREY-CHAMBERTIN, respective labels. Almost ageless. Both flourishing with new generation. Tiny volumes, esp GCS, huge prices deliver quality not value. Try D-P's BOURGOGNE Rouge to gain hint of GC quality.

L'Etoile takes its name from tiny star-shaped fossils you find among the vines.

Dujac, Dom C d'O ★★★→★★★★ MOREY-ST-DENIS grower originally noted for sensual reds that aged into haunting beauty, from village Morey to outstanding GCS: CLOS DE LA ROCHE, CLOS ST-DENIS, ÉCHÉZEAUX. Slightly firmer style today. ***Whites*** from Morey, PULIGNY. Eco-friendly winery (2023). Splendid tasting room (2025). Lighter merchant wines: D Fils & Père, DOM Triennes (COTEAUX VAROIS).

Durban, Dom S Rh ★★→★★★ Top MUSCAT de BEAUMES-DE-VENISE from beautiful, solitary vyds at height, veteran family; delicious, long-lived (20 yrs+). Steady BEAUMES (r), trim IGP dry Muscat, VIOGNIER.

Dureuil-Janthial Burg ★★ Vincent D-J runs highly regarded DOM in RULLY: fresh, appealing whites; attractive, juicy reds. No disappointments: Maizières (r/w), PC Meix Cadot (w). Seek out if C D'O now beyond budget.

Duroché, Dom C d'O ★★★→★★★★ Pierre D's deft approach yields richness, depth on one hand, elegance, finesse on other; all seamlessly blended with age. Also small NÉGOCE operation, joint venture with DANBURY RIDGE in UK.

Duval-Leroy Champ ★★★ Family-owned, over 200 ha. Focus CHARD crus. Improved Prestige BLANC DE BLANCS, Femme de CHAMP (GC 08 BRUT, Rosé). Fleur de Champ GC 02 04 08. ***Clos des Bouveries*** 06' 08. Chef de CAVE, pioneering Sandrine Logette.

Échézeaux C d'O ★★★ 02' 05' 09' 10' 12' 15' **16 17** 18 19' 20' 21 22' 23 24 GC next to CLOS DE VOUGEOT, but different style: lacy, ethereal, scintillating. Pixellated ownership, 38 ha, 59 owners. Value, in context of GC prices: ARNOUX-LACHAUX, Bizot, Coquard-Loison-Fleurot, DRC, DUJAC, EUGÉNIE, G NOËLLAT, GRIVOT, GROS, LIGER-BELAIR, MÉO-CAMUZET, ***Mugneret-Gibourg***, ROUGET, TREMBLAY. Also Berthaut-Gerbet, ***Guyon***, Lamarche, Millot, MUGNERET, Naudin-Ferrand, Tardy.

Edelzwicker Al ★ DYA Blended, entry-level fresh white: HUGEL Gentil, Meyer-Fonné.

Egly-Ouriet Champ ★★★→★★★★ Family affair in GC Ambonnay, Francis E heading 4th generation. Outstanding VIEILLES VIGNES: Les Crayères BLANC DE NOIRS. Also NV PC Les Prémices. Fashionable (and brilliant) COTEAUX CHAMPENOIS; CUVÉE des Grands Côtés 18 19 20. Also late-release VP (Vieillissement Prolongé), variant on RD theme. Fantastically subtle take on PINOT N.

Elian da Ros, Dom SW Fr ★★★→★★★★ Almost single-handedly created reputation of CÔTES DU MARMANDAIS, rare AOP e of SAUTERNES. Trained with ZIND H; est 1997. Excellent bio wines: BX varieties, local speciality Abouriou.

Entraygues-le-Fel and Estaing SW Fr ★→★★ DYA Two tiny, obscure AOP neighbours, nr-vertical terraces above Lot V. Cool climate, hard to find, but worth it (esp w). Bone-dry CHENIN BL v.gd: ★★ DOMS Laurent Mousset (r, esp La Pauca, v.gd rosé), Méjanassère, ★★ Nicolas Carmarans.

Entre-Deux-Mers Bx ★→★★ DYA Often gd-value dry white BX from between rivers Garonne and Dordogne. New red AOP from 23 (stricter rules than BX SUPÉRIEUR), available 25. Best: CHX BONNET, de Fontenille, Haut-Rian, La Mothe du Barry CUVÉE French Kiss, Landereau, La Peyre, Lauduc, Marjosse, Nardique-la-Gravière, Sainte-Marie, ***Tour de Mirambeau***, Thieuley, Turcaud, Vignol.

Escaravailles, Dom des S Rh ★★→★★★ Foremost CAIRANNE and RASTEAU name, high vyds. Daughter Madeline conjures sparkling fruit. Top Roaix Village (SYRAH); Rasteaus Ad Argillam (part amphorae), Héritage 1924 (rich); VDN; great CÔTES DU RH (r/w).

Escarelle, Ch l' Prov ★★★ CÔTEAUX VAROIS-EN-PROV; nature res; elegant, aromatic rosés. Croix d'Engardin (oaked, can age); Les Deux Anges gd.

Esclans, Ch d' Prov ★★→★★★ Self-styled architect of "rosé renaissance", Sacha Lichine has built high-profile rosé brands, most for export. Whispering Angel big everywhere. Top: Garrus GRENACHE/ROLLE, oaked, expensive, will age. Les Clans, partially oaked, v. stylish. Part-owned by LVMH.

Esmonin, Dom Sylvie C d'O ★★★ No-holds-barred style, ample, rich, whole-bunch vinification. Best: CLOS ST-JACQUES (DOM's back garden), GEVREY-CHAMBERTIN VIEILLES VIGNES. Slightly below radar, hence gd value (CÔTES DE NUITS-VILLAGES).

Estabel, La Cave de l' Ldoc ★★★ Top CABRIÈRES co-op: v.gd rosé; Fulcrand Cabanon CLAIRETTE even better. Super value. Fragrant, fine Cantate de Garrigue (r).

Etoile, L' Jura AOP for stony CHARD, SAVAGNIN on limestone and marl, often oxidative. VIN JAUNE, VIN DE PAILLE also allowed but not reds (sold as AOP CÔTES DU JURA). ★: Baud, Mouillard. ★★→★★★: ***Montbourgeau***.

Eugénie, Dom C d'O ★★★→★★★★ Artemis Estates, also CLOS DE TART, BOUCHARD (latter's CÔTE DE NUITS vyds transferred here). Intense, dark; enlivened by more whole-bunch vinification. Outstanding CLOS DE VOUGEOT, GRANDS-ÉCHÉZEAUX.

Faiveley, Dom Burg ★★→★★★★ Vibrant NUITS DOM; 200 yrs in 2025, marked by donation of 0.17 ha of CLOS DE VOUGEOT to HOSPICES DE BEAUNE. Run by siblings Erwan and Eve F. Polished style, sweet fruit. Leading light in CÔTE CHALONNAISE, but save up for top CHAMBERTIN-CLOS de Bèze, CHAMBOLLE-MUSIGNY, CORTON ***Clos des Cortons***, NUITS. Also DOM BILLAUD-Simon (CHAB).

Faugères Ldoc ★★★ AOP in Cevennes foothills, unique schist terroir, much organic. *Garrigue*-scented, poised reds. Will age. Elegant whites from GRENACHE BL, MARSANNE, ROUSSANNE, VERMENTINO. Drink CH de Ciffre, DE LA LIQUIÈRE. DOMS Ancienne Mercerie, BARDI-ALQUIER, CÉBÈNE, Chenaie, des Trinités, Estanilles, Grézan, LA SARABANDE, Léon Barral, Mas d'Alezon, Mas Gabinèle, Méteore, Ollier-Taillefer, St Antonin.

Felettig, Gilbert & Christine C d'O ★★★ CHAMBOLLE-MUSIGNY through and through, with some holdings to n and s. Lovely, lively freshness, even in weak vintages. Delicious, value CLOS le Village, HAUTES-CÔTES DE BEAUNE En Vallerot (w).

Ferraton Père & Fils N Rh ★★★ HERMITAGE-based grower-merchant, CHAPOUTIER-owned, bio. Varied wines (N/S Rh). Quality gd to v.gd: CORNAS Patou, CROZES-HERMITAGE Grand Courtil (r/w 50/50% MARSANNE/ROUSSANNE), Le Reverdy (w, oak), Les Dionnières (r, elegance), ST-JOSEPH Bonneveau (r, true terroir). LAUDUN (w) gd. Top Hermitage Le Méal plot sold to J-L CHAVE (2025).

Fèvre, William Chab ★★★→★★★★ Biggest owner of CHAB GCS: outstanding Bougros Côte Bougerots and Les CLOS. Small yields, no expense spared. GCs can be splendid, age-worthy; humbler wines more exciting than previously. DBR Lafite-owned. Visitor-friendly. Also N&G Fèvre (GC Preuses, PC Vaulorent).

Fiefs Vendéens Lo ★→★★★ 21 22 23 (25) Minor Atlantic AOP; whites (mostly CHENIN BL) have delicious Ligérian flavours and oceanic salinity. Bright, breezy reds from CAB FR, GAMAY, NÉGRETTE, more. Try ***Saint Nicolas*** (VDF), Mourat.

Fitou Ldoc ★★→★★★ Remote, oft-forgotten AOP. Enclave within CORBIÈRES. Great value, rugged, chalky, windswept; schist inland. Seek out old vines, mostly CARIGNAN. Try CHX de Nouvelles, Grand Guilhem, Champs des Soeurs; DOMS Bertrand-Bergé, de la Rochelierre, DU VENT, JONES, Lérys, Mas des Caprices.

Fixin C d'O ★★→★★★ 10' 12' 14 15' 16 17 18 19' 20' 21 22' 23 24 Now worthy of mention in same breath as GEVREY. Continuing improvement. Structured reds, previously hearty but gaining charm. Best vyds: Arvelets, CLOS de la Perrière, Clos du Chapitre, Clos Napoléon. Top locals: Berthaut-Gerbet, Gelin, Joliet, Naddef. Also gd: Bart, CLAIR, FAIVELEY, MORTET. Watch.

Fleurie Premiers Crus? Not yet, but in the long pipeline, since 2024.

Fleurie Beauj ★★→★★★ 15' 18' 19' 20' 21 22' 23 24 Approachable cru BEAUJ: scented, strawberry fruit. Charm in a glass. PCS applied for, will be yrs. Classic: CHX BEAUREGARD, Chatelard, de Poncié; DOMS Brun, Chignard; CLOS de la Roilette, Depardon, DUBOEUF, Métrat, co-op. Naturalists: Balagny, Dutraive, Métras, Pacalet, Sunier. New: Chapel, Clos de Mez, Dom de Fa, ***Hoppenot***, LAFARGE-Vial.

Fontanel, Dom Rouss ★★★ Go-ahead DOM: Arrels (r), classy MAURY Sec; VDNS Maury Grenat, moreish; RIVESALTES Ambré, nutty, orange-peel delight.

Fourrier, Dom C d'O ★★★★ GEVREY DOM producing sensual vibrant reds, magical fruit flavours, hard to fault. Age beautifully. Best: CLOS ST-JACQUES, Combe aux Moines (complete with monk sculpture in vyd), GRIOTTE-CHAMBERTIN. Magnificent wines, even in lesser yrs. Also Bass Phillip (*see* Australia).

Francs-Côtes de Bordeaux Bx ★★ 19 20 22 23 (25) Tiny CÔTES AOP next to CAS; also wants independent status. Fief of Thienpont (PAVIE MACQUIN) family. Mainly red; MERLOT-led (60%). Some gd white (Charmes-Godard, Puyanché). Try Ad Francos, Cru Godard, Franc-Cardinal, La Prade, Marsau, ***Puygueraud***.

Fronsac Bx ★★→★★★ 18 19' 20' 22 23 (25) Great-value, hilly AOP w of POM. MERLOT-led on clay-limestone; mid-term ageing potential. Top CHX: Arnauton, DALEM, de la Huste, Fontenil, George 7, Haut-Carles, ***La Dauphine***, La Rivière, LA VIEILLE CURE, LES TROIS CROIX, Mayne-Vieil (CUVÉE Alienor), ***Moulin Haut-Laroque***, Plain-Point, Villars. *See also* CANON-FRON.

Fronton SW Fr ★★ 20 22 23 (24) AOP n of Toulouse. Home to NÉGRETTE (violets, cherries, licorice); often blended with SYRAH. Best known, vibrant, fruity, purple-hued: ★★★ CHX Baudare, Bouissel, Caze; ★★ CH BELLEVUE-LA-FORÊT, ***du Roc***; La Colombière, Laurou, Plaisance. Also gd: ★ Boujac, Clamens, Viguerie de Belaygues. No AOP for whites yet.

Fuchs, Henri Al ★★★ Organic Ribeauvillé winery (est 1922), 4th generation. Outstanding SYLVANER VIEILLES VIGNES 19 20 21 (late-ripening Weinbaum site); v.gd RIES GC Kirchberg de Ribeauvillé.

Fuissé, Ch Burg ★★→★★★ Smart operation in POUILLY-FUISSÉ. Concentrated, can be lavish. Top: Combettes, Le CLOS, ST-VÉRAN (fresh). Also BEAUJ crus.

Gagnard C d'O ★★★ Widespread family in CHASSAGNE. Long-lasting wines, esp BÂTARD, Caillerets from Jean-Noël G; while Blain-G, Fontaine-G have full range, incl rare CRIOTS-BÂTARD, MONTRACHET itself – gd value all round. Don't ignore tasty Chassagne reds. Hard to go wrong with any Gagnard.

Gaillac SW Fr ★→★★ On Tarn River, stylistically most diverse AOP of SW. Cornucopia of grapes: (r) Braucol (Fer), Duras, SYRAH; (w) LEN DE L'EL, MAUZAC. Prunelard gaining ground for red, while Ondenc (w) has legendary status at ***Plageoles***. Quality variable but also look for ★★★ CHX Lastours, ***L'Enclos des Roses***; DOMS Causse-Marines, DE BRIN, d'Escausses, La Ramaye, La Vignereuse, Le Champ d'Orphée, Peyres-Roses, Rotier. Perlé is refreshing, summery white with slight prickle; can be delicious. Co-ops do it well, cheaply.

Ganevat Jura ★★★→★★★★ CÔTES DU JURA bio superstar. Single-vyd CHARD (Chalasses, Grands Teppes), Melon à Queue Rouge (CUVÉE Marguerite, Chard with red stems, some pre-phylloxera vines), SAVAGNIN (VIGNES de Mon Père, in barrel 10 yrs+). Also elegant reds. Anne et Jean-François G NÉGOCE business.

Gangloff, Yves N Rh ★★★ Rock-star (literally) CONDRIEU grower; high demand for musky, rich, textured wines. Also CÔTE-RÔTIES Barbarine (younger vines, dark, smoky), Sereine Noire (deep, complex); gd ST-JOSEPH (r/w).

Garrabou, Dom Ldoc ★★★ Smart AOP LIMOUX CHARD; racy L'Estrade CHENIN BL IGP. Intense MALBEC Le Gouffre de Diable, needs time.

Gayda, Dom Ldoc ★★★→★★★★ Innovative, smart bio estate nr LIMOUX. Expert use of IGP with blends across LDOC-ROUSS. Flagship Chemin de Moscou. Altre Cami, classy Rouss terroir range. Figure Libre, complex mono-CÉPAGES CHENIN BL (w), CAB FR (r). La Villa Mon Rêve, exquisite La Livinière.

GC (Grand Cru) Official term meaning different things in different areas. One of top Burg vyds with its own AOP. In AL, one of 51 top vyds, each now with own rules. In ST-ÉM, 60% of production is St-Ém GC, often run of the mill. In MÉD, five tiers of GC CLASSÉS. In CHAMP, top 17 villages are GCs. Since 2011 in Lo for QUARTS DE CHAUME; emerging system in LDOC. Take with pinch of salt in Prov.

Gérard Bertrand Ldoc ★★★★ A LDOC powerhouse. Ex-rugby-international Gérard took on family's CH de Villemajou in CORBIÈRES, now 17 estates. Ambitious move to bio. Ch l'Hospitalet (LA CLAPE), CLOS d'Ora (La Livinière), iconic rosé at Clos du Temple (CABRIÈRES). NÉGOCIANT arm covers 32 AOC, IGP.

Gérin, Jean-Michel N Rh ★★★ 19' 20' **21'** 22' 23' 24' 25' Youthful energy, 15-ha CÔTE-RÔTIE DOM, well-placed schist-granite vyds. Les Grandes Places (coiled depth), Côte Brune (2–7% VIOGNIER, complex). Also La Landonne (deep), La Viallière (style). Some oak. Two gd CONDRIEU.

Gevrey-Chambertin C d'O ★★→★★★★ 05' 09' 10' 12' 15' 16 17 18 19' 20' 21 22' 23 24 Major AOP, 2nd only to VOSNE in CÔTE DE NUITS hierarchy. Reds of substance, structure, up to great CHAMBERTIN and GC cousins. Style less forbidding today, best brilliant. Top PCS: Cazetiers, Combe aux Moines, Combottes, CLOS ST-JACQUES. Value from single-vyd village (En Champs, La Justice), VIEILLES VIGNES: ASTRELLES, BACHELET, BOILLOT, ***Burguet***, Damoy, Drouhin-Laroze, DUGAT, Dugat-Py, DUROCHÉ, ESMONIN, ***Faiveley***, FOURRIER, Guillon, Harmand-Geoffroy, Heresztyn-Mazzini, LEROY, Magnien (H), Marchand-Grillot, MORTET, ***Rebourseau***, ROSSIGNOL-TRAPET, Roty, ***Rousseau***, Roy, SÉRAFIN, ***Trapet***; gd merchants.

Gigondas S Rh ★★→★★★ 09' 10' 12' 13' **15' 16' 17' 18** 19' 20 21 22' 23 24' 25 Breezy, serious red; from 23 white (mainly CLAIRETTE) too. Pretty, *garrigue* vyds on stony, clay-sand plain and dramatic Alpine, limestone hills; GRENACHE, plus SYRAH, MOURVÈDRE. Pine, menthol-fresh length. Try Boissan, Bosquets (modern, oak), Brusset, Cayron (character), CH de Montmirail, CH DE ST COSME (oak), ***Clos des Cazaux*** (value), CLOS du Joncuas (organic), DOM ***Famille Perrin*** (incl classy Tourelles), Goubert, Gour de Chaulé (crystalline), Grapillon d'Or, LA BOUÏSSIÈRE (robust), Les Pallières, Longue Toque, Mas des Restanques (organic), Moulin de la Gardette (organic), Notre Dame des Pallières, P AMADIEU (consistent, long life), PESQUIER (*garrigue* authenticity), Piéblanc (organic), Pourra, ***Raspail-Ay*** (ages), Roubine, **St Gayan** (long life), Santa Duc (stylish), Semelles de Vent (handmade), Teyssonières (elegant). Heady rosés.

Gilbert, Philippe Lo ★★→★★★ Leading DOM in MENETOU-SALON; bio; exemplary (r/w). Try Les Chandelières (r/w), 35/44 Rangs (r) 19 20 21 22 23 (25).

Gilles, Guillaume N Rh ★★★ 19' 20' 21' 22' 23' 24' 25' Handmade, mineral, true CORNAS, repay patience (stylish Chaillot). Also CÔTES DU RH, GAMAY, ST-PÉRAY.

Gimonnet, Pierre Champ ★★★★ Didier and Olivier G make beautifully consistent CHARD on N Côte des Blancs, 28 ha, mainly GCS, PCS centred on Cuis. Testament to merits of old-vine Chard. Great-value Le Perlé de Gimonnet 18' 19 20. Special Club, complex expression of great Chard for long ageing 15 17' 19 20. Oger GC (glorious) departure from philosophy of assemblage 15' 16. Ditto Chouilly 12 16, Cramant GC 12 16'.

Girardin, Vincent C d'O ★★★ MEURSAULT-based NÉGOCIANT, part of BOISSET. Whites v.gd: CORTON-CHARLEMAGNE (value). Reds recently improved. Son Pierre-Vincent at impressive new winery in Meursault; real promise.

Givry Burg ★★→★★★ 15' 17 18' 19' 20' 21 22' 23 24 Age-worthy CÔTE CHALONNAISE reds, substantial but balanced. Rare whites. Best (r): CELLIER AUX MOINES, CLOS Salomon, ***Faiveley***, F Lumpp, Joblot, Masse, Thénard.

Goisot Burg ★★ Leading bio producer: single-vyd ST-BRIS (SAUV BL); Côtes d'Auxerre (CHARD, PINOT N). Racy, mineral, perky. ALIGOTÉ outstrips all: enduring delight.

Goldert Al Exceptional AL marl-limestone GC; rich, v. aromatic wines. Some of Al's best GEWURZ, MUSCAT, SYLVANER (Ernest BURN, ZIND HUMBRECHT).

Gonon, Dom N Rh ★★★ 15' 16' 17 18' 19' 20' 21' 22' 23' 24' 25' Two brothers work organically in 10-ha, terraced, granite-heartland ST JOSEPH vyds. Wines pursued by hipsters, prices heady. Mainly whole-bunch, old 600-litre casks, floral-spiced red. SYRAH from a higher place and rich, complex 50–80-yr-old-vines ***Les Oliviers*** (80% MARSANNE, brilliant *à table*), both live 20 yrs.

Gosset Champ ★★★★ Oldest house (1584), C18 bottle design. Based in AŸ, Cointreau-owned. Chef de CAVE, enigmatic Odilon de Varine. Outstanding ***Celebris Extra Brut*** 04 07' 08 12. Rosé 07 08 12 just as gd. Sublime Les Célébrissimes 95'; long-aged 12 and 15 Ans de Cave a Minima (incl rosé). Excellent double act: BLANC DE BLANCS, Millésime 12'. Plus Grand Millésime 15' 16. Limited-edition CUVÉE Suzanne.

Gouges, Henri C d'O ★★★ Days of forbidding concentration at Gouges are over. Wines beautifully crafted in lighter iteration; still compelling. Great PCS: CLOS des Porrets, Vaucrains, esp Les St-Georges. Excellent ***white Nuits*** (PINOT BL, aka "Pinot Gouges"). Visitor-friendly, snazzy website.

Graillot, Dom Alain N Rh ★★★ 19' 20' 22' 23 24' 25' CROZES-HERMITAGE, organic stony plain vyds, whole-bunch vinification. Smoky, dark-fruited red: La Guiraude special selection, mini HERMITAGE, 15 yrs+. Crozes (w, tender), ST-JOSEPH (r). Alain's son Maxime makes DOM des Lises (early drinking, small-quantity, old-vines merchant Crozes), Equis (CORNAS, St-Joseph).

Gramenon, Dom S Rh ★★→★★★ 23' 24' 25 Daring organic pathfinder since 70s; *garrigue* vyds, bio (2007). GRENACHE *en finesse*, v. low sulphur. CÔTES DU RH as it should be: La Papesse (30s Grenache), La Sagesse (Grenache), Poignée des Raisins (happy hour), Sierra du Sud (SYRAH).

Grande Rue, La C d'O ★★★ 05' 06 09' 10' 12' 15' 16 17 18 19' 20' 21 22' 23 24 MONOPOLE of DOM Lamarche, GC between LA ROMANÉE-CONTI, LA TÂCHE. Quality, consistency better under Nicole Lamarche. Light and long, not broad and deep.

Grands-Échézeaux C d'O ★★★★ 93 96' 99' 02' 05' 09' 10' 12' 15' 17 18 19' 20' 21 22'

23 24 Superlative GC next to CLOS DE VOUGEOT, but with a MUSIGNY silkiness, 9 ha. Almost always step up from ÉCHÉZEAUX. Top: BICHOT (CLOS Frantin), Coquard-Loison-Fleurot, ***DRC***, DROUHIN, EUGÉNIE, Millot, NOËLLAT G.

Gratien & Meyer / Alfred Gratien Champ ★★★→★★★★ (BRUT) **15' 18' 19** 20. Bijou idiosyncratic house, Henkell Freixenet-owned. Chef de CAVE Nicolas Jaegar loves old barriques. Brut NV; MV CUVÉE 565 (consecutive yrs 07–11), also magnum, 9 yrs' ageing; CHARD-led Prestige ***Cuvée Paradis Brut*** 12 **13' 15 16** 18. Also Gratien & Meyer in SAUMUR.

Graves Bx ★→★★ **20 22 23** (25) Appetizing fresh SAUV/SÉM (dr w), grainy CAB SAUV, MERLOT; Graves Supérieures denotes *moelleux*. "Ambassadeur de Graves" selected CHX. Some of best value in BX today. Top chx: ARCHAMBEAU, Brondelle, Caillivet, CHANTEGRIVE, Cheret Pitres, CLOS Bourgelat, ***Clos Floridène***, CRABITEY, de Cérons, Grand Enclos du Ch de Cérons, Haura, Lagrange, Liber Pater, Portets, RAHOUL, ***Respide Medeville***, Roquetaillade La Grange, Seuil, Torteau Chollet, ***Vieux Ch Gaubert***, Villa Bel-Air.

Graves de Vayres Bx ★ DYA Tiny AOP within E-2-M zone. Red, white, *moelleux*.

Grés de Montpellier Ldoc ★★★ Gained own AOC in 2023: LDOC terroir nr Montpellier. Intense red with lift from sea breezes. Nearby St-Georges d'Orques similar. DOMS Bas d'Aumelas, de Blanville, de L'Engarran, de Roquemale, de Saumarez, Henry, La Magdelaine, La Marfée; CLOS des Nines, Mas de Lunés, MAS DU NOVI.

Grignan-les-Adhémar S Rh ★→★★ AOP, stony, woods-lined *garrigue*, se of Montélimar, 1170 ha. Best red shows herbs, punch, value; drink 4–5 yrs. Leaders: DELAS (value); CHX Bizard, La Décelle (also CÔTES DU RH w); DOMS de Bonetto-Fabrol, de Montine (jolly r, gd w/rosé, also Côtes du Rh r), Grangeneuve best (serious VIEILLES VIGNES), St-Luc.

Wine and music? Check the grand piano in the cellars at Gros Frère & Soeur.

Griotte-Chambertin C d'O ★★★★ **96' 99' 02'** 05' **09' 10' 12'** 15' 16 17 18' 19' 20' 21 22' 23 24 Small GC, CHAMBERTIN neighbour, lighter structure. Juicy red fruit, ageing potential: DROUHIN, DUGAT, DUROCHÉ, FOURRIER, Ponsot (L). Not widely seen.

Gripa, Dom Bernard N Rh ★★★ **18' 19' 20' 21' 22'** 23' 24' 25' Extreme-elegance whites: ST-JOSEPH Le Berceau (60-yr+ MARSANNE), ***St-Péray Les Figuiers*** (class, interest). Also red St-Joseph Le Berceau (60-yr+ SYRAH). Bernard died in 2026.

Grivault, Albert C d'O ★★★ Family DOM, 150th anniversary 2029. Excellent, GC-quality MEURSAULT PC CLOS des Perrières MONOPOLE, unfolds slowly, lingers. More approachable Clos du Murger no slouch.

Grivot, Jean C d'O ★★★→★★★★ Leading VOSNE DOM. Superb range of PCS (esp Beaux Monts, NUITS Boudots) topped by GCS CLOS DE VOUGEOT, ÉCHÉZEAUX, RICHEBOURG. Beautiful wines. Refined style, days of heft over beauty gone.

Groffier C d'O ★★★→★★★★ Leading MOREY DOM, though most vyds in CHAMBOLLE-MUSIGNY. Two glorious versions of PC LES AMOUREUSES. Bewitching style dazzles. Flavour-packed yet delicate. Nicolas G hardly putting a foot wrong.

Gros, Doms C d'O ★★★→★★★★ VIGNERON family in VOSNE. Stylish wines from Anne, esp RICHEBOURG, also CUVÉE Marine. Now joined by children Julie and Paul Tollot-Gros. Succulent reds from Michel (CLOS de Réas), Anne-Françoise (now in BEAUNE), Gros Frère & Soeur (CLOS DE VOUGEOT En Musigni) and gd-value HAUTES-CÔTES DE NUITS. Also Anne's DOM Gros-Tollot in MINERVOIS. Some vyds changed hands within family (2022). Hard to go wrong with Gros.

Gros Plant du Pays Nantais Lo ★→★★ **23** (25) Old-school AOP for Gros Plant (FOLLE BLANCHE), occasionally anodyne alternative to MUSCADET. Try LIEUBEAU, LUNEAU-PAPIN. MUSCADET usually more interesting.

Guigal, Ets E N Rh ★★→★★★★ Celebrated still family affair based on constant hard work, attention to detail. Oaked reds. Grower-merchant at CÔTE-RÔTIE (dark La Landonne, stylish La Mouline, rich La Turque, 42 mths oak; owns DOM de Bonserine), plus CONDRIEU, CROZES-HERMITAGE, HERMITAGE (Ex Voto), ST-JOSEPH (VIGNES de l'Hospice), CHÂTEAUNEUF CH de Nalys (improving), top TAVEL Ch d'Aquéria (elegant, note new Héritage). Owns VIDAL-FLEURY. ***Astounding-value Côtes du Rh*** (r/w/rosé). Best whites: Condrieu, Condrieu La Doriane (oak), Hermitage, St-Joseph Lieu-Dit St-Joseph.

Hautes-Côtes de Beaune / Nuits C d'O ★★→★★★ (r) 18' 19' 20' 21 22' 23 24 (w) 17' 18 19' 20' 21 22' 23 24 BOURGOGNE AOP for villages in hills behind main C D'O vyds. Climate change means wines no longer coarse, gaining charm, elegance. Sweet spots: villages of Arcenant, Meloisey, Nantoux, plateau above CÔTES DE NUITS. Try Carré, Champy (Boris), CHEVROT, Devevey, DOM de la Douaix, Faure, Hoffmann-Jayer, Jacob, LEPRINCE, Naudin (Claire), Parigot, Vantey. Best to come.

Haut-Médoc Bx ★★→★★★ 18 19' 20 22 23 (25) Prime source of dry, digestible CAB/MERLOT reds. Usually gd value. Plenty of CRUS BOURGEOIS. Wines usually sturdier in n; finer in s. Five Classed Growths (BELGRAVE, CAMENSAC, ***Cantemerle***, ***La Lagune***, LA TOUR-CARNET). Five Crus Bourgeois Exceptionnels (de Malleret, du Taillan, ***Malescasse***, Paloumey, REYSSON). Also BEAUMONT, Bel Air Gloria, CISSAC, CITRAN, ***de Lamarque***, Doyac, LANESSAN, LIVERSAN, SÉNÉJAC, ***Sociando-Mallet***.

Haut-Poitou Lo ★→★★ 22 23 (25) Minor TOURAINE AOP for white (SAUVS BL/Gr), red/rosé (mostly CAB FR). Best fruity, drink young: La Tour Beaumont, Villemont.

Hauvette, Dom Prov ★★★★ Lawyer-turned-VIGNERONNE Dominique H makes sublime wines at bio DOM: IGP Alpilles; Jaspe ROUSSANNE, Amethyste CINSAULT.

Heidsieck, Charles Champ ★★★★ Totemic house, wines exquisite. ***NV Brut*** all purity, subtle yet ripe complexity. Peerless ***Blanc des Millénaires*** 04 06 07 14'. Great Vintage 12' 14 16 18. Older La Collection Crayères 83 90 95 96. Returning icon ***Champ Charlie*** MV, res wines from 96, 09. BLANC DE BLANCS NV keenly priced. Ditto Vintage Rosé 06' 07 08. New chef de CAVE Emilien Erard; Cyril Brun gone to Ferrari fizz in Italy.

Heitz C d'O ★★★ Chaudenay base, new winery in MEURSAULT. Gentle purity marks classy reds. Pure, poised whites. Driven by Armand H's remarkable energy.

Hengst Al Marl-limestone-sandstone GC, powerful but refined: GEWURZ (ZIND H); AUXERROIS, PINOT GR (JOSMEYER). Now one of three AL PINOT N GC sites (A MANN).

Henriot Champ ★★★→★★★★ Two changes in ownership in past 3 yrs; 1st Artemis and now co-op Terroirs et VIGNES de CHAMP (TEVC). Newish chef de CAVE Alice Tétienne continues to impress. BLANC DE BLANCS de CHARD NV; BRUT 08 09 12 15 Brut Rosé 09. Exceptional prestige CUVÉE ***Hemera*** 05 06 08 13'. New from AVIZE: L'Inattendu 16 18. Imperious Chard Perpetual Res Cuvée 38, now on 6th Edition (E6), blending wines from 90–12, magnum only.

Hermitage N Rh ★★★→★★★★ 05' 06' 07' 09' 10' 11' 12' 13' 15' 16' 17' 18' 19' 20' 21' 22' 23' 24' 25' (10 15 20 25 brilliant.) Majestic hill, mighty wine (r/w), quite hard to sell. Mixed terroir of Massif Central and Alps makes grandest, most complex, brooding SYRAH and nutty, oily, sometimes obstinate white (MARSANNE, some ROUSSANNE), best left for 7 yrs+, decanted. Best: Alexandrins, Belle (organic), ***Chapoutier (bio, magic w)***, Colombier (value), Darnaud, DELAS, Faurie (last vintage 20), GUIGAL, Habrard (w), ***J-L Chave***, PAUL JABOULET AÎNÉ, Philippe & Vincent Jaboulet (r/w), SORREL (top Le Gréal r, rich Les Rocoules w), Tardieu-Laurent (r/w). TAIN co-op gd (Gambert de Loche r, stylish VIN DE PAILLE w).

Hertz, Albert Al ★★→★★★★ 15' 17' 18' 19' Father/son team make v.gd bio GEWURZ (Eichberg GC 18, VT 15), PINOT GR (Zinnkopflé GC 18), SYLVANER (Eguisheim 18); can be uneven. Unforgettable SGNS.

Horizon, Dom de l' Rouss ★★★ Forensically linear, terroir wines from ROUSS. Old-vine, bio CARIGNAN, GRENACHES Gr/N, MACCABEO under IGP CÔTES CATALANES; gd-value Mar y Muntanya (r/w).

Hospices de Beaune C d'O Look beyond hype and razzmatazz of annual charity auction of CUVÉES from Hospices' 61 ha for BEAUNE's hospital. No longer a triumph of spectacle over substance, much improved. Acts as trade barometer; winemaker Ludivine Griveau doing fine job. Organic. Quality high, prices too; it's charity. Try BEAUNE cuvées, VOLNAYS or expensive GCS (r) CORTON, ÉCHÉZEAUX, MAZIS-CHAMBERTIN; (w) BÂTARD-MONTRACHET.

Hudelot C d'O ★★★ VIGNERON family in CÔTE DE NUITS. H-NOËLLAT (VOUGEOT) is top class, esp outstanding, refined GCS ROMANÉE-ST-VIVANT, RICHEBOURG, while H-Baillet (CHAMBOLLE) gets noticed with impressive reds.

Huet, Dom Lo ★★★★ Leading VOUVRAY DOM. Single-vyd ***Clos du Bourg***, Le Haut Lieu, Le Mont. All (dr/sw) age magnificently 89' 90' 02' 03 10 14' **16 17 18' 19 20'** 22' 23 (25); v.gd fizz.

Hugel & Fils Al ★★★→★★★★ Famed late-harvest, esp GEWURZ, RIES VT, SGN **08'** 10' 16 17. Superb Ries Schoelhammer 10 13 17 (GC SCHOENENBOURG); unforgettable, 1st VT Schoelhammer 15. Outstanding Gewurz Sporen 17. Don't miss Grossi Laüe ("great growth") 15'. New delicious SYLVANER Classic 24.

IGP (indication géographique protegée) Potentially most dynamic category in France (150+ regions), scope for experimentation. Replacing VdP, but new terminology still not accepted by every area. Zonal names most individual, eg. CÔTES DE GASCOGNE, Côtes de Thongue, Pays des Cévennes, Haute Vallée de l'Orb, among others. Enormous variety in taste, quality; never ceases to surprise.

Irancy Burg ★★ 17 **18'** 19 21 22' 23 24 Firm red nr CHAB from PINOT N and rustic local César. At best, punches above weight. Best vyds: Mazelots, Palotte. Try Cantin, Ferrari, GOISOT, ***Maison Chapelle***, Renaud, Richoux. Value.

SW is largest non-contiguous French region. Marcillac to Irouléguy: 500 km.

Irouléguy SW Fr ★→★★★ 18' 19 20 22 23 **(24)** Frontier AOP in Pyrénées, most remote in France. More likely to hear Basque than French. Excellent whites based on PETIT COURBU, both MANSENGS; gd reds based on Axéria (CAB FR), TANNAT. Rediscovered vines like Arrouya (Manseng N), Erremaxaoua. Best: Bordaxuria, ***Brana***, ★★★ ***Dom Arretxea***, Ilarria. Also v.gd co-op (Xuri w).

Isère Tiny but dynamic region between Rh and SAV; organic. Seek out indigenous grapes like Jacquère, Persan, Verdesse and v. rare Étraire de La Dhuy. ★★: Jérémy Bricka, Rutissons. ★★★: Thomas Finot.

Jaboulet Aîné, Paul N Rh Former Rh flag-bearer, international in style, price. Grower-merchant, organic vyds at CONDRIEU, CORNAS, CÔTE-RÔTIE, CROZES-HERMITAGE, HERMITAGE, ST-JOSEPH. Red: polished, smart, safe. Best: Hermitage ★★★★ La Chapelle (legendary 61 78 90; some revival since 2010, try 22). Also Cornas St-Pierre, Crozes Thalabert (can be stylish), Roure. Withdrawn from S Rh, except sound CÔTES DU RH (r/w). White: neat, fresh, drink most young; pricey Hermitage La Chapelle.

Jacquart Champ ★★★ Simplified range from co-op-turned-brand; focus on what it does best: PC Côte des Blancs CHARD. Fine BLANC DE BLANCS 13' **14** 19'. Rosé 12 **13** 14' impresses, as do entry-level NV CUVÉE Mosaïque, prestige Cuvée Alpha 10 14'. Villers-Marméry Blanc de Blancs 16' for essence of underrated village.

Jacquart, André Champ ★★★→★★★★ BLANC DE BLANCS specialist Marie Doyard. Flagship ***Mesnil Experience*** GC. Vertus Experience PC. Magic Vintage trio **18** 19 20 (also 02 12). Additional CUVÉES from AVIZE and local vyd, magnificent Chétillons. Admirable Solera too. Fantastic location, exploited with elegance. Use of barrels and lees-stirring; a particular style. Still on the up.

Jacquesson Champ ★★★★ Superlative Dizy house; precise, v. dry wines. Sold by Chiquet bros to Artemis Group (Pinault family). Outstanding single-vyd Avize CHAMP Caïn **12'** 13 14. Corne Bautray (CHARD). Dizy **09** 10' **12** 13'. Terres

Rouges 13 14. Innovative numbered *NV cuvées* 730' *et seq* 744 745' 746. Focus on character of each harvest rather than consistency yr on yr. Will it continue under new ownership? Try Dégorgement Tardif 7 Series too; somewhat rare. Owns 30 ha, covers majority of needs.

Jadot, Louis Burg ★★→★★★ Long-est BEAUNE merchant (1859): 130 ha = 200+ wines. Powerful white, wide range red. Big holdings in BEAUJ, C D'O, MÂCON incl POUILLY-FUISSÉ (DOM Ferret), MOULIN-À-VENT (CH des Jacques); GCS gaining more conviction.

Jamet, Dom N Rh ★★★★ 05' 09' 10' 12 13' 14 15' 16' 17' 18' 19' 20' 21 22' 23' 24' 25' Feast on rocks! Jean-Paul and Corinne J craft marvellous CÔTE-RÔTIE, notably long-lived: Classic, Côte Brune (30 yrs+). High-quality CÔTES DU RH (r/w), COLLINES RHODANIENNES (r), also age well.

Jasmin, Dom N Rh ★★★ Small, much-respected CÔTE-RÔTIE DOM, two daughters now present. Giroflarie, fine, scented, burgundian, evolves well; Oléa (oak); gd-value COLLINES RHODANIENNES (r/w).

Jasnières Lo ★→★★★ Underrated AOP on the Loir, tiny enclave within COTEAUX DU LOIR. Pure CHENIN BL 16' 18' 19 20' 22 23 (25). ***Bellivière*** leads (beautiful dr/sw). Also Maisons Rouges, Roche Bleue.

Jobard C d'O ★★★ VIGNERON family in MEURSAULT. Antoine J for elegant wines with Meursault "ballast": long-lived CHARMES, Genevrières, Poruzots; superb BOURGOGNE Bl; reds from former DOM Mussy (POMMARD). Rémi J for immediately class: Poruzots. Valentin J impressing too.

Joguet, Charles Lo ★★→★★★★ Leading CHINON DOM on top form with Kevin Fontaine: CLOS du Chêne Vert, ***Clos de la Dioterie*** 89' 03' 05' 09 10 15' 16 18' 19 20 22' 23 (25). Also underrated Varennes du Grand Clos.

Jones, Dom Rouss ★★★ Englishwoman Katie J, champion of old, abandoned vines. Excellent CÔTES CATALANES. Try CARIGNAN Gr, La Perle, or any FITOU.

Josmeyer Al ★★★→★★★★ Siblings Isabelle and Celine Meyer run Wintzenheim bio AL pioneer. Top-ten Al RIES, PINOT GR GCS Brand, Hengst 10' 13 14 16 17' 18' 19 22'; Al's best AUXERROIS "H" 21' 22'. Rain-plagued 24: no Ries Brand or H.

Juliénas Beauj ★★★ 18' 19' 20' 21 22' 23 24 Hilly BEAUJ cru at n of region. Structured, age-worthy, to convince those who doubt ageability, esp CLIMATS Beauvernay, Capitans, etc. Try Audras (CLOS de Haute Combe), Aufranc, Besson, Burrier, CH BEAUREGARD, CH FUISSÉ, DOM Granit Doré, Perrachon.

Jurançon SW Fr (sw) 18 19 20 22 23 (24) (dr) 18' 19 20 22 23 (24) AOP nr Pau; terraced, contoured vyds. Excellent dry based on GROS MANSENG, late-harvest sweet PETIT MANSENG. ★★★★: ***Camin Larredya***. ★★★: ***Clos Lapeyre***, CLOS Larrouyat; DOMS ***Cauhapé***, Guirardel. ★★: CH Jolys, Clos Benguères; Doms Bellegarde, Bordenave, Castéra, Nigri, Uroulat. ★: Gan co-op, gd value. *See* CABIDOS.

Kientzler, Andre Al ★★→★★★★ High-acid, pure, mineral RIES, SYLVANER; sensual GEWURZ GC Kirchberg 16 17' 18' 19 20. Also v.gd: VT and entry-level MUSCAT.

Kirrenbourg Al ★★★ Successor to much-loved Martin Schaetzel. Some great crus, given deep pockets of restaurateur owner Marc Rinaldi. Talented Samuel Tottoli (also of Hurst) makes wines. Superb GC SCHLOSSBERG 19 20; v.gd PINOT BL 22.

Kreydenweiss, Marc Al ★★→★★★★ Age-worthy limestone GC Moenchberg PINOT GR and black-schist Kastelberg RIES 10 17' ★★★★ 18' 19; bio for decades. Also in COSTIÈRES DE NÎMES.

Krug Champ ★★★★ Supremely prestigious; LVMH-owned. Grande CUVÉE Edition 172 based on 16. Grande Cuvée Rosé E26 E27 E28 ***Vintage*** 02 04 06' 08 11; Rosé; CLOS D'AMBONNAY 95' 96 98' 00 02 06'; ***Clos du Mesnil*** 02 03' 04 06' 08; Krug Collection 85 88 89 90 95 00' 08. Rich, nutty, oak-fermented; highest quality, ditto price. Chef de CAVE Julie Cavil, quiet radical?

Kuentz-Bas Al ★★→★★★ Organic/bio. Outstanding SYLVANER 13 15 17' 20 22'.

CUVÉE Caroline GEWURZ VT 09 12 17, winery's most balanced, though CUVÉE Jeremy SGN richer, more famous.

Labet, Dom Jura ★★★→★★★★ Sought-after CÔTES DU JURA organic family estate in Rotalier. Vibrant single-vyd CHARDS: En Chalasse, La Bardette, Les Varrons; exceptional SAVAGNINS. Also PINOT N, Poulsard, TROUSSEAU, classic VIN JAUNE, great MACVIN.

Labranche-Laffont, Dom SW Fr ★★★→★★★★ Organic estate in same family hands since French Revolution. Now run by Christine Dupuy, 1st female winemaker in MADIRAN. Gentler, long maceration to tame TANNAT's notorious fierce tannins. Some parcels 140 yrs+, ungrafted, pre-phylloxera.

Ladoix C d'O ★★ (r) 17 18' 19' 20' 21 22' 23 24 (w) 15 17' 18 19' 20' 21 22' 23 24 Perky whites (PC Grechons): Chevalier, ***Faiveley***, Loichet. Fresh red (PC Joyeuses): Capitain-Gagnerot, ***Ch de Meursault***, Mallard, Naudin-Ferrand, Ravaut. Value.

Lafage, Dom Rouss ★★→★★★ Jean-Marc L, 7th-generation VIGNERON, gd winemaker and marketeer. Impressive, consistent ROUSS range; AOP/IGP. Centenaire (w), Fundació (r), Miraflors (rosé) standout.

Lafarge, Michel Burg ★★★ VOLNAY bio DOM run by Frédéric L, now joined by next generation Clothilde, Eléonore, Max. Try PCS CLOS du CH des Ducs, Clos des Chênes. Fine BEAUNE (w Clos des Aigrots, r Grèves). In FLEURIE, Lafarge-Vial. Wines delightful in youth, then close down; time needed. Quirky ALIGOTÉ too.

Lafon, Dom des Comtes Burg ★★★→★★★★ Celebrated bio MEURSAULT DOM now run by cousins Léa and Pierre L. Try PCS Genevrières, Perrières; GC MONTRACHET. VOLNAY ***Santenots***, one of CÔTE DE BEAUNE's best reds; Dominique L's own-label BEAUNE, Volnay, Meursault. Also Héritiers du Comte L from Mâconnais.

On Schlossberg granite, Riesling tastes like terroir delivering a lecture.

Lafond Roc-Epine, Dom S Rh ★★★ Leading LIRAC, TAVEL, organic/bio, active sons; expressive crisp fruit. Tavel La Relève rosé (low sulphur) major interest, gd Lirac (r/w), CHÂTEAUNEUF (r) *vin de terroir*.

Laguiche, Marquis de C d'O ★★★→★★★★ Largest owner of MONTRACHET (2 ha/25%); fine PC CHASSAGNE, both made for yrs by DROUHIN.

Lahaye, Benoît Champ ★★★ Cerebral bio producer; GC Bouzy. ***Cuvée Violaine*** Base 13 15 18 19; Le Jardin de La Grosse Pierre Base 15 17 18' 19. Quintessence of PINOT N CHAMP. Also CUVÉE Naturessence (Pinot N/CHARD). Flagship BLANC DE NOIRS Extra BRUT NV. Fascinating Rosé de Maceration and, counterintuitively, wonderfully rich BLANC DE BLANCS. Most wines *de facto* vintages but labelled NV.

Lalande de Pomerol Bx ★★→★★★ 18 19 20 22 23 (25) Satellite neighbour of POM; similar but less depth, class; can be value. Largely MERLOT planted in communes of L de P and Néac. Top CHX: Annereaux, Chambrun (Le Bourg), Enclos de Viaud, Garraud, Grand Ormeau, Haut-Chaigneau, Jean de Gué, La Chenade, LA FLEUR DE BOÜARD, La Sergue, Les Cruzelles, ***Les Hauts Conseillants***, Moncets, Pavillon Beauregard, Sabines, Siaurac, ***Tournefeuille***.

Lallier Champ ★★★→★★★★ Artisan CHAMP from GC AŸ. Reflexion R 16 19 20 21'. Lovely Oger CHARD too. Interesting parcels Les Sous, Loridon, Ouvrage. Collection Memoire 08 10' 12 14. Campari group-owned. Dynamic chef de CAVE Dominique Demarville ex-VEUVE CLICQUOT. On way up.

Lamy C d'O ★★★ Peerless ST-AUBIN, DOM Hubert L, run by Olivier L. Master of high-density planting. Fastidious viticulture. Whites strikingly tight-coiled in youth, tense, reserved, decanting essential. Reward cellaring. Tasty reds too. Also L-Caillat (intense w), L-Pillot in CHASSAGNE.

Landron, Domaines Lo ★★→★★★ Ever-popular MUSCADET DOM, reins now passed from Jo to daughter Hélène. Top CUVÉE is cru communal prototype ***Fief du Breil*** 16 17 18 20 23 (25), also ***Amphibolite***. Worth trying.

Langlade Ldoc ★★★★ Retired doctor Elizabeth van der Bent makes extraordinary, burg-style AOP LDOC: depth yet delicacy from 3.5-ha DOM w of Nîmes.

Languedoc Biggest wine region in France, from Nîmes towards Perpignan, inland to Carcassonne and LIMOUX. AOP covers much of region; specific terroirs allowed to append name: CABRIÈRES, PÉZENAS, Quatourze, St-Georges d'Orques, St-Saturnin. Other AOPs incl FAUGÈRES, FITOU, GRÈS DE MONTPELLIER, MINERVOIS, MONTPEYROUX, ST-CHINIAN. CLAIRETTE du LDOC tiny AOP for white, Malepère. Top of hierarchy: crus incl CORBIÈRES-Boutenac, LA LIVINIÈRE, PIC ST-LOUP, LA CLAPE, TERRASSES DU LARZAC. Usual Ldoc grapes: (r) CARIGNAN, CINSAULT, GRENACHE, MOURVÈDRE, SYRAH; (w) GRENACHE BL, ROUSSANNE, VERMENTINO, but many others. IGP d'Oc covers whole region, regional IGPs too, source of quaffers and gd-quality, quirky wine from producers who don't follow AOP rules.

Lanson Champ ★★★ Major house, BCC-owned (PAILLARD). Black Label NV, Le Vintage Brut on a roll 08 12 13, Rosé NV. Prestige ***Noble Cuvée*** 04 06 08, NC BLANC DE BLANCS 07 08, NC Rosé 06 08. Vintage 02 04. Single-vyd Brut CLOS Lanson 08 09 12. Now some malo: rounder style. Extra Age series gd. Brilliant Chef des CAVES Hervé Danton. Purchased Heidsieck MONOPOLE from Vranken for €500m (2025/26).

Lapierre, Marcel Beauj ★★★ In vanguard of sulphur-free movement. Magnificent when on song, stern core wrapped in sweet fruit: BEAUJ, MORGON.

Laplace family SW Fr Oldest and at one time only producer of MADIRAN. Still at top. Best: ★★★ ***Ch d'Aydie***, needs time. Odie d'Aydie less so. Beautifully polished, less extracted than before; ★ Les Deux Vaches easy intro to TANNAT, lighter, rounder. Excellent ★★★ PACHERENCS (dr/sw). Sweet fortified Maydie (think BANYULS) gd with chocolate. Also gd-value IGP.

Larmandier, Guy Champ ★★★ Epitome of BLANC DE BLANCS apéritif elegance. Based Vertus, but best wine GC Cramant. Excellent Perlée NV, old-vine Signé François 13 14, GC BLANC DE NOIRS. Vertus PC trad, reliable.

Larmandier-Bernier Champ ★★★★ Exemplary CHARD-dominated range from Côtes des Blancs. Longitude and Latitude BLANCS DE BLANCS. Zero-dosed Terre de Vertus 14' 15 16 17, great value; renamed ***Vieilles Vignes de Levant*** (was de Cramant) 08 12 13 14' 15. Pierre and Sophie a formidable team. Long-standing bio tilt. Natural yeasts, low dosage.

Laroche Chab ★★→★★★ Major player in CHAB. Flagship St-Martin-blend Vieille Voye, special CUVÉE from 1.7-ha holding nr Vaillons; Rés de l'Obédience made from strict selection of GC Blanchots. Winemaker Grégory Viennois involved in NÉGOCIANT IRANCY project. Also Mas La Chevalière (LDOC).

Lascaux, Ch de Ldoc ★★→★★★ PIC ST-LOUP bio DOM, 15th generation: (w) Les Pierres d'Argent, taut, fragrant; (r) La Carra, powerful, brimming with terroir.

Latour, Louis Burg ★★→★★★ BEAUNE merchant. Winery sunk into Hill of CORTON. Own cooperage. Rich, age-worthy CORTON-CHARLEMAGNE, far superior to other whites. Also Mâconnais, ARDÈCHE (all CHARD). Reds improved: GCS (Corton, ROMANÉE-ST-VIVANT) deliver occasional splendour. Also Henry Fessy in BEAUJ.

Latricières-Chambertin C d'O ★★★★ 99' 05' 09' 10' 12' 15' 16 17 18' 19' 20' 21 22' 23 24 Small (7.3 ha) GC next to CHAMBERTIN, not as structured, smooth tannins, yet can age well. Best: ARNOUX-LACHAUX, BIZE, Drouhin-Laroze, Duband, DUROCHÉ, FAIVELEY, LEROY, Remy, ROSSIGNOL-TRAPET, TRAPET.

Laudun S Rh ★→★★ 23 24' 25 AOP, ex-CÔTES DU RH-VILLAGE (2024), but doubts as limited choice of DOMS. Whites (35%, v. high for region), accomplished, elegant, drink-young, mainly CLAIRETTE, GRENACHE BL. Red-fruit, spicy reds, much SYRAH, fluent rosés. Direct wines from Maison Sinnae co-op (was Laudun-CHUSCLAN). Best: Dom Pelaquié (stylish w). Also gd: CHX Courac, de Bord; Doms Carmélisa (ex-footballer), Duseigneur (bio), Maravilhas (bio), Olibrius (tiny), FERRATON (w).

Laureau, Damien Lo ★★→★★★★ Leading SAVENNIÈRES DOM: ***Roche-aux-Moines*** 14' 15' 16' 18 20 22 23 (25). Classic Bel Ouvrage, Les Genêts. New Chambourcier.

Laurens, Dom SW Fr ★★★→★★★★ Leading light of MARCILLAC AOP. Single parcels based on Mansois (FER SERVADOU): Claus d'Ifer, La Bruyère Le Dernier Lion.

Laurent Miquel Ldoc ★★→★★★ Family-owned large estate in ST CHINIAN but most under IGP. Best: LDOC VIOGNIERS. Great-value Nord-Sud, Solas. La Vérité, dead ringer for CONDRIEU at half the price. Now trying same for ALBARIÑO.

Laurent-Perrier Champ ★★★→★★★★ Important family-owned house (Nonancourt); No. 5 in CHAMP by volume. BRUT NV La CUVÉE (CHARD-led) perfect apéritif; v.gd skin-contact Rosé. Fine V 08 12' 14 15. Grand Siècle multi-vintage on form, now released as a numbered "Iteration"; latest I 26 (12 08 07) and I 24 in magnum. Peerless ***Alexandra Rosé*** 98 04 12. Interesting new MV Héritage, res from 4 yrs, youngest 19. Also DELAMOTTE, SALON.

Lauzeta, Dom La Ldoc ★★★ Low-intervention, bio DOM in remote, *garrigue*-strewn N ST CHINIAN. Corteza (r/w/rosé) complex for entry level, Mezura more heft. La Lauzeta (r), impressive length, schistous backbone.

Lavantureux Chab ★★→★★★ Go-to source for impressive PETIT CHAB, CHAB: single-vyd Vauprin. Also PC Vau de Vey, BOURGOGNE Epineuil reds.

Leccia, Yves Cors ★★★→★★★★ Small, bio; thrilling, intense. Backs local varieties incl rare Biancu Gentile. AOP PATRIMONIO El Croce, YL range IGP Île de Beauté.

Leclapart, David Champ ★★★★ High priest of bio, 3 ha in CHARD stronghold in Montagne. Barrel-fermented, oak sourced at LEFLAIVE; min sulphur, mainly zero dosage: ***L'Artiste Blanc de Blancs*** 13 18 19 20; L'Amateur, L'Aphrodisiaque, L'Apôtre, L'Astre.

Leclerc Briant Champ ★★★★ Impressive Épernay house, NÉGOCE displaying quality inclinations of top grower; bio, guided by guru Hervé Jestin. Excels at every level. NV BRUT Rés, deep-sea-matured Abyss 16 17 18 19', Le CLOS des Trois Clochers 15' 16 18, intriguing oak-aged Blanc de MEUNIERS 13 16 18. ***Ch d'Avize*** BRUT ZERO 12 14 15. La Croisette CHARD (Cumières). US owners (Royal Champagne Hotel).

Leflaive, Dom Burg ★★★→★★★★ Legendary PULIGNY-MONTRACHET DOM, back on form since 17. Quintessence of vinous elegance. Outstanding GCS CHEVALIER, MONTRACHET; ***fabulous PCs*** Combettes, Folatières, Pucelles, etc. Hard to fault when on song. Try S Burg range. Beware premoxed older yrs, esp in auction.

Leflaive, Olivier C d'O ★★★ White specialist NÉGOCIANT at PULIGNY-M. Lovely BOURGOGNE Les Sétilles and all levels up to own GC vyds. Reds improving. Also classy, friendly visitor welcome, no Gallic hauteur here.

Lendemain, Dom du Rouss ★★★ Mireille Ribière herbalist, VIGNERONNE since 2018, works fabulous bio estate. CÔTES CATALANES (w) Jeunes Pousses, intense, delicate Grenache Gr. Genese, top CARIGNAN. Lovely dry MUSCAT.

Leprince Burg ★★→★★★ Marvellous, entry-level ALIGOTÉ Frédéric L's calling card, perky-fruity masterclass in what can be achieved with this grape. Numerous other delights in range too. Try VOSNE, GEVREY-CHAMBERTIN. Below radar.

Leroux, Benjamin C d'O ★★★ BEAUNE-based NÉGOCIANT equally at home in red or white; C D'O only, strengths (w) in MEURSAULT with increasing DOM and (r) BLAGNY, GEVREY, VOLNAY. Rock-solid consistency, built on yrs of experience. Subtle labels: subtle wines. Sure buy at all levels.

Leroy, Dom C d'O ★★★★ Lalou Bize L, bio pioneer, delivers extraordinary reds, more impressive than charming, from tiny yields in VOSNE and from DOM d'Auvenay (more w). Once tasted, never forgotten. Ludicrously expensive. Investor territory.

Leroy, Richard Lo ★★★★ Cult ANJOU DOM, VDF (2008), yet Richard remains regional figurehead. Top: ***Les Noëls de Montbenault***, ***Les Rouliers***. Excellent wines, pricey but worth it; some bottle variation with age.

Liger-Belair, Comte C d'O ★★★★ VOSNE DOM. Comte Louis-Michel L-B exudes assurance, as do his brilliantly ethereal wines. Impressive range, led by fabulous MONOPOLE LA ROMANÉE. Also GCS CLOS DE VOUGEOT, ÉCHÉZEAUX, GRANDS-ÉCHÉZEAUX. La Cuverie wine bar (eclectic selection), guest rooms.

Liger-Belair, Thibault C d'O ★★★→★★★★ Succulent bio burg from generics up to Les St-Georges (to be upgraded to GC?), GC RICHEBOURG. Structured, serious ALIGOTÉ. Stellar old-vine, single-vyd MOULIN-À-VENT. Thibault talks the talk, his wines walk the walk, always satisfying. Eco-friendly winery.

Lignier C d'O ★★★ MOREY-ST-DENIS family. Understated, stylish, old vines from Laurent L (DOM Hubert L), esp CLOS DE LA ROCHE; Virgile L-Michelot, v.gd range; Dom Georges L, fresh, bordering on austere, try CLOS ST-DENIS.

Limoux Ldoc ★★★ Coolest part of LDOC, nr Carcassonne, AOPS for (r/w/sp). Cradle of fizz since 1531: gd-value, appley BLANQUETTE (aka MAUZAC) de Limoux, also CRÉMANT, more CHARD, CHENIN. Méthode Ancestrale is original pét-nat. Don't miss stylish still white AOP Limoux (CHARD, CHENIN BL, Mauzac), must be barrel-aged. Red AOP: MERLOT, plus SYRAH, GRENACHE, Cabs. PINOT N in Crémant and for IGP Haute Vallée de l'Aude. Try CHX de Gaure, Rives-Blanques; DOMS de Baronarques, Begude, de Fourn, de l'Aigle, DE MOUSCAILLO, GARRABOU; J Laurens, J-L Denois, MAISON ANTECH, Plô Roucarels, VIGNOBLE Nicolas Therez.

Liquière, Ch de la Ldoc ★★★ AOP FAUGÈRES, bio estate, never disappoints. Les Amandières (r/w/rosé) terrific value. Cistus old vines (r/w). Malpas top SYRAH. Les Racines (w), racy blend of five LDOC grapes.

Lirac S Rh ★★→★★★ 19' 22' 23 24' 25 Similar stony terroir to CHÂTEAUNEUF, across river, four villages, boosted by recent Châteauneuf owners bringing dashing fruit, tempo. Savoury, plummy, spiced red (6 yrs+) best. Try CHX Boucarut (organic, revived), de Bouchassy (gd w), de Manissy (organic/bio), DE MONTFAUCON (top age-worthy CLAIRETTE w, incl CÔTES DU RH), Mont-Redon, St-Roch; DOMS Carabiniers (bio), ***de la Mordorée*** (organic, best w, Reine des Bois r), Giraud, Joncier/Mont-Redon (bio), LAFOND ROC-EPINE (organic/bio), La Lôyane, La Rocalière (bio, clear fruit), Maby (Fermade, gd w), Maravilhas (bio), MARCOUX (stylish), Plateau des Chênes; CLOS DU MONT-OLIVET, Famille P Usseglio, Mas Isabelle (lovely, handmade), Rocca Maura (esp w), R Sabon. Whites fresh, herbal, gd depth, run 6 yrs. Table rosés gd: Romain le Bars (character).

Listrac-Médoc H-Méd ★★→★★★ 18 19 20 22 23 (25) Much-improved AOP for savoury red BX; now more fruit, depth and MERLOT due to clay soils. Also gd whites under AOP Bx (Le Merle Blanc de Ch Clarke). Best CHX: Cap Léon Veyrin, CLARKE, FONRÉAUD, FOURCAS-DUPRÉ, FOURCAS-HOSTEN, Lafon, l'Ermitage, LESTAGE, MAYNE-LALANDE, Reverdi, SARANSOT-DUPRÉ.

Long-Depaquit Chab ★★★ BICHOT-owned CHAB DOM with famous flagship brand, GC La Moutonne. Much recent improvement. Don't ignore, esp for value.

Lorentz, Gustave Al ★★→★★★ Bergheim grower-merchant; approachable, easy-going wines: v.gd RIES GC Altenberg de Bergheim 12 13 14 16 18 19. Best: VT, SGN (esp ***Gewurz***).

Lorenzon Burg ★★→★★★ Bruno L is maestro of MERCUREY. Meticulous viticulture: high-trained vines, high-density planting, self-described as *un travail de haute couture*. Intensely flavoured, memorable wines.

Lorgeril, Vignobles Ldoc ★★★ Family estates based at 400-yr-old CH Pennautier nr Carcassonne. Poised, gd-value CABARDÈS; classy Ch de Ciffre FAUGÈRES; gd Borie Blanche MINERVOIS LA LIVINIÈRE (r).

Loupiac Bx ★★ 18 19 22 23 (25) Minor SÉM-dominant *liquoreux*. Lighter, fresher than SAUT. Some can age. Top CHX: CLOS Jean, ***Dauphiné-Rondillon***, ***de Ricaud***, du Cros, Grand Plantier, ***Loupiac-Gaudiet***, Noble.

Luberon S Rh ★→★★ 24 25 Hilly, parched, fancy tourist area; 3000 ha, terroir bit *ordinaire*, altitude to 450m (1476ft) helps. Push-button oaked wines a pity, but young newbies making gd, personal VDF: Alexandre Dalet, DOM des Passages, Laura Aillaud. SYRAH lead role, crisp fruit. Whites certainly on the up, esp if low oak. Best: CH de la Canorgue (organic). Also gd: Chx Clapier, Edem, Fontvert (bio, gd w), La Verrerie, Puy des Arts (w), Ravoire, St-Estève de Neri (improving); Doms de la Citadelle (organic), Fontenille (organic), La Cavale, Le Novi (terroir), Marrenon, Maslauris (organic), Val-Joanis; top-quality/value La Vieille Ferme (w/rosé) from Famille Perrin.

Luneau-Papin, Dom Lo ★★★★ Probably leading DOM in MUSCADET: great, tightly defined single-vyd CUVÉES from Pierre-Marie and Marie L-P. Best: ***L d'Or*** 05 07' 10 12' 14 16 19 20 23 (25). Excelsior drinks just as well.

Lussac-St-Émilion Bx ★★ 20 22 23 (25) Most n of ST-ÉM satellites; lightest in style. Top CHX: Barbe Blanche, Bellevue, Courlat, de la Grenière, DE LUSSAC, des Landes, La Rose-Perrière, Le Rival, LYONNAT, Mayne-Blanc.

Macle, Dom Jura ★★★ Legendary producer of CH-CHALON VIN JAUNE for long ageing. Expanding range of CÔTES DU JURA CHARD-led whites, plus supreme MACVIN.

Mâcon-Villages Burg ★★→★★★ 18 19' 20' 21 22' 23 24 Chief appellation for Mâconnais whites. Individual villages may also use own names, eg. Mâcon-Lugny. Co-ops at Lugny (3-litre bag-in-box), Terres Secrètes, Viré for value, plus ***brilliant grower wines*** from Guffens-Heynen, Guillot, Guillot-Broux, Maillet, Merlin, Paquet and C D'O-based DOMS BOILLOT (J-M), ***Lafon***, LEFLAIVE. Also major NÉGOCIANTS ***Drouhin***, LATOUR, etc. Flavours improving. Explore.

Macvin Jura AOP, not Scottish. Grape juice fortified by oak-matured local marc to make apéritif (s/sw) or dessert wine of 16–18% abv. Usually white, can be red or rosé. Best by far are organic. Try Labet, Montbourgeau.

Madeloc, Dom Rouss ★★★★ Grower in N Rh, Pierre Gaillard's deft touch evident in top COLLIOURE DOM; works with daughter Elise. Sarral (r) masterclass in GRENACHE. Penya (w, Grenache Gr/Rolle), no less fine.

Madiran SW Fr ★★→★★★★ 15' 16 18 19 20 22 23 (24) Gascon AOP, France's home of TANNAT grape. Worthy reds in range of styles with many keepers. Try ★★★ CHX BOUSCASSÉ, ***Montus*** (owner BRUMONT has 15% entire AOP), Laffitte-Teston, ***Laplace***. Wide ranges from ★★★ Chx Arricaud-Bordès, de Gayon; DOMS Berthoumieu, Capmartin, Damiens, Dou Bernés, ***Labranche-Laffont***, Laffont, ***Pichard***; CLOS Basté. Doms ★★ Barréjat, ★★ Crampilh, Maouries not far behind. Laougue is new kid and looking gd.

Magnon, Maxime Ldoc ★★★→★★★★ Deft, BEAUJ-like CORBIÈRES; Burg native, high vyds, bio. Campagnès (r), stunning CARIGNAN (100-yr-old vines); Rozeta (r), elegant, spicy fruit-bomb.

Mailly Grand Cru Champ ★★★→★★★★ Top co-op, all GC grapes. Prestige/Heritage CUVÉE des Echansons 09 12 13', for ageing. Sumptuous Echansons Rosé 14 16 18. Impressive Magnum Collection series. ***L'Intemporelle*** 15 16 17' 18. EXTRA BRUT Millésimé 18' 19, v. reliable. Poétique de la Terre BLANC DE NOIRS Variation VIII. Top zero-dosage Nature 13. Incredibly well run by Xavier Millard. Now B Cert accreditation too.

Mann, Albert Al ★★→★★★★ Barthelmé family-owned Wettolsheim bio estate. Pure GCS HENGST, SCHLOSSBERG 17' 20' 23; RIES Epicentre, unforgettable 22' 23'. One of AL's two best PINOT N producers: Hengst 22 23, Les Stes Claires 15 18' 19. Amazing MUSCAT VT 19 (VT 23 as gd, but label reads "L'Ottonel" only); refined GC Steingrubler GEWURZ 22.

Maranges C d'O ★★→★★★ 18' 19' 20' 21 22' 23 24 Ever-improving name to watch. Pleasant rusticity replaces coarseness; age well. Try PCS Boutière, CLOS Roussots, Croix Moines, Fussière. Best: ***Bachelet-Monnot***, CASSIOPÉE, ***Charleux***, ***Chevrot***, Giroud, MATROT, Rouges Queues. Value.

Marchand-Tawse C d'O ★★★ Grower-NÉGOCE in NUITS. Widely travelled Pascal M shows deft touch. Style now refined rather than robust. Harmonious. Minute production of sublime MUSIGNY. (Incorporates DOM Maume.)

Marcillac SW Fr ★★ 19 20 22 23 (24) Aveyron AOP based on Mansois (aka FER SERVADOU). Stunning valley, terraced vyds, alt 500m+ (1640ft+). Medium-bodied, modest alc, spicy reds, great freshness. Brilliant with food, esp charcuterie, cheese and of course *aligot* (mashed potato, garlic, an unhealthy amount of cheese). Obscure but worth seeking out. ★★ ***Dom du Cros*** largest independent grower (gd w IGPS too), also DOMS des Boissières, des Costes Rouges, ***Laurens***, Le Mioula. Excellent co-op. Recent heatwave vintages outstanding.

Marcoux, Dom de S Rh ★★★ Rich reds with style, 1st bio CHÂTEAUNEUF. Classic (r), upfront fruit; VIEILLES VIGNES (1900 GRENACHE, sand-clay), prolonged, kaleidoscopic. Elegant white; spiced, forthright LIRAC La Lorentine (r).

Margaux H-Méd ★★→★★★★ 15' 16' 18 19' 20' 22' 23 (25) Most s MÉD communal AOP. Famous for elegance, fragrance; reality more diverse. Top: BRANE-CANTENAC, DURFORT-VIVENS, FERRIÈRE, GISCOURS, ISSAN, KIRWAN, LASCOMBES, MALESCOT ST EXUPÉRY, MARGAUX, PALMER, PRIEURÉ-LICHINE, RAUZAN-SÉGLA. Value: ANGLUDET, Arsac, Deyrem Valentin, LA TOUR DE MONS, Mongravey, Paveil de Luze, SIRAN.

Marionnet, Henry Lo ★★→★★★ 22' 23 (25) Iconic TOURAINE DOM, varied range. ***Provignage*** (pricy), leading example of Romorantin; ditto GAMAY in Les CÉPAGES Oubliées, Première Vendange (great value).

Maris, Ch Ldoc ★★★ Groundbreaking bio estate in LA LIVINIÈRE. Cool eco winery. SYRAH-dominant Les Amandiers, *garrigue*-scented Les Planels shine.

Marsannay C d'O ★★→★★★ (r) 15' 17 18' 19' 20 21 22' 23 24 Most N AOP of CÔTE DE NUITS. PCS in (long) pipeline (eg. CHAMP Salomon, CLOS du Roy, Longeroies). Further village-level vyds added in 2019, eg. Le Chapitre. Satisfying, fruit-laden reds, from energetic producers: ***Audoin***, Bart, ***Bouvier***, CHARLOPIN, CH DE M, CLAIR, Derey, Fournier, ***Pataille***; remarkable rosé needs 1–2 yrs; whites improving. Reputation still lags behind burgeoning reality. To follow.

Mas, Doms Paul Ldoc ★★→★★★ Jean-Claude M owns/manages 2400 ha in LDOC-ROUSS. Working on bio, low sulphur. IGP gd value, canny marketing with different labels for export: Arrogant Frog, Astelia, Côté Mas, La Forge, Les Tannes, Les VIGNES de Nicole. Owns Crès Ricards in TERRASSES DU LARZAC, Martinolles in LIMOUX; CHX Lauriga in ROUSS, Capendu in CORBIÈRES, Villegly in MINERVOIS.

Mas Amiel Rouss ★★★→★★★★ Leading MAURY, Côtes du ROUSS, IGP. Look for Altaïr (w), Origine, Vers le Nord, Vol de Nuit from v. old CARIGNAN/GRENACHE, others. Plus excellent VDN from young, fruity *grenat*, to venerable RANCIO 20–40-yr-old Maury aged in 60-litre glass demijohns, intensely sweet and savoury. Sublime.

Mas Cal Demoura Ldoc ★★★★ Outstanding bio estate next to MAS JULLIEN in TERRASSES DU LARZAC. Terre de Jonquières (r), all five LDOC varieties in perfect harmony. Some of Midi's best single-parcel wines: Feu Sacré, Fragments (r).

Mas de Daumas Gassac Ldoc ★★★→★★★★ Emblematic LDOC estate, Guibert family, self-styled GC of LDOC. Famed for CAB SAUV-based age-worthy reds. Perfumed white (CHENIN BL blend) arguably better; super-CUVÉE Émile Peynaud (r); rosé Frizant; v.gd Vin de Laurence (SW MUSCAT/SERCIAL).

Mas de Libian S Rh ★★ Must-try bio CÔTES DU RH, VDF S ARDÈCHE. Wines of character, mainly GRENACHE (r) with racy fruit. Try Khayyâm, La Calade (MOURVÈDRE); gd white.

Mas du Novi Ldoc ★★★ Once part of Cistercian abbey, now leading light in GRÉS DE MONTPELLIER; bio. Powerful Ô de Novi, Prestigi (r). Masterful SYRAH/VIOGNIER N de Novi. Stylish IGP CHARD.

Mas Jullien Ldoc ★★★★ Flagship estate in TERRASSES DU LARZAC, mercurial Olivier J. Outstanding Lous Rougeos (LDOC varieties at 400m/1312ft). Autour de Jonquières (MOURVÈDRE/CARIGNAN), Carlan, États d'Âme. Sublime, mineral Carignan Bl (w).

Mas Llossanes Rouss ★★★ Highest vyds in ROUSS (700m/2297ft): bio, elegant. Pure SYRAH, Pur CARIGNAN, super varietal expression; Au Dolmen, Dotrera gd red blends; Pur Chasan (w) unique, rare IGP CÔTES CATALANES.

Mas Sibert Ldoc ★★★★ Tiny, natural DOM, Swiss winemaker. Unfiltered/unfined VDF from un-LDOC grapes ALBARIÑO, PETITE ARVINE, MERLOT, PETIT VERDOT. Saramon dark rosé, SANGIOVESE-based, groovy. Playful, pink, pét-nat 20 Ans dans la Bulle.

Massif d'Uchaux S Rh ★★ 23 24 25 Leading CÔTES DU RH-VILLAGE, patchwork of pine-tree vyds, a little altitude, so crisp, spiced reds, best unadorned, stylish. Try CH St-Estève (gd old-vine VIOGNIER); DOMS ***Cros de la Mûre*** (big character; gd-value CÔTES DU RH r), de la Guicharde, La Cabotte (bio, precision), Renjarde.

Matrot Burg ★★★ Sisters Elsa and Adèle M oversee commendable improvement in quality at MEURSAULT DOM. Vigorous but civil flavours. Equally gd in red (BLAGNY, VOLNAY Santenots) and white (Meursault Blagny, Charmes, Les Perrières; PULIGNY PCS). Bracing, grapefruit-pith ALIGOTÉ. Prices not wild for C D'O. Watch.

Maury Rouss ★★→★★★ Village beneath Cathar Castle Quéribus, gives name to two distinct AOPS. Sweet VDN from GRENACHES N/BL/Gr (on island of schist, ambré, tuilé) and RANCIO. Maury SEC (dr r). MAS AMIEL leader for both; CH de l'Ou; DOMS FONTANEL, de Lavail, DES SOULANES, LAFAGE, of the Bee, Pouderoux; Maury co-op.

Got €500,000 spare? You could buy 1 ha of Burg Grand Cru. If everybody's asleep.

Mazis- (or Mazy-) Chambertin C d'O ★★★★ 96' 99' 05' 09' 10' 12' 15' 16' 17 18 19' 20' 21 22' 23 24 GEVREY-CHAMBERTIN GC upper (splendid) and lower parts separated by road. Best: Bernstein, DUGAT-Py, FAIVELEY, HOSPICES DE BEAUNE, LEROY, MARCHAND-TAWSE, MORTET, REBOURSEAU, ROUSSEAU.

Mazoyères-Chambertin C d'O ★★★★ Usually sold as CHARMES-CHAMBERTIN, hence below radar. Adjacent to MOREY-ST-DENIS, style more spicy, less amplitude than Charmes. Try DUGAT-Py, MARCHAND-TAWSE, MORTET, Perrot-Minot, Taupenot-Merme.

Médoc Bx ★★ 19 20 22 23 (25) AOP for reds in n part of Méd peninsula. Sturdy, savoury. Lots of CRUS BOURGEOIS. Can be gd value; be selective. New white AOP (2025). Top CHX: Castera, CLOS Manou, d'Escurac, Fleur La Mothe, GREYSAC, La Cardonne, ***La Tour-de-By***, LES ORMES-SORBET, LOUDENNE (Le Ch), Lousteauneuf, ***Patache d'Aux***, POITEVIN, ***Potensac***, PREUILLAC, Ramafort, ***Rollan-de-By*** (HAUT-CONDISSAS), TOUR HAUT-CAUSSAN, Vieux Robin.

Meffre, Gabriel S Rh ★★→★★★ Merchant, safe buy; owns GIGONDAS DOM Longue Toque (Hommage GM, solid VACQUEYRAS r). CHÂTEAUNEUF (incl small doms), VACQUEYRAS St-Barthélemy. Oaky Laurus range: ST-JOSEPH (r), HERMITAGE (w).

Mellot, Alphonse Lo ★★→★★★★ Imposing SANCERRE DOM. Broad range (r/w), some of Sancerre's best. ***Edmond*** (w) 16' 17 18 19 20 21 22 23 (25), ages well; En Grands Champs (r); Génération XIX (r/w); single-vyd CUVÉES.

Menard, Pierre Lo ★★→★★★ Vibrant name in ANJOU. Fabulous, ever-changing portfolio of ANJOU BL. ***Clos des Mailles*** 17 18 19 20 21 22 23 (25), Pluton, Quarts des Noëls, Varenne de Chanzé. Super COTEAUX DU LAYONS Chaos, Cosmos.

Menetou-Salon Lo ★★→★★★ 20' 21 22 23 (25) AOP for SAUV BL, PINOT N on Kimmeridgian limestone. SANCERRE neighbour and lookalike. Value, some quality: DOM PELLÉ, I&P Clément, LA TOUR ST-MARTIN, PHILIPPE GILBERT, Teiller.

Méo-Camuzet C d'O ★★★★ Noted VOSNE DOM: exemplary CLOS DE VOUGEOT, CORTON, also CROS PARANTOUX, RICHEBOURG. Glorious GC quartet. Value from M-C Frère & Soeur. Interesting HAUTES-COTES (w) CLOS St-Philibert.

Mercurey Burg ★★→★★★ 15' 17 18' 19' 20' 21 22' 23 24 Major CÔTE CHALONNAISE village. Hearty to harmonious (r); aromatic (w): BICHOT, Champs de l'Abbaye, ***Ch de Chamirey (Clos du Roi)***, CH ***Philippe Le Hardi***, DOM de Suremain, FAIVELEY, Génot-Boulanger, Juillot-Theulot, LORENZON, M Juillot, Raquillet. Value.

Merlin Burg ★★→★★★ Olivier M, flag-carrier for the Mâconnais, plus sons. Top: MÂCON La Roche Vineuse Les Cras, expanding POUILLY-FUISSÉ range, MOULIN-À-VENT La Rochelle. Co-owner CH des Quarts with Dominique LAFON. Value.

Mesclances, Ch les Prov ★★★ Farmed by same family since C16, delicious rosé from La Londe, terroir of CÔTES DE PROV. Try GRENACHE DOM St Honorat, Faustine more ambitious. Romane (w), crisp VERMENTINO. Silky reds too.

Mesnil-sur-Oger, Le Champ Top Côte des Blancs village, v. long-lived CHARD: ANDRÉ JACQUART, PIERRE PÉTERS; eponymous co-op with grape contracts to die for. Famous CLOS dating from 1698. Needs 10 yrs+. Top vyd: Les Chétillons.

Méthode champenoise Champ The trad method of putting bubbles into CHAMP by re-fermenting in the bottle. Outside Champ region, makers must use terms "classic method" or *méthode traditionnelle*.

Meunier-Centernach, Dom Paul Rouss ★★★→★★★★ Organic, horse instead of tractor, low-intervention wines vinified in old co-op. Chorèmes CÔTES DU ROUSS: (w) haunting Grenache Gr, MACCABEO; (r) perfumed, silky CARIGNAN. Falguayra MAURY Grenat VDN.

Meursault C d'O ★★★→★★★★ 09' 10' 12 14' 15 17' 18 19' 20' 21 22' 23 24 Potentially great full-bodied whites from PCS: Charmes, Genevrières, Perrières, more linear from hillside vyds Narvaux, Tesson, Tillets. Try Ballot-Millot, BOILLOT, Boisson-Vadot, BOUZEREAU, ***Ch de Meursault***, COCHE-DURY, ***de Montille***, Ente, F COCHE, Fichet, ***Girardin***, GRIVAULT, ***Javillier***, JOBARD, ***Lafon***, ***Latour-Giraud***, LEROUX, ***Matrot***, Michelot, Mikulski, ***P Morey***, PRIEUR, Rougeot, ***Roulot***. Also de Cherisey for Meursault-BLAGNY.

Meursault, Ch de C d'O ★★★ A 67-ha bio estate, buzzing with vitality. Tasty reds: BEAUNE, POMMARD, VOLNAY. Impressive whites: MEURSAULT. BOURGOGNE Bl, PULIGNY PC v.gd. Magnificent restoration of l'Ancienne Cuverie, to vinify GCS, PCS. (Hosts annual Paulée de Meursault.) Also CH de MARSANNAY.

Milhau-Lacugue, Ch Ldoc ★★★ Jean L makes joyously fruity, herb-scented ST-CHINIAN from 60 ha nr Beziers. CUVÉE Magali, gd value; Les Truffières, savoury, autumnal. IGP VERMENTINO, bargain.

Minervois Ldoc ★★→★★★ Undulating AOP; gently fruity, herbal red from SYRAH, GRENACHE, MOURVÈDRE, CARIGNAN. Some stylish white, rosé: CHX Coupe-Roses, d'Agel, Donjon, de Homs, Gourgazaud, Guery, La Grave, La Tour Boisée, Oupia, Paumarhel, St-Jacques d'Albas, Senat, Villerambert-Julien; DOM A Gros & J-P Tollot; Abbaye de Tholomiès, Borie-de-Maurel, CAILHOL-GAUTRAN, CLOS Centeille; Laville-Bertrou, Pierre Cros, PIERRE FIL. La Livinière cru, fine, long-lived red: Clos d'Ora (GÉRARD BERTRAND), Combe Blanche, COUDOULET, de l'Ostal, GAYDA, MARIS, Piccinini, Ste Eulalie excel. St Jean de Minervois, delicious fresh MUSCAT VDN: Barroubio, Clos du Gravillas, Montahuc.

Mirabeau, Maison Prov ★★→★★★ Stylish, well-packaged CÔTES DE PROV rosé, bought-in fruit, by Stephen and Jeany Cronk. Brands Etoile, Pure gd. DOM Res from own vyds a further step up. Focus on regenerative viticulture.

Mirabel, Dom Ldoc ★★★→★★★★ Under-the-radar bio DOM in far n of PIC ST-LOUP. Samuel and Vincent Feuillade let wines do the talking. Some of best value in appellation. Top: Les Éclats (SYRAH/MOURVÈDRE/CINSAULT/GRENACHE from "shattered" limestone). Les Bancels (r).

Mis en bouteille au château / domaine Bottled at CH, property, or estate. Note *dans nos caves* (in our cellars) or *dans la région de production* (in the area of production) often used but mean little.

Moët & Chandon Champ ★★★★ Largest CHAMP house by far. Fresher, drier BRUT

Imperial NV, dosage conspicuously lowered. Rare prestige CUVÉE MCIII "solera" superseded by ***Collection Impériale Creation No. 1*** (NV or MV of seven vintages), philosophy of "haut oenologie". Outstanding ***Grand Vintages Collection*** 12 13' 15' 16 showcase for urbane chef de CAVE Benoît Gouez. Historic vintages released simultaneously (currently 00 09). *See also* DOM PÉRIGNON.

Monbazillac SW Fr 18 19 20 21 22 23 BERGERAC sub-AOP: Sauternes-style sweet, with more MUSCADELLE. ★★★★ ***Tirecul-la-Gravière***; ★★★ CLOS des Verdots, L'Ancienne Cure, Les Hauts de Caillavel, co-op ***Ch de Monbazillac***; ★★ CHX de Belingard-Chayne, Grande Maison, Kalian, Le Faget, Monestier la Tour, Pech La Calevie, Pécoula. Neighbour SAUSSIGNAC makes similar wines.

Monopole A vyd in single ownership. Usually prestigious, and not common, in Burg, eg. LA ROMANÉE. Only five GC monopoles in C D'O.

Montagne-St-Émilion Bx ★★ 19 20 22 23 (25) Largest ST-ÉM satellite. Solid reputation. Arbo, Beauséjour, CLOS de Boüard, Clos de la Barbanne, Croix Beauséjour, Faizeau, La Couronne, Maison Blanche, Roudier, Simon Blanchard, Teyssier, Tour Bayard, Vieux Bonneau, Vieux CH Palon, ***Vieux Ch St-André***.

Montagny Burg ★★ 17 18 19' 20' 21 22' 23 24 CÔTE CHALONNAISE village, crisp whites, best of which punch above reputation, mostly in hands of CAVES DE BUXY; also LOUIS LATOUR, O LEFLAIVE. Try Aladame, Berthenet, Cognard, Feuillat-Juillot, ***Lorenzon***. Worth checking, deserves greater recognition. Value.

Montez, Stéphane N Rh ★★★ Aka DOM Monteillet, v.gd granite SYRAHS. COLLINES RHODANIENNES (r/w), CONDRIEU Chanson (complex, patience), CÔTE-RÔTIE (Bons-Arrêts, Grandes Places), ST-JOSEPH (Papy).

Montfaucon, Ch de S Rh ★★★ Rodolphe de Pins conjures v. stylish, handmade LIRAC: (r) 50s-GRENACHE based; (w) remarkable, complex, ancient-vine CLAIRETTE (lives long). Two v. correct CHÂTEAUNEUF reds.

Monthélie C d'O ★★→★★★ 15' 16 17 18' 19' 20' 21 22' 23 24 Crisp, chewy reds, grown uphill from VOLNAY, improving. Les Duresses best PC. Also ***Ch de Monthélie*** (de Suremain), Changarnier, Dubuet, Dujardin, Garaudet. Whites interesting (hillside sites). A little off the beaten track, hence value.

Montille, de C d'O ★★★ A VOLNAY name, though now MEURSAULT-based. Supple intensity in reds: BEAUNE, CÔTE DE NUITS (Malconsorts), POMMARD (Rugiens, Pézerolles), Volnay (Taillepieds). Impressive whites: CORTON-CHARLEMAGNE, Meursault, PULIGNY-MONTRACHET Caillerets. Glorious BOURGOGNE CHARD. Bracing PINOT N. Both value. Also Sta Rita Hills (California), Hokkaido (Japan).

Montlouis sur Loire Lo ★★→★★★★ 16 17 18 19' 20' 21 22' 23 (25) AOP facing VOUVRAY, also CHENIN BL (dr/sw/sp); soils more clay, flint than limestone. Seriously gd wines, similar energy but more tender. Try Chanson, CHIDAINE, Delecheneau, Rocher des Violettes, ***Taille aux Loups***.

Mont-Olivet, Clos du S Rh ★★★ Absolutely authentic CHÂTEAUNEUF reds, 26-ha family DOM. Evolve well, v. consistent quality. Regular CUVÉE (80% GRENACHE), *garrigue* influences; Papet (1904 Grenache), velvet, intricate, worth study; gentle white. Also gd CÔTES-DU-RH, LIRAC (r).

Montpeyroux Ldoc ★★★→★★★★ Cru nr Montpellier promoted to own AOP (2025). Innovative DOM D'AUPILHAC. Try also Chabanon, Divem, Jasse-Castel, Joncas, Mas d'Amile, Villa Dondona, serious co-op.

Montrachet (or Le Montrachet) C d'O ★★★★ 02' 04 05 08 09' 10 12 14' 15 17 18 19' 20' 21 22' 23 24 A GC vyd straddling PULIGNY-CHASSAGNE boundary, hence both claimed it. *Should* be greatest white burg for intensity, richness of fruit and reverberating length. Top: BOUCHARD, COLIN, DRC, LAFON, LAGUICHE (DROUHIN), LEFLAIVE, RAMONET, SAUZET. Temper expectations to avoid disappointment.

Montus, Ch SW Fr ★★★★ 15' 16 17 18 19 20 22 23 (24) Alain BRUMONT's flagship property, famous for long-extracted oak-aged wines. Long-lived all-TANNAT reds, much prized by lovers of old-fashioned MADIRAN. Classy (sw/dr w) barrel-raised PACHERENC-DU-VIC-BILH. La Tyre (tiny plot), Prestige equal to Classed Growths.

Mordorée, Dom de la S Rh ★★★ 16' 19' 20 22' 23' 24' 25 Top DOM at TAVEL, impetus for appellation, bio/organic rosés with drive, local ID. Also LIRAC La Reine des Bois (value r, gd w). CHÂTEAUNEUFS La Dame Voyageuse (r), La Reine des Bois (incl 1929 GRENACHE). Nifty VDF La Remise (r/w/rosé).

Moreau Chab ★★→★★★ Widespread family, esp ***Dom Christian M***, noted for PC Vaillons CUVÉE Guy M and superlative GC Les CLOS des Hospices. Louis M, worth exploring; DOM M-Naudet for longer keeping. Much-improved ***J Moreau*** (now incl J&S Dauvissat), BOISSET-owned.

Moreau C d'O ★★★→★★★★ Outstanding CHASSAGNE PCS from Alex and Benoît M (former DOM Bernard M). Age-worthy, fine La Cardeuse (r). Appealing, value range of SANTENAY, MARANGES from David M. Neither related to CHAB dynasty.

Morey, Doms C d'O ★★★→★★★★ VIGNERON family in CHASSAGNE. Can hardly go wrong here: Caroline M and husband Pierre-Yves COLIN-M, MARC (En Virondot), Sylvain, Thibault M-Coffinet (LA ROMANÉE), Thomas (excellent w), Vincent (more ample style). Also Pierre M in MEURSAULT for BÂTARD, BOURGOGNE CHARD.

Morey, Marc C d'O ★★★ Made by Marc M's granddaughter, Sabine Mollard. (Corks branded "by Sabine".) Elegant, refined. Gentle persistence. No razzmatazz or hoopla here, just quiet assurance. Delicious ALIGOTÉ.

Morey-St-Denis C d'O ★★★→★★★★ 02' 05' 09' 10' 12' 15' 16' 17 18 19' 20' 21 22' 23 24 The Janus appellation, caught between GEVREY's grandeur and CHAMBOLLE's grace. Deserves better recognition for wines of vigour with spicy note, age well; GCS CLOS DE LA ROCHE, CLOS DES LAMBRAYS, CLOS DE TART, CLOS ST-DENIS. Top: ARLAUD, CLOS DE TART, DOM des Lambrays, ***Dujac***, GROFFIER, ***H Lignier***, Perrot-Minot, PONSOT, ROUMIER, TREMBLAY. Also gd: AMIOT, Castagnier, Coquard-Loison-Fleurot, LIGNIER-Michelot, Magnien, Remy, Taupenot-Merme. Interesting whites, esp PC Monts Luisants. Relative value.

Morgat, Eric Lo ★★★→★★★★ Leading SAVENNIÈRES dom. Style evolved past 20 yrs. Currently tense, mineral, defined (older vintages more oaky). Try CLOS Sertaux, ***Fidès*** 14' 15' 18 20 21 22 23 (25). Fine ANJOU BL Litus.

Morgon Beauj ★★★ 15' 17 18' 19' 20' 21 22' 23 24 Large BEAUJ cru famed for long-lived wines. Volcanic slate of Côte du Py makes meaty, structured wine; clay of Les Charmes for accessible, smoother drinking. Try ***Burgaud***, CH de Pizay, Ch des Lumières (JADOT), ***Desvignes***, ***Foillard***, Gaget, Godard, ***Lapierre***, Piron, Sunier. It's Morgon 1st, Beauj 2nd. (Watch for change in nomenclature.)

Mortet C d'O ★★★→★★★★ Arnaud M on song with elegant, refined reds from BOURGOGNE Rouge to CHAMBERTIN. Key wines GEVREY-CHAMBERTIN Mes Cinq Terroirs; PCS Champeaux, Lavaut St-Jacques. Also separate Arnaud M label, equally impressive: CHARMES- and MAZOYÈRES-CHAMBERTIN. Thierry M: lighter, finessed style, but with gravitas too; overshadowed, worth following.

Moueix, J-P & Cie Bx Respected Libourne-based NÉGOCIANT and proprietor, family-owned. CHX BELAIR-MONANGE, HOSANNA, LA FLEUR-PÉTRUS, LAFLEUR-GAZIN, ***La Grave à Pomerol***, LATOUR-À-POMEROL, ***Trotanoy***. Also Dominus Estate (*see* US).

Moulin-à-Vent Beauj ★★★ 09' 11' 15' 18' 19' 20' 21 22' 23 24 Leading BEAUJ cru, not as elevated or hilly as its neighbours; Rh spiciness but matures towards PINOT flavours; can resemble C D'O red at 10 yrs old+. Increasing interest in single-vyd bottlings: Ch des Jacques, ***Ch de Moulin-à-Vent***, DOMS Janin, Janodet, Labruyère, ***Merlin*** (La Rochelle), Rottiers. *See also* C d'O producers: BICHOT (Rochegrès), L BOILLOT (Brussellions), T LIGER-BELAIR (Rouchaux).

Moulin Caresse, Ch SW Fr ★★ Family-owned property, nine generations, organic; BERGERAC, MONTRAVEL. Excellent value (r/w/rosé/sw).

Moulin de la Gardette S Rh ★★★ 16' 19' 20 21' 23' 24' 25 Organic, pine-tree encircled, 10-ha GIGONDAS, true *garrigue*-herb expression, local freshness, allow time. Petite Gardette, big value. Tradition, heart-on-sleeve GRENACHE, 20 yrs+. Oaked Ventabren is brave, firm.

Moulis H-Méd ★★→★★★ 18 19 20 22 23 (25) Tiny inland AOP w of MARGAUX. Honest, gd-value wines; best can age. Top CHX: Anthonic, BISTON-BRILLETTE, BRANAS GRAND POUJEAUX, ***Chasse-Spleen***, Dutruch Grand Poujeaux, ***Gressier Grand Poujeaux***, Lalaudey, La Mouline, MAUCAILLOU, ***Mauvesin Barton***, ***Poujeaux***.

Mourgues du Grès, Ch S Rh ★★→★★★ 23' 24' 25 Cast-iron-quality COSTIÈRES DE NÎMES, organic, early drinking. Brimming rosé (Dorés, Galets Rouges, Rosés). Firmer bio Capitelles; deep Terre d'Argence (SYRAH, ages well), Terre de Feu (GRENACHE).

Mouscaillo, Dom de Ldoc ★★★ In LIMOUX at 450m (1476ft), bio; 2nd-generation Camille and Thomas Fort take new direction. Limoux Bl, gorgeous CHARD/CHENIN BL/Mauzac. Jura-like Chard Sisyphus. One of LDOC's best IGP PINOT N. New, delicious CRÉMANTS.

Mugneret C d'O ★★★→★★★★ VOSNE family. Sublime wines of grace, gentle vigour from Georges M-Gibourg (from BOURGOGNE to RUCHOTTES-CHAMBERTIN). Try village Vosne from quintet of vyds. Guesthouse La Maison de Jacqueline. Cousins at DOM Gérard M doing equally well. Also Dom Mongeard-M.

Mugnier, J-F C d'O ★★★★ Leading, celebrated grower of CHAMBOLLE-MUSIGNY ***Les Amoureuses***, ***Musigny***. Don't miss PC Fuées. Finesse, seamless harmony, never shouty; thinkers' wines. MONOPOLE NUITS CLOS de la Maréchale (note reversed "a" in "la" on labels, replicates error on wrought-iron vyd sign). No longer sells young vintages of magnificent MUSIGNY, to avoid infanticide.

Burgundy's Monts Luisants has triple identity: part village, part PC, part GC.

Mumm, GH & Cie Champ ★★★ Revitalized house, Pernod Ricard-owned; chef de CAVE Yann Munier. Increasingly gd RSRV series; Mumm de Verzenay BLANC DE NOIRS 13 14' 15 16, BLANC DE BLANCS (formerly Mumm de Cramant) 12' 13 15, CUVÉE Lalou 08 13. RSRV 4.5. Cordon Rouge NV improved: PINOT-led weight with tension.

Muré / Clos Saint Landelin Al ★★★→★★★★ DOM Muré is estate; Maison Muré NÉGOCIANT arm. Top: PINOT N (CUVÉE V 15' 18' 23; CLOS St Landelin 23), CRÉMANTS. Outstanding SYLVANER Steinstuck, Cuvée Oscar 17 18 19 22', PINOT GR 17' 18 22, GEWURZ 19 22 from iron-rich Clos St Landelin (12-ha MONOPOLE in GC Vorbourg), up-and-coming SYRAH.

Muscadet Lo ★→★★ 22' 23 24 (25) MUSCADET is the generic AOP; trade up to zonal AOPs for true joy: Coteaux de la Loire (Champ Chapron) is decent, Côtes de Grandlieu (Haut-Bourg, Herbauges) better, but MUSCADET SÈVRE ET MAINE best.

Muscadet Crus Communaux Lo ★★→★★★ 10 12' 14 16 18 19 20 22 23 (25) MUSCADET's cru system; defined terroirs, low yields, long lees-ageing give complexity. Seven ratified: CH-Thébaud, Clisson, Gorges, Goulaine, Le Pallet, Monnières-St Fiacre, Mouzillon-Tillières. Try Lieubeau, LUNEAU-PAPIN, PÉPIÈRE. Three more crus coming: Champtoceaux, La Haye Fouassière, Vallet.

Muscadet Sèvre et Maine Lo ★→★★★ 16 19' 20' 22' 23 24 (25) Top AOP for both zesty drink-young and high-quality age-worthy MUSCADET. Try Bonnet-Huteau, Brégeon, Chereau-Carré, Bruno Cormerais, Gunther-Chereau, Haute-Fevrie, Jérémie Huchet, LANDRON, Lieubeau, ***Luneau-Papin***, ***Pépière***, Vincent Caillé.

Musigny C d'O ★★★★ 96' 99' 02' 05' 09' 10' 12' 15' 17 18 19' 20' 21 22' 23 24 Most beautiful red burg; the queen to CHAMBERTIN's king. Fragrance made flesh. Deceptive delicacy cloaks sinuous power. Wonderful persistence. Has it all. Never refuse, if someone else is paying. Best: DE VOGÜÉ, DROUHIN, FAIVELEY, JADOT, LEROY, ***Marchand-Tawse***, ***Mugnier***, PRIEUR, ROUMIER, VOUGERAIE.

Nature Unsweetened, esp for CHAMP: no dosage. Fine if v. ripe grapes, raw otherwise. Vin Nature = natural wine; *see* A Little Learning.

Négly, Ch La Ldoc ★★★ Prominent LA CLAPE estate, impressive range from salty Brise Marine (w), La Côte, La Falaise (r) for everyday, to icon La Porte du Ciel (SYRAH), MOURVÈDRE-based L'Ancely.

Négociant-éleveur Merchant who "brings up" (ie. matures) the wine.

Noblaie, Dom de la Lo ★★→★★★ Fine CHINON DOM, winemaker Jérôme Billard. Single-vyds: Chiens Chiens, Les Blancs Manteaux (best, vinified in ancient limestone vat), ***Pierre de Tuf*** 05' 09 10' 15' 18' 19 20 21 22' 23 (25). Also v.gd: Chante le Vent, La Part des Anges (w Chinon).

Noëllat C d'O ★★★ Noted VOSNE family. Maxime Cheurlin at DOM Georges N on top form: NUITS Boudots, Vosne Petits-Monts, GC ÉCHÉZEAUX, also gd-value lesser appellations, succulent fruit hallmark. Continuing improvement from cousins at ***Michel N*** (Vosne Les Suchots). *See also* HUDELOT-N in VOUGEOT.

Nuits-St-Georges C d'O ★★→★★★★ 99' 02' 05' 09' 10' 12' 15' 16 17 18 19 20 21 22' 23 24 Three-part, major AOP: Premeaux vyds for elegance (various CLOS: de la Maréchale, des Corvées, des Forêts, St-Marc); centre for dense, classic, plummy wines (Cailles, Les St-Georges, Vaucrains); VOSNE side for finesse (Boudots, Cras, Murgers, Richemone). Heavy-handedness now increasingly thing of past; Nuits treads lighter today. Worth exploring. Top: ARNOUX-LACHAUX, CATHIARD, CHEVILLON, ***Faiveley***, GOUGES, GRIVOT, LEROY, ***Liger-Belair***, ***Mugnier***. Also try Ambroise, ARLOT, Chauvenet, Chicotot, Confuron, Gavignet, Lechéneaut, Ledy, Machard de Gramont, MARCHAND-TAWSE, Michelot, Millot, Perdrix, RION.

Odyssée, Dom Rouss ★★★ Well-travelled Vincent Carreras makes sublime min-intervention La Belle Echappé (w, MACCABEO), Sanction (r, GRENACHE).

Ogereau, Dom Lo ★★→★★★ Leading old-school ANJOU DOM run by Emmanuel O. ANJOU BL (Bonnes Blanches, La Martinère, Vent de Spilite), SAVENNIÈRES (L'Enthousiasme), v.gd. ANJOU-VILLAGES (100% CAB SAUV) ***Côte de la Houssaye*** 09 10 15 18 19 20 22 23 25, a class apart. Also COTEAUX DU LAYON, QUARTS DE CHAUME.

Ogier, Stéphane N Rh ★★★ 20' 21 22' 23' 24' 25' High-profile CÔTE-RÔTIE DOM; dashing fruit, oaking, crunchy tannins, several v. small, plot-specific (Bertholon, Leyat). Top: Belle Hélène (50s SYRAH, majestic, time), Côte Blonde (perfumed), La Viallière (iron). IGP Seyssuel (r, schist truth), VDF Syrah, VIOGNIER.

Ollieux Romanis, Ch Ldoc ★★★★ Top-quality CORBIÈRES bio DOM: Tradition (r/w/rosé) gd value; Prestige (r/w, oaked, stylish) a step up. Superb Atal Sia, shows Boutenac terroir. CUVÉE Or, opulent, sun-drenched.

Oratoire St Martin, Dom de l' S Rh ★★★ 20' 22' 23 24' 25 Prime CAIRANNE, historic bio vyds; CH Mont-Redon-owned (CHÂTEAUNEUF). Reds, clear fruit, classy content: Haut Coustias (vines c.70 yrs), Les Douyes (1905 GRENACHE/MOURVÈDRE). Genuine *garrigue* table whites (from two S Rh, two N Rh varieties): Haut-Coustias, Rés Seigneurs.

The Loire: running red

Once the go-to region for those on the hunt for a little acidity in their whites, but climate change has resulted in a paradigm shift. Warm vintages (18 20 22 25) tend to produce whites brimming with mouthfilling texture and delicious flavour, but they miss the acid cut of old. The silver lining is that gd phenolic maturity in reds is more regular, reliable and the region is now home to reds full of ripe tannin. Try dark, brooding CAB SAUV Côte de la Houssaye from DOM OGEREAU, black-olive-scented Pavillon du Grand CLOS from YANNICK AMIRAULT, or swish CHINON from Baudry-Dutour's CH de la Grille to see what I mean.

Ostertag, Dom Al ★★★ Top bio estate now run by Arthur O. Terroir-driven Muenchberg RIES 10 14 18'. Trend-setting barrique-fermented, rich Muenchberg PINOT GR 15. Excellent SYLVANER VIEILLES VIGNES 15 18' 19'.

Overnoy, Maison Jura AOP ARBOIS-PUPILLIN. Otherworldly ★★★→★★★★ CHARD, SAVAGNIN, ★★ PLOUSSARD, TROUSSEAU/Ploussard. Other Jura Overnoy estates are cousins.

Pabiot, Jonathan Lo ★★★→★★★★ Iconic, trad POUILLY-FUMÉ DOM. Terroir-defined CUVÉES led by (Kimmeridgian) ***Luminance*** 19' 20' 21 22 23 (25); (Portlandian) Aubaine also often tiptop. Léon & Elisa CUVÉES gd value.

Pacherenc du Vic-Bilh SW Fr ★★→★★★ White AOP contiguous with MADIRAN. GROS/PETIT MANSENG (dr/sw). Made by most Madiran growers, but note ★★ CHX Arricau-Bordes (PRODUCTEURS PLAIMONT), d'Aydie, de Mascaaras. Best: PETIT COURBU (dr w) from ALAIN BRUMONT.

Paillard, Bruno Champ ★★★→★★★★ Top quality; est 1981; Bruno P heads LANSON-BCC group; cerebral daughter Alice took over in 2018, with impressive results. BRUT and Rosé Première CUVÉE NV plus long-aged Cuvée 72; Prestige ***NPU*** 02' 03 04 08 09; BP assemblage 08 09 12' 15; BLANC DE BLANCS 09 13' 14; 40-yr-old Perpetual Res nurtures the Première Cuvée (up to 50%).

Palette Prov ★★★ Tiny AOP nr Aix. GRENACHE, MOURVÈDRE; floral, age-worthy reds, fragrant rosés; intriguing forest-scented whites, also oddities like FURMINT. Try trad, serious CH SIMONE, Crémade, HENRI BONNAUD.

Palmer & Co Champ ★★★→★★★★ Exemplary co-op, enviable patchwork of vyds. PINOT N-dominated. Inspired leadership by Rémi Vervier; reliable BRUT Rés. Powerful NV Amazone; ***Grands Terroirs*** 03 12 15'. Excellent BLANC DE BLANCS too. Magnum 13 superb.

Paradis, Les Vignes de Sav ★★→★★★ Above Lac Léman (Lake Geneva), IGP Vin des Allobroges (shunning AOP); organic/bio estate uses eggs, amphorae to bring v. best from CHASSELAS, plus CHENIN BL, SAVAGNIN.

Partagé, Dom Sav ★★→★★★ Tiny organic/bio DOM of Gilles Berlioz in CHIGNIN. Energetic ★ Altesse, ★★ Jacquère, ★★★ MONDEUSE. Range of various ★★★ Chignin-Bergeron (ROUSSANNE).

Pascal, J C d'O ★★★ Look hard enough, and value can still be found in C D'O. Pascal's BOURGOGNE C d'O CHARD offers unrivalled quality at fair price. Move up to PULIGNY village for even greater delight. Uber-reliable and somewhat undiscovered wines.

Pas de l'Escalette, Dom du Ldoc ★★→★★★ Exciting TERRASSES DE LARZAC. Ze CINSAULT, exuberantly fruity. Las Clapas (r/w) consistently gd, intense.

Pataille Burg ★★★ Wild-haired guru Sylvain P is MARSANNAY's standard-bearer. Excellent single-vyd red (whole bunches), white (site-specific ALIGOTÉ), rosé (Fleur de PINOT), low sulphur, long ageing. Excitement in every bottle.

Paternal, Dom du Prov ★★→★★★ Santini bros make consistently elegant (w) CASSIS. Also gd BANDOL, CÔTES DE PROV.

Patrimonio Cors AOP in N CORS with cru status, along with AJACCIO. Sumptuous reds, fresh rosé from NIELLUCCIO, VERMENTINO for white. Lots of organic.

Pauillac H-Méd ★★★→★★★★ 10' 15 16' 18' 19' 20' 22' 23 (25) Communal AOP in N MÉD with 18 Classed Growths, incl LAFITE, LATOUR, MOUTON. Famous for long-lived wines, the acme of CAB SAUV. Other top CHX: CLERC MILON, DUHART-MILON, GRAND-PUY-LACOSTE, LYNCH-BAGES, PICHON BARON, PICHON LALANDE, PONTET-CANET. Investment, progression at GRAND-PUY DUCASSE, PÉDESCLAUX.

Pays d'Oc, IGP Ldoc ★→★★★ Huge IGP, covering whole of LDOC-ROUSS; 58 authorized grape varieties and counting. Full spectrum: simple, easy-drinking varietals to high-quality, cutting-edge: CALMEL & JOSEPH, GÉRARD BERTRAND, Jeanjean, GAYDA, PAUL MAS; co-ops Anne-de Joyeuse, Foncalieu.

PC (Premier Cru) First Growth in BX; 2nd rank of vyds (after GC) in Burg; 2nd rank in Lo: one so far, COTEAUX DU LAYON Chaume.

Pécharmant SW Fr ★★→★★★ 18 19 20 22 23 (24) BERGERAC inner AOP on edge of town. Iron, manganese in soil generate biggest, longest-living wines of area. Veteran ★★★: CH DE TIREGAND, DOM du Haut-Pécharmant, l'Ancienne Cure. ★★: CHX Beauportail, Corbiac, du Rooy, Terre Vieille; Dom des Bertranoux.

Pech Redon, Ch Ldoc ★★★ Highest DOM in LA CLAPE, bio, low yields. Top: La Centaurée (BOURBOULENC/CLAIRETTE). L'Epervier (r/w) gd value.

Pélican, Dom du Jura ★★★ VOLNAY'S MARQUIS D'ANGERVILLE venture nr ARBOIS; bio vyds incl those from retired legend Jacques Puffeney, give pristine range.

Pellé, Dom Lo ★★→★★★ Exemplary MENETOU-SALON DOM. Large range of single-vyd CUVÉES: (in w) Le Carroir, ***Les Blanchais*** 19 20 21 22 23 (25), VIGNES de Ratier; (in r) Le Carroir, Les Cris 18 19 20 22 23 (25), rarely seen Coeur de Cris.

Pena, Ch de Rouss ★★ Tiny co-op of 20 families making cracking, approachable wines. Try Ninet de Pena ("little stone" in Catalan), IGP CÔTES CATALANES.

Pépière, Dom de la Lo ★★→★★★★ 14 18 19' 20 23 MUSCADET name to know. Wines frequently best there are. Top: Briords (old vines, ages well). Try ***Clisson***, CH-Thébaud, Gorges, Monnières-St-Fiacre.

Pernand-Vergelesses C d'O ★★★ (r) 10' 12 15' 17 18' 19' 20' 21 22 23 24 (w) 14' 15' 17' 18' 19' 20' 21 22' 23 24 Village hosting w-facing part of CORTON-CHARLEMAGNE. Other vyds e-facing, thus hard to assign a catch-all commune style. Different vyds thrive in each colour: (r) Île des Vergelesses; (w) Combottes, Sous Frétille. Local DOMS CHANDON DE BRIAILLES, Dubreuil-Fontaine, RAPET, Rollin.

The oldest known fossilized vine leaf dates from 56 million years ago.

Perret, André N Rh ★★★ 19' 20' 21 22' 23' 24' 25' Top-class CONDRIEU DOM, go buy! Three whites: bright, fruity Classic; stylish, mineral-laced CLOS Chanson; deep, rolling, intriguing Chéry. ST-JOSEPH (r/w): (r) Classic, upfront fruit; serious old-vine Les Grisières, smoky, engaging. COLLINES RHODANIENNES (r/w) gd.

Perrier, Joseph Champ ★★★ Fine family-run CHAMP house with v.gd PINOTS N/M vyds, esp in own Cumières DOM. Prestige CUVÉE Joséphine 12'; BRUT Royale NV more focused with lower dosage. Distinctive, tangy BLANC DE BLANCS 13' 17' 19 20. Cuvée Royale 12 15' 16 18; older Blanc de Blancs vintages age well, esp 95. Anniversarial Cuvée 200 15. Owner Jean-Claude Fourmon easing reins to son.

Perrier-Jouët Champ ★★★ The 1st (in C19) to make dry CHAMP for UK; strong in GC CHARD; deluxe ***Belle Époque*** in painted bottle 08 12' 13 15; BRUT NV; Blason de France NV Brut and Rosé; Belle Époque Rosé 13 14' 15; Belle Époque BLANC DE BLANCS 12 13 14' 15. Chef de CAVE (2020) Séverine Frerson.

Pesquié, Ch S Rh ★★ Central name at VENTOUX. Organic/bio vyds; gd range clear-drinking, polished reds, attractive whites: Terrasses, IGP Mediterranée Paradou.

Pesquier, Dom du S Rh ★★★ *Garrigue*-in-glass GRENACHE-fuelled GIGONDAS, real grassroots truth, bingo! Value, consistency. Genuine (r) CÔTES DU RH, VACQUEYRAS.

Pessac-Léognan Bx ★★★→★★★★ 15 16 18 19' 20' 22 23 (25) AOP for best part of N GRAVES, incl all Crus Classés: DOM DE CHEVALIER, HAUT-BAILLY, HAUT-BRION, LA MISSION HAUT-BRION, PAPE CLÉMENT, SMITH HAUT LAFITTE, etc. Aspiring unclassified: LES CARMES HAUT-BRION. Firm, full-bodied, earthy reds; BX's finest dry whites. Try also BOUSCAUT, COUHINS-LURTON, LARRIVET HAUT-BRION.

Péters, Pierre Champ ★★★★ Superb Côte des Blancs estate; Rodolphe P outstanding winemaker. ***Les Chétillons*** longest-lived CHARD in CHAMP 08 09 12 13 14' 15 16 17. Project with CH DE BEAUCASTEL: Fleur de Miraval (ER I, II, III: Exclusivement Rosé, not late Queen). CUVÉE Montjolys 16. Also L'Esprit BLANC DE BLANCS 19; unforgettable Rés Oubliée.

Petit Chablis Chab ★ DYA Refreshing mini-CHAB from outlying vyds mostly not on Kimmeridgian clay. Don't ignore from best producers: BILLAUD, BROCARD, DAUVISSAT, Defaix, LAVANTUREUX, Pommier, RAVENEAU; co-op LA CHABLISIENNE.

Pézenas Ldoc Only AOP LDOC on basalt, volcanic soil. Red GSM blends. Enchanting, historic town. Try Mas Gabriel (bio), PAUL MAS. Also DOMS Allegria, des Aurelles, de Nizas, Les Trois Puechs, Magellan, Prieuré St Jean de Bebian, Villa Tempora.

Philipponnat Champ ★★★→★★★★ Influential house Mareuil-sur-AŸ, PINOT N style. LANSON-BCC group-owned, but Charles P hands on. NV BRUT (renamed Rés Perpétuelle), NV Rosé, CUVÉE 1522 13 15 16 18. Majestic single-vyd ***Clos des Goisses*** 08 09 12 13 14' 15 16. Goisses Juste Rosé 12 13 14' 15. And from within Goisses, Les Cintres 08 09 12. Exceptional late-disgorged Vintage CLOS des Goisses LV (Long Vieillissement) 95 96 99. Rare Léon 08 14, Rémissionne 09 12 15.

Picpoul de Pinet Ldoc ★→★★★ Relatively obscure 20 yrs ago, now LDOC's most popular AOP. DYA, PICPOUL (dr w), crisp, refreshing, salty tang from vyds bordering Med. Think riper version of MUSCADET. Perfect apéro or with seafood. Co-ops Florensac, l'Ormarine, Pomerols brilliant value, also DOMS de Belle Mare, des Lauriers, Félines-Jourdan, Font-Mars, La Croix Gratiot, Petit Roubié, Reine Juliette, St Martin de la Garrigue.

Pic St-Loup Ldoc ★★★★ AOP n of Montpellier with dramatic scenery dominated by eponymous peak. Higher, cooler, wetter; more elegance to wines; 50% min SYRAH plus GRENACHE, MOURVÈDRE. Reds for ageing, rosé gd; white potential considerable but still AOP LDOC or IGP Val de Montferrand. Growers: CHX CAZENEUVE, de Lancyre, de LASCAUX, de Valflaunès, La Roque, Puech-Haut; CLOS de la Matane, Clos Marie; DOMS de l'Hortus, MIRABEL, Pegaline; Bergerie du Capucin, Le Chemin des Rêves, Mas Bruguière, Mas Gourdou, Mas Peyrolle. Tiny co-op, eight growers, Hommes & Terres du Sud v.gd.

Pieretti, Dom Cors ★★★ Small estate in windswept Cap CORSE, n of Bastia. Lina Pieretti-Venturi makes top rosé on schist soils, delicious MUSCAT (r/sw). Star: Marine (w), predictably perfect with seafood.

Pierre-Bise, Ch Lo ★★→★★★★ Famed ANJOU DOM now run by René Papin. Focus now more on dry than sweet. Top ANJOU BL, ROCHE-AUX-MOINES, SAVENNIÈRES age well. Small v.gd range of COTEAUX DU LAYON, QUARTS DE CHAUME 07' 09 10 11' 13 14' 15 16 17 18' 22 23 (25), snap up older vintages without hesitating. Also gd red, fizz.

Pierre Fil, Dom Ldoc ★★★ MINERVOIS; USP MOURVÈDRE with carbonic maceration. Top Dolium and CUVÉE M superb, reward ageing. Drink *garrigue*-scented Orebus while waiting.

Pillot C d'O ★★★ CHASSAGNE family, all branches on form: F&L P (sound all round), Jean-Marc P (esp CLOS St-Marc) and Paul P (Grandes Ruchottes, LA ROMANÉE, etc.). Appealing red Chassagne PCs from all three.

Pinard, Vincent Lo ★★→★★★ Exciting SANCERRE; vibrant and cellar-worthy wines. Single-vyd Le CHÂTEAU 20 21 22 23 (25), ***Le Grand Chemarin***, Le Petit Chemarin. Also classy reds: Charlouise, Vendanges Entières.

Pinelli, Dom Cors ★★→★★★ Marie-Charlotte P, young talent at family DOM, PATRIMONIO; Campo Vecchio (r), Impassitu MUSCAT, VDF (sw).

Pinon, François & Julien Lo ★★★★ Top VOUVRAY DOM run by Julien P (2021). Off-dry wines a speciality (Les Trois Argiles, Silex Noir), but ***Deronnières*** proves the dom's worth in dry. Fine fizz, and long history of super *moelleux*: CUVÉE Botrytis (under late François) 89' 90' 96' 02 03 05' 09 10 14 18' 19' 20 22.

Piper-Heidsieck Champ ★★★→★★★★ Surging wave of quality, newish chef de CAVE Emilien Boutillat. Dynamic BRUT Essentiel with more age, less sugar. Vintage back on form 08 12 14 16' 18. Hors Serie late-disgorged, 71 82 released so far.

Place de Bordeaux, La Bx Internal BX NÉGOCIANT marketplace. Négociants buy through brokers, sell to other merchants, or to you and me.

Plageoles, Dom SW Fr ★★★ Fervent custodians of trad GAILLAC varieties, styles, incl rare Ondenc (base of ★★★ Vin d'Autan), ★★ Prunelard (r, deep, fruity), Verdanel (dr w, oak-aged), seven sub-varieties of MAUZAC. Lovely reds, Braucol (FER SERVADOU), Duras. Vin de Voile (10 yrs age), superb Amontillado-like (*see* Spain) MAUZAC.

Plaisance, Ch de Lo ★★→★★★ Fine DOM skilfully run by Vanessa Cherruau. Focus moved from sweet to dry. Exemplary mineral ANJOU BL: La Grande Pièce, Ronceray, Zerzilles 19 20 **21 22 23** (25).

Plan de Dieu S Rh ★★ 22' 23 **24' 25** Top village, Mistral wind-lashed stony alluvial plain, can require irrigation, mainly GRENACHE. Robust spice-tannin, some more elegant recently. Nice broad choice. Leaders: CH la Courançonne, CLOS St Antonin (50s Grenache), Le Plaisir; DOMS APHILLANTHES (bio), Arnesque, Durieu (stylish), Espigouette (grass roots), Favards (organic), FERRATON, Grand Retour, La Bastide St Vincent, Longue Toque, Martin (full, trad), Pasquiers (organic), St-Pierre (60s Grenache, trad).

Pol Roger Champ ★★★★ Family-owned Épernay house, *sine qua non* of elegance. BRUT Rés NV excels, dosage lowered since 2012; Brut Vintage **15' 16 18**; Rosé 09 15 16 18 19; BLANC DE BLANCS **08** 09' **12 13 15'** also ***Pure*** (no dosage). Sumptuous keeper ***Cuvée Sir Winston Churchill*** 02 **09 12 13 14' 15** 18. More focus on Vinothèque. Long-standing head Patrice Noyelle died in 2025.

Pomerol Bx ★★★→★★★★ 15 16' **18' 19' 20'** 22' 23 (25) Tiny, pricey AOP; MERLOT-led, plummy to voluptuous, but long life. Top CHX on clay, gravel plateau: L'ÉGLISE-CLINET, L'ÉVANGILE, LA CONSEILLANTE, LA FLEUR-PÉTRUS, LE PIN, PETRUS, TROTANOY, ***Vieux Ch Certan***. LAFLEUR now VDF (2025). Relative value from BOURGNEUF, CLOS du Clocher, FEYTIT-CLINET.

One in every 20,000 Champagne bottles will explode spontaneously. Take care.

Pommard C d'O ★★★→★★★★ 96' 99' **05'** 09' 10' **12** 15' 16' 17 18 19' 20' 21 22' 23 24 As with NUITS, reputation for heft over grace is increasingly outdated. Best PC: Epenots (grace), Rugiens (power). Try Noizons at village level. Top: BICHOT (DOM du Pavillon), CH de Pommard, Clerget, Commaraine, COMTE ARMAND, DE COURCEL, DE MONTILLE, HOSPICES DE BEAUNE, J-M BOILLOT, Launay-Horiot, Lejeune, Parent, Rebourgeon-Mure, Violot-Guillemard. Relative value.

Pommery Champ ★★→★★★ Historical house with spectacular cellars but now few vines; brand owned by Vranken. BRUT ROYAL NV steady bet, no fireworks; Rosé NV; Brut 12' 13 14 15. Apanage 1874 range more promising: BLANC DE BLANCS/NOIR, Brut. Once-outstanding CUVÉE Louise slowly regaining ground 02 **04 05 06'**. Celebrated Le CLOS de Pompadour **02 03 04**, a fading beauty.

Ponsot, Dom C d'O ★★→★★★★ Famed MOREY-ST-DENIS DOM. Rock-face in cellar with dangling vine roots. Largest landholder in ***Clos de la Roche***, 3.35 ha, marvellous wine. Exceptional PC Monts Luisants, benchmark ALIGOTÉ.

Ponsot, Laurent C d'O ★★→★★★★ Man who made DOM PONSOT wines for 30 yrs left family business to create own haute-couture label nearby (2016). Kept sharecropping contracts, incl amazing CLOS ST-DENIS, GRIOTTE-CHAMBERTIN. Buying vines and developing whites in new purpose-built winery (Gilly).

Pouilly-Fuissé Burg ★★→★★★ 14' 15 17 18 **19'** 20' 21 22' 23 24 Top AOP of Mâcon. Variety of styles, choose what suits: rounded, intense (can be lush) whites from around Fuissé, more mineral, linear in Vergisson. Offers value compared to C D'O. Top: Barraud, ***Bret***, Carette, ***Ch de Beauregard***, CH DE FUISSÉ, CH des Quarts, Ch des Rontets, Cornin, Ferret, Forest, Lassarat, ***Merlin***, Paquet, Renaud, Robert-Denogent, Rollet, ***Saumaize***, Saumaize-Michelin, VERGET.

Pouilly-Fumé Lo ★★→★★★★ 19' 20' 21 **22' 23** (25) AOP for SAUV BL sitting on the opposite bank of the Loire to SANCERRE. Similar terroirs, as nervy. Most drink young but best cellar-worthy. Try JP AGISSON, Bouchot, CAILBOURDIN, LOUIS-BENJAMIN DAGUENEAU; (VDF) ***Jonathan Pabiot***, Masson-Blondelet, Michel Redde.

Pouilly-Vinzelles Burg ★★ 15 17 18 19' 20' 21 22' 23 24 POUILLY-FUISSÉ neighbour, close in quality. New PCS (2024): Les Longeays, Les Pétaux, Les Quarts. Best: CH de V, DROUHIN, ***Soufrandière*** (Bret), Valette. Volume from CAVE des GCS Blancs. For when C D'O challenges budget.

Pousse d'Or, Dom de la C d'O ★★★ Substantial VOLNAY DOM; choice holdings in CÔTE DE NUITS too, esp CHAMBOLLE-MUSIGNY. Lovely, pure Volnay PCS. Amphorae for portion of some wines: lighter "weave" in texture. Some impressive whites.

Premières Côtes de Bordeaux Bx ★→★★ 22 23 (25) Same zone as CADILLAC-CÔTES DE BX but sweet whites only; SÉM-dominated *moelleux*. Generally early drinking. Try CHX Crabitan-Bellevue, Marsan, Rozier-Morillons.

Prieur, Dom Jacques C d'O ★★★ Major MEURSAULT estate. Magnificent range of vyds across C D'O, incl fabulous GCS: CHAMBERTIN, MONTRACHET, MUSIGNY... More verve, excitement would be welcome. New project Labruyère-Prieur in Burg. Famille Labruyère-owned (also MOULIN-À-VENT; CHAMP; CH ROUGET, BX).

Producteurs Plaimont SW Fr ★→★★★ France's most dynamic co-op: CÔTES DE GASCOGNE, MADIRAN, SAINT MONT (best). Champions of SW vines: MANSENGS, PETIT COURBU, TANNAT, pre-phylloxera finds. All colours, styles, mostly ★★, outstanding value. Top: ★★★ Le Faîte. Colombelle, entry level (w/rosé).

Propriétaire-récoltant Champ Owner-operator, literally owner-harvester. Does not buy in fruit.

Provence Rosé powerhouse, 89% of production. Pale, dry, some v. complex. Most from three AOPS: COTEAUX D'AIX-EN-PROV, CÔTES DE PROV, VAROIS-EN-PROV (and subzones). Don't overlook reds: AOPs BANDOL, BAUX-DE-PROVENCE standout. Intriguing white: CASSIS. IGP Alpilles and rare Bellet.

Puech-Haut, Ch Ldoc ★★→★★★ AOP LDOC St Drézéry. Powerful Prestige (r/w), Tête de Belier (r/w/rosé); swish wine, packaging. IGP Argali rosé gd value. Owns ★★★ PIC ST-LOUP CH Lavabre.

Puisseguin St-Émilion Bx ★★ 20 22 23 (25) Most e of four ST-ÉM satellites; MERLOT-led; meaty but firm. Top: CHX BEAUSÉJOUR, Branda, Clarisse, de l'Anglais, de Puisseguin Curat, de Roques, DES LAURETS, Fongaban, Guibeau (Noé), Haut-Bernat, La Mauriane, Soleil.

Puligny-Montrachet C d'O ★★★→★★★★ 09 10' 12 14' 15 17' 18 19' 20' 21 22' 23 24 Fine-boned, tingling white burg, often finest of all. Deceptive delicacy cloaks memorable intensity, bewitching attraction. Curiosity red too. Outstanding PCS, esp Caillerets, Champ Canet, Combettes, Folatières, Pucelles, plus fabled MONTRACHET GCS. Try ***Carillon (F&J)***, ***Chartron***, Chavy, ***Dom Leflaive***, ***Drouhin***, Ente, ***J-M Boillot***, ***O Leflaive***, ***Pascal***, Pernot family, ***Sauzet***, Thomas-Collardot.

Py, Dom Ldoc ★★★ On n flank of Mt Alaric, nr Carcassonne; bio. Antoine (r/w) expressive, approachable CORBIÈRES. Succulent PINOT N IGP.

Quarts de Chaume GC Lo ★★★→★★★★ 07' 09 10 11' 13 14' 15 16 17 18' 22 (25) Iconic sweet AOP on banks of Layon. Sadly much of crop now vinified dry (sw just doesn't sell). Try classic, high-quality, botrytized: BAUDOUIN, BAUMARD, BELARGUS, Bergerie, Forges, OGEREAU, ***Pierre-Bise***, PLAISANCE.

Quenard Sav Six separate Q estates in CHIGNIN, incl (all ★★) super-reliable A&M Q, excellent J-F Q, small-but-lovely organic P&A Q. All offer top ROUSSANNE (Chignin-Bergeron), Jacquère, MONDEUSE. Try J-F Q Persan.

Quincy Lo ★★ 21 22' 23 (25) Small AOP for SAUV BL W of SANCERRE. More texture, generosity. Many gd-value options from Domaines Tatin (under Ballandors, Tatin, Tremblay labels; single-vyd CUVÉES best in appellation), also Adèle Rouzé, Jacques Rouzé, Lecomte, Mardon, Villalin.

Ramonet, J-C C d'O ★★★→★★★★ Distinctive, often ethereal white: magnificent

CORTON-CHARLEMAGNE. Excellent, age-worthy reds remain largely under radar, ***value***. J-C now joined by daughters. Watch for new label from Noël R's sons.

Rancio Rouss Indicates complex, high-toned flavours from extended, oxidative ageing, often in demijohns outside. Similar to Tawny Port, or Bual Madeira. Associated specifically with BANYULS, MAURY, RASTEAU, RIVESALTES. Superb wines, unbelievable value.

Rangen Al Uniquely steep, volcanic, hot, most s GC of AL at Thann. Top: ZIND HUMBRECHT PINOT GR CLOS St Urbain 08' 10' 17' 21' (world's greatest dr Pinot Gr), SCHOFFIT RIES St-Théobald 15' 17'. As of 2025, three new owners: DEISS, Thomas Mack (Ch Ollwiller), Trapet (taking over 4 ha ex-Wolfberger).

Rapet, Père & Fils C d'O ★★→★★★ On hill of CORTON, 4 ha+ form substantial base for significant family DOM of 25 ha. Styles from lush, plump CORTON-CHARLEMAGNE to nervy, mineral ALIGOTÉ. Largely unheralded, gd value.

Rare Champ ★★★★ 02 06 07' 08 12 13 14 Was part of PIPER-HEIDSIECK, now separate. Little made; outstanding. Wins many blind tastings.

Rasteau S Rh ★★ 19' 20 22' 23 24' 25 GRENACHE-led (r) with body mass, rolling delivery, prominent tannins, spice; some now more refined, agreeably elegant, drink earlier. Clay soils, so gd in hot, dry yrs. BEAURENARD (bio, major, ages: Argiles Bleues), CAVE Ortas/Rhonéa, CH La Gardine (old Grenache), Ch du Trignon, Famille Perrin; DOMS Beau Mistral, Collière (handmade, style), Combe Julière (robust), Coteaux des Travers (bio), Elodie Balme (soft), ESCARAVAILLES (bright fruit), Girasols, Gourt de Mautens (supreme character, IGP from 2010), Gramiller (organic), Grand Nicolet (bold, character), Grange Blanche, M Boutin (handmade, organic), Rabasse-Charavin, Soumade (sleek), ***St Gayan***, Trapadis (bio). Grenache dessert VDN, lives v. well, quality rising, more refined: DOMS Banquettes, Bressy Masson, Combe Julière, Coteaux des Travers, Escaravailles, Trapadis. Also gd CÔTES DU RH (r).

Vosges Mtns keep rain off Alsace: dry climate means lots of organic vineyards.

Raveneau Chab ★★★★ World-renowned CHAB family, using classic methods for ***extraordinary long-lived wines***; unfathomable depth without undue weight. Excellent value (except in secondary market). Try PC Butteaux, Chapelot, Vaillons and GC Blanchots, Les CLOS. Cellar for as long as patience permits, then revel.

Rayas, Ch S Rh ★★★★ 05' 06' 07' 08' 09' 10' 11' 12' 15' 16' 17' 19' 20' 21' 22' 23' 24' 25' Mystical, off-piste, 12-ha CHÂTEAUNEUF estate with sandy, tree-sheltered, almost-garden plots, late harvesting, simple winemaking. Translucent, caressing, spicy, scented reds (100% GRENACHE), age wonderfully (30 yrs+). Owner Emmanuel Reynaud died in 2025. White Rayas (CLAIRETTE, GRENACHE BL) rich, locked away, v.gd over 20 yrs+. Also *en finesse* separate plot, Pignan. Top CH Fonsalette CÔTES DU RH, incl compelling, complex SYRAH (long life). Decant all; each an occasion for joy; no 18 (mildew). In VACQUEYRAS, Ch des Tours, gd VDP.

Ray-Jane, Dom Prov ★★★→★★★★ AOP BANDOL. Third of vyds 100 yrs+; de Sanary (90% CLAIRETTE), floral, elegant; Le Falun (r), intensity, silky power.

Rebourseau, Dom Henri C d'O ★★★ Resurgent GEVREY name: major investment from Bouygues family (CH MONTROSE, CLOS ROUGEARD). Splendid new winery; 13 ha incl significant GCS. Sumptuous, sweet-fruit style. Best to come.

Regnié Beauj ★★ 19 20' 21 22' 23 24 Most recent BEAUJ cru. Mixed reputation, potential still to be harnessed. Starting to get some gd growers now: Burgaud, Chemarin, de la Plaigne, Dupré, Rochette, Sunier (A), Sunier (J). Watch.

Reuilly Lo ★★→★★★ 21 22' 23 (25) Minor AOP; stylistically similar to SANCERRE (r/w/rosé), esp from Kimmeridgian soils. White (SAUV BL), red (PINOT N), unique rosé (PINOTS GR and/or N). Try Claude Lafond, Denis Jamain, Jacques Rouzé.

Riceys, Les Champ Key AOP in AUBE for notable Rosé des Riceys, PINOT N rosé.

Producers: A Bonnet, Brice, Jacques Defrance, Morize. Excels, almost counterintuitively, in warm yrs, *viz* **09 15' 18** 19 20 22 25. Source, unsurprisingly, of COTEAUX CHAMPENOIS.

Richaud, Dom S Rh ★★★ High-profile, organic CAIRANNE, genuine *garrigue* reds, multi-variety use, drive and dark-fruit thrust: classy Ebrescade (high MOURVÈDRE, 20 yrs). Correct white, gd CÔTES-DU-RH (r).

Richebourg C d'O ★★★★ 02' 05' 09' **10' 12'** 15' 16 17 18' 19' 20' 21 22' 23 24 VOSNE GC, ROMANÉE-CONTI neighbour. Magisterial; extraordinary structure, depth, endless waves of flavour. Sonorous name, sonorous wine. Try ***DRC***, GRIVOT, GROS, HUDELOT-NOËLLAT, LEROY, LIGER-BELAIR (T), MÉO-CAMUZET.

Rion C d'O ★★→★★★ Related DOMS in NUITS, VOSNE. Patrice R for excellent Nuits CLOS St-Marc, Clos des Argillières, CHAMBOLLE-MUSIGNY. Daniel R for Nuits and Vosne PCS, now being split between family members. Vosne-based A&B R, visitor-friendly (easily found on main road). All dependable, value.

Rivesaltes Rouss ★★→★★★ Underappreciated VDN, various styles: Ambré, RANCIO/ Hors d'Age, Rosé, Tuilé. Mostly GRENACHE, except MUSCAT de Rivesaltes AOP, fragrant, youthful. Try Boucabeille, des Chênes, des Schistes, DOM CAZES, Puig-Parahy, Rancy, Sarda-Malet, Valmy, Vaquer. Excellent co-op, Arnaud de Villeneuve. *See also* ROUSS VDNs BANYULS, MAURY.

R&L Legras Champ ★★★ Essence of Chouilly CHARD from flamboyant Julien Barbier (punts of bottles bright red like certain shoes); longevity, filigree finesse, esp St Vincent BLANC DE BLANCS GC **08** 12 13, Présidence VV GC **08 12** 13 **14'**.

Roc, Dom Le SW Fr ★★ Organic estate in FRONTON run by multi-talented Ribes family. Crunchy red based on NÉGRETTE; lovely white from rare Bouysselet.

Roc des Anges, Le Rouss ★★★★ Sublime innovative DOM, mosaic of terroirs in ROUSS. Stellar lineup: Llum Grenache Gr; CARIGNAN 1903 (122-yr-old vines); IGP CÔTES CATALANES.

Roches Neuves, Dom des Lo ★★★→★★★★ Only real challenger to SAUMUR-CHAMPIGNY crown. Fine (r/w): (r) CLOS de L'Échelier, Les Mémoires 16 18 **19 20** 22 23 (25); (w) ***Clos Romans*** 16 **18 19** 20 22 23 (25).

Rodez, Eric Champ ★★★ Flamboyant former mayor of Ambonnay; wines equally flamboyant, taste for oak; 6 ha. Complex Grands Vintages; also CUVÉE des Crayères, fascinating Les Beurys maceration PINOT N Rosé 13 **14 16'**.

Roederer, Louis Champ ★★★★ Family ownership par excellence (Rouzaud). Enviable vyds, largest bio holdings. Brilliant chef de CAVE Jean-Baptiste Lecaillon. BRUT Premier NV phased out for MV Collection, **242 243** 244 245. BLANC DE BLANCS **16 17' 18** 19. Vintage LR **15 16'** 17. Far-from-disagreeable Cristal 08 **09** 12 **13 14 15 16**, Cristal Rosé 08 **09** 12 **13 14 15**. ***Cristal Vinothèque Bl, Rosé*** 95. Brut NATURE Philippe Starck (all Cumières 12 **15'** 19). ***Late Release Vintage*** 95 **96 97 99** 00. Also CH PICHON LALANDE, DEUTZ.

Rolland, Michel Bx Veteran international consultant, MERLOT specialist. Own wines: The Rolland Collection. Michel Rolland died in 2026.

Rolly Gassmann Al ★★★ Outstanding now bio DOM, mostly off-dry, rich, luscious wines (and v. many of them); maybe too sweet for some. Outstanding SGNS. Mineral RIES, rich SYLVANER 13 **16** 17' 18 19'.

Romanée, La C d'O ★★★★ 09' 10' 12' 15' 16' **17** 18' 19' 20 21 22' 23' 24 Tiniest GC in VOSNE, 0.85 ha, MONOPOLE of COMTE LIGER-BELAIR. Upslope neighbour of ROMANÉE-CONTI. Exceptionally fine, perfumed, intense. Matchless beauty. Vines planted n–s, unusual for C D'O. Superlative burg, superlative price.

Romanée-Conti, La C d'O ★★★★ 90' 93' 96' 99' 00 02' 05' 09' **10'** 12' 14' 15' 16' 17 18' 19' 20' 21 22' 23' 24 VOSNE GC, DRC MONOPOLE. Grandest name in all Burg (and world); needs long ageing before reverberating splendour unfolds. When on song, no superlative captures its haunting delight. Magnificence made wine.

Romanée-St-Vivant C d'O ★★★★ 90' 99' 02' 05' 09' 10' 12' 15' 16' 17 18' 19' 20' 21 22' 23' VOSNE GC, downslope from ROMANÉE-CONTI. Seductive perfume, delicate but intense. Less magisterial, perhaps more beautiful, than famous neighbours. Try ARLOT, ARNOUX-LACHAUX, CATHIARD, DRC (holding greater than all others combined), Follin-Arbelet, HUDELOT-NOËLLAT, J-J Confuron, LATOUR, LEROY, Poisot. Hard to fault, delivers boundless delight, in right hands.

Romanin, Ch Prov ★★★ Leading bio DOM in BAUX-EN-PROV, worth visiting for magnificent cathedral cellar. Grand vin (r/w), equally majestic.

Rosé de Loire Lo ★→★★ DYA Large, multi-regional rosé AOP: dry alternative to CABERNET D'ANJOU, ROSE D'ANJOU. Usually Grolleau-based. Try Bablut, Bergerie, CADY, Passavant.

Rossignol-Trapet C d'O ★★★→★★★★ Brothers Nicolas and David R-T doing great job. Forget hearty GEVREY stereotype and revel in light-footed yet intense, memorable flavours. Healthy holdings of GCS, esp CHAMBERTIN; gd value across range from GEVREY VIEILLES VIGNES up. BEAUNE vyds from Rossignol side.

Rostaing, Dom N Rh ★★★→★★★★ 10' 12' 13' 15' 16' 17' 18' 19' 20' 21' 22' 23' 24' 25' Classy CÔTE-RÔTIE, top name: five mineral-cool, tight wines from prime plots, all v. elegant, restrained, low-level oak, wait 6 yrs+, decant. Genuine Ampodium (value), complex, top-class Côte Blonde (5% VIOGNIER), Côte Brune, also La Landonne (20–25 yrs), occasional Viallière. Linear CONDRIEU, also IGP COLLINES RHODANIENNES (r/w), LDOC Puech Noble (r/w).

Rouget, Dom C d'O ★★★ Renamed as DOM R rather than Emmanuel R, with new generation refreshing dom famed for Henri Jayer connection and CROS PARANTOUX vyd. Style more robust than in Jayer era. Not as ethereal.

Roulot, Dom C d'O ★★★→★★★★ Outstanding MEURSAULT DOM. Poised, precise, never flashy. Now holding back some wines for later release. Great PCS: CLOS des Bouchères, Perrières. Value from top village sites Luchets, Meix Chavaux (Clos du Haut Tesson). Don't miss AUXEY-DURESSES, BOURGOGNE Bl.

Roumier, Georges C d'O ★★★★ Reference DOM for BONNES-MARES and other ***brilliant Chambolle*** (incl Amoureuses, Cras) from Christophe R, now joined by nephews Alexis, Clément. Long-lived but attractive early. Hard to fault. Silly prices for MUSIGNY, secondary market. Best value: MOREY CLOS de la Bussière.

Rouquette sur Mer, Ch Ldoc ★★★→★★★★ Impressive LA CLAPE estate, vyds, *garrigue* by beach. ***Arpège*** (w), crisp, herbal, terrific value. L'Esprit terroir-benchmark red. Le CLOS de la Tour, top MOURVÈDRE.

Rousseau, Dom Armand C d'O ★★★★ Legendary GEVREY-CHAMBERTIN DOM: fragrant, majestic, age-worthy GCS. Best Chambertin, though rivalled by own CLOS de Bèze. Celebrated PC CLOS ST-JACQUES. Village wines less commanding.

Roussette de Savoie Sav AOP, same area as AOP SAV; mostly organic; 100% ALTESSE, age to 5 yrs+. ★: Dupasquier, Lupin. ★: Orchis. ★★: Chevillard, Côtes Rousses (bio). ★★★: Prieuré St-Christophe.

Roussillon Often linked with LDOC, and incl in AOP Ldoc, but has distinct Catalan ID. From Pyrénéan foothills to Med. Different soils, topography attract innovative producers; some brilliant wines. Lots of old vines, tiny yields, intense. GRENACHE is key. Largest AOP CÔTES DU ROUSS, gd-value spicy reds. Original, sometimes stunning, trad VDN (BANYULS, MAURY, RIVESALTES). Also serious age-worthy table wines (r/w). *See also* COLLIOURE, CÔTES DU ROUSS (VILLAGES), Maury (SEC). IGP excellent CÔTES CATALANES, Côte Vermeille.

Ruchottes-Chambertin C d'O ★★★★ 02' 05' 09' 10' 12' 15' 16 17' 18' 19' 20' 21 22' 23 24 Small (3.3 ha) GC. Forbidding when young; ethereal, great finesse when mature: MUGNERET-Gibourg, ROUMIER, ROUSSEAU. Also gd: CH de MARSANNAY, F Esmonin, H Magnien, Marchand-Grillot, Pacalet. LAMBRAYS from 2021.

Ruinart Champ ★★★★ Oldest CHAMP house (1729). Brilliant chef de CAVE Fréd

Panaïotis died in diving accident; replaced by Caroline Fiot. R de Ruinart BRUT NV; Ruinart Rosé NV; R de Ruinart Brut 15 16. BLANC DE BLANCS now MV Blanc Singulier Editions 17 18 19. Prestige DOM Ruinart Blanc de Blancs 02 04' 06 07 09 10 13. No 08 made, shame. Gastronomic ***DR Rosé*** 90 96 98' 02 04 07 09. Move to age under cork.

Rully Burg ★★→★★★ (r) 17 18 19' 20' 21 22' 23 24 (w) 17' 18 19' 20' 21 22 23 24 CÔTE CHALONNAISE village. Ultra-reliable, seldom disappoints. Appealing (w), fruity (r). Best vyds: Grésigny, Pucelle, Rabourcé. Try BRIDAY, Champs l'Abbaye, Devevey, ***de Villaine***, DOM de la Folie, DROUHIN, ***Dureuil-Janthial***, FAIVELEY, ***Jacqueson***, Jaeger-Defaix, Jobard (C), Leflaive (O). ***Picamelot*** for top CRÉMANT.

Sablet S Rh ★★ 24' 25 Successful, easy-to-drink CÔTES DU RH-VILLAGE on often sandy soils (sable = sand); some, cooler high terraces nr GIGONDAS. Pretty red-berry fruit, mainly GRENACHE, some darker. Try co-op CAVE le Gravillas, Crève Coeur (organic/bio); CHX Cohola (organic), du Trignon (stylish); DOMS de Boissan (organic, full), Les Goubert (r/w), Pasquiers (organic, deep, best). Filled whites gd, for apéritifs/table: Boissan (ages well), Notre Dame des Pallières, ST GAYAN.

St-Amour Beauj ★★ 19' 20' 21 22' 23 24 Most n cru, mixed soils, character. Much wine sells on name alone. Try Cheveau, DOM de Fa, Patissier, ***Pirolette***, Revillon.

St-Aubin C d'O ★★★ (w) 14' 15 17' 18 19' 20' 21 22' 23 24 ***Increasingly complex white***; St-A PC now merits comparison with big three: CHASSAGNE, PULIGNY, MEURSAULT. Also juicy, easy-drinking red. Best vyds: ***Chatenière***, ***En Remilly***, ***Murgers Dents de Chien***. Best growers: BACHELET (JC), COLIN (Joseph, Marc), COLIN-MOREY, ***Lamy***, Larue. Value Prudhon. On exciting upward curve.

Project Volta: major Burgundy study of white wines' proclivity to oxidize.

St-Bris Burg ★ Unique AOP for SAUV BL in N Burg. Fresh, simple, lively, but can age (de Moor). Also gd: Bersan, Davenne, Felix, GOISOT, Simonnet-Febvre, Verret.

St-Chinian Ldoc ★★→★★★ AOP of two halves. Schist in hillier n, mineral, taut reds; crus Berlou (mostly CARIGNAN), Roquebrun (mostly SYRAH). Clay-limestone in rolling s, fuller, rounder. Underrated, seek out. Usual suspects Syrah, GRENACHE, Carignan, MOURVÈDRE. White from GRENACHE BL, MARSANNE, ROUSSANNE, VERMENTINO. Roquebrun co-op excels; CHX Cazal Viel, Castigno; DOMS Borie la Vitarèle, Canet-Valette, Comps, des Jougla, La Dournie, LA LAUZETA, LA LINQUIÈRE, La Madura, Les Eminades, MILHAU-LACUGE, Navarre, Rimbert; CLOS Bagatelle, Mas Champart, Mas de Cynanques, Quartironi de Sars, Viranel.

St Cosme, Ch de S Rh ★★★ 09' 10' 12' 13' 14' 15' 16' 17' 18' 19' 20' 21' 22' 23 24' 25 Energetic, high-quality bio GIGONDAS estate; spiced reds, pine notes, drive, live long. Seek: CÔTES DU RH Les Deux Albion (r), Gigondas Classique (authentic, value), Hominis Fides (1902 GRENACHE, complex), Le Poste (class). Owns CH de Rouanne (VINSOBRES). Upmarket N Rh merchant range (CONDRIEU, CÔTE-RÔTIE).

Ste-Anne, Dom S Rh ★★ Notable CÔTES DU RH-VILLAGE DOM on limestone above St-Gervais; low profile, seriously deep wines, pioneer in 60s/70s (so old vines). Reds of character, prosper with age: Mourillons (mostly SYRAH), Rouvières (60s MOURVÈDRE), live 15 yrs+. Refined, superior VDF from 1977 VIOGNIER.

Ste-Croix-du-Mont Bx ★★ 19 20 22 23 (25) Tiny AOP for sweet white. Soils consist of fossilized oysters. Best: rich, creamy, can age. Top CHX: Bel Air, Crabitan-Bellevue, des Arroucats, du Mont, La Caussade, La Rame, ***Loubens***.

St-Émilion Bx ★★→★★★★ 15' 16 18 19' 20' 22' 23 (25) Big MERLOT-led AOP on BX's Right Bank; CAB FR also strong. Many GCS, mixed quality. Collective environmental projects. Top designation St-Ém PREMIER GRAND CRU CLASSÉ (14 in 2022 classification). Warm, full, rounded style but much diversity due to terroir, winemaking and blend. Best firm, v. long-lived. Top CHX: ANGÉLUS, AUSONE, CANON, CHEVAL BLANC, FIGEAC, PAVIE.

St-Estèphe H-Méd ★★→★★★★ 10' 15 16' 18 19' 20' 22' 23 (25) Most n communal AOP in MÉD. Gravel, but more limestone, clay. Solid, structured wines for ageing. Five Classed Growths: CALON SÉGUR, COS D'ESTOURNEL, COS LABORY, LAFON-ROCHET, MONTROSE. Top unclassified estates: CAPBERN, DE PEZ, Laffitte Carcasset, LE BOSCQ, LE CROCK, MEYNEY, ORMES-DE-PEZ, PHÉLAN SÉGUR, TRONQUOY.

Ste-Victoire Prov ★★→★★★ Subzone of CÔTES DE PROV, majority rosé. Limestone slopes of Montagne Ste-V: much-needed freshness in hotter yrs. DOMS de St Ser, des Diables, Gassier, Mas de Cadenas, St Pancrace. IGP Dom Richeaume.

St Gayan, Dom S Rh ★★★ 05' 07' 10' 15' 16' 17' 18' 19' 20' 21 22' 23 24' 25 High-rank, v. consistent GIGONDAS. *Garrigue*, take-time red, top value: Origine (80% GRENACHE), RASTEAU Ilex. White CHÂTEAUNEUF, SABLET L'Oratory.

St-Georges-St-Émilion Bx ★★ 19 20 22 23 (25) Smallest ST-ÉM satellite; 24 growers. Sturdy, structured. Best CHX: Cap St-Georges, CLOS Albertus, Haut St-Georges, Macquin, St-André Corbin, St-Georges, Tour du Pas-St-Georges.

St-Joseph N Rh ★★→★★★ 15' 16' 17' 18' 19' 20' 21 22' 23 24' 25' Granite SYRAH of character, v.gd replacement for expensive CÔTE-RÔTIE etc. Lots of choice. Original vyds nr Tournon: red-fruit detail, smoke-crispness, need time; further n nr Chavanay, 2nd-wave vyds, more black fruit, pepper, oak. Way more character than most CROZES-HERMITAGE: CHAPOUTIER (Les Granits), ***Gonon*** (brilliant), ***Gripa***, GUIGAL (VIGNES de l'Hospice), ***J-L Chave*** (class). Also gd: Alexandrins, Amphores (bio), A PERRET (Grisières), B Jolivet (watch), Boissonnet, Chèze, Courbis (modern), Coursodon (racy), E Darnaud (bespoke), DELAS, Farge, Faury (fab 24), FERRATON, F Villard, Gaillard (CLOS de Cuminaille), Gouye (trad), Iserand (handmade), J Cécillon, J-B Souillard, J&E Durand, Marsanne (trad), Monier-Perréol (bio), MONTEZ, P-J Villa (style), P Marthouret, S Blachon (trad), Sept Lunes (bio), Vallet, Vins de Vienne, Y CUILLERON. Interesting ***white (mainly Marsanne)***: A PERRET, Barge, ***Chapoutier*** (Les Granits), Curtat, Faury, ***Gonon*** (evolves well), Gouye (trad), ***Gripa***, Guigal, Pilon, Vallet, Y Cuilleron.

Steep Alsace slopes: tractors venture into vyds only with written medical permission.

St-Julien H-Méd ★★★→★★★★ 10' 15 16' 18 19' 20' 22' 23 (25) Epitome of harmonious, fragrant, savoury red; v. consistent mid-MÉD communal AOP; 11 classified (1855) estates own most of vyd area; incl DUCRU-BEAUCAILLOU, GRUAUD-LAROSE, LÉOVILLES (x3). Second wines (Connetable de TALBOT) gd bet.

Saint Mont SW Fr ★★ (r) 18 19 20 22 23 (24) AOP en route to Pyrénées with some Atlantic influence. Red similar to MADIRAN, but often softer, less intense. White blends: pithy Arrufiac. PRODUCTEURS PLAIMONT makes almost all. ★★★ ***Ch de Sabazan***. Fantastic value. Don't miss Marciac Jazz Festival July/Aug.

St Nicolas de Bourgueil Lo ★→★★★ 15' 16 17 18' 19' 20 22' 23 (25) Fine AOP for CAB FR, neighbouring BOURGUEIL; stylistically indistinguishable. Easydrinking from sandy soils, cellar-worthy from gravels, limestone, clay: Cotelleraie, Frédéric Mabileau, Xavier Amirault, ***Yannick Amirault***.

St-Péray N Rh ★★→★★★ 24' 25' White-only AOP opposite Valence; hilly, high granite, also limestone. MARSANNE/ROUSSANNE blends with finesse, cool fruit; much recent planting, core quality gd. Sparkling also, drunk by Wagner when composing: A Voge, Pic & CHAPOUTIER, R Nodin, TAIN co-op. Best still white: Chapoutier (Hongrie), Clape (pure), Colombo, ***du Tunnel*** (style), Gripa (best; 60s ROUSSANNE Figuiers), J&E Durand, J Michel, L Fayolle, Lorient, R Nodin (old-vine Suchat), Tain co-op, Vins de Vienne, Voge (Fleur de Crussol, oak), Y CUILLERON (Biousse).

St-Pourçain Lo, Mass C ★→★★★ 22' 23 (25) Minor AOP nr Vichy; CHARD, SAUV BL; acid-fresh Tressalier (aka Sacy) most interesting. GAMAY/PINOT N (r/rosé) less intriguing. Try ***Bérioles***, Terres d'Ocre, VIGNERONS de St-Pourçain.

St-Romain C d'O ★★→★★★ (w) 17' 18 19' 20' 21 22' 23 24 ***Crisp whites*** from picturesque side valley of CÔTE DE BEAUNE, rising to 400m (1312ft). Gaining in stature, gd value by Burg standards. Best vyds: Combe Bazin, Sous la Roche, Sous le CH. Specialists: ***Alain Gras***, de Chassorney, ***H&G Buisson*** (outstanding). Fresh reds.

St-Véran Burg ★★ 19 20' 21 22' 23 24 AOP either side of POUILLY-FUISSÉ. Best sites in Davayé. CH de Beauregard, Chagnoleau, Corsin, Deux Roches, Litaud, Merlin; gd-value DUBOEUF, Poncetys, Terres Secrètes co-op. Watch for DROUHIN.

Salitis, Ch de Ldoc ★★ At crossroads of Atlantic and Med influences nr Carcassonne; bio. CABARDÈS SYRAH/MERLOT/CAB FR, a real steal. Rosé eminently gd value too.

Salon Champ ★★★★ Original BLANC DE BLANCS, from LE MESNIL in Côte des Blancs. Tiny quantities. Long-lived, luxury prices. On song recently, quality once again catching up with reputation, *viz* 96 97' 02 04' 08 10 12 13 14' 15. *See* DELAMOTTE. Both owned by LAURENT-PERRIER.

Sancerre Lo ★→★★★★ 19' 20 21 22 23 (25) AOP renowned for SAUV BL, but PINOT N (r/rosé) also gd. White range from simple drink-now to cellar-worthy with great acidity. Try Alphonse Mellot, Claude Riffault, CLOS la Néore, COTAT (FRANÇOIS or Pascal), DOM Delaporte, François Crochet, ***Gérard Boulay***, HENRI BOURGEOIS, J-M Roger, JP Agisson, Lucien Crochet, P&N Reverdy, Paul Prieur, Pierre Martin, VACHERON, ***Vincent Pinard***.

Sang des Cailloux, Dom Le S Rh ★★★ 16' 18' 19' 20' 21 22' 23 24' 25 Top VACQUEYRAS, bio, grass-roots thrust. Peppery, *garrigue*, mostly GRENACHE (r). Classic red, gd fruit, rotates name: Floureto (25), Azalaïs (24), Doucinello (23). High-grade, deep, complex Lopy (r) merits time. Sturdy, table-necessary Un Sang Bl (w) suits garlic dishes.

Sansonnière, La Ferme de Lo ★★→★★★ Cult ANJOU DOM; low-intervention guru Mark Angeli, son Martial and pal Bruno Ciofi. Dry CHENIN BL all VDF (2006). Try blended ***La Lune*** 08 09 10 12 14' 16 21' (22) (23) (25), single-vyds Coteau du Houet, Les Fouchardes, Les Vieilles des Blanderies. Red, rosé more variable.

Santenay C d'O ★★★ 15' 16 17 18 19' 20' 21 22' 23 24 At s end of COTE DE BEAUNE, fine red, lovely white. Best vyds: CLOS de Tavannes, Clos Rousseau, Gravières (r/*w*). Local producers: ***Bachey-Legros***, ***Capuano-Ferreri***, ***Ch Philippe le Hardi***, CHEVROT, Girardin (Justin), Jessiaume, MOREAU, ***Muzard***, ***Olivier***, VINCENT. Also gd: Giroud, JADOT (incl DOM Prieur-Brunet), LAMY. Evenstad for CÔTE DE NUITS (r).

Sarabande, Dom La Ldoc ★★→★★★ Australian/Irish couple, impressive FAUGÈRES. Les Espinasses powerful SYRAH-based. ROUSSANE/MARSANNE stylish, schist.

Saumur Lo ★→★★★★ 19' 20' 21 22' 23 (25) AOP and region, latter home to AOPs SAUMUR-CHAMPIGNY, Saumur Le Puy-Notre-Dame (both r); range from simple fare to stunning cellar-worthy wines, also rare Coteaux de Saumur (sw). White (CHENIN BL) can be v. fine. Try Antoine Sanzay, Arnaud Lambert, CLOS DE L'ÉCOTARD, ***Clos Rougeard***, Guiberteau, Le Porte Saint Jean, Nerleux, ROCHES NEUVES, Rocheville, Targé, Théo Blet, Villeneuve, Yvonne.

Saumur-Champigny Lo ★★→★★★★ 05' 10' 15' 16 17 18' 19 20 22' 23 (25) Famed AOP in SAUMUR for CAB FR. Usually more structured, complex than SAUMUR. Try Antoine Sanzay, Arnaud Lambert, ***Clos Rougeard***, Guiberteau, Hureau, Nerleux, ROCHES NEUVES, Rocheville, Villeneuve, Yvonne.

Saussignac SW Fr ★★→★★★ 18' 19 20 22 23 (24) Tiny AOP enclave of BERGERAC adjoining MONBAZILLAC, best challenge SAUTERNES. ★★★ DOMS de Richard, La Maurigne, ***Les Miaudoux***, Lestevenie. ★★ CHX Le Chabrier, Le Payral, Le Tap.

Sauternes Bx ★★→★★★★ 13 14 15' 16' 18 19 20 22 23 24 (25) AOP making France's best *liquoreux* from "noble rotted" grapes. Luscious, golden; drink young or aged. Classified (1855): GUIRAUD, ***Lafaurie-Peyraguey***, LA TOUR BLANCHE, RAYNE VIGNEAU, RIEUSSEC, SUDUIRAUT, YQUEM. Unclassified: ***Fargues***, ***Gilette***, ***Raymond-Lafon***.

Sauzet, Etienne C d'O ★★★→★★★★ Leading PULIGNY DOM. Superb range of PCS (Combettes, Champ Canet best) and GC BÂTARD-M. Concentrated, lively, bio, age-worthy. Magnificent BOURGOGNE Bl. (Sublime MONTRACHET from bought grapes.) Slick tasting room, glorious view across vyds.

Savennières Lo ★★→★★★★ 14' 15 16 18 19 20 22' 23 (25) Famed AOP in ANJOU, once sweet, now (almost) always dry. Wines from schist, complex, ageable; from sand, drink young. Try BAUDOUIN, BAUMARD, BELARGUS, Bergerie, ***Boudignon***, Closel, DOM FL, Epiré, LAUREAU, Mahé, MORGAT, OGEREAU, PIERRE-BISE, Soucherie.

Savennières Roche-aux-Moines Lo ★★★→★★★★ 10' 14' 15 16 18 19 20 22' (23) (25) Pinnacle of SAVENNIÈRES, dry CHENIN BL, 35-ha AOP. Best are stunning, mineral, packed with cellar potential: ***Dom aux Moines***, FL, Forges, LAUREAU, PIERRE-BISE.

Savigny-lès-Beaune C d'O ★★→★★★ 10' 15' 18' 19' 20' 21 22' 23 24 Village next to BEAUNE; similar wines, more excitement recently, while remaining gd value. Top vyds: Dominode, Guettes, Lavières, Vergelesses. Growers: A Guyon, ***Bize***, Camus-Bruchon, ***Chandon de Briailles***, Chenu, Girard, Guillemot (w), Pavelot, RAPET, ***Tollot-Beaut***. Exceptional CUVÉES: CLAIR, DROUHIN, JP Guyon, LEROY.

Savoie AOP Alpine wines, two-thirds white, mostly organic; 20 crus incl APREMONT, ARBIN, AYZE, Chautagne, CHIGNIN, Jongieux, St Jean de la Porte; regional AOPs incl CRÉMANT de Sav, ROUSSETTE DE SAV, SEYSSEL; 25 grapes (r) mainly GAMAY, MONDEUSE, Persan, PINOT N; (w) Altesse, CHARD, CHASSELAS, Gringet, Jacquère, ROUSSANNE. ★★: Baraterie, ***Giachino***. ★★: A Berlioz (bio), Chevillard, Côtes Rousses (bio). ★★→★★★★: Prieuré St-Christophe (last vintage of Michel Grisard 14, now in talented hands of Giachino, old vintages magical). New thrilling DOMS. ★: Albatros, Archer. ★★: Sonjon. ★★→★★★: C Houillon, Ça Boit Libre. *See* QUENARD.

Schlossberg Al Famous since C15 but officially est 1975, AL's 1st ever GC. Glorious RIES from ALBERT MANN, PAUL BLANCK, TRIMBACH, WEINBACH.

Schlumberger, Doms Al ★★★→★★★★ Huge private estate (owns c.1% all AL vyds); GCS Kessler, Kitterlé, Saering. Superb Saering RIES **08** 17' 18 19, but GEWURZ tops, esp VT CUVÉE Christine (unforgettable 76'; 20' excellent) and SGN Cuvée Anne (masterpiece 89'). New, v.gd Ries CLOS St Leger 17 19 vies with TRIMBACH CLOS STE-HUNE as most expensive Al.

Schoenenbourg Al Historic Riquewihr GC famous for RIES. (Voltaire owned vines here.) Top: HUGEL Ries Schoelhammer. Fine VT, SGN Ries DOPFF AU MOULIN.

Schoffit, Dom Al ★★★★ Rare winery situated in Colmar. Contrast RIES RANGEN CLOS St-Théobald 10' **17'** **18'** 20' (volcanic) and Ries GC Sommerberg 13 15 **16** 17' (granite). Superb VT, SGN. Harth CHASSELAS VIEILLES VIGNES, AL best. Hard-to-find pure SYLVANER.

Sec Literally means dry, though CHAMP so called is medium-sweet.

Old flavours for a new climate

At the forefront of climate change, LDOC-ROUSS and SW France growers are increasingly turning to ancient or abandoned varieties to adapt. Whites doing well incl BOURBOULENC in LA CLAPE (tastes of salted almonds), rare Carignan Gr (v. late-ripening, low alc) in FITOU, Rouss; PIQUEPOUL in all guises (uplifting w; floral rosé; light r). Old stalwart reds are seeing a new lease of life: GRENACHE (cherries, spice), CARIGNAN (keeps freshness). GAILLAC is a veritable open-air library of resurgent varieties: Prunelart (r, dark plums), DURAS (r, robust, peppery), Ondenc (w, quince, lemon). Braucol aka FER SERVADOU (r, tannic, spicy) retains moderate alc and high acidity, esp in MARCILLAC. Seek v. rare CAMARALET (w, pungent, musky) from JURANÇON, blended with Mansengs.

Séguret S Rh ★★ 23 24' 25 Picture-postcard hillside village in Rh-Villages top three; heated plain, cool heights. Led by GRENACHE, peppery, direct, berried red; cosy white. Try CH la Courançonne (gd w); DOMS Bosquets (w), Crève Coeur (handmade, organic, bio), de Cabasse (hotel), de l'Amauve (sleek, organic, gd w), Fontaine des Fées (organic), Garancière (organic/bio), Maison Plantevin (organic), Malmont (rosé), Mourchon (depth), Pourra (character).

Selosse, Anselme Champ ★★★★ Influential grower, prophet no longer in wilderness. Vinous, oxidative style, oak-fermented. Son Guillaume adding finesse: Version Originale vibrant after 7 yrs on lees. NV BRUT Initial and rare Substance (solera style; *see* Spain). Contraste BLANC DE NOIRS. Côte des Blancs parcels: lieux-dits Les Carelles, Le Bout du Clos, ***La Côte Faron*** Blanc de Noirs. Much of range NV, but Millésime 08 **09 10' 12** 13.

Selz, Albert Al ★★★→★★★★ King of SYLVANER, with vyds in Mittelbergheim's clay-calcareous GC Zoztenberg. Outstanding 19 20 22; also v.gd RIES 19', marvellous late-harvest. Son Jeremy now joined.

Sérafin, Dom C d'O ★★★ Niece Frédérique in charge, continuing Christian S recipe: deep colour, intense flavours, new wood. Wines need age. Full throttle, structured. For GEVREY traditionalists. Dense, vibrant Cazetiers (DOM's back garden), CHARMES-CHAMBERTIN, Gevrey-Chambertin VIEILLES VIGNES.

Sérol, Dom Lo ★★★ 18' 19 20' **21 22'** 23 (25) Leading DOM in CÔTE ROANNAISE AOP. GAMAY planted on granite, basalt soils gives beautifully fresh but dense, shapely wines. Top, dark, cellar-worthy: Millerands, Oudan, Perdrizière. Others (Eclat de Granite), drink youngish.

Seyssel Sav Small regional AOP, long history. Light white, fizz (Altesse, Molette). Try ★ Caves de Seyssel (esp Royal Seyssel).

SGN (Sélection des Grains Nobles) Al Term coined by HUGEL for AL equivalent of German Beerenauslese. Today, *grains nobles* mostly made with noble rot-affected grapes, not just v. sweet grapes that meet legal SGN requirement.

Sichel & Co Bx Notable BX merchant: Sirius a top brand. Family-run. Interests in CHX ANGLUDET, Argadens, Daviaud, PALMER.

Sigoulès, Les Vignerons de SW Fr Much-improved source for BERGERAC, incl top CLOS d'Yvigne.

Simone, Ch Prov ★★★ Historic estate outside Aix, where Churchill painted Mont STE-VICTOIRE. Rougier family for c.200 yrs. AOP PALETTE; n-facing slopes on limestone with clay and gravel give freshness. Seek age-worthy whites; iconic rosé, elegant reds from GRENACHE, MOURVÈDRE, with rare grape varieties Castet and Manosquin (r).

Sipp, Louis Al ★★→★★★ Trades in big volumes of young wines, but also two GC: fine RIES Kirchberg **13 16**; luscious GEWURZ Osterberg VT 09 **15 16** 18 19.

Sipp-Mack Al ★★→★★★ Large range of lively, easy-drinking, dry, mineral wines, but not last word in concentration. Caroline S at helm now: lovely RIES GC Rosacker, expansive PINOT GR best.

Sorg, Bruno Al ★★★ Small grower at Eguisheim, GCS Florimont (RIES **13 14** 16' great 17'), PFERSIGBERG (MUSCAT) 18'. Immaculate eco-friendly vyds.

Sorrel, Dom N Rh ★★★→★★★★ **18'** 19' 20' 21 22' 23' 24' 25' Small 3rd-generation HERMITAGE grower; hillside truth, depth; more refined since 19 under Guillaume. Top: Le Gréal (r, mighty, long life), Les Rocoules (w, rich, a wonder at 10 yrs+). Also gd: old-vine CROZES-HERMITAGE (r/w).

Soulanes, Dom des Rouss ★★★ Tucked below Cathar castle of Quéribus, Daniel and Cathy Laffite have for 20 yrs been quietly making some of ROUSS's best-value wines. Jean Pull (r), crunchy; Sarrat del Mas (r), more serious. Great MAURY VDN.

Sousa, De Champ ★★★ Erick and daughters enter 2nd decade as bio heroes in AVIZE. CUVÉE Les Caudalies BLANC DE BLANCS **GC** 08 **10 13'** 14 15. Well-named

Cuvée Umami **09 12 13** GC Blanc de Blancs Rés consistently excellent. Also 3A from three Grand Crus. Can you guess which? Hunt; they all begin with the letter A!

Sur lie "On the lees", as in MUSCADET. Bottled straight from vat: zest, body, character.

Tâche, La C d'O ★★★★ 90' 93' 96' 99' 02' 03 05' 09' 10' 12' 15' 16' **17** 18' 19' 20' 21 22' 23 24 VOSNE GC, DRC MONOPOLE. Firm but always appealing in youth, a merry-go-round of flavour. Develops extraordinary complexity and allure with time, floral and perfumed. Can age for decades – then, fairest of all DRCs?

Taille-aux-Loups, Dom de la Lo ★★★→★★★★ 14' 15 16 17' 18 **19' 20'** 21 22' 23 (25) MONTLOUIS SUR LO's top DOM. Jean-Philippe Blot continues father's legacy with *éclat*. Brilliant MONTLOUIS, VOUVRAY (latter all VDF), barrel-fermented, dry, a touch burgundian; only get better with age. Try CLOS Michet, Clos Mosny, Les Hauts de Husseau, Remus. Don't miss Triple Zéro (top Lo sp).

Tain, Cave de N Rh ★★→★★★ Superior co-op, legacy vyds, incl 25% of all HERMITAGE. Hermitage red gd to v.gd: Gambert de Loche (best, gd depth, value). Rich Hermitage Au Coeur des Siècles (w, incl 1900s MARSANNE, value). ST-JOSEPH (r/w), ST-PÉRAY, clear drinking Bio (organic) range (St-Joseph r, CROZES w); others technical, can be dull. Gourmand Marsanne VIN DE PAILLE.

Taittinger Champ ★★★→★★★★ Family-run Reims house. BRUT NV, Rosé NV, Brut Vintage Collection Brut **89** 95'. Luxury ***Comtes de Champagne*** 08 **09 12 13** 14'. Comtes Rosé **12' 13** 14. NV GC: Les Folies de la Marquetterie, Prélude. Children Clovis and Vitalie now key. *See* DOMS Evremond (England), Carneros (US).

Tarlant Champ ★★★→★★★★ Marne family in Oeuilly, 12th generation. ***Zero Brut Nature***; BAM!, CUVÉE Louis, Entracte. Impressive BRUT Rés. Bone-dry style.

Tasque, Dom La Ldoc Small bio DOM in MINERVOIS, but most IGP. Easy-drinking SYRAH-led Appia; old-vine CARIGNAN; intriguing ASSYRTIKO.

Tavel S Rh ★★ 24' 25 Attractively red-hued, full-bodied rosé; proper wine, from *garrigue* soils, across River Rhône from CHÂTEAUNEUF, centred on GRENACHE, CINSAULT, aided by white grapes (CLAIRETTE) for suave texture, oiliness. Should be herbal; can drink all through a meal. Best continue well 3–4 yrs. Now some escapist, PROV-apéritif style. Top: CHX Aquéria (v. stylish), de Manissy (organic/bio), La Genestière (organic), Ségriès, ***Trinquevedel*** (refined, organic); DOMS A Hote (organic, handmade), Corne-Loup, ***de la Mordorée*** (top, bio), des Carabiniers (bio), LAFOND ROC-EPINE (organic/bio), Maby (Prima Donna), Moulin-la-Viguerie (low sulphur), Rocalière (bio); Alain Jaume, GUIGAL, L'Anglore (no sulphur, character), R Le Bars (low sulphur), Tardieu-Laurent (organic, full), VIDAL-FLEURY, Vignerons de Tavel (Lauzeraies, value).

Tempier, Dom Prov ★★★→★★★★ Iconic BANDOL: Lucien and Lulu Peyraud revived AOP in 30s. Outstanding intensity, poise, depth. Benchmark CUVÉE Classique; single-vyds Cabassaou, La Tourtine, pure expressions of MOURVÈDRE; v.gd rosé.

Terrasses du Larzac Ldoc ★★★→★★★★ Packed full of great LDOC DOMS, 1st-rate terroir. Warm days, cool nights; geologically complex AOP producing intense yet exhilarating reds. Attracts innovative growers, small plots of vines; 50%+ organic/bio. Try CH de Jonquières; DOMS de La Rés d'O, de Malavielle, de Montcalmès, du PAS DE L'ESCALETTE; La Peira, Le Clos du Serres, L'Écriture, MAS CAL DEMOURA, Mas Combarèla, Mas Conscience, Mas d'Agamas, Mas des Brousses, MAS JULLIEN. Neighbouring AOP Ldoc St-Saturnin: Doms Archimbaud, Virgile Joly.

Thénard, Dom Burg ★★→★★★★ Large holding of MONTRACHET, 1.8 ha, mostly sold to DOMS, NÉGOCIANTS. Also v.gd reds from home base in GIVRY.

Thévenet, Jean Burg ★★★ Top Mâconnais purveyor of rich, some semi-botrytized CHARD: ***Dom de la Bongran***'s CUVÉE Levroutée. Also DOMS de Roally, Emilian Gillet. Opulent flavours, distinctive style, doesn't chime with today's zeitgeist.

Thiénot, Alain Champ ★★★ Young. Ever-improving quality. BRUT NV; Brut Rosé NV; Vintage Stanislas BLANC DE BLANCS 02 04 06 08'. Voluminous VIGNE aux Gamins (single-vyd AVIZE 08 09 10). CUVÉE Garance CHARD 07 08. Interesting Garance Blanc des Rouges 08 10 12 13. "Le 3" tourism hub. Release of Immersion Collection celebrates 40 yrs. Owns CANARD-DUCHÊNE, CH Ricaud (LOUPIAC).

Thivin, Ch Beauj ★★★ Geoffray family makes great CÔTE DE BROUILLY. Single-vyd bottlings cover soil types. Wide variety of grapes in experimental plots.

Tiregand, Ch de SW Fr ★★★ Leading estate in PÉCHARMANT. Age-worthy BX-style reds, greater freshness, distinctive SW twist; v. small but excellent SAUV BL. New owners 2023 after nearly 200 yrs in St-Exupéry family.

Tissot Jura Dominant family around ARBOIS. Jacques T (volume). ★: Jean-Louis T (value). ★★★→★★★★: ***Stéphane T*** (also as A&M Tissot), bio with top single-vyd CHARD (plus Rose Massale; w made from rare pink Chard mutation), SAVAGNIN Ouillé, Sous Voile, VIN JAUNE, brooding reds, brilliant CRÉMANT du Jura selections. T-Maire, unrelated BOISSET brand.

Tollot-Beaut C d'O ★★★ CÔTE DE BEAUNE grower with 20 ha in BEAUNE (Grèves, CLOS du Roi), CORTON (Bressandes), SAVIGNY (MONOPOLE PC Champ Chevrey) and CHOREY-LÈS-BEAUNE (Pièce du Chapitre). Benchmark DOM for consistent quality at attractive prices. Appealing wines, can age. Also CORTON-CHARLEMAGNE.

Touraine Lo ★→★★★ Region and AOP (easy-going r/w). Some more serious, even age-worthy, esp sub-AOPs: Amboise, Azay-le-Rideau, Mesland (all CHENIN BL-led), Chenonceaux (SAUV BL, CÔT), Oisly (Sauv Bl). Best: ***Echardières***, Garrelière, Gosseaume, Grosbois, J-F Mérieau, Joël Delaunay, La Grange Tiphaine, MARIONNET, Ricard, Roussely. Also Touraine-Noble-Joué (triple-Pinot rosé AOP).

The freezing point of wine is roughly -0.5°C per degree of alcohol.

Tour des Gendres, Ch SW Fr ★★★ Top BERGERAC, bio, siblings Gilles and Margaux de Conti (related to ALBERT DE C). Mostly BX varieties, interesting additions CHENIN BL, SAVAGNIN. Outstanding Anthologia, single-parcel, old-vine SAUV BL.

Tour Saint-Martin, La Lo ★★→★★★ Fine DOM in MENETOU-SALON run by Bertrand Minchin. SAUV BL: Fumet, Honorine 21 22 23 (25). PINOT N ages surprisingly well. VALENÇAY for value.

Trapet C d'O ★★★→★★★★ Long-est GEVREY DOM but nothing fuddy-duddy here; bio: eye-catching COTEAUX BOURGUIGNONS to majestic GC CHAMBERTIN, plus AL by marriage. Sons Pierre, Louis trying glass globes, steel barrels, eggs.

Tremblay, Dom Cecile C d'O ★★★ Wines of harmony and persistence. Style firmer recently. Concentrated, structured ÉCHÉZEAUX, also lovely village VOSNE from two plots.

Trévallon, Dom de Prov ★★★★ Famous DOM at LES BAUX; daughter Ostiane now in charge. No GRENACHE, only CAB SAUV/SYRAH, so labelled as IGP Alpilles. Huge reputation fully justified: meticulous viticulture, whole-bunch fermented, age-worthy. Rare barrique-aged MARSANNE/ROUSSANNE. Timeless. Picasso-like labels.

Trimbach, FE Al ★★★★ Peerless CLOS STE-HUNE 67' 71' 75' 89'; VT and VT Hors Choix 90' (still great) 13 17' 18 19' 21' 22' 23' (classic); almost-as-gd (much cheaper) ***Frédéric Emile*** 10 12 13 14 16 17' 20' 21 22' 23'. Improved RIES SCHLOSSBERG, exceptional 20 21' 22' 23'. Brand 24' best Trimbach cru-labelled wine of yr. Underrated, fresh PINOT GR: superb Osterberg 15' 24. Knockout Ries-like SYLVANER Weinbaum from Trottacker lieu-dit, ages spectacularly well.

Tunnel, Dom du N Rh ★★★ Stéphane Robert makes four leading ST-PÉRAY, notably rich, stylish Prestige, Pur Blanc (30s MARSANNE, serious, develops). Plush, upfront CORNAS (Pur Noir, 1900s SYRAH), ST-JOSEPH (r).

Tursan SW Fr Mostly DYA AOP in LANDES. ★★★ super-chef Michel Guérard makes lovely wines in chapel-like cellar at CH de Bachen, but not trad Tursan. Real thing from ★★ DOM de Perchade. Lovely dry white from ★★ Dom de Cazalet (two MANSENGS plus rare local Baroque). Worthy co-op rather outclassed.

U Stiliccionu, Dom Cors ★★★→★★★★ Live-wire Sébastien Poly makes some of best SCIACCARELLO at 7-ha bio estate in AJACCIO: crunchy Antica; exquisite Sottu Scala. Emy-Lidia, fine VERMENTINO.

Vacheron, Dom Lo ★★→★★★ One of SANCERRE's top. Entry-level gd but best are single-vyds: Chambrates, Guigne-Chèvres, Le Paradis, ***Les Romains*** 15 16 17 19 21 22 23 (25). Also v.gd: cellar-worthy PINOT N, Belle Dame.

Champagne corks, unleashed, travel at 50 km/h, without prejudice.

Vacqueyras S Rh ★★→★★★ 16' 18 19' 20 22' 23 24' 25 Robust, warm lands; spiced, tannic GRENACHE-powered red from nr GIGONDAS; suits big flavours, game. Lives 10 yrs+. CHX de Montmirail, ***des Tours*** (fine elegance, RAYAS stable); CLOS de Caveau (organic), ***Clos des Cazaux*** (v.gd value); DOMS Amouriers (organic), Archimbaud-Vache, CHARBONNIÈRE, Famille Perrin, Font de Papier (organic), Fourmone (fine), Garrigue (grassroots), Grapillon d'Or, Monardière (organic, top rank), Montirius (bio), Montvac (organic), Ouréa (organic), Roucas Toumba (organic, much character), SANG DES CAILLOUX (organic/bio, esp Lopy), Semelles de Vent (handmade), Verde; P AMADIEU. Grounded, table whites: Ch des Roques, Clos des Cazaux, Fourmone, Mas des Restanques, Montvac (finesse) Sang des Cailloux.

Val de Loire Lo ★→★★ Main regional IGP in Lo. Mostly minor wines (DYA). Occasional gem: YANNICK AMIRAULT Bâtard-Princesse CHENIN BL (BOURGUEIL).

Valençay Lo ★→★★ 22' 23 (25) Peripheral Touraine AOP, GD value. Easy-drinking SAUV BL/CHARD or CÔT/GAMAY/PINOT N blends: Domaines Minchin (from Bertrand at LA TOUR SAINT MARTIN), Lafond, Preys, Sinson.

Valréas S Rh ★★ 24' 25 CÔTES DU RH-VILLAGE in rolling country of N Vaucluse, basket of lavender, olive, truffles, wine; 450 ha, high vyds, quality rising. Spiced, red-fruited, mainly GRENACHE; attractive white (GRENACHE BL, CLAIRETTE etc). Try CH la Décelle, CLOS Bellane incl Val des Rois (organic, gd w), Mas de Ste-Croix; DOMS des Grands Devers, du Séminaire (organic, pure r), Prévosse (organic).

VdF (Vin de France) Replaces Vin de Table, but with mention of grape variety, vintage. Often blends of regions with brand name. Can be source of unexpected delights if talented winemaker uses this category to avoid bureaucractic hassle, eg. Mark Angeli, Y CUILLERON VIOGNIER. ANJOU, S ARDÈCHE hotbeds of VdF.

VDN (vin doux naturel) Rouss Original fortified wines. BANYULS, MAURY, RIVESALTES can be outstanding. Speciality of ROUSS based on GRENACHES BL/Gr/N. Sweet, lower alc than Port, either richly fruited or oxidative styles. Top, esp aged RANCIOS: sublime, great value. MUSCAT, reductive styles from BEAUMES DE VENISE, FRONTIGNAN, Lunel, RIVESALTES, ROUSS; St Jean de MINERVOIS more refreshing.

VdP (Vin de Pays) *See* IGP.

Vendange Harvest. **VT (Vendange Tardive)** Late-harvest; AL equivalent to German Auslese but usually higher alc.

Venoge, de Champ ★★★ Venerable house, LANSON-BCC-owned; articulate boss in Gilles de la Bassetière. Cordon Bleu Extra-BRUT, CUVÉE des Princes, Vintage BLANC DE BLANCS 13' 16 17. Prestige Cuvée Louis XV 06 08 14, BLANC DE NOIRS 12 14'. Less Anglophone following than deserved.

Vent, Dom du Ldoc ★★ Natalie and Benjamin Boyer worked all over France, in LDOC since 2022. Cracking start. Perfumed, delicate Comme un Souffle FITOU, floral, zippy VERMENTINO IGP Aude. MUSCAT de Rivesaltes fine too. Watch.

Ventoux S Rh ★★ 24 25 Widespread 5440-ha AOP surrounding Mont Ventoux: diverse soils, hot low plains, fresh heights. Some top DOMS: value red, gd selection names. GRENACHE/SYRAH from perky, stand-at-bar style to deeper, peppery; quality rising. Neat, clear rosé. Stylish white (more oak). Best: CH

Unang (organic, gd w), Ch Valcombe, Chêne Bleu (oak, rosé), CLOS de Trias, Clos des Patris (organic), Gonnet, La Ferme St Pierre (w/rosé, organic), La Vieille Ferme (r, value, also VDF), St-Marc, Terra Ventoux, Vignerons Mont Ventoux; Doms Allois (organic), Anges, Berane, Brusset, Cascavel, Champ-Long, Croix de Pins (gd w), du Tix, Fondrèche (organic), Grand Jacquet, Martinelle (organic, stylish), Murmurium, Olivier B (organic), PESQUIÉ (superior), Piéblanc (organic, fresh depth), Pigeade, St-Jean du Barroux (organic, character, incl w), Terres de Solence, Tix, Verrière, VIDAL-FLEURY, Vieux Lazaret, VIGNOBLES Brunier (70s Grenache); co-op Bédoin.

Vernay, Dom Georges N Rh ★★★★ 23' 24' 25' Must try, wonderful, expensive CONDRIEU from Christine and Emma V: restraint, finesse. Terrasses de l'Empire ***apéritif de luxe***; Chaillées d'Enfer, precise richness; Coteau de Vernon, subtle, total class, lives 20 yrs+. CÔTE-RÔTIE, ST-JOSEPH (r), tight, red-fruited; superior IGP COLLINES RHODANIENNES (r/w).

Veuve Clicquot Champ ★★★★ Historical house. Improving Yellow Label NV; 5% oak. Impressive DEMI-SEC NV. Vintage Rés **12 15**. Luxe La Grande Dame (GD) **12' 15** 18. Older vintages of GD stay course, *viz* 04' (no 02, deemed too muscular for GD). GD Rosé **12** 13 **15'**. Affable, capable chef de CAVE Didier Mariotti.

Veuve Fourny Champ ★★★→★★★★ Superb archetypal Côte des Blancs specialist, delightful bros (Charles-Henry and Emmanuel). Sustainable (HEV-certified) in Vertus. CUVÉE R, Monts de Vertus both Extra BRUT. BLANC DE BLANCS PC **15 17'** 18 19, NV exceptional value. Historic CLOS Faubourg Notre Dame.

Vézelay Burg ★→★★ Age 1–2 yrs. Lovely location (with abbey) in NW Burg. Promoted to full AOP for tasty whites from CHARD. Also try revived MELON (COTEAUX BOURGUIGNON), light PINOT (generic BOURGOGNE). Best: DOM de la Cadette, des Faverelles, Elise Villiers, La Croix Montjoie.

Vidal-Fleury N Rh ★→★★★ Merchant-grower at CÔTE-RÔTIE (1781), GUIGAL-owned. Top red by far: distinguished, profound ***La Chatillonne*** (from Blonde, 12% VIOGNIER, all new oak, leave min 7 yrs). Decent CAIRANNE (r), gd CHÂTEAUNEUF (w), tidy CÔTES DU RH (w/rosé), GIGONDAS, rich MUSCAT de BEAUMES-DE-VENISE, VENTOUX.

Vieilles vignes Old vines. Can give extra depth, complexity. Internationally considered to be 35 yrs+; many growers claim age at 25 yrs, which is absurd.

Vieux Télégraphe, Dom du S Rh ★★★ 05' 07' **09' 10'** 12' 14' **15'** 16' **17' 18'** 19' 20' 21 23' 24' 25 Benchmark, high-quality estate, in gd form; large-stone, windy-plateau soils; slow to evolve, dark, terroir-herbal red CHÂTEAUNEUF. Top two wines: La Crau (complex, long life; no 22), Piedlong (aromatic, silky). High-interest, true-*garrigue*, Med-table-white ***La Crau*** (complex if aged), CLOS La Roquète (fine). Also owns spicy, intricate GIGONDAS DOM Les Pallières.

Vignelaure, Ch de Prov ★★★→★★★★ Top estate for reds, AOP COTEAUX D'AIX EN PROVENCE; CAB SAUV, SYRAH at 300m (984ft), depth, freshness. Will age 10 yrs. Rosé up to 5 yrs; intriguing ROUSSANNE, Rolle, SÉM.

Burgundy or Bourgogne? The world uses Burg. The French prefer Bourg.

Vigne or vignoble Vineyard (vyd), vineyards (vyds). **Vigneron** Vine-grower.

Vignoble du Rêveur Al ★★★ Project by Mathieu DEISS and Emanuelle Milan using Mathieu's maternal family vines. Dry, food-friendly, pure, bio field blends in Bennwihr; won't make a horse faint, like many "natural" wines. Superb Pierre Sauvages, Singulier **17' 18** 20 21.

Vigouroux, Georges SW Fr Top name in CAHORS, instrumental in reviving AOP. Estates incl Haute Serre and Mercues. Generations have changed; wines seem to be getting better after slightly dull period.

Villaine, de Burg ★★→★★★ Pierre de Benoist, nephew of Aubert de V, crafts impressive range, numerous appellations: age-worthy BOUZERON (ALIGOTÉ), calling card; RULLY, Les Saint-Jacques (w); CÔTE CHALONNAISE, La Digoine (r).

Villeneuve, Ch de Lo ★★→★★★ 18' 19' 20' **22'** 23 (25) Underrated DOM. Jean-Pierre Chevallier now handed reins to daughters. Whites: delicious SAUMUR, fine SAUMUR-CHAMPIGNY. Les Cormiers (w), Le Grand Clos (r) age beautifully.

Vilmart & Cie Champ ★★★→★★★★ Exemplary grower farming 11 ha of PC in unfashionable Montagne village Rilly. Oak fermentation. Long-serving chef de CAVE Laurent Champs. Superb Coeur de CUVÉE 13 **15'** **16**, Grand Cellier d'Or **18** 19 20. Also Rubis Rosé, "basic" Grand Cellier; PC Grande Rés, impeccable. Neat range.

Vincent, Jean-Marc C d'O ★★★ Viticulturist at heart, spending countless hrs in vyds. Excellent, age-worthy whites; v.gd reds (Gravité). Check daring, full-bodied, multi-vintage ALIGOTÉ blend Soler-Al. Now joined by daughter Anaïs.

Vincent, Pierre C d'O ★★★ Now est own name in AUXEY-DURESSES (ex-DOM LEFLAIVE, VOUGERAIE). Small CUVÉES of some 20 appellations, from ALIGOTÉ to CORTON-CHARLEMAGNE. Many old vines; pure, delicate wines. Challenging prices.

Vin de paille From grapes dried before pressing, so concentrated sweetness, acidity; esp in Jura, also HERMITAGE.

Vin gris Pale pink. "Oeil de perdrix" means much the same; so does "blush".

Vin jaune Jura ★★→★★★★ Speciality of Jura; inimitable golden wine. SAVAGNIN, 6 yrs+ barrel without topping up, develops flor like Sherry but no added alc. Ages for decades. Sold in unique 62cl clavelin bottles. Top spot, CH-CHALON has own AOP; S TISSOT specializes in single-vyd bottlings. Bourdy in old vintages. *See also* ARBOIS, CÔTES DU JURA, L'ETOILE.

Vinsobres S Rh ★★ 19' 22' 23 **24'** 25 Low-profile AOP; signs of life from owners Perrin and CH Rouanne. Appealing, fresh, lightly spiced SYRAH, gd hillside, high-plateau vyds; best stylish, age 10 yrs. New DOMS emerging. Leaders: CAVE la Vinsobraise (Diamant N), Ch Rouanne (plot-specific), CLOS Volabis (organic); Doms Autrand (stylish), Chaume-Arnaud (bio, v.gd, incl w), Constant-Duquesnoy, du Tave, Famille Perrin (***Hauts de Julien*** top, ages well; Cornuds, value), Jaume (full, age well), Moulin (trad, gd r/w), Serre Besson (gd VdF), Vallot (bio).

Vins Schaal Al ★★★ Husband and wife Julian and Sophie S each have own labels. Julian GC only, labels carry dominant mineral: ROSACKER, Calcaire; RANGEN, Volcanique. Sophie lieu-dits mostly (and S African Born of Fire). Organic J Schaal RIES GCS BRAND, SOMMERBERG 24; Sophie Schaal GEWURZ, PINOT N 24.

Viré-Clessé Burg ★★ 17' 18 19' **20'** 21 22' 23 24 AOP, two of best white villages of MÂCON. Exuberant rich style, esp from Quintaine area, sometimes late-harvest. Try ***Bonhomme***, Chaland, DOM de la Verpaille, Gandines, Gondard-Perrin, Guillemot-Michel, J-P Michel, THÉVENET and all gd Mâconnais NÉGOCIANTS.

Visan S Rh ★★ 24' 25 On-the-move CÔTES DU RH-VILLAGE, highish vyds: peppered, mostly GRENACHE red; some supple, plenty organic. White decent. DOMS Au 7ème CLOS, Bastide, Coste Chaude, Dieulefit (bio, low sulphur, v.gd), Florane (bio, v.gd), Fourmente (bio, esp Nature), Guintrandy (full), Montmartel, Philippe Plantevin, Roche-Audran (organic/bio, gd CÔTES DU RH), VIGNOBLE Art Mas.

A single Savagnin seed

One single 900-yr-old seed found at an archaeological site in Orléans is genetically the same as SAVAGNIN (one of France's most ancient varieties?). It's either a parent or offspring of PINOT N. (Shall we bet on which is oldest?) Savagnin is also a grandparent of CAB SAUV and (probably) a parent of PETIT MANSENG and GRÜNER V. Quite a family.

Vogüé, Comte Georges de C d'O ★★★★ Patrician CHAMBOLLE estate with lion's share of MUSIGNY. Winemaker Jean Lupatelli using more whole bunches, making style more accessible in youth; also plot-by-plot vinification. Unique, splendid ***Musigny Bl***. Noble Marc de Bourgogne.

Volnay C d'O ★★★→★★★★ 05' 09' 10' 15' 16 17' 18 19 20 21 22' 23 24 Top CÔTE DE BEAUNE reds, prone to hail. The s echo of CHAMBOLLE-MUSIGNY, similar grace, satin charm (challenged by hot vintages), slightly more structure. Wonderful evolution with age. (Ban on weedkillers in PC vyds.) Best vyds: Caillerets, Champans, CLOS des Chênes, Santenots (more clay), Taillepieds and MONOPOLES Clos de la Bousse d'Or, Clos de la Chapelle, Clos des Ducs, Clos du CH des Ducs. Growers: BOULEY, D'ANGERVILLE, ***de Montille***, LAFARGE, ***Pousse d'Or***. Also v.gd: ***Bitouzet-Prieur***, Buffet, Clerget, Glantenay, H BOILLOT, HOSPICES DE BEAUNE, LAFON, Rossignol.

Vosne-Romanée C d'O ★★★→★★★★ 90' 93' 96' 99' 02' 05' 09' 10' 12 15' 16' 17 18 19' 20' 21 22' 23 24 Most patrician village in Burg, with celebrated GCS and outstanding PCS Beaumonts, Brûlées, Malconsorts, Suchots etc. Should always be special and regularly sublime, often with a haunting note of sweet incense. No excuses for anything less. Just question of price... Top: ARNOUX-LACHAUX, Bizot, CATHIARD, Coquard-Loison-Fleurot, DRC, EUGÉNIE, GRIVOT, GROS, Lamarche, LEROY, LIGER-BELAIR, MÉO-CAMUZET, MUGNERET, NOËLLAT, ROUGET. Try also Clavelier, ***Confuron-Gindre***, Forey, Guyon, Tardy.

Vougeot C d'O ★★★ 02' 05' 09' 10' 12' 15' 16 17 18 19' 20 21 22' 23 24 Mostly GC as CLOS DE VOUGEOT (variable, improving). Also village, PCS Les Cras, Les Petits Vougeots, MONOPOLES ***Clos Blanc de V*** (outstanding w, compares favourably with DE VOGÜÉ MUSIGNY w), ***Clos de la Perrière***. Try ***Bertagna***, Clerget, ***Fourrier***, GROS (A), HUDELOT-NOËLLAT, LEROUX, ***Vougeraie***.

Vougeraie, Dom de la C d'O ★★★→★★★★ BOISSET's vyd holdings; bio. Fine-boned, perfumed, whole-bunch-vinified GCS, esp ***Bonnes-Mares***, CHARMES-CHAMBERTIN, MUSIGNY. Fine white: superb, age-worthy ***Clos Blanc de Vougeot***, four GCs incl Charlemagne. Bought Duc de Magenta CHASSAGNE vyds (2021); organic (2024).

Vouvray Lo ★→★★★★ (dr) 18' 19' 20' 21 22 23 (25) (sw) 47' 89' 90' 02' 03 05 08' 09 10 11' 15' 16 17 18' 20' 22 23 (25) Famed AOP for CHENIN BL. All styles: dry (bright, mineral); off-dry (super with acid/sugar harmony); sweet (can be astonishing); sparkling (great from top DOMS, others can disappoint). Try AUBUISIÈRES, Autran, Brunet, CHAMPALOU, ***Clos Naudin***, FRANÇOIS CHIDAINE (VDF), FRANÇOIS & JULIEN PINON, Gaudrelle, HUET, Meslerie, Perrault-Jadaud, TAILLE-AUX-LOUPS (VdF), Vigneau-Chevreau, ***Vincent Carême***.

Weinbach, Dom Al ★★★★ World's best GEWURZ SGN (Furstentum GC 22 superb). Exceptionally elegant, pure gastronomic wines: MUSCAT 22' 23, SYLVANER 19' 20, RIES GC SCHLOSSBERG (Cuve Ste Catherine 22 24 exceptional, from best plots at mid-slope), PINOT GR Altenbourg 10' 13' 17' 18' 19' 21'. Talented Théo Faller makes superlative wines, all styles (even superb orange). Slowly changing/adding many wine names to French (Caracolles, Les Treilles du Loup).

Zind Humbrecht, Dom Al ★★★★ Arguably best bio AL winery; stellar RIES, GEWURZ, PINOT GR from GCS Brand, HENGST, GOLDERT, RANGEN, plus MUSCAT GC Goldert (Al's best along with Ernest BURN's). CLOS Windsbuhl (not GC) Ries, Pinot Gr great too: splendid 21 22, classic 19, sumptuous 18.

Zotzenberg Al Only GC for SYLVANER (should be many more). Different geological-era limestone marls give full, fresh, age-worthy wines. Best: Albert Seltz, BOECKEL, Hirtz, Rieffel.

Zusslin, Valentin Al ★★★ Much-admired 13th-generation bio estate; saline, chiselled. Marly-sandstone CLOS Libenberg MONOPOLE (4 ha, top of Pfingstberg hill; v.gd 17 18 23), Pfingstberg GC RIES (spectacular 18).

Châteaux of Bordeaux

Abbreviations used in the text:

Bar	Barsac
Bx	Bordeaux
Cas	Castillon-Côtes de Bx
E-2-M	Entre-Deux-Mers
Fron	Fronsac
H-Méd	Haut-Médoc
L de P	Lalande de Pomerol
List	Listrac
Marg	Margaux
Méd	Médoc
Mou	Moulis
Pau	Pauillac
Pe-Lé	Pessac-Léognan
Pom	Pomerol
Saut	Sauternes
St-Ém	St-Émilion
St-Est	St-Estèphe
St-Jul	St-Julien

Whither Bordeaux at this juncture in time? Grubbing-up has reduced the vineyard area to around 85,000 ha, down from 103,000 ha in 2023. And there's probably more to come. Small producers – particularly at generic level – are still suffering, but the surface area is now closer to market demand. At lower price points, the market indicates a desire for Crémant de Bordeaux, dry white and rosé, with red still struggling. Producers need to be innovative (single-variety cuvées, a modern approach to soften tannins, low/no-alcohol, etc.) or offer an established brand to succeed. In the mid-level, value-for-money range (Cru Bourgeois and equivalent) there's still a demand from established consumers who appreciate the distinctive Bordeaux taste at attractive

Châteaux of Bordeaux entries also cross-refer to France

prices. As to the Grands Crus, the prestige and quality are there, but sales in today's global market remain difficult. Châteaux are holding more stock and releasing older vintages later, which should be good news for consumers if the price is right. The same applies to en primeur, the 2025 vintage possibly a watershed year. Potentially a very fine vintage; the châteaux just have to get it right. Otherwise it's the end of the futures market as we know it.

Heat and drought were the climatic markers of 2025, along with precocity. It was one of the three hottest in the past 30 years (with 03 22), and there was practically no rain from May until 29 August, when 30–70 mm (1–3 in) fell. Yet the wines have a balanced, Bordeaux feel with ample fruit and fresh aromas. Alcohol appears lower than in 22 20 19 18. Yields were tiny (like the berries), good for concentration but not volume. Luckily there are plenty of vintages for drinking now: the luscious 09s are tempting at whatever level; the 08s have come into their own; the 10s are opening, as are the "classic" 14s. For early drinking, try the often-charming 12s or underrated 11s, which have improved with bottle-age.

Of recent years, the softer 17s will be the first to broach. Mature vintages to look for are 96 (best Médoc), 98 (particularly Right Bank, Graves), 00 01 (Right Bank, but don't dismiss Médoc), 02 04 06. The splendid 05s are also opening, although patience is still a virtue here. Dry white Bordeaux remains consistent in quality and value: the 25s are powerful but balanced. Fine white can age as well as white burgundy, providing there's acidity and freshness. And Sauternes continues to offer an array of remarkable years: 25 looks to have excellent potential. Even moderate years like 08 14 16 offer approachability and a fresher touch, while great years, 09 11 15 17, have concentration and a hedonistic charm that make them indestructible..

A, Dom de l' Cas ★★ 18 19 20 22 23 24 CAS property owned by STÉPHANE DERENONCOURT and wife Christine. Consistent quality.

Agassac, D' H-Méd ★★ 18 19 20' 22 23 In S H-MÉD. Modern, accessible. Gérard Jicquel owner (2021).

Aiguilhe, D' Cas ★★ 18 19 20 22 23 Large von Neipperg-owned estate. MERLOT-led (90%) ***power, finesse***. Some ageing potential. Also a BX white (100% SAUV BL).

Andron-Blanquet St-Est ★★ 18 19 20 Last vintage 21. Integrated into COS LABORY.

Angélus St-Ém ★★★★ 12 14 15' 16' 17 18' 19' 20 21 22' 23 24 25 Declined classification in 2022. Dark, rich, sumptuous (40%+ CAB FR). More finesse from 19. Second label: Carillon d'Angélus. Also No. 3 d'Angélus and BX red Tempo d'Angélus; all made in state-of-the-art winery.

Angludet Marg ★★ 16' 18' 19 20 22 23 25 Owned by NÉGOCIANT SICHEL; Benjamin S winemaker. Lots of PETIT VERDOT in blend. Fragrant, stylish. Value.

Archambeau Graves ★★ (r) 20 22 (w) 23 24 Family-owned property at Illats; 20 ha in a single block; organic methods. ***Fruity dry white***; fragrant reds; all gd value.

Arche, D' Saut ★★ 16 17 18 20 21 22 23 24 Much-improved Second Growth. Visitor-friendly.

Armailhac, D' Pau ★★★ 15' 16' 17 18 19 20 22' 23 25 (MOUTON) ROTHSCHILD-owned Fifth Growth. New chai in 2022. Fair value.

Aurelius St-Ém ★★ 19 20 21 Top CUVÉE from go-ahead ST-ÉM CO-OP; MERLOT/CAB FR (80/20%), new oak. Ready when released.

Ausone St-Ém ★★★★ 08 09' 10' 12 14 15' 16' 17 18' 19' 20' 21 22 23 24 25 Tiny, illustrious CH owned by Vauthier family. Declined classification in 2022, so now just basic ST-ÉM. Only 1500 cases; vyds s- and se-facing, sheltered; lots of

BORDEAUX

CAB FR (65% in 24). Long-lived wines with volume, texture, finesse. At a price. Second label: Chapelle d'Ausone (new label from 22). FONBEL, ***La Clotte***, MOULIN ST-GEORGES same stable.

Balestard la Tonnelle St-Ém ★★ 16 18 19 20 22' 23 25 Capdemourlin-owned property on limestone plateau. More CABS FR/SAUV these days (44% in 24).

Barde-Haut St-Ém ★★→★★★ 16 18 19' 20 22 23 24 MERLOT-led GRAND CRU CLASSÉ; s-facing vyd in one block. Clay-limestone terroir. Modern touch.

Bastor-Lamontagne Saut ★★ 17 19 21 22 23 24 25 Much-improved Preignac estate; SÉM/SAUV BL; organic. New ownership (2018). Elegant, pure; gd form since 21.

Batailley Pau ★★★ 11 12 15 16 17 18 19' 20 21 22 23 24 Relatively gd value, CAB SAUV-led (81% in 24) Fifth Growth.

Beaumont H-Méd ★★ 19 20 22 23 Large CRU BOURGEOIS Supérieur. Approachable early. Usually gd value. Eric Boissenot consults.

Beauregard Pom ★★★ 15 16 18 19' 20' 22 23 Much improved; organic; modern winery. MERLOT-led/CABS FR/SAUV. New manager Lauren Laudrin (2025).

Beauséjour St-Ém ★★★ 15 16 17 18' 19' 20' 22 23 24 25 Tiny PREMIER GRAND CRU CLASSÉ (B). Owned by Joséphine Duffau-Lagarrosse and Courtin family (Clarins cosmetics). New *cuvier* in 2024 and more finesse.

Beau-Séjour Bécot St-Ém ★★★ 14 15 16 17 18 19 20' 21 22 23 24 25 Distinguished PREMIER GRAND CRU CLASSÉ (B) on limestone plateau. Family-owned. More terroir-driven these days, but still gd ageing potential.

Beau-Site St-Est ★★ 18 19 20 22 23 BORIE-MANOUX-owned. Supple, fresh, accessible. Axel Marchal consults.

Bélair-Monange St-Ém ★★★ 12 14 15 16' 17 18 19 20 21 22 23 24 25 PREMIER GRAND CRU CLASSÉ (B) on limestone plateau and côtes. MOUEIX-owned. Mainly MERLOT (98% in 24). Huge investment in vyd and Herzog & de Meuron-designed winery. Refined style; more intensity, precision these days.

Belgrave H-Méd ★★ 15 16 18 19 20 21 22 23 DOURTHE-owned Fifth Growth (since 1979). Understated but consistent (60% CAB SAUV). Value.

Bellefont-Belcier St-Ém ★★ 16 17 18 19' 20 21 22 23 24 25 Much-improved GRAND CRU CLASSÉ on s côtes. Owned by VIGNOBLES K.

Belle-Vue H-Méd ★★ 17 18 19 20 In S H-MÉD. Dark, dense but firm. Australian-owned (TWE) since 2021.

Berliquet St-Ém ★★ 15' 16' 18 19' 20 21 22 23 24 25 Improving GRAND CRU CLASSÉ on plateau and côtes. Same stable as CANON. To watch.

St-Émilion classification – 2022 edition

The 2022 classification incl a total of 85 CHX: 14 PREMIERS GRANDS CRUS CLASSÉS and 71 GRANDS CRUS CLASSÉS. FIGEAC received promotion, joining PAVIE as the only Premiers Grands Cru Classés (A), ANGÉLUS, AUSONE and CHEVAL BLANC having officially withdrawn from the classification. There were no other changes at Premier Grand Cru Classé (B) level, barring the absence of LA GAFFELIÈRE, which had also withdrawn. New to status of Grand Cru Classé were Badette, Boutisse, CLOS Badon Thunevin, Clos Dubreuil, Clos St-Julien, La Confession, Corbin Michotte (declassified in 2012), Croix de Labrie, La Croizille, Lassègue, MANGOT, Montlabert, Montlisse, ROL VALENTIN, Tour Baladoz and TOUR SAINT CHRISTOPHE. Among the absentees from the 2012 classification, Grand Pontet, L'Arrosée and Tertre Daugay are now all part of newly created QUINTUS. Others withdrew (LA CLOTTE, QUINAULT L'ENCLOS), and some were absorbed by a sister property (Les Grandes Murailles by CLOS FOURTET). Classification is reviewed every 10 yrs, so next, theoretically, in 2032.

Bernadotte H-Méd ★★ 18' 19 20 23 Hong Kong-based ownership. CAB SAUV/MERLOT/PETIT VERDOT. Savoury; gd value.

Beychevelle St-Jul ★★★ 14 15' 16' 17 18 19' 20 21 22 23 24 25 Sizeable Fourth Growth owned by Castel and Suntory. Wines of consistent ***elegance*** rather than power. Visitor-friendly (13 rooms and La Table de Beychevelle).

Blavia is the new name for Blaye AOP. Inspiring?

Biston-Brillette Mou ★★ 18 19 20 22 CRU BOURGEOIS Supérieur (2024) owned by CH de Malleret (H-MÉD). Attractive, early drinking and gd value. MERLOT/CAB SAUV (50/50%).

Bonalgue Pom ★★ 15 18 19 20 22 23 Much-improved MERLOT/CAB FR (90/10%) POM from sand, gravel, clay soils; gd value for AOP. Same stable as Les Hauts Conseillants (L DE P).

Bonnet Bx ★★ (r) 19 20 22 (w) DYA Forged by André Lurton; now run by son Jacques. Large producer of some of best E-2-M white and red (oak-aged Rés) BX. Also COUHINS-LURTON, LA LOUVIÈRE.

Bon Pasteur, Le Pom ★★★ 15' 16 18 19 20 21 22 23 24 Tiny cru on ST-ÉM border. MERLOT/CAB FR (80/20%). Ripe, opulent, seductive, but ages well; c.20,000 bottles/yr.

Boscq, Le St-Est ★★ 16' 18' 19' 20 22 23 24 DOURTHE-owned, consistently great value. MERLOT-led (52% in 24).

Bourgneuf Pom ★★ 15' 16' 17 18 19' 20 21 22 23 24 25 Vayron family-owned (1840). Subtle, savoury wine; gd value for POM.

Bouscaut Pe-Lé ★★★ (r) 16' 18 19 20 21 22 (w) 21 22 23 24 Classed Growth. Structured, MERLOT-led reds. Sappy, age-worthy SAUV BL/SÉM ***whites***. Organic, certified 2024.

Boyd-Cantenac Marg ★★★ 15 16 18 19 20 22 25 Tiny (17 ha) Cantenac-based Third Growth. Guillemet family-owned (1932). CAB SAUV-based. Needs time. Second label: La Croix de Boyd-Cantenac.

Branaire-Ducru St-Jul ★★★ 15 16' 17 18' 19 20 21 22 23 24 25 Consistent Fourth Growth; regularly gd value; ageing potential. Modern, gravity-fed *cuvier* (2022).

Branas Grand Poujeaux Mou ★★ 16' 18 19 20' 22 23 Neighbour of CHASSE-SPLEEN, POUJEAUX. Now 25-ha vyd. Rich, modern style. Hubert de Boüard consults.

Brane-Cantenac Marg ★★★→★★★★ 14 15' 16' 17 18 19' 20 22 23 24 Second Growth owned by Lurton family since 1925; CAB SAUV-led (70%+)/CARMENÈRE (1%). Classic, fragrant MARG to age. New parcel selection Mosaïque from 21.

Brillette Mou ★★ 18 19 20 Reputable DOM on gravelly soils. Acquired and integrated into CHASSE-SPLEEN in 2023.

Cabanne, La Pom ★★ 16' 18 19 20 22 23 24 MERLOT-dominant (94%) DOM on w slope. Generally earlier-drinking.

Caillou Saut ★★ 15' 18 19 22 23 24 Family-owned Second Growth BAR for pure *liquoreux;* 100% SÉM. Second label: Les Erables.

Calon Ségur St-Est ★★★★ 12 14 15' 16' 17 18' 19' 20 21 22 23 24 25 Third Growth on top form; more CAB SAUV these days (82% in 24). Powerful but fine, complex. Second label: Le Marquis de Calon.

Cambon la Pelouse H-Méd ★★ 18 19 20 21 Big, reliable. Australian-owned (TWE).

Camensac, De H-Méd ★★ 15 16 18' 19 20 22 Sizeable Fifth Growth in N H-MÉD. Owned by Merlaut family (CHASSE-SPLEEN, GRUAUD-LAROSE). Steady improvement. Second label: La Closerie de Camensac.

Canon St-Ém ★★★★ 12 14 15' 16' 17 18' 19' 20 21 22' 23 24 25 Esteemed PREMIER GRAND CRU CLASSÉ (B), vyd on limestone plateau. Wertheimer-owned (BERLIQUET, RAUZAN-SÉGLA), so investment. MERLOT/CAB FR (70/30%). Elegant, complex, long ageing. Five-vintage limited-edition case (2025). Second label: Croix Canon.

BORDEAUX

Canon-la-Gaffelière St-Ém ★★★ 14 15 16 17 18 19' 20 22 23 25 PREMIER GRAND CRU CLASSÉ (B) on s foot slope. MERLOT/CAB FR/CAB SAUV blend. Stylish, impressive. Organic. Von Neipperg family-owned (1971).

Cantemerle H-Méd ★★★ 14 15 16 18 19' 20 22 23 25 Large Fifth Growth in S H-MÉD. Replanted over past 40 yrs. New gravity-fed *cuvier* with 114 tanks in 2025 (was 40). On gd form; gd value.

2024 tough for organics: Alcée, Dom de Chevalier, Le Crock stopped conversion.

Cantenac-Brown Marg ★★★ 15 16' 18 19' 20 21 22 23 24 25 Third Growth being revamped. New gravity-fed winery from 2023 with 70 tanks. More voluptuous, refined these days. CAB SAUV-led (70% in 24). José Sanfins long-term manager. Second label: BriO de Cantenac-Brown.

Capbern St-Est ★★ 15' 16' 17 18 19 20 21 22 23 24 25 Same ownership/team as CALON SÉGUR; CAB SAUV-led (70% in 24); gd form and value.

Cap de Mourlin St-Ém ★★ 15 16 18 19 20 22 GRAND CRU CLASSÉ on n slopes. Estate's origins date from 1647. MERLOT-led/CAB FR/CAB SAUV. Firm, tannic. Also BALESTARD LA TONNELLE.

Carbonnieux Pe-Lé ★★★ 16' 18 19' 20 21 22 23 24 Classed Growth GRAV, owned by Perrin family (1956). Sterling red/white; large volumes of both. Fresh ***whites***, 65% SAUV BL, eg. 22 23 24. Red can age. Old-vine white (100% SÉM) CUVÉE 1741 in 20. Second label: La Croix de Carbonnieux.

Carles, De Fron ★★ 18 19 20 22 23 Haut-Carles is prestige CUVÉE; MERLOT/CAB FR/MALBEC (90/5/5%) blend.

Carmes Haut-Brion, Les Pe-Lé ★★★ 15 16' 17 18' 19' 20' 21 22' 23 24 25 Tiny property in heart of Bordeaux city; CABS FR (48% in 24)/SAUV-led, structured but suave. Part whole-bunch vinification. Second label: Le C des Carmes Haut-Brion.

Caronne Ste Gemme H-Méd ★★ 18 19 20 Now integrated into LA TOUR CARNET; CAB SAUV-led; fresh, structured; 21 last vintage.

Carruades de Lafite Pau ★★★ Second label of CH LAFITE. Second Growth prices. Accessible but can age. Organic, certified 2024.

Carteau Côtes-Daugay St-Ém ★★ 18 19 20 22 Small s-facing GRAND CRU ST-ÉM. MERLOT-led (70%), supple, gd value.

Certan de May Pom ★★★ 15' 16' 17 18 19' 20 21 22 23 24 Prime site on POM plateau. Much improved. Elegant, age-worthy.

Chantegrive, De Graves ★★→★★★ 18 19 20' 21 22 23 Large estate at Podensac; quality and value. MERLOT/CAB SAUV/PETIT VERDOT red. CUVÉE Caroline is top, ***fragrant white*** 22 23 24.

Chasse-Spleen Mou ★★★ 16' 17 18 19' 20 21 22 23 24 25 Well-known CH owned by Céline Villars. Often impressive, long-maturing; classical structure, fragrance. Visitor-friendly, contemporary art exhibition.

Chauvin St-Ém ★★ 18' 19' 20' 21 22' 23 24 25 Consistent GRAND CRU CLASSÉ owned by Sylvie Cazes. Fruit, freshness, balance.

Cheval Blanc St-Ém ★★★★ 12 13 14 15' 16' 17 18' 19' 20' 21 22 23 24 25 Declined classification in 2022. Superstar, easier to love than buy. Agro-ecological approach in vyd. MERLOT/CAB FR/CAB SAUV. Firm, fragrant, verging on POM. Delicious young; lasts a generation. Second label (r/w): Le Petit Cheval.

Chevalier, Dom de Pe-Lé ★★★★ 10' 12 14 15' 16' 17 18' 19' 20 21 22 23 24 25 Reliable Classed Growth owned by Bernard family. Elegant, finely textured red. Impressive, complex, long-ageing white 20 21 22 23 24 25. Organic conversion temporarily suspended. Second label (r/w): L'Esprit de Chevalier.

Cissac H-Méd ★★ 16' 18 19 20 22 23 Large CRU BOURGEOIS Supérieur in N H-MÉD, owned by Vialard family. CAB SAUV/MERLOT/PETIT VERDOT/MALBEC. Structured but more fruit than in past.

Citran H-Méd ★★ 16 18 19 20 22 24 Sizeable S H-MÉD estate owned by Merlaut family (1996). Approachable early.

Clarence de Haut-Brion, Le Pe-Lé ★★★ 12 14 15 16' 17 18 19' 20 21 22 23 25 Second label of CH HAUT-BRION (was Bahans Haut-Brion). Usually MERLOT-led (45.7% in 24), stylistically similar to *grand vin*. More approachable but can age.

Clarke List ★★→★★★ 15 16' 18 19 20 21 22 23 MERLOT-led (70%) cru; now greater length, precision. New *cuvier* 2022. Also gd Le Merle Blanc du CH Clarke (dr w).

Clerc Milon Pau ★★★ 12 14 15 16' 17 18' 19' 20 21 22 23 24 Fifth Growth owned by (MOUTON) ROTHSCHILD; CAB SAUV-based (66% in 24). Powerful but harmonious; consistent quality at a price.

Climens Bar ★★★★ 09' 10' 11' 12' 13' 14 15 16' 19 22 23 Classed Growth; Frédéric Nivelle long-time winemaker. Concentrated, vibrant acidity; ageing potential guaranteed; bio. No 17 18 20 21 (frost). Second label: Les Cyprès. Also dry whites (100% SÉM) Lilium, Asphodèle, Petite Lily.

Clinet Pom ★★★ 14 15' 16' 17 18 19 20 21 22 23 24 25 Property run by Ronan Laborde since 2004. MERLOT-led (80%)/CAB SAUV. Sumptuous, modern, to age. Second label: Fleur de Clinet.

Clos de l'Oratoire St-Ém ★★ 15 16' 18 19 20 22 23 Supple GRAND CRU CLASSÉ; 80% MERLOT. Von Neipperg-owned. Organic.

Clos des Jacobins St-Ém ★★→★★★ 14 15' 16' 17 18 19 20 22 23 Côtes GRAND CRU CLASSÉ owned by Decoster family. MERLOT-led (80%)/CAB FR/CAB SAUV; powerful, modern style. Also CH la Commanderie.

Clos du Marquis St-Jul ★★→★★★ 14 15' 16' 17 18' 19' 20 21 22 23 24 25 Owned by Domaines Delon (LÉOVILLE LAS CASES, NÉNIN); gd ST-JUL character; more length these days. New *cuverie* in 2023.

Clos Floridène Graves ★★ (r) 18' 19 20 22 23 (w) 22 23 24 Dubourdieu family-owned/run. SAUV BL/SÉM from limestone, ***fine modern white***; vibrant, CAB SAUV-led red. Also DOISY-DAËNE, Haura, REYNON.

Clos Fourtet St-Ém ★★★ 14 15' 16' 18 19 20 21 22 23 PREMIER GRAND CRU CLASSÉ (B) on limestone plateau owned by Cuvelier family. MERLOT-led (80%+)/CAB FR/CAB SAUV. Classic, stylish ST-ÉM. Consistently gd form. Second label: La Closerie de Fourtet.

Clos Haut-Peyraguey Saut ★★★ 15 16 17 18 19 20 21 22 23 24 First Growth in Bommes. Owned by magnate Bernard Magrez (2012). Harmonious wines; majority SÉM (80%) with SAUV BL. Second label: Symphonie.

Clos l'Église Pom ★★★ 14 15' 16 18 19 20 22 23 Tiny (5.9 ha) plateau estate run by Hélène Garcin and Patrice Levêque. MERLOT/CAB FR (80/20%) on clay-gravel. Seductive, will age.

To water or not to water?

Irrigation for BX AOPS is banned (as it is for AOPs throughout France), except in the case of young plants and when special permission is given. But climate change with increased heat and drought is putting greater stress on the vine. Such are the difficulties that in 2025 CH LAFLEUR, one of Bx's most expensive wines, announced it was leaving the comfort of the POM appellation for the more liberal VDF category. Lafleur has the renown to go its own way, but what direction for the more modest? The debate has raged since: defined character and terroir under strict appellation rules or more freedom to combat today's challenging conditions? And even if there was greater leniency, water sources are scarcer these days, and individual finance has to be guaranteed. There's no clear-cut solution.

Clos Puy Arnaud Cas ★★ 16' 18 19' 20' 22 23 24 Leading CAS estate run with passion by Thierry Valette. Vibrant wines with plenty of energy; bio; MERLOT-led/CABS FR/SAUV.

Clos René Pom ★★ 15' 16 18' 19 20 22 Owned by Garde family. MERLOT-led with spicy MALBEC (10%); sandy-gravel soils. Classical rather than modern; can age.

Clotte, La St-Ém ★★→★★★ 16' 17 18 19' 20 21 22' 23 24 25 Top-flight ST-ÉM. Owned by Vauthier family (AUSONE). Recent renovation.

Conseillante, La Pom ★★★★ 12 14 15' 16' 17 18 19' 20 22 23 Nicolas family-owned for over 150 yrs. Some of noblest, most fragrant POM. Organic practices. Marielle Cazaux winemaker.

Corbin St-Ém ★★ 16' 18 19 20 22 23 GRAND CRU CLASSÉ owned by Anabelle Crus; gd value. Relatively accessible. Visitor-friendly.

Cos d'Estournel St-Est ★★★★ 11 12 13 14 15' 16' 17 18 19' 20' 21 22 23 24 25 Big Second Growth owned by magnate Michel Reybier. Refined, suave, long-ageing. Pricey SAUV BL-dominated white. Second label (r/w): Les Pagodes de Cos (engraved bottle for 30th anniversay, 2024).

Cos Labory St-Est ★★→★★★ 14 15 16' 18 19 20 21 22 23 24 25 Small Fifth Growth; acquired by Michel Reybier (COS D'ESTOURNEL) 2023. Savoury, usually gd value.

Coufran H-Méd ★★ 16' 18 19 20 22 24 Atypical: 85% MERLOT (since 20s). Supple wine but can age. Older vintages at the CH.

Couhins-Lurton Pe-Lé ★★→★★★ (r) 16 18 19 20 22 23 (w) 21 22 23 24 *Fine white*, tense, long-lived pure SAUV BL. MERLOT-led red. Jacques Lurton-run since 2018.

Couspaude, La St-Ém ★★★ 15 16 18 19 20 22 23 GRAND CRU CLASSÉ on limestone plateau. MERLOT-led/CAB FR/CAB SAUV.

Coutet Saut ★★★ 14' 15 16 17' 18 19' 20 21 22 23 24 25 First Growth; majority SÉM. Baly family-owned. Consistently v. fine. CUVÉE Madame: v. rich, old-vine selection 97 01 03 09. Dry white Opalie (SAUV BL/Sém) v.gd.

Couvent des Jacobins St-Ém ★★ 14 15 16' 18 19' 20 22 23 GRAND CRU CLASSÉ in town of St-Émilion; trad ST-ÉM; organic.

Crabitey Graves ★★ (r) 18 19 20 22 23 (w) 20 22 23 Arnaud de Butler owner. Harmonious CAB SAUV-led reds; small volume of lively SAUV BL-dominant white.

Crock, Le St-Est ★★ 15 16' 18 19' 20 22 23 CRU BOURGEOIS Exceptionnel. Firm but polished. Organic conversion suspended. Also LÉOVILLE POYFERRÉ.

Croix, La Pom ★★ 15 16 18 19 20 22 Owned by NÉGOCIANT Joseph Janoueix (1974). MERLOT-led (90%)/CAB FR.

Croix de Gay, La Pom ★★★ 15 16 18 19 20 22 23 Tiny MERLOT-dominant (95% in 23) vyd on gravelly soils. Rich, round.

Croix du Casse, La Pom ★★ 15' 18 19 20 23 Supple, early drinking. MERLOT/CAB FR (70/30%) on sandy/gravel soils. Castéja-owned (BORIE-MANOUX).

Cru Bourgeois – 2025 edition

The 2025 edition of the three-tier classification incl a total of 170 CHX: 120 CB, 36 CB Supérieur, 14 CB Exceptionnel. All candidates had to have environmental certification – HVE level 2 for CB and 3 for higher (Haute Valeur Environnementale). The five vintages tasted were 17–21, and all candidates had to present wines for the blind tasting, whatever level desired. Also, all those wishing to use the CB certificate needed to present their wines in bottles that weigh no more than 390g (a reduction of 22% on the previous max weight). Classified CB Exceptionnel: Chx Castera, d'Arsac, de Malleret, du Taillan, la Cardonne, Laffitte Carcasset, Laujac, LE CROCK, MALESCASSE, Mongravey, Paloumey, Paveil de Luze, Reverdi, REYSSON. Classification organized every 5 yrs.

Croizet-Bages Pau ★★ 15 16' 18 19 20 22 23 24 Striving, CAB SAUV-led (70% in 24) Fifth Growth; 27 ha on Bages plateau. Steady improvement in recent yrs.

Cru Bourgeois Méd Three-tier classification in 2025 (CB, CB Supérieur, CB Exceptionnel). 170 CHX all told. *See* box, opposite.

Cruzelles, Les L de P ★★ 15' 16' 17 18 19' 20 21 22 23 24 25 Consistent, expressive, gd-value. MERLOT-led (85% in 24). Same stable as L'ÉGLISE-CLINET.

Production of Crémant de Bordeaux now at 15 million bottles/year. Worth trying.

Dalem Fron ★★ 16 17 18' 19 20 21 22 23 MERLOT-dominated (95% in 23) property. Smooth, ripe, fresh. Eric Boissenot has consulted since 2019.

Dassault St-Ém ★★ 15 16 18' 19 20 22 23 24 Rich, modern GRAND CRU CLASSÉ on sandy soils. MERLOT-led (66%). Dassault-owned (1955); CH Faurie de Souchard integrated in 2022. Second label: D de Dassault.

Dauphine, De La Fron ★★→★★★ 15 16 18' 19 20 22 23 24 A reference in FRON. Expansion, renovation over past 25 yrs. Organic. Second label: Delphis. Also BX white, rosé.

Dauzac Marg ★★→★★★ 15 16' 17 18' 19 20 21 22 Busy Fifth Growth at Labarde. Dense, rich, dark. Also Aurore, Labastide and ungrafted Franc de Pied (100% CAB SAUV).

Desmirail Marg ★★→★★★ 14 15 16' 18 19 20 22 23 Discreet Third Growth; fine, delicate. Also La Perle white (BLANC DE NOIRS) from 2023.

Destieux St-Ém ★★ 15 16 18 19 20 22 23 24 GRAND CRU CLASSÉ. MERLOT-based; firm, powerful, modern. Limestone-clay soils.

Doisy-Daëne Bar ★★★ 14 15' 17' 18' 19 20 22 23 24 25 ***Fine, sweet*** but tangy BARS. Pure SÉM. L'Extravagant 17' 18' 19' 22 23 intensely rich, expensive, 100% SAUV BL CUVÉE. Also Doisy-Dubroca (SAUT).

Doisy-Védrines Bar ★★★ 14 15' 16' 17 18' 19 20 22 23 24 25 ***Long-term fave***; delicious, gd value; SÉM/SAUV BL/MUSCADELLE.

Dôme, Le St-Ém ★★★ 17 18 19 20 22 Micro-wine; rich, modern, powerful. Majority old-vine CAB FR (80%). Circular, Norman Foster-designed cellar. Visitor-friendly.

Dominique, La St-Ém ★★★ 15 16' 17 18' 19 20 21 22 23 24 GRAND CRU CLASSÉ. MERLOT-led (85% in 24); complex and refined. Visitor-friendly (restaurant). Also Nuances (rosé).

Ducru-Beaucaillou St-Jul ★★★★ 12 14 15' 16 17 18' 19' 20' 21 22 23 Outstanding Second Growth. Bruno Borie owns. Majors in CAB SAUV (82% in 22). Excellent form; classic cedar-scented claret for long ageing.

Duhart-Milon Rothschild Pau ★★★ 14 15 16' 17 18' 19' 20 21 22 23 25 Fourth Growth owned by LAFITE ROTHSCHILD; CAB SAUV-dominated (78% in 24); v. fine quality. Organic, certified 2024.

Durfort-Vivens Marg ★★★ 14 15' 16' 17 18' 19' 20' 21 22 23 24 25 High-flying Second Growth; recent yrs tiptop; CAB SAUV-led (94.5% in 24). Organic, bio. Three CUVÉES *parcellaires* (Les Plantes, Le Plateau, Le Hameau).

Eglise, Dom de l' Pom ★★ 14 15 16 18 19 20 22 Owned by BORIE-MANOUX. MERLOT-led/CAB FR. Clay/gravel soils of plateau. Consistent, fleshy of late. Also CROIX DU CASSE, TROTTEVIEILLE.

Église-Clinet, L' Pom ★★★★ 11' 12 14 15' 16' 17 18 19' 20' 21 22 23 24 25 Tiny, top-flight. Great consistency; full, concentrated, fleshy but expensive. MERLOT-led (90%). Needs time; long ageing.

Evangile, L' Pom ★★★★ 14 15' 16' 17 18' 19' 20' 21 22 23 24 25 ROTHSCHILD (LAFITE)-owned (1990). MERLOT-led, but more CABS FR/SAUV these days; more finesse. Organic. Second label: Blason de L'Evangile.

Fargues, De Saut ★★★ 11' 13 14 15' 16' 17' 18 19 20 21 22 23 25 Philippe de Lur Saluces at helm. Unclassified but top quality; rich, refined, age-worthy. No 12 24.

Faugères St-Ém ★★→★★★ 15 16' 18 19' 20 22 23 24 Sizeable GRAND CRU CLASSÉ owned by Silvio Denz since 2005. Rich, bold, modern wines. Sisters Péby Faugères, Cap de Faugères (CAS).

Ferrand, De St-Ém ★★→★★★ 14 15 16 18 19 20 22 23 24 25 Big GRAND CRU CLASSÉ. Organic. More CAB FR (25% in 24) these days; more finesse.

Liber Pater 2015 (VdF), indigenous Bx varieties, £36,000/bottle. Not that free.

Ferrande Graves ★★ 18 19 20 22 Sizeable (100 ha) property owned by Castel. Easy-going MERLOT/CAB SAUV; creamy SÉM/SAUVS BL/Gr.

Ferrière Marg ★★★ 14 15 16' 18 19 20 22 23 24 25 Small CAB SAUV-led Third Growth. Organic, bio. Dark, firm, perfumed.

Feytit-Clinet Pom ★★→★★★ 14 15 16' 18 19' 20 22 23 Owner Jeremy Chasseuil's 25th vintage in 24. MERLOT/CAB FR. Top form; rich, seductive. Relatively gd value.

Fieuzal Pe-Lé ★★★ (r) 16' 18' 19' 20 21 22 23 (w) 21 22 23 Classified estate. Full-bodied SAUV BL/SÉM. Rich, firm MERLOT/CAB SAUV/PETIT VERDOT.

Figeac St-Ém ★★★★ 08 09' 10' 12 14 15 16' 17 18' 19' 20' 21 22 23 24 25 PREMIER GRAND CRU CLASSÉ (A) on a roll. Owned by Manoncourt family. Gravelly vyd with unusual 70% CABS FR/SAUV. Now richer, but always elegant; needs long ageing. "1er Cru Classé A" on label from 2022.

Filhot Saut ★★ 13 14 15 18 20 22 23 Second Growth run by Gabriel de Vaucelles; SÉM/SAUV BL/MUSCADELLE. Richer, purer in recent yrs.

Fleur Cardinale St-Ém ★★ 15 16' 18 19' 20' 21 22 23 24 GRAND CRU CLASSÉ, Decoster family-owned. Ripe, unctuous and modern. MERLOT/CABS FR/SAUV. Also Croix Cardinale.

Fleur de Boüard, La L de P ★★→★★★ 16' 18 19 20 22 23 Dark, dense, modern. Special CUVÉE Le Plus: 100% MERLOT barrel-aged 33 mths, more extreme. State-of-the-art winery. Visitor-friendly.

Fleur-Pétrus, La Pom ★★★★ 14 15 16 17' 18 19' 20' 21 22 23 24 25 J-P MOUEIX property on plateau. Sizeable (18.7 ha) for POM. MERLOT-led with unusual PETIT VERDOT (0.5% in 24). Refined, long-ageing.

Fombrauge St-Ém ★★→★★★ 15 16' 18 19 20 22 23 24 Substantial GRAND CRU CLASSÉ. Origins in C16. Bernard Magrez-owned since 1999. Rich, dark, creamy, opulent. Magrez Fombrauge is special CUVÉE.

Fonbadet Pau ★★ 15 16' 18 19' 20' 22 23 24 Small non-classified estate; gd value, less long-lived but reliable. Second label: Harmonie.

Fonbel, De St-Ém ★★ 16 18 19 20 22 23 24 25 Consistent, juicy, fresh, gd-value ST-ÉM. MERLOT-led/CAB SAUV/CARMENÈRE.

Fonplégade St-Ém ★★ 15 16' 18' 19 20' 22 23 24 GRAND CRU CLASSÉ, Adams family-owned; bio. Fruit, balance these days.

Fonréaud List ★★ 15 16' 17 18 19 20 22 23 Consistent, satisfying, savoury; CAB SAUV-led (55% in 23). Next-generation Chanfreau (Guillaume, Loïc) at helm.

Fonroque St-Ém ★★★ 16 18 19 20' 21 22 23 24 25 Côtes GRAND CRU CLASSÉ; bio; MERLOT-led/CAB FR. Medium-bodied, mineral, fresh.

Fontenil Fron ★★ 16 18' 19 20 22 23 24 Owned by Dany and MICHEL ROLLAND. Ripe, chocolatey, opulent.

Forts de Latour, Les Pau ★★★★ 12 14 15 16' 17 18 19' 20 22 Second label of CH LATOUR; authentic PAU flavour in slightly lighter format. Second Growth price. Primeur sales finished; only released when deemed ready to drink (19 in 2025), but another 10 yrs often pays.

Fourcas Dupré List ★★ 15' 16' 18 19 20 22 24 25 New owner, investment from 2019. Fairly consistent; medium-bodied, dry, fresh.

Fourcas-Hosten List ★★→★★★ 16 17 18 19 20 22 23 Large estate owned by Hermès connections. Organic. Finesse, precision these days. Also dry white BX.

France, De Pe-Lé ★★ (r) 16' 18 19 20 22 23 24 (w) 21 22 24 CAB SAUV/MERLOT (50/50%); ripe and modern reds. Fresh and balanced SAUV BL/SÉM (80/20%); gd value.

Franc Mayne St-Ém ★★ 16 17 19' 20 22 23 24 25 Improving GRAND CRU CLASSÉ on côtes. 100% MERLOT. Fresh, structured. Visitor-friendly.

Gaby Fron ★★ 16 18 19' 20 22 Well-sited CANON-FRON estate; C18 CH. MERLOT-dominated; organic.

Gaffelière, La St-Ém ★★★ 15 16' 17 18 19' 20 21 22 23 24 25 Top ST-ÉM; declined classification in 2022. Investment, improvement; part of vyd replanted. MERLOT with lots of CAB FR (40%); on fine, elegant form.

Garde, La Pe-Lé ★★ (r) 18 19 20 21 22 23 24 (w) 22 23 24 Unclassified, owned by DOURTHE; supple. More CAB SAUV, finesse from 23. Tiny production SAUV BL/SÉM (97/3% in 24). Axel Marchal consults.

Gay, Le Pom ★★★ 14 16 17 18' 19' 20 21 22 23 24 25 Plateau POM; gravel/clay soils. MERLOT/CAB FR (81/19% in 24). Rich, suave, ageing potential. Also La Violette.

Gazin Pom ★★★ 15' 16' 18' 19' 20 22 23 Large DOM on plateau. 5th-generation de Baillencourt at helm. On gd form; generous (90% MERLOT), long-ageing.

Gilette Saut ★★★ 86 88 89 90 96 97 99 01 Extraordinary small Preignac CH. Stores its sumptuous wines untouched in concrete vats for 18–20 yrs; c.400–500 cases/yr. Vintages back to 53.

Giscours Marg ★★★ 14 15 16' 17 18' 19' 20' 21 22 23 24 25 Substantial Third Growth; veteran-manager Alexander van Beek. Full-bodied, long-ageing MARG; CAB SAUV-led (60%), recent vintages on song. Second label: La Sirène de Giscours.

Glana, Du St-Jul ★★ 16' 18 19' 20 22 24 Unclassified; CAB SAUV/MERLOT (69/31% in 24). Undemanding, robust, value. Owned by Jean-Paul Meffre and his sons. Second label: Pavillon du Glana.

Gloria St-Jul ★★→★★★ 14 15 16' 17 18 19' 20 21 22 23 24 25 Domaines Henri Martin property; CAB SAUV/MERLOT/CAB FR/PETIT VERDOT (56/32/7/5% in 24). Unclassified but sells at Fourth Growth prices. On superb form.

Grand Corbin-Despagne St-Ém ★★→★★★ 15 16' 18' 19' 20' 21 22 23 24 25 GRAND CRU CLASSÉ discerningly run by François Despagne (7th generation), gd value. Aromatic now, with riper, fuller edge. Organic. Le Chemin (POM) sister estate. Second label: Petit Corbin-Despagne.

Grand Cru Classé St-Ém 2022: 71 classified; reviewed every 10 yrs (next in 2032).

Grand Mayne St-Ém ★★★ 15 16' 17 18 19' 20 22 23 24 Consistent GRAND CRU CLASSÉ on côtes and pied de côtes. MERLOT/CAB FR (70/30% in 24), full-bodied, structured. Second label: Filia.

Grand-Puy Ducasse Pau ★★★ 15' 16' 18 19' 20 22 23 24 25 Fifth Growth, steady rise in quality; CAB SAUV/MERLOT/PETIT VERDOT (59/36/5%). New state-of-the-art winery with suspended vats. Visitor-friendly. Second label: Prélude.

Grand-Puy-Lacoste Pau ★★★ 12 14 15' 16' 17' 18' 19' 20 21 22 23 24 25 Fifth Growth famous for CAB SAUV-driven PAU to lay down; vyd in one block around CH. New gravity-fed *cuvier* in 2025.

Grave à Pomerol, La Pom ★★★ 14 15 16' 17 18 19' 20 21 22 23 Small J-P MOUEIX

Tall Ships

In 2027, Bordeaux hosts the start of the Tall Ships Race, one of the most prestigious races in the world for large historic sailing ships. The annual Bordeaux Fête le Vin tasting extravaganza will coincide, and from July 7 to 11 you'll be able to wander along the quais and taste and eat at pavilions while gawping at a host of three- and four-masted ships on the water. You can visit the ships too. No stowing-away, mind.

property on gravel soils with fine clay; gd value for POM. 100% MERLOT. Refined wines; can age.

Greysac Méd ★★ 18 19 20 22 23 Fine, fresh, consistent. MERLOT/CAB SAUV/CAB FR/PETIT VERDOT. Sister Rollan de By.

Gruaud-Larose St-Jul ★★★★ 14 15' 16' 17 18' 19' 20' 22' 23 24 25 One of biggest, best-loved Second Growths. CAB SAUV-led (81% in 24). Vigorous claret to age. Organic. On song. Second label: ***Sarget de Gruaud-Larose***.

Magnum of Lafite 1870, $387,500 at Zachys, New York, Oct 2025. £30,000+/glass.

Guadet St-Ém ★★ 15 16' 18 19 20 22 Tiny GRAND CRU CLASSÉ on the limestone plateau; bio; fresh. Also CRÉMANT.

Guiraud Saut ★★★ 11' 13 14 16' 17 19 20 22 23 24 25 Classed Growth SAUT; organic. More SAUV BL than usual. Ex-YQUEM winemaker-manager. Two dry whites: G de Guiraud, Grand Vin Blanc Sec.

Gurgue, La Marg ★★ 15 16' 18 19 20 22 23 Organic, bio; CAB SAUV/MERLOT/PETIT VERDOT. Light but fine.

Hanteillan, D' H-Méd ★★ 18 19 20 22 23 Sizeable property at Cissac-Médoc. Reliable, early drinking. New owner 2023.

Haut-Bages-Libéral Pau ★★★ 14 15' 16 18 19' 20' 21 22 23 24 25 Much-improved Fifth Growth; CAB SAUV-led (94% in 24); organic, bio. Reasonable value. Owned by Claire Villars-Lurton.

Haut-Bailly Pe-Lé ★★★★ 12 14 15' 16' 17 18' 19' 20' 21 22 23 24 25 Top-quality Classed Growth. Refined, elegant, CAB SAUV-led (58% in 24). New visitor centre (2025). Second label: Haut-Bailly II (was La Parde de H-B).

Haut-Batailley Pau ★★★ 14 15 16' 17 18' 19' 20' 22 23 24 25 Fifth Growth owned by Cazes family (LYNCH-BAGES); vyd doubled to 41 ha since 2018. On top form. Second label: Verso.

Haut-Bergeron Saut ★★ 18 19 20 21 22 Family-owned, 9th generation. Consistent, unclassified. Mainly SÉM (90%). Rich, opulent and gd value. Second label: CH Fontebride.

Haut-Bergey Pe-Lé ★★→★★★ (r) 15 16' 19 20' 22 23 (w) 23 Paul Garcin owns. Organic, bio. More fruit, freshness these days. Also Cuvée Paul (r/w).

Haut-Brion Pe-Lé ★★★★ 08 09' 10' 11' 12 13 14 15' 16' 17' 18' 19' 20' 21 22 23 24 25 Only non-MÉD First Growth in list of 1855, owned by American Dillon family since 1935; 1st written reference 1521. Prince Robert de Luxembourg titular head. Deeply harmonious, wonderful texture; for many, top choice of all. A little ***sumptuous dry white*** (SAUV BL/SÉM) for tycoons: 20 21 22 23 24 25. Also La Clarté (w) from both H-B and LA MISSION HAUT-BRION. Second label: LE CLARENCE DE HAUT-BRION (previously Bahans H-B). Restaurant Le Clarence in Paris.

Haut Condissas Méd ★★★ 19' 20 22 23 Top wine from Jean Guyon stable (GREYSAC, Tour Seran). Exuberant, modern. MERLOT (60%)/PETIT VERDOT/CABS SAUV/FR.

Haut-Marbuzet St-Est ★★→★★★ 15 16 17 18 19' 20' 21 22 23 Situated between MONTROSE and COS D'ESTOURNEL; Duboscq family-owned. Easy to love, but unclassified; 60%+ sold directly by CH. Unctuous, matured in 100% new oak. MERLOT/CAB SAUV/PETIT VERDOT/CAB FR. Second label: Mac Carthy.

Haut-Sarpe St-Ém ★★ 15' 16' 18 19 20 22 GRAND CRU CLASSÉ owned by Joseph Janoueix; MERLOT (70%)/CAB FR; ripe, modern.

Hosanna Pom ★★★★ 15 16' 17 18 19' 20' 21 22 23 25 Tiny vyd in heart of plateau. Clay/gravel soils, iron-rich subsoil. MERLOT (70%), old-vine CAB FR (30%). No 24 (grey rot). Power, complexity, balance; needs time.

Issan, D' Marg ★★★ 12 14 15' 16' 17 18' 19' 20 21 22 23 24 Third Growth. Fragrant, CAB SAUV-led (65%) wines that age. Unusual dry white VDF (VIOGNIER/ROUSSANNE/MARSANNE/Rolle). Second label: Blason.

Jean Faure St-Ém ★★ 15 16 18' 19' 20' 22 23 GRAND CRU CLASSÉ neighbour of CHEVAL BLANC. Organic. CAB FR-led (5% MALBEC), fresh, elegant. Second label: La Réserve.

Kirwan Marg ★★★ 16' 18 19' 20' 21 22 23 24 25 Third Growth owned by Schÿler family. Freshness, finesse, charm; CAB SAUV-led (68% in 24). Dry white VDF (100% CHARD). Second label: Charmes.

Labégorce Marg ★★→★★★ 14 15 16' 17 18' 19 20 21 22 23 24 Substantial unclassified property; CAB SAUV-led (50%). Nathalie Perrodo owns. Ripe, modern but fresh. Second label: Zédé de Labégorce.

Lafaurie-Peyraguey Saut ★★★ 11 14 15' 16' 17 18 19 20 21 22 23 24 Leading First Growth (1855). Rich, harmonious, sweet. SÉM (100% in 23 24). Tiny volume. Second label: La Chapelle. Also Grand Vin Sec (dr w).

Lafite Rothschild Pau ★★★★ 08 09' 10' 11' 12 13 14 15' 16' 17 18' 19' 20' 21 22 23 24 25 Big (112 ha) First Growth of famously elusive perfume, style; never great weight, although more dense, sleek these days. Lots of CAB SAUV (96% in 24). Great vintages need keeping for decades. More affordable, approachable (MERLOT-led) Anseillan. Second label: CARRUADES DE LAFITE. Own cooperage. Also DUHART-MILON, L'EVANGILE, RIEUSSEC; WILLIAM FÈVRE (CHAB).

Lafleur Pom ★★★★ 11 12 13 14 15' 16' 17' 18' 19' 20 21 22 23 24 25 Superb but tiny; Guinaudeau family-owned. Elegant, intense, to age. Expensive. Labelled VDF from 2025. Second label: ***Les Pensées***.

Lafleur-Gazin Pom ★★ 15 16' 18' 19 20' 21 22 23 24 J-P MOUEIX-owned (2021). Small, gd value; 100% MERLOT; elegant, fresh.

Lafon-Rochet St-Est ★★★ 14 15' 16' 17 18' 19 20' 21 22 23 24 25 Fourth Growth owned by Jacky Lorenzetti (LILIAN LADOUYS, PÉDESCLAUX). On gd form; firm but zesty. Organic, certified 2024. Second label: Les Pélerins de Lafon-Rochet.

Lagrange St-Jul ★★★ 12 14 15' 16' 17 18 19' 20 21 22 23 24 Large (118 ha) Third Growth owned by Suntory. Serious investment. Consistent, fresh; CAB SAUV-driven (84% in 24). Dry white Les Arums de Lagrange. Second label: Les Fiefs de Lagrange (gd value). Also Pagus de Lagrange (H-MÉD).

Lagrange Pom ★★ 16' 17 18 19 20 21 22 23 J-P MOUEIX-owned; on n edge of plateau. 100% MERLOT; supple, round, accessible; gd value. No 24 (rot).

Lagune, La H-Méd ★★★ 12 14 15' 16' 17 19 20 21 22 23 24 25 Substantial Third Growth in far s of MÉD. On gd form; fine-edged with structure, depth. Organic, bio. Delphine Frey now at helm.

Lamarque, De H-Méd ★★ 15 16 18 19' 20 22' 23 Medium-sized estate owned by Gromond family. Competent, savoury, mid-term, value wines; CAB SAUV/ MERLOT/PETIT VERDOT. Second label: D de Lamarque.

Lanessan H-Méd ★★ 16' 17 18 19' 20 22 23 Reliable, gd-value claret. Part of TWE (*see* Australia); future projects, investment.

Langoa Barton St-Jul ★★★ 14 15' 16' 17 18' 19' 20 21 22 23 24 Small Third Growth sister CH to LÉOVILLE BARTON; CAB SAUV/MERLOT/CAB FR; charm, elegance, with ageing potential.

Larcis Ducasse St-Ém ★★★ 10 14 16' 17 18 19' 20 21 22 23 24 25 PREMIER GRAND CRU CLASSÉ on s côtes. On top form; wine to mature; MERLOT (85% in 24). David Suire at helm (as LAROQUE).

Irish whiskey aged in Bx barrels for "Bordeaux finish". Return of the wild geese?

Larmande St-Ém ★★ 15 16 18' 19' 20 22 23 GRAND CRU CLASSÉ owned by La Mondiale insurance. MERLOT-led. Sound but lighter weight; accessible.

Laroque St-Ém ★★→★★★ 15 16 18' 19' 20' 21 22 23 24 Large GRAND CRU CLASSÉ. MERLOT (98%); terroir-driven (limestone).

Larose-Trintaudon H-Méd ★★ 18 19' 20 22 Largest vyd in MÉD (202 ha). Generally for early drinking. Large new cellars in 2025. Also Larose Perganson.

Laroze St-Ém ★★ 15 16' 18' 19' 20 21 22 23 24 GRAND CRU CLASSÉ on sandy-gravel soils. MERLOT/CABS FR/SAUV/PETIT VERDOT. Lighter, but fruit, freshness, balance.

Larrivet Haut-Brion Pe-Lé ★★★ (r) 14 16' 18' 19 20 21 22 23 24 Unclassified; 70-ha vyd. CABS SAUV/FR/MERLOT. Refined red. Rich, creamy, SAUV BL-led ***white*** 22 23 24. Charlotte Mignon new manager. Second label (r/w): Les Demoiselles.

Lascombes Marg ★★★ 10' 14 15' 16' 17 18 19' 20 21 22 23 24 25 Large Second Growth; chequered history. Rich, opulent. Style change from 23; more MARG elegance. New 100% MERLOT La Côte from 22; pricey. Second label: Chevalier de Lascombes.

Latour Pau ★★★★ 05' 06 08 09' 10' 11 12 13 14 15' 16' 17 18' 19' 20' 21 22 23 First Growth considered grandest statement of BX. Pinault family-owned. Profound, intense, almost immortal in great yrs; even weaker vintages have unique taste and run for many yrs. Sustainable and organic. Only old vines, average age 60 yrs. Ceased en primeur sales 2012; wines now only released when considered ready to drink (16 in 2025 and a 2nd portion of 12). Second label: LES FORTS DE LATOUR. ***Third label: Pauillac***; even this can age 20 yrs.

Latour à Pomerol Pom ★★★ 14 15' 16' 17 18 19' 20 21 22 23 24 25 J-P MOUEIX-owned from 2024. 100% MERLOT; consistent, well structured, balanced; can age.

Latour-Martillac Pe-Lé ★★→★★★ (r) 14 15' 16 18' 19 20 21 22 23 Cru Classé owned by Kressmann family. Fresh, fragrant red. Appetizing ***white*** 22 23 24. Usually gd value. White Grapecap 1884 (mainly SÉM).

Laurets, Des St-Ém ★★ 18 19 20 22 Edmond de Rothschild Heritage wine. Large estate in PUISSEGUIN ST-ÉM. Mainly MERLOT. Supple, early drinking.

Laville Saut ★★ 18 19 22 Non-classified Preignac estate; SÉM-dominated (90%); lush, gd value, botrytized. Jean-Christophe Barbe owns.

Léoville Barton St-Jul ★★★★ 10' 11 12 14 15' 16' 17 18' 19' 20' 21 22 23 24 25 Second Growth. 200 yrs of Barton ownership in 2026; Lilian B with daughter Mélanie and son Damien in charge. Harmonious, classic, long-ageing claret; CAB SAUV-dominant (92% in 24). New gravity-fed *cuvier* shared with LANGOA-BARTON. Second label: La Rés de Léoville Barton.

Léoville Las Cases St-Jul ★★★★ 09' 10' 11' 12 13 14 15' 16' 17 18' 19' 20' 21 22 23 24 25 Largest Léoville and original "Super Second" owned by Jean-Hubert Delon (NÉNIN, POTENSAC). Elegant, complex wines for long ageing. New *cuverie* in 2023. Second label: Le Petit Lion.

Léoville Poyferré St-Jul ★★★★ 10' 11' 12 13 14 15' 16' 17 18' 19' 20' 21 22 23 24 Second Growth owned by Cuvelier family. "Super Second" level; dark, rich, spicy, long-ageing; CAB SAUV-led (64% in 24). Second label: Pavillon de Léoville Poyferré. Also Moulin Riche.

Lestage List ★★ 18 19' 20 22 24 Owned by Vignobles Chanfreau (FONRÉAUD). Firm, ripe, toasty. Dry white La Mouette.

G'day, Bordeaux

Australian wine giant Treasury Wine Estates (TWE, *see* Austrailia), owner of PENFOLDS, has brought its particular vision of winemaking to the MÉD. In the early 2020s, the company acquired CHX BELLE-VUE, CAMBON LA PELOUSE, Gironville and LANESSAN (all H-MÉD), providing potentially around 185 ha of vines for various projects. So far, these have incl two blended French Winemaking Trial CUVÉES: FWT 585 (CAB SAUV/MERLOT/PETIT VERDOT) and FWT 543 (CAB SAUV/SYRAH) made from own and bought-in grapes and labelled VDF. Lanessan becomes the focal point for all projects but will continue to make an estate wine, with investment planned for a new chai and facilities to develop wine tourism. The New World harnessing the Old.

Lilian Ladouys St-Est ★★ 16' 17 18' 19' 20 22 23 Lorenzetti family-owned; sizeable estate (*see* LAFON-ROCHET). Organic. MERLOT-led (66% in 24). Full but fine. Second label: La Devise de Lilian.

Liversan H-Méd ★★ 18 19 20 22 23 CRU BOURGEOIS Supérieur in N H-MÉD. MERLOT/CAB SAUV; round, savoury, early drinking.

Loudenne Méd ★★ 18 19' 20 22 Large estate owned by Christophe Gouache. Landmark C17 pink-washed *chartreuse* by river. Supple reds, MERLOT/CAB SAUV; SAUV BL-led white; rosé; Au Naturel (no sulfites).

Louvière, La Pe-Lé ★★★ (r) 15 16' 17 18 19 20 21 22 23 (w) 22 23 24 VIGNOBLES André Lurton property (run by son Jacques). Excellent 100% SAUV BL; savoury MERLOT-led/CAB SAUV.

Lussac, De St-Ém ★★ 19 20 22 24 Top estate in LUSSAC-ST-ÉM. MERLOT-led/CAB FR. Supple, accessible red.

Lynch-Bages Pau ★★★★ 10' 11 12 13 14 15 16' 17 18 19' 20' 21 22 23 24 25 Large (106 ha) estate; always popular, far higher than its Fifth Growth rank; pricier. Rich, dense CAB SAUV-led (70% in 24), for ageing. New winery in 2020. Second label: Echo de Lynch-Bages. ***Blanc de Lynch-Bages*** (gd SAUV BL-led w).

Lynch-Moussas Pau ★★ 15 16 18 19' 20 22 23 24 BORIE-MANOUX Fifth Growth; CAB SAUV-led (78% in 24). Less gravitas than top PAU, but improving.

Lyonnat St-Ém ★★ 18 19 20 22 Sizeable LUSSAC-ST-ÉM estate, Milhade family-owned. MERLOT-led (90%); consistent. Also Les Lionnes (100% Merlot).

Malartic Lagravière Pe-Lé ★★★ (r) 15' 16' 17 18 19' 20' 21 22 23 24 25 (w) 21 22 23 Classed Growth owned by Bonnie family. Rich, appetizing red; fresh, creamy ***white*** (majority SAUV BL). Visitor-friendly. Also Gazin Rocquencourt.

Malescasse H-Méd ★★ 18 19 20 22 23 CRU BOURGEOIS Exceptionnel owned by VIGNOBLES Austruy. Ripe, fleshy, polished.

Malescot St Exupéry Marg ★★★ 15' 16' 17 18' 19 20 21 22 23 24 25 Third Growth owned by Zuger family. Ripe, fragrant, finely structured.

Malle, De Saut ★★★ 11' 12 14 16' 17' 18 19 Second Growth. Medium-bodied SAUT. Changes with new ownership (24). New dry white M.

Mangot St-Ém ★★ 16 18 19 20 22 23 24 GRAND CRU CLASSÉ; vyd in e of ST-ÉM; clay-limestone. MERLOT/CAB FR/CAB SAUV. Organic, bio.

Margaux, Ch Marg ★★★★ 10' 11 12 13 14 15 16' 17 18' 19' 20' 21 22 23 24 25 First Growth; most seductive, fabulously perfumed, consistent, long ageing; CAB SAUV-dominated (93% in 24). Alexis Leven-Mentzelopoulos titular head. Second label: Pavillon Rouge 16' 17 19 20 21 22 23 24 25. Third label: Margaux du CH Margaux. ***Pavillon Blanc*** (100% SAUV BL) best white of MÉD 22 23 24 25. Second label (from 22): Pavillon Blanc Second Vin.

Marojallia Marg ★★★ 18' 19' 20 22 Micro-CH; big, rich, un-MARG-like wines. Absorbed into MARQUIS DE TERME in 2023.

Marquis d'Alesme Marg ★★→★★★ 15 16 17 18 19 20 22 23 24 Third Growth revived by Perrodo family. Investment: upward curve. Wines: MARG on lush side; CAB SAUV-led. Visitor-friendly.

Marquis de Terme Marg ★★→★★★ 14 15 16' 17 18' 19' 20 21 22 23 Fourth Growth. Investment, progression in recent yrs, but solid side of MARG. Visitor-friendly.

Maucaillou Mou ★★ 15' 16' 17 18 19' 20 21 22 23 Dourthe family-owned. Consistent, medium-term; CAB SAUV-led. Second label: No. 2 de Maucaillou.

Mayne Lalande List ★★ 16 18 19 20 23 Lartigue family-owned. Full, finely textured.

Mazeyres Pom ★★ 16' 18 19' 20 21 22 23 Lightish but consistent. Earlier-drinking, MERLOT/CAB FR/PETIT VERDOT. Organic, bio.

Méaume Bx ★★ 19 20 22 23. Consistent BX SUPÉRIEUR. Johnson-Hill family-owned. Rés du CH from oldest vines.

Meyney St-Est ★★→★★★ 12 15' 16' 17 18' 19' 20' 21 22 23 24 25 Big river-slope vyd,

BORDEAUX

Claret, but not as we know it
The name Claret is now official, with its own AOP. It's to be used for lighter red, but is not to be confused with *clairet*, which is dark rosé. You're keeping up, aren't you? The idea is to appeal to a younger generation that apparently likes fruitier, low-tannin wines with some sweetness: up to 7g/l residual sugar will probably be allowed. It can be sold from Dec of the vintage yr. Let's hope it works.

superb site next to MONTROSE. Structured, age-worthy; CAB SAUV-led, but lots of PETIT VERDOT; gd value. Organic, certified 24. Second label: Prieur de Meyney.

Mission Haut-Brion, La Pe-Lé ★★★★ 08 09' 10' 11 12 13 14 15' 16' 17' 18' 19' 20' 21 22 23 24 25 Unofficial sixth First Growth owned by DOM Clarence Dillon. Considerable investment over past 40 yrs. Consistently grand-scale, full-blooded, long-maturing. Second label: La Chapelle de la Mission. Magnificent SÉM-led white: previously Laville Haut-Brion; renamed La Mission Haut-Brion Blanc 21' 22 23 24 25. Second label: La Clarté.

Monbousquet St-Ém ★★★ 15 16' 18 19 20 21 22 23 GRAND CRU CLASSÉ on sand and gravel plain; 30 yrs' investment by Perse family (*see* PAVIE). MERLOT-led (60%). Voluptuous. Second label: Angélique de Monbousquet.

Monbrison Marg ★★→★★★ 15' 16 17 18 19 20 21 22 Tiny property owned by Laurent Vonderheyden. CAB SAUV-led (81% in 22). Delicate, fragrant.

Mondotte, La St-Ém ★★★→★★★★ 14 15' 16 17 18 19' 20' 22 23 24 25 Tiny (4.5 ha) PREMIER GRAND CRU CLASSÉ on limestone-clay plateau. Old-vine (average 60 yrs) MERLOT/CAB FR (75/25%); intense, powerful. Organic since 14.

Montrose St-Est ★★★★ 10' 12 13 14 15' 16' 17 18' 19' 20' 21 22 23 24 25 Second Growth with riverside vyd. Famed for forceful, long-ageing claret (1979–85 were lighter). Bouyges bros-owned. *Grand vin* from Terrace 4 vyd only from 23; new wine, Terrasse III, from Terrace 3 vyd from 24. Second label: ***La Dame de Montrose.***

Moulin du Cadet St-Ém ★★ 15' 16 18' 19' 20' 22 23 24 25 Tiny GRAND CRU CLASSÉ; 100% MERLOT. Structured, lithe, fresh. Sister SANSONNET.

Moulinet Pom ★★ 18 19 20 22 Large CH for POM: 18 ha on clay and gravel soils. Lighter MERLOT/CAB FR (90/10%).

Moulin Haut-Laroque Fron ★★ 16 18' 19' 20' 21 22 23 Leading FRON. MERLOT-led (65%)/CAB FR/CAB SAUV/MALBEC. Consistent, can age.

Moulin Pey-Labrie Fron ★★ 18 19 20' 22 CANON-FRON owned by Hubau family. MERLOT/MALBEC (95/5%); organic, natural. Can age.

Moulin St-Georges St-Ém ★★★ 15' 16' 17 18' 19' 20 22 23 24 25 Vauthier family (AUSONE)-owned (1921). Lively, fresh, harmonious; gd value.

Mouton Rothschild Pau ★★★★ 08' 09' 10' 11 12 13 14 15' 16' 17' 18' 19' 20' 21 22 23 24 25 Rothschild-owned (1853). Most exotic, voluptuous of PAU First Growths; at top of game; CAB SAUV-led (93% in 24). White Aile d'Argent (SAUV BL/SÉM) now more graceful. Second label: ***Le Petit Mouton.*** Also CLERC MILON, D'ARMAILHAC.

Nairac Bar ★★ 11 13 15 16 17 18 22 23 24 Second Growth run by Les Grands Chais de France since 2022. No wine in 19 20 21. Rich but fresh, SÉM-led.

Nénin Pom ★★★ 12 14 15' 16' 17 18' 19' 20' 21 22 23 24 25 Domaines Delon-owned (LÉOVILLE LAS CASES). Less generous than some POM but length, structure. MERLOT-led/CABS FR/SAUV. Second label: Fugue de Nénin.

Olivier Pe-Lé ★★★ (r) 15 16' 18 19' 20 21' 22 23 24 (w) 21 23 24 Vast DOM; C16 CH. Structured red, juicy white. Organic from 24. Second label (r): Le Dauphin.

Ormes de Pez St-Est ★★ 14 15' 16' 17 18' 19 20' 22 23 24 25 Cazes family (LYNCH-BAGES)-owned; CAB SAUV/MERLOT/PETIT VERDOT/CAB FR. Cool, classic, age-worthy.

Ormes Sorbet, Les Méd ★★ 18 19 20 22 23 24 Reliably consistent MÉD cru. Boivert family-owned (1764); CAB SAUV-led (65% in 24). Elegant, gently oaked.

Palmer Marg ★★★★ 10' 11 12 14 15' 16' 17 18' 19' 20' 21 22' 23 24 25 Third Growth on par with "Super Seconds" (occasionally Firsts). Voluptuous wine of power, complexity, much MERLOT (41% in 24). Organic, bio, environmental. Sells 50% en primeur, releases rest at 10 yrs (15 in 2025). Second label: ***Alter Ego de Palmer***.

Pape Clément Pe-Lé ★★★★ (r) 14 15' 16' 17 18' 19' 20 22 23 24 (w) 22 23 24 Historic estate in Bordeaux suburbs, owned by Bernard Magrez since 1985. Dense, long-ageing reds. Tiny production of rich, SAUV BL-led white. Visitor-friendly. Second label (r/w): Clémentin.

Patache d'Aux Méd ★★ 18 19 20 22 23 Sizeable CRU BOURGEOIS Supérieur owned by Advini; CAB SAUV/MERLOT/PETIT VERDOT; savoury, gd value.

Pavie St-Ém ★★★★ 09' 10' 12 14 15' 16' 17 18 19' 20' 21 22 23 24 25 Owner Gérard Perse (*see* MONBOUSQUET) died in 2025. PREMIER GRAND CRU CLASSÉ (A) the summit of his achievement. Intense, powerful, for long ageing; recent vintages less extreme (more CABS FR/SAUV). Second label: Arômes de Pavie.

Pavie Decesse St-Ém ★★★ 12 14 15' 16 17 18 19' 20' 21 Former GRAND CRU CLASSÉ now integrated into PAVIE. Tight, tannic, needs time.

Pavie Macquin St-Ém ★★★ 14 16' 17 18' 19' 20' 21 22 23 24 25 PREMIER GRAND CRU CLASSÉ (B); vyd in one block on limestone-clay; MERLOT-led (84% in 24)/CABS FR/SAUV. Sturdy, needs time. Second label: Les Chênes de Macquin.

Pédesclaux Pau ★★ 14' 15 16' 18 19' 20 22 23 24 25 Underachieving Fifth Growth transformed by owner Jacky Lorenzetti. Organic. Ex-LAFITE winemaker at helm from 2025. Increasingly more refined.

Petit Village Pom ★★★ 15' 16' 17 18' 19 20' 22 23 24 25 Much improved. Atypical 40% CABS FR/SAUV. Organic. Now greater precision. Second label: Le Petit.

Petrus Pom ★★★★ 09' 10' 11' 12 13 14 15' 16' 17 18' 19' 20' 21 22 23 24 25 (Unofficial) First Growth of POM: MERLOT solo *in excelsis*. 11.5-ha vyd on blue clay gives massively rich, concentrated wine for long ageing, at a price; c.30,000 bottles/yr.

Pey La Tour Bx ★★ 20 22 23 24 Large DOURTHE property (135 ha). Quality-driven generic BX. Two red CUVÉES: Rés du CH (90% MERLOT) top.

Peyrabon H-Méd ★★ 18 19 20 22 23 Savoury CRU BOURGEOIS Supérieur in N H-MÉD; owned by Castéja family (*see* LYNCH-MOUSSAS).

Pez, De St-Est ★★★ 14 15' 16' 17 18' 19' 20 21 22 23 24 Dense, reliable, for ageing; vyd in one block. Second label: 2nd Pez.

Phélan Ségur St-Est ★★★ 14 15' 16' 17 18' 19' 20 21 22 23 24 25 Reliable, top-notch, unclassified CH with Irish origins. Long, supple style; CAB SAUV-led (68% in 24). Visitor-friendly. Second label: Frank Phélan.

Pibran Pau ★★ 15 16' 18' 19' 20 21 22 23 Tiny (17 ha) PAU property. Earlier-drinking, almost 50/50% MERLOT/CAB SAUV.

Pichon Baron Pau ★★★★ 09' 10' 11 12 14 15' 16' 17 18' 19' 20 21 22 23 24 25 AXA-owned. Second Growth on flying form. Powerful, long-ageing PAU at a price; CAB SAUV-led (87% in 24). Second labels: Les Tourelles de Longueville, Les Griffons de Pichon Baron. Dry white Les Griffons Grand Vin Blanc Sec (100% SÉM).

Bordeaux branch of 67 Pall Mall wine bar: 5000 wines, 7000-bottle wine tower.

Pichon Longueville Comtesse de Lalande (Pichon Lalande) Pau ★★★★ 11 12 14 15' 16' 17 18' 19' 20' 21 22 23 24 25 ROEDERER-owned Second Growth; 102 ha with 100 plots. Always among top performers; long-lived wine of famous breed. More elegance, less power than PICHON BARON. More CAB SAUV in recent yrs (83% in 24). Second label: ***Rés de la Comtesse***.

Pin, Le Pom ★★★★ 11 12 14 15 16' 17 18' 19' 20' 21 22 23 24 25 Original BX cult wine owned by Jacques Thienpont since 1979. Only 2.8 ha. MERLOT (100%) on deep gravel and sand. Almost as rich as its drinkers; prices out of sight. Aged in new oak barrels. Potential to age. Also L'If (ST-ÉM), L'Hêtre (CAS).

Plince Pom ★★ 15 16' 18 19 20 22 23 Lighter POM on sandy soils; earlier drinking. MERLOT-led (85% in 23)/CAB FR.

Pointe, La Pom ★★ 15' 16' 18 19 20 21 22 23 24 Large, well-run estate; less intense than top POM. MERLOT-led (79% in 23)/CAB FR.

Poitevin Méd ★★ 17 18 19 20 22 23 CRU BOURGEOIS Supérieur. Consistent quality, value. Organic. Also dry white, rosé.

Pontet-Canet Pau ★★★★ 10' 14 15 16' 17 18' 19' 20 21 22 23 24 25 Large, bio, Tesseron family-owned Fifth Growth. Radical improvement has seen prices soar; CAB SAUV-led (52% in 24). Lighter bottles from 2022 (glass weight 490g). Classic PAU but generous, refined.

Potensac Méd ★★→★★★ 15 16' 17 18' 19' 20' 21 22 23 24 25 Firm, long-ageing, gd value; CAB SAUV, MERLOT and lots of old-vine CAB FR (22% in 24). Owned by Domaines Delon (*see* LÉOVILLE LAS CASES).

Pouget Marg ★★ 14 15' 16 18 19 20 22 23 Tiny Fourth Growth sister of BOYD-CANTENAC; CAB SAUV-led. Sturdy; needs time. Second label: Antoine Pouget.

Poujeaux Mou ★★ 14 15' 16' 17 18' 19 20 22 23 24 Large MOU estate; CAB SAUV-led (50% in 24). Full, robust, ageing potential.

Premier Grand Cru Classé St-Ém 2022: 14 classified, two ranked (A) and 12 (B). *See* box, p.108.

Pressac, De St-Ém ★★ 16' 17 18' 19' 20' 21 22 23 24 GRAND CRU CLASSÉ e of St-Émilion town. MERLOT-led; ripe, full, engaging.

Preuillac Méd ★★ 18 19' 20 22 23 Savoury, structured CRU BOURGEOIS Supérieur. MERLOT/CAB SAUV/CAB FR/PETIT VERDOT. Solid, value.

Prieuré-Lichine Marg ★★★ 14 15' 16' 17 18' 19' 20' 22 23 24 Fourth Growth owned by Ballande group. Parcels in all five MARG communes; CAB SAUV-led (65% in 24). Fragrant; on gd form. Second label: Confidences. Also gd Le Blanc (w). Visitor-friendly.

Puygueraud Bx ★★ 18' 19 20 22 23 24 Leading CH of tiny FRANCS-CÔTES DE BX AOP. MERLOT-led; top yrs can age a bit. MALBEC/CAB FR-based George; dry white (SAUVS BL/Gr). Fire in storage cellar in 2025.

Quinault L'Enclos St-Ém ★★→★★★ 18' 19' 20 22 23 24 25 Same team/owners as CHEVAL BLANC. MERLOT-led, but more CABS SAUV/FR these days (37% in 24), with more CAB SAUV planted in 2025; added freshness, finesse.

Quintus St-Ém ★★★ 15 16' 17 18' 19' 20' 22 23 24 25 Same stable as HAUT-BRION. Composed of ex-Tertre Daugay, L'Arrosée and Grand Pontet vyds. *Grand vin* 21% of production in 24 (smallest ever). Gaining in stature; expensive. Second label: Le Dragon de Quintus. Third label: St-Émilion de Quintus.

Rabaud-Promis Saut ★★→★★★ 13 14 15' 16 17' 18 19 20 23 Family run First Growth (1855); SÉM-led; quality, gd value.

Rahoul Graves ★★ (r) 18 19 20 21 22 23 24 Reliable, MERLOT-led (54% in 24); gd-value white SÉM-dominated 22 23 24 25.

The Médoc sees white

2025 saw the 1st vintage of the new AOP MÉD white. Producers in the peninsula's two existing regional (Méd, H-MÉD) and six communal AOPs are allowed to make it, from SAUV BL, SÉM, MUSCADELLE and Sauvignon Gr. Up to 5% in the vyd, 10% in the blend (individually or together) of experimental varieties ALVARINHO, Floréal, Liliorila, Sauvignac and Souvignier Gr are also permitted. An environmental certificate is mandatory and chemical weeding forbidden, and 30% of the production must be aged in wood for at least 3 mths. Currently there are 70 CHX and c.170 ha eligible for the new AOP. Let's see if it works.

Ramage la Batisse H-Méd ★★ 19 20 23 CRU BOURGEOIS Supérieur at St-Sauveur-en-Médoc; CAB SAUV, MERLOT, lots of PETIT VERDOT.

Rauzan-Gassies Marg ★★★ 15 16' 18 19 20' 22 23 Second Growth; CAB SAUV-led (90% in 23). Some improvement but still lacks a little finesse.

Rauzan-Ségla Marg ★★★★ 11 12 14 15' 16' 17 18' 19' 20' 21 22 23 24 25 Leading Second Growth; owned by Wertheimers of Chanel; Nicolas Audebert manager. Fragrant, structured CAB SAUV-led (63.5% in 24). Second label: Ségla.

90% of Bordeaux wine boxes are Galician pine. (What makes a Galician pine?)

Raymond-Lafon Saut ★★★ 14 15' 16' 17' 18 19 20 22 23 Unclassified SAUT, but First Growth quality. Rich, complex, gd value. Second label: Jeunes Pousses.

Rayne Vigneau, De Saut ★★★ 14 15' 16' 17 18' 19' 20 22 23 24 25 Substantial First Growth; SÉM-led (74% of vyd). Suave, age-worthy. Visitor-friendly. Second label: Madame de Rayne.

Respide Médeville Graves ★★ (r) 19 20 22 (w) 21 22 23 Tiny property. Part of VIGNOBLES Gonet-Médeville. Elegant red, fresh ***white***.

Reynon Bx ★★ Leading CADILLAC-CÔTES DE BX estate; Dubourdieu family-owned. MERLOT-led 20' 22 23 24; BX white SAUV BL (DYA).

Reysson H-Méd ★★ 19 20 22 23 24 CRU BOURGEOIS Exceptionnel owned by DOURTHE. Mainly MERLOT on limestone-clay. Consistent; rich but fragrant.

Rieussec Saut ★★★★ 14 15' 16' 17 18' 19 20 21 22 First Growth, substantial vyd in Fargues (85 ha), owned by (LAFITE) Rothschild; SÉM-led, rich, dense. Special bottle with resealable cork (21). Second label: Carmes de Rieussec.

Rivière, De la Fron ★★ 18 19 20 21 22 23 Largest (65 ha), most impressive FRON property. New investment-fund owner in 2025. MERLOT-led; fresh, more refined these days. Visitor-friendly.

Roc de Cambes Bx ★★★ 15' 16' 17 18 19 20 21 22 23 24 François Mitjavile's undisputed leader in CÔTES DE BOURG; MERLOT/CAB SAUV (80/20%). Savoury, opulent, pricey. Can age. Also DOM de Cambes.

Rochemorin, De Pe-Lé ★★ (r) 18' 19 20 22 24 (w) 23 24 Sizeable (68 ha) property owned by VIGNOBLES André Lurton. Fleshy, MERLOT-led, earlier-drinking red; aromatic white (100% SAUV BL). Fairly consistent quality.

Rol Valentin St-Ém ★★ 15' 16' 18 19 20' 21 22 GRAND CRU CLASSÉ; MERLOT-led/MALBEC (7%). Ripe, modern, structured.

Rouget Pom ★★ 15 16' 18 19 20 22 23 24 Sizeable (for POM) estate on n edge of plateau. Labruyère family-owned. Organic (2023). MERLOT-led/CAB FR. Powerful, unctuous. Second label: Le Carillon de Rouget.

St-Georges St-Ém ★★ 16 18 20 22 23 24 This vyd represents 25% of ST-GEORGES AOP. MERLOT-led (80%)/CABS FR/SAUV (10% each); vyds average age 40 yrs; gd wine sold direct to public.

St-Pierre St-Jul ★★★ 14 15' 16' 18' 19' 20 22 23 24 25 Tiny Fourth Growth; CAB SAUV-led, stylish, consistent, classic. Organic (2024). Second label: Esprit de St-Pierre.

Sales, De Pom ★★ 16 18 19' 20' 22' 23 24 Biggest vyd of POM (47.6 ha). Investment, improvement. Honest, drinkable; can age; value. Marie-Laure Latorre new manager. Second label: CH Chantalouette.

Sansonnet St-Ém ★★→★★★ 16' 17 18 19' 20 21 22 23 24 25 Plateau-based GRAND CRU CLASSÉ. MERLOT-led/CABS FR/SAUV. Modern but refreshing.

Saransot-Dupré List ★★ 16 18 19 20 22 23 A LIST cru owned by Yves Raymond. Firm, generous. Also gd dry white BX.

Sénéjac H-Méd ★★ 16' 18 19' 20' 22 23 Cru in S H-MÉD (Pian). Gravel soils. Consistent, well balanced. Visitor-friendly.

Serre, La St-Ém ★★ 16' 18' 19' 20' 22 23 Small GRAND CRU CLASSÉ on limetone plateau. MERLOT/CAB FR; fresh, consistent, stylish.

BORDEAUX

Sigalas Rabaud Saut ★★★ 13 16 17' 18 19' 21 22 23 24 Tiny First Growth; 100% SÉM, ***v. fragrant and lovely***. Second label: Le Lieutenant de Sigalas. Also a non-alc sweet "wine".

Siran Marg ★★→★★★ 14 15' 16' 17 18' 19' 20 22 23 24 25 Unclassified MARG. Substance, fragrance, can age. MERLOT/CAB SAUV/PETIT VERDOT; 22 label a tribute to Queen Elizabeth II. Second label: S de Siran.

"Blouge", red/white grapes, growing trend: co-fermented Cab Fr/Sauv Bl (A Lurton).

Smith Haut Lafitte Pe-Lé ★★★★ (r) 12 14 15' 16' 17 18 19' 20 21 22 23 24 25 (w) 22 23 24 25 Celebrated Classed Growth with spa hotel (Caudalie). Full, ripe, sappy white; precise, generous red. Organic. New visitor centre Gaïa in 2025. Second labels: Le Petit Haut Lafitte (r/w), Les Hauts de Smith (r/w).

Sociando-Mallet H-Méd ★★★ 14 15' 16' 17 18 19' 20 22 23 24 Large (83 ha), unclassified but esteemed estate. MERLOT/CABS SAUV/FR on gravel hillock. Wines for ageing. Second label: La Demoiselle de Sociando-Mallet.

Sours, De Bx ★★ Large property owned by Jack Ma of Alibaba fame. Quarry range: (r) MERLOT-led; (w) SAUV BL.

Soutard St-Ém ★★★ 15 16' 17 18' 19' 20' 22 23 24 ***Potentially excellent*** GRAND CRU CLASSÉ on limestone plateau. MERLOT-led/CABS FR/SAUV/MALBEC. Massive investment, making strides in recent yrs. Visitor-friendly.

Suduiraut Saut ★★★★ 14 15' 16' 17' 19' 20' 21 22 23 24 25 AXA property. One of v. best SAUT: 100% SÉM, luscious, pure, long, age-worthy. Second labels: Castelnau de Suduiraut, Lions de Suduiraut (fruitier). Dry wines: VIEILLES VIGNES, Pur Sém, entry-level Lions de Suduiraut.

Taillefer Pom ★★ 16 18' 19 20' 22 23 Bernard MOUEIX-owned. Lighter weight but refined. Usually gd value.

Talbot St-Jul ★★★ 14 15 16 17 18 19 20 21 22 23 24 25 Substantial ST-JUL Fourth Growth (110 ha); CAB SAUV-led (70% in 24). Wine rich, age-worthy, ***consummately charming, reliable.*** Approachable SAUV BL-based Caillou Bl. Second label: Connétable de Talbot (more approachable).

Tertre, Du Marg ★★★ 15' 16' 17 18' 19' 20 21 22 23 24 25 Fifth Growth isolated s of MARG; CAB SAUV-led (75% in 24). Fragrant and structured. Also Tertre Blanc VDF (CHARD/SAUV BL/VIOGNIER/GROS MANSENG). Second label: Les Hauts du Tertre.

Tertre Roteboeuf St-Ém ★★★★ 14' 15' 16' 17 18' 19 20 21 22 23 24 25 Tiny, unclassified côtes star at St-Laurent-des-Combes. Lush, concentrated, toasty; frightening prices. Also v.gd ROC DE CAMBES.

Thieuley Bx ★★ An E-2-M supplier of consistent-quality AOP BX (r/w); run by Sylvie and Marie Courselle. Also gd Bx CLAIRET.

Tour Blanche, La Saut ★★★ 14 15 16' 17 18' 19' 20 21 22 23 24 25 Excellent First Growth owned by Région Nouvelle-Aquitaine. Rich, bold, powerful, on sweeter end of scale; SÉM-dominant. Second label: Les Charmilles.

Tour Carnet, La H-Méd ★★★ 14 15 16' 18' 19' 20 21 22 23 Large Fourth Growth owned by Bernard Magrez (*see* FOMBRAUGE, PAPE CLÉMENT) since 2000. MERLOT-led; ripe, sweet, savoury. Dry white BX (SÉM/SAUV BL). Second label: La Mémoire de La Tour Carnet.

Tour de By, La Méd ★★ 16' 18 19' 20' 22 23 Substantial estate in N MÉD nr Begadan. Popular, sturdy, reliable; CAB SAUV-led (60%); can age.

Tour de Mons, La Marg ★★ 15' 16' 18' 19 20 22 23 Owned by Perrodo family (MARQUIS D'ALESME). MERLOT-led; upward curve; value.

Tour du Haut Moulin H-Méd ★★ 16' 18 19 20 22 In N H-MÉD; Tzora Vyds-owned (2024). Classic wines; structured, age-worthy.

Tour du Pas St-Georges St-Ém ★★ 18 19 20 22 23 ST-GEORGES-ST-ÉM cru, Delbeck family-owned; wines made by FLEUR DE BOÜARD. MERLOT/CAB FR; classic style.

Tour Figeac, La St-Ém ★★ 16' 18' 19' 20 22 23 GRAND CRU CLASSÉ neighbour of FIGEAC. MERLOT/CAB FR; fine, floral; organic.

Tour Haut-Caussan Méd ★★ 18 19 20 22 23 Small cru owned by VIGNOBLES Courrian; CAB SAUV/MERLOT on clay-limestone. Consistent, value.

Tournefeuille L de P ★★ 18 19 20 22 Reliable; MERLOT-led (62%); round, firm, fleshy. Also CUVÉE La Cure.

Tour Saint Christophe St-Ém ★★ 18 19 20 22 23 24 GRAND CRU CLASSÉ; MERLOT-led (80% in 24). VIGNOBLES K-owned (BELLEFONT-BELCIER). Also Le Rey (CAS).

Trois Croix, Les Fron ★★ 18' 19' 20 22 23 24 Léon family; MERLOT/CAB FR; gd-value.

Tronquoy St-Est ★★★ 14 15' 16' 17 18' 19' 20 21 22 23 Was Tronquoy-Lalande until 2019. Consistent, satisfying. Not sold en primeur.

Troplong Mondot St-Ém ★★★ 14 15' 16 17 18' 19' 20 21 22 23 24 25 PREMIER GRAND CRU CLASSÉ (B) on limestone plateau. Lots of investment: new winery, restaurant. Major style change from 17; more elegance, freshness. MERLOT-led (85% in 24)/CABS SAUV/FR (13/2%). Second label: Mondot.

Trotanoy Pom ★★★★ 14 15' 16' 17 18' 19' 20 21 22 23 24 25 Jewel in J-P MOUEIX crown; MERLOT/CAB FR (99.5/0.5% in 24) on clay-gravel; dense, powerful, long-ageing.

Trottevieille St-Ém ★★★ 14 15 16' 17 18' 19' 20 22 23 24 PREMIER GRAND CRU CLASSÉ (B) owned by BORIE-MANOUX. Greater consistency; wines long, fresh, structured; lots of CAB FR (46% of vyd). Axel Marchal consults. Second label: Dame de Trottevieille.

Valandraud St-Ém ★★★★ 14 15' 16' 17 18 19' 20 21 22 23 24 25 PREMIER GRAND CRU CLASSÉ (B). Garage wonder turned First Growth. MERLOT-led (85% in 24). Formerly super-rich; now dense and balanced. Also Virginie de V, V Bl.

Vieille Cure, La Fron ★★ 18' 19' 20 22 23 24 Leading FRON estate; appetizing, fruit-evident, MERLOT-led. Value.

Vieux Château Certan Pom ★★★★ 12 13 14 15' 16' 17 18' 19' 20' 21 22 23 24 One of the great POMS. Different in style from neighbour PETRUS; ***elegance, harmony, fragrance***. Plenty of old-vine CABS FR/SAUV one of reasons. Great consistency; long-ageing. Second label: La Gravette de Certan (young vines).

Vieux Château St-André St-Ém ★★ 18 19 20 22 23 24 25 Small cru in MONTAGNE-ST-ÉM. Berrouet family-owned; ***gd value***; MERLOT-led (85% of vyd).

Villegeorge, De H-Méd ★★ 18 19 20 22 Tiny S H-MÉD owned by Marie-Laure Lurton; CAB SAUV/MERLOT/PETIT VERDOT. Light but elegant.

Vray Croix de Gay Pom ★★★ 15 16' 17 18' 19' 20' 22 23 24 Tiny vyd on POM plateau. More finesse of late. New cellar in 2025. Organic and bio practices. Also CALON SÉGUR.

Yquem Saut ★★★★ 05' 06' 07 08 09' 10' 11' 13' 14 15' 16' 17' 18' 19 20 21' 22 King of sweet, *liquoreux* wines. Owned by LVMH. Strong, intense, luscious; kept 2 yrs in barrel. Most vintages improve for 15 yrs+, some live 100 yrs+ in transcendent splendour; 100 ha in production (75/25% SÉM/SAUV BL). No Yquem made 51 52 64 72 74 92 2012. Project to be carbon neutral by 2035. Makes small amount (c.830 cases) off-dry (5g/l sugar) Sauv Bl/Sém (75/25%) "Y" (pronounced "ee-grec"). Organic.

Y wouldn't you?

Fancy doing a bit of seasonal work picking at YQUEM? There are 140 seasonal pickers. Average age: 60. More than a third are over 70; more than half are women. They have to be available seven days a week during the harvest but are only paid on the days they pick. The harvest may run for 2–3 mths, with up to seven passages through the vyd. But they probably get a gd lunch.

Italy

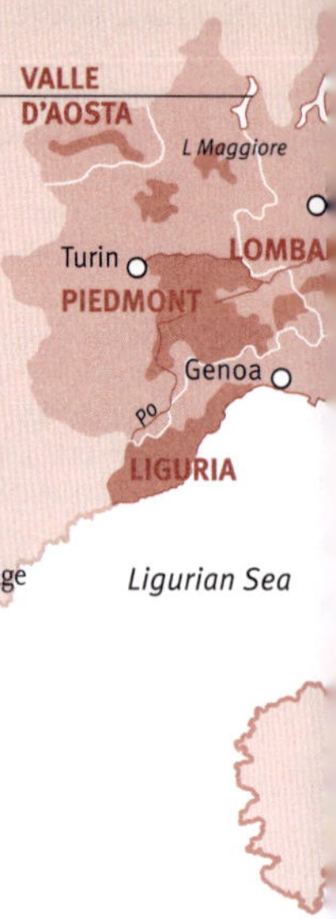

More heavily shaded areas are the wine-growing regions.

Abbreviations used in the text:

Ab	Abruzzo	Mol	Molise
Bas	Basilicata	Pie	Piedmont
Cal	Calabria	Pu	Puglia
Cam	Campania	Sar	Sardinia
E-R	Emilia-Romagna	Si	Sicily
FVG	Friuli Venezia Giulia	T-AA	Trentino-Alto Adige
Lat	Latium	Tus	Tuscany
Lig	Liguria	Umb	Umbria
Lom	Lombardy	VdA	Valle d'Aosta
Mar	Marches	Ven	Veneto

Over the past ten years, the acceleration of climate change has profoundly affected Italian viticulture. Rising temperatures, more frequent heatwaves and droughts, reduced rainfall, unexpected frost and hail, and shifting seasonal patterns are redefining the balance between sugar ripeness and phenolic and aromatic ripeness. Areas that were too cold in the past are now looking rather good, and some that were once highly thought of are facing new difficulties.

Northern and Alpine regions are among the main beneficiaries. The Alta Langa has warmer yet breezy summers, so Pinot Noir and Chardonnay get properly ripe and give more complex base wine for sparkling. In foothill areas like Carema, higher temperatures help Nebbiolo (Picotendro) ripen more evenly, with sweeter tannins and more expressive aromatic profiles. In Alto Piemonte (Lessona, Gattinara, Boca, etc.), warming has reduced cold, rainy vintages. The wines are more consistent, while still fresh and mineral. Nebbiolo now ripens more reliably. In Trentino and Alto Adige, vineyards above 500–600 metres (1640–1969 feet, pretty high) are looking terrific; ripening is improved with better balance between acidity and alcohol, though cool-climate varieties now need to be planted hundreds of metres higher up than before.

Further south, the picture is less good. Since 2015, Chianti Classico has faced hotter, drier summers with low water reserves, penalizing lower areas and warmer exposures, resulting in wines with higher alcohol and lower freshness. Higher zones of Gaiole, Radda and Lamole have an advantage. Brunello di Montalcino struggles with excessive alcohol and less acidity in spots that face south or west; facing north, or being higher up, helps. There's more detail about winners – and

those we should be looking for – on p.134. Western and southern Sicily, Puglia and parts of coastal Tuscany (Bolgheri, Maremma) suffer prolonged drought, water shortages and rising alcohol levels at the expense of balance and freshness. Veneto and Emilia-Romagna face more hail and heatwaves, reducing yields and quality. On Etna, lower vineyards and southern slopes risk overripeness; higher is better.

So: good news so far for the north, which is riper. Less good for central and southern areas, which are riper than they want to be and short of water. The solution here: adapt grape varieties, and plant higher.

Recent vintages

Amarone, Veneto & Friuli

2025 Ven: difficult, gd whites. FVG: high quality (r/w), medium quantity.
2024 Ven: complicated, gd whites. FVG: high quality (r/w), low quantity.
2023 Ven: better than expected in difficult yr. FVG: uneven; better whites.
2022 Ven: dry, gd quality. FVG: v.gd quality. Better than expected.
2021 Ven: dry, v.gd quality, less quantity. FVG: vgd quality, uneven volume.
2020 Ven: balanced, gd quality, quantity. FVG: wet June, uneven, better whites.
2019 Low quantity. Ven: gd for Amarone, Soave. FVG: fair quality.
2018 Optimal weather conditions; gd for quantity, quality, esp fresh whites.

Campania & Basilicata

2025 Balanced, gd quality, quantity (r/w).
2024 Warm, gd quality, quantity (r/w).
2023 V. difficult: downy mildew, hail. Small crop. What escaped is gd.
2022 Cam: classic, v.gd quality (r/w). Bas: warm, classic, v.gd.
2021 Cam: balance, quality, less quantity (best r). Bas: late harvest, classic, v.gd.
2020 Similar to 19. Classic, balanced but lower quantity; gd (r/w).
2018 Rainy, but whites fresh, lively; sleek reds (Aglianico best).

Marches & Abruzzo

2025 Mar: gd quality (esp w), medium quantity. Ab: gd quality, quantity.
2024 Mar: complicated, low quantity. Ab: v. difficult due to drought.
2023 V. difficult: downy mildew; small crop; better for whites.
2022 Mar: similar to 21, uneven. Ab: dry, better than 21. Both best for red.
2021 Hot, dry late vintage, gd quality but low yields; gd for late-ripening grapes.
2020 Uneven; quality peaks; wet June, fresh weather; late-ripening grapes gd.
2019 Difficult yr. Rainy, cold spring. Low quantity, medium quality.
2018 Patchy spring. More balanced than 17; v. high volume, gd quality (r/w).

Piedmont

2025 Quality, quantity gd. Alto Piemonte: v.gd quality, low quantity.
2024 Complicated, uneven, lower alc, gd quality. Alto Piemonte: less quantity.
2023 Better than expected, though still difficult. Alto Piemonte v.gd.
2022 Better than expected, uneven quantity, gd quality.
2021 Gd, despite warm dry summer; gd quality, less quantity.
2020 Classic, 19 better balance, but elegant; better Barbera than Nebbiolo.
2019 Classic, more balanced than 18. Lower quantity but higher quality.
2018 Despite difficult spring, potentially classic Barolo, Barbaresco.
Earlier fine vintages: (drink or keep) 21 19 16 13 10 06 04 99; (mature) 12 11 09 08 07 05 03 01 00 98 97 96.

Tuscany

2025 Quality, quantity v.gd. Balanced.
2024 Challenging. Style as in 90s. Elegance more than power.
2023 Complicated but promising, crop reduction, but gd quality.
2022 Better than expected, high quality; gd structure, acidity for Sangiovese.
2021 V.gd (even if warm, dry) mainly for Sangiovese (better: fresher sites).
2020 V.gd, but complicated. Less power, alc than 19; elegant.
2019 Maybe one of best since 2000. Classic, balanced; gd quality, quantity.
2018 Reds gd: of steely personality, age-worthiness.
Earlier fine vintages: (drink or keep) 21 20 19 16 15 11 10 01 99; (mature) 09 08 07 06 04 00 97 95.

Abate Nero T-AA ★★★ Roberta Lunelli runs artisanal winery, devoted to sparkling Trento. Top: Domini, Domini Nero, RISERVA Cuvée dell'Abate. Waiting for new Brut Riserva Luciano Lunelli.

Abbona, Anna Maria Pie ★★★ Freshness, elegance and strong territorial identity for Anna Maria's wines. Top: ALTA LANGA, BAROLO San Pietro (also RISERVA), Dogliani SUPERIORE (Maioli, San Bernardo).

Abrigo, Orlando Pie ★★★ Giovanni A continues work to promote Treiso terroir. Some of most mineral, steely, refined BARBARESCOS. Top: Meruzzano (and RISERVA), Montersino, CN III (100% NEBBIOLO rosé).

Adanti Umb ★★★ A historic benchmark for Montefalco DOC. Top: MONTEFALCO SAGRANTINO (Il Domenico, Passito). Montefalco Rosso RISERVA, GRECHETTO v.gd.

Aglianico del Taburno Cam ★→★★★ DOCG Around Benevento. Generally cooler microclimate than TAURASI. Spicier notes (leather, tobacco), herbs, higher acidity than other AGLIANICOS. Best: Cantina del Taburno (Apis, Delius), La Rivolta (Taburno Aglianico, Terra di Rivolta). Also gd: Fontanavecchia (RISERVAS: Grave Mora, VIGNA Cataratte).

Aglianico del Vulture Bas ★→★★★ DOC(G) 15 **16** **18** 19 20 21' DOC after 1 yr, SUPERIORE after 3 yrs, RISERVA after 5. From slopes of extinct volcano Monte Vulture; soils with high content of clay-rich tuff. More floral (violet), dark fruits (plum), smoke, spice than other AGLIANICOS. Top: Elena Fucci. Then try Basilisco, Cantina di Venosa, Cantine del Notaio, Donato d'Angelo, Grifalco, Mastrodomenico (Likos), Paternoster. Also gd: Mustocarmelitano, Terre degli Svevi.

Alba Pie Truffles, hazelnuts and PIE's, if not Italy's, most prestigious wines: Alba, BARBARESCO, BARBERA D'ALBA, BAROLO, DOLCETTO d'Alba, NEBBIOLO D'ALBA.

Alessandri, Massimo Lig ★★★ One of best with Pigato grape. Top: Pigato Vigne Veggie (35-yr-old vines), Viorus (VIOGNIER/ROUSSANNE). Also v.gd: Granaccia, Ligustico (SYRAH/Granaccia, aka GARNACHA), Pigato, Puro (ROUSSANNE) and VERMENTINO.

Alessandria, Fratelli Pie ★★★ Since 1870 top BAROLO producer in VERDUNO. Best crus: Monvigliero, Gramolere, San Lorenzo. Barolo di Verduno and Verduno Pelaverga Speziale v.gd.

Almondo, Giovanni Pie ★★★★ Top ROERO estate. Best: Roero ARNEIS Bricco delle Ciliegie, Rive del Bricco, Roero Bric Valdiana (r). Outstanding FREISA.

Alta Langa Pie ★★★ DOCG The 1st METODO CLASSICO made in Italy, since mid-C19 in "underground cathedrals". Vintage only, and simply CHARD, PINOT N. Best: COCCHI-BAVA, Contratto (For England Blanc de Noirs, Millesimato), ETTORE GERMANO. Then try BANFI, Bera, Borgo Maragliano, Brandini (Blanc de Blancs), Cascina Cerutti, Colombo (Blanc de Blancs, Rosé), Del Tetto (PN+CH, RISERVAS), Enrico Serafino (Zero Pas Dosé, M+M 18 Perpetuelle Sbagliato, Zero 140), Fontanafredda VIGNA Gatinera (120, 108 and 84 Mesi) and Blanc des Blancs, Gancia (120 Mesi, 60 Mesi), Il Falchetto, MARCALBERTO, Marco Capra, Mirafiore (Blanc de Noirs), Monsignore, Paolo Berruti (now Echi di Vigna), PODERI COLLA, RIZZI, ROBERTO GARBARINO, San Biagio.

Alto Adige (Sudtirol) T-AA DOC Mountainous region with Bolzano its chief city (Austrian until 1919); arguably best Italian whites today but also underrated reds. Germanic vines dominate. GEWURZ, KERNER, SYLVANER, but PINOT GR too. Probably world's best PINOT BIANCO. PINOT N often overoaked; ***Lagrein*** in gd yrs.

Alto Piemonte Pie Cradle of PIE quality in C19 (40,000 ha). Acidic soil, exposure, climate and altitude diversity, ideal for many different NEBBIOLO expressions (here called Spanna). Main DOC(G): BOCA, BRAMATERRA, Colline Novaresi, Coste della Sesia, Fara, GATTINARA, Ghemme (Antichi Vigneti di Cantalupo, Ioppa, Rovellotti), LESSONA, Sizzano, Valli Ossolane. Many outstanding wines. Actually, rarely 100% Nebbiolo: small additions of Croatina, Uva Rara, Vespolina common.

ITALY

Ama, Castello di Tus ★★★★ Among 1st to produce single-vyd CHIANTI CLASSICO. Top: Gran Selezione VIGNETO Bellavista 22 21; La Casuccia 22 21. Also v.gd: RISERVA Montebuoni, San Lorenzo. MERLOT L'Apparita 21 20, one of Italy's three best.

Amarone della Valpolicella Ven ★★→★★★★ DOCG 12' 15' 16' 18 19' 20 21' (22) CLASSICO area (from historic zone), Val d'Illasi and Valpantena (from extended zone) can make unique world-class reds from raisined grapes. Alas, many less than what they should be, despite hype. Choose carefully. (*See* VALPOLICELLA, and box p.157.)

Ambra, D' Cam ★★★ On Ischia; fosters rare local native grapes. Best: single-vyd Frassitelli, new Pietra Martone (w, 100% Biancolella). Also v.gd: (w) Forastera, Ischia Bianco; (r) La VIGNA dei Mille Anni (blend).

Antinori, Marchesi L&P Tus ★★→★★★★ Top CHIANTI CLASSICO (***Badia a Passignano***, TENUTE); two excellent SUPER TUSCANS (TIGNANELLO, SOLAIA) and Prunotto (PIE BAROLOS); gd FVG (JERMANN), La Braccesca, MONTALCINO (Pian delle Vigne).

Argiano, Tenuta di Tus ★★★→★★★★ Since 1580. High-quality BRUNELLOS (RISERVA, VIGNA del Suolo 21 20); trad-style Brunello; single-vyd, modern Riserva. Also v.gd: Bx blend Argiano 21.

Argiolas Sar ★★★ Top producer, native island grapes. Outstanding crus: Iselis (MONICA, Nasco), ***Turriga*** ★★★★, ***Vermentino*** di SARDEGNA (Cerdeña) and top Antonio 100 (CANNONAU PASSITO). Bovale Korem, Cannonau RISERVA Senes, CARIGNANO del Sulcis (Is Solinas), VERMENTINO (Is Argiolas).

Arnaldo Rivera Pie ★★★ From 2013, top-quality range of Terre del BAROLO co-op. Small parcels (<0.5 ha) in prestigious Barolo crus. Best: Barolo Bussia, Monvigliero, Rocche dell'Annunziata, Vignarionda and Cannubi.

Attimis Maniago, Conte d' FVG ★★★ One of best trad estates; standout FRIULANO, MALVASIA, RIBOLLA, Pignolo, SCHIOPPETTINO; Tazzelenghe knockout.

Avignonesi Tus ★★★ Large bio estate. ***Italy's best Vin Santo***. Top: VINO NOBILE single-vyd Grandi Annate, Poggetto di Sopra. Also gd MERLOT Desiderio.

Azelia Pie ★★★ Distinctive, elegant BAROLOS from Scavino family. Some of best

Top Barbaresco by MGA

BARBARESCO has four main communes, four distinct styles: **Barbaresco** most complete, balanced. Growers incl Asili (BRUNO GIACOSA, CA' DEL BAIO, CERETTO, PRODUTTORI DEL BARBARESCO), Martinenga (MARCHESI DI GRÉSY), Montefico (Produttori del B, ROAGNA), Montestefano (Giordano Luigi, Produttori del B, Rivella Serafino), Ovello (CANTINA del Pino, ROCCA ALBINO), Pajè (Roagna); Pora (Ca' del Baio, MUSSO, Produttori del B), Rabaja (BRUNO GIACOSA, BRUNO ROCCA, CASTELLO DI VERDUNO, GIUSEPPE CORTESE, Produttori del B), Rio Sordo (Cascina Bruciata, Cascina delle Rose, MUSSO, Produttori del B), Roccalini (Cascina Roccalini), Roncaglie (PODERI COLLA). **Neive** most powerful, fleshiest. Albesani (Cantina del Pino, CASTELLO DI NEIVE, MASSOLINO), Basarin (MARCO E VITTORIO ADRIANO, Giacosa Fratelli, Negro Angelo, PAITIN, SOTTIMANO), Bordini (La Spinetta), Currà (Bruno Rocca, Sottimano), Gallina (Castello di Neive, Ceretto, La Spinetta, Lequio Ugo, ODDERO), Serraboella (Cigliuti, PAITIN). **San Rocco Seno d'Elvio** readiest to drink, soft. Rocche Massalupo (Lano, TENUTA Barac), Sanadaive (Marco e Vittorio Adriano). **Treiso** freshest, most refined. Bernardot (Ceretto), Bricco di Treiso (PIO CESARE), Marcarini (Ca' del Baio), Montersino (ORLANDO ABRIGO, Rocca Albino), Nervo (RIZZI), Pajoré (Rizzi, Sottimano), Rombone (Fiorenzo Nada, Luigi Oddero).

crus. Top: Bricco Fiasco, Cerretta, Margheria, RISERVA Bricco Voghera, San Rocco. Also v.gd: BARBERA D'ALBA, LANGHE NEBBIOLO.

Azienda agricola / agraria Estate (large or small) making wine from its own grapes.

Badia a Coltibuono Tus ★★★ One of top CHIANTI CLASSICO producers; organic. Buy every wine, great terroirs spell non-stop success (new Cetamura, Chill). Also v.gd: Montebello (blend of nine historic CHIANTI grapes), RISERVA Cultus, SANGIOVETO.

Banfi (Castello or Villa) Tus ★★→★★★ Giant of MONTALCINO. Top: limited-production POGGIO all'Oro, great BRUNELLO. Also v.gd: ALTA LANGA (Aurora 100 Mesi, new Blanc de Blancs), Moscadello.

Barale, Fratelli Pie ★★★ Historic BAROLO winery, est 1870. Classic, among best. Top crus: Bussia (also RISERVA), Cannubi, di Barolo, Castellero. Also v.gd: BARBARESCO Serraboella.

Barbaresco Pie ★★→★★★★ DOCG 13 14 15 16' 18 19 20' 21' Often better than BAROLO, Barbaresco's lesser reputation is undeserved. When spot-on, the gracefulness, age-worthiness and perfumed intensity are like those of no other wine in Italy – the world, really. Min 26 mths' ageing, 9 mths in wood; at 4 yrs becomes RISERVA. Two main types of soil: Serravalian (alternation of sandy levels and grey silty marls), on average, elegant and v. perfumed wines, not too fleshy; Tortonian (blue-grey marls with more or less sand), v. structured wines (mainly in Barbaresco, Neive). (For top crus/producers, *see* box, opposite.)

Barbera d'Alba Pie DOC Unique, luscious, sultry Barbera, quite different from d'Asti's nervier, higher-acid version. AZELIA, BREZZA, BROVIA, GB BURLOTTO, CAVALLOTTO, CLERICO DOMENICO, CORREGGIA, CONTERNO FANTINO (Vignota), Cortese, Fratelli Revello, ETTORE GERMANO (della Madre), GD VAJRA, MASSOLINO, Paolo Conterno, PODERI ALDO CONTERNO (Conca Tre Pile), PODERI COLLA, Renato Corino, ROAGNA, SOTTIMANO, TREDIBERRI, VIETTI (Scarrone VIGNA Vecchia) make benchmarks. COGNO's Pre-Phylloxera is *hors classe*.

Barbera d'Asti Pie Huge DOCG, encompassing v. different soils (from sandy to marly) and climatic characteristics. Wines vary, but usually high acidity and fruity notes. Superiore: higher quality (but often overoaked). (*See also* NIZZA.) Best: BRAIDA, BAVA, L'Armangia, MARCHESI DI GRÉSY, Marchesi Incisa della Rocchetta, SCARPA (La Bogliona), TENUTA Olim Bauda (Le Rocchette). Also v.gd: Bersano, Cascina Castlet, Crivelli, Gianni Doglia, Marchesi Alfieri (Alfiera), ODDERO, Spertino, Tenuta Garetto, ***Vietti*** (La Crena), Vinchio Vaglio (Vigne Vecchie).

Barolo Pie DOCG 10' 11 12 13' 15 16' 17 19' 20 21' "King of wines and wine of kings", 100% NEBBIOLO. 2000-ha zone. Must age 38 mths before release (5 yrs for RISERVA), of which 18 mths in wood. Best are age-worthy, able to join power and elegance, with alluring floral scent and sour red-cherry flavour. Now most is single vyd, but trad a blend of vyds from different communes. The concept of "cru" is replaced (in Barolo and BARBARESCO at least) by subzones known officially as MGAs (menzioni geografiche aggiuntive). Currently Barolo has 11 village mentions and 170(!) additional geographical mentions. Often underrated: Village MGA ("Barolo del Comune di...") best way to understand different Barolo terroirs. Best: "di Barolo" (FRATELLI BARALE, ROAGNA, SCARZELLO), "di Castiglione" (BOROLI, Monchiero Fratelli, Rocche Viberti), "di Diano d'Alba" (Bricco Maiolica), "di Grinzane" (Canonica), "di La Morra" (CIABOT BERTON, GIANNI GAGLIARDO, Marcarini TREDIBERRI), "di Monforte" (Diego Conterno, Fortemasso, Ruggeri Corsini), "di Novello" (Le Strette), "di Serralunga" (Boasso, ETTORE GERMANO, GIOVANNI ROSSO, Luigi Vico, MAURO VEGLIO, Paolo Manzone, RIVETTO), "di VERDUNO" (DIEGO MORRA, FRATELLI ALESSANDRIA). Three main types of soil: Messinian (chalk-sulphur formation), readier to drink, more open Barolo, w slope of La Morra; Serravalian (greyish yellow/red

ITALY

Top Barolos by MGA

Here are a few top crus and their best producers: **Bricco Boschis** (Castiglione Falletto) CAVALLOTTO (RISERVA VIGNA San Giuseppe). **Bricco delle Viole** (BAROLO) GD VAJRA, MARENGO, VIBERTI. **Bricco Rocche** (Castiglione Falletto) CERETTO. **Briccolina** (Serralunga) RIVETTO. **Brunate** (La Morra, Barolo) Ceretto, FRANCESCO RINALDI, GIUSEPPE RINALDI, MARENGO, ODDERO, VIETTI. **Bussia** (Monforte) ALDO CONTERNO (Gran Bussia e Romirasco), ARNALDO RIVERA, Ceretto, EINAUDI, GIACOMO FENOCCHIO (also Riserva 90 Dì), Oddero (Vigna Mondoca), PODERI COLLA (Dardi Le Rose). **Cannubi** (Barolo) BREZZA, Giacomo Fenocchio, LUCIANO SANDRONE, PIRA E FIGLI – CHIARA BOSCHIS, Einaudi, Virna. **Cerequio** (La Morra, Barolo) BOROLI, GAJA, Vietti. **Falletto** (Serralunga) BRUNO GIACOSA (Riserva Vigna Le Rocche). **Francia** (Serralunga) GIACOMO CONTERNO (Cascina Francia and Monfortino). **Ginestra** (Monforte) CONTERNO FANTINO (Sorì Ginestra and Vigna del Gr), DOMENICO CLERICO (Ciabot Mentin). **Lazzarito** (Serralunga) ETTORE Germano (Riserva), GIANNI GAGLIARDO, VIETTI. **Monprivato** (Castiglione Falletto) GIUSEPPE MASCARELLO (Mauro). **Monvigliero** (VERDUNO) Arnaldo Rivera, CASTELLO DI VERDUNO, DIEGO MORRA, EINAUDI, FRATELLI ALESSANDRIA, GB BURLOTTO, PAOLO SCAVINO, Viberti. **Mosconi** (Monforte) Conterno Fantino, Domenico Clerico, Pira e Figli – Chiara Boschis, PIO CESARE. **Ornato** (Serralunga) Palladino, Pio Cesare. **Ravera** (Novello) ELVIO COGNO (Bricco Pernice), GD VAJRA, VIETTI. **Rocche dell'Annunziata** (La Morra) Arnaldo Rivera, Paolo Scavino (Riserva), Ratti, Rocche Costamagna, FRANCESCO RINALDI, TREDIBERRI. **Rocche di Castiglione** (Castiglione Falletto) BROVIA, Oddero, ROAGNA, Vietti. **Sarmassa** (Barolo) Bergadano, Brezza, Scarzello. **Vigna Rionda** (Serralunga) Ettore Germano, GIOVANNI ROSSO, Figli Luigi Oddero, MASSOLINO VR, Oddero. **Villero** (Castiglione Falletto) Boroli, BROVIA, GIACOMO FENOCCHIO, Giuseppe Mascarello. And the Barolo of BARTOLO MASCARELLO blends together Cannubi San Lorenzo, Ruè and Rocche dell'Annunziata. A sommelier's delight.

looser calcareous marl soil and sands), Castiglione Falletto (bold), Monforte (structure), Serralunga (power); Tortonian (blue-grey compact marl soil and calcareous sands, younger), Barolo (grace), La Morra (fragrance). Newcomers to follow: La Contrada di Sorano. (For top crus and producers, *see* box, above.)

Barone Pizzini Lom ★★★ A top FRANCIACORTA estate; bio. Best: Animante (also LA, Long Ageing), Brut Naturae 19 21, RISERVA Bagnadore Dosaggio Zero 15 16'.

Bartoli, Marco De Si One of best estates in all Italy. Marco spent his life promoting "real" MARSALA, his must be tried. Top: Vecchio Samperi. Also v.gd: Grappoli del GRILLO, ZIBIBBO (Pietranera), Zibibbo di PANTELLERIA ***Bukkuram*** (sw).

Benanti Si ★★★★ This family turned world on to ETNA Bianco SUPERIORE. ***Pietramarina*** 19' 20' 21 one of Italy's best whites, Contrada Rinazzo 21' 23', new Contrada Monte Serra. Top: (r) Etna RISERVA (Rovittello, Serra della Contessa) 18' 19' 20, Selezione Contrade (Calderara Sottana, Cavaliere, Dafara Galluzzo, Monte Serra, Rinazzo) 22 23'. Also v.gd: Lamorèmio and Noblesse 48 Mesi (sp).

Berlucchi, Guido Lom ★★★ Created FRANCIACORTA with Franco Ziliani in 1961, hence names of wines. Top: 61 Nature, 61 Nature Blanc de Blancs, 61 NV Extra Brut, Palazzo Lana Extreme, new RISERVA Franco Ziliani.

Bertinga Tus ★★★ Estate in Gaiole, CHIANTI. Best: Volta (MERLOT) 16 19'. Also v.gd: Bertinga (SANGIOVESE/Merlot) 18'. Original.

Biondi-Santi Tus ★★★★ Invented BRUNELLO. High quality, high in acid, tannin requiring decades to develop fully.

Bio Vio Lig ★★★ Top Ponente estate, superstar winery; Aimone and daughter Caterina. Outstanding Pigato Bon in da Bon 23 24; v.gd Marené, Pigato Grand-Père 23, 4C ROSATO.

Bisol Ven ★★★ Owned by FERRARI's Lunelli family; quality leader in PROSECCO. Top: CARTIZZE, Rive di Campea, Rive di Guia. Also v.gd: Molera, Relio.

Boca Pie 16' 18 19 DOC *See* ALTO PIEMONTE. Potentially among greatest reds resurfaced thanks to Christoph Kunzli (LE PIANE). Blend of NEBBIOLO (70–90%), incl up to 30% Uva Rara and/or Vespolina. Volcanic quartz porphyry soils. Needs long ageing. Best: ***Le Piane***. Carlone Davide, Castello Conti gd.

Bolgheri Tus DOC Mid-Maremma, on w coast, cradle of many expensive SUPER TUSCANS, mainly based on French varieties 16' 19' 20 21'. Big name, excellent quality. Top: MASSETO (100% MERLOT), ORNELLAIA (FRESCOBALDI), San Guido (SASSICAIA, original Super Tuscan). Also v.gd: Campo alla Sughera, Fabio Motta (Le Gonnare r/w), GAJA (Ca' Marcanda), GRATTAMACCO, LE MACCHIOLE, Michele Satta (Marianova, Piastraia).

Borgo del Tiglio FVG ★★★★ Nicola and son Mattia, top COLLIO estate. Top: Black Label collection 16' 19' 21, CHARD, Collio FRIULANO RONCO della Chiesa, MALVASIA Selezione, Rosso della Centa, Studio di Bianco esp impressive.

Borgogno, Virna Pie ★★★ Family estate run by Virna B and sister Ivana. Great-value BAROLO from famous crus: Cannubi, Sarmassa 16' 19 21'. Also v.gd: BARBERA D'ALBA, BARBARESCO Montersino, Barolo Noi.

Boroli Pie ★★★ Achille now runs this winery, devoted to BAROLO. Best: Brunella (monopole), Cerequio, Villero and new Barolo di Castiglione.

Bosco, Tenute Si ★★★ Small ETNA estate owned by Sofia B, high quality. Best: Vico Prephylloxera (r, new w). Also v.gd: Piano dei Daini (r/w/rosé).

Botte Big barrel, anything from 6–250 hl, usually 20–50, trad Slavonian but increasingly of French oak. To traditionalists, ideal vessel for ageing wines without adding too much oak smell/taste.

Braida Pie ★★★ If BARBERA D'ASTI is known today, it's thanks to Bologna family, world ambassadors for it. Top: Ai Suma, Bricco della Bigotta 16' 19 21, Bricco dell'Uccellone. Also v.gd: Montebruna. GRIGNOLINO d'Asti Limonte one of best (Limonte GB bigger, esp age-worthy). New TIMORASSO.

Bramaterra Pie 16' 19' 20 21 DOC Volcanic porphyry, marine deposits: most variegated in terms of soils. Wines tend to be lighter, less massive than other ALTO PIEMONTE DOC. Top: Antoniotti Odilio, PROPRIETÀ SPERINO.

Brezza Pie ★★★→★★★★ Organic. Certainty for those who love trad BAROLOS. Great value, from famous crus Cannubi 19, Castellero, Sarmassa (RISERVA VIGNA Bricco 19' 21'); v.gd BARBERA, LANGHE NEBBIOLO; outstanding FREISA.

Brolio, Castello di Tus ★★★ Since 1141 run by Ricasoli family. Historic estate of CHIANTI CLASSICO. Outstanding Gran Selezione 18' 19' 21 (Castello di Brolio, Ceniprimo, Colledilà, Roncicone).

Brovia Pie ★★★→★★★★ Since 1863, classic BAROLOS in Castiglione Falletto. Organic. Top: Ca' Mia 20 21', Garblèt Sue, Rocche 20 21', Villero. Also v.gd: DOLCETTO d'ALBA Solatio. New sparkling Antersè (BARBERA/NEBBIOLO/FREISA).

Bruna Lig ★★★ An est Pigato name. Best: Russeghine, U Baccan. Also v.gd: Majè.

Brunello di Montalcino Tus 07 10' 12 **13** 15' 16' 19' 20 21' DOCG World-famous, but quality all over the shop. When gd, memorable and ageless, archetypal SANGIOVESE. Problems derive mostly from greedily enlarged production area (a ridiculous 2000 ha+), much less than ideal for fickle Sangiovese and world-class wines. Recent push to turn wine into a blend has been successfully stopped (thus far, at least). Generally speaking, MONTALCINO's soils vary from the limestone-rich Galestro of the n sector (wines are sleeker, more floral and mineral, generally higher acidity), to the loamier, siltier sandy clays

Best of Brunello

Any of the below provide satisfying BRUNELLO DI MONTALCINO; the top get a ★: ★ Altesino, ★ Baricci, ★ BIONDI-SANTI, Campogiovanni, ★ Canalicchio di Sopra, Canalicchio di Sotto, Caparzo, ★ CAPRILI, Casanova di Neri, ★ CASE BASSE, Castelgiocondo, ★ CASTELLO DI Argiano, ★ CASTELLO ROMITORIO, CASTIGLION DEL BOSCO, Ciacci Piccolomini, ★ COL D'ORCIA, ★ Collemattoni, Cortonesi, ★ Costanti, ★ Cupano, Donatella Cinelli, ★ Franco Pacenti, ★ FULIGNI, ★ GIANNI BRUNELLI, Giodo, Giuseppe Gorelli, Il Colle, ★ IL MARRONETO, Il Paradiso di Manfredi, La Gerla, LE CHIUSE, ★ Le Potazzine, ★ Le Ragnaie, LE RIPI, Lisini, ★ MASTROJANNI, ★ PIAN DELL'ORINO, Pieve di Santa Restituta, POGGIO ANTICO, ★ POGGIO DI SOTTO, San Filippo, ★ Salvioni, SESTA DI SOPRA, Silvio Nardi, Siro Pacenti, ★ Stella di Campalto, TALENTI, ★ TENUTA IL POGGIONE, TENUTA di Sesta, Uccelliera, Val di Suga.

of the s (wines broader, more powerful). (For top producers, *see* box, above.)

Bucci Mar ★★★★ Villa Bucci RISERVA one of Italy's ten best whites 16' **17 18** 21' 22'. All wines quasi-Burgundian, v. elegant, esp complex VERDICCHIOS. All age splendidly; v.gd red Pongelli. Outstanding Vintage Collection. Now owned by Veronesi family, with La Giuva (Ven), Podere Guardia Grande (SAR), Tenimenti Leone (Lat).

Burlotto, Commendatore GB Pie ★★★★ Fabio Alessandria maintains his ancestor Commander GB Burlotto's (among 1st to make/bottle BAROLO, 1880) high quality and focus. Top: Barolo Monvigliero and Cannubi 19' 21', FREISA 21' 23. Acclivi, Castelletto (Barolos), VERDUNO Pelaverga also outstanding.

Bussola, Tommaso Ven ★★★★ Self-taught maker of some of the great AMARONES, RECIOTOS, RIPASSOS of our time. The great Bepi QUINTARELLI steered him; he steers his two sons. Top TB selection 10' 11 12' 13.

Ca' del Baio Pie ★★★ Family estate; best-value producer in BARBARESCO. Outstanding Asili (RISERVA too), Vallegrande Vecchie Viti 19' 20 21. Also v.gd: Autinbej, LANGHE RIES, Pora, Vallegrande.

Ca' del Bosco Lom ★★★★ Arguably Italy's best METODO CLASSICO fizz, famous FRANCIACORTA estate owned by Zanella family and Santa Margherita Group. Innovative, avant-garde; immersive sensory room. Outstanding, unforgettable Dosage Zéro Annamaria Clementi Riserva (rosé too) 13' 14 15 16' and new Annamaria Clementi RS 1980 (aged 40 yrs+). Great Cuvée Prestige (Edizione RS). Vintage Collection 17' 18 (Dosage Zéro, Dosage Zéro N) practically as gd. Excellent CHARD, Bx-style red Maurizio Zanella, PINOT N.

Cadinu, Francesco Sar ★★★ Micro size, mega quality. Top: CANNONAU di SARDEGNA (Ghirada Elisi, Ghirada Fittiloghe). Also v.gd: Mattìo (w, rare Granatza).

Caiarossa Tus ★★★ Dutch-owned (Ch Giscours; *see* Bordeaux) estate, n of BOLGHERI. Excellent Caiarossa Rosso 20' 21' 22, plus reds Aria 22, Pergolaia 21.

Ca' La Bionda Ven ★★★ Some of finest VALPOLICELLA. Top: AMARONE, CORVINA.

Calcagno Si ★★★→★★★★ Lilliputian size and Brobdingnagian quality from ETNA family estate. Outstanding mineral NERELLO MASCALESE. Top reds: Arcurìa, Calderara, Feudo di Mezzo. Also v.gd: EB SUPERIORE Primazappa (w), Romice delle Sciare (rosé).

Calì, Paolo Si ★★★ Passionate Paolo C makes numerous wines typical of Vittoria's sandy terroir. Top: CERASUOLO DI VITTORIA new single-vyd Forfice, Niscia, Pruvuletta, Manene **16'** 17 18' 21 22'. Also v.gd: Blues (w GRILLO), Frappato, NERO D'AVOLA (r), Mood (rosé/sp).

Caluso / Erbaluce di Caluso Pie ★★→★★★ DOCG Morainic soils giving v. interesting and mineral wines. Can be still, sparkling or sweet (Caluso PASSITO).

Top: FERRANDO (Cariola), Giacometto, TAPPERO MERLO (Kin, sp). Also v.gd: Cieck (Misobolo), Favaro (Le Chiusure), Gnavi (VIGNA Crava, sp Turbante), LUCA LEGGERO (Rend Nen, Turciaura), Orsolani, San Martin (Memento), Scelte di Vite (also sp 36 mths), SORPASSO. Outside DOCG: MONTE MALETTO, Sopravvento (Changes, Rebel Rebel).

Campania Some of Italy's greatest and most age-worthy whites, terroir-driven, full of character. Reds unfortunately less consistent: overripe grapes, too much oak, with some remarkable exceptions. Few international varieties cloud native grapes panorama. FIANO DI AVELLINO may well be Italy's best white zone, TAURASI makes better and better reds. Try BENITO FERRARA, Caggiano, Cantine Astroni, CANTINE Lonardo, CANTINE MAZZELLA, ***Colli di Lapio***, Contrada Salandra, D'AMBRA, De Angelis, Di Prisco, FATTORIA LA RIVOLTA, FEUDI DI SAN GREGORIO, Galardi, Guastaferro, I FAVATI, Il Cancelliere, La Sibilla, Luigi Maffini, ***Marisa Cuomo***, MASTROBERARDINO, Molettieri, Perillo, Pierlingeri, Pietracupa, QUINTODECIMO, Reale, Rocca del Principe, Sarno 1860, SORRENTINO, Terredora, TRAERTE. MONTEVETRANO: world-class, international, mostly CAB SAUV.

Canalicchio di Sopra Tus ★★★★ Top-ten BRUNELLO estate. Francesco Ripaccioli keen observer of terroir, MONTALCINO typicity. Top: Brunello RISERVA 16' 19', single-vyd La Casaccia 19' 20, Montosoli 20' 21. Also v.gd: Brunello, ROSSO DI MONTALCINO.

Cantina A cellar, winery or even a wine bar.

Capezzana, Tenuta di Tus ★★★ Organic production from noble Bonacossi family that made Carmignano's reputation. Excellent Carmignano (Trefiano, Villa di Capezzana), UCB (SANGIOVESE), Ghiaie della Furba (Bx blend). Exceptional VIN SANTO, one of Italy's five best.

Caprai Umb ★★★→★★★★ MONTEFALCO leader thanks to Marco C. Top: Montefalco 25 Anni 19 20'. Also v.gd: Collepiano (less oak), GRECHETTO Grecante, Montefalco Rosso RISERVA 21', Valdimaggio.

Caprili Tus ★★★ Family-run; based on Alfo Bartolommei's experience. Top BRUNELLO: classic 19 20', RISERVA Adalberto 16'. Also v.gd: Moscadello.

Carema Pie ★★★ DOC **12' 14 16** 18' 19' 20' 21' (22) (23) Only 22 ha, n of Turin. Steep terraces, morainic agglomerate soils for light, mineral, intense, outstanding NEBBIOLO. Top: FERRANDO, MONTE MALETTO, SORPASSO. Also v.gd: Milanesio, Murajè, Produttori Nebbiolo di Carema (esp RISERVA), Sopravvento.

Carpineti, Marco Lat ★★★ Phenomenal bio whites from little-known Bellone, GRECOS Giallo/Moro varieties. Benchmark Moro; Ludum (top sticky).

Cartizze Ven ★★★→★★★★ DOCG 16' **18'** 19' 21 At 107 ha, this PROSECCO super-cru is 2nd-most expensive vyd land in Italy, after BAROLO; v. steep hills in heart of Valdobbiadene showcase just how great Prosecco DOCG can be. Usually on sweet side due to fully ripe grapes. Best: Adami, Andreola, BISOL, Bortolomiol, Col Vetoraz, Le Colture, NINO FRANCO, Ruggeri, Silvano Follador.

Case Basse Tus ★★★★ Gianfranco Soldera's children keep up similar lofty level of iconic BRUNELLO. Long-oak-aged. Rare, precious.

Castel de Paolis Lat ★★→★★★ One of leading quality estates in Lat. Best: Frascati SUPERIORE, Donna Adriana (VIOGNIER/MALVASIA del Lazio).

Castel Juval, Unterortl T-AA ★★★ Distinctive, crystalline. Best: WEISSBURGUNDER old-vine Himmelsleiter 23 24. Also v.gd: RIES (Windbichel) 21 22' 23', MÜLLER-T, PINOT N RISERVA, new SAUV BL.

Castell' in Villa Tus ★★★ CHIANTI CLASSICO estate in extreme sw of zone. Wines of class, trad, excellence; v. age-worthy. Top: RISERVA.

Castello Romitorio Tus ★★★→★★★★ Filippo Chia makes some of BRUNELLO's sleekest, most perfumed wines. Top: single-vyd Filo di Seta (also RISERVA) 19' 21, classic Brunello. Also v.gd: Metafisica (w blend), Romitoro 20 21' (r), ROSSO DI MONTALCINO.

Castiglion del Bosco Tus ★★★ One of best organic BRUNELLO. Top: Campo del Drago 20' 21', RISERVA Millecento 19'. Cecilia Leoneschi made possibly 1st single-vyd ROSSO DI MONTALCINO (Deimassi, Gaugggiole, L'America).

Caudrina Pie ★★★→★★★★ Romano Dogliotti makes one of best MOSCATO D'ASTI. Top: Asti La Selvatica, La Galeisa. Also gd: La Caudrina, NIZZA Montevenere.

Cavallotto Pie ★★★★ Organic. Solid reference for trad BAROLO, in Castiglione Falletto. Outstanding RISERVA VIGNA San Giuseppe, Riserva Vignolo. Also v.gd: BARBERA D'ALBA SUPERIORE, FREISA, LANGHE NEBBIOLO. Waiting for new cru of Barolo.

Cave Mont Blanc VdA ★★★ Quality co-op at foot of Mont Blanc, with ungrafted indigenous 60–100-yr-old Prié Bl vines. Organic. Outstanding sparkling. Top: Blanc de Morgex et de la Salle Rayon and cru La Piagne (oaked), sparkling (Blanc du Blanc, Cuvée des Guides, Cuvée du Prince, XT).

Cenatiempo Cam ★★★ Pasquale C, one of most talented on ISCHIA. Volcanic soils, sea breezes, charming wines. Best: (w) Biancolella Kalimera, Ischia Bianco Lefkòs; (r) Mavros (Piedirosso).

Cerasuolo d'Abruzzo Ab ★ DOC DYA ROSATO version of MONTEPULCIANO D'AB. Can be brilliant. Best (by far): TIBERIO, VALENTINI. Also v.gd: Masciarelli – Villa Gemma, Terraviva, Torre dei Beati, Valle Reale. Also gd: Barone Cornacchia, Cataldi Madonna, De Fermo, I Fauri, Illuminati, La Valentina, Praesidiumo.

Cerasuolo di Vittoria Si ★★→★★★ 14 16 18' 19' 20 21' Blend of Frappato/NERO D'AVOLA. Only SI DOCG, in se, around city of Vittoria, best terroir for Frappato. Top: GULFI, PAOLO CALÌ. Also v.gd: COS, OCCHIPINTI ARIANNA, PLANETA, Valle dell'Acate.

Ceretto Pie ★★★★ Leading organic/bio producer: (BARBARESCO) Asili 19' 21' 22 23', Bernadot 21' 22, Gallina 22' 23; (BAROLO) Bricco Rocche 19' 20' 21', Brunate 19' 21', Bussia 19' 20 21', Cannubi San Lorenzo, Prapò and new Rocche di Castiglione 19' 21'. Plus LANGHE Bianco Blange (ARNEIS). Classic, elegant.

Cerruti, Ezio Pie ★★★ Small estate in gd area for MOSCATO. Best: sweet Sol, naturally dried Moscato. Also v.gd: dry Fol.

Cesanese (Comune and di Affile) Lat ★→★★★ Two grapes: Comune (more common in Olevano Romano area, s of Lat), d'Affile (in Affile and Piglio). Three wines: C del Piglio, try Casale della Ioria (Torre del Piano); C di Affile, try Colline di Affile (Le Cese); Olevano Romano C, try DAMIANO CIOLLI. Outstanding Colacicchi (Cesanese Tufano IGT).

Chianti Tus ★→★★★ DOCG When gd, delightfully delicious, easy-going and food-friendly fresh red. Modern-day production zone covers most of TUS; v. big differences in topography, climate and soils among various Chianti denominations. RÙFINA is only terroir of quality comparable to historic Chianti production zone (now called CHIANTI CLASSICO).

Chianti Classico Tus ★★→★★★ DOCG 15 16' 18' 19 20' 21' No wine in Italy has improved more over past 20 yrs+, now often 100% SANGIOVESE. More than 500

Who makes really good Chianti Classico?

CHIANTI CLASSICO is a large zone with hundreds of producers, so picking the best is tricky. Top get a ★: ★ CASTELLO DI AMA, ★ BADIA A COLTIBUONO, ★ BROLIO, ★ CASTELL' IN VILLA, ★ CASTELLO DI MONSANTO, ★ Castello di Querceto, ★ CASTELLO DI VOLPAIA, ★ FELSINA, ★ FONTODI, ★ I Fabbri, ★ Ipsus, ★ ISOLE E OLENA, ★ Le Cinciole, ★ Mazzei, ★ QUERCIABELLA, ★ RIECINE, ★ Rocca di Montegrossi, ★ SAN GIUSTO A RENTENNANO, Castello di Radda, Castello la Leccia, Cinciano, Palagio di Panzano, Tenuta di Perano (FRESCOBALDI), Vecchie Terre di Montefili, ★ Villa Calcinaia.

producers means inconsistent quality, but best are among Italy's greatest. Made in historic (high, rocky) CHIANTI production zone between Florence and Siena in nine townships. Climate varies greatly from n to s sectors, three main soil types – Alberese (whitish marls), Galestro (clay schist) and macigno (mix of sands and compacted sands) – so potentially wines are v. different from each other. From 2019, new UGAs (unità geografiche aggiuntive) only for Gran Selezione (new top level, above RISERVA). (For top producers, *see* box, opposite.)

Chiuse, Le Tus ★★★ Simonetta BIONDI-SANTI (great-granddaughter of Ferruccio) runs small but great family estate: classic, BRUNELLO RISERVA, ROSSO DI MONTALCINO.

Ciabot Berton Pie ★★★ Marco Oberto and wife Federica; best value in La Morra. Top: BAROLO 1961, di La Morra; crus Roggeri, Rocchettevino have distinctive single-vyd characters, LANGHE NEBBIOLO, BARBERA D'ALBA.

Cinque Terre, CS Lig ★★→★★★ **16'** 18 19' 22 Quality co-op in beautiful area. Top: Cian Auti, Costa da Posa, Sciacchetrà (sw, one of Italy's best stickies).

Ciolli, Damiano Lat ★★★ One of most interesting in central Italy. Best: RISERVA Cirsium, 100% CESANESE DI AFFILE, 80-yr-old vines. Also v.gd: Botte 22 (Trebbiano Verde aka VERDICCHIO/Ottonese), Silene.

Cirò Cal ★→★★★ DOC 19' **20** 22 Brisk strong red from Cal's main grape, Gaglioppo, or light, fruity white from GRECO (DYA). Best: ***Librandi***, IPPOLITO 1845. Also v.gd: 'A Vita, Caparra & Siciliani, Cataldo Calabretta.

Classico Term for wines from a restricted, usually historic and superior-quality area within limits of a commercially expanded DOC. *See* CHIANTI CLASSICO, SOAVE, VALPOLICELLA, VERDICCHIO DEI CASTELLI DI JESI, numerous others.

Clerico, Domenico Pie ★★★→★★★★ Influential BAROLO innovator, modernist producer of Monforte d'ALBA: crus Bussia Briccotto (only 1000 bottles), Ginestra (Ciabot Mentin, Pajana), Mosconi (Percristina only in best yrs **10' 11'** 14' 15'). Also v.gd: Barolo Aeroplanservaj (from Baudana cru), LANGHE NEBBIOLO (Capisme-e).

Clivi, I FVG ★★★ Wealth of old vines (FRIULI COLLI ORIENTALI, COLLIO), up to 90 yrs. Pure, age-worthy, mineral whites – ranking with Italy's best. Top: FRIULANO, MALVASIA, also outstanding dry Verduzzo.

Cocchi-Bava Pie ★★★ Since 1891 producer of vermouth. Top Cocchi: ALTA LANGA (Pas Dosé, Toto Corde, new Espressione Bianc and Noir), Vermouth Storico di Torino and Extra Dry. Top: BARBERA D'ASTI Stradivario, BAROLO Scarrone, NIZZA Piano Alto, Ruchè, Serre di San Pietro (NEBBIOLO).

Cogno, Elvio Pie ★★★★ Top estate; super-classy, austere, elegant BAROLOS from Ravera cru. Best: Bricco Pernice, Ravera, RISERVA VIGNA Elena 16' 17 19' 20' (NEBBIOLO Rosé clone). Also v.gd: Anas-Cëtta (100% Nascetta), BARBERA D'ALBA Bricco Merli, Barolo Cascina Nuova.

Col d'Orcia Tus ★★★ Top-quality MONTALCINO estate (3rd-largest) owned by Francesco Marone Cinzano. Best: BRUNELLO Nastagio 13 16 19', Brunello RISERVA POGGIO al Vento 15 16'. Also v.gd: Brunello, Ghiaie Bianche (CHARD), Moscadello di Montalcino.

Colla, Poderi Pie ★★★★ Family-run, with experience of Beppe C. Classic, trad and age-worthy. Top: BARBARESCO Roncaglie, BAROLO Bussia, LANGHE Bricco del Drago, new RISERVA Beppe Colla and Bonmè (vermouth). Also v.gd: ALTA LANGA Pietro Colla, NEBBIOLO D'ALBA, PINOT NERO, RIES.

Colli = hills (singular: colle). **Colline** (collina) = smaller hills. *See also* COLLIO, POGGIO.

Colli di Lapio Cam ★★★ Clelia Romano's estate makes Italy's ***best Fiano***. Outstanding FIANO Clelia. Also v.gd: GRECO DI TUFO, TAURASI Andrea.

Colli di Luni Lig, Tus ★★→★★★ DOC nr Spezia **18 19' 20** 21 Albarola, VERMENTINO whites; SANGIOVESE-based reds, easy-drinking charm. Top: Giacomelli, LUNAE, OTTAVIANO LAMBRUSCHI, TERENZUOLA. Also v.gd: Il Monticello, La Baia del Sole, La Pietra del Focolare, Zangani.

Collio FVG ★★→★★★★ DOC 18' 19 **21'** Famous white denomination, unfortunately moved steadily to nonsensical Collio Bianco blend rather than highlight terroir differences of its communes, incl coolish San Floriano and Dolegna, warmer Capriva. Happily, Collio boasts glut of talented producers with new generations bringing new energy. Best: BORGO DEL TIGLIO, Damijan Podversic (top w: MALVASIA, RIBOLLA, Kaplja e Nekaj), Doro Princic, Gravner, I CLIVI, LIVIO FELLUGA, ***Schiopetto***. Also v.gd: Alessandro Pascolo, Attems, Ca' Ronesca, Castello di Spessa, Drius, Gradis'Ciutta, Isidoro Polencic, Primosic, Radikon, Ronc dai Luchis, RONCO dei Tassi, RUSSIZ SUPERIORE, Toros, Venica & Venica, VILLA RUSSIZ.

Colombera, La Pie ★★★ Elisa Semino, "queen" of TIMORASSO. Top: DERTHONA (Il Montino, Santacroce), Monleale (100% BARBERA).

Colombo, Gianluca Pie ★★★ A v. promising young winemaker. Top: BAROLO, VERDUNO. Also v.gd: Langhe NEBBIOLO, PINOT N.

Colterenzio, CS / Schreckbichl T-AA ★★★ Cornaiano-based main player among ALTO ADIGE co-ops. Top whites: CHARD Lafóa, SAUV BL, PINOT BL Berg 22' 23, LR **19** 20' **21**. Lafóa reds: CAB SAUV 22', PINOT N. Outstanding SAUV BL RISERVA Gran Lafóa 21 22'. Cru range v.gd.

Conegliano Valdobbiadene Ven ★★ DOCG DYA Name for top PROSECCO: may be used separately or together. Extremely steep hills; quality should be better. Top: Adami, BISOL, Bortolomiol, Col Vetoraz, Gemin, Marchiori, Masottina, NINO FRANCO, Ruggeri, Silvano Follador, Sorelle Bronca, Zucchetto. Also v.gd: Andreola, Biancavigna, Bosco del Merlo, Fratelli Bortolin, Le Colture.

Conterno, Aldo Pie ★★★★ Top estate of Monforte d'ALBA, 25 ha for only 80,000 bottles of highest quality. Granbussia 06' 10' **12'** **14** 15', iconic expression of BAROLO's greatness and one of best. Top: Barolos Cicala, Colonello, esp Romirasco; Bussiador CHARD. Also v.gd: BARBERA D'ALBA, LANGHE NEBBIOLO, Quartetto (r blend).

Conterno, Giacomo Pie ★★★★ 04' 08 10' 13 14' 15 19 Monfortino, one of best wines of Italy. Outstanding BARBERA, BAROLO. Owns Nervi in GATTINARA.

Conterno Fantino Pie ★★★→★★★★ Organic. One of top producers of excellent modern-style BAROLO crus at Monforte, aims to valorize each single different vyd of MGAs: Castelletto (VIGNA Pressenda), Ginestra (Vigna Sorì Ginestra, Vigna del Gris), Mosconi (Vigna Ped). Bastia CHARD (one of PIE's best), Ginestrino, iconic Monprà (NEBBIOLO/BARBERA).

Contini Sar ★★★ Benchmark VERNACCIA DI ORISTANO, oxidative-styled whites (like dry Sherry, *see* Spain). Antico Gregori one of Italy's best whites. Amazing Flor 22, RISERVA; gd I Giganti (r).

Summit of Etna

Some of Italy's most exciting wines come from this famous volcano. Vines grow up to 1000m (3281ft) on SI's e coast. *Contrada* is Si's way to express cru: differences in soil, altitude and age of lava flows. Of Etna's 133 *contrade*, the greatest number are in Castiglione di Sicilia (46), Randazzo (25) and Linguaglossa (10). Following producers make gd to great wine; the top get a ★: Alberelli di Giodo, ★ BENANTI, Calabretta, ★ CALCAGNO, Cottanera, Cusumano Alta Mora, DONNAFUGATA, ★ FRANK CORNELISSEN, ★ GIROLAMO RUSSO, Graci (Arcuria, Feudo di Mezzo), ★ GULFI, ★ I Custodi dell'Etna, ★ I VIGNERI, Palmento Costanzo, ★ PIETRADOLCE, Statella (Pignatùni Vecchie Vigne), TASCA D'ALMERITA, TENUTE BOSCO (VIGNA Vico), ★ TENUTA DELLE TERRE NERE, ★ TENUTA DI FESSINA, Tornatore (Pietrarizzo, Trimarchisa), ★ VINI FRANCHETTI.

Cordero di Montezemolo Pie ★★★ Organic; est 1340, 19th generation. Elegant, long-lasting. Top: BAROLO Enrico VI (cru Villero), Gattera, Monfalletto. Also v.gd: BARBERA D'ALBA Sup Funtanì, CHARD.

Cornelissen, Frank Si ★★★★ One of ETNA's top producers, esp for red. Practically all crus outstanding. Don't miss Magma (from vyd at 910m/2986ft, planted in 1910), usually SI's most expensive wine, and Munjebel crus CS, SC, Cuvée VA (r/w) and Perpetuum (using perpetual solera).

Coroncino, Fattoria Mar ★★★ Organic, trad estate, specialist in VERDICCHIO DEI CASTELLI DI JESI. Top: Cenobita, Gaiospino (also Fumè), Stracacio, Stragaio. Coroncino v.gd.

Correggia, Matteo Pie ★★★ Organic. Leading ROERO: RISERVA Rochè d'Ampsej 17 18 19' 21, Roero ARNEIS, Val dei Preti. Plus BARBERA D'ALBA (Marun), Roero Arneis Val dei Preti (aged 6 yrs). Also v.gd: ALTA LANGA Severina, Apapà (100% NEBBIOLO).

Corte Fusia Lom ★★★ Daniele and Gigi are passionate, talented, young. Elegant, pleasing, terroir FRANCIACORTA. Top: Brut, Millesimato Dosaggio Zero, single-vyd Orfano, Saten.

Cretes, Les VdA ★★★ Costantino Charrère is father of modern VDA viticulture, saved many forgotten varieties. Top ***Petite Arvine***, and new La Sabla 50 Anni (r blend); Cuvée Bois CHARD (one of Italy's best), Fumin, Neige d'Or (w blend), Torrette.

Cristo di Campobello, Baglio del Si ★★→★★★ Bonetta family estate just e of Agrigento. Top: GRILLO La Luci, NERO D'AVOLA Lu Patri. New METODO CLASSICO (100% Grillo). Solid wines.

Crotta di Vegneron, La VdA ★★→★★★ Quality co-op in Chambave. Top: La Griffe des Lions line (Fumin, Nus MALVOISIE). Also v.gd: Chambave MUSCAT Attente, Chambave Superieur, 4478 Nobleffervescence (sp).

CS (cantina sociale) Cooperative winery.

Cuomo, Marisa Cam ★★★★ Fiorduva is ***one of Italy's greatest whites*** 19' 21 22'. Top: (r) RISERVAS (Furore, Ravello); (w) Furore, Ravello.

Cupertinum Pug ★★→★★★ Quality CS since 1935. Best: Copertino Rosso (RISERVAS, Settantacinque), NEGROAMARO (also sw).

Custodi delle Vigne dell'Etna, I Si ★★★ Estate run by Mario Paoluzi. Top: (r) ETNA Aetneus, RISERVA Saeculare; (w) Contrada Caselle.

Dal Forno Bros Ven ★★★→★★★★ Michele and Luca DF took over historic Trabucchi winery (AMARONE, Galante, Recioto, RISERVA Cent'Anni, VALPOLICELLA SUPERIORE) and launched new project Comaroto (Amarone, Valpolicella).

Dal Forno Romano Ven ★★★★ VALPOLICELLA, AMARONE, RECIOTO (latter not identified as such any more) v. high quality; vyds outside CLASSICO zone but wines great.

Derthona Pie ★→★★★ TIMORASSO grown only in COLLI Tortonesi. One of Italy's most ***interesting whites***, like v. dry RIES from Rheinhessen (*see* Germany). Best: Boveri Giacomo (Lacrime del Bricco, Piazzera), LA COLOMBERA (Il Montino), Mariotto (Pitasso), Ricci, ROAGNA, TENUTA della Cascinassa, VIGNETI MASSA, VIETTI.

Di Barrò VdA ★★★ Small family estate, top quality from typical VDA grapes. Best: (r) Mayolet, Torrette Sup (Ostro); (w) Petite ARVINE.

DOC / DOCG Quality wine designation: *see* box, p.159.

Donnafugata Si ★★→★★★ Classy range: (r) ETNA Rosso (Contrada Fragore, Marchesa, Sul Vulcano), Mille e Una Notte, Tancredi; (w) Chiaranda, Lighea. Also v. fine: MOSCATO PASSITO di PANTELLERIA Ben Ryé 15' 16' 19' 21.

Due Terre, Le FVG ★★★ Small family-run FRIULI COLLI ORIENTALI estate. Top: Sacrisassi Rosso (SCHIOPPETTINO/REFOSCO). MERLOT, Sacrisassi Bianco (w) v.gd.

Einaudi, Luigi Pie ★★★ Founded late C19 by ex-president of Italy, 52-ha estate in Dogliani. Solid BAROLOS from Bussia, Cannubi, Monvigliero, Terlo, Villero. Also v.gd: Barolo Ludo, Dogliani from VIGNA Tecc.

Enoteca Wine library; also shop or restaurant with ambitious wine list. There is a national enoteca at the *fortezza* in Siena.

Etna Si ★★→★★★★ DOC (r) 13' 14' **15** 16' 18 19' 20' 21' 22 Remarkable development; 900 ha on n slopes, high-altitude, volcanic soils. Etna Rosso typically NERELLOS MASCALESE/Cappuccio (90/10%); Bianco can be pure CARRICANTE or incl CATARATTOS Comune or Lucido and others varieties. (*See also* box, p.138.)

Favati, I Cam ★★★ Rosanna Petrozziello runs high-quality family winery. Top: Etichetta Bianca (w label range): FIANO 19' 21', GRECO 20, TAURASI.

Fay Lom ★★★ Run by Fay family in VALTELLINA since 1971. Alpine wines. Top: SFORZATO (RONCO del Picchio), Valgella (Carterìa RISERVA, Il Glicine).

Felline Pug ★★★★ Gregory Perucci pioneered rediscovery of PRIMITIVO, Susumaniello vines. Top: PRIMITIVO DI MANDURIA (Cuvée Anniversario, Dunico, Giravolta, ZIN). Also v.gd: Verdeca (w), Edmond Dantès 36 Mesi (sp VERMENTINO), Pietraluna (NEGROAMARO), Sum (Susumaniello), Polignano rosé (PRIMITIVO/Negroamaro/Susumaniello).

Felluga, Livio FVG ★★★→★★★★ Consistently fine, age-worthy FRIULI COLLI ORIENTALI, esp blends Abbazia di Rosazzo 19 21', Terre Alte 20' 21' 22. Also Bianco Illivio, FRIULANO (Sigar), ***Pinot Gr*** (Curubella), SAUV BL Potentilla, Sossó (MERLOT/REFOSCO), PICOLIT (Italy's best?).

Felsina Tus ★★★ CHIANTI CLASSICO estate of distinction in se of zone. Best (100% SANGIOVESE): Gran Selezione Colonia, classic RISERVA Rancia, IGT Fontalloro.

Fenocchio, Giacomo Pie ★★★→★★★★ Small but outstanding Monforte d'ALBA-based BAROLO cellar; trad style. Crus: Bussia (also RISERVA 90 Dì), Cannubi, Catsellero, Villero. Outstanding FREISA, one of Italy's 2–3 best.

Ferrando Pie ★★★→★★★★ Historic, iconic producer of outstanding Caluso Cariola (one of best), CAREMA Black Label 15' 19 20 21'. Also v.gd: C White Label.

Ferrara, Benito Cam ★★★ One of Italy's best GRECO DI TUFO producers (Terra d'Uva, VIGNA Cicogna). Talent shows in excellent TAURASI (Vigna Quattro Confini).

Ferrari – Tenute Lunelli T-AA ★★★★ TRENTO maker of one of two best Italian METODO CLASSICOS. Outstanding Giulio Ferrari RISERVA del Fondatore 06' 08' 09' 12 (also Rosé), new Collezione 07. Also v.gd: Riserva Lunelli, Perlè range. TENUTE Lunelli: Castelbuono, Umb (MONTEFALCOS Carapace Lunga Attesa, Lampante Riserva); Margon, T-AA (Chard, Pinot N); Podernovo, TUS.

Fessina, Tenuta di Si ★★★→★★★★ One of youngest, top ETNA estates. Elegant. Best: EB A' Puddara (w), Il Musmeci (r/w), Il Musmeci Rosso RISERVA Speciale di Roberto e Silvia. Also v.gd: Erse Moscamento 1911 (r).

Feudi di San Gregorio Cam ★★★ Much-hyped CAM producer. DOCGS: FIANO DI AVELLINO (Pietracalda 20 23), GRECO DI TUFO (Cutizzi 23), TAURASI (RISERVA Piano di Montevergine 17 18'). Look for ***FeudiStudi*** range.

Feudo di San Maurizio VdA ★★★★ Outstanding wines from rare native grapes CORNALIN, Mayolet, Vuillermin; last two among Italy's greatest reds. Try (w) GEWURZ, PETITE ARVINE; (r) Torrette (and SUPERIORE), Ch de Sarre (NEBBIOLO).

Feudo Montoni Si ★★★★ Exceptional estate in upland E SI. Best: NERO D'AVOLA Lagnusa, Vrucara. Try (w) CATARRATTO del Masso, GRILLO della Timpa; (r) Perricone del Core; (sw) PASSITO Bianco. Authentic.

Fiano di Avellino Cam ★★→★★★★ DOCG **16'** 18 19' 20 21' 22 (23) Can be either steely (most typical) or lush. Best: CANTINA del Barone, Ciro Picariello, COLLI DI LAPIO, Contrada, Joaquin, FEUDI SAN GREGORIO, I FAVATI, Marsella, MASTROBERARDINO, Pietracupa, Rocca del Principe, QUINTODECIMO, TENUTA Sarno, TRAERTE (Vadiaperti).

Fino, Gianfranco Pug ★★★★ Greatest PRIMITIVO, old, low-yielding bush vines. Outstanding Es 16 19' 22, among Italy's top 20 reds, Es Selezione Red Label. Also v.gd: Jo (NEGROAMARO), Se (Primitivo).

Florio Si ★★★ Historic quality maker of MARSALA. Specialist in Vergine Secco. Best: RISERVA Donna Franca, New Geography range and its narrative labels (Premium, Exclusive). Also v.gd: Vino Florio (100% GRILLO).

Fongaro Ven ★★★★ METODO CLASSICO Lessini Durello (100% Durella). High quality, even higher acidity, age-worthy. Top: RISERVAS (Brut, Pas Dosé), new Degorgement Tardif. Also v.gd: Pas Dosé.

Fonterutoli Tus ★★★ Historic CHIANTI CLASSICO estate of Mazzei family at Castellina. Characterful. Chianti Classico GS: Badiola, Castello Fonterutoli, Vicoregio 36, outstanding Ipsus 16' 19 21 (Caggio vyd). IGT Siepi 19' 21 22 (SANGIOVESE/MERLOT). Owns TENUTA di Belguardo (Maremma), Zisola (SI).

Fontodi Tus ★★★★ One of v. best CHIANTI CLASSICOS: Filetta di Lamole, Flaccianello (100% SANGIOVESE); Gran Seleziones San Leolino, VIGNA del Sorbo. Also v.gd: Fontodi Bianco, IGT Case Via SYRAH (among best TUS Syrah).

Foradori T-AA ★★★ Outstanding ***Teroldego***, lovely macerated, amphora-aged Incrocio Manzoni, Nosiola. TEROLDEGOS Morei, Sgarzon (also amphora-aged Cilindrica), Nosiola Fontanasanta (w). Top remains Teroldego-based Granato 19' 20 21.

Franchetti, Vini Si ★★★→★★★★ Contributor to fame of ETNA (was Passopisciaro), run by Franchetti (*see* TENUTA DI TRINORO). Outstanding Rosso Franchetti (PETIT VERDOT/CESANESE DI AFFILE), NERELLO MASCALESE single *contrada*. Best: Contradas C, G, S (R also v.gd). New Contrada PC (CHARD).

The name Chianti appears in official documents as early as 1398.

Franciacorta Lom ★★→★★★★ DOCG 15 16' 17 19 (20) Italy's zone for top-quality METODO CLASSICO. Soils extremely complex (50+ types). Two large sectors: e generally most elegant, freshest; w generally broadest, richest. Top: BARONE PIZZINI, CA' DEL BOSCO, CORTE FUSIA, GUIDO BERLUCCHI, MOSNEL, TERRA MORETTI (Bellavista, Contadi Castaldi), UBERTI, VILLA. Also v.gd: Cola, Castello Bonomi, Cavalleri, Corte Aura, Ferghettina, Gralò, Lantieri de Paratico, Lo Sparviere, Majolini, Ricci Curbastro, Villa Crespia.

Franco, Nino Ven ★★★→★★★★ PROSECCOS that age surprisingly well. Among finest: Grave di Stecca, Riva di San Floriano. Excellent CARTIZZE.

Frascole Tus ★★→★★★★ Small organic estate. Top: CHIANTI RÙFINA, VIN SANTO.

Frescobaldi Tus ★★★→★★★★ Ancient noble family, leading CHIANTI RÙFINA pioneer at NIPOZZANO estate (look for ★★★ ***Montesodi***), also BRUNELLO from Castelgiocondo estate, MONTALCINO. Sole owner of LUCE estate (Montalcino), MASSETO (BOLGHERI), TENUTA Perano (top: CHIANTI CLASSICO Gran Selezione Rialzi), ORNELLAIA. Also vyds in COLLIO (Attems), Maremma (Ammiraglia), Montespertoli (Castiglioni), Gorgona Island (state prison). Now co-owner of TENUTA TERRE NERE.

Friuli Colli Orientali FVG ★★→★★★★ DOC 15 16' 18 19' 20 21' (23) (was COLLI Orientali del Friuli) Hilly area of FVG next to COLLIO. Unlike latter, not just whites, but outstanding reds, v.gd stickies from likes of red Pignolo, REFOSCO dal Peduncolo Rosso, SCHIOPPETTINO, Tazzelenghe and white MALVASIA Istriana, RIBOLLA GIALLA, PICOLIT, Verduzzo, FRIULANO. Top: Grillo Iole, I CLIVI, LA VIARTE, LIVIO FELLUGA, MEROI, MIANI, RONCHI DI CIALLA, VIGNA PETRUSSA. Also v.gd: Aquila del Torre, Butussi, D'ATTIMIS, Ermacora, Gianpaolo Colutta, Gigante, Jacuss, La Sclusa, LE DUE TERRE, Nadalutti, Polencic, Specogna, Volpe Pasini (Zuc di Volpe range). Ramandolo DOCG, best sweet Verduzzo (Anna Berra, Giovanni Dri). Picolit can be Italy's best sweet: Aquila del Torre, Livio Felluga, Marco Sara, RONCHI DI CIALLA, VIGNA Petrussa.

Friuli Isonzo FVG ★★★ DOC (previously just Isonzo) One of world's best flatland wine denominations. High-alc, powerful, rich, unfailingly complex whites from gravel-rich, clay-loam soils and hot mesoclimate. Best: LIS NERIS, RONCO DEL GELSO, VIE DI ROMANS. Also gd: Brandolini, Drius, Pierpaolo Pecorari.

Friuli Venezia Giulia FVG A ne region hugging Slovenian border, home to Italy's best whites (along with ALTO ADIGE). Hills to ne give best, but alluvial seaside regions (DOC from Annia, Aquilea, Latisana) improving markedly. DOCs Carso, COLLIO, F COLLI ORIENTALI, F ISONZO best.

With 36-month-aged Parmigiano, drink Passito di Pantelleria. North and south.

Frizzante Semi-sparkling, up to 2.5 atmospheres, eg. MOSCATO D'ASTI, much PROSECCO, LAMBRUSCO and the like.

Fucci, Elena Bas ★★★★ AGLIANICO DEL VULTURE Titolo (55–70-yr-old vines in Mt Vulture's Grand Cru, one of Italy's 20 best), RISERVA, SUPERIORE. Also v.gd: Pink Edition, Sceg. Organic

Fuligni Tus ★★★★ Outstanding, trad: BRUNELLO (top RISERVA), ROSSO DI MONTALCINO.

Gagliardo, Gianni ★★★ High-quality BAROLOS. Best: Castelletto, Lazzarito VIGNA Preve, Monvigliero, Mosconi. Iconic, v.gd Fallegro (Favorita). Owns TENUTA Garetto (Monferrato).

Gaja Pie ★★★★ Old family firm at BARBARESCO led by eloquent Angelo G; daughter Gaia G following. One of Italy's top. Best: Barbaresco (Costa Russi, Sorì San Lorenzo, Sorì Tildìn, classic Barbaresco), BAROLO (Conteisa, Sperss). Splendid CHARD (Gaia e Rey). Also owns Ca' Marcanda in BOLGHERI (Camarcanda, Magari, Promis), Pieve di Santa Restituta in MONTALCINO. Waiting for new white.

Garbarino, Roberto Pie ★★★ One of most talented young producers of ALTA LANGA DOCG. Top: Le Rapide (PINOT N/CHARD). Also v.gd: Il Viaggio (Chard), La Sorgente (Pinot N). New RIES and rare Rossese Bianco.

Gattinara Pie 13' 15 16' **18** 19' **20** 21' (23) Best known of a cluster of ALTO PIE DOC(G)s based on NEBBIOLO. Steep hills; wines suitable for long ageing. Best: Antoniolo, CANTINA del Signore, Iarretti Paride, Nervi, Torraccia del Piantavigna, TRAVAGLINI. *See also* Alto Piemonte.

Gavi / Cortese di Gavi Pie ★→★★★ DOCG At best, subtle dry white CORTESE. Best: Castellari Bergaglio (Rovereto, Rolona), LA SCOLCA, Nicola Bergaglio (Minaia). Also v.gd: ***Bruno Broglia*** – La Meirana, Castello di Tassarolo, Chiarlo, Enrico Serafino (Maneo, Poggio della Rupe), La Giustiniana, La Mesma, Villa Sparina.

Germano, Ettore Pie ★★★★ Serralunga estate run by Sergio G and family. Top BAROLOS: Cerretta, Riserva Lazzarito, Barolo Prapò, Del Comune di Serralunga, outstanding VIGNA Rionda. Also v.gd: ALTA LANGA (also RISERVAS Blanc de Noirs, Blanc de Blancs, both 65 mths), BARBERA D'ALBA SUPERIORE della Madre, LANGHE RIES Hérzu (one of Italy's best).

Ghizzano, Tenuta di Tus ★★★ Historic bio estate on Pisa's hills; non-interventionist. Best: (r) Nambrot (Bx blend), Il Ghizzano. New Mimesi Project (r/w).

Giacosa, Bruno Pie ★★★★ Now run by daughter Bruna; wines still top. Splendid iconic trad-style BARBARESCOS (Asili, Rabajà), BAROLOS (Falletto, Falletto VIGNA Rocche). Top wines (ie. RISERVAS) get famous red label. Amazing METODO CLASSICO Brut (one of best in PIE), ROERO ARNEIS (w), Valmaggiore (r).

Ginestre, Le Pie ★★★ Barbara Audasso runs historic family estate; gd value. Top: BAROLO Sottocastello di Novello (also RISERVA), LANGHE NEBBIOLO.

Gini Ven ★★★ Gini family since 1500s; bio. Best: SOAVE CLASSICO Contrada Salvarenza Vecchie Vigne, La Froscà 19' 20 21'. Also v.gd: AMARONE RISERVA Scajari, RECIOTO DI SOAVE, white Camillo.

Girlan, Cantina T-AA ★★★ Quality co-op. Top: Solisti (CHARD Curlan; PINOT NS Trattmann, VIGNA Ganger; VERNATSCH), Flora (PINOT BL) ranges.

Giuseppe Cortese Pie ★★★ A trad producer of outstanding BARBARESCO Rabajà (also RISERVA). Also gd Barbaresco, LANGHE NEBBIOLO, Scapulin (CHARD).

Grattamacco Tus ★★★ Owned by Colle Massari Group; historic estate (2nd in BOLGHERI). Long line of outstanding wines (salinity, power): Bolgheri Grattamacco (r, c.15% Sangiovese; w, Vermentino) 17' 18 20', L'Alberello, Montecucco Rosso RISERVA.

Greco di Tufo Cam ★★→★★★ DOCG 18 19' 21' (23) Better versions among Italy's best whites (tannic, oily) made with local GRECO (different from Cal's also outstanding Greco Bianco). Best: Bambinuto, BENITO FERRARA, Di Meo (Vittorio), Di Prisco, Pietracupa, QUINTODECIMO, TRAERTE (Vadiaperti). Also v.gd: CANTINA dei Monaci, Colle di San Domenico, COLLI DI LAPIO, FEUDI DI SAN GREGORIO, I FAVATI, MASTROBERARDINO, SALVATORE MOLETTIERI.

Grifalco Bas ★★★→★★★★ Small estate in high-quality Ginestra and Maschito subzones; wines of purity, trad. Best: AGLIANICO DEL VULTURE SUPERIORE Daginestra, Damaschito.

Grignolino Pie DYA Two DOCS: Grignolino d'ASTI, Grignolino del Monferrato Casalese. At best, light, perfumed, crisp, high in acidity, tannin. D'Asti: Bersano, BRAIDA, Cascina Tavijin, Crivelli, Incisa della Rocchetta, Spertino, TENUTA Garetto, Tenuta Santa Caterina (also Monferace). M Casalese: Accornero (Bricco del Bosco, Vigne Vecchie), Bricco Mondalino, Castello di Uviglie, Piero Vellano, PIO CESARE.

Guerrieri Rizzardi Ven ★★→★★★ Noble family. Top: AMARONE (Calcarole, 3 Cru, Villa Rizzardi), Bardolino (Montebaldo). Also v.gd: SOAVE CLASSICO Costeggiola.

Gulfi Si ★★★★ Best NERO D'AVOLA in SI; 1st to bottle single-*contrada* (cru) wines in Eloro DOC Pachino (in se of Sic). Organic. Top *contrade*: Baroni, Bufaleffi, Maccari, Sanlorè; iconic Nerojbleo. Also v.gd: (r) CERASUOLO DI VITTORIA CLASSICO, ETNA Reseca, Pinò (PINOT N); (w) Carjcanti.

Gussalli Beretta, Agricole Lom ★★→★★★ Group with properties in best regions: Castello di Radda (CHIANTI CLASSICO), Fabio Motta (BOLGHERI), Fortemasso (LANGHE), Lo Sparviere (FRANCIACORTA), Steinhaus (ALTO ADIGE).

IGT (indicazione geografica tipica) Increasingly known as IGP (indicazione geografica protetta). (*See* box, p.159.)

Inama Ven ★★★→★★★★ Important producer in COLLI Berici, Soave. Some of denomination's best: Soave CLASSICO (Carbonare, Du Lot, Foscarino, new I Palchi Grande Cuvée), CARMENÈRE RISERVA Oratorio di San Lorenzo, Bradisismo (r blend).

Ippolito 1845 Cal ★★→★★★ Since 1845 in heart of CIRÒ. Best: Cirò Bianco Mare Chiaro (GRECO Bianco); Cirò Rosato Mabilia, red Cirò (Liber Pater, RISERVA COLLI del Mancuso).

Ischia Cam ★★→★★★ DOC DYA Island off Naples, green volcanic tuff soils, own grape varieties (w: Biancolella, Forastera; r: Piedirosso, also found in CAM). Best for Biancolella: Frassitelli, VIGNA del Lume vyds. Top: CANTINE MAZZELLA, CENATIEMPO, D'AMBRA. Also v.gd: Crateca, Giardini Arimei (Arcipelago Muratori), Tommasone, Perrazzo.

Isole e Olena Tus ★★★★ Top CHIANTI CLASSICO estate, owned by the EPI group. Superb red IGT Cepparello 17' 19' 20 22. Outstanding CHARD, Chianti Classico, VIN SANTO.

Italy grows over a quarter of all the grape varieties in the world.

Kaltern, Cantina T-AA ★★★ Quality co-op. Best: Quintessenz range (PINOT BL, Kalterersee). Also v.gd: Selezioni. Look for limited-edition Kunst Stück (celebrating grape that best interprets vintage), new Brut Nature (sp).

Köfererhof T-AA ★★★★ Great whites: KERNER, SYLVANER; PINOT GR (new K); excellent MÜLLER-T (R), new CHARD K.

Lageder, Alois T-AA ★★★ Famous ALTO ADIGE producer. Exciting single-vyds:

CHARDS Gaun, Löwengang; GEWURZ Am Sand; CAB SAUV Cor Römigberg; PINOT N Krafuss; MCM (MERLOT Vecchie Viti).

Lagrein Alto Adige T-AA ★★→★★★ DOC 16' 18 19' 20 21' (23) Alpine red: deep colour, rich palate (plus bitter hit at back); refreshing pink ***Kretzer rosé***. Top: ALTO ADIGE: CANTINA Bolzano (Taber), CS TERLANO, CS COLTERENZIO , CS TRAMIN, IGNAZ NIEDRIST, LAGEDER, MURI GRIES, TIEFENBRUNNER.

Lambruschi, Ottaviano Lig ★★★ One of best COLLI DI LUNI VERMENTINO producers: Costa Marina, SUPERIORE. Also v.gd: Il Casale.

Lambrusco E-R ★→★★★ DYA The 17 different Lambrusco grapes (five mostly planted) make for highly distinct wines. When gd, delightful fresh, lively, fizzy red that pairs divinely with rich, fatty fare. DOCS: Best: **Grasparossa** Cleto Chiarli (Enrico Cialdini), Moretto (Monovitigno and VIGNA Canova), Pederzana (Canto Libero Semi Secco), ***Vittorio Graziano*** (Fontana dei Boschi); **Maestri** Ceci, Dall'Asta; **Marani** Medici Ermete; **Salamino** Cavicchioli, Luciano Saetti, Medici Ermete; **Sorbara** Cavicchioli (Cristo Secco, Cristo Rose), Cleto Chiarli (Antica Modena Premium), Medici Ermete, PALTRINIERI. Casali (blend).

Langhe Pie The hills of central PIE, home of BAROLO, BARBARESCO, etc. DOC name for several Pie varietals plus Bianco and Rosso blends.

Langhe Nebbiolo Pie ★★→★★★ Like NEBBIOLO D'ALBA (85%+ Nebbiolo) but from a wider area: LANGHE hills. Unlike N d'Alba, may be used as a downgrade from BAROLO or BARBARESCO. Try ALDO CONTERNO, AZELIA, BREZZA, BURLOTTO, Cascina Roccalini, CIABOT BERTON, CLERICO, DIEGO MORRA, ETTORE GERMANO, FRANCESCO RINALDI, GIACOMO FENOCCHIO, GIOVANNI ROSSO (Ester Canale), GIUSEPPE RINALDI, LUCA MARENCO, MASSOLINO, TREDIBERRI, VERSIO.

Leggero, Luca Pie ★★★ Young, talented producer. Top: CALUSO Rend Nen, NEBBIOLO Maura Nen. Also v.gd: Caluso Turciaura, Nebbiolo La Vila.

Lessona Pie DOCG *See also* ALTO PIEMONTE 10 13' 16' 18 19' 20 21' (23) NEBBIOLO (at least 85%); mostly clay-free marine sandy soils, rich in minerals. Elegant, age-worthy, fine bouquet, long savoury taste. Best: PROPRIETÀ SPERINO. Also v.gd: Colombera & Garella, La Prevostura, Massimo Clerico, Noah, TENUTE Sella.

Librandi Cal ★★★ Top producer pioneering research into Cal varieties. Best: CIRÒ (***Riserva Duca San Felice*** ★★★), IGT Asylia (GRECO Bianco), Efeso (w Mantonico), Gravello (CAB SAUV/Gaglioppo), Megonio (r Magliocco).

Liguria ★→★★★ Narrow ribbon of extreme mtn viticulture produces memorable (w) PIGATO, VERMENTINO, (r) ROSSESE DI DOLCEACQUA. Riviera di Levante (in e): CS CINQUE TERRE, De Battè, Giacomelli, La Baia del Sole, LUNAE, OTTAVIANO LAMBRUSCHI, TERENZUOLA. Riviera di Ponente (in w): BIO VIO, BRUNA, Ka' Manciné, Maccario, Maria Donata Bianchi (Pigato Diana, Vermentino), MASSIMO ALESSANDRI, TENUTA di Selvadolce (Pigato), Terre Bianche, Terre Rosse, Vis Amoris (Pigato Sogno, sp Zero). For Ormeasco di Pornassio (r Ligurian DOLCETTO biotype): Cascina Nirasca, Fontanacota, Lorenzo Ramò, Lupi. *See also* ROSSESE DI DOLCEACQUA.

Lis Neris FVG ★★★ Top ISONZO white. Best: Confini, Fiore di Campo, Gris, Picol.

Luce Tus ★★★ FRESCOBALDI's estate. Lovely BRUNELLO DI MONTALCINO; SANGIOVESE/ MERLOT 17' 18 21' for oligarchs.

Lugana ★★→★★★ DOC DYA Much-improved white of S Lake Garda, rivals gd SOAVE next door. Main grape, Turbiana (was TREBBIANO di Lugana). Best: Ca' dei Frati (esp ***Brolettino***), Cavalchina, Corte Sermana (Due Rive, RISERVA), Zeni. Also gd: MONTE DEL FRÀ, TOMMASI, ZENATO.

Lunae, Cantine Lig ★★★ Bosoni family-owned, in COLLI DI LUNI. Terroir-expressive: VERMENTINO (Cavagino, Etichetta Nera, Numero Chiuso). Rare Vermentino Nero v.gd.

Lungarotti Umb ★★→★★★ Leading producer of TORGIANO. Stars: DOC Rubesco,

DOCG RISERVA ***Monticchio*** 15' 16 18 20'. Also Giubilante, MONTEFALCO SAGRANTINO, Sangiorgio (SANGIOVESE/CAB SAUV), VIGNA Il Pino (VERMENTINO/GRECHETTO/TREBBIANO).

Macchiole, Le Tus ★★★★ Organic. One of few native-owned wineries of BOLGHERI, Best: Paleo Rosso (CAB FR) one of Italy's best, Messorio (MERLOT).

Malvasia delle Lipari Si ★★★ DOC Luscious sweet, from one of many MALVASIA varieties. Best: Caravaglio, Casa Pedrani, Marchetta, TASCA D'ALMERITA – TENUTA Capofaro (Dydime, VIGNA di Paola).

Malvirà Pie ★★★→★★★★ Top ROERO producer. Organic. Best single-vyd: (r/w) Renesio, Trinità; (w) Saglietto. New ARNEIS RISERVA Saglietto.

Manduria (Primitivo di) Pug ★★→★★★ DOC Cradle of PRIMITIVO, alias ZIN; gutsy, alc, can be Porty. Best: FELLINE, GIANFRANCO FINO, MORELLA. Also v.gd: Conti Zecca, Feudi di San Marzano, Leone de Castris, Pirro Varone, Zicari. For Gioia del Colle: PIETRAVENTOSA, Polvanera, Tenute Chiaromonte.

Manincor T-AA ★★★ On Lake Caldaro, bio. Strong personality. Top: Liebenaich (SAUV BL), Mason di Mason (PINOT N), Castel Campan (Bx blend). Also v.gd (w): La Contessa (Terlaner), Sophie (blend).

Marcalberto Pie ★★★ Reference for lovers of sparkling ALTA LANGA. Top new RISERVAS dedicated to Caterina Rivella (and rosé). Also v.gd: Blanc de Blancs, Nature.

Marchesi di Grésy Pie ★★★ Historic BARBARESCO (1797), Martinenga cru (monopole). Best: Gajun, Martinenga, RISERVA Camp Gros. Also v.gd: BARBERA D'ASTI Monte Colombo.

Marenco, Luca Pie ★★★ Young talent between Barolo, Novello; terroir-driven. Top: Nascetta del Comune di Novello (w); BAROLOS Bergera-Pezzole, La Volta. Also v.gd: DOLCETTO, NEBBIOLO.

Region with most DOPs? Piedmont. 70+ DOCs and DOCGs. Time to stop.

Marengo Pie ★★★ Marco M is one of most talented BAROLO producers. Top: Bricco delle Viole, Brunate, Classico (and new Stefano), NEBBIOLO D'ALBA Valmaggiore.

Marrone, Agricola Pie ★★★ Small estate, gd-value BAROLOS. Top: Bussia, Castellero, Pichemej. Also ARNEIS, BARBERA D'ALBA SUPERIORE, Favorita, San Carlo (r).

Marroneto, Il Tus ★★★→★★★★ Alessandro Mori, son Iacopo; top MONTALCINO estate. Top: BRUNELLO Madonna delle Grazie. Also v.gd: Brunello, Rosso di M Selezione Iacopo.

Marsala Si ★→★★★★ DOC Once-famous fortified of SI. Can be dry to v. sweet; best is bone-dry Marsala Vergine. Top: MARCO DE BARTOLI (Vecchio Samperi, VIGNA La Miccia), FLORIO.

Mascarello Pie ★★★★ Two iconic BAROLO producers: Bartolo M, of Barolo (daughter Maria Teresa continues father's highly trad path), outstanding FREISA, BARBERA D'ALBA, LANGHE NEBBIOLO; Giuseppe M, of Monchiero (son Mauro now makes), v. fine, trad-style Barolo from great ***Monprivato*** vyd in Castiglione Falletto.

Masi Ven ★★→★★★ Archetypal yet innovative Verona producer, led by inspirational Sandro Boscaini; v.gd Rosso Veronese ***Campo Fiorin*** and Osar (Oseleta). Top AMARONES: Campolongo di Torbe, Costasera. Masi Wine Estates: Canevel (CARTIZZE, Valdobbiadene Campofalco), Conti Bossi Fedrigotti (Fojaneghe Bx blend, Trento Conte Federico), Serego Alighieri (Amarone Vaio Armaron).

Maso Martis T-AA ★★★ Stelzer family-owned. Organic TRENTO reference. Top: Dosaggio Zero RISERVA, Madame Martis Dosaggio Zero Limited Edition, Monsieur Martis Rosé (PINOT M). Also v.gd: AL-MA 800 MÜLLER-T.

Massa, Vigneti Pie ★★★ Walter M key figure in white TIMORASSO renaissance. Top: Coste del Vento, Montecitorio, Sterpi. Also v.gd: Anarchia Costituzionale (MOSCATO Bianco); BARBERAS Bigolla, Monleale.

Masseto Tus ★★★★ 15' 16' 18 19' 20' 21' 23' (24) Owned by FRESCOBALDI, now own winery. Outstanding Masseto (MERLOT) one of best Italian reds. Also v.gd: Massetino (Merlot/CAB FR).

Massolino Vigna Rionda Pie ★★★ One of finest BAROLO estates, in Serralunga. Top: long-ageing VIGNA Rionda RISERVA (also Black Label). Excellent Margheria, Parafada, Parussi, new BARBARESCO Albesani.

Mastroberardino Cam ★★★ Historic top-quality producer of mtn Avellino province. Top: More Maiorum (GRECO/FIANO), Stilema range, ***Taurasi*** (Radici RISERVA).

Mastrojanni Tus ★★★ Classic BRUNELLOS from Castelnuovo dell'Abate. Top: VIGNA Loreto, Vigna Schiena d'Asino. Also v.gd: ROSSO DI MONTALCINO.

Mattoni, Lorenzo Umb ★★★ Young talent in Umb. Best: MONTEFALCO 15 16' 18, Trebbiano Spoletino (w, unrelated to TREBBIANO Toscana).

Mazzella, Cantine Cam ★★★ High-quality winery on ISCHIA. Top: single-vyd Biancolella VIGNA del Lume. Also v.gd: Forastera, Ischia Biancolella Enaria Spadara, Villa Campagnano (w blend).

Meroi FVG ★★★ Dynamic estate. Top: CHARD Dominin, FRIULANO, MALVASIA Zittelle Durì, RIBOLLA GIALLA, SAUV BL Zitelle Barchetta; REFOSCO Dominin.

Metodo classico (MC) or tradizionale Italian for "Champagne method".

Miani FVG ★★★★ Enzo Pontoni is Italy's best white-wine maker. Top: FRIULANO (Buri, Filip), RIBOLLA GIALLA Pettarin, SAUV BL Zitelle. Also v.gd: CHARD Zitelle, Sauv Bl Saurint, MERLOT, REFOSCO Buri.

Mirizzi and Montecappone Mar ★★★→★★★★ Two estates owned by Gianluca

Climate change: the winners

If you want winners, look for these (w to e and s). **Boca** (LE PIANE). **Carema** (FERRANDO, Monte Malletto, SORPASSO): in CAREMA, NEBBIOLO now ripens more regularly, so less vegetal character and tannic harshness typical of cold vintages prior to 10; silky tannins, elegance, balance. **Gattinara** (Antoniolo, Nervi-Conterno, TRAVAGLINI): more stable climate improved phenolic ripeness and tannin sweetness without affecting freshness; finesse, balance. **Lessona** (PROPRIETÀ SPERINO). **Alto Adige – Pinot N** (Bozen, ELENA WALCH, Girlan, Gottardi): high-altitude vyds now ripen better, so goodbye to rusticity, dryness; elegance, fresher fruit. **Collio – Friulano, Ribolla Gialla, Sauv Bl, Malvasia Istriana** (Boro del Tiglio, Primosic, SCHIOPETTO, VIE DI ROMANS): less summer rain, higher temps have improved aromatic complexity, structure. **Montepulciano d'Ab** (TIBERIO, VALENTINI): more regular ripening, softer and less green tannins; in the hilly and high hill areas (250–450m/ 820–1476ft: Loreto Aprutino, Ofena, Tocco da Casauria); finer tannins, cleaner fruit, more balanced profile and greater stability across vintages. **Fiano di Avellino** (COLLI DI LAPIO, Di Meo): late-ripening FIANO now ripens more easily and with less risk of diluted vintages, so has greater aromatic complexity, structure, while maintaining freshness. **Taurasi** (Lonardo, MASTROBERARDINO, Perillo): v. late-ripening AGLIANICO loves warmer seasons; greater consistency, more regular phenolic ripeness; more mature, silky tannins. **Etna** (BENANTI, Passopisciaro): more regular ripening of NERELLO MASCALESE, greater reliability of vintages. CARRICANTE, esp on e side (Milo), likes drier summers with stable temperatures; excellent acidity, greater aromatic depth. Other improving areas incl altitudes of 800–1000m (2625–3281ft), with slower ripening, more complexity, refinement (Passopisciaro, Solicchiata), districts in n and ne (Calderara, Feudo di Mezzo, Pietramarina) making more balanced wines.

Mirizzi; VERDICCHIO DEI CASTELLI DI JESI. Mirizzi on marly sandstone, deep slopes; organic, trad winemaking: Ergo, Ergo Sum RISERVA, Millesimè Pas Dosè, TT Totus Tuus (Grenache). Montecappone on calcareous clay; reductive winemaking: Federico II, Riserva Utopia.

Molettieri, Salvatore Cam ★★★ Outstanding RISERVA VIGNA Cinque Querce, TAURASI; gd FIANO DI AVELLINO Apianum, GRECO DI TUFO.

Molino, Mauro Pie ★★★ High-quality BAROLO producer in La Morra. Top: Conca. Excellent: Bricco Luciani, Gallinotto, La Serra.

Monacesca, Fattoria La Mar ★★★ Family-run; top VERDICCHIO DI MATELICA. Best: RISERVA Mirum **18' 19'** 21, Terra di Mezzo (longer ageing). Outstanding Mirum 30 Year (multi-vintage blend). Also v.gd: Criptico (VERDICCHIO/CHARD), Ecclesia Brut (sp Verdicchio).

Monsanto, Castello di Tus ★★★ Historic, top-quality CHIANTI CLASSICO. Top: Il Poggio Gran Selezione (1st single-vyd) 18 19' 20', iconic RISERVA, IGT Fabrizio Bianchi (w CHARD, r SANGIOVETO Grosso).

Montalcino Tus Hilltop town, Siena province; fashionable, famous for concentrated, expensive BRUNELLO and more approachable, better-value ROSSO DI MONTALCINO, both still 100% SANGIOVESE.

Monte del Frà Ven ★★→★★★ Bonomo family-owned; v.gd value. Top: AMARONE (Lena di Mezzo, RISERVA), Custoza (Bonomo Sexaginta, Ca' del Magro). Also v.gd: Bardolino (Bonomo), LUGANA.

Montefalco Sagrantino Umb ★★★→★★★★ DOCG **16'** 18 19 20' Sweet PASSITO best; drier version is powerfully tannic red, requiring optimal ripening. Top: ADANTI, Antano Milziade, Antonelli San Marco, Bea, CAPRAI, Colpetrone, TENUTE LUNELLI – Castelbuono (Lampante, Carapace Lunga-Attesa), LORENZO MATTONI, Ruggeri. Also v.gd: Bellafonte, Bocale, Lungarotti, Pardi, Romanelli, Tenuta Alzatura, Terre dei Capitani.

Monte Maletto Pie ★★★ Young, v. talented Gian Marco Viano. Best: CAREMA Sole e Roccia, single-vyds La Costa, Le Rue.

Montepulciano d'Abruzzo Ab ★★→★★★ DOC (r) **15** 16' 18 19 20' 21' Thanks to new generation of winemakers, Ab's wines (MONTEPULCIANO, TREBBIANO D'AB too) never been better. Reds: light, easy-going or structured, rich. Best: Cataldi Madonna (Piè delle Vigne, Tonì), Praesidium, TIBERIO, Torre dei Beati, ***Valentini*** (age-worthy), Valle Reale.

Montevertine Tus ★★★★ Organic estate in Radda. Top: IGT Le Pergole Torte 19' 20' 21' 22', world-class, pure, long-ageing SANGIOVESE. Also v.gd: Montevertine.

Montevetrano Cam ★★★ Iconic CAM AZIENDA, run by passionate Silvia Imparato. Superb IGT Montevetrano (AGLIANICO/CAB SAUV/MERLOT). Also v.gd: Core Bianco (FIANO/GRECO), Rosso (Aglianico).

Morella Pug ★★★→★★★★ Gaetano M and wife Lisa Gilbee make outstanding PRIMITIVO (La Signora, Mondo Nuovo, Old Vines) from c.90-yr-old vines. Also v.gd: Mezzogiorno (FIANO), Mezzarosa rosé (Primitivo/NEGROAMARO).

Morellino di Scansano Tus ★→★★★ DOCG 18 19' 20 21' (24) Maremma's famous SANGIOVESE-based red is better when cheerful, light than overoaked, gritty. Best: Fattoria dei Barbi, ***Le Pupille*** (plus RISERVA), MORISFARMS, PODERE 414, POGGIO ARGENTIERA, Roccapesta, TENUTA Belguardo.

Morisfarms Tus ★★★ One of 1st new-age producers of TUS Maremma. Top: iconic IGT Avvoltore (rich SANGIOVESE/CAB/SYRAH), MORELLINO DI SCANSANO (regular, RISERVA). Also VERMENTINO, Rosato Rosamundi.

Morra, Diego Pie ★★★ Young talented winemaker. Top: BAROLO crus (di Verduno, Monvigliero, San Lorenzo di V), VERDUNO Pelaverga. Also v.gd: Barolo Zinzasco, LANGHE NEBBIOLO.

Moscato d'Asti Pie ★★→★★★ DYA Similar to DOCG Asti, but usually better grapes;

lower alc, lower pressure, sweeter, fruitier, often small producers. Best DOCG MOSCATO: Cadgal (Vite Vecchia), ***Caudrina*** (La Galeisa), Forteto della Luja, L'Armangia, Mongioia, ***Saracco***, Vignaioli di Santo Stefano. Also v.gd: BRAIDA, GD VAJRA, RIZZI.

Mosnel Lom ★★★→★★★★ Barzanò family-run, in FRANCIACORTA (1836). Organic. Elegance, complexity, long-ageing: EBB, Nature, Pas Dosé RISERVA, Riedizioni Late Release Vintage.

In Pantelleria, Zibibbo grapes grow low, seem to play hide-and-seek in the sand.

Muri Gries T-AA ★★→★★★ Monastery in Bolzano suburb of Gries; trad and still top producer of LAGREIN ALTO ADIGE DOC. Best: Abtei Muri, Klosteranger.

Musso Pie ★★★ Musso family-run (1929). Underrated: BARBARESCOS Pora (also RISERVA), Rio Sordo.

Nals Margreid T-AA ★★★ Small quality co-op making mtn-fresh whites (esp PINOT BIANCO Sirmian from porphyritic soil), CHARD RISERVA, v.gd Nama.

Nebbiolo d'Alba Pie ★★→★★★ DOC 15 16' 18 19' 20' 21' (100% NEBBIOLO) Sometimes a worthy replacement for BAROLO/BARBARESCO, though it comes from a distinct area between the two. Best: BREZZA, BRUNO GIACOSA, CERETTO, Hilberg-Pasquero, LUCIANO SANDRONE, ORLANDO ABRIGO, PAITIN, PODERI COLLA.

Neive, Castello di Pie ★★★ Historic estate, owns single greatest cru of all BARBARESCO, famous Santo Stefano (Albesani MGA). Top: Gallina, Santo Stefano (also RISERVA). Also v.gd: Albarossa, Barbarossa.

Niedrist, Ignaz T-AA ★★★ LAGREIN Berger Gei RISERVA **17' 18 19** 21' is reference. Also RIES, WEISSBURGUNDER (Berg, Limes), BLAUBURGUNDER Riserva. Also v.gd: CHARD (vom Kalk), SAUV BL (Limes, Porphyr & Kalk), Trias (w blend).

Nipozzano, Castello di Tus ★★★→★★★★ FRESCOBALDI estate, excellent CHIANTI RÙFINA. Top: VIGNA Montesodi RISERVA 18' 19' 21', Riserva (and Vecchie Viti). Also v.gd: Mormoreto (Bx blend).

Nittardi Tus ★★→★★★ Reliable source of quality modern CHIANTI CLASSICO (Casanuova di Nittardi, RISERVA). German-owned; oenologist Carlo Ferrini.

Nizza Pie ★★→★★★ DOCG (100% BARBERA) Only from best-exposed sites of 19 villages around town of Nizza Monferrato; also RISERVA. Needs time. Best: BAVA, BERSANO, Cacina Garitina (900, RISERVA), Chiarlo (La Court), Doglia Gianni, L'Armangia (Titon, Riserva Vignali), La Barbatella, ODDERO, Olim Bauda (and Riserva), TENUTA Garetto, Villa Giada, Vinchio Vaglio.

Nössing, Manni T-AA ★★★★ Outstanding benchmark GRÜNER V, KERNER, MÜLLER-T Sass Rigais, SYLVANER.

Occhio di pernice Tus "Partridge's eye". Type of VIN SANTO made predominantly from black grapes, mainly SANGIOVESE. ***Avignonesi's is definitive.***

Occhipinti, Arianna Si ★★★ Cult producer, deservedly so; organic. Top: CERASUOLO DI VITTORIA CLASSICO Grotte Alte, Il Frappato.

Oddero, Poderi e Cantine Pie ★★★★ Traditionalist La Morra estate for excellent BAROLO (Brunate, Bussia RISERVA, Villero, outstanding VIGNA Rionda Riserva, new Capalot in best yrs), BARBARESCO (Gallina) crus, plus other serious PIE; v.gd-value RIES.

Ornellaia Tus ★★★★ 15 16' 18 19' 20' 21' 22 23' (24) Fashionable, indeed cult, estate nr BOLGHERI owned by FRESCOBALDI. Top (Bx grapes/method): Bolgheri DOC Ornellaia, Ornellaia Bianco (SAUV BL/VIOGNIER). Also gd: Le Serre Nuove, POGGIO alle Gazze (w).

Orvieto Umb ★→★★★ DOC DYA One of few noble-rot areas of Italy. Sweet late-harvest can be memorable. Off-dry Amabile less in favour today but delicious. Top: Barberani (Luigi e Giovanna, sw Calcaia), Decugnano dei Barbi, Palazzone, Sergio Mottura (Lat). Also v.gd: Paolo e Noemia d'Amico.

Ottin VdA ★★★ Elio O one of top interpreters of VDA terroir. Best: PETITE ARVINE Nuances, PINOT N (also L'Emerico), Torrette Superieur.

Paitin Pie ★★★ Pasquero-Elia family bottling BARBARESCO since C19. Today back on track, "real" Barbaresco from cru Serraboella in large barrels. Star: Sorì Paitin Vecchie Vigne. Also v.gd: new Barbaresco (Basarin, Faset), BARBERA D'ALBA (Campolive), NEBBIOLO D'ALBA.

Paltrinieri E-R ★★→★★★ One of top three LAMBRUSCOS; among 1st to produce 100% L di Sorbara. Best: La RISERVA, Leclisse, Secco Radice.

Pantelleria Si ★★★ Windswept, black-earth (volcanic) SI island off Tunisian coast, famous for superb MOSCATO d'Alessandria stickies. Dense, intense PASSITO. Try Coste Ghirlanda, MARCO DE BARTOLI (Bukkuram), DONNAFUGATA (Ben Ryé), Ferrandes, Vinisola (A'mmare, Arbaria, Zefiro).

Parusso, Armando Pie ★★★ Excellent BAROLO. Best: Bussia (and RISERVAS Munie, Rocche), Mariondino. Also v.gd: Mosconi, Perarmando.

Passito Si, Tus, Ven Ancient, characteristic style: grapes dried briefly under harvest sun (in s) or over wks/mths in airy attics (*appassimento*). Best-known versions: AMARONE/RECIOTO, VALPOLICELLA/SOAVE (Ven); VIN SANTO (TUS); Pantelleria (SI). Try Loazzolo, MONTEFALCO, ORVIETO, Torcolato. Never cheap.

Pavese Ermes VdA ★★★ One estate, one grape: Prié Bl, ungrafted vines up to 1219m (4000ft). Top: Blanc de Morgex et de la Salle (Classic, Le 7 Scalinate, Nathan), Ninive (sw), MC Pavese (sp XLVIII and LX, mths of ageing).

Petrolo Tus ★★★ DOC Valdarno di Sopra. Luca Sanjust is an artist, painter and passionate winemaker. Top: Boggina A and C (SANGIOVESE), Galatrona (MERLOT) 19' 20' 21'.

Petrussa, Vigna FVG ★★★ Small, high quality. Best: PICOLIT, Richenza (indigenous w grapes, old vines), SCHIOPPETTINO di Prepotto (and RISERVA).

Pian dell'Orino Tus ★★★★ Small MONTALCINO estate, committed to bio. BRUNELLO seductive, technically perfect; Rosso nearly as gd. Many epic wines.

Piane, Le Pie ★★★★ Christoph Kunzli, one of best ALTO PIEMONTE. Top: (r) BOCA 16' 17' 18 20', single-vyd Antonio Cerri 18', Plinius; (w) Bianko, Eos (Erbaluce). Also v.gd: Maggiorina, Mimmo (NEBBIOLO/Croatina), Nebbiolo, Piane (Croatina).

Picolit FVG ★★→★★★ DOCG **13** 15' 16' **17** 18 20' 21' (24) Potentially Italy's best sweet (most air-dried grapes; rare late-harvests even better), but plagued by poor versions that don't speak of the grape. Texture ranges from light, sweet (rare) to super-thick (passito). Best: Aquila del Torre, d'Attimis, I Comelli, LIVIO FELLUGA, Marco Sara, Perusini, RONCHI DI CIALLA, Valentino Butussi, VIGNA PETRUSSA. Also v.gd: Ermacora, Girolamo Dorigo, Paolo Rodaro.

Piedmont / Piemonte In ne, bordering France to the w. Turin is capital. Main areas: ALTO PIEMONTE, Monferrato, LANGHE, ROERO. With TUS, Italy's most important region for quality (10% of all DOC[G] wines). No IGTS allowed. Grapes incl BARBERA, Brachetto, CORTESE, DOLCETTO, FREISA, GRIGNOLINO, MALVASIA di Casorzo, Malvasia di Schierano, MOSCATO, NEBBIOLO, Ruchè, TIMORASSO. *See also* BARBARESCO, BAROLO.

Carlo Alberto, king of Sar, Piedmont (1798–1849), liked Barolo sweet. As did many.

Pieropan Ven ★★★★ Andrea and Dario P run winery; organic. Cru ***La Rocca*** still ultimate oaked SOAVE; Calvarino best of all. Outstanding Calvarino 5 (blend of yrs). Also v.gd: AMARONE, RECIOTO DI SOAVE (Le Colombare).

Pietradolce Si ★★★★ Faro bros in key ETNA crus, often pre-phylloxera vines. Top: (r/w) Archineri; (r) Barbagalli, Feudo di Mezzo, Rampante, Santo Spirito; (w) Sant'Andrea (100% CARRICANTE). Precise.

Pietraventosa Pug ★★★ Small family estate, one of top producers of PRIMITIVO di Gioia del Colle. Top: Allegoria, RISERVA, Rosé Est-Rosa.

ITALY

Pievalta Mar ★★★ Founded by BARONE PIZZINI, bio. Top: VERDICCHIO DEI CASTELLI DI JESI (RISERVA San Paolo, Tre Ripe, sp Perlugo).

Pio Cesare Pie ★★★ Veteran ALBA producer; BAROLO, BARBARESCO in modern (barrique) and trad (large cask-aged) versions. NEBBIOLO D'ALBA esp gd, ***a little Barolo at half the price.*** Best: Single-vyd (Bricco, Mosconi, Ornato), Classic (Pio, dedicated to Pio Boffa) collections. Also gd: Barolo Chinato, vermouth.

Pira e Figli – Chiara Boschis Pie ★★★★ Organic. Top: Cannubi 19' 20' 21', Mosconi 19' 21', Via Nuova 16' 19'. Also v.gd: BARBERA D'ALBA SUPERIORE, LANGHE NEBBIOLO. Must visit.

Italy has a native grape for every day of the year, plus: 540+ officially recognized.

Planeta Si ★★★ Leading SI estate, vyds all over island, incl Menfi (GRILLO Terebinto), Noto (NERO D'AVOLA Santa Cecilia, PASSITO di Noto), Vittoria (CERASUOLO Dorilli, Frappato), most recently on ETNA (NERELLO MASCALESE Eruzione 1614). Also gd: Cometa (FIANO). Reliable.

Podere Tus Small TUS farm, once part of a big estate.

Poggio Tus Means "hill" in TUS dialect. **Poggione** means "big hill".

Poggio Antico Tus ★★★ Paola Gloder looks after 32-ha estate, one of highest in MONTALCINO (500m/1640ft). Restrained, consistent, at times too herbal.

Poggio Argentiera Tus ★★★ In Maremma, TUA RITA-owned: fresh, drinkable. Best: Capatosta (95% SANGIOVESE), MORELLINO DI SCANSANO.

Poggio di Sotto Tus ★★★★ Small MONTALCINO estate, with big, well-deserved reputqtion. Top: BRUNELLO 17' 19 20' and RISERVA 18' 19', ROSSO, trad character with idiosyncratic twist.

Poggione, Tenuta Il Tus ★★★ MONTALCINO estate, in s. Consistently excellent BRUNELLO (RISERVA VIGNA Paganelli 19'), Rosso; v.gd VIN SANTO.

Potazzine, Le Tus ★★★★ Gorelli family just s of MONTALCINO; organic, vyd quite high. Outstanding, serious, v. drinkable BRUNELLO **18** 19' 20' (and RISERVA 15' 19'), Rosso. Try at family restaurant.

Prà Ven ★★★★ Leading SOAVE CLASSICO: Colle Sant'Antonio, Monte Grande, Staforte. Excellent AMARONE (15 top), VALPOLICELLA La Morandina.

Produttori del Barbaresco Pie ★★★ One of Italy's earliest, best co-ops. Excellent trad, classic BARBARESCO, plus crus Asili 16' 17' '21, Montefico 17' 20' 21', Montestefano 16' 20' 21', Ovello 16', Rabajà 16' 20' 21'. Super value.

Proprietà Sperino Pie ★★★★ Top estate of LESSONA. One of best of ALTO PIEMONTE run by Luca De Marchi. Outstanding BRAMATERRA, LESSONA 18' 19' 20' (and RISERVA Covà 15' 17' 19'). Also v.gd: 'L Franc (one of best Italian CAB FR), Rosa del Rosa (NEBBIOLO/Vespolina rosé), Uvaggio (r blend).

Prosecco Ven ★→★★ DOC(G) DYA Prosecco is the wine, GLERA the grape variety. Quality is higher in Valdobbiadene and Conegliano (DOCG zones).

Puglia The "heel" of Italy. Many gd-value reds from Bombino Nero, NEGROAMARO, PRIMITIVO, Susumaniello, UVA DI TROIA. Bombino Bianco, aromatic Minutolo, Verdeca most interesting whites. Castel del Monte, Gioia del Colle Primitivo, PRIMITIVO DI MANDURIA, SALICE SALENTINO best denominations.

Querciabella Tus ★★★ Top CHIANTI CLASSICO estate, bio since 2000. Best: Batàr (CHARD/PINOT BL) **19' 20 21'**, Chianti Classico (Gran Selezione, RISERVA), IGT Camartina (CAB SAUV/SANGIOVESE) **16' 17' 19'** 21'. Also v.gd: Mongrana (VIOGNIER/VERMENTINO), Palafreno (MERLOT).

Quintarelli, Giuseppe Ven ★★★★ Arch-traditionalist artisan producer of sublime VALPOLICELLA, RECIOTO, AMARONE (RISERVA in best yrs) **15' 17** 18', new AMARONE Tre Terre. Daughter Fiorenza and sons now in charge, altering nothing.

Quintodecimo Cam ★★★→★★★★ Oenology professor-winemaker Luigi Moio's beautiful estate. Outstanding Grande Cuvée Luigi Moio (w blend native grapes),

TAURASI (VIGNA Grande Cerzito, Vigna Quintodecimo, new Grand Cru Luigi Moio). Also v.gd: AGLIANICO, FALANGHINA, FIANO D'AVELLINO, GRECO DI TUFO.

Ragnaie, Le Tus ★★★ Makes trad BRUNELLOS revealing essence of SANGIOVESE. Top: Casanovina Montosoli, Passo del Lume Spento, VV.

Recioto della Valpolicella Ven ★★★→★★★★ DOCG 15' 18' Sweet-wine marketing problems mean this trad Italian beauty is being made less and less. Shame, esp as always much better than many disappointing overly sweet/tannic AMARONES. Top: Brigaldara, Roccolo Grassi, Secondo Marco, TEDESCHI, TOMMASO BUSSOLA.

Recioto di Soave Ven ★★★→★★★★ DOCG SOAVE from half-dried grapes: sweet and fruity, slightly almondy; sweetness is cut by high acidity. ***Drink with cheese.*** Best: Anselmi, Coffele, GINI, PIEROPAN, SUAVIA, Tamellini. Often v.gd: Ca' Rugate, Pasqua, PRÀ, Trabuchi.

Redalmo Ven ★★★ Elisa and Mattia run family estate in Val d'Alpone and Berici Hills. Top: GARGANEGA, Rosso Veneto (100% MARSELAN, rare in Italy).

Refosco (dal Peduncolo Rosso) FVG ★★ 15 16' 18 19' 20 21' (24) Most planted native red grape of region. Best from FRIULI COLLI ORIENTALI DOC. Top: MIANI, Ronchi di Cialla, VIGNA PETRUSSA, Volpe Pasini. Also gd: Jacuss, La Viarte, LIVIO FELLUGA, MEROI.

Revello, Fratelli Pie ★★★ Small family estate, delicious BAROLO from some of La Morra's best crus (Conca, Gattera, Rocche dell'Annunziata), new Cerretta; v.gd L'Insieme (NEBBIOLO/BARBERA/CAB SAUV).

Riecine Tus ★★★→★★★★ SANGIOVESE specialist at Gaiole since 70s. Riecine di Riecine, La Gioia (100% Sangiovese) potentially outstanding; gd Tresette (MERLOT). Now entirely run by talented Alessandro Campatelli.

Rinaldi, Francesco Pie ★★★ Paola and Piera R make classic, elegant BAROLOS. Top: Brunate, Cannubi (also RISERVA), Rocche dell'Annunziata. Also v.gd: Classic Barolo, LANGHE FREISA, NEBBIOLO.

Rinaldi, Giuseppe Pie ★★★ Marta and Carlotta R produce some of most iconic LANGHE: FREISA; BAROLOS Brunate, Bussia, Tre Tine; LANGHE NEBBIOLO.

Ripi, Podere Le Tus ★★★ MONTALCINO, bio, 35 ha, two opposite slopes: BRUNELLO Cielo D'Ulisse 20' on w; Amore e Magia 20', Brunello Lupi e Sirene 19' on e. Also v.gd: R di M Sogni e Follia.

Riserva Wine aged for a statutory period, usually in casks or barrels.

Rivetto Pie ★★★ Talented young Enrico R; bio. Top: BAROLOS Briccolina, di Serralunga. Also v.gd: Langhe Nascetta (w), LANGHE NEBBIOLO, Kaskal (sp).

Rivolta, Fattoria La Cam ★★★ Paolo Cotroneo, in ancient farm on ne slope of Taburno, since 1998. Best: AGLIANICO del Taburno (Terra di Rivolta), Sogno di Rivolta (GRECO/FIANO/FALANGHINA). Also v.gd: Coda di Volpe, Falanghina.

Rizzi Pie ★★★→★★★★ In the heart of the ***Treiso*** area, Enrico and Jole Dellapiana run this organic estate. Top: Barbaresco Pajorè, Rizzi RISERVA Boito. Also v.gd: ALTA LANGA, Barbaresco (Nervo, Rizzi), MOSCATO D'ASTI. Mineral, steely.

With tiramisù (if you must eat it – ed), drink Aleatico dell'Elba.

Roagna Pie ★★★★ Old vines, massal selection, organic, wild yeast, long maceration and long ageing in large oak casks. Outstanding BARBARESCO Crichet Pajet (and RISERVA) 13' 14 15' 16', BAROLO and Barbaresco Vecchie Viti ("old vines") ranges, Riservas, with a black label. More than v.gd: Solea (CHARD/NEBBIOLO), TIMORASSO Montemarzino, Barbaresco (Albesani, Faset, Gallina, Pajè), Barolo (Del Comune di Barolo, Pira, Rocche di Castiglione).

Rocca, Albino Pie ★★★→★★★★ Foremost producer of elegant, sophisticated BARBARESCO: Cottà, Ovello VIGNA Loreto, Ronchi; RISERVAS (Cottà, Ronchi).

Rocca, Bruno Pie ★★★→★★★★ Family estate run by Francesco and Luisa, Bruno's children. BARBARESCO with more trad style. More elegance than power.

Top: Currà, Maria Adelaide, Rabajà, RISERVAS. Also v.gd: BARBERA D'ASTI, LANGHE NEBBIOLO.

Roero Pie ★★★ DOCG 13 15 16' 18 19' 20 21' Wilder, cooler than LANGHE. Three main soils (sandy, marls, clay) produce profoundly different Nebbiolos (refined tannins, elegance, freshness, aromatics). ARNEIS, NEBBIOLO. Best: ANGELO NEGRO, BRUNO GIACOSA, GIOVANNI ALMONDO, Hilberg Pasquero (Sul Monte, Mon Suri), MALVIRÀ, MATTEO CORREGGIA. Also v.gd: Alberto Oggero, Bajai, Cordero Gabriele, Cornarea, Deltetto, Ghiomo, Manuele Priolo, Rosavica-Benotti, Valfaccenda.

Trentino-Alto Adige has vineyards higher than many ski slopes: 1000m (3281ft)+.

Ronchi di Cialla FVG ★★★→★★★★ Leading FVG estate, in Cialla subzone of FRIULI COLLI ORIENTALI; Rapuzzi family-run, devoted to local old native grapes. Best: Ciallabianco (RIBOLLA GIALLA/Verduzzo/PICOLIT), Picolit di Cialla, SCHIOPPETTINO. Also v.gd: REFOSCO dal Peduncolo Rosso di Cialla, Sol (dr Picolit).

Ronco Term for a hillside vyd in NE Italy, esp FVG.

Ronco del Gelso FVG ★★★→★★★★ Tight, pure ISONZO. Regional benchmarks: FRIULANO Toc Bas, MALVASIA VIGNA della Permuta, PINOT GR Sot lis Rivis. Latimis (w blend), RIES Schulz, MERLOT, all v.gd.

Rosato General Italian name for rosé. Other rosé names incl Chiaretto from Lake Garda; CERASUOLO from Ab; Kretzer from ALTO ADIGE.

Rossese di Dolceacqua, or Dolceacqua Lig ★★→★★★ DOC 16' 18 19' Interesting reds. Intense, salty, spicy; greater depth of fruit than most. Best: Ka' Manciné, Maccario-Dringenberg (Curli, Luvaira, Posaù, Sette Cammini), TENUTA Anfosso. Also v.gd: Poggi dell'Elmo, Terre Bianche (Bricco Arcagna).

Rosso, Giovanni Pie ★★★ Davide R is talented interpreter of Serralunga BAROLO. Best: Ester Canale Rosso LANGHE NEBBIOLO; Barolos Cerretta, di Serralunga, Serra, Vignarionda. Also v.gd: ROERO ARNEIS, Langhe Nebbiolo. In ETNA too: new EB Contrada Pietra Marina.

Rosso di Montalcino Tus ★★→★★★ 13 15 16 18 19' 20 21 DOC for earlier-maturing wines from BRUNELLO, usually from younger or lesser vyd sites; bargains exist.

Rosso Piceno / Piceno Mar ★→★★ DOC 18 19 (20) Blend of MONTEPULCIANO (35%+)/SANGIOVESE (15%+). SUPERIORE means it comes only from far s of region. Top: BUCCI, Cocci Grifoni, MONTECAPPONE (Utopia). Also v.gd: Aurora, Clara Marcelli, Saladini Pilastri, Velenosi.

Rùfina Tus ★★→★★★ 16' 18 19 22' Most n subzone of CHIANTI, e of Florence, is by far best and most interesting non-CHIANTI CLASSICO denomination. Highest of all Chiantis, so refined, age-worthy. Soils are varied and incl limestone, sand, Galestro, Alberese, marly clays and others. Top: Colognole, Fattoria il Capitano, Fattoria Lavacchio, Frascole, Grignano, I Veroni, NIPOZZANO (*see* FRESCOBALDI), Ormaevini, Podere Il Pozzo, ***Selvapiana***, Travignoli.

Russiz Superiore FVG ★★→★★★ LIVIO FELLUGA's brother Marco est vyds in various parts of FVG. Now run by Marco's granddaughter Ilaria. Wide range. Best: Col Disôre (COLLIO Bianco blend), PINOT GRIGIO. Also v.gd: PINOT BIANCO RISERVA.

Russo, Girolamo Si ★★★→★★★★ Giuseppe R is one of three or four best ETNA producers. Among 1st on Etna to bottle crus separately. Top: (r) Caldera Sottana, Feudo, Feudo di Mezzo, San Lorenzo; (w) Nerina, San Lorenzo.

Sabbioni, Podere Mar ★★★ Best Ribona (grape, also called Maceratino) in Italy: della Famiglia. Also v.gd: ROSSO PICENO.

Salento Pug ★→★★★ Home to Italy's best rosé from NEGROAMARO (alongside Ab's CERASUOLO from MONTEPULCIANO). Plus v.gd red Negroamaro, with a bit of help from MALVASIA Nera, and now red from local Susumaniello. Best: Conti Zecca (Nero, Rodinò), CUPERTINUM, Leone de Castris (Five Roses); Rosa del Golfo (VIGNA Mazzi classic, rosé). *See also* SALICE SALENTINO.

Salice Salentino Pug ★★→★★★ DOC 16' 17 19' 20 21' Best known of Salento's too many NEGROAMARO-based DOCS. RISERVA after 2 yrs. Top: Agricole Vallone, Leone de Castris (Riserva). Also v.gd: Cantele, Due Palme, Mocavero. For ROSATO: Candido, FELLINE, Leone de Castris, Rosa del Golfo.

Salvioni Tus ★★★★ (aka La Cerbaiola) Iconic small, highest-quality MONTALCINO estate. BRUNELLO, ROSSO DI MONTALCINO among v. best available.

Sandrone, Luciano Pie ★★★→★★★★ Modern-style ALBA. Deep BAROLOS: Aleste (was Cannubi Boschis), Le Vigne 17' 19' 21', Vite Talin. Also gd: NEBBIOLO D'ALBA Valmaggiore.

San Felice Tus ★★★ Historic winery, owned by Gruppo Allianz, run by Leonardo Bellaccini. Fine: CHIANTI CLASSICO and RISERVA POGGIO Rosso from Castelnuovo Berardenga. Also gd: BRUNELLO DI MONTALCINO Campogiovanni, IGT ***Vigorello*** (1st SUPER TUSCAN, from 1968).

San Giusto a Rentennano Tus ★★★★ Top CHIANTI CLASSICO; organic. Outstanding IGTS La Ricolma (MERLOT), ***Percarlo*** (SANGIOVESE) 16' 18 19 20' 21' 22; Chianti Classico (and RISERVA Le Baroncole); Vin San Giusto (PASSITO). New Fuori Misura (ROSATO).

San Leonardo T-AA ★★★★ Top Trentino estate of Marchesi Guerrieri Gonzaga. Main wine is Bx blend, ***San Leonardo*** (now released 1 yr later) 16' 17' 18 19 20'. Also v.gd: RIES, CARMENÈRE, Villa Gresti (MERLOT/Carmenère), TRENTO (sp Cuvée Pietra, RISERVA Privata).

San Lorenzo, Fattoria Mar ★★★ Age-worthy VERDICCHIOS from Montecarotto, bio/organic. Top: Campo delle Oche (also Integrale), Il San Lorenzo Bianco. Also v.gd: Il San Lorenzo Rosso (SYRAH), Le Oche, VIGNA La Gattara (r).

San Michele Appiano T-AA ★★★ Historic co-op; ***mtn-fresh whites*** a speciality brimming with varietal typicity, drinkability. Best: Appius (selected by Hans Terzer) 19' 20', Sanct Valentin, The Wine Collection. Also v.gd: Schulthauser PINOT BL.

Santadi Sar ★★★ Best SAR co-op (and one of Italy's), esp for Carignano del Sulcis (Rocca Rubia RISERVA, ***Terre Brune***). Also v.gd: VERMENTINO DI SARDEGNA (Cala Silente), Villa di Chiesa (w blend), Latinia (PASSITO).

Saracco, Paolo Pie ★★★★ Top MOSCATO D'ASTI; v.gd CHARD, LANGHE RIES, PINOT N.

Sardinia / Sardegna Italy's 2nd-largest island is home to world-class whites and reds. Look for: VERMENTINO DI GALLURA, VERMENTINO DI SARDEGNA (fruitier, less mineral), Sherry-like VERNACCIA DI ORISTANO, NURAGUS, Nasco, Semidano. CANNONAU (GARNACHA), CARIGNANO, most famous reds. Bovale, MONICA, Pascale just as gd.

Sartarelli Mar ★★★ High-quality VERDICCHIO DEI CASTELLI DI JESI CLASSICO. Top: Balciana, Milletta RISERVA, Tralivio.

Sassicaia Tus ★★★★ 10' 13' 15' 16' 18 19' 20' 21' 22' 23 (24) Single-vyd DOC (BOLGHERI), a CAB (SAUV/FR) made on First Growth lines by Marchese Incisa della Rocchetta at Tenuta San Guido. More elegant than lush, made for age – and often bought for investment – but hugely influential in giving Italy a top-quality image; 16 extremely elegant, one of best recent yrs.

In Sardinia, some Cannonau vineyards 150 yrs old+. Very long-lived people too.

Satta, Michele Tus ★★★ Virtually only BOLGHERI grower to succeed with 100% SANGIOVESE (Cavaliere). Best: BOLGHERI Marianova 18' 19' 21', Piastraia.

Scarpa Pie ★★★ Historic trad winery in NIZZA Monferrato. Top: BARBERA D'ASTI La Bogliona 15' 16' 17' 19' 20', Barolo (Tettimora, new Monvigliero), VERDUNO Pelaverga. Also v.gd: BARBARESCO Tettineive, Brachetto.

Scarzello Pie ★★★ Classic, refined BAROLO. Top: Boschetti, Sarmassa. Also v.gd: BARBERA D'ALBA, LANGHE NEBBIOLO.

Scavino, Paolo Pie ★★★ Modernist BAROLO producer of Castiglione Falletto: Bric del Fiasc, Monvigliero, Prapò, Ravera, Rocche dell'Annunziata.

Schiava Alto Adige T-AA ★ DOC DYA Schiava (VERNATSCH in German): blend of the three main Schiava varieties (Gentile, Grigia, Grossa). Used to make DOC wines called Lago di Caldaro, St-Magdalener (Santa Maddalena). Light- to medium-bodied, v. fresh, pleasant red. Best: cs Bolzano, Caldaro, GIRLAN, Merano.

Oldest wine ever found in Italy dates to c.6000 years ago, from Sicily.

Schiopetto, Mario FVG ★★★ Legendary late COLLIO pioneering estate now owned by Rotolo family; v.gd DOC FRIULANO, SAUV BL, ***Pinot Bl***, RIBOLLA GIALLA and IGT blend Blanc des Rosis, etc.

Scolca, La Pie ★★★ Among 1st to make GAVI known in world, with legendary Black Label. Best: Gavi dei Gavi (Black Label, Limited Edition), Soldati D'Antan (and SPUMANTE Millesimato).

Sella & Mosca Sar ★★→★★★ Major SAR grower-merchant. *See* TERRA MORETTI.

Selvapiana Tus ★★★★ RÙFINA organic estate among Italian greats. Best: RISERVA Bucerchiale, IGT Fornace; but even ***basic Chianti Rùfina is a treat***. Also fine red Petrognano, Pomino, Riserva VIGNETO Erchi.

Sesta di Sopra Tus ★★★ High-quality BRUNELLO (top RISERVA), ROSSO DI MONTALCINO.

Sesti – Castello di Argiano Tus ★★★ Distinctive, refined yet flavourful BRUNELLOS from Sesti family estate; trad-style. CLASSICO Brunello, RISERVA Phenomena equally gd, if different.

Sforzato / Sfursat Lom ★★★ DOCG Sforzato di VALTELLINA is made AMARONE-like, from air-dried NEBBIOLO grapes. Ages beautifully. Best: FAY (RONCO del Picchio). Also v.gd: Dirupi (Vino Sbagliato), Mamete Prevostini (Albareda, Corte di Cama), Nino Negri (Cinque Stelle), Triacca. *See* VALTELLINA.

Sicily The Med's largest island, modern source of exciting original wines and value. Native grapes (r Frappato, NERELLO MASCALESE, NERO D'AVOLA; W CARRICANTE, CATARRATTO, Grecanico, GRILLO, INZOLIA), plus internationals. The vyds are on flatlands in w, hills in centre, volcanic altitudes on Mt Etna. (*See also* ETNA.)

Soave Ven ★★→★★★ DOC Famous, hitherto underrated Veronese white. Soils: mix of mainly volcanic or calcareous elements. Wines from volcanic soils of CLASSICO zone can be intense, saline, v. fine, quite long-lived. Best: PIEROPAN, GINI, INAMA, PRÀ, SUAVIA. Also v.gd: Agostino Vicentini (Il Casale), Casato 1922, Coffele (Alzari), Filippi, Nardello, Roccolo Grassi (Broia). *See also* RECIOTO.

Solaia Tus ★★★★ 15 16' **18** 19' 20 21' 22 (23) CAB SAUV/SANGIOVESE by ANTINORI; needs age.

Sorpasso Pie ★★★ Vittorio Garda is one of the most talented young winemakers in PIE. Top: CALUSO, CAREMA (and single-vyds Neirere, Siei, Vigne Alte). Elegant and refined.

Sorrentino Cam ★★→★★★ Benni S makes top (r/w) Lacryma Christi (5 Viti, VIGNA Lapillo). Best: AGLIANICO Don Paolo (r), Caprettone (Benita 31), Catalò (w).

Sottimano Pie ★★★→★★★★ Family estate. One of most inspired in BARBARESCO (Basarin, Cottá, Currá, Fausoni, Pajoré), Riserva 10' 13' 16'. Also v.gd: BARBERA D'ALBA, DOLCETTO d'ALBA, LANGHE NEBBIOLO.

Speri Ven ★★★ VALPOLICELLA family estate; organic; trad style. Top: AMARONE Sant'Urbano, RECIOTO DELLA VALPOLICELLA (La Roggia).

Spumante Sparkling.

Strette, Le Pie ★★★ Makes gd-value BAROLO: B di Novello, Bergera Pezzole, Corini Pallaretta. Also LANGHE Nas-cëtta del Comune di Novello (single-vyd Pasinot).

Suavia Ven ★★★ Tessari sisters make v. refined SOAVE CLASSICO: Le Rive (GARGANEGA), Massifitti (TREBBIANO di Soave), Soave Classico (and Monte Carbonare).

Südtirol T-AA German name for ALTO ADIGE.

Superiore Wine with more ageing than normal DOC and 0.5–1% more alc. May indicate a restricted production zone, eg. ROSSO PICENO Superiore.

Super Tuscan Tus Wines of high quality and price developed in 70s/80s to get around silly laws then prevailing. Now, esp with Gran Selezione on up, scarcely relevant. Wines still generally considered in Super Tuscan category, strictly unofficially: BERTINGA, Ca' Marcanda, Flaccianello, Guado al Tasso, Messorio, ORNELLAIA, Redigaffi, SASSICAIA, SOLAIA, TIGNANELLO.

Tappero Merlo Domenico Pie ★★★ Roots in the past, eyes to the future and Erbaluce grape as life partner. Top: Acini Perduti (blend), ERBALUCE DI CALUSO (sp Cuvée des Paladins, Kin). Also v.gd: Bohemien (PASSITO).

Tasca d'Almerita Si ★★★ New generation runs historic TENUTE. Top: (r) Regaleali (NERO D'AVOLA-based ***Riserva del Conte***); (w) CHARD VIGNA San Francesco, Nozze d'Oro. Also v.gd: Capofaro (MALVASIA delle Lipari – Didyme, Vigna di Paola), Sallier de la Tour (SYRAH La Monaca), Tascante (ETNA r – Contrada Rampante, Contrada Sciaranuova Vigna Vecchia), Whitaker (GRILLO Mozia).

Taurasi Cam ★★★ DOCG 13 15 16' 19' 20 21' (24) The 1st DOCG in S Italy. Best is AGLIANICO of CAM. None so potentially ***complex, demanding, ultimately rewarding***. With 17 communes, four subzones: nw, w, Taurasi, s. Top: Contrade di Taurasi, Guastaferro (and RISERVA VV Primum), MASTROBERARDINO, QUINTODECIMO, SALVATORE MOLETTIERI. Also v.gd: BENITO FERRARA, COLLI DI LAPIO, Contrada Vini, Di Prisco, Fratelli Urciuolo, I FAVATI, Perillo, Pietracupa, Rocca del Principe, Tecce, Terredora.

Tavignano, Tenuta di Mar ★★★ Organic. One of best VERDICCHIO DEI CASTELLI DI JESI. Top: Misco (and RISERVA), new Dosaggio Zero (sp). Also v.gd: Villa Torre.

Tedeschi Ven ★★★ Bevy of v. fine VALPOLICELLA, AMARONE. Best: Amarones Capitel Monte Olmi, La Fabriseria, Maternigo; RECIOTO Capitel Monte Fontana. Also v.gd: Valpolicella Capitel Nicalò, new Ga.Ry. (GARGANEGA/RIES).

Tenuta An agricultural holding (*see* under name – eg. CAPEZZANA, TENUTA DI).

Terenzuola Lig, Tus ★★★ Passionate, talented Ivan Giuliani makes some of best wines in Cinque Terre, COLLI DI LUNI. Top: Colli di Luni-VERMENTINO (Fosso di Corsano, I Pini di Corsano), rare Vermentino Nero (r). Also v.gd: Cinque Terre Bianco, Sciacchetrà.

Terlano, Cantina di T-AA ★★★★ High-quality co-op, benchmark PINOT BL. Outstanding LAGREIN RISERVA Porphyr, Pinot Bl Riserva Vorberg, ***Terlaner I*** Grande Cuvée (Pinot Bl/SAUV BL/CHARD), ***Rarity*** (Pinot Bl aged 10 yrs+: 09' 10' 11 12'), Sauv Bl Quarz, Terlaner Nova Domus. Also v.gd: GEWURZ Lunare, iconic Terlaner (Pinot Bl/Sauv Bl/Chard).

Teroldego Rotaliano T-AA ★★→★★★ DOC Trentino's best local grape makes seriously tasty wine on flat Campo Rotaliano. Top: ***Foradori***. Also gd: Cipriano Fedrizzi (Due Vigneti), Dorigati (Diedri), Zeni.

Marsala: first Italian wine to be exported widely, thanks to Brits in C18.

Terra Moretti Lom, Sar, Tus ★★★→★★★★ Three regions, six estates owned by Moretti family. In FRANCIACORTA: Bellavista with chef de cave Richard Geoffroy, ex-Dom Pérignon (top Pas Operé, Vittorio Moretti; v.gd new Alma Assemblage 1, Teatro alla Scala Brut), Contadi Castaldi (new Pinònero RISERVA 2017, Zéro). In SAR: Sella & Mosca (top r CAB SAUV Marchese di Villamarina, Tanca Farrà, CANNONAU Mustazzo; top w Torbato Terre Bianche Cuvée 161, VERMENTINO DI GALLURA Monte Oro; v.gd new Tintas range, VERMENTINO, Cannonau). In TUS: Acquagiusta La Baiola, Petra (Petra, Quercegobbe), Teruzzi (VERNACCIA DI SAN GIMIGNANOS Isola Bianca, Riserva Sant'Elena).

Terre Nere, Tenuta delle Si ★★★★ Marc de Grazia (and new partner Lamberto FRESCOBALDI) shows great wine can be made from CARRICANTE, NERELLO, on coveted n side of Mt Etna. Top: Cuvée delle Vigne Niche, Guardiola, pre-phylloxera La VIGNA di Don Peppino. New ER Bocca d'Orzo (monopole), EB SUPERIORE – Contrada Salice.

Teularju Sar ★★★ Family estate, dedicated to CANNONAU and its ancient biotypes. Top: crus (*ghiradas*) Cara'Gonare, Ocruarana.

The highest wine in Italy? Valle d'Aosta, at 1200m (3937ft)+. Some valley.

Tiberio Ab ★★★★ Outstanding TREBBIANO D'AB Fonte Canale (60-yr-old vines), one of Italy's best whites; MONTEPULCIANO D'AB (single-vyds Archivio, Colle Vota); CERASUOLO D'AB (one of Italy's best ROSATOS); PECORINO (also new single-vyd Quarmarì).

Tiefenbrunner T-AA ★★★→★★★★ Christof T runs one of most historic estates in Turmhof Castle in S ALTO ADIGE. Wide range of mtn-fresh white and well-defined red varietals, esp 1000m- (3281ft-)high MÜLLER-T ***Feldmarschall*** (one of Italy's best whites: **18 20** 22'), now also late-harvest. Top VIGNA range: CHARD Au, SAUV BL Rachtl, CAB SAUV Toren. Linticlarus range v.gd: Chard (esp new RISERVA), LAGREIN, PINOT N.

Tignanello Tus ★★★ 16' 17 19' 20' 21' **22** 23 Dense SANGIOVESE/CAB SAUV blend, from ANTINORI.

Tommasi Ven ★★★ Now 4th generation, elegant wines. Top: AMARONE (RISERVA Ca' Florian, iconic De Buris), LUGANA Riserva Le Fornaci, VALPOLICELLA Rafael. Classic. Also in Bas (Paternoster), Oltrepò Pavese (TENUTA Caseo), PUG (Masseria Surani), Ven (Filodora).

Torgiano Umb ★★ DOC ★★→★★★ DOCG RISERVA 13 15 16' **19'** 20 21' Range gd to excellent reds: LUNGAROTTI ***Vigna Monticchio*** Rubesco Riserva, keeps many yrs.

Torrette VdA ★→★★★ DOC Blend based on Petit Rouge and other local varieties. Best: Torrette Superieur. Also gd: Anselmet, D&D, DI BARRÒ, Didier Gerbelle, FEUDO DI SAN MAURIZIO, Grosjean, LES CRETES, LO TRIOLET, OTTIN.

Traerte Cam ★★★ Raffaele Troise, v. talented maker of Torama, one of Italy's best whites (100% Coda di Volpe Bianca). Top: GRECO DI TUFO Tornante, GRECO Fuori Limite Le Vecchie Vigne, FIANO DI AVELLINO Aipierti.

Tramin, Cantina T-AA ★★★ Quality co-op with benchmark GEWURZ. Outstanding Epokale **09' 13' 16'** 17', Nussbaumer, Terminum, Troy (CHARD), Unterebner (PINOT GR). Best: Selezioni range, highest expression.

Travaglini Pie ★★★ Solid producer of GATTINARA. Best: RISERVA (new VIGNA Ronchi), Tre Vigne. Also v.gd: Coste della Sesia, Gattinara, METODO CLASSICO Nebolé (NEBBIOLO).

Trebbiano d'Abruzzo Ab ★→★★★★ DOC DYA Generally crisp, simple, but TIBERIO's (Fonte Canale) and VALENTINI's are ***two of Italy's greatest*** whites. Also v.gd: Talamonti, Valle Reale. And gd: Ciavolich, Cingilia, Marramiero.

Trediberri Pie ★★★ Dynamic. Top: BAROLO Rocche dell'Annunziata (value). Also v.gd: BARBERA D'ALBA, Barolo Berri, Dogliani, LANGHE NEBBIOLO.

Trento T-AA ★★→★★★★ DOC High-quality METODO CLASSICO. Top: ABATE NERO, FERRARI, MASO MARTIS, SAN LEONARDO. Also v.gd: Cembra (Oro Rosso), Cesarini Sforza, Letrari.

Trinoro, Tenuta di Tus ★★★★ Individualist TUS red estate, pioneer in DOC Val d'Orcia. Heavy accent on Bx grapes in flagship TENUTA di Trinoro, also in Camagi, Magnacosta, Palazzi, Tenagli. *See also* VINI FRANCHETTI (ETNA).

Triolet, Lo VdA ★★★ Try PINOT GR; PETITE ARVINE, GEWURZ, MUSCAT, Fumin, Torrette.

Tua Rita Tus ★★★★ As new BOLGHERI in 90s, 1st producer of possibly Italy's greatest MERLOT in Redigaffi **15' 16' 18' 19'** 21' 22'; outstanding Bx blend ***Giusto di Notri***, SYRAHS Keir (amphora), Per Sempre. Also POGGIO ARGENTIERA in Maremma (best: Capatosta, MORELLINO DI SCANSANO).

Tuscany / Toscana Home of world's top SANGIOVESE. CHIANTI CLASSICO, BRUNELLO DI MONTALCINO, RÙFINA best, but BOLGHERI just as gd and world-class for international grapes (CAB FR, MERLOT), and SASSICAIA (CAB SAUV) most famous.

Uberti Lom ★★★→★★★★ Historic estate, excellent interpreter of FRANCIACORTA'S terroir. Outstanding Comarì del Salem, Dequinque (blend of 02–19), Quinque (blend of 5 yrs). Also v.gd: Dosaggio Zero Sublimis RISERVA, Francesco I.

Vajra, GD Pie ★★★→★★★★ Leading BAROLO producer in Vergne. Outstanding Bricco delle Viole, LANGHE FREISA Kyè. Also gd: Langhe RIES, Barolos (Coste di Rose, Ravera), DOLCETTO Coste & Fossati, Serralunga's Baudana Barolos (Cerretta).

Valentini, Edoardo Ab ★★★★ Collectors seek CERASUOLO D'AB, MONTEPULCIANO D'AB, TREBBIANO D'AB **18' 19' 20'**; among Italy's v. best. Age-worthy, trad.

Valle d'Aosta ★★→★★★ DOC Italy's smallest region makes some of its best reds/whites, but hard to find. Soil of morainic origin (heterogeneous glacial deposits of gravel sands). Famous names: Arnad-Montjovet, Blanc de Morgex (w/sp from Prié Bl), Chambave (local biotype of MUSCAT), Donnas (NEBBIOLO-based), Nus MALVOISIE (with PINOT GR), Torrette (r mostly Petit Rouge). Lovely wines from (r) Cornalin, Mayolet, Premetta; (w) CHARD, PETITE ARVINE.

Valle Isarco T-AA ★★ DYA ALTO ADIGE DOC for mainly whites made along Isarco (Eisack) River, ne of Bolzano. Top: Abbazia di Novacella, Eisacktaler, KÖFERERHOF, Kuenhof, MANNI NÖSSING. KERNER best, GEWURZ, MÜLLER-T, RIES, SILVANER v.gd

Vallerosa Bonci Mar ★★★ Historic estate famous for VERDICCHIO (pioneer of sp). Top: RISERVA Pietrone, San Michele, trad-method Caterina.

Valpolicella Ven ★→★★★★ DOC(G) Light, easy-going red (Valpol), medium-bodied to powerfully alc, rich, tannic (AMARONE) and super-sweet (RECIOTO). Popular RIPASSO, between Valpol and Amarone, but few noteworthy. (*See* box, below.)

Valpolicella Ripasso Ven ★★→★★★ DOC 13 15 16 18 19' 20 21' In huge demand, so changes from 2016. Used to be only from VALPOLICELLA SUPERIORE re-fermented (only once) on RECIOTO or AMARONE grapeskins to make a more age-worthy wine. Now can blend 10% Amarone with standard Valpol and call it Ripasso. Best: Brigaldara, BUSSOLA, CA' LA BIONDA, PRÀ, SPERI, Tamburino Sardo, TEDESCHI, TOMMASI, ZENATO.

Valtellina Lom ★→★★★ DOC/DOCG Rare e-w valley, just s of Swiss border. Soils are sandy-loamy. Home of CHIAVENNASCA. Best labelled Valtellina SUPERIORE (five subzones: Grumello, Inferno, Maroggia, Sassella, Valgella), *see* SFORZATO. Top: ArPePe (Grumello RISERVA Sant'Antonio, Inferno Fiamme Antiche, Sassella Rocce Rosse), Dirupi, FAY, Mamete Prevostini (Sassella Sommarovina).

Venissa Ven ★★★ Owned by BISOL family. Beautiful vyd on island of Mazzorbo in Venice lagoon. Top: Venissa (100% rare w Dorona). Also v.gd: Rosso Venissa (Bx blend). Unique wines.

Valpolicella: the best

Time to take gd VALPOLICELLA more seriously. AMARONE DELLA VALPOLICELLA and RECIOTO DELLA VALPOLICELLA are now DOCG, while RIPASSO has new rules. Following producers make gd to great (★) wine: Allegrini, Begali, Bertani, BOLLA, Boscaini, ★ Brigaldara, BRUNELLI, ★ BUSSOLA, Ca' la Bianca, ★ Ca' La Bionda, Ca' Rugate, Campagnola, CANTINA Valpolicella, Castellani, ★ Comaroto, Corteforte, Corte Sant'Alda, CS Valpantena, ★ DAL FORNO ROMANO, DAL FORNO BROS, ★ GUERRIERI RIZZARDI, La Giuva, Le Ragose, La Giuva, Le Salette, ★ MASI, ★ Mazzi, MONTE DEL FRÀ, Nicolis, ★ PRÀ, ★ QUINTARELLI, ★ Roccolo Grassi, Secondo Marco, ★ Serego Alighieri, ★ SPERI, ★ Stefano Accordini, ★ TEDESCHI, Tenuta Santa Maria, ★ TOMMASI, ★ Trabucchi, Venturini, ★ Viviani, ZENATO, Zeni, ★ ZÝMĒ.

ITALY

Verdicchio dei Castelli di Jesi Mar ★★→★★★ Versatile white from nr Ancona on Adriatic; light and quaffable or sparkling or structured, complex, long-lived (esp RISERVA DOCG, min 2 yrs old), usually lighter and more floral than those of Matelica. Montecarotto more structured. Cupramontana more vibrant. Also CLASSICO. Best: ***Bucci***, La Staffa, Marotti Campi, MIRIZZI, MONTECAPPONE, SARTARELLI, TENUTA DI TAVIGNANO, VALLEROSA BONCI. Also v.gd: Casalefarneto, CORONCINO, Garofoli Podium, PIEVALTA, Serra Fiorese), Edoardo Dottori (Kochlos, Nardì), FATTORIA SAN LORENZO, TENUTA dell'Ugolino, Vignamato.

Verdicchio di Matelica Mar ★★→★★★ Higher acidity, more body, alc, intense minerality than Jesi; longer-lasting though less easy-drinking young. Lower-lying vyds on alluvial soils; higher hillsides more complex soils. RISERVA is likewise DOCG. Top: Belisario (Cambrugiano), Bisci, Borgo Paglianetto (Jera Riserva, Petrara, Vertis), Collestefano, LA MONACESCA.

Verduno Pie ★★★ DOC DYA Berry and herbal flavours. Top: ARNALDO RIVERA, DIEGO MORRA, CASTELLO DI VERDUNO, FRATELLI ALESSANDRIA, GB BURLOTTO, GIANLUCA COLOMBO. Also v.gd: Cadia, I Brè, PODERI EINAUDI, Reverdito, SCARPA.

Verduno, Castello di Pie ★★★ Husband-and-wife team producing v.gd terroir-driven BARBARESCOS Rabajà, Rabajà-Bas and BAROLOS Massara, Monvigliero (also RISERVA), VERDUNO Basadone.

Vermentino di Gallura Sar ★★★ DOCG More flinty and saline than VERMENTINO DI SARDEGNA. Different soils characterized by pink granite (rarity in Italy) with high acidity and minerality. Maybe best in Italy. Top: Cantina di Gallura (Canayli), Capichera (Santigaini, VT), CS del Vermentino (Funtanaliras), Masone Mannu (Costarenas, Petrizza, Roccaìa), Mura (Sienda), Pala (Stellato), Paolo Depperu (Ruinas), SELLA & MOSCA (Monteoro), Surrau.

Vermentino di Sardegna Sar ★★ DOC DYA From anywhere on SAR; generally fruitier (less structured) and offer earlier, uncomplicated appeal compared to VERMENTINO DI GALLURA. Best: ARGIOLAS, Deiana, Mora e Memo, Podere Guardia Grande (Saldenya, Saldenya 85), Quartomoro, ***Santadi***, ***Sella & Mosca***.

Vernaccia di Oristano Sar ★→★★★★ DOC Flor-affected wine, similar to light Sherry (*see* Spain), a touch bitter and full-bodied. Delicious with bottarga. Must try. Top: CONTINI (***Antico Gregori***, Flor 22, RISERVA), Silvio Carta. Also v.gd: Fratelli Serra, Josto Puddu.

Vernaccia di San Gimignano Tus ★★→★★★ Better at entry level than RISERVA. Top: Fontaleoni (VIGNA Casanuova), Giovanni Panizzi, Guicciardini Strozzi/Fattoria di Cusona (1933), La Lastra, Sono Montenidoli (Fiore), Turizzi (Sant'Elena).

Versio, Francesco Pie ★★★ Young talented winemaker in BARBARESCO. Top: refined Barbaresco, new BAROLO di Serralunga. Also v.gd: FREISA, Dogliani, LANGHE NEBBIOLO.

Vevey Albert, Maison VdA ★★★ From vyds at 1000m+ (3281ft), Vevey bros make some of best Blanc de Morgex et de la Salle (Priè Bl). Blanc Flapi (PASSITO) v.gd.

Viarte, La FVG ★★→★★★ Organic estate of FRIULI COLLI ORIENTALI; v.gd terroir-driven FRIULANO, SCHIOPPETTINO di Prepotto, Tazzelenghe.

Viberti Pie ★★★ High-quality, classic BAROLO (Bricco delle Viole, La Volta, Monvigliero, San Pietro), RISERVAS. Also v.gd: BARBERA D'ALBA, LANGHE NEBBIOLO.

Vie di Romans FVG ★★★★ Gianfranco Gallo has taken his ISONZO estate to top status. Outstanding Climat range (six CHARDS, from six sites), Flors di Uis blend, Isonzo PINOT GR Dessimis, MALVASIA, SAUV BLS Piere, Vieris. Also v.gd: MERLOT (Voos dai Ciamps), PINOT N (Vie di Romans).

Vietti Pie ★★★★ Organic estate at Castiglione Falletto owned by Krause Group. Characterful. Textbook BAROLOS: Brunate, Cerequio, Lazzarito, Monvigliero, Ravera, Rocche di Castiglione, Villero RISERVA. Also v.gd: BARBERA D'ALBA, BARBERA D'ASTI, BARBARESCO (Rabajà Riserva, Roncaglie), DERTHONA.

Vigna (or vigneto) A single vyd, generally indicating superior quality.

Vigneri, I Si ★★★★ ETNA estate run by Salvo Foti (greatest expert on NERELLO MASCALESE and all Etna varieties) and his sons. Focus on bush-trained vines, native grape varieties, respect for the land. Outstanding Etna Bianco SUPERIORE (Palmento Caselle, VIGNA di Milo), Etna Rosso (Vinupetra, Viti Centenarie). Also v.gd: Aurora (w), I Vigneri (r), Vinudilice (rosé/sp).

Villa Crespia Lom ★★★ Family estate in FRANCIACORTA, organic. Top: Brut Millè RISERVA, Dosaggio Zero Numero Zero, Riserva del Gelso. Also v.gd: Brut Millè.

Villa Franciacorta Lom ★★★→★★★★ Owned by Bianchi family, in small medieval hamlet (C15) in FRANCIACORTA. Consistent. Best sparkling: Diamant Pas Dosè, Emozione Brut Millesimato, Selezione RISERVA.

Villa Russiz FVG ★★★ Historic estate for DOC COLLIO, v.gd CHARD, FRIULANO, PINOTS BL/GR, SAUV BL, MERLOT (de la Tour selections).

Vino Nobile di Montepulciano Tus ★★→★★★ 15 16' 18 19' **20** 21' The 1st Italian DOCG (1980). Prugnolo Gentile (SANGIOVESE)-based, from TUS town MONTEPULCIANO (distinct from grape). Recent focus on single vyds. Complex, long-lasting Sangiovese expression; often tough, drying tannins. Top: AVIGNONESI, Boscarelli (Costa Grande, Nocio, RISERVA Sotto Casa), Dei (Bossona, cru Madonna della Querce), La Braccesca, Poliziano, Salcheto. Also gd: Bindella, Fattoria del Cerro, Fattoria della Talosa, Montemercurio, Valdipiatta. Riserva after 3 yrs.

Vin Santo / Vinsanto / Vino Santo T-AA, Tus ★★→★★★★ DOC Sweet PASSITO, usually TREBBIANO, MALVASIA and/or SANGIOVESE in TUS (Vin Santo), Nosiola in Trentino (Vino Santo). Versions from Tus extremely variable, anything from off-dry and Sherry-like to sweet and v. rich. May spend 3–10 unracked yrs in small barrels called *caratelli*. ***Avignonesi's is legendary***; plus CAPEZZANA, FELSINA, FRASCOLE, ISOLE E OLENA, Rocca di Montegrossi, SAN GIUSTO A RENTENNANO, SELVAPIANA, Villa Sant'Anna, Villa di Vetrice. *See also* OCCHIO DI PERNICE.

Volpaia, Castello di Tus ★★→★★★ Top CHIANTI CLASSICO at Radda, organic. Best: Balifico (SANGIOVESE/CAB SAUV), Chianti Classico RISERVA, Gran Selezione Coltassala (Sangiovese/Mammolo).

Walch, Elena T-AA ★★★→★★★★ Sisters Karoline and Julia carry on winery founded by mother with passion, talent. Top: Kastelaz, Ringberg vyds, Grande Cuvée (Beyond the Clouds, Kermesse), PINOT N Res Aton.

Zenato Ven ★★★ Garda wines: v. reliable, sometimes inspired. Also AMARONE, LUGANA, SOAVE, VALPOLICELLA. Look for RISERVA Sergio Zenato.

Zýmē Ven ★★★→★★★★ Celestino Gaspari was disciple of GIUSEPPE QUINTARELLI; est his own winery 1999. Best: Harlequin (blend), AMARONE DELLA V RISERVA La Mattonara, RECIOTO DELLA V CLASSICO Amandorlato, Kairos (blend). Also v.gd: Oseleta, SYRAH, From Black to White (w).

What do the initials mean?

DOC (denominazione di origine controllata) controlled denomination of origin, cf. AOP in France.

DOCG (denominazione di origine controllata e garantita) "G" = "guaranteed". Italy's highest quality designation. Guarantee? It's still caveat emptor.

IGT (indicazione geografica tipica) geographic indication of type. Broader and more vague than DOC, cf. IGP in France.

DOP / IGP (denominazione di origine protetta / indicazione geografica protetta) "P" = "protected". The EU's DOP/IGP trump Italy's DOC/IGT.

MGA (menzione geografica aggiuntiva) or UGA (unità geografica aggiuntiva), eg. subzone, cf. cru in France.

ITALY

Germany

Abbreviations used in the text:

Bad	Baden
Frank	Franken
Hess	Hessische Bergstrasse
M-M	Mittelmosel
M Rh	Mittelrhein
Mos	Mosel
Na	Nahe
Pfz	Pfalz
Rhg	Rheingau
Rhh	Rheinhessen
Sa-Un	Saale-Unstrut
Sachs	Sachsen
Würt	Württemberg

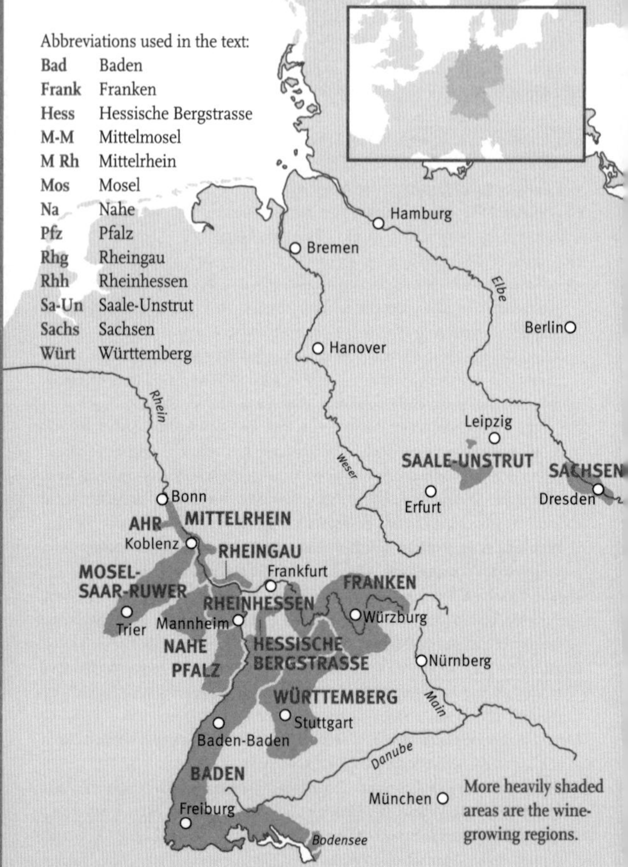

More heavily shaded areas are the wine-growing regions.

German wine has been a success story over the past 30 years, unparalleled in terms of quality. Nevertheless, there will be less German wine in future. If the estimates of the German wine-growers' association prove true, a third less. Many wineries are having trouble finding successors. Sons and daughters can earn more money in industry, with regular working hours and without having to worry that a single night of frost or a single hailstorm will wipe out their earnings. Let's keep our fingers crossed that, despite all this, the steep slopes that characterize the landscape along the Mosel, Rhine, Nahe, Neckar and Main, Elbe, Saale and Unstrut Rivers will be preserved. And with every sip, let's remind ourselves that these pleasures cannot be taken for granted: their production needs passion, diligence and resilience – and wine-growers who show these virtues day after day after day.

Recent vintages

Baden, Franken, Württemberg

Germany's s regions produce wines capable of ageing too: white and red Pinots from Bad, Frank Silvaner, and Ries, Pinot N, Lemberger from Würt improve for 5–10 yrs if from gd producers.

2025 Rain complicated harvest. The further s, the more difficult.
2024 Challenging (frost, mildew). Dense, aromatic; low quantities.
2023 Rollercoaster season with happy end, v.gd whites.
2022 Hot, dry: Pinot N of class, surprising freshness; whites more variable.
2021 Cool summer, plenty of rain. Exceptional whites, middling reds.
Earlier fine vintages: 19 16 15 12 10 (Pinot N) 07 05 97 90 83 71 64 59.

Mosel, Saar, Ruwer

Don't drink them too young. Certainly, Mosels are delicious v. soon after bottling, but to enjoy their max complexity, allow Grosses Gewächs (GG) a min of 3 yrs, Kabinett 3–5 yrs, Spätlese 5–7 yrs, Auslese 7–10 yrs.

2025 Early, quick harvest, low quantity, variable quality. Fine sweet wines.
2024 Frost diminshed quantity (by up to 80%), esp Saar, Ruwer; overall sound quality.
2023 Conditions improved just in time and lasted: mid-weight wines of fine balance.
2022 Another dry, hot summer. Sept rain complicated harvest.
2021 Mildew and rain led harvest into Nov, lighter wines, outstanding freshness, balance.
Earlier fine vintages: 19 18 15 12 11 09 08 07 05 04 03 01 99 97 95 94 93 90 89 88 76 71 69 64 59 53 49 45 37 34 21.

Rheingau, Nahe, Pfalz, Ahr, Rheinhessen, Mittelrhein

Rhg tends to be longest-lived of all German regions, improving for 15 yrs or more, but best Ries from Rhh, Na and Pfz can last as long – and this applies not only to Spätlese and Auslese; GGs undoubtedly have potential to age for 10 yrs+ too. The same holds for Ahr V reds.

2025 Early, quick harvest; mixed results. Ahr, Pfalz v. promising (esp red); Rhg, Nahe balanced sweet up to TBA.
2024 Devastating frost in Na, Ahr, parts of M Rh, Rhg. Plus mildew: mixed bag.
2023 Ries better than Pinot N, but tight selection crucial.
2022 Hot, dry yr, mixed results for whites. Cool nights in autumn. Outstanding Pinot N.
2021 Classical yr like those of 80s, gd acidity, moderate alc, intense flavours.
2019 Drought, heatwaves, rain. Excellent Ries with gd acidity.
2018 Record summer, powerful wines. Growers allowed to acidify.
2017 Roter Hang and Mittelhaardt outstanding: freshness combined with extract.
Earlier fine vintages: 12 11 09 08 05 03 02 01 99 98 97 96 93 90 83 76 71 69 67 64 59 53 49 45 37 34 21.

Acham-Magin Pfz ★★★ Family estate at FORST; vines in Kirchenstück, Jesuitengarten, Pechstein (outstanding 24'). Organic; crisp, age-worthy. Also restaurant, continuously open since 1712.

Adams, Simone Rhh ★★★ Leading estate of INGELHEIM – contributed to renaissance of this ancient town with its calcareous soils. Best: single-vyd PINOT N Auf dem Haun and Pares, fine whites too.

Adelmann, Graf Würt ★★→★★★ Estate in idyllic Schaubeck castle (est 1297). Elegance is key: Süssmund RIES, Oberer Berg LEMBERGER, Götzenberg PINOT N.

Adeneuer, JJ Ahr ★★★ Prime producer, best usually Gärkammer, from enclave in famous Kräuterberg, planted with ancient Kastenholz clone of PINOT N.

Ahr Small river valley s of Bonn; PINOT N of outstanding complexity from slate. Terrible flood in July 2021 destroyed buildings and equipment, but not the steep slopes – 22 likely best vintage ever produced. Best: ADENEUER, BERTRAM-BALTES, Brogsitter, BURGGARTEN, DEUTZERHOF, KREUZBERG, KRIECHEL, MEYER-NÄKEL, NELLES, POLLIG SCHMIDT, Riske, SCHUMACHER, SERMANN, STODDEN. Also gd co-ops: Dagernova, Mayschoss-Altenahr.

Aldinger, Gerhard Würt ★★★→★★★★ Outstanding family estate at Fellbach nr Stuttgart. Reliable (RIES, LEMBERGER, PINOT N), inventive: Brut Nature SEKT, TROLLINGER ALTE REBEN Blanc de Noirs. Wines often yeasty when young, but age exceptionally well.

Alte Grafschaft, Weingut Bad, Frank ★★→★★★ New estate in 400-yr-old cellars at Kreuzwertheim on River Main, vyds there (outstanding Kaffelstein PINOT N) and neighbouring BAD district TAUBERTAL (Satzenberg RIES).

Alte Reben Old vines. But no min age.

Amtliche Prüfungsnummer (APNr) Official test number for quality wine. Useful for discerning different lots of AUSLESE a producer has made from the same vyd. Otherwise, little significance.

Assmannshausen Rhg ★★→★★★★ Steep Höllenberg (45 ha) produces delicate ***Spätburgunder*** (ageing potential 50 yrs+). Growers: Allendorf, Berg, BISCHÖFLICHES WEINGUT RÜDESHEIM, CHAT SAUVAGE, HESSISCHE STAATSWEINGÜTER, KESSELER, König, KRONE, KÜNSTLER, SOLVEIGS, SAALWÄCHTER.

Aus Ersten Lagen Rhh Initially introduced by VDP RHH as "Ortswein aus Ersten Lagen", indicating village wine grown in classified vyds. Funnily enough, no Erste Lage single-vyd wines in Rhh.

Aust, Karl Friedrich Sachs ★★★ Fine family estate (brilliant TRAMINER, PINOT N) nr Dresden, brand-new winery at foot of steep, terraced Goldener Wagen vyd.

Ayl Mos ★→★★★ All vyds known since 1971 by name of historically best site: Kupp. Growers: BISCHÖFLICHE WEINGÜTER TRIER, ***Lauer***, Vols, ZILLIKEN.

Bacharach M Rh ★→★★★ Small, idyllic Rhine-side town; centre of M RH RIES. Growers: BAER, JOST, Kauer, RATZENBERGER.

Baden Huge sw region; former Grand Duchy; 15,000 ha over 300 km. Nine districts, v. different conditions, eg. BODENSEE, KAISERSTUHL, MARKGRÄFLERLAND, ORTENAU.

Baer M Rh ★★→★★★ Former Bastian estate, taken over and enlarged by Baer family (wine merchants and pharmacists), vyds farmed by hand, concentrated, taut wines to age (1st vintage 21). Watch.

Barth, Wein- und Sektgut Rhg ★★→★★★ Family estate at HATTENHEIM, 22 ha; specializes in finely chiselled RIES SEKT from single vyds (Hassel, Schützenhaus).

Bassermann-Jordan Pfz ★★★ Famous historic estate producing powerful RIES from DEIDESHEIM and FORST: GGS often sweeter than its peers.

Battenfeld-Spanier Rhh ★★★★ Passionate HO Spanier (*see also* KÜHLING-GILLOT) is leading grower in calcareous sites at Hohen-Sülzen, Mölsheim and ZELLERTAL (auction RIES about to get cultish); bio. Brilliant Brut Nature SEKT. Outstanding even in difficult 24.

Becker, Friedrich Pfz ★★★★ Age-worthy, terroir-driven PINOT N from S PFZ, wines can age decades (Heydenreich, Kammerberg). Friedrich Wilhelm B continues work of father Friedrich (died in 2025).

Becker, JB Rhg ★★→★★★ Delightfully old-fashioned, cask-aged (and long-lived) dry RIES, SPÄTBURGUNDER at Walluf and Martinsthal. Mature vintages (back to 90s) great value.

Bercher Bad ★★★ KAISERSTUHL family estate, long experience in barrique ageing PINOTS BL/GR/N, GGS now aged one more yr in bottle before sale.

Bergdolt Pfz ★★★ Organic estate at Duttweiler, known for food-friendly WEISSBURGUNDER GG Mandelberg. Now also amazing SEKT (Fluxus Extra Brut, Blanc de Blanc Brut Nature).

Bergweiler-Prüm Mos ★★★ Project of Erni LOOSEN with his grandfather's vines and cellar at WEHLEN, sold only through Place de Bx (*see* France). From 0.55 ha in SONNENUHR, usually one *Fuder* each of dry ALTE REBEN, KABINETT, AUSLESE. Vines 130 yrs old, no machines in vyd or cellar, grass mowed by hand, basket press from 1910. Fairly priced.

Bernhart Pfz ★★★ Gerd B and son Marius at Schweigen, S PFZ: dense, straightforward, classically structured PINOT varieties (r/w).

Bernkastel M-M ★→★★★★ Centre of M-M, misrepresented by Kurfürstlay GROSSLAGE (avoid!). Rightly famous sites for rich, complex RIES: Alte Badstube am Doctorberg, Badstube, DOCTOR, Graben, Johannisbrünnchen, Lay.

Bertram-Baltes Ahr ★★★ Shooting stars in AHR, engaged in regenerative viticulture – eg. no more plastic in vyd or cellar; cover crops, sheep. Fresh, racy, almost slim SPÄTBURGUNDER from prime vyds.

Bischel Rhh ★★★ VDP family estate in Appenheim, outstanding RIES GGS Heerkretz, Hundertgulden, Scharlachberg.

Bischöfliches Weingut Rüdesheim Rhg ★★★ Not to be confused with BISCHÖFLICHE WEINGÜTER TRIER: 9 ha of best sites in ASSMANNSHAUSEN, RÜDESHEIM. Age-worthy, dense ***Pinot N***. Cellarmaster Peter Perabo vinified legendary vintages at KRONE previously.

Bischöfliche Weingüter Trier Mos ★★ 120 ha of potentially 1st-class historic donations. Reliability a concern, but seems to be improving: gd Res range (Apotheke RIES TROCKEN 19').

Bocksbeutel Frank Belly-shaped bottle dating back to C18, today only permitted in FRANK and village of Neuweier, BAD. (*See* box, below.)

Bodensee Bad Idyllic district of S BAD and on (particularly dynamic) Bavarian shore of Lake Constance, at altitude: 400–580m (1312–1903ft). Dry, elegant MÜLLER-T, light, firm SPÄTBURGUNDER.

Böhme & Töchter Sa-Un ★★→★★★ Rising star in e, top vyds at Freyburg (Unstrut) and purist winemaking shape expressive PINOTS (BL/GR/N), culinary CHARD, mineral RIES.

Boppard M Rh ★→★★★ Wine town of M RH with GROSSE LAGE Hamm, an amphitheatre of vines. Growers: Heilig Grab, Lorenz, M Müller, Perll, WEINGART. Unbeatable ***value***.

Brauneberg M-M ★★★→★★★★ Excellent full RIES from Juffer and Juffer-Sonnenuhr

The whole truth about the Bocksbeutel

It's often claimed that the bulbous bottles used by trads in FRANK for SILVANER are modelled on the shape of a billy goat's testicles. Somewhat repulsive, isn't it? However, the German word *Bock* (male goat) is by no means the origin of "BOCKSBEUTEL". The term is in fact derived from N German *Bookesbüdel*: a C14 invention, when priests, doctors, scholars, merchants carried a bag on their belts with the book most important to their profession sewn into it. You could say that the "book bag" was the smartphone of its day. When this utensil went out of fashion, its name was transferred to the bulbous bottle – for a trad object that you can carry with you at all times, or perhaps even should. Sublime irony – an attitude as complex as a gd Silvaner.

vyds. Growers: ***F Haag***, KESSELSTATT, M Conrad, MF RICHTER, Paulinshof, Sankt Nikolaus Hospital, SCHLOSS LIESER, THANISCH, ***W Haag***.

Bremer Ratskeller Town-hall cellar in N Germany's commercial town of Bremen, founded in 1405, UNESCO World Heritage Site. Oldest wine is a barrel of 1653 RÜDESHEIMER Apostelwein.

Breuer Rhg ★★★→★★★★ Exquisite RIES from RAUENTHAL, RÜDESHEIM and LORCH. Nonnenberg transforms austerity into age-worthiness, Berg Schlossberg **90' 93' 96' 97' 02' 08' 12' 13' 14** 15' 16 17' 18 19 20 21' has depth at 12% alc, Pfaffenwies full of floral elegance.

Buhl, Reichsrat von Pfz ★★★ Historic PFZ estate at DEIDESHEIM. After several changes in cellar, unstable – but signs of things turning round.

Bürgerspital zum Heiligen Geist Frank ★★★→★★★★ Charity founded 1316. Long-time director Robert Haller has retired, but continuity for whites trad-made from best sites in/around WÜRZBURG, eg. SILVANER GG from monopoly Stein-Harfe **15' 16' 17' 18' 19' 20' 21'** 22 23', RIES Randersacker Pfülben and STEIN-BERG.

Burggarten Ahr ★★★ PINOT N from best sites in lower AHR, tight, aromatic (esp Alte Lay, Burggarten, Kräuterberg). Family runs hotel at Heppingen.

Bürklin-Wolf, Dr Pfz ★★★→★★★★ Finely chiselled RIES full of finesse from 30 ha of best MITTELHAARDT vyds, incl FORST (Jesuitengarten, Kirchenstück, Pechstein), Ruppertsberg (Gaisböhl), WACHENHEIM (Rechbächel); bio. Forerunner of VDP classifcation (1994).

Busch, Clemens Mos ★★★★ Steep Pündericher Marienburg farmed by hand, bio. Seven GGS from different parcels, eg. Felsterrasse (mineral, deep), Raffes (power, balance), Rothenpfad (silky, balsamic). Also Res range (2 yrs' barrel-ageing). Son Johannes taken over.

Castell'sches Fürstliches Domänenamt Frank ★★★ Ferdinand Fürst zu Castell vigorously increases quality: SILVANER GG Schlossberg **15' 16 17'** 18 19' 20', sold only 5 yrs after harvest, ERSTE LAGE Silvaners outstanding value.

Chat Sauvage Rhg ★★★→★★★★ Dense PINOT N from ASSMANNSHAUSEN, JOHANNISBERG, LORCH, RÜDESHEIM; crisp CHARD. And no RIES!

Christmann Pfz ★★★→★★★★ VDP President Steffen C, bio pioneer, now joined by daughter Sophie, PINOT N expert. Estate owns only classified vyds. Also CHRISTMANN & KAUFFMANN.

Christmann & Kauffmann Pfz ★★★ SEKT estate, est 2019 by Sophie and Steffen C and ex-Bollinger cellarmaster (*see* France) Mathieu K. Triple-digit codes on labels starting with "1": RIES-based, starting with "2": PINOTS N/BL/CHARD-based.

Clüsserath, Ansgar Mos ★★★ Tense TRITTENHEIMER Apotheke RIES from Eva Clüsserath-WITTMANN (married to Philipp W). KABINETTS delicious.

Corvers-Kauter Rhg ★★★ Organic estate at Mittelheim, 37 ha, textbook dry RIES from MARCOBRUNN, RAUENTHAL (Baiken), RÜDESHEIM, occasionally also TBA; PINOT N from ASSMANNSHAUSEN.

Crusius, Dr Na ★★★ Family estate at TRAISEN, holdings in prime vyds Bastei, Felsenberg, Kupfergrube. Young Rebecca C changes style to drier, more mineral, gd eye on balance.

Dautel Würt ★★→★★★★ Christian D produces outstanding CHARD, PINOTS BL/N, LEMBERGER, in Burgundian spirit.

Deidesheim Pfz ★★→★★★★ Centre of MITTELHAARDT (also economically). Top: BASSERMANN-JORDAN, Biffar, BUHL, BÜRKLIN-WOLF, CHRISTMANN, Fusser, MARGARETHENHOF, MOSBACHER, SECKINGER, Siben, Stern, VON WINNING. Also gd co-op.

Der Ring Mosel 1899 Mos Formerly Bernkasteler Ring, one of two MOS growers' associations organizing an auction every Sept, eg. MOLITOR, THANISCH Erben Müller-Burggraef.

Germany's quality levels

The official range of qualities and styles in ascending order is (take a deep breath):

1 **Wein** Formerly known as Tafelwein. Light wine of no specified character, mostly sweetish.

2 **ggA (geschützte geographische Angabe)** or protected geographical indication, formerly known as LANDWEIN. Dryish wine with some regional style. Mostly a label to avoid, but some thoughtful estates use the Landwein designation to bypass official constraints.

3 **gU (geschützte Ursprungsbezeichnung)** or protected designation of origin. Replacing QUALITÄTSWEIN. Up to now, only six small-scale appellations in the narrower sense of the word approved by the EU.

4 **Qualitätswein** Dry or sweetish wine with sugar added before fermentation to increase its strength, but tested for quality and with distinct local and grape character. Don't despair.

5 **Kabinett** Lightest of German wines, dry/dryish, unsugared, subtle yet long-lived, production complicated by climate change: altitude vyds needed, and early, speedy picking.

6 **Spätlese** Late-harvest. One level riper and sweeter than KABINETT. Needs to be aged for 5 yrs at least. Dry SPÄTLESE (or what could be considered as such) is today mostly sold under Qualitätswein designation (even if not sugared).

7 **Auslese** Wines from selective picking of super-ripe bunches affected by noble rot (*Edelfäule*). Unctuous, but – trad – elegant rather than super-concentrated; 99% are sweet, but specialists (JB BECKER, Koehler-Ruprecht) show Auslese TROCKEN can be elegant too.

8 **Beerenauslese (BA)** Luscious sweet wine from exceptionally ripe, individually selected berries concentrated by noble rot.

9 **Eiswein** Made from frozen grapes with the ice (ie. water content) discarded, thus v. concentrated: of BA ripeness or more. Outstanding Eiswein vintages: **98 02 04 08**. Less and less produced in past decade: climate change is Eiswein's enemy.

10 **Trockenbeerenauslese (TBA)** Sweetest, most expensive category of German wine; extremely rare, viscous and concentrated, with dried-fruit flavours. Made from selected dried-out berries affected by noble rot (botrytis). Half-bottles a gd idea.

Deutzerhof Ahr ★★★ PINOT N from AHR V with body and density; GGS (Eck, Mönchberg), Res range (Grand Duc). Sensational 22 FRÜHBURGUNDERS (Herrenberg, Mönchberg).

Diel, Schlossgut Na ★★★→★★★★ Caroline D reliably produces exquisite ***GG Ries***, best is usually Burgberg. Magnificent SPÄTLESEN, serious ***Sekt*** Cuvée Mo, Goldloch RIES.

Doctor M-M Emblematic steep vyd at BERNKASTEL, place where TBA was invented 1921 by THANISCH. Unique balsamic-flavoured RIES from 3.2 ha, five owners: both Thanisch estates, WEGELER (1.1 ha), Lauerburg and local Heiligen Geist charity (0.26 ha, leased until 2033 to MOLITOR, SCHLOSS LIESER).

Dolde, Helmut Würt ★★→★★★ Some of Germany's highest vyds (up to 530m/1739ft), meticulously managed by retired grammar-school teacher. Great SILVANERS; delicate, age-worthy SPÄTBURGUNDER (brilliant 22' Fass 2).

Dönnhoff Na ★★★★ Outstanding in every respect: solid basic wines, excellent GGS (balance, ageing potential), and fruity and nobly sweet wines of great distinction. In 24, many vyds affected by frost.

Egon Müller zu Scharzhof Mos ★★★★ 59 71 83 90 01 03 15 18 19 20 21 22 23 24 Legendary SAAR family estate at WILTINGEN, treasury of old vines. Racy SCHARZHOFBERGER RIES among world's greatest: sublime, vibrant, immortal. ***Kabinetts*** feather-light, long-lived (but meanwhile costly).

Einzellage Individual vyd site. Never to be confused with GROSSLAGE.

Emrich-Schönleber Na ★★★ Precise RIES GG from Monzingen, in upper NA V, esp Halenberg and auction wine Auf der Ley.

Erden M-M ★★★→★★★★ Village in M-M with a Roman wine press worth seeing. Red-slate soils give RIES (dr/sw), rare spiciness, delicacy. GROSSE LAGE: Prälat, Treppchen. Growers: Bremer Ratskeller, Erbes, JJ Christoffel, LOOSEN, MAX F RICHTER, MERKELBACH, MOLITOR, Mönchhof, Rebenhof, Schmitges.

Erste Lage Classified vyd, 2nd-from-top level in VDP classification, similar to Burgundy's Premier Cru.

Erzeugerabfüllung Analogous to GUTSABFÜLLUNG, but also allowed on co-op labels.

Escherndorf Frank ★★★ Village with steep GROSSE LAGE Lump ("scrap" – as in tiny inherited parcels). Marvellous ***Silvaner***, RIES (dr/sw). Growers: Fröhlich, H SAUER, R SAUER, Schäffer, zur Schwane.

Eser, August Rhg ★★→★★★ Fine Oestrich family estate known for emphatically dry but elegant RHG RIES; gd PINOT N too.

Feinherb Imprecisely defined trad term for wines with around 10–30g/l sugar. After 2–5 yrs age, fine food matches, esp curries or chilli-influenced dishes.

Forst Pfz ★★→★★★★ Famous MITTELHAARDT village; Kirchenstück was PFZ's highest-taxed vyd on 1828 tax map. Pechstein, Jesuitengarten, Ungeheuer vyds almost equally outstanding. Top: ACHAM-MAGIN, BASSERMANN-JORDAN, BÜRKLIN-WOLF, H Spindler, MARGARETHENHOF, MOSBACHER, VON BUHL, VON WINNING, WOLF.

Franken / Franconia Frank Region of distinctive dry wines, esp SILVANER, often bottled in round-bellied flasks (BOCKSBEUTEL).

Fricke, Eva Rhg ★★★ Dense, full, even silky RIES from 17 ha at KIEDRICH, LORCH.

Full Rhh ★★→★★★ Deeply mineral RIES (Silberberg, Zellerweg am Schwarzen Herrgott) from RHH part of ZELLERTAL.

Fürst, Weingut Frank ★★★★ ***Spätburgunders*** 97' 03' 05' 09 10' **15' 16'** 17 18' 19 20 21 22 23 of great finesse from red sandstone (most dense, Hundsrück; most powerful, Schlossberg; most typical, Centgrafenberg). Tight CHARD in burgundian style, underrated RIES, rich but fresh FRÜHBURGUNDER, tiny quantities delicious CHARD SEKT (Brut Nature). No small wines at this estate.

Gallais, Le Mos EGON MÜLLER ZU SCHARZHOF 2nd estate, with 4-ha monopoly Braune Kupp at WILTINGEN. AUSLESEN can be exceptional.

Grosse Lage / Grosslage: spot the difference

Up to now, German wine labels can say GROSSLAGE or GROSSE LAGE. They are not the same: the former is a mix of usually hundreds of ha of secondary vyds, the latter refers to the exact opposite – to a top single vyd, an EINZELLAGE, a German "Grand Cru", according to the classification set up by growers' association VDP. Until now, a *Grosslage* could disguise itself as a single vyd: who would know if Forster Mariengarten is an *Einzellage* or a *Grosslage*? (It's Gross.) But luckily, this is not the end of the story: after 2026, a *Grosslage* name is no longer allowed to be mentioned together with a village name. Instead of Forster Mariengarten, it must be written: region Mariengarten. The term *Bereich* will also be replaced by region. *Bereich* means district within an *Anbaugebiet* (region). *Bereich* on a label should equally be treated as a flashing red light; the wine is a blend from arbitrary sites within that district.

Geisenheim Rhg Town primarily known for Germany's university of oenology and viticulture. GROSSE LAGE Rothenberg (WEGELER) is one of RHG's best.

GG (Grosses Gewächs) "Great/top growth". The top dry wine from a VDP-classified GROSSE LAGE.

Goldkapsel / Gold Capsule Mos, Na, Rhg, Rhh Designation (and bottle seal) mainly for AUSLESE and higher; v. strict selection of grapes, which should add finesse and complexity, not primarily weight and sweetness. Lange Goldkapsel (Long Gold Capsule) even better. Not a legal term.

Graach M-M ★★→★★★★ Small village between BERNKASTEL and WEHLEN. GROSSE LAGE vyds: Domprobst, Himmelreich, Josephshöfer. Growers: ***JJ Prüm***, Kees-Kieren, KESSELSTATT, LOOSEN, MAX F RICHTER, MOLITOR, SA PRÜM, SCHAEFER, ***Selbach-Oster***, Studert-Prüm, WEGELER.

Grans-Fassian M-M ★★★ Catharina Grans, 13th generation, has treasure of prime sites at TRITTENHEIM, PIESPORT and Leiwen. Kitsch-free and age-worthy RIES (dr/sw), drive, balance.

Griesel & Compagnie Hess ★★★ SEKT start-up (2013) at Bensheim, known for crisp, dry style. Top: Dosage Zero PINOTS BL/N from single-vyds Fürstenlager, Höllberg (both granite). Single-vyd RIES Sekt to come.

Gröhl Rhh ★★★ Family estate celebrated 400 yrs in 2025. Young Johannes G advocates early picking for bitingly acidic RIES (Pettenthal TROCKEN); tight-knit PINOT N (Hölle 22), salty 1625 Grande Cuvée Brut Nature.

Grosse Lage Top level of VDP classification, but only for VDP members. Dry wine from a *Grosse Lage* site is called GG. Note: not on any account to be confused with GROSSLAGE. Stay awake, there.

Grosser Ring Mos Group of top (VDP) MOS estates, whose annual Sept auction at TRIER sets world record prices.

Grosslage Term destined, maybe even intended, to confuse: a collection of secondary vyds without identity. Not on any account to be confused with GROSSE LAGE. Newest legislation stipulates term "region" must precede *Grosslagen* name; mention of village together with *Grosslage* (eg. Piesporter Michelsberg) no longer permitted, but transition period lasted until 2026.

Gunderloch Rhh ★★★→★★★★ Historical NACKENHEIM estate portrayed in Carl Zuckmayer's play *Der fröhliche Weinberg* (1925). Deeply mineral Rothenberg RIES both TROCKEN (GG 17' **18' 19'** 20 21' 22 23' 24) and sweet. New VERSTEIGERUNGSWEIN/GG from Rothenberg parcel Fenchelberg. ***Kabinett Jean-Baptiste*** is perfect match for spicy dishes.

Gut Hermannsberg Na ★★★ Ex-Prussian state dom at NIEDERHAUSEN, now private. RIES GGS need time to develop: fine RES range (Hermannsberg and Kupfergrube). Stylish guesthouse.

Gutsabfüllung Estate-bottled, and made from own grapes.

Gutswein Entry-level wine, no vyd or village designation, but only producer's name. Ideally, produced from own grapes, but not always the case.

Gutzler Rhh ★★★ Reliable, versatile: refined Morstein RIES, dense SILVANER, subtle SPÄTBURGUNDERS from Gundersheim and Westhofen. Also plot of historical Liebfrauenstift-Kirchenstück at Worms.

Haag, Fritz Mos ★★★★ BRAUNEBERG's top estate; Oliver H is more modern in style than father Wilhelm. *See* SCHLOSS LIESER.

Haag, Willi Mos ★★→★★★ BRAUNEBERG family estate, led by Marcus H. Old-style RIES, mainly sweet, rich but balanced, inexpensive.

Haart, Reinhold M-M ★★★→★★★★ Best estate in PIESPORT, with important holding in famous Goldtröpfchen ("gold droplet") vyd. RIES PRÄDIKAT ***racy, copybook Mos.***

Haidle Würt ★★★→★★★★ Moritz H uses cool climate of Remstal area for distinctive freshness. Outstanding LEMBERGER GGS Berge, Gehrnhalde, RIES Pulvermächer.

Halbtrocken Medium-dry with 9–18g/l unfermented sugar, inconsistently distinguished from FEINHERB.

Hallgarten Rhg ★★→★★★★ Some of highest vyds in RHG (up to 200m/656ft above River Rhine); Hendelberg, Jungfer sites more and more sought after with climate change. Growers: FÜRST LÖWENSTEIN, KÜHN, H Nicolai, PRINZ, Querbach, SPREITZER.

Hattenheim Rhg ★★→★★★★ Town famous for *Brunnen* ("well") vyds (Nussbrunnen, Wisselbrunnen), with water-bearing layers underneath and legendary STEINBERG high above village. Estates: BARTH, HESSISCHE STAATSWEINGÜTER, Kaufmann, Knyphausen, Ress, Schloss Reinhartshausen, SPREITZER.

Heger, Dr Bad ★★★→★★★★ Young Rebecca H sets accents in steep slopes of Achkaren, IHRINGEN by picking earlier. Best parcel selections: Häusleboden PINOT N from old Clos de Vougeot (*see* France) cuttings, planted 1956; Winklerberg Vorderer Berg (PINOTS BL/GR/N).

Heitlinger / Burg Ravensburg Bad ★★→★★★ Two leading estates of Kraichgau, N BAD, under same ownership: Heitlinger more elegant (PINOT N), Burg Ravensburg full-bodied (BLAUFRÄNKISCH).

Hermann, Dr Mos ★★★ Top estate at ERDEN, vyds also in ÜRZIG, new VDP member (2025). Best known for magnificent sweet Prädikatsweine, KABINETT to TBA.

Hessische Bergstrasse Germany's smallest wine region (460 ha), n of Heidelberg, cool climate (proximity of Odenwald low mtn range), geologically v. interesting.

Hessische Staatsweingüter Hess, Rhg ★★→★★★★ State dom with vinotheque in KLOSTER EBERBACH; 210 ha in top sites all along RHG and HESSISCHE BERGSTRASSE. Management change 2025.

Hey, Weingut ★★★ Leading estate in e, at Naumburg, SA-UN. Impressive RIES, PINOTS BL/GR GGS from steep Steinmeister vyd.

Heymann-Löwenstein Mos ★★★ Family estate known for terroir-minded, nonconformist RIES from steep terraces at WINNINGEN. Sold to wine merchant and investors 2025. Reinhard L consults for transition period.

Hochheim Rhg ★★→★★★★ Town e of main RHG, on River Main, rich RIES from loess and limestone soils, best usually Domdechaney, Hölle, Kirchenstück. Growers: Domdechant Werner, Flick, HESSISCHE STAATSWEINGÜTER, Himmel, Im Weinegg, KÜNSTLER, Rosenkranz.

Hock A trad English term for Rhine wine, derived from HOCHHEIM.

Hövel, Weingut von Mos ★★★ Historical Saar estate, founded 1803, with substantial vyd holding (3.8 ha) of SCHARZHOFBERG and monopolies Hörecker (0.6 ha) and Hütte (5.8 ha). Closed early 2026 after economically challenging yrs. Watch out for what's left of superb 22s.

Huber, Bernhard Bad ★★★→★★★★ PINOT N ALTE REBEN, Sommerhalde, Wildenstein have generous fruit – and world fame. Same holds for Julian H's tight, demanding CHARD.

Ihringen Bad ★→★★★ Village in KAISERSTUHL known for fine PINOTS N/GR/BL on steep volcanic Winklerberg. Top: DR HEGER, Konstanzer, Michel, Stigler.

Immich-Batterieberg Mos ★★→★★★ Handcrafted, balanced RIES, mostly dry, from Enkirch's rocky Batterieberg vyd (shaped by "batteries" of dynamite in C19).

Ingelheim Rhh ★★→★★★★ Town with limestone banks under vyds; historic fame for PINOT N. C19 *Trousset* encyclopedia puts it on par with Volnay, Pommard, Vosne, Chambolle-Musigny (*see* France). Dynamic estates: ADAMS, Baum-Barth, Bettenheimer, Dautermann, NEUS, Schloss Westerhaus, SAALWÄCHTER, WASEM, Werner.

Iphofen Frank ★★→★★★ Well-ageing SILVANER from gypsum soils in E FRANK (Steigerwald = altitude). Growers: Arnold, Emmerich, JULIUSSPITAL, Popp, RUCK, Seufert, Vetter, Von der Tann, Weigand, WELTNER, ***Wirsching***, Zehntkeller.

Johannisberg Rhg ★★→★★★★ Legendary SCHLOSS JOHANNISBERG has made town's name synonymous with RIES; other wineries incl CHAT SAUVAGE, JOHANNISHOF (Eser), Prinz v. Hessen, Schamari-Mühle. GROSSLAGE (avoid!): Erntebringer.

Johannishof (Eser) Rhg ★★→★★★ Family estate; vyds at JOHANNISBERG, Rüdesheim, Winkel: RIES, perfect balance of ripeness, steely acidity. Back vintages available.

Jost, Toni M Rh ★★★ Leading estate in BACHARACH, M RH. Monopoly Hahn. Inexpensive Devon S TROCKEN; KABINETT; FEINHERB.

Jülg Pfz ★★→★★★★ Dense, long-ageing PINOT N (15' SCHWEIGEN ORTSWEIN, splendid form 2025), sharply mineral CHARD, SAUV BL from limestone.

Juliusspital Frank ★★★ Ancient WÜRZBURG charity, top vyds all over FRANK, firmly structured ***dry Silvaners*** that age well. New directors 2023 and 2025.

Kaiserstuhl Bad Extinct volcano nr Rhine in S BAD, notably warm climate, black soil. Altitudes up to 400m (1312ft). PINOTS BL/N of class. Unique PINOT GR: Kaiserstuhl is for Pinot Gr what Provence (*see* France) is for rosé.

Kanzem Mos ★★★ SAAR village with steep GROSSE LAGE vyd Altenberg. Growers: BISCHÖFLICHE WEINGÜTER TRIER, Cantzheim (plus guesthouse), VAN VOLXEM, VON OTHEGRAVEN.

Karthäuserhof Mos ★★★ Historic RUWER estate with emblematic neck-only label. New team led by Mathieu Kauffmann (ex-Bollinger, *see* France) and Dominik Völk (ex-VAN VOLXEM) continues glory days. New achievement: great RIES SEKT.

Keller, Franz Bad *See* SCHWARZER ADLER.

Keller, Klaus Peter Rhh ★★★★ Star of RHH, cultish for terroir-driven ALTE REBEN RIES G-Max from undisclosed (calcareous) parcel, and GGS Hubacker, Morstein. Also Ries from NIERSTEIN (Hipping, Pettenthal), M-M (PIESPORT Schubertslay).

Kesseler, August Rhg ★★★★ A man like a *Gesamtkunstwerk*: grower, oenologist, marketing genius and strategist: ASSMANNSHAUSEN PINOT N of great distinction, longevity. Powerful, balanced RIES from LORCH, RÜDESHEIM. Long-time employees follow his path.

Kesselstatt, Reichsgraf von Mos ★★ Top vyds on Mosel and tributaries, 50 ha; after difficult yrs now improving.

Kiedrich Rhg ★★→★★★★ Top village, almost monopoly of WEIL estate. Other growers (FRICKE, Knyphausen, PRINZ VON HESSEN) own only small plots. Famous church and choir.

Kloster Eberbach Rhg Atmospheric C12 Cistercian abbey in HATTENHEIM, where *The Name of the Rose* was filmed. Domicile of HESSISCHE STAATSWEINGÜTER.

Klumpp Bad ★★★ Top family estate in Kraichgau, N BAD, led by bros Markus and Andreas K, esp fruit-driven PINOT N, refined PINOT GR from Rothenberg vyd at Bruchsal, and Unteröwisheim Kirchberg CHARD. Also inexpensive Hand in Hand series together with Markus K's wife Meike Näkel (MEYER-NÄKEL).

Can PIWIs age?

Some organic wine-growers believe that viticulture will only survive with fungus-resistant grape varieties, in German known as PIWIS (*Pilzwiderstandsfähig*). Other growers condemn these hybrid crosses between *Vitis vinifera* and resistant American *Vitis* species as overly simplistic and uninspiring. What insights can be gained from tasting a 1959 (top yr) Léon Millot (PIWI) from GROSSE LAGE ASSMANNSHAUSEN Höllenberg – at that time an experimental cultivation by the HESSISCHE STAATSWEINGÜTER? Malt, slate, a hint of coffee. Creamy attack, fine tannin, medium-bodied; a fine, not overpowering acidity, tactile-mineral on the finish, tobacco and rum flavours. Both views of PIWIs are somehow confirmed – but overall, this is a truly remarkable wine.

Knebel Mos ★★★ Family estate in top form at WINNINGEN. Refined TBA, seriously crafted, dense dry wines, esp Uhlen RIES GG.

Knewitz Rhh ★★★ Big RHH success story: from unknown to VDP star in less than 15 yrs. Stylish CHARD Res, extract-laden RIES Hundertgulden 17' 18 19' 20' 21' 22' 23' 24'. Organic.

Knipser Pfz ★★★→★★★★ Top estate in N PFZ, best for age-worthy PINOT N (best selection RdP 14' 15' 18' 19' 20'), discreetly oaked CHARD and specialities like ancient grape Gelber Orleans or quaffable CLAIRETTE (Bx-blend rosé). Now also "ten yrs after" series: GEWURZ, RdP, Cuvée X, SYRAH, all 15 marketed 2025.

Johann Philipp Bronner quotes "Eremitage" planted at Würzburg 1839: Marsanne?

Königin Viktoriaberg Rhg ★★→★★★ Historic RIES vyd at HOCHHEIM, today run by Flick estate, Wicker. After 1845 visit, Queen Victoria granted owner right to rename vyd as "Queen-Victoria-mountain".

Kopp Bad ★★★ In ORTENAU, bio estate and fine restaurant (with livestock farming) nr Baden-Baden city. Tight CHARD; dense, mineral PINOT N.

Kranz, Weingut Pfz ★★★→★★★★ Top organic estate at Ilbesheim with its limestone reef Kalmit. Tight, mineral RIES, PINOTS BL/N – and superb Blanc de Noirs Brut Nature SEKT. Kerstin and Boris K now assisted by son Xaver.

Kreuzberg, HJ Ahr ★★★→★★★★ Perfectionist producer, some of most elegant AHR V reds: Devonschiefer R PINOT N, Oben im Eigelstal FRÜHBURGUNDER GG.

Kriechel, Peter Ahr ★★→★★★ Fine family estate at Ahrweiler. Round, full SPÄTBURGUNDER: Kräuterberg GOLDKAPSEL.

Krone, Weingut Rhg ★★★ Famous SPÄTBURGUNDER estate with a treasure of old vyds in ASSMANNSHAUSEN (Juwel 15', Höllenberg 22'), run by WEGELER.

Kühling-Gillot Rhh ★★★★ Top bio estate, run by Caroline Gillot and husband HO Spanier. Best in outstanding range of ROTER HANG RIES: GG Rothenberg Wurzelecht from ungrafted vines.

Kühn, Peter Jakob Rhg ★★★→★★★★ Obsessive bio vyd management and long macerations shape ***nonconformist but exciting*** RIES. Many novelties: GGS RÜDESHEIM Berg Schlossberg, RAUENTHAL Baiken; great SEKT. Landgeflecht, Schlehdorn to be discontinued.

Kuhn, Philipp Pfz ★★★→★★★★ Outstanding estate at Laumersheim, N PFZ: RIES (Saumagen, Schwarzer Herrgott), age-worthy SPÄTBURGUNDER, terrific specialities CHARD, SAUV BL, VIOGNIER.

Künstler Rhg ★★★→★★★★ Gunter K's family estate at HOCHHEIM has vyds and GGS in every part of RHG, incl ex-Schönborn vyd in MARCOBRUNN; trad, reliable style. Wines need, and reward, time.

Kuntz, Sybille Mos ★★★ Progressive bio estate at Lieser. Pioneer of MOS TROCKEN; intense wines, one of each ripeness category (for gastronomy). Now also Natural.

Kurek, Jonas Würt ★★→★★★ Young grower on Bavarian shores of BODENSEE. Trained with Bernhard and Julian HUBER, makes outstanding Seehalde PINOT N.

Laible, Andreas Bad ★★★ Crystalline dry RIES, fine TRAMINER from Durbach's Plauelrain vyd (granite). Younger brother Alexander has own estate.

Landwein Technically "ggA" (*see* box, p.180), meant to label wines with only broadly defined origin. Now popular among ambitious growers to avoid narrow-minded official quality testing. Best known: Brenneisen, Enderle & Moll, Forgeurac, Greiner, Höfflin, Nieger, Vorgrimmler, WASENHAUS, ZIEREISEN (all BAD); Drei Zeilen, Vetter, Weigand (FRANK); Schmitt (RHH); Konni & Evi (SA-UN).

Lauer Mos ★★★ Fine, precise SAAR RIES: tense and poised. Parcel selections from huge Ayler Kupp vyd incl salty, phenolic Schonfels and ethereal-spicy Lambertskirch (auction).

Leitz, Josef Rhg ★★★ Important RÜDESHEIM estate, 160 ha, producing anything from respectable discount RIES to outstanding GGS. Inexpensive, reliable Eins-Zwei-Dry label, and soundly produced de-alc wines.

Lippold, Dr Mos ★★→★★★ Dr Enno L was manager at Deinhard; now holds 1 ha in ÜRZIG's Würzgarten. Refined SEKT (RIES Brut Nature 14), delicious Würzgarten Grand Cru Weltersberg AUSLESE Gold 18. Export only.

Loewen, Carl Mos ★★★ RIES of complexity, best vyd Longuicher Maximin Herrenberg (planted 1896, ungrafted). Entry-level Ries Varidor too: excellent ***value***.

Loosen, Weingut Dr M-M ★★→★★★★ Legendary estate for textbook M-M RIES led by Ernst L. Reliable entry-level (even Dr L from bought-in grapes), nine different GGS and four Res. Tradition range KABINETT, SPÄTLESE with less sweetness and prolonged barrel-ageing (3, 5, 8 yrs). Cultish Prälat AUSLESE. More projects, estates: BERGWEILER-PRÜM, Villa Wolf (PFZ); Maison Perron de Mypont (Burgundy); Appassionata, J Christopher (Oregon, US); Ch Ste Michelle (Washington State, US).

Lorch Rhg ★→★★★ Village in extreme w of RHG, conditions more M RH-like than Rhg-like. Best: BREUER, CHAT SAUVAGE, FRICKE, KESSELER, SOLVEIGS, von Kanitz.

Löwenstein, Fürst Frank, Rhg ★★→★★★ Classic RIES from HALLGARTEN (RHG); Ries, SILVANER from ultra-steep Homburger Kallmuth (FRANK).

Marcobrunn Rhg Historic 7-ha VDP-classified GROSSE LAGE in Erbach. Potential for rich, long-lasting RIES. Growers: CORVERS-KAUTER, HESSISCHE STAATSWEINGÜTER, Höhn, Knyphausen, KÜNSTLER, PRINZ, Schloss Reinhartshausen, von Oetinger.

Margarethenhof Pfz ★★★ Up-and-coming family estate in FORST, organic. Classy RIES from Jesuitengarten, Pechstein, Ungeheuer vyds; also serious GUTSWEIN and ORTSWEIN.

Markgräflerland Bad District s of Freiburg, cool climate nr Black Forest, limestone soils. Typical GUTEDEL a pleasant companion for local cuisine. PINOT varieties increasingly successful.

Markgräfler Winzer Bad ★→★★★ Innovative MARKGRÄFLERLAND co-op (915 ha) with distinctive approach to quality, led by former LVMH (*see* Moët & Chandon, France) manager. Best: DER series (CHARD, GUTEDEL, PINOT N).

Mathis, Gebrüder – Kalkbödele Bad ★★★ Young couple (3rd generation) making wine from vyds next to a lime plant. Excellent PINOT N parcel selections: spicy Hohrain, fragrant Rosenloch. Also gd: CHARD, PINOT BL, SEKT.

Maximin Grünhaus Mos ★★★★ For generations, stronghold of herb-scented, ***delicate, long-lived Ruwer Ries (dry and sweet)***. But creamy WEISSBURGUNDER, chiselled PINOT N (Abtsberg GG 22) have what it takes to become legends.

May, Rudolf Frank ★★★ SILVANER at its best, reliable entry-level, sophisticated, oak-influenced GGS, ultra-rare Kniebrecher from estate's oldest vines.

Merkelbach M-M ★★→★★★ Tiny estate at ÜRZIG, 1.4 ha. Brothers Alfred and Rolf (died in 2024 and 2023 respectively) M handed over day-to-day business to SELBACH-OSTER, but wine still made in bros' cellar.

Renovation of vineyard walls at Walporzheim, Ahr: 64,000 m² brickwork, €30m.

Meyer-Näkel Ahr ★★★→★★★★ AHR V flagship estate, now in conversion to organic. Sisters Meike and Dörte N produce even more refined SPÄTBURGUNDER GGS than late father Werner (died in 2025), all can age 5–10 yrs+: Kräuterberg, Pfarrwingert, Hardtberg, Silberberg, Sonnenberg. Also in Portugal (Quinta da Carvalhosa), S Africa (Zwalu, with Neil Ellis).

Michel Bad ★★★ Father Josef and son Robin M bring max elegance, freshness from Achkarren's and IHRINGEN's warm terroir, combined with loads of extract. Try 23': Schlossberg PINOT GR, Hinter Winklen SPÄTBURGUNDER.

Minges Pfz ★★→★★★ Purist, steely RIES from prime S PFZ vyds (Schäwer, Unterer Faulenberg). Delicate GEWÜRZ AUSLESE too.

Mittelhaardt Pfz North-central and best part of PFZ, incl DEIDESHEIM, FORST, RUPPERTSBERG, WACHENHEIM; largely planted with RIES.

Mittelmosel Central and best part of MOS, a RIES Eldorado, incl BERNKASTEL, BRAUNEBERG, GRAACH, PIESPORT, WEHLEN, etc.

Mittelrhein M Rh ★★→★★★ Dramatically scenic Rhine area, nr tourist magnet Loreley. ***Steely, underrated Ries.*** Today's vyds only quarter of the size (460 ha) in 1980.

Molitor, Markus M-M, Mos ★★★→★★★★ Perfectionist producer, trad winemaking from 120 ha in 24 EINZELLAGEN; almost 100 different bottlings/yr. Capsules indicate degree of sweetness (white = dry, green = off-dry, golden = sweet). *See also* DOMÄNE SERRIG.

Mosbacher Pfz ★★★ Some of best GG RIES of FORST, refined rather than massive; trad ageing in big oak casks; breathtaking 24' Langenmorgen GG.

Mosel ★→★★★★ Growing area for lightest of German RIES, 8536 ha, 62% Ries. Conditions on RUWER and SAAR tributaries (also subsumed under "Mosel" in wine law) significantly different.

Münzberg Pfz ★★→★★★ Tight PINOTS BL/GR, CHARD from limestone in S PFZ. Best usually Schlangenpfiff Pinot Bl GG.

Nackenheim Rhh ★→★★★★ ROTER HANG village famous for ***Rhh's richest Ries,*** superb TBA from Rothenberg on red shale. Top: ***Gunderloch,*** KÜHLING-GILLOT, Marbé-Sans, SCHÄTZEL.

Nahe Tributary of the Rhine, dynamic region (4249 ha); handful of famous (DIEL, DÖNNHOFF, EMRICH-SCHÖNLEBER, GUT HERMANNSBERG, JB SCHÄFER, SCHÄFER-FRÖHLICH) and dozens of lesser-known but trustworthy producers, excellent ***value.*** Great soil variety.

Neipperg, Graf von Würt ★★★→★★★★ One of most reliable estates in all Germany, strongold of elegance (LEMBERGER, SPÄTBURGUNDER), but also PINOT BL, RIES. Aus dem Reifekeller series has appropriate bottle-age. Count Philipp N's uncle Stephan makes wine at Canon-la-Gaffelière (*see* Bordeaux) and elsewhere.

Nelles Ahr ★★★ Family estate, est 1479: ancestor paid high rent for Landskrone vyd plot. Splendid 22 Burggarten, Landskrone, Schieferlay SPÄTBURGUNDER.

Neus Rhh ★★★ Revived historic estate at INGELHEIM, v.gd. CHARD (Schlossberg), excellent PINOT N (best: Pares) in reductive style.

Niederhausen Na ★★→★★★★ Village known for RIES from Hermannshöhle vyd and neighbouring steep slopes. Growers: CRUSIUS, ***Dönnhoff,*** GUT HERMANNSBERG, Jakob Schneider, Mathern.

Nierstein Rhh ★→★★★★ Avoid by any means GROSSLAGE Gutes Domtal designation. Genuine Nierstein RIES is rich, complex from prime sites on red soil:

How flavour changes

How do German wines and their flavours change with climate change? To sum it up: (1) less acidity (not necessarily welcome for RIES); (2) more tannin (welcome to a certain extent for all reds and some whites); (3) less apple and citrus fruit and more "yellow" and tropical fruit flavours in whites like Ries, SILVANER, PINOT BL; (4) almost no more almond flavour and rather cherry or black fruit than red fruit in SPÄTBURGUNDER, or even plum. Plum should be a flashing red light in Spätburgunder: it has been harvested too late. Important note: these four rules of thumb describe trends and are not absolute truths, as winemakers respond to global warming and adapt viticulture, picking dates and winemaking – thus securing the freedom to achieve the style they desire.

Hipping, Oelberg, Pettenthal. Growers: Bunn, Gehring, GRÖHL, GUNDERLOCH, Guntrum, Hofmann, Huff (both), KELLER, KÜHLING-GILLOT, Manz, SCHÄTZEL, ST-ANTONY, Strub.

Ockfen Mos ★★→★★★ SAAR village known for GROSSE LAGE Bockstein. Historic Geisberg now re-cultivated (VAN VOLXEM).

Odinstal, Weingut Pfz ★★→★★★ Highest vyd of PFZ, 150m (492ft) above WACHENHEIM; bio, low-tech vinification bring pure PINOT BL, RIES, SILVANER, sometimes with (well-dosed and clean) touch of Vin Nature. Also PINOT N from Herxheim.

Traffic on Monster Mosel Bridge: 7 vehicles/min. Cost: €500m, ruined vineyards.

Oechsle Scale for sugar content of grape juice. Until 90s, more Oechsle meant better wine. But climate change has altered game.

Oppenheim Rhh ★→★★★ Village s of ROTER HANG with different soil (limestone) and no direct Rhine influence. Growers: GRÖHL, Guntrum, Kissinger, KÜHLING-GILLOT, Manz. Spectacular C13 church.

Ortenau Bad ★★→★★★ District around and s of city of Baden-Baden. Mainly RIES (locally called Klingelberger), SPÄTBURGUNDER from granite soils and often steep slopes.

Ortswein The 2nd rank up in VDP's pyramid of qualities: a village wine, many bargains. *See* AUS ERSTEN LAGEN.

Östreicher, Richard Frank ★★★ Organic viticulture, low-intervention winemaking: concentrated CHARD Rossbach, flinty SILVANER Maria im Weingarten, smoky PINOT BL Hölzlein, burgundian Katzenkopf PINOT N 23'.

Othegraven, von Mos ★★★ Family estate owned by German TV star Günther Jauch; important holdings in superb Altenberg at KANZEM. KABINETT and SPÄTLESE VERSTEIGERUNGSWEIN among SAAR's finest.

Palatinate Pfz English for PFALZ.

Pfalz Germany's 2nd-largest region, 23,793 ha, balmy climate, Lucullian lifestyle. Legendary MITTELHAARDT RIES; outstanding S PFZ PINOTS N/BL, plus CHARD. ZELLERTAL now fashionable: cool climate.

Piesport M-M ★→★★★★ Village in M-M for rich, aromatic RIES from famous Goldtröpfchen vyd. Growers: GRANS-FASSIAN, Hain, Joh Haart, Julian Haart, KP KELLER, KESSELSTATT, Loersch, ***Reinhold Haart***, SANKT URBANS-HOF, SCHLOSS LIESER. Avoid GROSSLAGE Michelsberg.

Pollig Schmidt Ahr ★★★ Side project of a roofer and an accountant at Ahrweiler, exciting low-tech PINOT N from 2 ha in best sites (Alte Lay, Rosenthal).

Prädikat Legally defined category of ripeness at harvest. *See* QMP and box, p.165.

Prinz, Weingut ★★★ Distinctly fresh, elegant RIES from HALLGARTEN's altitude vyds; organic. KABINETT GOLDKAPSEL can be magnificent. Now also MARCOBRUNN.

Prüm, JJ Mos ★★★★ 59 71 76 83 90 03 11 15 18 19 20 21 22 23 24 Legendary WEHLEN estate; also BERNKASTEL, GRAACH. Delicate but extraordinarily long-lived wines with finesse, recognizable character.

Prüm, SA Mos ★★→★★★ Old estate at WEHLEN. Noticeable improvements since Saskia Antonia P took over. Fine AUSLESEN 24 (Himmelreich, Lay).

QbA (Qualitätswein bestimmter Anbaugebiete) "Quality Wine", controlled as to area, grape(s), vintage. May add sugar before fermentation (chaptalization). Intended as middle category, but VDP obliges its members to label their best dry wines (GGS) as QbA. The new EU name gU is scarcely found on labels (*see* box, p.180).

QmP (Qualitätswein mit Prädikat) Top category, six levels according to ripeness of grapes: KABINETT to TBA. (*See* box, p.165.) No sugaring of must or other forms of enrichment allowed.

Ratzenberger M Rh ★★★ Approachable style of M RH RIES, and occasionally magnificent BA, TBA.

Rauenthal Rhg ★★→★★★★ ***Spicy, austere but complex*** RIES from inland slopes. Baiken, Gehrn, Rothenberg vyds contain GROSSE LAGE, ERSTE LAGE parcels, while neighbouring Nonnenberg (monopoly of BREUER) is unclassified, despite its equal quality.

Raumland Rhh ★★★ SEKT house, deep cellar, full range of fine cuvées; 1st Sekt-only estate to become VDP member. Best: CHARD Grande Res Brut Nature (disgorged after 10 yrs+), Triumvirat cuvée, sensational (and rare) MonRose 07' 09' 12'.

Every 5th bottle of German wine is Sekt: 250 million bottles/year – and rising.

Rebholz, Ökonomierat Pfz ★★★→★★★★ Top S PFZ estate: bone-dry, best usually RIES GG Kastanienbusch from red schist, also outstanding CHARD, SPÄTBURGUNDER.

Reinecker Bad ★★→★★★ SEKT pioneer in BAD, VDP member since 2025. Best: single-vyd PINOT N Brut Natures (Römerberg, Schäf, Steingässle).

Restsüsse Unfermented grape sugar remaining in (or added in the form of süssreserve to) wine to give it sweetness. Can range from 1g/l in TROCKEN to 300g/l in TBA.

Rheingau Birthplace of RIES, famous for substantial, age-worthy wines with steely backbone (dr/sw). Soils are either pyhillite, schist, quarzite (in mtn villages) or limestone, loess, river sediments nr Rhine. Only 3200 ha (8th-largest region). Small but increasing amounts of SPÄTBURGUNDER.

Rheinhessen Germany's largest region by far (27,499 ha), between Mainz and Worms. Much *Fasswein* (bulk wine), but also treasure trove of well-priced wines from wide range of precious soils.

Richter, Max F M-M ★★→★★★ Fine, reliable M-M estate wealthy in prime vyds at BRAUNEBERG, ERDEN, GRAACH, WEHLEN: full, aromatic RIES (dr/sw).

Rings Pfz ★★★→★★★★ Dense, emphatically fresh RIES (Kallstadt Saumagen), SPÄTBURGUNDER (Leistadt Felsenberg) from prime sites in N PFZ.

Roter Hang Rhh ★★→★★★★ Leading RIES area of RHH (NACKENHEIM, NIERSTEIN). Name ("red slope") refers to the soil – former desert floor from geological era of Rotliegend – that gives wines a characteristic smoky aroma.

Ruck, Johann Frank ★★★ Spicy, age-worthy RIES, SCHEUREBE, SILVANER, TRAMINER from IPHOFEN.

Rüdesheim Rhg ★★→★★★★ Tourist magnet in RHG. Unique RIES from Berg (mtn) vyds on slate (Kaisersteinfels, Roseneck, Rottland, Schlossberg). Full but never clumsy, esp gd in off-yrs. Best: Allendorf, BISCHÖFLICHES WEINGUT RÜDESHEIM, ***Breuer***, CHAT SAUVAGE, CORVERS-KAUTER, HESSISCHE STAATSWEINGÜTER, JOHANNISHOF, ***Kesseler***, KÜNSTLER, ***Leitz***, Prinz von Hessen, Ress.

Ruwer Mos ★★→★★★★ Tributary of Mosel nr TRIER, cool and late-ripening, esp renowned for dry RIES. Best: Beulwitz, Karlsmühle, KARTHÄUSERHOF, KESSELSTATT, MAXIMIN GRÜNHAUS.

Saale-Unstrut Small but fine ne region (853 ha) around confluence of these two rivers 50 km w of Leipzig. Terraced vyds have Cistercian origins. Best: Böhme, BÖHME & TÖCHTER, Born, Gussek, HEY, Kloster Pforta, Konni & Evi (LANDWEIN), Pawis, Proppe. Local growers' association Breitengrad51 sets high standards to promote terroir focus of wines.

Saalwächter, Carsten Rhh ★★★ Shooting star at INGELHEIM; outstanding SILVANER Grauer Stein, elegant CHARD, delicate PINOT N (ASSMANNSHAUSEN, Ingelheim).

Saar Mos Tributary of Mosel, bordered by steep slopes. Most austere, steely, ***brilliant Ries*** of all, consistency favoured by climate change, but frost remains perpetual threat.

Sachsen Region in Elbe V around Meissen and Dresden. Characterful dry whites, with TRAMINER a speciality. Best: AUST, Drei Herren, F Fourré, Gut Hoflössnitz, Rothes Gut, SCHLOSS PROSCHWITZ, SCHLOSS WACKERBARTH, Schuh, SCHWARZ, ZIMMERLING.

St-Antony Rhh ★★→★★★ NIERSTEIN organic estate. Exceptional vyds, known for sturdy, ageable ROTER HANG RIES, BLAUFRÄNKISCH, PINOT N. Steep slopes all worked by hand.

Salm, Prinz zu Na, Rhh ★★→★★★ Owner of Schloss Wallhausen, vyds there and at BINGEN (RHH); ex-president of VDP.

Salwey Bad ★★★→★★★★ Leading KAISERSTUHL estate, forerunner of fresher PINOTS N/GR style (from 2008). Best: GGS Henkenberg Pinot Gr (21'), Steingrubenberg CHARD and Kirchberg PINOT BL, Henkenberg and Kirchberg Pinot N.

Sankt Urbans-Hof Mos ★★★ Large family estate (50 ha) led by Nik Weis, vyds along M-M and SAAR; vine nursery too. Limpid RIES: Goldtröpfchen KABINETT 24'; Laurentiuslay GG 22'; Goldtröpfchen TBA 23', impeccably pure, racy, age well.

Sauer, Horst Frank ★★★ Man who put FRANK on sweet-wine map. Sensational BA, TBA from ESCHERNDORF's steep Lump vyd. Daughter Sandra now in charge.

Sauer, Rainer Frank ★★★ Top family estate, seven different dry SILVANERS from ESCHERNDORF's steep slope Lump. Best: GG am Lumpen, and L.

Schaefer, Willi Mos ★★★→★★★★ Small (4.8 ha) but outstanding family estate, MOS RIES at its best, pure, crystalline, feather-light and long-lasting. Christoph S cultivates dozens of tiny parcels, mainly in GRAACH, also Wehlener SONNENUHR.

Schäfer, Joh. Bapt. Na ★★★ Handcrafted, low-intervention RIES mainly from Dorsheim (GGS Goldloch, Pittermännchen). Brilliant KABINETT too.

Schäfer-Fröhlich Na ★★★→★★★★ Family estate in NA, spontaneously fermented RIES of great intensity; GGS Bockenau Felseneck (despite frost, monumental 24'), Kupfergrube, Schlossböckelheim Felsenberg.

Scharzhofberg Mos ★★→★★★★ Superlative SAAR vyd, 28 ha: a rare coincidence of microclimate, soil and human intelligence to bring about perfection of RIES. Estates: BISCHÖFLICHE WEINGÜTER TRIER, EGON MÜLLER, KESSELSTATT, VAN VOLXEM, VON HÖVEL, VEREINIGTE HOSPIZIEN.

Schätzel Rhh ★★★ VDP member with prime ROTER HANG vyds, advocating regenerative viticulture and low-alc, low-sulphur, tannic RIES, aged in cask, under flor and/or in a kind of solera (*see* Spain). Steiner (= NIERSTEINER) ORTSWEIN gd intro to this idiosyncratic world. Also gd trad KABINETT.

Schlipf, Weingut am Bad ★★★ Brothers Christoph and Johannes Schneider excel in S MARKGRÄFLERLAND with GUTEDEL (El Fayoum, no added sulphur) and PINOT N.

Schlör Bad ★★★ Best grower in remote TAUBERTAL, perhaps only world-class red from SCHWARZRIESLING (aka PINOT M): Fyerst 1476 Res. Also v.gd: PINOTS BL/N.

Schloss Johannisberg Rhg ★★★→★★★★ Historic RHG estate and Metternich mansion, place where SPÄTLESE was invented (1775); 100% RIES, owned by Henkell (Oetker group). Seal colour indicates wine type. Currently on top form and in conversion to organic. Ex Bibliotheca Subterranea and Goldlack TROCKEN are pricey, but entry-level Gelblack shows nobility of site too.

Germany's northernmost vyds: on islands Sylt, Föhr, Rügen, and at Strande nr Kiel.

Schloss Lieser M-M ★★★★ Thomas Haag, elder brother of Oliver H (FRITZ HAAG) makes painstakingly elaborate RIES (dr/sw) from BRAUNEBERG, Lieser (Niederberg Helden), PIESPORT, WEHLEN. Sensational SPÄTLESE VERSTEIGERUNGSWEIN 24' from leased plot of BERNKASTEL's DOCTOR. Hotel Lieser Castle has no ties to wine estate.

Schloss Neuweier Bad ★★★ A C16 castle and some of BADEN's best RIES vyds on porphyry soils. Remarkable Late Release series: Mauerberg Ries 19, Heiligenstein PINOT N 16. Hotel and lovely restaurant with terrace.

Schloss Ortenberg Bad ★★★ Historic N BAD (ORTENAU) estate, 45 ha, steep slopes on granite, taken over 2021 by hotelier Thomas Althoff (Schloss Bensberg, St James's Hotel & Club). Remarkable progress: Spitalberg SPÄTBURGUNDER GROSSES GEWÄCHS 22. Erste Lage PINOT BL/GR, CHARD bargains.

Schloss Proschwitz Sachs ★★→★★★ New team brings notable improvements in Prince zur Lippe's 70-ha estate. Top: WEISSBURGUNDER, SPÄTBURGUNDER, delicious TRAMINER Brut SEKT.

Schloss Rattey ★→★★★ Hotel and winery in ne state of Mecklenburg-Vorpommern, 30 ha, important investment, remarkable dry Solaris.

Schloss Vaux Rhg ★★→★★★ Renowned SEKT house, co-owned by PRINZ ZU SALM. Best known for single-vyd RIES Sekt: Marcobrunn Brut 19'.

Schloss Wackerbarth ★★→★★★ Saxon state dom on outskirts of Dresden, restaurant, park, events, 190,000 visitors/yr. Best: ALTE REBEN, Protze RIES TROCKEN, TRAMINER SPÄTLESE, all from Radebeul's Goldener Wagen vyd. Also v.gd: Bussard Royal Res SEKT.

Schnaitmann Würt ★★★→★★★★ Excellent barrel-aged reds from Fellbach nr Stuttgart. Whites (eg. RIES, SAUV BL), SEKT (Evoé!) tasty too. Burgundy-inspired TROLLINGER ALTE REBEN.

Schneider, Markus Pfz ★★→★★★ Full range of soundly produced, trendily labelled PFZ wines. Joint venture with Kaapzicht Estate in Stellenbosch (*see* S Africa).

Schneider, Reinhold & Cornelia Bad ★★★ Fine family estate at Endingen, KAISERSTUHL. Delightfully old-fashioned GRAUBURGUNDER labelled "Ruländer"; v.gd SPÄTBURGUNDER; Res range shows great capacity to age (PINOT BL II 12, CHARD 12, Rosé 18).

Schoppenwein Café (or bar) wine, ie. wine by the glass.

Schumacher, Paul Ahr ★★★ Perfectionist grower at Marienthal, only 4 ha. Age-worthy PINOT N: Kräuterberg **12 13 15' 16 17'** 18 19' 20' 21 22', Rosenthal (Magna Essentia), Trotzenberg. FRÜHBURGUNDER Alegria 22', depth, appeal.

Schwarz, Martin Sachs ★★★ Perfectionist grower (6 ha) at Meissen: CHARD, RIES, PINOT N, and, believe it or not, NEBBIOLO. Best vyd is reclaimed (2009–11) Friedstein at Radebeul on granite.

Schwarzer Adler Bad ★★★→★★★★ Michelin-starred restaurant and top estate at Oberbergen, KAISERSTUHL: PINOTS N/BL/GR and CHARD to show France is nr.

Schwegler Würt ★★★→★★★★ Family estate, 15 ha, red blends full of charcter: Beryll, Granat, Saphir. Powerful CHARD.

Seckinger Pfz ★★→★★★ Three brothers from Niederkirchen/MITTELHAART making name for RIES from DEIDESHEIM in style of Vin Nature but without becoming too extreme. Organic.

Seeger Bad ★★★→★★★★ Fine family estate nr Heidelberg. Thomas S, 12th generation, is PINOT N expert, but CHARD, SAUV BL, BLAUFRÄNKISCH equally remarkable. Daughter Anna Marie has own series: subtle Pinot N 23.

Seehaldenhof Würt ★★→★★★ Gifted young grower Simon Hornstein making name for CHARDS Seehalde (*allegro ma non troppo*), Sonnenbichl (*largo*) from Bayerischer BODENSEE. Trained at FÜRST.

Sekt ★→★★★★ German sparkling. Avoid cheap offers: bottle fermentation is not mandatory. Serious producers: ALDINGER, BARTH, BATTENFELD-SPANIER, BERGDOLT, BREUER, BUHL, DIEL, DR LIPPOLD, F John, GRIESEL, GUT HERMANNSBERG, H Bamberger, HEYMANN-LÖWENSTEIN, KARTHÄUSERHOF, PJ KÜHN, LAUER, Leiner, MAX F RICHTER, Melsheimer, MOLITOR, RAUMLAND, REINECKER, Schembs, Schloss Sommerhausen, SCHLOSS VAUX, SCHWARZER ADLER, Solter, S Steinmetz, Strauch, WAGECK, WEGELER, Wilhelmshof, ZILLIKEN.

Selbach-Oster M-M ★★★ Scrupulous family estate with excellent vyd portfolio, known for classic style and focus on sweet PRÄDIKAT wines.

Sermann, Lukas Ahr ★★→★★★ Young grower in Altenahr. Superb: Im Eck PINOT N ALTE REBEN (30–80 yrs), RIES TROCKEN from ungrafted vines. Relaxed restaurant.

Serrig, Domäne Mos ★★★→★★★★ Former state dom at Serrig, 25 ha in one piece. After 2016 acquisition, MARKUS MOLITOR started tremendous work of conversion, reconstruction. Only two wines, slightly off-dry Vogelsang GROSSE LAGE, and Vogelsang KABINETT. Sold on Place de Bx (*see* France).

Solveigs Rhg ★★→★★★★ PINOT N from red slate at ASSMANNSHAUSEN, LORCH; only 2 ha, organic, low-tech winemaking. Best plots: Micke **13'** **15'** **16'** 18' 19' 20' 21 22', Present **09'** **12** **13'** **15'** **16'** 18' 19' 20' 21 22'.

Sonnenuhr M-M Sundial; vyd name at BRAUNEBERG, Pommern, WEHLEN, Zeltingen.

Sorentberg Mos ★★→★★★ Steep slope in cool side valley nr Reil, fallow for decades until 2014, 1000 old vines on red slate, 3.5 ha newly planted. Terrible frost 24, but lovely back vintages.

Spreitzer Rhg ★★★ Deliciously ***racy, harmonious*** RIES from vyds in HATTENHEIM, Mittelheim, Oestrich. Mid-price range ALTE REBEN a bargain. Breathtaking TBA (Eiserberg 23' 24'), EISWEIN.

Staatlicher Hofkeller Frank ★★→★★★ Bavarian state dom with 115 ha of vyds; cellars in WÜRZBURG's baroque residence. Recently significantly improved.

Staatsweingut / Staatliche Weinbaudomäne State wine estates or doms exist in BAD (IHRINGEN, Meersburg), NA (Bad Kreuznach), PFZ (Neustadt), RHG (HESSISCHE STAATSWEINGÜTER), RHH (OPPENHEIM), SACHS (Wackerbarth), SA-UN (Kloster Pforta), WÜRT (Weinsberg).

Steinberg Rhg ★★★ Walled-in vyd above HATTENHEIM, est by Cistercian monks 700 yrs ago: a German Clos de Vougeot (*see* France). Monopoly of HESSISCHE STAATSWEINGÜTER. Best parcels have unique soil: clay with fragments of decomposed schist in various colours.

Stein-Berg Frank Best parcels of famous Stein vyd at WÜRZBURG (39 ha out of 71 ha), since 2020 acknowledged by EU as gU (in sense of AOP, *see* France).

Steintal, Weingut Frank ★★★ SPÄTBURGUNDER from Klingenberg in modern style: dense, fleshy, influenced by ageing in barrels and on lees.

Steinwein Frank Wine from WÜRZBURG's best vyd, Stein. Goethe's favourite. Only six producers: BURGERSPITAL, JULIUSSPITAL, L Knoll, Meinzinger, Reiss, STAATLICHER HOFKELLER. Hugh J once tasted the 1540 vintage.

Stodden Ahr ★★★→★★★★ Alexander S is master of tannin extraction; AHR SPÄTBURGUNDER with density, potential; best usually ALTE REBEN, Herrenberg GG.

Sturm, Martin M Rh ★★→★★★ Journalist turned grower-winemaker; perfectionistic CHARD, RIES, PINOT N from most n part of M RH. Organic.

Südpfalz Pfz On Alsace border, S PFZ, known for Pinots (r/w).

German vintage notation

The vintage notes after entries in the German section are mostly given in a different form from those elsewhere in the book. If the vintages of a single wine are rated, or are for red wine regions, the vintage notation is identical to the one used elsewhere (*see* p.6). But for regions, villages or producers, two styles of vintage are indicated.

Bold type (eg. **22**) indicates classic, ripe vintages with a high proportion of SPÄTLESEN and AUSLESEN; or in the case of red wines, gd phenolic ripeness and must weights.

Normal type (eg. 23) indicates a successful but not outstanding vintage. Generally, German white wines, esp RIES, can be drunk young for their intense fruitiness or kept for a decade or even two to develop their potential aromatic subtlety and finesse.

Taubertal Bad, Frank, Würt ★→★★★ Cool-climate river valley, divided by Napoleon into BAD, FRANK, WÜRT sections. SILVANER (limestone soils), local red Tauberschwarz. Hofmann, SCHLÖR, gd co-op at Beckstein.

Thanisch, Weingut Dr M-M ★★★ BERNKASTEL estate, founded 1636, famous for its share of DOCTOR vyd. After family split in 1988, two homonymous estates: Erben (heirs) Müller-Burggraef, powerful, more modern; Erben Thanisch (VDP), elegant, classical.

Thörle Rhh ★★★ Brothers Christoph and Johannes T known for dense RIES Hölle TROCKEN, racy KABINETT, rich Probstey SILVANER, delicate SPÄTBURGUNDER.

Trier Mos Largest city n of Alps in C3, n capital of ancient Rome on crossroads of MOSEL, RUWER and SAAR. Almost no vyds within city limits, but charitable estates with cellars among awesome Roman remains.

Trittenheim M-M ★★→★★★ Racy, textbook M-M RIES if from gd plots within extended Apotheke vyd. Growers: A CLÜSSERATH, Clüsserath-Weiler, E Clüsserath, F-J Eifel, GRANS-FASSIAN, Loersch, Milz.

Trocken Dry. Defined as max 9g/l unfermented sugar. Generally, the closer to France, the more Trocken wines.

Ürzig M-M ★★★→★★★★ MOS village on red sandstone and red slate, famous for ungrafted old vines and ***unique spicy Ries*** from Würzgarten vyd. Growers: Berres, Christoffel, Erbes, DR LIPPOLD, ***Loosen***, MERKELBACH, ***Molitor***, Mönchhof, Rebenhof.

Van Volxem Mos ★★★ Historic SAAR estate, spectacular castle-like new cellar building in a Saar loop nr WILTINGEN. Low yields from top sites (SCHARZHOFBERG and Gottesfuss of Wiltingen, Bockstein and restored, formerly fallow Geisberg of Ockfen) bring about monumental, mostly dry RIES.

VDP (Verband Deutscher Prädikatsweingüter) Influential association of 200 premium growers setting highest standards. Look for its eagle insignia on wine labels and for GG logo on bottles. VDP wine is usually a gd bet. President is Steffen CHRISTMANN.

Vereinigte Hospizien Mos ★★→★★★ Association of charities at TRIER with excellent vyds and spectacular cellar dating back to Roman times. Sound quality and improving: SCHARZHOFBERG SPÄTLESE 23.

Versteigerungswein ★★★★ Wines of extraordinary quality, auctioned off by one of the historic growers' associations (ie. Ring Mosel or VDP), easily recognized by a sticker on bottle stating auction from which bottle was purchased.

Wachenheim Pfz ★★★ Celebrated village with, according to VDP, no GROSSE LAGE vyds. See what you think. Top growers: Biffar, BÜRKLIN-WOLF, Karl Schäfer, ODINSTAL, WOLF, Zimmermann (bargain).

The Frühburgunder paradox

FRÜHBURGUNDER, aka Pinot Noir Précoce, is a mutation of PINOT N that ripens 2–3 wks earlier. Before climate change, this property was attractive – even if Frühburgunder's strong susceptibility to rot limited its spread. Now, since German growers also have to harvest SPÄTBURGUNDER early to prevent it from becoming jammy, growing Frühburgunder no longer seems to make any sense. But climate change is not that simple. In 2022, a warm, dry yr, Germany produced better Frühburgunder than ever before. How is that possible? The key lies in a dry August. The grapes were perfectly healthy, and winemakers were able to produce extract-rich, fresh wines. "The 22s are magnificent," comments Frühburgunder expert KATRIN WIND. "Now we have to harvest around 20/25 August, but so what?"

Wachtstetter Würt ★★→★★★ LEMBERGER with depth, distinction; trad local cuisine in family restaurant.

Wageck Pfz ★★★ Family estate at Bissersheim; CHARD, PINOT N (best: Geisberg), SEKT and Portugieser ALTE REBEN (planted 1931).

Wagner-Stempel Rhh ★★★ Seriously crafted RHH wines from Siefersheim nr NA border. Best: usually powerful RIES GGS Heerkretz. Excellent Res SILVANER, v.gd SPÄTBURGUNDER.

Wasem Rhh ★★→★★★ INGELHEIM family estate, trad for FRÜHBURGUNDER, but RIES (Elsheim Blume), PINOT N equally remarkable.

Wasenhaus Mos ★★★ Burgundy-inspired PINOT N Bellen, Kanzel and PINOT BL Möhlin from limestone sites in MARKGRÄFLERLAND, all farmed by hand, all labelled LANDWEIN.

Wassmer, Fritz Bad ★★★ One of finest producers of Pinot varieties in Breisgau, esp powerful Herbolzheim Kaiserberg CHARD, PINOT N. Recently, tauter style, less rich than before.

Wassmer, Martin Bad ★★★ Top producer of Pinot varieties in MARKGRÄFLERLAND, esp tight, vertical Dottingen Castellberg CHARD, PINOT N.

Weedenborn Rhh ★★★ Expert in SAUV BL, altitude vyds bring density, freshness without superficiality.

Wegeler M-M, Rhg ★★→★★★★ Important estate in Oestrich and BERNKASTEL plus a stake in the famous KRONE estate of ASSMANNSHAUSEN. Geheimrat J (TROCKEN RIES blend from best RHG sites 83' 85' 95' 00 **15'** **17** 19 21') on par with GGS. Old vintages available: Vintage Collection.

Wehlen M-M ★★★→★★★★ Wine village with legendary steep SONNENUHR vyd expressing RIES from slate at v. best: rich, fine, everlasting. Top: BERGWEILER-PRÜM, JJ PRÜM, Kerpen, KESSELSTATT, LOOSEN, MAX F RICHTER, MOLITOR, Pauly-Bergweiler, SA PRÜM, Sankt Nikolaus Hospital, SCHLOSS LIESER, SELBACH-OSTER, Studert-Prüm, THANISCH, WILLI SCHAEFER, WEGELER.

Wehrheim, Dr Pfz ★★★ SÜDPFALZ family estate known for outstanding Kastanienbusch Köppel RIES, PINOT N, Mandelberg WEISSBURGUNDER.

Weil, Robert Rhg ★★★★ Outstanding estate in KIEDRICH, v. consistent quality. GROSSE LAGE vyd Gräfenberg gives superb sweet KABINETT to TBA, and age-worthy GG. New super-premium parcel selections: Monte Vacano (by subscription and auction), Monte Nostrum (through Place de Bx, *see* France).

Weingart M Rh ★★★ Passionate grower at Spay, vyds in BACHARACH, BOPPARD. Refined, steely but balanced RIES, low-tech in style, superb value.

Weingut Wine estate.

Weissherbst Pale-pink wine, made from a single variety, often SPÄTBURGUNDER; v. variable quality.

Weltner, Paul Frank ★★★ Family estate at Rödelsee in cool, high-altitude Steigerwald. Densely structured, age-worthy SILVANER from underrated Küchenmeister vyd. Advocate of BOCKSBEUTEL (*see* box, p.163).

Wiltingen Mos ★★→★★★★ Heartland of the SAAR. SCHARZHOFBERG crowns a series of GROSSE LAGE vyds (Braune Kupp, Braunfels, Gottesfuss, Kupp). ORTSWEIN usually a bargain.

Wind, Katrin Pfz ★★→★★★ Shooting star at Arzheim, S PFZ. Straightforward but nuanced: RIES; Kalmit FRÜHBURGUNDER, SPÄTBURGUNDER.

Winning, von Pfz ★★★→★★★★ DEIDESHEIM estate, prime vyds and at FORST. ***Ries of great purity***, terroir expression, fermented in partly new *Fuder* casks. Recently increased focus on CHARD (KO **23'** from famous RIES site Kalkofen), PINOT BL.

Winningen Mos ★★→★★★ Lower MOS town nr Koblenz; powerful dry RIES. GROSSE LAGEN: Röttgen, Uhlen. Top: Fries, HEYMANN-LÖWENSTEIN, KNEBEL, Kröber, Materne & Schmitt, R Richter.

Wirsching, Hans Frank ★★★ Renowned estate in IPHOFEN known for classically structured dry RIES, ***Silvaner***. Occasionally crystal-clear BA, TBA: breathtaking Julius-Echter-Berg Ries TBA 22'.

Wittmann Rhh ★★★→★★★★ Leading bio estate; pure, zesty dry RIES GGS Brunnenhäuschen, Kirchspiel, Morstein 08 11 12' 15 16 17 18 19' 20 21' 23' 24'. Top: Morstein ALTE REBEN selection La Borne. Also v.gd: PINOT N (Steingrube ERSTE LAGE).

Wöhrle Bad ★★★ Organic pioneer (30 yrs+) in Breisgau, BAD. Top GGS: Kirchgasse GRAUBURGUNDER, SPÄTBURGUNDER; Teufelslochgasse CHARD.

Wöhrwag Würt ★★★ Family estate at Untertürkheim (district of Stuttgart), long known for some of best RIES in WÜRT. Now also successful with LEMBERGER, PINOT N, Bx blend ***Cuvée X***, always fresh, elegant.

Württemberg Dynamic s region nr Stuttgart, many young growers eager to experiment. Best: usually LEMBERGER, SPÄTBURGUNDER and red blends. Light, bright trad TROLLINGER renaissance. Mainly red region, only 30% white varieties, RIES needs altitude vyds.

Würzburg Frank ★★→★★★★ Great Baroque city on the Main, famous for its best vyd Stein (STEINWEIN, STEIN-BERG).

Zellertal Pfz ★★→★★★★ Area in N PFZ, high, cool; recent gold rush: BATTENFELD-SPANIER, KP KELLER, PHILIPP KUHN have bought in Zellertal's best vyd Schwarzer Herrgott or neighbouring RHH plot Zellerweg am Schwarzen Herrgott. Local estates: Full, Janson Bernhard.

Ziereisen Bad ★★→★★★★ Outstanding estate in MARKGRÄFLERLAND, advocating LANDWEIN. Best: SPÄTBURGUNDERS from small plots (RH, S, TAL). Jaspis = old-vine selections. Top: GUTEDEL 10[4] (provocatively priced at €125) has great terroir expression.

Zilliken, Forstmeister Geltz Mos ★★★→★★★★ Long-est SAAR family estate and founding member of VDP, with unique track record of mature fruity and noble sweet ***Ries from Saarburg Rausch*** and Ockfen Bockstein. Dorothee Z follows father's path of elegance, delicacy.

Zimmerling, Klaus Sachs ★★★ Small, perfectionist estate, VDP, one of 1st to be est after Berlin Wall came down. Best vyd: Königlicher Weinberg ("King's vyd") at Pillnitz nr Dresden.

EU terminology

Germany's part in new EU classification involves, firstly, abolishing the term Tafelwein in favour of plain **Wein** – this is, up to now, the only visible change on labels. LANDWEIN is still called Landwein, even if its bureaucratic name would be **geschützte geographische Angabe (ggA)**, or protected geographical indication. Brussels generally allows continued use of est designations. **Geschützte Ursprungsbezeichnung (gU)**, or protected designation of origin, should technically be replacing QUALITÄTSWEIN and QUALITÄTSWEIN MIT PRÄDIKAT but is, up to now, mainly in place for large geographical units such as AHR, BAD, FRANKEN, etc. Since it's hard and time-consuming (4–6 yrs) to get recognition for a village- or vyd-specific gU, only seven such gUs were in place by end of 2026: Bürgstadter Berg (*see* WEINGUT FÜRST), Iphofen Berg (*see* WIRSCHING), WINNINGEN Uhlen (parcel-specific Blaufuesser Lay, Laubach, Roth Lay, *see* HEYMANN-LÖWENSTEIN), WÜRZBURGER STEIN-BERG and Monzinger Niederberg (NA). The existing predicates – SPÄTLESE, AUSLESE and so on (*see* box, p.165) – stay in place; the rule for these styles hasn't changed and isn't going to.

Luxembourg

Vineyards (1295 ha) are on the upper Moselle but have more in common with Chablis than Piesport: limestone soils; 90% are white, usually with some sweetness; every fourth bottle is Crémant.

Alice Hartmann ★★★→★★★★ Rich, slightly off-dry RIES from prime sites (Wormeldange Koeppchen).

Aly Duhr ★★★ Well-made Koeppchen RIES (organic), serious PINOT N Barrique 22.

Bernard-Massard ★→★★★ Big producer, esp Crémant. Top: Ch de Schengen/Thill, Clos des Rochers. Sekt in Germany too.

Charta Luxembourg 16 independent growers, high standards (cover crops in vyd, yield max 60hl/ha, no chaptalization).

Domaine & Tradition Leading growers' association, eight members, high quality.

Gales ★★→★★★ Reliable producer, cellar labyrinth worth seeing. Classical DOMAINE & TRADITION whites, stylish Crémant.

Kox, R&L ★★★ Avant-garde: planting trees in the vyd (Orchard series); Crémant without added sulphur, trad wines gd too.

Krier-Welbes ★★→★★★ Organic, linear, dry: Bech-Kleinmacher Falkenberg RIES 23'.

Molling, Bob ★★→★★★ Young grower; distinctly fresh, bone-dry RIES, PINOT GR spontaneous fermentation. Roots: orange-lite.

Pauqué, Ch ★★★→★★★★ Abi Duhr's RIES come close to those of German neighbours (Sous la Roche-Rue, "15hl"), but also barrel-fermented AUXERROIS (Clos du Paradis), CHARD (Clos de la Falaise).

Rezbergh ★★ Ambitious Crémant start-up. Watch.

Schram ★★→★★★ SYLVANER (Kurschels), Franken-like (*see* Germany) Keuper soils.

Sunnen-Hoffmann ★★★ Organic. Aromatic concrete-egg RIES Wintrange Felsbierg, dense, aromatic PINOT GR Insolite (partly destemmed by hand).

Vinsmoselle ★→★★★ Union of co-ops, 550 ha, incl Crémant Poll-Fabaire. Variable quality. Vignum-series can be v.gd: Vignum Crémant (53 mths on lees).

Other good estates: Bentz, Cep d'Or, Desom, Gloden, Häremillen, Kohll-Leuk, Krier Frères, Mathis Bastian, Ruppert, Schmit-Fohl, Schumacher-Lethal.

Belgium

Belgium has eight PDOs, two PGIs and c.1000 ha of vineyards, spread out over all provinces. Chardonnay is the most planted variety, followed by Pinot Noir, Johanniter, Pinot Gris, Auxerrois, Solaris, Souvignier Gris and Meunier. Because of the challenging climate, volumes differ greatly between vintages, and the significance of disease-resistant hybrids continues to rise, primarily in Wallonia. Vibrant traditional-method sparkling and still whites make up the majority of production, while sparkling rosés and pét-nats are increasingly noteworthy. Most wines sell locally.

Try ***Aldeneyck***, Beekborne, Bioul, Bon Baron, Bousval, Bruut, Chant d'Eole, ***Chapitre***, Chenoy, Clos d'Opleeuw, Cruysem, d'Hellekapelle, Degavre, Den Nachtegael, Domaine W, Entre-Deux-Monts, Fumal, Genoels-Elderen, Gloire de Duras, Haksberg, Hoenshof, Kitsberg, Falize, Lijsternest, Meerdael, Mérula, Mont des Anges, Nobel, Oud Conynsbergh, Petrushoeve, Ravenstein, Ruffus, Schorpion, Steinberg, ten Gaerde, Terroir Terwaer, Valke Vleug, Vandersteene, Vandeurzen, ***Vin de Liège***, Waes, Wijnfaktorij.

Spain

Abbreviations used in the text:

SPAIN

Alel	Alella
Alic	Alicante
Ara	Aragón
Bier	Bierzo
Bul	Bullas
Cád	Cádiz
Can	Canary Islands
C-La M	Castilla-La Mancha
C y L	Castilla y León
Cat	Catalonia
C de Bar	Conca de Barberá
Cos del S	Costers del Segre
Emp	Empordà
Ext	Extremadura
Gal	Galicia
Jum	Jumilla
La M	La Mancha
Mál	Málaga
Mall	Mallorca
Man	Manchuela
Mén	Méntrida
Mont-M	Montilla-Moriles
Mont	Montsant
Mur	Murcia
Nav	Navarra
Pen	Penedès
Pri	Priorat
P Vas	País Vasco
R Bai	Rías Baixas
Rib Sac	Ribeira Sacra
Rib del D	Ribera del Duero
Rio	Rioja
R Ala	Rioja Alavesa
R Alt	Rioja Alta
R Or	Rioja Oriental
Rue	Rueda
Som	Somontano
U-R	Utiel-Requena
Vald	Valdeorras
Vcia	Valencia

PORTUGAL

Alen	Alentejo
Alg	Algarve
Bair	Bairrada
Bei Int	Beira Interior
Dou	Douro
Lis	Lisboa
Mad	Madeira
Min	Minho
Set	Setúbal
Tej	Tejo
Vin	Vinho Verde

Change is happening in Spain, and it's nothing to do with climate change. This is all about the human factor. In the early years of Spain joining the EU, its wine industry began to blossom as winemakers travelled and returned, full of ideas and rule-breaking. The country began what it is not an exaggeration to call a golden age. People revived the ignored grape varieties, they married new winemaking techniques (stainless steel, concrete eggs) with old (amphorae, *foudres*). They produced internationally respected white wines. They brought some areas to international attention, notably Priorat, but also Rías Baixas, Valdeorras, Ribeira Sacra, among others. Now, more than a quarter of century later, these greats are approaching retirement age or have already retired. In Priorat, Álvaro Palacios has introduced his daughter to the business; at La Rioja Alta, Guillermo de Aranzabal (Junior) has taken over from his father; in Jerez, the irrepressible *hacedor de vinos* (winemaker) at González Byass, Antonio Flores, has been introducing his daughter to the soleras; at Pazo de Señorans, Marisol Bueno's work is being carried on by her daughter; in Penedès, the Gramona cousins have

taken charge of the sparkling wine giant formerly run by Leo's late father Xavier (who died so suddenly) and Roc's dad Jaume (still alive and well). Generational change is never easy, and some wineries introduce an independent CEO if there's no appropriate candidate in the family. In Navarra, the Ochoa sisters have confidently run the family business following a well-planned handover from their parents. What each of these examples suggests is that there is a promising wind of change in Spain, with new ideas and imagination, often bolstered by a master's degree in the US and/or internships in wineries internationally.

Recent Rioja vintages

2025 Complicated yr. Time will tell on quality; lower yields may help sell through Rio's overstocks.
2024 Cool, wet vintage; low production. Those who harvested early best.
2023 Difficult: drought. Lower yields. Quality depends on producer.
2022 A few v. hot summer days. Lower yields. Generally lighter wines.
2021 V. attractive. Drink now or with fine ageing potential.

2020 Difficult yr with mildew. Not for long ageing.
2019 Low yield, overall fine quality. Some wines outstanding.
2018 Gd yr with generous yields, fresher, lighter styles.
2017 Dramatic frost. What was left can be v.gd. Enjoy soon.
2016 Largest harvest since 05, well-balanced wines, plenty to like.

Aalto Rib del D ★★★→★★★★ Stylish classics: Aalto, PS, VERDEJO (w blend) from MARIANO GARCÍA. Owner Masaveu also has Enate (SOM), Fillaboa (R BAI), Leda (C Y L), Murua (RIO), Pagos de Araiz (NAV); v.gd Asturias cider (Valverán).

Abadía Retuerta C y L ★★→★★★ No expense spared at VINO DE PAGO: glossy spa hotel, Michelin restaurant next door to RIB DEL D. Serious single-vyd reds: SYRAH, CAB SAUV, PETIT VERDOT. Also gd: Le Domane (w), modern Winemaker's Collection. Novartis-owned.

Águila, Dominio del Rib del D ★★→★★★★ Welcome new face of RIB DEL D: fine, intense. Field-blend Peñas Aladas, exceptional; fresh pale *clarete*; Albillo, v.gd.

Álava / País Vasco / Basque Country ★→★★★★ Stretching s from the TXAKOLIS of the Atlantic to RIO, Álava is home to a people with a proud history and their own language. Young, trad R Ala wines use carbonic maceration; R Ala known for old vines, different village characters. Campaigns for regional identity encouraging some producers to break from Rio to unite under Ala umbrella.

Alba en Ribera Rib del D ★★ Estate's 1st release 2024, red portfolio growing. Alba (ex-Tesla Holland), daughter of RIO expert; gd pedigree, clever marketing. Watch.

Algueira Rib Sac ★★→★★★★ Exceptional producer in RIB SAC, expert in extreme viticulture on vertiginous river bank, v. fine selection of elegant wines from local varieties. Outstanding Merenzao (aka Jura's TROUSSEAU), almost burgundian; Pizarra (MENCÍA on slate).

Alicante ★→★★★ Spiritual home of MONASTRELL: spicy reds and rare, trad, unfortified ***Fondillón***. Dry white from formerly unloved MOSCATEL de Alejandría; local (r) Giró. Top: GUTIÉRREZ DE LA VEGA, PEPE MENDOZA CASA AGRÍCOLA, COLECCIÓN DE TONELES CENTENARIAS, El Sequé (ARTADI), Les Freses, Murviedro.

Allende, Finca R Alt ★★→★★★★ Top (in all senses) BODEGA at BRIONES in merchant's house with tower looking over town to vyds, run by irrepressible Miguel Ángel de Gregorio. Outstanding white.

Almacenista Man, Sherry Stockholder; cellars wines for BODEGAS to increase or refresh stocks. Important in MANZANILLA production. Can be terrific. Few left; many have changed direction and now sell direct to consumers: El Maestro Sierra, GUTIÉRREZ COLOSÍA.

Alma de Carraovejas C y L, R Bai, Rib, Rib del D, Rio ★★→★★★★ Exceptional project, started in RIB DEL D (Milsetentayseis, PAGO DE CARRAOVEJAS), now across Spain. Founded/acquired blue-chip bodegas: Aiurri (RIO), Marañones (GREDOS), Ossian (C Y L), Tricó (R BAI), VIÑA MEÍN – EMILIO ROJO (RIBEIRO). Also owns Ambivium, Michelin-starred restaurant in Peñafiel.

Alvear Ext, Mont-M ★★→★★★★ Historic; superb array of PX in MONT-M; gd FINO CB and Capataz (lovely sw SOLERA 1927); unctuous DULCE Viejo; v. fine vintage. Pioneering range of still wines aged under FLOR. Palacio Quemado is in Ribera del Guadiana.

Amaren R Ala ★★→★★★ Sidekick of Luis Cañas winery, est 1995 with powerful, oaky wines. Next generation now exploring old vines/varieties (Amaren 60 MALVASÍA Riojana), concrete tanks, winemaking. Refined single-vyd reds.

Añada Vintage yr.

Antídoto Rib del D ★★ Another pioneer of elegance in RIB DEL D, Bertrand Sourdais, reveals delicacy, purity of Soria province. Old-vine TEMPRANILLO. Charming Le Rosita ROSADO.

Anza R Ala ★★ Elegance from Diego Magaña, part of impressive, well-travelled new generation in RIO.

Aragón Mighty medieval kingdom, stretching s from Pyrénées, home to DOPS CALATAYUD, CAMPO DE BORJA, CARIÑENA, Som. Once a land of bulk wine, co-ops, now gaining attention for new generation recuperating old vines, esp GARNACHA, Moristel (r).

Arfe, Bodegas Sherry ★★★ Single-mindedly, Luis Arroyo built business making one wine: unstoppable medal-winner PALO CORTADO de la Cruz de 1767.

Arizcuren Rio ★★→★★★ Engaging Javier A trained as architect, designs wineries in RIO, incl own urban BODEGA in downtown Logroño (worth a visit, one of 200 trad cellars hollowed into a riverside hill in Quel town). Specializes in GARNACHAS at altitude from R OR, Mazuelo (CARINEÑA; relatively rare as single variety in Rio) and amphora wine.

Ars Laietà-Alta Alella Cava, Pen ★★→★★★★ Family business with toes in Med, closest to Barcelona. Excellent CAVAS, Dolç Mataró (sw r MONASTRELL). Organic. Also Celler de les Aus: min-intervention, no-added-sulphur wines. ELABORADOR INTEGRAL.

Artadi Ala, Alic, Nav, P Vas ★★→★★★★ Juan Carlos López de Lacalle makes wine within RIO DOP but prefers to label with ÁLAVA origin. Single-vyd focus: luxuriant La Poza de Ballesteros; dark, stony El Carretil; outstanding El Pisón. Also in ALIC (r El Sequé), NAV (r Artazuri, ROSADO DYA). Izar-Leku TXAKOLÍ (w) from Getaria.

Artuke Rio ★★→★★★ Family's wines transformed by bros Arturo and Kike de Miguel. One of new generation of "Rioja 'n' Rollers" now seriously gd. Exponent of villages in R Ala. Gloriously elegant, subtle use of large oak. Two top single vyds: El Escolladero, on limestone; La Condenada, on iron-rich sandstone.

Brisat: Catalan term for white wine with skin maceration. Orange, in other words.

Arzuaga C-La M, Rib del D ★→★★ Classic BODEGA on Golden Mile; hotel-restaurant to match. Fan d'Oro, rare encounter with CHARD in RIB DEL D. Also VINO DE PAGO, Pago Florentino (Malagón, Ciudad Real).

Axarquía Mál Beautiful mtn region inland from MÁL, worth a visit, renowned for sweet wines: BENTOMIZ, Jorge Ordóñez, Sedella, TELMO RODRÍGUEZ.

Barbadillo Cád, Man ★→★★★★ From supermarket to superb. Astonishingly fine portfolio. Sherry guru Armando Guerra works with Montse Molina seeking out specialities from cellars, incl unfortified PALOMINO. Pioneered MANZANILLA EN RAMA. Top-of-range Reliquía, esp AMONTILLADO, PALO CORTADO. Innovating in whites. Glorious As de Mirabras Sumatorio, delicate Manzanilla. Also Vega Real (RIB DEL D), BODEGAS Pirineos (SOM).

Belondrade C y L, Rue ★★→★★★ Consistent leader in VERDEJO as it should be but so rarely is. Didier B was early (1994) exponent of finesse in RUE, and lees ageing. Impressive Les Parcelles shows benefits of 5 yrs' age.

Bentomiz, Bodegas Mál ★★→★★★ Dutch by birth, Spanish by adoption: Clara (winemaker) and André (chef) are welcoming hosts in Axarquía. Sweet MOSCATEL, MERLOT. Rare dry Romé (rosé). New: CAVA with PENEDÈS grapes and Bentomiz *licor de expedición*. Fine restaurant.

Bhilar, Bodegas R Ala ★→★★ David Sampedro Gil is a single-minded pioneer in El Villar. Focus on vyds, old vines, bio. Whites are textured, reds show elegance. Phinca Revilla Sexto Año spends 6 yrs in oak, homage to trad whites of RIO. *See* ETÉREA KRIPAN.

Bideona R Ala ★→★★ Promising project (backed by two MWs), reflects specific terroirs. Founded when RIO prevented use of village name on wines not made in that village, so Bideona uses abbreviations, eg. V1BN4 (Villabuena). Part of Península Viticultores (C Y L, CEBREROS, GREDOS, TXAKOLÍ de Bizkaia).

SPAIN

Bierzo ★→★★★★ Looking for a different flavour in Spain? Find it in aromatic, mid-weight, often crunchily fresh reds from MENCÍA in nw. On slate soils they become perfumed, ***Pinot-like***. The DOP shot to international fame with RAÚL PÉREZ and Ricardo Pérez Palacios (no relation). Look for CÉSAR MÁRQUEZ, DESCENDIENTES DE J PALACIOS, Raúl Pérez, plus Dominio de Tares, Losada, Luna Berberide, Mengoba, MICHELINI, Peique, Veronica Ortega. Also fine GODELLO (w).

Bimbache Can ★★ If you are on a walking tour of El Hierro, smallest of the Canaries, check out this promising project. Local varieties, vividly fresh whites, small in quantity, big in ambition.

Xarel·lo grape is v. high in the antioxidant resveratrol. Cava as a health supplement?

Bodega A cellar; a wine shop; a business making, blending and/or shipping wine.

Butt Sherry 600-litre barrel of long-matured American oak used for Sherry. Filled 5/6 full, allows space for FLOR to grow, protecting wine from oxygen and consuming nutrients. Trend for wineries – and whisky distillers – to use former butts for maturation for Sherry influence – eg. CVNE Monopole Clásico, BARBADILLO Mirabras.

Calatayud Ara ★→★★ Full-bodied red GARNACHAS grown at altitude. Also GARNACHA BL. Historic region with many old vines. Try Cuevas de Arom (from Fernando Mora MW of BODEGAS FRONTONIO), ESCOCÉS VOLANTE, Raíces Ibericas, San Alejandro, VINTAE (Garnacha Olvidada).

Campo de Borja Ara ★→★★ Self-proclaimed "Empire of GARNACHA". Heritage of old vines; gd-value Garnacha, now starting to show serious quality: Alto Moncayo, Aragonesas, Borsao.

Campo Viejo Rio ★ Australian-owned bestselling CAVA, RIO brand.

Canary Islands ★→★★★★ Seven main islands, nine DOPS. Tenerife has five of them. Favourite of vine-hunters: unusual varieties, old vines, distinct microclimates, volcanic soils, unique pruning, until recently untouched by phylloxera. Diverse varieties incl dry white LISTÁN (aka PALOMINO) and Listán Negro, Marmajuelo, Negramoll (TINTA NEGRA), Vijariego. MOSCATELS, MALVASÍAS, incl fortified El Grifo from Lanzarote. Top: Borja Pérez, ENVINATE, SUERTES DEL MARQUÉS, Viñátigo. In volcano-hit La Palma: Victoria Pecís Torres (esp Malvasía Volcánica). Lanzarote: EL GRIFO, Titerok-Akaet. Gran Canaria: Agala, CARMELO PEÑA, Lava, TAMERÁN. Tourism may rule, but v. fine wines to be found.

Cangas ★→★★ Isolated DOP in wild Asturias. Unique varieties USP: fresh Albarín Blanco; crunchy red Albarín Negro, Verdejo Negro and, most promising, Carrasquín. Try Dominio de Urogallo, Monasterio de Corias, Siluvio, VidAs.

Can Sala Cava ★★★★ Exceptional CAVA from Ferrer family, founders of FREIXENET. Cava de Paraje focused on PARELLADA. ELABORADOR INTEGRAL.

Cariñena Ara ★→★★ DOP and name of grape variety. Oldest DOP in Ara (1932). Co-op country (Grandes Vinos, San Valero) transforming. Leader: local JORGE NAVASCUÉS. Also Care, Libre y Salvaje. Bold, characterful, value. Visit Cariñena wine museum: underground cellars in Almonacid de la Sierra.

Casa Castillo Jum ★★→★★★★ One of Spain's greats, José María Vicente, proves JUM can be tiptop. Family business high up in *altiplano*. Outstanding MONASTRELLS, esp PIE FRANCO.

Castell d'Encús Cos del S ★★→★★★ Shades of a philosopher-king, Raül Bobet (also of PRI FERRER BOBET) is constantly planning. At over 1000m (3281ft) he can make ***superbly fresh, original wines.*** Grapes fermented in C12 granite *lagares.* Acusp PINOT N, Ekam RIES, Thalarn SYRAH all classics.

Castilla y León ★→★★★ Spain's largest wine region. Diversity means exciting discoveries. DOPS: Arlanza, Arribes, BIER, Cigales, RUE, Sierra de Salamanca (one to watch, with red Rufete grape), Tierra de León, Tierra del Vino de Zamora,

TORO, Valles de Benavente, Valtiendas. Catch-all IGP Vino de la Tierra de C y L can be source of v. fine wines: Barco del Corneta, Máquina y Tabla. Top: ABADÍA RETUERTA, MARQUÉS DE RISCAL (VERDEJO), Mauro, Ossian, Prieto Pariente. Reviving unique grapes: Cenicienta, Juan García, Puesta en Cruz.

Castillo de Cuzcurrita R Alt ★★ Lovely walled vyd and castle, v. fine RIO. Inky, pure, single-vyd Tilo.

Castillo Perelada Emp, Nav, Pri, Rio ★→★★ Glossy tourist destination: hotel, casino, Michelin restaurant, striking winery. Vivacious value CAVAS. Also modern red blends. Rare 12-yr-old, SOLERA-aged Garnatxa de l'EMPORDÀ. Also Chivite (NAV), Viña Salceda (RIO), now being transformed by David González; v. promising.

Catalonia Vast umbrella DOP, covers whole of Cat: seashore, mtn, in-between. Top chefs and top BODEGAS. Actual DOP too large to have identity.

Cava Ext, Rio, Vcia ★→★★★ Spain's trad-method sparkling; 90%+ made in PEN (also EXT, RIO, VCIA). Youngest, min 9 mths' age. Cava de Guarda Superior (min 18 mths), incl all older wines, certified organic (2025); Res (min 18 mths), Gran Res (min 30 mths), single-vyd Cava de Paraje (min 36 mths). Brut Nature v. common in top categories; XAREL·LO now v. highly rated for ageability. Regulatory changes and subregional categories partly driven by actions of breakaway producer groups. Among top: ALTA ALELLA, CAN SALA, CODORNÍU, JUVÉ Y CAMPS, MESTRES. ELABORADOR INTEGRAL.

SPAIN

Cebreros C y L ★→★★ Youthful (2017) DOP illustrating dynamic development of GREDOS, with distinct zones identifying themselves. As elsewhere, GARNACHA (r) dominates; also Albillo Mayor (w). Look for Daniel Ramos, Rico Nuevo, Ruben Díaz, Soto Manrique, TELMO RODRÍGUEZ.

Celler del Roure Vcia ★→★★ Interested in TINAJAS? Then visit this BODEGA in S VCIA. Impressive underground cellar of vast *tinajas* buried up to necks; gd, fresh, elegant. Cullerot, Parotet, Safrà from local varieties. Many old houses in Alforins district have trad *tinajas*, none quite so remarkable as this.

Cerrón, Bodegas Jum ★★→★★★ Enthusiastic Cerdán bros working with family's v. old vines at up to 960m (3150ft); bio. Transforming image of JUM.

Chipiona Sherry Sandy coastal zone, source of MOSCATEL. Best: floral delicacies, far less dense than PX.

Clàssic Penedès Pen Category of DOP PEN for trad-method fizz: min 15 mths' ageing, organic grapes. Members incl Albet i Noya, Colet, Loxarel, Mas Bertrán.

Clos Mogador Pri ★★→★★★ René Jnr's father, René Barbier, is one of PRI's founding quintet and mentor to many. One of 1st wineries to gain a Vi de Finca designation. Lovely Manyetes CARIÑENA. Gratallops Vi de Vila ROSADO (1st vintage 2021), vinous treat.

Codorníu Raventós Cos del S, Pen, Pri, Rio ★→★★★★ Former family business now owned by venture capital; sign of CAVA's troubled times. Single-vyd/variety Cavas de Paraje v. fine. Elsewhere, Legaris in RIB DEL D, v.gd village wines; Raimat in COS DEL S, Europe's largest organic estate; Bodegas Bilbaínas in RIO, bestseller VIÑA Pomal. Jewel is outstanding PRI SCALA DEI (part owns). Visit Art Nouveau Cava winery.

Pét-nat popular with young Penedès makers. Might make Xarel·lo doubly healthy.

Colección de Toneles Centenarios Alic ★★★★ Superb aged FONDILLÓN: forgotten casks discovered, revived, commercialized under brand Luis XIV; v. limited release. Also excellent dry wines from local varieties, vermouth.

Consejo Regulador Organization that controls a DOP; each DOP has its own. Quality as inconsistent as wines they represent: some bureaucratic, others enterprising.

Contador ★★→★★★ Rapidly became an icon of modern, polished RIO from vyds across R Ala. Contador is eponymous wine, v. fine, succulent fruit integrated with French oak. Predicador the little brother. La Cueva del Contador bold, richly textured. Elegant Alma originally made for Place de Bx (*see* France).

Contino R Ala ★★→★★★★ Estate incl one of RIO's great single vyds. Winemaker Jorge NAVASCUÉS developing tiptop range. CVNE-owned.

Corpinnat Cat ★★→★★★★ Independent group of producers of trad-method fizz, more stringent regulations than CAVA; 21 members and growing. Leaders: GRAMONA, RECAREDO.

Cortijo de los Aguilares Mál ★→★★★ Proves PINOT N can be made in Andalusia. How? Because vyds nr Ronda are at 900m (2953ft). GRACIANO; Tadeo PETIT VERDOT and TINAJA all v.gd. Lovely Breñal (GARNACHA BL/VIOGNIER/Vijiriega).

Costers del Segre ★→★★★ Geographically divided DOP combines mountainous CASTELL D'ENCÚS and lower-lying Castell del Remei, Raimat.

Cota 45 Sherry ★★ From thoughtful, ever-interesting SANLÚCAR winemaker RAMIRO IBÁÑEZ. Understands different PAGOS, works with scarce old varieties. Always something new. Co-author with Willy Pérez of xthe book that will be the last word on JEREZ and its pagos. *See* M ANT DE LA RIVA, WILLY PÉREZ.

Crianza Declaration of wine age – not quality – in RIO. Indicates use of oak. Must be min 2 yrs old; reds min 1 yr in oak barrels, whites and ROSADOS min 6 mths.

Cuentaviñas Rio ★★ Personal project of Eduardo Eguren, son of Marcos (SIERRA CANTABRIA), in Peciña (San Vicente de la Sonsierra). Old-vine (1923) El Tiznado.

CVNE R Ala, R Alt ★★→★★★★ One of RIO's great names. Pronounced *"coo-neh"*, Compañia Vinícola del Norte de España, founded 1879. Four Rio wineries: CONTINO, CVNE (incl Real de Asúa), Imperial, VIÑA Real. Most impressive at top end. Also in CAVA (Roger Goulart), R Bai (La Val), RIB DEL D (Bela), VALDEORRAS (Virgen del Galir).

De Alberto Rue ★★★ Exceptional demijohn- and SOLERA-aged oxidative VERDEJO: caramel and walnut, vanilla and raisin.

Dinastía Vivanco R Alt ★→★★ Family business in Briones known for varietal wines and ***outstanding wine museum*** in Briones. Impressive trad-method sparkling RIO.

DO / DOP (denominación de origen / protegida) DOP replaced former DO category.

Dominio de Atauta Rib del D ★★→★★★★ Star among elegant wines of RIB DEL D's Soria province. Pre-phylloxera vyds; v. different from typically bold wines of DOP.

Dominio do Bibei Rib Sac ★★→★★★ Schist and granite dominate steep vyds, influencing blends of local red varieties: Lacima, Lalama. GODELLO stars in Lapena, Lapola.

Dulce Sweet. Can be late-harvest, botrytis, or fortifed, red or white. Top: ARS LAIETÀ-ALTA ALELLA, BENTOMIZ, GUTIÉRREZ DE LA VEGA, OCHOA, TELMO RODRÍGUEZ, TORRES and, of course, SHERRY and MONT-M.

Elaborador Integral Cava Top category of CAVA producers who grow, vinify, age wine on own estate. Currently 19 producers, incl ARS LAIETÀ-ALTA ALELLA, CAN SALA, JUVÉ Y CAMPS, PARÉS BALTÀ, VINS EL CEP.

El Escocés Volante Ara, Cal ★→★★★ Scot Norrel Robertson MW was flying winemaker in Spain, hence the brand. Focus on old-bush-vine GARNACHA grown at altitude, often field blends. Individual, characterful wines, part of movement transforming ARA; v. fine, single parcels.

El Grifo, Bodegas Can ★→★★ Historic winery with over 250 yrs of unbroken winemaking on Lanzarote. Specializes in MALVASIA Volcánica (dr/sw w).

El Puerto de Santa María Sherry Few BODEGAS remain, incl GUTIÉRREZ COLOSÍA, OSBORNE (gd wine bar). Puerto FINOS are less weighty than JEREZ, not as "salty" as SANLÚCAR. Lustau's EN RAMA trio shows differences of Sherries aged in the three different towns.

El Reventón C y L ★★→★★★ Argentine arrivals in GREDOS: Adrianna Catena and wunderkind Alejandro Vigil purchased vyd from DANI LANDI. Expect gd things.

Empordà Cat ★→★★ One of number of centres of creativity in CAT, incl CASTILLO PERELADA, Celler Martí Fabra, Pere Guardiola, Vinyes dels Aspres. Sumptuous natural sweet wine from Celler Espolla: SOLERA GRAN RES.

Enclòs de Peralba, L' Pen ★★→★★★ Impressive project of GRAMONA cousins Leo and Roc; elegant, refined still XAREL·LOS, red, ancestral-method fizz. Watch.

Envínate Alm, Can, Rib Sac ★→★★★ Sparkling quartet of winemakers unlocking lesser-known regions: Almansa (Albahra), RIB SAC (Lousas), Tenerife (Táganan).

Equipo Navazos Man, Mont-M, Sherry ★★★→★★★★ Pioneering collection by academic Jesús Barquín and Sherry-maker Eduardo Ojeda working as négociants, bottling individual BUTTS. Not just JEREZ: v. fine MONT-M selections; also vermouths and aged vinegar.

Etérea Kripan R Ala ★→★★ Personal project of Melanie Hickman, partner of David Sampedro of BODEGAS BHILAR; bio. Phinca Hapa Blanco (v. fine), Sasikume (fascinating, delicate) from (illegal) TROUSSEAU grapes.

Extremadura For tourists, magnets are conquistador city of Trujillo and Roman city of Mérida. But linger: Extremadura has some ambitious projects, esp HABLA, Pago de los Balancines, Palacio Quemado (*see* ALVEAR), Pentateuco. Ribera del Guadiana is DOP. Almendralejo, "city of CAVA", v. distant subzone of DOP Cava.

Faustino Rib del D, Rio ★→★★ One of the famous names of RIO's boom yrs. With some 650 ha of vyd, it makes wines in all classic categories. Celebrating 160 yrs; winery by UK architect Norman Foster + Partners. Also Marqués de Vitoria (Rio), Portia (RIB DEL D).

Fernando de Castilla Sherry ★★→★★★★ Gloriously consistent quality. Antique range all qualify as VOS or VORS, but label doesn't say so. Complex Antique FINO is fortified to historically correct 17% abv. OLOROSO, PX Singular v.gd. Plus v. fine brandy, vermouth, vinegar. Favoured supplier to EQUIPO NAVAZOS.

Must visit for dog-lovers: Pago de los Balancines (Ext), breeds huge mastiffs.

Ferrer Bobet Pri ★★→★★★★ Gloriously velvety CARIGNAN. Sergi F and Raúl B (*see* CASTELL D'ENCUS) enter 3rd decade of focused brilliance. Exceptional Selección Especial and sweet wine. Winery worth a visit.

Flor Sherry Spanish for "flower": refers to the layer of *Saccharomyces* yeasts that typically grow and live on top of FINO/MANZANILLA Sherry in a BUTT 5/6 full. Flor consumes oxygen and other compounds ("biological ageing") and protects wine from oxidation. It grows a thicker layer nearer the sea at EL PUERTO and SANLÚCAR, hence finer character of Sherry there. VINO DE PASTO often aged for a short time with flor.

Florido, César Sherry ★→★★★ Master of MOSCATEL, sadly underrated sweet Sherry. Gloriously scented, succulent: Dorado, Especial, Pasas. Based in CHIPIONA.

Fondillón Alic ★→★★★★ Fabled unfortified *rancio* semi-sweet wine from overripe MONASTRELL. Matured in oak for min 10 yrs; some SOLERAS of great age. Unfairly fallen out of fashion, production shrinking too fast: Brotons (v. fine 64' 70'), MG Wines, COLECCIÓN DE TONELES CENTENARIOS, Fundación María Teresa.

Forjas del Salnés R Bai ★★→★★★★ Gerardo Méndez renowned for lovely ALBARIÑO: Leirana Genoveva, Sálvora (centenarian vines on granite). Top: O Raio do Vella, young vines (12 yrs), great energy.

Freixenet Cava, Pen ★→★★ Best known for black-bottled Cordón Negro CAVA. Plus: Morlanda (PRI), Solar Viejo (RIO), Valdubón (RIB DEL D), Vionta (R BAI). Also Finca Ferrer (Argentina), Gloria Ferrer (US), Katnook (Australia). Owned by sparkling giant Henkell.

Frontonio Ara ★→★★★ Fernando Mora MW continues to make waves with old-vine GARNACHAS N/BL; also v.gd MACABEO.

Fulcro R Bai ★★→★★★ Manuel Moldes, literal *garagiste*, makes exceptional, mineral,

SPAIN

saline, maritime ALBARIÑO, expressive of sand, granite soils. Aliaxe (r blend), powerful, crunchy.

Galicia Spain's nw corner. Isolation has ensured rare varieties. Outstanding whites, esp RAFAEL PALACIOS; growing number of fascinating crisp reds: ALGUEIRA, DESCENDIENTES DE J PALACIOS, QUINTA DA MURADELLA, Zarate (*see* MONTERREI, R BAI, RIB SAC, RIBEIRO, VALDEORRAS). Recent arrival: Anonimas Viticultoras, project run by two women making wine across region.

García, Mariano & Sons Bier, C y L, Rib del D, Rio Mariano G is fixture in N and NW Spain. For many yrs winemaker at VEGA SICILIA. Co-founded Aalto (RIB DEL D) and launched Mauro (C Y L). He and sons Alberto, Eduardo also run Garmón Continental (Rib del D), San Román (TORO), Baynos (RIO), Valeyo (BIE).

Genérico Rio If there's no age category shown on the RIO bottle – such as RES – then it's a *genérico*. *Genéricos* need not follow all DOP rules on ageing (such as barrel size, min ageing). Unattractive, unhelpful name, but can be v.gd. Case of needing to know producer.

Gil, José R Ala ★★→★★★ Rapidly rising star in R Ala, with precise single parcels El Bardallo, La Canoca. Plenty more to come.

Gómez Cruzado Rio Tiny historic BODEGA in Haro. Focus on GARNACHA and cool Alto Najerilla V: Pancrudo. Fine aged Montes Obarenes (w). Long overlooked, but transformed by David González and Juan Bautista (ex-TELMO RODRÍGUEZ).

González Byass Cava, Cád, Rib del D, Rio, Sherry ★→★★★★ Family business (1845). Cellarmaster Antonio Flores is debonair presence, born in the winery; daughter Silvia also a winemaker. From the ***Tío Pepe*** SOLERA, Flores extracts fine EN RAMA and ***glorious Palmas series***. Consistently gd. Exceptional 1975 AMONTILLADO. Boutique hotel (1st hotel in a working BODEGA in JEREZ). Other wineries: Beronia (RIO), Pazos de Lusco (R BAI), fresh Vilarnau (CAVA), VIÑAS del Vero (Som); Dominio Fournier (RIB DEL D); plus (not so gd, but popular) Croft Original Pale Cream Sherry. Finca Moncloa, close to Jerez, produces still reds.

Gramona Cat, Pen ★★→★★★★ Specialist in long-aged trad-method sparkling, esp

Altitude: going up

Climate change has scrambled that old rhyme: the rain in Spain now comes not on the plain but in catastrophic downpours on the coast and the islands. Or it does not come at all, leading to equally catastrophic yrs of drought. In this time of change, growers need to escape the scorching sun and unexpected plagues of green mosquitoes or mildew. Planting in higher vyds gives longer ripening, avoiding any jammy characters. In the cliche of "sunny Spain", there are strikingly cool-tempered wines to be found. Even CAVA producers – whose Brut Nature wines are crisp – are looking to the hills of PEN. The Riojanos are planting as high as they can, up to 700–800m (2297–2625ft), to sites once thought to be only gd for whites. The Garnachistas of the SIERRA DE GREDOS, n of Madrid, relish the coolness of the elevation and the granite soils. Europe's highest vyds are in the CAN. These island wines offer refreshing salinity from their ocean exposure and volcanic soils. To find the fresh reds of mainland Spain, look to the nw. The MENCÍAS of BIER, the Caiño Tintos and Merenzaos of RIB SAC are varieties that bring a welcome contrast to weighty extracted reds. Still, there are always exceptions. Ars Laietà-Alta Alella is just 2 km from the Med, just n of Barcelona, hardly above sea level. Yet its vines are cooled daily by the sea breezes. No taste of sun-baked wines here. The historic exception is JEREZ, esp SANLÚCAR; v. low-lying vyds and BODEGAS encourage humidity and a saline character.

Enoteca, ***III Lustros, Celler Batlle***. Co-founder of CORPINNAT; bio, also still wines. Run by next-generation cousins Leo and Roc G. *See* L'ENCLÒS DE PERALBA.

Gran Reserva In RIO, red Gran Res ages min 5 yrs, of which min 2 yrs in 225-litre barrel, min 2 yrs in bottle. Whites, ROSADOS age min 4 yrs, of which 6 mths in barrel. Older vintages can be great value. Note: age no guarantee of quality.

Gredos, Sierra de C y L ★→★★★★ The mtn region nw of Madrid. Renowned for new-wave GARNACHA. Best: pale, ethereal. DOPS gradually appearing: CEBREROS, Madrid, MÉN. Try 4 Monos, Bernabeleva, Canopy, Comando G, DANIEL GOMEZ JIMÉNEZ-LANDI, Marañones, TELMO RODRÍGUEZ, Vitícola Mentridana.

Guímaro Rib Sac ★★→★★★ Pedro Rodríguez makes crunchy reds with spicy, savoury character; trad winemaking, varieties. *Guímaro* means "rebel" (relates to historic event) but describes individual approach.

Guita, La Man ★→★★★ Classic ***Manzanilla*** distinctive for sourcing fruit from vyds close to maritime SANLÚCAR. Grupo Estévez-owned (also VALDESPINO).

Gutiérrez Colosía Sherry ★→★★★ Rare remaining riverside BODEGA in EL PUERTO. Family business. Excellent old PALO CORTADO.

Gutiérrez de la Vega Alic ★→★★★ Remarkable BODEGA specializing in sweet wine. In ALIC, but not DOP, after disagreement over regulations. Expert in MOSCATEL, FONDILLÓN. Daughter Violeta now leading business alongside own project Curii (with partner Alberto Redrado, focus on Giró r).

Habla, Bodegas Ext ★→★★ Impressive estate: vyds, prime cattle, horses in conquistador country. Distinctive series of red varietals numbered from 1. Plus curiosities, incl white aged underwater.

Hidalgo, Emilio Sherry ★★★→★★★★ Outstanding family bodega. All wines (except PX) start by spending time under FLOR. Excellent unfiltered 15-yr-old La Panesa FINO, thrilling 50-yr-old AMONTILLADO Tresillo 1874, rare Santa Ana PX 1861.

Hidalgo-La Gitana Man ★★→★★★★ Historic (1792) SANLÚCAR firm. MANZANILLA La Gitana, popular favourite. Top: classic single-vyd Pastrana Pasada, verging on AMONTILLADO. Outstanding VORS, incl Napoleon Amontillado, Triana PX.

Ibáñez, Ramiro Mont-M, Sherry Winemaker (COTA 45), SANLÚCAR native, leading thinker in returning Sherry country to v. best of its old ways. Co-author with WILLY PÉREZ of book on JEREZ history and PAGOS. Influential consultant to ALVEAR (MONT-M), VIÑA CORRALES (PETER SISSECK). Member TERRITORIO ALBARIZA.

IGP (indicación geográfica protegida) Quality category less strict than DOP. Covers immense geographical possibilities; may incl prestigious producers, non-DOP by choice to be freer of inflexible regulation and to use other grapes.

Jerez de la Frontera Capital of Sherry region. DOP is Jerez-Xérès-Sherry. MANZANILLA has own DOP: M-SANLÚCAR DE BARRAMEDA.

Joven Young, unoaked wine.

Jumilla Mur ★→★★★ Arid vyds in mtns n of Mur with heritage of old MONASTRELL vines; esp gd when young, unoaked. Top: CASA CASTILLO. Also gd: CERRÓN, El Nido, Juan Gil, VIÑA Elena.

Juvé y Camps Cava, Pen ★★→★★★ Consistently gd CAVA. Family business. Stalwart is RES de la Familia (though qualifies as GRAN RES), La Capella is Cava de Paraje, released with decade of ageing. ELABORADOR INTEGRAL.

Lagar de Santa Magdalena Mont-M ★→★★ Charming BODEGA (est 1831). Lively young Blanco Natural, v.gd long-aged FINO Pasado, AMONTILLADO. Worth a visit.

Lalomba Rio ★→★★★ Ambitious winery of RAMÓN BILBAO. Paradise of concrete tanks, with two single-vyd reds and Provençal-style ROSADO.

La Mancha C-La M ★→★★ Don Quixote country; Spain's least impressive (except for its size) wine region, s of Madrid. Key source of grapes for distillation to brandy, particularly neutral AIRÉN. Too much bulk wine, yet excellence still possible: Martínez Bujanda's Finca Antigua, newbie Verum.

Landi, Dani C y L, Mén ★★→★★★ Daniel Gómez Jiménez-Landi, pioneer in new generation of GARNACHA producers, making wines at higher altitude across GREDOS (CEBREROS, Mén, etc.). *See also* EL REVENTÓN.

López de Heredia R Alt ★★→★★★★ Haro's oldest (1877), a family business in the BARRIO DE LA ESTACIÓN with wines that have become a cult. Famous "Txori-toki" tower and Zaha Hadid-designed shop. See how RIO was made (as it still is, here). Cubillo is younger range with GARNACHA; darker Bosconia; delicate, ripe ***Tondonia***. Whites have seriously long barrel- and bottle-age; GRAN RES ROSADO is like no other. No shortcuts here.

Lupier, Dom Nav ★→★★★ Put NAV and its GARNACHA back on map, rescuing old vines: exceptional, bold El Terroir, ethereal La Dama; bio. RAÚL PÉREZ in charge.

Lustau Sherry ★★★→★★★★ Benchmark Sherries from JEREZ, SANLÚCAR, EL PUERTO. Only BODEGA to make EN RAMA from three Sherry towns. Consistently excellent.

Málaga ★→★★★ From the Med to the mtns, in five zones, Mál surprises; sweet wines of course. TELMO RODRÍGUEZ revived ancient glories with subtle, sweet ***Molino Real***. Jorge Ordóñez Barrel-aged No. 3 Old Vines Moscatel, gloriously succulent. BENTOMIZ, unique varieties (r/w, dr/sw). But dry wines too: VICTORIA ORDÓÑEZ has excellent dry mtn whites from PX and MOSCATEL.

Mallorca ★→★★★ Uneven quality, some v.gd, some simply prestige projects. Can be high-priced and hard to find off island: 4 Kilos, Ánima Negra, Biniagual, Binigrau, Can Ribas, Mesquida Mora, Miquel Gelabert (wide array), Soca-Rel, Son Bordils, Toni Gelabert, Tramuntana Vinyes del Formentor. Reds blend trad varieties (Callet, Fogoneu, Mantonegro) plus CAB, SYRAH, MERLOT. Whites improving fast. DOPS: Binissalem, Pla i Llevant.

Manchuela ★→★★★ Take another look: Juan Antonia PONCE, quietly superb, working with BOBAL and field blends. Also revitalized Finca Sandoval.

Marqués de Cáceres R Alt, R Bai, Rue ★→★★ Famous for introducing French techniques in 70s. Young white, rosé. Modern Gaudium; classic GRAN RES. Also R BAI, RUE.

Marqués de Murrieta R Alt, R Bai ★★★→★★★★ Two styles, classic and modern: Castillo Ygay GRAN RES one of RIO's trad greats. Gran Res Blanco **12**, latest release. Dalmau, impressive glossy modern Rio. ***Capellania***, fresh, taut, complex white, one of Rio's v. best. Primer Rosé (MAZUELO), v. pale, crisp. In R BAI, relaunched Pazo de Barrantes shines gloriously; La Comtesse, brilliantly intense.

Marqués de Riscal C y L, R Ala, Rue ★★→★★★★ Riscal is living history of RIO, able to put on a tasting of every vintage going back to 1st, 1862. Take your pick of styles: reliable RES, modern Finca Torrea, balanced GRAN RES. Powerful ***Barón de Chirel Res***. Tapias sold on Place de Bx (*see* France). Marqués launched RUE (1972) and today makes vibrant DYA SAUV BL, VERDEJO (Barón de Chirel Verdejo), though prefers to put wines in C Y L not Rue. Eye-popping Frank Gehry hotel attached to Rio BODEGA.

Márquez, César Bier ★★→★★★ Nephew of RAÚL PÉREZ rapidly building exceptional reputation: outstanding El Val (w GODELLO); single-vyd El Rapolao (r).

Mas Doix Pri ★★→★★★★ Treasure is old vines, esp superb CARIÑENA (grape). Top: all blueberry and velvet, astonishingly pure, named after yr vyd was planted *1902*, one of few Gran Vinya Clasificada ***Tossal d'en Bou***. Also v. fine: old-vine GARNACHA *1903* ***Coma de Casas***. Murmuri, Salix (w).

Mas Martinet Pri ★★→★★★ Sara Pérez is daughter of one of original PRI quintet. Vociferous, adventurous, ready to try new approaches. Husband also Pri aristocracy René Barbier Jnr.

Mendoza, Abel R Ala ★★→★★★ For knowledge of RIO villages and varieties, Abel and Maite M have few equals. Discover no fewer than five varietal whites. Grano a Grano are only-the-best-berry-selected TEMPRANILLO and GRACIANO.

Merino, Miguel R Alt ★★ Son of famous father with same name, Miguel Jnr growing the winery: classics, yes, but also varietal Mazuelo, single-vyd wines.

Mestres, Cava Pen ★★→★★★ Specialist in aged CAVAS; 1st producer of Brut Nature Cava, in 1945. Fascinating Cavateca series with different disgorgement dates, and time in bottle.

Michelini i Muffato Bier, Rio ★★ The Michelinis (parents) from Argentina have old-vine project in BIER. Son Matías in RIO at Dominio de Challao.

Monasterio, Hacienda Rib del D ★★→★★★ PETER SISSECK co-owns/consults, where he 1st started in RIB DEL D. More accessible in price than his DOMINIO DE PINGUS.

Monterrei Gal ★→★★★ Small DOP on Portuguese border, with traces of Roman winemaking. Best by far: QUINTA DA MURADELLA.

Montilla-Moriles Mont-M ★→★★★ Andalusian DOP nr Córdoba. Unfairly still in JEREZ's shadow; PX makes unfortified dry FINOS but also sweet wines from sun-dried grapes. *Albariza* soils. Best wines superbly rich, some long-ageing in SOLERA. Trend for dry whites aged in large amphorae. Top: ALVEAR, PÉREZ BARQUERO, TORO ALBALÁ. Important source of PX for use in Jerez DOP.

Montsant Cat ★→★★★ Tucked in around PRI; gd-value neighbour. Fine GARNACHA BL (Acústic). Reds worth exploring: Can Blau, Capçanes, Domènech, Espectacle, Joan d'Anguera, Mas Perinet, Masroig, Venus la Universal.

Muga R Alt ★★→★★★★ Family business with siblings, cousins. Two styles: classical GRAN RES ***Prado Enea***; modern, powerful ***Torre Muga, Aro***. Pale ROSADO, elegant white, lively trad-method sparkling.

Phylloxera now spotted in phylloxera-free Tenerife. The Canary in the coal mine.

Mustiguillo Rib del D ★★→★★★ Toni Sarrión led renaissance of BOBAL grape, also Merseguera (w); created VINO DE PAGO Finca El Terrerazo with top Quincha Corral. Also at Hacienda Solano (RIB DEL D).

Navarra ★→★★★ Formerly in shadow of neighbour RIO. Early focus on international varieties confused its identity. Today's GARNACHA revival relaunching region. Try Artazu, Aseginolaza & Leunda, DOM LUPIER, Gonzalo Celayeta, OCHOA, Tandem, VIÑA ZORZAL. Also sweet MOSCATELS.

Navascués Ara Jorge N, working wonders all over N Spain, esp with GARNACHA. Runs family winery in CARIÑENA, Mas de Mancuso. Top: eponymous Mas de M, great value. Popular Cutio. At CVNE, technical director for CONTINO (RIO), VIRGEN DEL GALIR (VALD), advises VIÑA ZORZAL (NAV).

Nivarius Rio ★★ The 1st winery in RIO dedicated to white. Focus on local varieties, altitude; also single vyds (Finca La Nevera MATURANA BL), pét-nat and v.gd Lía (trad-method sp).

Numanthia Toro ★★→★★★★ One of TORO's heavyweights. Founded by Egurens of SIERRA CANTABRIA, who sold to LVMH. Exceptional, powerful wines gradually becoming more elegant. Top: Termanthia, comes round with 10 yrs of age.

Ochoa Nav ★→★★ Ochoa *padre* led modern growth of NAV, with focus on CAB, MERLOT. Winemaker daughter Adriana calls her range 8a, a play on her surname, incl Mil Gracias GRACIANO; Asti-like sparkling MdO; classic MOSCATEL.

Ontañón R Baj ★★ Family business, classic/modern, plus vyds in RIB DEL D, RUE. Queirón is boutique winery in Quel (R OR), v.gd experimental vinifications.

Ordóñez, Bodegas Jorge Mál ★★ Glorious portfolio of sweet MOSCATEL. Launched 2004 by Austrian Alois Kracher and Jorge and VICTORIA O.

Ordóñez, Victoria Mál ★→★★★ Independent-minded former medical doctor rescuing old vyds, making v. fine wines in Montes de MÁL. Vividly fresh dry whites from MOSCATEL, PX. Pure, fresh reds.

Osborne Sherry ★★→★★★★ Historic BODEGA in EL PUERTO, treasure trove, incl AOS AMONTILLADO, PDP PALO CORTADO. Owns former Domecq VORS incl 51–1a

Amontillado. FINO Quinta and mature Coquinero Fino typical of town. Wineries in RIO (Montecillo), RUE, RIB DEL D.

Pago / Vino de Pago / Grandes Pagos *Pago* is a vyd, ie. Sherry's *pago* Miraflores and *pago* Balbaína. **Vino de Pago** is officially the top category of DOP; actually, not always. Typically, Vinos de Pago are estates in less famous zones. Not to be confused with **Grandes Pagos**, the network of mainly family-owned estates. Some are Vinos de Pago, but not all.

Palacio de Fefiñanes Gal ★★→★★★★ Reliable R Bai ALBARIÑO. Two superior styles: barrel-fermented 1583 (yr winery was founded, oldest of DOP); super-fragrant, lees-aged III. Visit palace/winery at Cambados.

Palacios, Álvaro Bier, Pri, Rio ★★★→★★★★ Almost single-handedly built modern reputation of Spanish wine through obsession with quality. One of quintet that revived PRI. L'Ermita on a magical hilltop site helped place Spain on the modern fine-wine map. He has driven classifications from village to Grand Cru: Gran Vi de Vinya. In RIO, at Palacios Remondo, transforming reputation of R OR and its GARNACHAS. Complex Plácet (w) originally created by brother RAFAEL P. Top: Quiñón de Valmira from slopes of Monte Yerga. In BIER with nephew Ricardo at DESCENDIENTES DE J PALACIOS. Lola, Álvaro's daughter, has now joined her father and uncle in the business.

Palacios, Descendientes de J Bier ★★★→★★★★ MENCÍA at its best. Ricardo Pérez P, Álvaro's nephew, grows old vines on steep slate. Floral Pétalos, Villa de Corullón gd value; Las Lamas and Moncerbal are different soil expressions, one clay, one rocky. Exceptional ***La Faraona*** (only one barrel), grows on tectonic fault; bio.

Palacios, Rafael Vald ★★★→★★★★ Impossible to find fault with Rafael's wines. In VALDEORRAS, focus on GODELLO across many rocky parcels (*sortes*). Lovely Louro do Bolo; As Sortes, a step up; ***Sorte O Soro***, surely Spain's best white. Sorte Antiga (old vines), v. delicate orange wine, Sorte Souto (tiny production, late harvest).

Order Manzanilla in most of Spain and you'll get camomile tea. Not what you want.

Parés Baltà Cava, Pen ★★→★★★ Dynamic family led by Marta Casas proving ageability of XAREL·LO. Expert with brisat (orange), amphora wines. Electio (Xarel·lo), still lively at 12 yrs. ELABORADOR INTEGRAL.

Pasto, Vino de Sherry ★→★★★ White from the Sherry zone, from Sherry grapes but unfortified, revival of a former style. Grapes may be sun-dried for a day, then wine aged in Sherry casks. Have distinct *albariza* (chalky) soil character and may have FLOR aromas. Growing in popularity. Delicate introduction to Sherry: M ANT DE LA RIVA, COTA 45, LUIS PÉREZ La Escribana.

Pazo de Señorans Gal ★★★ Consistently excellent ALBARIÑOs from glorious R BAI estate. Outstanding Selección de Añada, min 30 mths on lees, proof v. best Albariños age beautifully.

Peña, Carmelo Can ★→★★ One of new generation putting Gran Canaria on map. CV incl RAÚL PÉREZ, Puro Rofe (Lanzarote), Niepoort (*see* Portugal). Two projects: Bien de Altura (Gran Canaria, incl Ikewen), mineral, fresh; Jable de Tao (Lanzarote), saline, crunchy.

Penedès Cat ★→★★★★ Region w of Barcelona, most diverse of CAT. Mix of soils, mix of varieties, a little mixed in message. XAREL·LO should be star; 1st DOP to be 100% organic. Best: Agustí Torelló Mata, Alemany i Corrio, Can Rafols dels Caus, Enric Soler, GRAMONA, Jean León, Pardas, PARÉS BALTÀ, TORRES. Fizz has own CLASSIC PEN category.

Pepe Mendoza Casa Agrícola Alic ★★→★★★ Left family wine business (Enrique M) decade ago to launch personal project with great success. Top: Fierroca. Elegant Giró (r), MONASTRELL, MOSCATEL. Pequeñas Producciones experimental range.

Pérez, Raúl Bier ★★→★★★★ A star, but avoids celebrity. Renowned for finesse, nonintervention. Provides generous house-room for new winemakers in cellar in BIER. Magnet for visiting (eg. Spanish, Argentine) winemakers. Outstanding Vizcaina Mencías; ***El Rapolao*** exceptionally pure. Other projects incl DOM LUPIER.

Pérez, Willy Sherry With RAMIRO IBÁÑEZ leading return to old ways in JEREZ, researching and reviving practices, trads, rare varieties, terroirs – and jointly writing the history. Interest in unfortified PALOMINO. Projects incl M ANT DE LA RIVA. Founder member TERRITORIO ALBARIZA.

Pérez Barquero Mont-M ★→★★★ Leading producer of MONT-M; Gran Barquero FINO, AMONTILLADO, OLOROSO; La Cañada PX. Supplier to EQUIPO NAVAZOS.

Pie franco Ungrafted vine, on own roots. Typically on sandy soils where phylloxera cannot penetrate. Some 110 yrs+. Many in TORO, some in C Y L, CAN, RUE.

Pingus, Dominio de Rib del D ★★★→★★★★ One of RIB DEL D's greats. Tiny bio winery of Pingus (PETER SISSECK's childhood name), made with old-vine TINTO FINO, shows refinement of variety in extreme climate. Flor de Pingus from younger vines; Amelia is single barrel named after wife. PSI uses grapes from growers, long-term social project to encourage them to stay on land. *See also* HACIENDA MONASTERIO, SAN FRANCISCO JAVIER.

Pomares, Eulogio R Bai, Rib Sac ★★→★★★ No better way to understand R BAI and ALBARIÑO: eponymous project explores soils, styles of R Bai with great sensitivity.

Ponce Man ★★→★★★ Quietly spoken Juan Antonio P has single-mindedly transformed family business into pre-eminent producer in DOP. One of leaders building reputation of BOBAL; bio. PIE FRANCO bottling: PF.

Priorat ★★→★★★★ Some of Spain's finest. Named after former priory tucked under craggy cliffs. Key is *llicorella* (slate) soil, although there's clay too. Best show remarkable purity, finesse, sense of place; Pri has pioneered classification pyramid from village wines through Vi de Vila to Gran Vi de Vinya. After a period when CAB, SYRAH were thought best, producers have returned to trad CARIÑENA, GARNACHA and have toned down new oak.

Pujanza R Ala ★★→★★★ Carlos San Pedro famed for Añadas Frías VIURA. Name "cold vintages" may lack appeal, but crisp elegance defines aim to capture only coolest influences at 600m (1969ft). Also fine range of modern RIO (r).

Quinta da Muradella Monterrei ★→★★★ José Luis Mateo continues to charm and surprise. From some 15 ha in GAL's tiniest DOP he releases v. accomplished wines, from range of local grapes (r/w).

Ramón Bilbao R Bai, Rib del D, Rio, Rue, Vald ★→★★★ Part of huge Zamora company (producer of Licor 43). In RIO, centenary winery delivers classics but also fresh R OR GARNACHA. Sister winery Lalomba, paradise of concrete tanks, with single-vyd reds, pale ROSADO. Also in RUE, R BAI (v.gd Mar de Frades), bio Cruz de Alba (RIB DEL D). With latest purchase Godeval (VALD) gains dominance in key NW Spain white areas.

Raventós i Blanc Cat ★★→★★★ Pepe R led historic family business out of CAVA in 2012. Created Conca del Riu Anoia for high-quality sparklings with strict controls; bio: De Nit ROSADO, Mas del Serral, ringingly pure Textures de Pedra. Can Sumoi estate natural-wine project (2017): XAREL·LO, pét-nats.

Recaredo Pen ★★→★★★★ Outstanding trad-method sparkling, small family concern, celebrated centenary 2024. Wines aged under cork, not crown cap; still hand-disgorges. Top: precise, mineral ***Turó d'en Mota***, from vines planted 1940, ages brilliantly; classic RES Particular; Enoteca library releases. Member CORPINNAT. Celler Credo: still wines, low in alc, strikingly pure. All bio.

Remelluri, La Granja Nuestra Señora R Ala ★★→★★★ TELMO RODRÍGUEZ's family property; v. fine white blend; old-vine TEMPRANILLOS; exceptional old GARNACHA single-vyds, ethereal wines. Yjar a sell-out on Place de Bx (*see* France). Lindes de Remelluri is project with local growers, different parcels.

Remírez de Ganuza R Ala ★★→★★★ Fernando R de G (died 2024) hit 100-point jackpot with 04 GRAN RES from selected vyds around Samaniego. Classic reds remain but white Olagar Gran Res is outstanding. Juicy Iraila, 1st GARNACHA.

Reserva (Res) Has actual meaning in RIO. Reds: aged min 3 yrs, of which min 1 yr in oak of 225 litres and min 6 mths in bottle. Whites and ROSADOS: min 2 yrs age, of which min 6 mths barrel. Note: age does not guarantee quality.

Revert, Javier Vcia ★→★★★ Remarkably pure Med wines from family vyds, local grapes, eg. Tortosí, Trepadell and others. Three wines: Micalet, Sensal, Simeta, a benchmark.

Rías Baixas Gal ★→★★★★ Atlantic DOP in GAL split in five subzones, too many simple DYA. Best: FORJAS DEL SALNÉS, FULCRO, Martín Códax, PALACIO DE FEFIÑANES, Pazo de Barrantes (MARQUÉS DE MURRIETA), ***Pazo de Señorans***, Terras Gauda, Zárate. Land of *minifundia*, tiny landholdings. Until recently Spain's premier DOP for whites, now like RUE at risk of overproduction. ALBARIÑO is variety here; v. best can age, reaching burgundian elegance. A few reds, strikingly fresh, crisp.

Ribeira Sacra Gal ★★→★★★ Magical DOP with vyds running dizzyingly down to River Sil. Some impressive, original, crisp MENCÍA reds and other local vines at Adegas Moure, ALGUEIRA, Castro Candaz, DOMINIO DO BIBEI, GUÍMARO, Rectoral de Amandi, Regina Viarum. Worth a visit.

Ribeiro Gal ★→★★★ Historic region, famed in Middle Ages for Tostado (sw). Promising textured whites made from GODELLO, LOUREIRO, Treixadura. Some reds, fresh, crunchy. Top: Casal de Armán, Coto de Gomariz, Finca Viñoa, VIÑA MEÍN – EMILIO ROJO, XOSÉ LUIS SEBIO.

Ribera del Duero ★→★★★★ Ambitious DOP with great appeal in Spain, created 1982. Anything that incl Aalto, ALMA DE CARRAOVEJAS, DOMINIO DE PINGUS, VEGA SICILIA has to be serious. Originally dominated by domestic demand for oaky concentration. At last, elegance breaking through. Wineries in Soria (to e) provide most delicate wines (DOMINIO DE ATAUTA, Dominio de Es, DOMINIO DEL AGUILA). Also Alonso del Yerro, ARZUAGA, Cillar de Silos, Francisco Gómez, Garmón, Hacienda Solano, Marta Maté, Sei Solo, Tomás Postigo, Valduero. *See* C Y L neighbours ABADÍA RETUERTA, Mauro.

Rioja ★→★★★★ Spain's most famous wine region. Three subregions: R Ala, R Alt and R OR. Two key provinces: La Rioja and ÁLAVA, with NAV to e. Growing political differences between provinces and between producers and CONSEJO REGULADOR prompted some producers to leave (or consider leaving). Introduction of Viñedo Singular category was criticized but gradually est itself; trad-method sparkling permitted since 2017, small but promising: Bilbaínas, Conde Valdemar, URBINA, VIVANCO. New generation of producers shaking up trad image of Rio.

Rioja Alta, La R Ala, R Alt, R Bai ★★→★★★★ For lovers of classic RIO. Standard keeps going up. Top: Gran Res 904, ***Gran Res 890***. But rest of range from ***Ardanza*** down to Alberdi, Arana each carry classic house style; all qualify as Gran Res. Offer value for age, quality. Also owns R Ala modern-style Torre de Oña, R BAI Lagar de Cervera, RIB DEL D Àster. Hard to fault.

Rioja Oriental Rio Formerly Rioja Baja. Most e and largest subregion of RIO. Was poor relation, rapidly gaining attention for vyds at altitude, quality of GARNACHA. Best: ÁLVARO PALACIOS. Also gd: ARIZCUREN, Queirón (owned by ONTAÑÓN). Visit Quel town with cliffside cellars.

Riva, M Ant de la Sherry ★★→★★★ Project from WILLY PÉREZ, RAMIRO IBÁÑEZ based on abandoned De La Riva BODEGA. Exceptionally fine.

Roca, AT Cat, Pen ★★→★★★ Impressive father-and-son business, both named Agustí R. Top trad-method CLASSIC PEN AT Roca. Anima Mundi, no sulphur, TINAJA-aged, ancestral method; v. fine, expresses terroir.

Roda R Alt, Rib del D ★★→★★★ At far tip of BARRIO DE LA ESTACIÓN. TEMPRANILLO specialist: polished Cirsion, Roda, Roda I, approachable Sela. Now also white Roda I (VIURA, plus GARNACHA BL, MALVASIA aged in large French oak). Also in RIB DEL D: Corimbo (w), Corimbo I, La Horra.

Rosado Rosé. The trad dark rosados of NAV were defeated by Provence pinks. Spain fights back with pale hues, esp SCALA DEI's Pla dels Àngels (PRI), MARQUÉS DE MURRIETA's Primer Rosé (RIO), DOMINIO DEL ÁGUILA Pícaro Clarete (RIB DEL D), LALOMBA Finca Lalinde.

Rueda C y L ★→★★★ Spain's response to SAUV BL: zesty VERDEJO. Much straightforward DYA. Best: BELONDRADE y Lurton, Javier Sanz, José Pariente, MARQUÉS DE RISCAL, Murillo Chapirete, Naia. Exceptional SOLERA-aged DE ALBERTO. Gran Vino quality category for older vines still needs time to est.

Saca Sherry A withdrawal of Sherry from the SOLERA (oldest stage of ageing) for bottling. For EN RAMA wines, most common *sacas* are in *primavera* (spring) and *otoño* (autumn), when FLOR is richest, most protective.

Sánchez, Carlos R Ala ★★ Works with small growers and own plots, for spicy reds (Bienlarmé Lágrimas Bellas), citrus whites (Buradón).

Sánchez Romate Sherry ★★→★★★ Historic (1781) BODEGA with wide range, also sourcing and bottling rare BUTTS for négociants and retailers; 8-yr-old ***Fino Perdido***, nutty AMONTILLADO NPU, PALO CORTADO Regente, excellent VORS Amontillado and OLOROSO La Sacristía de Romate, unctuous Sacristía PX.

San Francisco Javier, Bodegas Sherry ★★★ PETER SISSECK'S BODEGA in JEREZ. FINO is VIÑA Corrales from PAGO Balbaína, 8–9-yr-old EN RAMA. Aim is single-vyd Sherries from organic vyds. Viña La Cruz is Fino-AMONTILLADO from Pago Macharnudo.

Martes of Wine: group of Rioja producers who meet on Tuesdays. MWs won't sue.

Sanlúcar de Barrameda Man, Sherry Town on River Guadalquivir. Port where Magellan, Columbus, admiral of Armada, set sail. Humidity in low-lying cellars encourages FLOR. Sea air said to encourage "saltiness". Wines aged here qualify for DOP MANZANILLA-Sanlúcar de Barrameda.

Scala Dei Pri ★★→★★★ Tiny vyds of "stairway to heaven" cling to craggy slopes. Part-owner CODORNÍU. Winemaker Ricard Rofes, leader in GARNACHA revival, expresses exceptional terrior, esp in single-vyd ***Mas Deu***, Sant'Antoni. Also unusual GARNACHA BLANCA/CHENIN BL.

Sebio, Xosé Lois Rib ★★→★★★ Once a bit of a wild child, now owns vyds; quality ladder from village to single vyd, working with local varieties. Village White, Red, fresh, crunchy blends. Salvaxe (w), peachy, brisk, complex.

Serdio Jerez ★★→★★★ New name in JEREZ, based on premises of Urium. Former TRADICIÓN people tracked down fine Sherries to build soleras: v. fine OLOROSO VORS, v.gd AMONTILLADO.

Sierra Cantabria R Ala, Toro ★★★ Exceptional family business run by bros Marcos (winemaker) and Miguel Ángel Eguren. Elegant, single-vyd, low-intervention: v. fine Amancio, Mágico. Señorio de San Vicente, Viñedos de Paganos (RIO); Teso la Monja (TORO). Next-generation cousins have own R Ala wineries: Eduardo (CUENTAVIÑAS), Koldo (Ukan).

Sierra de Toloño R Ala ★★ Sandra Bravo's wines are all about elevation, cool climate, purity; assisted by old vines, field blends, neutral oak and time in amphora. Bravo indeed.

Sisseck, Peter Rib del D, Sherry Dane who attracted world interest to RIB DEL D with DOMINIO DE PINGUS working magic on JEREZ. He says "Sherry is the best white wine in Spain". His purchase (with partner) of SAN FRANCISCO JAVIER, plus vyd in PAGO Balbaína, and commitment to wines from organically grown grapes has re-energized sector. Also at Ch Rocheyron (Bx).

Solera Sherry System for blending Sherry, less commonly Madeira (*see* Portugal), plus specialities such as DE ALBERTO Dorado and res wine of GRAMONA. Consists of topping up progressively more mature BUTTS with younger wines of same sort from previous stage, or *criadera*. With FINOS, MANZANILLAS it maintains vigour of FLOR. For all wines gives consistency; refreshes mature wines.

Suertes del Marqués Can ★→★★★ Discover new-wave Tenerife wines here. Unique local *trenzado* (plaited) vines. Owner Jonatán García currently makes 20 wines, all full of character. Edición 1 (r/w) v.gd. Worth a visit. Advises at Ocampo (Tacoronte-Acentejo), TAMERÁN.

Tamerán Can ★★ Impressive Gran Canaria project from local boy and former UK (Man City) football star David Silva, working with Jonatán García of SUERTES DEL MARQUÉS (Tenerife). Subtle, delicate, intense.

Telmo Rodríguez, Compañía de Vinos Mál, Rib del D, Rio, Toro, Vald ★★→★★★★ Telmo Rodríguez's family base is REMELLURI in RIO, but he and Pablo Eguzkiza work across Spain reviving old vines and traditions: in ALIC (Al-Murvedre), GREDOS (Pegaso), MÁL (***Molino Real*** MOSCATEL), RIB DEL D (Matallana), RUE (Basa), TORO (Dehesa Gago), VALDEORRAS (Gaba do Xil GODELLO, plus exceptional r single vyds). In Rio, BODEGA Lanzaga brings new life to old vyds, with village wines, exceptionally pure single-vyds. La Estrada, Las Beatas, Tabuérniga are stars. *See* REMELLURI.

Terra Alta Cat Top GARNACHA country, with 90% of CAT'S GARNACHA BLANCA vyds and 75% of Spain's. Deliciously complex, textured. Producers: Bárbara Forés, Celler Piñol, Edetària, Herencia Altés, Lafou.

Territorio Albariza Sherry Network of producers in JEREZ dedicated to *albariza* soils, and leading producers of VINO DE PASTO. Members incl Alejandro Muchada (Muchada-Leclapart), Forlong, Joaquin Gomez (Meridiano Perdido), M ANT DE LA RIVA, Pepe Blanco, Primitivo Collantes, RAMIRO IBÁÑEZ (COTA 45), SAN FRANCISCO JAVIER, WILLY PÉREZ (Luis Pérez). Visit Albariza en las Venas, Jerez bar selling many of these.

Terroir al Limit Pri ★★→★★★ Dominik Huber, based in Torroja village, might have been something of an angry young man but today shows true understanding of his vyds. Wines of infusion not extraction; great refinement.

Tihom Rio ★→★★ Former winemaker at MUGA, Jorge M's new project at entrance to BARRIO DE LA ESTACIÓN. Looks beyond VIURA, TEMPRANILLO to RIO's less usual varieties, blends. Wine bar on-site.

Tinaja Broadly same as amphora, but amphora has handles at the neck. Both made of clay. Vary greatly in size, and can be buried or, more usually, above ground. Often made from local clay. *See* A Little Learning.

Toro ★→★★★★ Small DOP on Duero. Famed for bold reds from Tinta del Toro (phenotype of TEMPRANILLO, similar but not identical). Today best more restrained, but still firm tannic grip. Glamour from VEGA SICILIA-owned Pintia, LVMH-owned NUMANTHIA, and early investor the Egurens of SIERRA CANTABRIA, now owners of Teso la Monja. San Román, owned by MARIANO GARCÍA and family, also working with GARNACHA and v.gd zesty MALVASÍA Castellana (w). Growing trend for Garnacha, a lighter alternative to trad reds. Try Dominio del Bendito, Fariña, Las Tierras de Javier Rodríguez, Matsu.

Toro Albalá Mont-M ★★→★★★★ Why is MONT-M not better known? Unique treasure trove of wines from PX, incl AMONTILLADO Viejísimo, sumptuous Don PX Convento Selección 31, v.gd GRAN RES 90.

Torres Cat, Pri, R Bai, Rib del D, Rio ★★→★★★★ Torres family never stops. After 150 yrs they might ease off, but no more. Miguel T Snr might be retired but takes lead on many eco fronts. Miguel Jnr engaged with business; sister Mireia technical director, runs Jean León. Clear pyramid of quality in wines. Top is

Torres Antología, outstanding Catalan terroir collection: Bx blend ***Res Real***, top PEN CAB ***Mas la Plana***; C DE BAR duo (burgundy-like ***Milmanda***, one of Spain's finest CHARDS, tiptop ***Grans Muralles*** blend of local varieties); single-vyd ***Mas de la Rosa*** will become Gran Vi de Vinya (top category of PRI) in due course. Also Camino de Magarín (RUE), La Carbonera (RIO), PAGO del Cielo (RIB DEL D), Pazo Torre Pezelas (R BAI). Also famous, consistent, gd-value portfolio, eg. Viña Sol. Pioneer in Chile. Marimar T est in Sonoma (US).

Tradición, Bodegas Man, Sherry ★★→★★★★ Fabulous collection of VOS/VORS Sherries. Must-visit for outstanding collection of Spanish art. Based on oldest-known Sherry house (1650), fascinating archives. Recent purchase of SANLÚCAR's historic Argüeso gives access to classic MAN, San León, plus glorious property to display art.

Txakolí P Vas ★→★★ Three DOPS: ÁLAVA, Bizkaya (serious depth, ageability), Getaria (known for DYA acidic wines with light spritz). Top: Ameztoi, Bat Gara, Doniene Gorrondona, Izar-Leku (from ARTADI), Txomín Etxaníz.

Urbina Rio ★★→★★★ For lovers of gloriously mature RIO. Seemingly bottomless store of fine aged wines.

Valdeorras Gal ★→★★★★ Warmest, most inland of GAL's DOPS, named after gold (*oro*) the Romans mined. GODELLOS more interesting than many ALBARIÑOS. RAFAEL PALACIOS's Godello miraculously gd. TELMO RODRÍGUEZ'S MENCÍA v. fine. Also Godeval, Valdesil.

Valdepeñas C-La M ★→★★ Big DOP of LA MANCHA. Historic favourite for value reds.

Valdespino Sherry ★★→★★★★ Inocente FINO from top Macharnudo single vyd is rare oak-fermented Sherry. Terrific dry AMONTILLADO Tío Diego; outstanding 80-yr-old ***Toneles*** MOSCATEL, JEREZ's v. best. Macallan whisky has 50% stake, ensuring supply of Sherry casks for whisky ageing.

Amphora or *tinaja*? An amphora has two handles at the neck. Tastes the same.

Valencia ★→★★ Take a look: higher-altitude old vines and min-intervention winemaking from Aranleon, Baldovar 923, CELLER DEL ROURE, El Angosto, Filloxera & Cia, JAVIER REVERT, Los Frailes, Rafael Cambra.

Vega Sicilia Rib del D, Rio, Toro ★★★★ Carries a heavy burden of history, its reputation placing it above fashion. In Alvarez family ownership for 40 yrs+. Wines built to last, but developing a notable elegance. Valbuena has 5 yrs in oak and bottle, Único has almost 10 yrs in oak of different sizes and in bottle. Star is outstanding RES Especial, NV blend of three vintages. Neighbouring Alión (modern take on RIB DEL D). Pintia (TORO) now much fresher. Macán (RIO), joint venture with Benjamin de Rothschild, going in right direction. Oremus in Tokaj (*see* Hungary), in addition to sweet wine, has electrically fresh dry FURMINTS Mandolás, Petracs. Latest project: Deiva (R BAI).

Viña Literally, a vyd.

Viña Meín – Emilio Rojo Rib ★★★ Rojo's eponymous wine is a Treixadura blend with thrilling freshness. Star of RIBEIRO, v. fine (r/w). Now owned by ALMA DE CARROVEJAS group. Rojo remains to advise.

Vinegar Mont-M, Sherry ★→★★★ The trad unwanted by-product of winemaking that Sherry and MONT-M producers did not wish to publicize. Yet top vinegars are gastronomic treats: FERNANDO DE CASTILLA, TORO ALBALÁ GRAN RES.

Vins el Cep Cava, Pen ★★→★★★ Four families dating back to C15; 1st producer of bio CAVA: Cava de paraje Claror. Still wines v.gd. ELABORADOR INTEGRAL.

Vintae Nav, Rib del D, Rio, Toro ★→★★★ Entrepreneurial pair from Badarán making v.gd-value RIO at LÓPEZ DE HARO, but also v.gd Bodega Classica GRAN RES (esp rosado). Brands: El Pacto (Rio); Aroa (NAV), Bardos (RIB DEL D), Matsu (TORO). Lively Logroño wine bar, Wine Fandango.

SPAIN

Sherry styles

Palomino Fino Dominant grape of Sherry zone. Strong trend to unfortified PALOMINO aka VINO DE PASTO, eg. COTA 45, Muchada-Leclapart, Primitivo Collantes.
Manzanilla From SANLÚCAR, v. dry, biologically aged. Serve cool with seafood, eg. I Think (EQUIPO NAVAZOS), LA GUITA.
Manzanilla Pasada With 7 yrs+, where FLOR is dying, starting to turn into AMONTILLADO; v. dry, complex, eg. LUSTAU's Almacenista Cuevas Jurado.
Fino Dry, biologically aged in any of the 8 Sherry towns (except Sanlúcar); weightier than MANZANILLA; min age 2 yrs (as Manzanilla), but only start drinking from 4 yrs. Trend for mature FINOS aged 7 yrs+, eg. SERDIO. Trend to cellar and age Finos and Manzanillas in bottle.
Fino Viejo JEREZ category, parallel to Manzanilla Pasada. Min 7 yrs+.
En Rama Sherry as if bottled directly from BUTT; not clarified or cold-stabilized, low filtration = max flavour. Understood to refer to Manzanilla and Fino, but any Sherry bottled this way is En Rama. SACA typically when flor is most abundant, in spring.
Amontillado Started as Fino, then protective flor died. Oxidative ageing gives complexity. Naturally dry, eg. Lustau Amontillado del Castillo. If more than 5g/l residual sugar, indicated by "medium" label.
Palo Cortado Between Amontillado and v. delicate OLOROSO. Each winery has own style, eg. BARBADILLO Reliquía, Fernando de Castilla Antique.
Oloroso Typically not originally aged under flor. Naturally ultra-dry, superbly savoury, even fierce. May be sweetened and sold as CREAM, eg. Emilio Hidalgo Gobernador (dr), Old East India (sw).
Cream Blend sweetened with grape must, PX and/or MOSCATEL. Can be excellent, eg. TRADICIÓN.
Pedro Ximénez (PX) Raisined sweet, from partly sun-dried PX grapes. Unctuous, decadent, bargain. Sip with ice cream, eg. Emilio Hidalgo Santa Ana 1861, Lustau VORS.
Moscatel Aromatic appeal, around half sugar of PX, eg. Lustau Emilín, VALDESPINO Toneles.
VOS / VORS Age-dated Sherries, some of treasures of Jerez. Wines assessed by carbon dating to be 20 yrs old+ are VOS (Very Old Sherry/ Vinum Optimum Signatum); 30 yrs old+ are VORS (Very Old Rare Sherry/Vinum Optimum Rare Signatum). Also 12-yr-old, 15-yr-old categories. Applies only to Amontillado, Oloroso, PALO CORTADO, PX. Some VORS wines softened with PX; sadly producers may overdo the PX.
Vintage / Añada Sherry with declared vintage. Runs counter to trad of SOLERA. Formerly private bottlings now winning public accolades, eg. WILLIAMS & HUMBERT series, Lustau Sweet Oloroso Añada 1997.

Williams & Humbert Sherry ★→★★★★ Historic BODEGA famed for classic brands: Dry Sack, Winter's Tale AMONTILLADO, As You Like It OLOROSO (sw). Among pioneers of organically grown Sherry (and Vintage).

Ysios Rio ★→★★ Visitors delight in undulating roof of Calatrava-designed winery. Polished single-vyd selections.

Zorzal, Viña Nav ★→★★★ Watch Xabi Sanz: entrepreneurial family business moving focus back to NAV: v.gd GRACIANO; fine old-vine GARNACHAS (Malayeto, Señora de la Alturas). Elegant new wine with Spain-born Swiss DJ Fredi Torres (Fitero).

Portugal

In Portugal, wine is part of a meal, and it is always seen as such, from the moment you plant a vineyard to the moment you open a bottle and pour a glass with your food. The huge geographic variety of this relatively small country built a vast array of wine styles, made from hundreds of grape varieties, many of them autochthonous. Wines are fiercely terroir-based, because they are designed for harmonious pairings with local cuisine. What's happening now is that reds are becoming lighter and more elegant, and whites more age-worthy and focused; and there's always another new Port category. And a healthy return to old traditions, supported by enlightened young producers, brings even more variety. The other good news is that Portugal is one of the countries where one finds good value at every price point.

Recent Port vintages

Don't think you have to age classic Vintage Port for half your lifetime. Yes, it will age for decades, but it's delicious young (just bottled; that sort of young) and it doesn't close up in the way it used to. Silkier tannins are one reason (better viticulture, better winemaking), and better spirit is the other. The rough stuff used for fortification in ye olden days is a thing of the past; and better spirit means better Port. Single-quinta vintages too can be drunk from release – and are delicious, believe me, and better with cheese than any unfortified red. Tawnies: drink with cheese, pâté, chocolate.

2025 Small harvest, great natural concentration, freshness.
2024 Exceptional harvest, v.gd concentration. Classic vintage potential.
2023 Increased production, great quality if picked before rain. Top: Nacional, Noval, Churchill's Gricha.
2022 Smaller quantities, hot, concentrated year. Top: Nacional, Noval, Churchill's Gricha, Capela do Vesuvio, Try: Taylor's Sentinels.
2021 Gd quality; gd weather conditions: mild July after fairly wet winter. Best: Graham's Stone Terraces, Noval, Nacional, Ramos Pinto.
2020 Challenging yr; tiny vols of v. concentrated Graham's, Warre's Vinhas Velhas, Vargellas, Noval, Nacional, Ventozelo, Gaivosa Amphitheatrum.
2019 Balance, freshness but less structure. Best: Niepoort, Noval (incl Nacional), Pintas, Vesúvio.
2018 Gd quality, declaration for some, esp Dou Superior. Best: Ferreira, Noval, Sandeman, Taylor's, Vesúvio.
2017 Superlative yr, widely declared; v. hot, dry, compared to historic 1945.
2016 Classic yr, widely declared. Great structure, finesse.
2015 Controversial yr; v. dry, hot. Declared by many (drink: Niepoort, Noval) but not Fladgate, Sogrape or Symington.
2014 Excellent from vyds that ducked September's rain; production low.
Earlier fine vintages: 13 11 09 07 03 00 97 94 92 91 87 83 80 77 70 66 63 45 35 31 27.

Recent table-wine vintages

2025 Hot summer, small crop, v. elegant, concentrated.
2024 Low rainfall, relatively cool temp; v.gd quality all round.
2023 Portugal avoided weather crisis; v.gd whites; elegant reds.
2022 V. v. dry; light, fruity whites; elegant low-alc reds.

2021 Quality, quantity; v.gd whites and fresh, elegant reds.
2020 Gd quantity overall; v.gd whites; pick your red producer.
2019 No rain, cool summer; v.gd quality all round. Keep.
2018 Heavy rains; v. low yields. Aromatic whites, concentrated reds.

Açor, Domínio do Dão ★★★ Deservedly acclaimed boutique project: stunning, modern, old-vine, cement/oak-aged Bical, ENCRUZADO, Jaen, Tinta Pinheira.

Açores / Azores ★→★★★★ Mid-Atlantic nine-island archipelago with three DOCS: Pico, Biscoitos, Graciosa; trad vyds on volcanic rock, shielded from salty winds by stone walls, in UNESCO-protected landscape. Rare, indigenous varieties incl Arinto dos Açores, Terrantez do Pico. Best are crisp, mineral, saline whites. Try ★★ Adega do Vulcão, ★★★ Azores Wine Company, ★★★ Cerca dos Frades, ★★★ Eruptio, ***Insula Vinus***, ★★ Magma, PICO WINES. Rare, late-harvest, non-fortified *licoroso* is luscious treat: ★★★★ ***Czar***.

AdegaMãe Lis ★→★★★ Modern estate n of Lisbon, owned by salt-cod group Riberalves. Fresh, bright, age-worthy Atlantic-influenced whites v.gd. Dory range (esp ARINTO, Viosinho) gd value. Top-notch Terroir oak-aged range (r/w).

Aldeia de Cima Alen ★★★ Auspicious project by Luisa Amorim (QUINTA NOVA NSC) blends region's heritage with modernity. High-quality (r/w), fresh terroir, old vines, alternative ageing (amphora, concrete, oak vats). Superb, age-worthy range (GARRAFEIRA, Myndru), v.gd RES.

Alentejo ★→★★★★ Large, popular, reliable, hot, dry region known for wheat, cork, olive oil and fruit-forward reds. Leader in sustainability initiatives. Subregional diversity allows for other styles: mineral, seaside Costa Vicentina (Cebolal, VICENTINO); fresh, high-altitude, old vyds PORTALEGRE (CABEÇAS DO REGUENGO, ★★ Fonte Souto, RUI REGUINGA, Teixinha, ★★★ Julian Reynolds); fresh Vidigueira (CORTES DE CIMA, ROCIM); earthy, ancient clay amphora VINHO DE TALHA DOC (XXVI Talhas, ROCIM). Also look for ADEGA MONTE BRANCO, ALDEIA DE CIMA, CARTUXA, ESPORÃO, HERDADE DOS GROUS, JOÃO PORTUGAL RAMOS, JOSÉ DE SOUSA, MALHADINHA NOVA, MOUCHÃO, MOURO. Classical red blend TRINCADEIRA/ ARAGONEZ, with ALICANTE BOUSCHET increasingly used. Don't overlook white.

Alorna, Quinta da Tej ★★ Historic noble estate known for majestic 300-yr-old tree. Consistent (r/w): rich, oak-aged Marquesa de Alorna; elegant RES das Pedras; single-variety and estate gd value.

Ameal, Quinta do Vin ★→★★★ Benchmark ESPORÃO-owned boutique estate. Organic, age-worthy LOUREIRO incl gd-value Bico Amarelo, racy single-vyd Solo Único, v.gd oaked ***Res***.

Andresen Port ★★→★★★★ Historic, boutique, Portuguese-owned house with superb TAWNIES: v.gd 20-yr-old; ethereal ***Colheitas*** **1900' 1910'** (bottled on demand) **68' 80' 91' 92' 97' 00' 03' 05'**. Pioneered age-dated WHITE PORTS: 10-, 20-, ***40-yr-old***.

Aveleda Vin ★→★★ Most popular, largest VIN, available worldwide. Now B-Corp, focused on sustainability. Makes gd-value, reliable white range, esp ALVARINHO, LOUREIRO. Owns top estate VALE D MARIA (DOU), ★★ D'Aguieira (BAIR), ★ Villa Alvor (Alg). A gd visitor centre nr Porto.

Bacalhôa Vinhos Alen, Lis, Set ★★→★★★ Large group with popular brands. Top: age-worthy, v.gd ***Quinta da Bacalhôa*** Bx blend incl CAB SAUV 1st planted 1974, also used in iconic red Palácio da Bacalhôa, cask-aged MOSCATEL DE SETÚBAL (incl rare Roxo); gd fruit-forward ALEN QUINTA do Carmo reds incl RES; gd-value white Catarina (SET). Owns several art museums.

Bágeiras, Quinta das Bair ★★★→★★★★ Reputed family-owned estate, using trad low-intervention methods, techniques. Top-notch old-vines ***Avô Fausto*** (r/w), ***Garrafeira*** (r/w), Pai Abel (r/w). Also gd-value RES, sparkling, entry level (r/w).

Bairrada ★★→★★★★ Atlantic-influenced DOC famous for world-class, age-worthy, structured BAGA (often v. old vines), charming whites and v.gd sparkling, esp Baga Bair. Best: *Bágeiras*, CAVES SÃO JOÃO, *Filipa Pato*, *Giz by Luis Gomes*, *Kompassus*, LUÍS PATO, *Mira do Ó*, ★★ Principal, ★★★ Sidónio de Sousa, *Vadio*. Unmissable local *roast suckling pig*.

Barbeito Mad ★★★★ Highly regarded 1946-founded firm. Owner Ricardo Freitas revolutionized MAD wines, focusing on elegance, perfect acidity. Unique, single-vyd, single-cask FRASQUEIRAS; outstanding 20-, 30-, 40-, 50-yr-old MALVASIAS, 50-yr-old BASTARDO; New 50-yr-old Familias. Also v.gd *table wines*.

Barca Velha Dou ★★★★ Portugal's most prized, sought-after red, 1st made 1952. Blend of low/high-altitude plots. Cellar release only in exceptional yrs, after 8–10 yrs in bottle: 91 95 99 00 04' 08' 11' 15. Too expensive? Second label: *Res Especial*, released in great-but-not-BV yrs 86' 89' 92' 94 97 01' 07' 09 14'. By CASA FERREIRINHA (SOGRAPE), smooth, deep, long and enticing, drink on release, but can improve in bottle for decades.

Blandy's Mad ★★→★★★★ Reputed family-run firm. *10-yr-old range* revamped, fresher, livelier. Superlative, rare, library of old stocks: FRASQUEIRA (BUAL 1920' 57' 66' 72' 76', MALMSEY 88' 77' 81' 91', SERCIAL 68' 75' 80' 88' 89' 90', *Terrantez* 75' 77' 80' 87', VERDELHO 76 79' 82'); v.gd 20-yr-old Malmsey, and COLHEITAS (Bual 96 08 09 10, Malmsey 99 04 07 10, Sercial 02 08 09 10, Verdelho 00 08 09 10). Superb *50-yr-old Malmsey*. Expensive, rare MCDXIX blends 11 yrs between 1863 and 2004. Unique 77 Listrão from Porto Santo Island. Popular, affordable RAINWATER. Atlantis table-wine range. Unmissable, historic *Funchal lodges*.

Boavista, Quinta da Dou ★★★★ Top Cima-Corgo estate, run by SOGEVINUS. Superb, age-worthy old field blends: 80-yr-old vines, single-vyd spicy Oratório, piney Ujo. Varietal range; seductive *Res*; oak-aged Vinha do Levante (w).

Bual (or Boal) Mad Classic grape for medium-sweet MAD: tangy, smoky; balances acidity/sweetness. Pairs exquisitely with aged hard cheeses or alone. Thrilling old vintages are a treasure.

Cabeças do Reguengo Alen ★★→★★★ Boutique estate, trad winemaking. Elegant, low-intervention range from high-altitude, v. old field blends in PORTALEGRE. Try Quartzo (w), Solstício (r). Cosy guesthouse.

Canteiro Mad Natural, slow-warming ageing in humid lodges; trad reserved for more expensive MAD (now also TINTA NEGRA). Superior to ESTUFAGEM.

Carcavelos Lis ★★★ Tiny, true hidden-gem seaside DOC. Unique, mouthwatering, gripping, off-dry fortified. Try Villa Oeiras.

Cardo, Quinta do Bei Int ★★→★★★ Historic 90-yr-old, high-altitude (750m/2461ft), bio estate, now revamped. Elegant, fresh range: top-notch Grande Res (w), single-vyd *Lomedo* (w), Pombal (r); gd-value Cardo, Res (r/w) labels.

It's festival time

If you happen to be in Portugal over a wkd, you might want to take in a wine festival, eg. Encontro Grandes Escolhas (Lisbon) and Essência do Vinho (Lisbon, Oporto, Funchal). Millésime (BAIR) and Brut Experience (LIS) showcase sparkling wines. Some towns hold festivals focusing on their home terroir: Melgaço, Monção (VIN); Alijó, Foz Côa (DOU); Pinhel (Bei Int). DÃO and ALEN organize events in Lisbon. Enophilo travels to several towns during the yr: Braga, Coimbra, Lisbon, Oporto, Vilamoura. Featuring art, music and a selection of alternative/low-intervention whites: Vinho ao Vivo (Lisbon), Simplesmente Vinho (Oporto), Vinho na Vila (Alen). Major distributors show their portfolio annually: Decante Vinhos, Garrafeira Soares, Vinalda.

Cartuxa, Adega da Alen ★★→★★★★ Historic, reputed ALEN firm run by Eugénio de Almeida Foundation. Home to flagship, full-bodied Pêra Manca (r); v.gd, age-worthy, best-buy ***Cartuxa Res***; v.gd single-variety Scala Coeli changes every yr.

Carvalhais, Quinta dos Dão ★★→★★★ SOGRAPE-owned classic DÃO estate. Benchmark, age-worthy: gd oak-aged, flinty ENCRUZADO; rich RES (***esp w***); earthy ***Alfrocheiro***; floral TOURIGA N; dense, top red Único; rich multi-vintage Branco Especial. Popular, gd-value Duque de Viseu, Grão Vasco.

Casa da Atela Tej ★★ Historic (C14) large estate; unique 75-yr-old plot of CASTELÃO (origin of top r). Native/international varieties range gd, esp CHARD, SYRAH, PETIT VERDOT, RES (r/w). Estate label gd value.

Casa Santos Lima Alen, Alg, Dou, Lis, Vin ★→★★ Large operator in six regions, incl AZORES. Varietal LIS range. Also ***Colossal***, ***Palha-Canas***, QUINTA das Setencostas, ***Touriz***; Al-Ria (Alg); Quinta de Porrais (DOU); all v.gd value.

Chocapalha, Quinta de Lis ★★★ Coastal family-run estate. Winemaker Sandra Tavares da Silva (WINE & SOUL) makes vibrant, mineral, saline ***whites*** (v.gd CHARD, RES, old-vine ARINTO CH, ARINTO Antigo from old vyds). Vinha Mãe v.gd; also gd-value red, esp CASTELÃO, and gd wine tourism.

Chryseia Dou ★★★★ Modern classic. Prestigious, consistent, fine, elegant TOURIGA-driven red. Born from SYMINGTON FAMILY ESTATES, Bruno Prats (Bx) partnership. ***Post Scriptum*** v.gd value.

Churchill's Dou, Port ★★★ Boutique, family-run, with v.gd ***reds*** (gd-value Churchill's Estates Grafite range, esp Grande RES). Top Port: Dry WHITE PORT, 20-yr-old, 30-yr-old, unfiltered LBV, VINTAGE PORT. Popular Meio Queijo. Guesthouse.

Cockburn's Port ★★→★★★ Refreshed, focus on younger clients, SYMINGTON-owned, consistently gd Port: Special RES aged longer in wood than others; vibrant LBV; v.gd single-QUINTA dos Canais; drier, fresher style of VINTAGE PORT.

Coelheiros, Tapada de Alen ★★★ Historic C15 estate, bottling since 1992, converting large vyds, orchard, forest to bio. Top-notch GARRAFEIRA; classy CAB SAUV/ALICANTE BOUSCHET (r), ARINTO/Roupeiro (w); gd-value Coelheiros (r/w).

Colares Lis ★★★ Historic DOC with windswept, ungrafted vines on sand. Europe's w-most vyds. Age-worthy; tannic Ramisco (r); crisp, saline MALVASIA (w). Try ★★ Adega Regional de Colares, ★★★ ***Baías e Enseadas***, ★★★ Chitas (w). Visit ***Viúva Gomes***, ★★★ Casal Santa Maria.

Colheita Mad, Port Single-yr TAWNY or WHITE PORT. Bottling date fine-printed on label (look for recent dates); nutty, oxidative, thrilling. Cask-aged: min 7 yrs, often 50 yrs+, rare superb 100 yrs+ bottled on demand. Best (serve chilled): ANDRESEN, Burmester, DALVA, GRAHAM'S, KOPKE, NIEPOORT, NOVAL, TAYLOR'S. Also in MAD, cask-aged min 5 yrs.

Cortes de Cima Alen ★★★→★★★★ Family-run estate undergoing bio revolution, now led by Anna Jørgensen (daughter of ALEN SYRAH pioneers). Revamped, repriced, fresher range: iconic 100% Syrah Incógnito; great ***Res*** (r), elegant Chaminé range, esp Atlantic-coast white. Also saline Lour-inho (ALVARINHO/LOUREIRO), Salino (r/w).

Cossart Gordon Mad ★★★ Oldest MAD shipper (1745), known for fine, drier style; v.gd single-yr bottlings. Try: COLHEITAS (VERDELHO 09'; Bual 89' 06'; MALMSEY 08' 95'); FRASQUEIRA (VERDELHO 75'). MADEIRA WINE COMPANY-owned.

Crasto, Quinta do Dou, Port ★★→★★★★ Prestigious C17 family-run estate with striking hilltop lodge. Reputed for single-vyd, field-blend reds ***Vinha da Ponte*** and Vinha Maria Teresa. Superb varietals, esp age-worthy TINTA RORIZ. Popular, gd value: rich old-vyd ***Res***, Dou Superior range.

Croft Port ★★→★★★ Historic C16 FLADGATE-owned VINTAGE PORT-focused house; v.gd-value, single-QUINTA ***Quinta da Roêda***. Superlative old-vine Sērikos 17. Popular treat Pink Rosé Port, Triple Crown. Visitor centre in Pinhão.

Crusted (Port) Wallet-friendly, delicious Port treat. Luscious, rare, age-worthy NV style. Blend of two or more vintage-quality yrs, aged up to 4 yrs in casks, 3 yrs in bottle. Forms deposit ("crust"), so decant. CHURCHILL'S, DOW'S, FONSECA, ***Niepoort***.

Dalva Port ★★★→★★★★ Quality-focused C19 house, 1st-class TAWNIES: gd-value 20-yr-old; superior 50-yr-old. Superb COLHEITAS; 10-, 20-, 30-, 40-, 50-yr-old white range, stunning ***golden white*** 52' 63' 71' 89'. Pure bio Port v.gd. Table wines gd value. Owned by GRANVINHOS.

Dão ★★→★★★★ Historic, granite-hills DOC. Fresh, elegant ENCRUZADO-based whites, food-friendly, elegant, age-worthy reds. Home of TOURIGA N. Classics: ★★ Boas Quintas, ★ Cabriz, ***Carvalhais***, ★★ Casa de Santar, ★ Lusovini, ***Pellada/Saes***. Try low-intervention ***António Madeira***, organic CASA DE MOURAZ (1st-class ***Druida***), characterful JOÃO TAVARES DE PINA WINES, ★ Casa Américo. Top designation, Dão Nobre ("noble"): ★★★ Vinha do Contador. Watch: ***Casa da Passarella***, DOMÍNIO DO AÇOR, TABOADELLA, TEXTURA.

DOC (denominação de origem controlada) Quality wine designation. Newer denomination DOP rarely used.

Dona Maria Alen ★★★★ Classic, reputed estate run by charismatic owner Júlio Bastos. Age-worthy range with native and French varieties v.gd. Foot-trodden, old-vine ALICANTE BOUSCHET reds, esp ***Grande Res***, ***Júlio B Bastos***; v.gd varietals (esp PETIT VERDOT), elegant Amantis; v.gd-value ***estate label***.

Douro ★→★★★★ Historic, dreamy UNESCO World Heritage Site made of hard-to-work steep hills. Tourists visit for river views, Port and quality table wine (Dou DOC). Powerful, structured reds; fine, high-altitude seductive whites. Three subregions (cooler Baixo Corgo, milder Cima Corgo and warmer, fast-expanding Dou Superior). Vinhas Velhas (old vines) now regulated: min 40 yrs+ old, low yields, min four varieties. Rare 100-yr+ field blends (30+ varieties) planted in terraces of unforgiving schist. Classics: ***Boavista***, ***Casa Ferreirinha*** (incl top ***Barca Velha***), ***Chryseia***, CHURCHILL'S, ***Crasto***, ***Infantado***, ***Noval***, ***Pintas***, QUANTA TERRA, QUINTA NOVA NSC, RAMOS PINTO, ***Vale Meão***, ***Vesúvio***. Best for elegance: ALVES DE SOUSA, Carolina, Conceito, Luis Seabra, Manoella, NIEPOORT, ***Poeira***. Watch: FOLIAS DE BACO, Invincible, QUINTA DE TOURAIS.

Dow's Port ★★★★ Historic, reputed, SYMINGTON-owned. Age-defying, drier-style VINTAGE PORT. Legendary yrs: 27 45 63 66 70. Recent yrs: 00' 03' 07' 11' 16' 17'. In non-declared yrs, v.gd single QUINTAS do Bomfim 19 20 21, ***Senhora da Ribeira*** 15 18 19 22. Plus v.gd 10-, 20-, 30-, 40-yr-old Tawnies, LBV. Pinhão highlight: classy ***Bomfim visitor centre***, v.gd ***restaurant***.

Duorum Dou, Port ★★→★★★ DOU Superior estate owned by JOÃO PORTUGAL RAMOS (ALEN). Top, aged several yrs pre-release ***O Leucura***; v.gd-value range with fine

Old, dry and rancio

What is *rancio*? It sounds like "rancid", as in butter; but in wine it's a bright, tense note that comes from long ageing in a hot, dry climate. A Portuguese word for it is *vinagrinho* ("little vinegar") – not actually vinegar, but a touch of that high-toned flavour. It is part long ageing, part oxidation, part volatile acidity, part the micro-reactions of sugars in wine over the yrs. And it's wonderful – lifting the wine, giving it energy and keeping it tasting fresh for decades. Fortified wine, that is. In table wine, it's a fault. But in MAD, in TAWNY Port, in Banyuls from France, in Sherry from Spain, it's glorious. However, it takes time, as well as the right conditions; rarely found in a wine under 30 yrs old. In Port, it is stronger in wines aged in the DOU Valley than in wines aged in GAIA, on the coast. Drier, you see.

Res, fruity Altitude (r/w); gd-value COLHEITA, LBV, Tons. Dense VINTAGE PORT from 100-yr-old vines v.gd.

Espera Wines Lis ★★ Low-intervention boutique winery run by winemaker Rodrigo Martins. Native-variety bio range v.gd: fresh, fruity CASTELÃO, Palheto; mineral ARINTO, Bical; skin-contact Curtimenta.

Esporão Alen ★★★ Dynamic, eco-focused firm. Vast, consistent wine and olive oil range. High-end, rare Torre do Esporão; fine GARRAFEIRA-like wood-aged Private Selection (creamy SEM w and rich, dense r). High-quality, fruit-focused, modern *Res (r/w)*. Popular Monte Velho. Visitor centre, restaurant v.gd. Interests in DOU (Murças), VIN (AMEAL).

Bifana (braised pork sandwich): found everywhere, eaten anytime. Go for lager.

Espumante Sparkling. Wallet-friendly gem. Best are age-worthy with BAGA BAIR quality designation. Try ***Abibes***, Aliança, CAVES SÃO JOÃO, Colinas (***Kompassus***), Marquês de Marialva, Poço do Lobo, São Domingos, VADIO (esp ***Perpetuum***). Távora-Varosa gd value, try ***Murganheira***. Great DOU ***Vértice***.

Esteban, Susana Alen ★★★ Galician (*see* Spain) trailblazer winemaker reviving v. old PORTALEGRE vyds. Fine, elegant: top Procura (two plots r, field-blend w); earthy CASTELÃO Sem Vergonha; fruity Aventura (r/w); oak-aged ★★★★ ***A Centenária***; exotic Vinyle; vibrant VINHO DE TALHA. Collaboration series: v.gd Sidecar; complex DOU Crochet, ALEN Tricot with Sandra Tavares da Silva (WINE & SOUL).

Estufagem Mad Sea voyage-inspired MAD ageing method (up to 50°C/122°F, min 90 days) for unique scorched-earth tang in entry-level wines.

Falua Tej ★→★★ French-owned estate with multi-region interests: Barão do Hospital auspicious VIN project (esp ALVARINHO, LOUREIRO); QUINTA de São José (v.gd DOU range); Quinta do Mourão (v.gd PORT stocks). Falua range incl gd-value Conde de Vimioso (RES a step up), gd Res (r/w, esp Sommelier Edition). Top: stony-soil Vinha do Convento (r/w).

Ferreira Port ★★★→★★★★ Historic, prestigious, SOGRAPE-owned. Stand-out VINTAGE PORT 11' 16' 18', top Vinhas Velhas 16', v.gd-value single-QUINTA do Porto **17' 19' 20'**, LBV. Elegant TAWNY v.gd value: Dona Antonia RES, 10-, ***20-***, 30-yr-old.

Ferreirinha, Casa Dou ★→★★★★ Large, highly reputed SOGRAPE-owned brand. Winemaker Luís Sottomayor makes iconic ***Barca Velha***, rare ***Res Especial***, age-worthy, 1st-class ***Quinta da Leda***, v.gd ***Castas Escondidas***, v.gd-value ***Vinha Grande***. Popular: Esteva, Papa Figos.

Fladgate Port Large, dynamic, independent, family-owned Port firm, expanding to table wine. Owns: leading Port brands CROFT, FONSECA, TAYLOR'S; multi-region table wines VIN (Palmeira, Pedra), DÃO Bella, BAIR Principal; growing travel empire incl hotels in GAIA, Lisbon, Pinhão, Porto; Michelin-starred The Yeatman; seven-museum WOW (World of Wine) Gaia visitor centre.

Folias de Baco Dou ★★ Run by winemaker Tiago Sampaio. High-altitude, low-intervention ***Uivo*** range (skin-contact Curtido) v.gd; fresh old-vine (r/w grapes) Renegado; low-alc Piquette.

Fonseca Port ★★★★ FLADGATE-owned house from 1815. Reputed, age-defying VINTAGE PORT 63' 70' 77' **94' 97' 11' 16' 17'**. Superb ***Fonseca Guimaraens*** 76' 91' **98' 01' 08' 13' 15' 18' 19' 22'**. Single-QUINTA Panascal; v.gd 20-, 40-yr-old TAWNY; Bin 27 popular, gd value.

Fonseca, José Maria da Alen, Set ★★→★★★★ Large, 190-yr-old, 7th-generation, family-run firm. Jewel in crown is fortified ***Moscatel de Setúbal***, esp stocks of old MOSCATEL: stunning ***20-yr-old Alambre*** and ***Moscatel Roxo***, lavish ***Superior*** 55' 66 71. Table-wine range: top-notch, dense Hexagon (r/w); gd-value single-variety DSF range; popular BSE, João Pires, Lancers, Periquita. Owns v.gd-value ALEN classic ***José de Sousa***.

Foz de Arouce Bei At ★★★ Hidden gem, esp classy older vintages. JOÃO PORTUGAL RAMOS's family-run Lousã outpost making age-worthy range: vivid *Cercial*, TOURIGA N/BAGA blend, top-notch old-Baga-vines *Vinhas Velhas*.

Frasqueira Mad Pinnacle of MAD wines. Aged for decades (min 20 yrs) in CANTEIRO, best over 100 yrs old. Single yr (aka Vintage), single (noble) variety. Bottling date on label. Best: BARBEITO, MADEIRA WINE COMPANY.

Gaia, Vila Nova de Dou, Port Historic home of major Port shippers, also walkable tourist attraction: working cellars, tasting rooms, cable car, boat tours, hotels, wine shops, museums (WOW), restaurants/bars (Enoteca 17·56, Espaço Porto Cruz, Vinum). Best: GRAHAM'S. Also: Cálem, CHURCHILL'S, COCKBURN'S, FERREIRA, NIEPOORT, POÇAS, RAMOS PINTO, SANDEMAN, TAYLOR'S.

Garrafeira Literally bottle (*garrafa*) storage. Designation for aged wine, esp ALEN, BAIR, DÃO. Reds aged for min 30 mths (often longer), min 1 yr in bottle. Whites need 12 mths, min 6 in bottle. Also, wine shop.

Giz by Luis Gomes Bair ★★★ Reputed project; century-old-vyds revival, low-intervention range: fine VINHAS VELHAS (r/w), esp BAGA; vibrant rosé; gd fizz.

Global Wines Bair, Dão ★★→★★★ Large DÃO-based firm. Owns: gd-value, popular Cabriz range, Casa de Santar (v.gd Res, superb Nobre); fine, age-worthy Vinha do Contador range (dense r; rare, creamy, organic Grand Jury w). In other regions: Encostas do DOU (Dou), Lourosa (VIN), Monte da Cal (ALEN) and QUINTA do Encontro (BAIR), incl visitor centre with striking architecture.

Graham's Port ★★★★ Highly reputed SYMINGTON-owned 200-yr-old house. Top-notch VINTAGE PORT 27' 63' 66' 85' 91' 94' 97 00' 03' 07' 11' 16' 17' 20' (delightful at release, heaven with age); lavish Stone Terraces 11' 15' 16' 17' 21'; single QUINTA (Malvedos 12 15 18' 19', new old-vines Tua). CRUSTED, LBV, RES RUBY Six Grapes all gd value. Superb, seductive 20-, 30-, 40-, 50-yr-old TAWNIES; luscious Single Harvest (COLHEITAS) collection 40' 50' 52' 61' 63' 69' 72' 82 94' 97 03. Ne Oublie VERY VERY OLD TAWNY is 1882 bottled history. Best-in-class *visitor centre, restaurant in Gaia*.

Granvinhos Port ★★★ Ex-Gran Cruz. Owns: reputable DALVA; DOU Ventozelo; Port's largest exporting brand Porto Cruz (volume, cocktails); Porto Presidential. Stylish museum, bar, hotel, restaurants in GAIA/Porto. La Martiniquaise-owned.

Grous, Herdade dos Alen, Dou ★★→★★★ Prestigious eco-focused estate: RES (rich, oak-aged w; ripe, fine r); fruity Moon Harvested, best-barrels 23 Barricas labels; thrilling cement-aged *Concrete*. Reputed wine tourism. Watch: DOU outpost QUINTA de Valbom.

Henriques & Henriques Mad ★★→★★★★ Leading MAD shipper, thrilling range: *20-yr-old (Malvasia, Terrantez)*, *50-yr-old* TINTA NEGRA; top-notch FRASQUEIRAS (some aged in bourbon barrels): BASTARDO 27, BUAL 00' 09, VERDELHO 32 57, SERCIAL 28 71' 01', Terrantez 54'. Entry-level range gd value; gd tasting room. La Martiniquaise-owned.

Vineyards on Madeira need c.900 man-hrs work p.a. Dou: c.500; Alen, c.150–200.

Infantado, Quinta do Dou, Port ★★★ Roseira family-owned, 100 yrs+ (est 1816). Estate *Res* (r) concentrated, yet elegant, polished. Ports always on dry side: acclaimed *Vintages*, classic, age-worthy; *Tawnies*, rich, long. Great *Rabigato* (w), rich, rewarding, zesty acidity. Recent release *50-yr-old Luis Roseira*, rare treat.

Insula Atlantis Azores ★★ Grower-winemaker Paulo Machado on his home island, Pico: creamy, crisp *Chão de Lava AA* (w); fragrant Chão de Sal (light r blend of r/w grapes).

João Tavares de Pina Wines Dão ★★→★★★ Rebel natural-wine pioneer, lost many vyds, stock to forest fires. Native-varieties range: classic, increasingly natural Torre, Terra de Tavares. Young, fresh, low-intervention: Rufia range, Tretas.

Justino's Mad ★→★★★★ Largest MAD shipper; lively wines. Winemaker Juan Teixeira blends trad, modernity. Gems: Terrantez *50-yr-old* and 78' (oldest in cask), MALVASIA 64' 68' 88' 97'. Try also Verdelho 98', SERCIAL 97', TINTA NEGRA 99'. Makes popular Broadbent label. Owned by La Martiniquaise.

Kompassus Bair ★★★★ João Póvoa, BAIR wine aristocracy. Classic BAGA, sometimes with TOURIGA N, sharp, polished, food-friendly. Balanced dry white. Iconic ***Private Collection*** incl immortal 91' red, stunning old-vine Baga. Great value estate, ***Res*** (both r/w). Range incl varietals (r/w, esp ***Tinto Cão***), high-end fizz. Watch.

Kopke Port ★★→★★★★ Oldest Port house (1638), now making DOU. Thrilling TAWNY (10-, 20-, 30-, 40-, *50-yr-old*, COLHEITAS 35' 40' onwards), exceptional WHITE PORT (esp now-rare *35'* 40' and 20-, 30-, 40-, *50-yr-old*). SOGEVINUS-owned.

LBV (Late Bottled Vintage) Port Budget-friendly, widely available alternative to VINTAGE PORT. Cask-aged 4–6 yrs (twice as long as VP) for early drinking. Best are age-worthy, unfiltered versions: FERREIRA, NIEPOORT, NOVAL, OFFLEY, RAMOS PINTO, SANDEMAN, TAYLOR'S, WARRE'S. Serve lightly chilled, alone or pair with chocolate, nuts, cheese, baked apples. Dare to serve it with steak au poivre.

Lisboa ★→★★★★ Underrated N Lisbon coastal region making great-value fresh, crisp, mineral whites (ARINTO-based) and age-worthy reds (CASTELÃO, SYRAH, TINTA RORIZ). Historic, microclimate COLARES subregion (MALVASIA, Ramisco). Quality-focused, dynamic, often bio producers balance large firms. Best: CHOCAPALHA, ***Monte Bluna***, top Syrah pioneer MONTE D'OIRO. Try also ADEGAMÃE, ★★ Pancas (age-worthy range), SANT'ANA. Young, often natural, producers to watch: ★★★ ***Baías e Enseadas***, ★★ ***Casal Figueira***, ★★ ***COZs***, ESPERA WINES, HUGO MENDES, ★★ Humus, ★★ Marinho, ★★ Olival da Murta, ★ Serradinha, ★★★ ***Vale da Capucha***, VIÚVA GOMES. Best to visit: ADEGAMÃE, MONTE D'OIRO, SANT'ANA.

Lobo de Vasconcellos Alen, Dou ★★★→★★★★ Family project of Manuel LV (CRASTO). Fresh, vibrant, terroir-driven ALEN LV and ***Res*** (r/w). ***Vinha do Norte*** is stellar DOU red from one of its best winemakers.

Lopes, Márcio Dou, Vin ★★→★★★ Rising-star winemaker. ***Pequenos Rebentos*** range (gd-value ALVARINHO/LOUREIRO); top Caminho; DOU (Permitido/Proibido).

Louro, Luis – Adega Monte Branco Alen ★★★ Family project, Portuguese varieties, ***Alento*** and esp ***Alento Res*** gd value. ***Monte Branco*** (r/w) top quality. Intense, pure, balanced, v. food-friendly. With co-winemaker Inês Capão, Lou and Ca are bottled experiments: different varieties, blends, sometimes multi-vintage.

Touriga Nacional, nationally

Lovers of BAIR might argue, but the most famous Portuguese grape is probably TOURIGA N. It most likely comes from DÃO; this is where the greatest genetic variation is found, and where there's a small village called Tourigo (as the grape is known in those parts). It is 1st recorded in 1822 so is not that old, but it has been busy: Touriga Francesa or Franca is its offspring, and also probably Touriga Fêmea (aka Touriga Brasileira). Touriga N's quality saw it planted nationwide, but it only reached the Douro once clones with more reliable yields became available. Old vyds in the Douro tend to have none; however, it is now fashionable for Portugal's table wines. What does its wine taste like? Tea and violets, esp violets. For a grand tour, try **Dou**: Carvalhas, CRASTO, NOVAL, VALLADO, Ventozelo, Zom; **Dão**: Casa Américo, Carrocel, Pedra Cancela, QUINTA das Marias, Santar Amores, TABOADELLA, Villa Oliveira; **Bair**: Aguieira, Primavera; **Bei Int**: Termos; **Tej**: Cabeça de Toiro, FALUA, Tyto Alba; **Lis**: ADEGAMÃE, Coragem; **Set**: Ameias; **Alen**: CORTES DE CIMA, ESPORÃO, Paço dos Infantes, Peceguina, ROCIM.

Maçanita, António Alen, Dou ★★→★★★★ Star winemaker-consultant, many projects, regions. Home ALEN: ***Enxarrama*** (r), ***Morgado de Oliveira*** (w), popular Sexy, seductive Fita Preta, v.gd Palpite, trad Chão dos Eremitas. AZORES: ***Terrantez do Pico***, old-vine Vinha dos Utras. Sister-led: Letra A, F range (DOU); rare, thrilling Porto Santo island range (MAD). Wine tourism in Alen, Dou, Azores.

There are 160 road tunnels on Madeira. Sunglasses off, sunglasses on...

Madeira ★→★★★★ Dramatic archipelago, island and DOC; cliff-hanging vines, mouthwatering wines, only eight firms making world-famous fortified. Quality starts at 10-yr-olds. In order of sweetness: SERCIAL (9–27g/l), VERDELHO (27–45g/l), BUAL (45–63g/l), MALMSEY (63–117g/l), all based on those grapes. More affordable, ubiquitous TINTA NEGRA. For all, high acidity ensures balance. Treasured decades-old stocks. Best: BARBEITO, MADEIRA WINE COMPANY. Also: ★ Borges, HENRIQUES & HENRIQUES, JUSTINO'S, PEREIRA D'OLIVEIRA, ★ Faria & Filhos, ★ Madeira Vintners. Watch: table wines rise, ★★ Atlantis, ★★ BARBEITO, ★★ Barbusano; unique smaller Porto Santo island wines.

Madeira, António Dão ★★★ Reputed French-born winemaker reviving v. old vyds (up to 120 yrs). Fine bio range: old-vine ***A Centenária***, A Palheira; eponymous label Vinha da Serra; v.gd ***Vinhas Velhas*** (r/w). Light, fruity Ainda Palhete.

Madeira, Rui Roboredo Bei Int, Dou ★★→★★★ High-altitude pioneer; DOU: v.gd mineral ***Pedra Escrita (r/w)***, top, eponymous old-vines label; Bei Int: great-value ***Beyra*** range, esp Jaen, ***Grande Res, Garrafeira***. Popular: Castello d'Alba.

Madeira Wine Company Mad Reputed, largest MAD firm, led by 7th-generation Chris Blandy. Owns BLANDY'S, COSSART GORDON, Leacock, Miles.

Malhadinha Nova, Herdade da Alen ★★★ Leading Soares-family S ALEN bio estate, high-end ***country house***; v.gd, age-worthy range, incl ***estate label***; rich, late-released Marias da Malhadinha; piney, dense ALICANTE BOUSCHET Menino António and CAB SAUV Pequeno João. Old-vine (1949) Vale Travessos (r/w) v.gd; single-variety, often single-vyd range gd. Watch: high-altitude PORTALEGRE outpost ★★★★ ***Teixinha*** growing range.

Malvasia (Malmsey) Mad Sweetest, richest of MAD's noble varieties. Sharp tang: thrilling, luscious crème brûlée, dark chocolate pair. Look for older yrs.

Mateus Rosé ★ Bestseller in a flask-shaped bottle. Fresh, off-dry spritzy rosé with dry edition. SOGRAPE-owned.

Mendes, Anselmo Vin ★★★→★★★★ "Mr ALVARINHO": benchmark minerality. Try lees-aged ***Contacto*** (now co-owned by SYMINGTON); v.gd-value, crisp Muros de Melgaço, Muros Antigos range; superb, flinty Parcela Única.

Mendes, Hugo Lis ★★ Dynamic, influential. Elegant multi-region range: LIS (Claret, CASTELÃO, Vital); Tej (FERNÃO PIRES); ALEN (VINHO DE TALHA). Eponymous label (r/w) gd value; gd skin-contact Underdog.

Menin Dou ★★→★★★ Firm to watch. Large investments, consultant star winemaker Tiago ALVES DE SOUSA. Classy range, incl RES (r/w), single-variety labels, top Grande Res, New Legacy and D Beatriz. Also HO Wines, gd value.

Menina d'Uva Trás M ★★ Natural-wine project by Parisian Aline Domingues, back to ancestral roots, old vyds. Elegant, native-varieties, low-intervention range, esp blend of Ciste (r/w grapes).

Mira do Ó Alen, Bair, Dão, Lis, Vin ★★★★ Dynamic project, eponymous winemaker Nuno MÓ. Low-intervention old-vines; elegant, precise. VIN: Sou ALVARINHO (with Joana Santiago). DÃO: top-notch ENCRUZADO ***Druida Res***, smooth ***Druida*** (r), deep, fresh ***Grande Druida*** (r); gd-value Caminhante, Vidente. BAIR: Project V Puro (partner João Soares) incl ***Aliás*** (r/w/rosé), Doravante (r/w), Outrora. Bucelas: Mira (v. mineral ARINTO). ALEN: Teima (r/w) from old vyds in PORTALEGRE.

Monte Bluna Lis ★★★ Classy Atlantic-influenced min-intervention project, high-altitude vyds n of Lisbon: superb ARAGONÊZ-based Blunissima; fine, elegant, rare-variety ***Tinta Miúda***; seductive ***Res*** and TicTac range.

Monte d'Oiro, Quinta do Lis ★★→★★★★ Family-owned, Atlantic-influenced, Hermitage-inspired bio estate. Superb range: SYRAH/VIOGNIER ***Res***; v.gd VIOGNIER ***Res***; 1st-class Ex Aequo SYRAH/TOURIGA N label; thrilling limited-edition 100% ***Arinto***. Entry-level range gd value.

Monte da Casteleja Alg ★★ Boutique winery keeping ancestral techniques alive (foot-treading, wooden vats). Elegant bio range. Visitor centre.

Great Port years are not necessarily great Douro table wine years. Don't assume.

Monte da Ravasqueira Alen ★★→★★★ Part of family-run WINESTONE group. Consultant David Baverstock (ex-ESPORÃO) makes quality range, esp Premium, ALICANTE BOUSCHET. Single-vyd Vinha das Romãs (r/w) gd value. Visitor centre.

Morgado do Quintão Alg ★★ Historic family-run bio estate focused on native varieties. Winemaker Joana Maçanita makes sandy-soil, old-vine range: NEGRA MOLE (elegant: rosé, *clarete*), CASTELÃO (estate r), amphora (blends both). Charming wine tourism.

Moscatel de Setúbal Set ★→★★★★ Thrilling, exotic, sweet MOSCATEL fortified treasure, esp richer ***Roxo***. Superlative ***Superior*** designation. Star: JOSÉ MARIA DA FONSECA (100-yr-old stocks). Also v.gd BACALHÔA VINHOS. Value: Palmela Wine Company, Piloto. Pair with crème brûlée, hard salty cheeses, or the right company.

Mouchão, Herdade do Alen ★★★ Historic family-run estate, introduced ALICANTE BOUSCHET to Portugal in C19. Fine foot-trodden range: large-barrel-aged ***estate red*** (1st bottled 1949, life-changing ★★★★ ***1990***); prestigious ALEN Tonel No. 3–4; v.gd-value perfumed ***Ponte*** (r), old-vine ***Dom Rafael*** (r/w).

Mouraz, Casa de Dão ★★ Vibrant range from bio pioneer: estate label; Planet Mouraz (esp natural Bolinha, *palhete* Nina); gd-value Air. Best: v.gd 80-yr-old field blend Elfa; top-notch 100-yr-old-vines Boot.

Mouro, Quinta do Alen ★★★ Impressive Estremoz estate. Vines barely trained, look wild; v.gd age-worthy flagship red; fruit-forward, ripe Zagalos RES. Unforgettable high-end Gold Label (r). Vinha do Mouro gd value.

Nicolau de Almeida Dou ★★★ Boutique project; descendants of Fernando NA, BARCA VELHA creator. Superb, seductive Monte Xisto; elegant Órbita, Oriente.

Nicolau de Almeida, Mateus Dou ★★→★★★ Star winemakers Mateus, wife Teresa Ameztoy; v.gd bio wines. Trans Douro Express mirrors DOU's subregions: cooler Baixo Corgo, balanced Cima Corgo, rich Dou Superior. Eremitas, 100% Rabigato, three plots. Cellar experiments Curral Teles.

Niepoort Bair, Dou, Dão ★★→★★★★ Run by influential DOU pioneer Dirk N and family. Fine, fresher-than-ever, age-worthy Dou range: 1st-class Batuta; ***Charme***; Coche (w); v.gd Redoma (esp ***Res*** w); single-vyd, structured Robustus; elegant 100% TINTA AMARELA; 130-yr-old-vines ***Turris***. Diálogo/Fabelhaft is gd-value globetrotter. Other regions: BAIR (GARRAFEIRA, Poeirinho, VV), DÃO (top-notch Lomba, gd-value Conciso), PORTALEGRE (Ximena), VIN (ADN). Port range v.gd, often superb: VINTAGE PORT 45' 87' 00' 15' 17' 19'; trad ***Pisca***; organic Bioma VV; great-value Crusted; unique demijohn-aged ***Garrafeira***; ethereal 1983 ***VV***; TAWNY v.gd (bottle-aged COLHEITAS). Book to visit private GAIA Niepoort cellar.

Noval, Quinta do Dou, Port ★★★★ Historic AXA-owned (1993) estate known for Port, table wines. Enjoyable-young v.gd ***Vintage*** released every yr; jewel-in-crown, pricey ***Nacional*** 00' 01' 03' 04' 11' 16' 17' 19' 21' 22' from ungrafted vines, just 200–250 cases/vintage; v.gd unfiltered LBV; superior ***Colheitas***, 20-, ***50-yr-old***. Try DOU: top-notch, expensive, single-plot, v. old field-blend Terroir Series; v.gd age-worthy RES (classic r, oak-aged ***Viosinho-based w***); gd-value Cedro (r/w); elegant, single-variety Tinto Cão, SYRAH, TOURIGA N. Passadouro range gd value.

Offley Port ★★ Historic C18 brand. Fruit-driven VINTAGE PORT, gd-value unfiltered LBV. Cocktail-ready Clink. SOGRAPE owned.

Pacheca, Quinta da Dou, Port ★→★★ Historic estate, pioneer of estate-bottled DOU; gd-value, esp RES. Owner group Terras & Terroir expanding: ★★ Caminhos Cruzados, esp Teixuga (DÃO), Ortigão (BAIR), Ribafreixo, Rocha (ALEN), Valle de Passos (Trás-os-Montes).

Passarella, Casa da Dão ★★→★★★★ Historic, boutique estate; star winemaker Paulo Nunes. Fine, late-release ***Vindima 09' 11'*** (80-yr-old field blend); classy Villa Oliveira range (TOURIGA N); bold, 80-yr-old-vine Pedras Altas; v.gd-value ***Fugitivo*** range (Vinhas Centenárias).

Pato, Filipa Bair ★★★ Star winemaker. Fine, v. old-vine BAGA reds: old, ungrafted-vines ***Nossa Missão***, elegant ***Nossa Calcario***. Fresh, mineral Bical whites: Nossa Calcario, Nossa Tola. Amphora-aged Post-Quercus v.gd.

Pato, Luis Bair ★★→★★★★ Opinionated, nonconformist, modern BAIR pioneer following rebellious family tradition. Father of FILIPA P. Fine range: ***age-worthy, single-vyd Baga*** (Barrio, ***Barrosa***, Pan) and ***Pé Franco*** (ungrafted) wines (bright, sandy-soil Ribeirinho); age-worthy whites (rich, single-vyd Vinha Formal, sharp Parcela Cândido, fine Ribeirinho). VINHAS VELHAS (r/w) v.gd value.

Pellada, Quinta da Dão ★★★★ Modern. ***Estate*** red as gd as it gets. ***Primus*** top white. Carrocel, 100% TOURIGA N from its birth terroir, complexity, elegance. Century-old vyds, varietals, combinations to explore. Great-value ★★ ***Quinta de Saes***.

Pereira d'Oliveira Mad ★★→★★★★ Vast stocks, on-demand FRASQUEIRA, many available at time-machine touristy cellar door. Always go for older wines; ask nicely for C19 vintages MOSCATEL 1875, SERCIAL 1875, Terrantez 1880, or rare BASTARDO 1927. Owns Barros e Sousa.

Pico Wines Azores ★★→★★★ Largest, oldest AZORES co-op makes consistent-quality volcanic range: Frei Gigante, Terras de Lava; v.gd salty, single-variety ARINTO/Terrantez do Pico/VERDELHO range. Top: ***Rola Pipa***, 100-yr-old-vine ***Gruta das Torres***. 10-yr-old Licoroso a treat.

Poças Dou, Port ★★→★★★ Centenarian, family-run firm with gd Port, dynamic table-wine range. Old Tawny stocks: fine 20-, ***30-, 50-yr-old***, COLHEITAS fabulous 90-yr-old+ 1918. VINTAGE PORT, LBV v.gd. Top: sumptuous, oaked Branco da Ribeira (w); dense Símbolo; new field-blend Vinha do Cerro. Also gd-value RES; ***Fora da Série*** range (Vinho da Roga).

Portalegre Alen ★→★★★ Old, now trendy n subregion; high-altitude, cooler-climate, old field-blend vyds. Best: ★★★ CABEÇAS DO REGUENGO, ★★★ RUI REGUINGA, ***Susana Esteban***, ★★ Tapada do Chaves. Trend followers: ESPORÃO, MALHADINHA (Teixinha), NIEPOORT, SOGRAPE (Série Ímpar), SYMINGTON (Fonte Souto).

Quanta Terra Dou ★★★ Underrated estate run by star winemakers Jorge Alves, Celso Pereira (VÉRTICE). Fine range: unique, oak-aged ***Gold Edition***; top-notch Grande Res (r/w); old-vines Inteiro; unique Phenomena PINOT N Rosé; Pouca Terra gd value. Book to visit DOU art centre.

Quinta Portuguese for estate. In ALEN, *herdade* or *monte*.

When did elderberry stop being used in Port? More recently than we think, I'm told.

Quinta Nova de Nossa Senhora do Carmo Dou ★★★→★★★★ Historic family estate, led by Luisa Amorim (cork family). Fine, rich, oaked Mirabilis (r/w); outstanding rich, layered Vinha Centenária range (100-yr-old vines: ***Tinta Roriz*** or TOURIGA N); superior 100-yr-old-vines Aeternus; v.gd-value rosé, ***Grainha*** (r/w). ***Charming hotel***, award-winning wine tourism. DÃO outpost: TABOADELLA. ALEN: ALDEIA DE CIMA.

Rainwater Mad Seductive chilled apéritif. Lighter, drier style of MAD estufa-aged min 5 yrs, usually TINTA NEGRA.

PORTUGAL

Ramos, João Portugal Alen ★★→★★★ Large, family-run, ALEN pioneer firm. Best: Marquês de Borba RES, and ***Vinhas Velhas***. Estremus, single-vyd range. Popular: Loios, Pouca Roupa. Value brands: Marquês de Borba, Vila Santa. Outposts: VIN, DOU (DUORUM), Beira Atlântico (FOZ DE AROUCE).

Ramos Pinto Dou, Port ★★★→★★★★ Historic Port estate, growing DOU range: silky Ervamoira; classy ***Duas Quintas Res*** (r/w); great-value Duas QUINTAS (r/w); popular Bons Ares. Best Port: 1st-class 20-yr-old; v.gd VINTAGE PORT, incl single-quintas Bom Retiro, Ervamoira. Champagne Roederer-owned (*see* France).

Real Companhia Velha Dou, Port ★→★★★ Founded 1756, now run by Pedro Silva Reis and sons. Diverse range: fine Carvalhas (esp v.gd old-vines r/w); international-variety/style Cidrô, incl popular oaked CHARD and seductive, fine ***Marquis*** (TOURIGA N/CAB SAUV); bio, native-variety Síbio; gd-value Aciprestes, Evel; best-in-class ***Grandjó*** late-harvest. Value Port brands: Carvalhas, Delaforce, RCV, Royal Oporto, Silva Reis. GAIA wine bar.

Reguinga, Rui Alen, Tej ★★★ Consultant's own v.gd brand. ALEN, PORTALEGRE: bio, high-altitude, old-vines ***Terrenus*** range, incl centenarian-vine ***Vinha da Serra*** (w). Rhône-inspired Tejo: ***Tributo***, Vinha da Talisca (w).

Reserve / Reserva (Res) Port Higher-quality designation, with rules varying by region. Often implies oak-ageing. Grande Res more demanding and much better. For Port bottled without age indication: often gd-value RUBY, TAWNY.

10% of population of Douro has left in past 15 years. Never an easy life there.

Rocim Alen ★★→★★★ Dynamic, family-run, increasingly bio firm. Also VINHO DE TALHA-revival pioneer. Top: fine Grande Rocim (dense, piney ALICANTE BOUSCHET r; firm, oaky ARINTO w), late-release Crónica #328, 1st-class ***Vinha da Micaela***. Clay-pot range v.gd: luxury-priced amphora-aged Júpiter Code 01; foot-trodden, polished ***Clay Aged*** (r); elegant Amphora (r/w). Also gd old-vine, single-vyd Olho de Mocho (r/w). Other regions: seductive old-field-blend DOU Bela Luz; fine DÃO ***O Estrangeiro*** (r/w), precise LIS Vale da Mata (r/w). Visitor centre in Vidigueira, ALEN.

Romeira, Quinta da Lis ★★ Popular, historic Bucelas estate. Fresh, mineral, ARINTO-based range v.gd value: Morgado Sta Catherina, Prova Régia. SOGRAPE-owned.

Rosa, Quinta de la Dou, Port ★★★ Classic, family-run estate. Value range by winemaker Jorge Moreira: La Rosa, ***Res*** (r/w); Passagem DOU Superior label. Best Port: v.gd LBV, 30-yr-old TAWNY, VINTAGE PORT. Riverside guesthouse, restaurant.

Rozès Dou, Port ★★ Vranken-Pommery (*see* France) PORT brand (gd DOU Superior LBV); gd Terras do Grifo range (fine RES, VINHAS VELHAS, Grande Res).

Ruby Port Major PORT style/category. Bottle-aged, fruitier (vs TAWNY), yrs in wood before bottling: VINTAGE PORT (2), LBV (4–6), RES (6). Also, most simple, young, cheap, often delicious sweet Port.

Sandeman Port ★★→★★★ Renowned house famous for caped-image "The Don", modern labels. VINTAGE PORT back on form; v.gd-value range: ***20-***, 30-, 40-, 50-yr-old TAWNY; unfiltered LBV. SOGRAPE-owned; DOU visitor centre, restaurant.

Sanguinhal, Companhia Agrícola do Lis ★★★ Historic estate incl QUINTAS Cerejeiras (***Grande Res r/w***), Sanguinhal (***Grande Escolha r/w***), S. Francisco. Old experimental vyds with dozens of varieties; trad blends from seaside terroir of DOC Óbidos, precise, focused. Best of old and new: (r) light, elegant, textured; (w) fragrant, delicate, saline. Food-friendly, age-worthy.

Sant'Ana, Quinta de Lis ★★ Idyllic, family-run bio estate known for crisp, saline whites: v.gd ALVARINHO, ARINTO, FERNÃO PIRES, esp pricey Marreco. Age-worthy reds. Rare, native ***Ramisco***.

São João, Caves Bair ★★ Historic firm famous for cellar releases, incl sparkling; BAIR (Frei João, Luiz Costa, Poço do Lobo); DÃO (Porta dos Cavaleiros r/w).

Seabra, Luis Dou, Vin ★★★ Reputed winemaker makes elegant, low-intervention, single-vyd range; DOU (v.gd Ilimitado r/w, Indie, ***Xisto Cru*** r/w); VIN (fine lees-aged ALVARINHO ***Granito Cru***).

Sercial Mad Grape variety for racy, tart, driest style of MAD. Great as apéritif; perfect with smoked fish, caviar, or fresh goat's cheese.

Setúbal, Península de Set ★→★★★ Seaside region s of Lisbon, home of world-class fortified MOSCATEL DE SETÚBAL. Table wines: look for crisp whites, sandy-soil reds, esp CASTELÃO. Best: BACALHOA, Brejinho da Costa, Horácio Simões, JOSÉ MARIA DA FONSECA, ★★ ***Pegos Claros***, ★ Piloto, ★★ Portocarro. Popular: Adega de Pegões, Casa Ermelinda Freitas.

Soalheiro, Quinta de Vin ★★→★★★ Leading ALVARINHO firm; gd-value Classico; mineral ***Granit***; v.gd, subtly barrel-fermented ***Primeiras Vinhas***; oaked RES.

Sogevinus Dou, Port ★→★★★★ Large Spanish-owned Port group, growing table-wine range: gd-value São Luiz range, esp unique Winemaker's Collection; high-end QUINTA DA BOAVISTA. Owns gd Port houses: ★★→★★★ Barros (v.gd-value COLHEITAS from every decade since 30s; v.gd 20-, 30-, 40-yr-old TAWNY); ★★★ Burmester (elegant, gd-value Tawny; 20-, 40-yr-old, amazing ★★★★ ***Colheitas***; delectable 30-, 40-yr-old WHITE PORTS); ★→★★ Cálem (bestseller, entry-level Velhotes; 10-, 40-yr-old Tawny); ★★★→★★★★ KOPKE. Visit: GAIA (three popular cellars); DOU (São Luiz guesthouse).

Sogrape Alen, Dou, Vin ★→★★★★ Largest wine firm in Portugal, global interests. Home of MATEUS ROSÉ. Fine 100-yr+ vines ***Legado***, ***Série Ímpar***, ALEN (gd-value ★★ Herdade do Peso), DÃO (CARVALHAIS), DOU (iconic ***Barca Velha***, ***Casa Ferreirinha***, QUINTA da Leda, others), LIS (v.gd-value QUINTA DA ROMEIRA), VIN (★ Azevedo). Port: FERREIRA, OFFLEY, SANDEMAN. Outposts: Argentina (Finca Flichman), Chile (Los Boldos), NZ (Framingham), Spain (LAN, Santiago Ruiz, Viña Mayor).

Sousa, Alves de Dou, Port ★★★ Family-run table-wine pioneer, large, dynamic range: v.gd, classic ***Quinta da Gaivosa***, unique multi-vintage ***Memórias***, RES Pessoal (r/w); fine, old field blends Abandonado, Vinha de Lordelo; refined Port. Value: Caldas, Oliveirinha, Vale da Raposa.

Sousa, José de Alen ★★→★★★ Historic estate keeping ALEN trad alive with largest (100+) TALHA collection in use: v.gd ***Mayor*** and ***J***. Spicy, ripe ***José de Sousa*** and RES v.gd value. JM DA FONSECA'S ALEN outpost.

Symington Family Estates Dou, Port ★★→★★★★ Historic, family-run B Corp-certified PORT firm (owns top brands COCKBURN'S, DOW'S, GRAHAM'S, Quarles Harris, Smith Woodhouse, WARRE'S). Growing table-wine range. Top: CHRYSEIA, fruit-driven VESUVIO, thrilling high-altitude DOU whites (Ilustres Desconhecidos range, ***Pequeno Dilema***). Altano RES, Pombal, Post Scriptum, VIN ***Contacto*** (alongside ANSELMO MENDES), all gd value. Fabulous historic 1890 GAIA lodge, visitor centre, restaurant. Outposts: high-altitude ALEN/PORTALEGRE Fonte Souto (fine Taifa w); new Vin range; co-owner of VÉRTICE, Hambledon (*see* England).

Taboadella Dão ★★★ Amorim-family DÃO project in Serra da Estrela microclimate. Classy range: top, oaked Grande Villae (r/w); seductive varietal RES range, (***Alfrocheiro***, ***Jaen***). Unoaked entry-level Villae v.gd value. Charming guesthouse.

Talha, Vinho de Alen DOC. 2000-yr-old clay-amphora trad undergoing revival. Vinification: some whole-bunch, 5–6-wk maceration in decades-old amphorae, now hunted treasures. Best: ★★ XXVI Talhas, esp ***Mestre Daniel***, ★★ Gerações da Talha, ★★ Herdade Grande, JOSÉ DE SOUSA, ★★ José Piteira, ROCIM.

Tawny Port ★→★★★★ Port style (alternative to RUBY). Entry-level RES (6 yrs in wood) a wallet-friendly treat. Age-dated, a big step up: 10-, **20-**, 30-, 40-, 50-yr-old; single-yr, cask-aged COLHEITAS up to 100 yrs, incl luscious, expensive ***Very Very Old Tawny*** (80-yr-old+). Top: ANDRESEN, Burmester, DALVA, GRAHAM'S, KOPKE, NIEPOORT, NOVAL, Otima (WARRE'S), POÇAS, RAMOS PINTO, SANDEMAN, TAYLOR'S,

Co-ops for value

Co-ops, if they're well run, are great sources of gd-value wine. These are the ones to look for. **Vin**: Monção, Ponte da Barca, Vercoope; **Dou**: Alijó, Favaios, Freixo de Numão, Santa Marta, Vila Real; **Bei Int**: Covilhã, Pinhel; **Bair**: Cantanhede; **Dão**: Mangualde, Penalva, Silgueiros, Tázem; **Azores**: Pico; **Lis**: Colares, Ventosa; **Tejo**: Cartaxo, Almeirim; **Set**: Pegões; **Alen**: Borba, CARMIM, Redondo, Vidigueira.

VASQUES DE CARVALHO. Crowd-pleaser: wood-aged, oxidative, nutty, sweet; perfect dessert on its own or with crème brûlée. Ready to drink on release, generally doesn't improve with bottle-age. Serve chilled to time-travel to DOU.

Taylor's Port ★★★★ Historic Port brand, FLADGATE's jewel in the crown. Pioneered LBV, dry WHITE PORT. Impressive range of top Port wines. VINTAGE PORTS 63' 66' 70' 77' 94' 97' 00' 03' 07' 11' 16'. In non-declared yrs: single QUINTAS (Terra Feita, ***Vargellas***), new Sentinel's. Rare, splendid ***Vargellas Vinha Velha*** from 70-yr+ vines. Outstanding ***Tawny range*** (some from stocks of reputable Krohn brand), esp 20-, 30-, 40-, 50-yr-old Golden Age, 1863' single-harvest, Scion, Kingsman Edition (average 90 yrs old); new VERY VERY OLD PORT, a luscious, decadent liquid treasure.

Textura Dão ★★→★★★ Family-owned Serra da Estrela estate; v.gd bio range (complex Pura w); v.gd Textura da Estrela; gd-value Encoberta, Pretexto.

Tourais, Quinta de Dou ★★→★★★ Redefining DOU. Close to river, going against conventional wisdom that higher = freshness. Red/white from rare Alvarelhão, BAGA, Jaen, PINOT N, Tinta Francisca, Touriga Brasileira. Innovative blends ***JABA*** (Jaen/ALICANTE BOUSCHET/ARINTO). Brands: Fúria, ***Lilipop***, ***Miura***, Tourónio.

Vadio Bair ★★★ Fine, consistent BAGA-focused boutique project; v.gd, classic ***Estate label***, Grande Vadio. Great ESPUMANTE ***Perpetuum***.

Vale D Maria, Quinta do Dou, Port ★★→★★★ Fine DOU range: v.gd ***estate label***, single-vyd Vinha do Rio, ***Vinha da Francisca*** and new top, rare cellar-release Vinha do Moinho. Oak-aged whites gd, esp Vinha do Martim; Dou Superior range gd value. Try Ports: LBV, RES, VINTAGE PORT, VERY OLD TAWNY. AVELEDA-owned.

Vale Meão, Quinta do Dou ★★★→★★★★ Historic, family-run estate. Fine range: sought-after eponymous top ***red***; v.gd single-vyd varietal range Monte Meão (Vinha dos Novos); gd-value Meandro (r/w); gd VINTAGE PORT.

Vallado, Quinta do Dou ★★★ Régua-based firm. Top: old-vine Coroa, ***Granja***, 100-yr-old-vine Adelaide (r). Great: ***Res*** (r/w), ***Touriga N***, gd-value estate red. Also organic DOU Superior. Port: thrilling, pre-phylloxera 1888 VERY OLD TAWNY; v.gd 10-, 20-, 30-, 40-, 50-yr-old TAWNY. Striking hotel, winery.

Valle Pradinhos Trás M ★★→★★★ Historic family-owned estate just n of DOU; v.gd, consistent quality range (r/w RES, ***Grande Res***).

Van Zellers & Co Dou, Port ★★★ Cristiano VZ's family project. Top: CV – Curriculum Vitae (r/w). Also v.gd VZ (r/w). Port: superb, stylish COLHEITA range 34 35 40 50 76; v.gd 10-, 20-, 30-, 40-, 50-yr-old TAWNY.

Vasques de Carvalho Dou, Port ★★★→★★★★ Boutique firm, est 2012 from inherited family cellars, stock, vyds. Liquid gold: fine, pricey, stylish ***10-, 20-, 30-, 40-, 50-yr-old Tawny*** and WHITE PORT; gd VINTAGE and DOU range. GAIA tasting room.

Verdelho Mad Classic MAD grape. Sweeter than SERCIAL, drier than BUAL. Versatile: gd with hard cheese, unique fusion with Japanese food or trad salt-cod dishes. Popular in Mad table wine.

Vértice Dou ★★★→★★★★ One of Portugal's best sparklers, ages well; v.gd-value Gouveio, ***Millésime***. Pricey, high-altitude PINOT N. Co-owned by SYMINGTON.

Very Very Old Tawny Port ★★★★ Bottled treasures, best ethereal, super-TAWNIES. Wood-aged for decades (min 80 yrs). Top: 1900, 1910 (ANDRESEN), 1918 (POÇAS),

5G (WINE & SOUL), Carvalhas Memories (RCV), Adelaide Tributa (Vallado), Coronation, Ne Oublie (GRAHAM'S), Scion, VV (NIEPOORT), VVOT (TAYLOR'S). Great deal: Roncão.

Vesuvio, Quinta do Dou, Port ★★★★ Magnificent, historic SYMINGTON-owned riverside QUINTA, book to visit. Fruit-driven DOU range: classy old-vine estate red; gd-value 2nd-tier Pombal. VINTAGE PORT still foot-trodden, on par with best, esp 100-yr-old-vines ***Capela***.

Vicentino Alen ★★ Atlantic-coast ALEN pioneer, making gd-value mineral, saline range: ALVARINHO, ARINTO, SAUV BL, PINOT N, SYRAH, entry-level label.

Vinevinu Vin ★ Founded 2024 by Luis Cerdeira (ex-SOALHEIRO) with son Manuel. Just released: ALVARINHO Génese, Alvarinho-based ***Almanua***, low-alc Guri. Watch.

Vinhas Velhas Old vineyards. Sought-after national treasure. Age/meaning varies by region, only regulated in DOU (min 40-yr-old vyds, min four-variety field blend, low yield).

Vinho Verde Vin ★→★★★ Portugal's most exported wines, known for spritzy freshness, increasingly for quality. Borders Galicia/Spain. Top ALVARINHO: ***Anselmo Mendes***, ★★ Barão do Hospital, ***Génese***, ***Luis Seabra***, MÁRCIO LOPES, ***Regueiro***, ★★ ***Santiago***, ***Soalheiro***. Top bio LOUREIRO: AMEAL, ★★ Aphros. Top Avesso: ★★ bio ***A&D***, ★★ Covela. Also try: Almanua, AVELEDA, ★ Azevedo, ★★ Casa de Cello, ★★ Casa de Vilacetinho. Large brands with cheap, off-dry, slightly fizzy wines: Adega de Monção, Adega Ponte da Barca, Casal Garcia, Gazela, Muralhas. White best, but red improved: Fedelho, ★★ QUINTA de Monforte.

Vintage Port Port Prestigious, one of world's greatest classics. Aged patiently in bottle after 2 yrs in wood. Old vintages 27' 45' 63' 66' 70' 77' are ethereal, a sweet treat when young. Made in v. finest yrs (aka "classic" or "declared" yrs), increasingly made back-to-back due to precision viticulture/winemaking. Underrated ***Single-quinta VPs*** made in non-declared yrs: Bomfim, Senhora da Ribeira (DOW'S), Guimaraens, Panascal (FONSECA), Malvedos (GRAHAM'S), Vargellas (TAYLOR'S). Rare, superlative ***special editions***: Capela (VESUVIO), Sērikos (CROFT), Stone Terraces (Graham's), Vinha da Pisca (NIEPOORT), Vargellas Vinha Velha (Taylor's). Throws deposit, always decant. Serve at 15–16°C (59–61°F).

Viúva Gomes Lis ★★★ Historic C19 COLARES estate. Baeta family bringing subregion back. Blend of trad, modernity on phylloxera-resistant sandy soils. Classic ***estate label*** v.gd: Ramisco (r), MALVASIA de Colares (w). Decades-old vintages still in shops. Experimental, low-intervention ***Pirata*** range.

Warre's Port ★★★★ SYMINGTON-owned historic PORT brand. Fresh, long-ageing ***Vintage*** (limited-edition VINHAS VELHAS), v.gd unfiltered LBV, elegant single-QUINTA ***Cavadinha***, racy 20-yr-old TAWNY Otima.

White Port Port Underrated category, often overshadowed by TAWNY. Undergoing revival with high-quality labels: age-dated 10-, 20-, 30-, 40-, or 50-yr-old v.gd (ANDRESEN, KOPKE, Quevedo, S Leonardo, Vieira de Sousa); superb, rare COLHEITAS (***Dalva***, ***Kopke***). Lágrima is cheap, v. sweet. Best cocktail: refreshing Port & Tonic (half/half).

Ancient Greeks passed wine R to L. Good excuse when Port passed the wrong way.

Wine & Soul Dou, Port ★★★★ Prestigious family-run estate. Fine range: complex, iconic (r) ***Pintas***; delicious, elegant, field-blend ***Pintas Character***, top-notch ***Manoella Vinhas Velhas***; Vinha Alecrim; (w) stunning oak-aged ***Guru***; crisp, high-atitidude ***Vinha do Altar***. Entry level (r/w) gd-value. Elegant Port: superlative 100-yrs+ VERY VERY OLD TAWNY 5G.

Winestone Alen, Dou, Lis, Port, Vin Ambitious group, owns MONTE DE RAVASQUEIRA (ALEN), Wiese & Krohn (PORT); QUINTA DE PANCAS (LIS); long-term loan of QUINTA do Côtto (DOU) and Paço do Teixeiró (VIN).

Switzerland

Abbreviations used in the text:

Aar	Aargau
Gris	Grisons
Luc	Lucerne
Neu	Neuchâtel
Schaff	Schaffhausen
Thur	Thurgau
Tic	Ticino
Val	Valais
Vd	Vaud
Zür	Zürich

At the risk of repeating ourselves here, Swiss viticulture is a gem. When it comes to their public appearance, however, Swiss growers are always lagging behind: while single vineyards are classified all over the world today, Switzerland's controlled appellations are almost always only for cantons and very seldom even for villages, let alone single vineyards. Nevertheless, many of the wines we recommend here are only available in quantities of some hundred bottles. You have to be quick to get your hands on one. And it definitely helps to live in Switzerland.

Recent vintages

2025 Mixed bag, hot summer, harvest rain, quality v. promising.
2024 Frost, mildew. What was left has gd quality.
2023 Another rollercoaster: rain at harvest, hail in Tic.
2022 Warm and dry yr, generally gd quantity, quality.
2021 Frost, hail, mildew: tiny crop. Lighter wines, sound quality, v.gd whites.
2020 Early, small, 20–40% less: uneven flowering, drought, v.gd quality.
Earlier fine vintages: 18 15 09 05 90; (Pinot N) 13 10; (Dézaley) 99 97.

Switzerland's leading organic vineyard is Neuchâtel: 60% surface certified.

Adank, Hansruedi Gris ★★★ Patrick A revamped fine family estate at FLÄSCH. Best: PINOT N (Spondis), sparkling Brut Nature.
Aigle Vd ★→★★★ Popular CHASSELAS AOC, best from Plantour hill. Be selective.
Amandiers, Caves des Val ★★★ Passionate Alexandre Delétraz grows vines at

Saillons and Fully: outstanding PETITE ARVINE Les Seyes, multi-layered SYRAH Franc de Pied, planted ungrafted on sandy soil.

AOC Equivalent of France's appellation contrôlée; 62 AOCs countrywide.

Auvernier, Ch d' Neu ★★→★★★ Castle and vyds (60 ha) owned by Grosjean family since 1604, a range of textbook NEU CHARD, CHASSELAS, OEIL-DE-PERDRIX, PINOT N (single-vyd Les Argiles, Les Grand'Vignes). Kairos series of special vinifications.

Bachtobel, Schlossgut Thur ★★★ Family estate (since 1784); refined PINOT N labelled 1–4 (higher number = better quality), new oenologist Aylin Bader (2025).

Bad Osterfingen Schaff ★★★ Since 1472, summer residence, wine estate and spa of abbots of nearby Rheinau Abbey. Today run by Meyer family, trad restaurant, PINOTS BL/N v. fine food matches.

Badoux, Henri Vd ★★ AIGLE Les Murailles (classic lizard label) most popular Swiss brand. Ambitious Lettres de Noblesse series (barrel-aged YVORNE).

Bern Capital and canton, wine villages on Lake Biel and Lake Thun. Top growers: Andrey, Johanniterkeller, Keller am See, Krebs & Steiner, Schlössli, Schott (bio).

Besse, Gérald Val ★★★ Fine family estate, organic. Steep terraces up to 600m (1969ft) bring crisp FENDANT Les Bans, elegant GAMAY Bovernier, rich ***Ermitage Les Serpentines*** (MARSANNE on granite, planted 1945).

Blass, Cantina Tic ★★→★★★ Up-and-coming; low- (but not no-) sulphur MERLOT: foot-trodden, juicy Vittorio; Regina more trad. Peppery CAB FR Pietro.

Bonvin 1858 Val ★★→★★★ Old name of VAL, intriguing local grapes: ***Nobles Cépages*** series (eg. HEIDA, PETITE ARVINE, SYRAH).

Bovard, Louis Vd ★★→★★★★ Keeper of the grail in World-Heritage-Site LAVAUX (La Médinette can age 20 yrs+). Other AOCs, varieties (incl CHENIN BL) also reliable.

Calamin Vd ★★★ GRAND CRU of LAVAUX, 16 ha of deep calcareous soils on a landslide. CHASSELAS tarter than nearby DÉZALEY.

Chablais Vd ★★→★★★ Wine region at upper end of Lake Geneva around AIGLE, YVORNE. Name from Latin *caput lacis*, head of the lake.

Chappaz, Marie-Thérèse Val ★★★→★★★★ Perfectionist bio estate. Best known for nobly sweet Ermitage (MARSANNE), Petite ARVINE; but dry wines equally gd.

Colombe, Dom La Vd ★★→★★★ At FÉCHY; bio. Young Laura Paccot expands her father Raymond's work: CHASSELAS Brez, terracotta-aged field-blend white (Curzilles), SAVAGNIN Amédée.

Constantin, Thierry Val ★★★ Passionate grower, 7 ha of steep slopes, top SYRAH Anastasi (ex-L'Odalisque).

Cortaillod Neu PINOT N stronghold on shores of Lake Neuchâtel, eponymous low-yielding local clone. Best: PORRET.

Côte, La Vd ★→★★★ A breadbasket of CHASSELAS: 2000 ha w of Lausanne on Lake Geneva, v. variable quality. Villages incl FÉCHY, Mont-sur-Rolle, Morges.

Cruchon Vd ★★★ In LA CÔTE, bio. Many SPÉCIALITÉS, ie. Savoyard (*see* France) grape Altesse, PINOT N Raissennaz.

Devinière, Dom de la Gen ★★→★★★ Organic family estate. Age-worthy: CHASSELAS, PINOT N, finesse; CAB SAUV, purity. Free series (no sulphur).

Dézaley Vd ★★★ LAVAUX GRAND CRU on steep slopes of Lake Geneva, 54 ha; planted in C12 by Cistercian monks. Potent CHASSELAS develops with age (7 yrs+). Best: DUBOIS, DUBOUX, ***Fonjallaz***, LEYVRAZ, ***Louis Bovard***, MONACHON, Ville de Lausanne.

Dôle Val ★→★★ VAL's answer to Burgundy's Passetoutgrains: PINOT N plus GAMAY for light, quaffable red.

Donatsch Gris ★★★ Pioneer Thomas D (died in 2024) paved way for son Martin. CHARD, PINOT N Unique collector's items.

Dubois, Frères Vd ★★→★★★ Age-worthy, silky DÉZALEY-Marsens Vase No. 4; fine Epesses Braise d'Enfer.

Duboux, Blaise Vd ★★★ Family estate in LAVAUX. Rich, mineral CALAMIN, DÉZALEY.

Wine regions
Switzerland has six major wine regions: VAL, VD, GENEVA, TIC, Trois Lacs (NEU, Bienne/BER, VULLY/Fribourg) and German Switzerland (Aar, GRIS, SCHAFF, St Gallen, Thur, ZÜR and some smaller wine cantons). The largest wine-growing canton by far is Val at 4564 ha.

Dutruy, Frères Vd ★★→★★★ Fine organic estate in LA CÔTE, LAVAUX, incl DÉZALEY, rare local red Plant Robez. Top old-vines-blend Les Romaines Res GAMAY.

Féchy Vd ★→★★★ Famous though unreliable AOC of LA CÔTE, mainly CHASSELAS.

Fendant Val ★→★★★ Rich VAL CHASSELAS; balsamic scent, low acidity, for fondue.

Fläsch Gris ★★★→★★★★ Village of Bündner Herrschaft, PINOT N from schist, limestone. Try ADANK, Hermann, Marugg families, HÖRLER. Top: ***Gantenbein***.

Flétri / Mi-flétri Late-harvested grapes for sweet/slightly sweet wine.

Fromm, Georg Gris ★★★ Top bio grower in MALANS: age-worthy single-vyd PINOT N.

Gantenbein Gris ★★★★ Top estate at FLÄSCH. Daniel and Martha G (now joined by Andreas Hütwohl) make CHARD, PINOT N of great distinction.

Geneva Gen ★→★★★ 1355 ha w of city Geneva nr French border. Best: Balisiers, Clos des Pins, DE LA DEVINIÈRE, GRAND'COUR, Les Hutins, Novelle.

Germanier, Jean-René Val ★★→★★★ Reliable FENDANT Les Terrasses, SYRAH Cayas, local AMIGNE from schist at Vétroz (dr/sw).

Gialdi Tic ★★→★★★ Prime producer in TIC. Bought-in grapes from small producers in mtn-altitude vyds: top MERLOT Sassi Grossi **13' 14 15 16'** 18' 19 20' (no 21) 22.

Glacier, Vin du (Gletscherwein) Val ★★★ A sort of Alpine "Sherry" from rare Rèze grape of Val d'Anniviers, aged in larch casks. Taste at Grimentz town hall.

Grain Noble ConfidenCiel Val Quality label for authentic sweet wines. Berries must be concentrated on vine.

Grand'Cour, Dom Gen ★★★ Leading estate of GENEVA, 25 varieties on 15 ha, outstanding CABS FR/SAUV blend Grand'Cour **13'** 15' 16' 17 18' 19' 20 22'.

Grand Cru Val, Vd Inconsistent term, used in VAL and VD, sometimes linked to specific varieties or restricted yields, or to designations like clos, ch, abbaye. Only few are classifications of a vyd site (eg. CALAMIN, DÉZALEY).

Grisons (Graubünden) A mtn canton, PINOT N king. Famous Bündner Herrschaft: four villages (FLÄSCH, Jenins, Maienfeld, MALANS): 6000 people, 329 growers.

Guichard, Valentin Zür ★★★ Small dom in obscure Säuliamt (piglet district) in canton of Zür. Valentin G worked in Burgundy; tiny amounts elegant PINOT N.

Hammel, Maison Val, Vd ★→★★★★ Merchant with 15 doms, incl L'Ovaille at YVORNE, and Dom de Crochet (Cuvée Charles Auguste SYRAH/CABS SAUV/FR).

Hauser, Urs Tic ★★→★★★ Career-changer makes balanced MERLOT (**18'** Stella) on slopes of Monte Ceneri.

Hörler, Silas Gris ★★→★★★ Chef-turned-winemaker: rich CHARD Valäris, tight-knit PINOT N Carsilias.

Hubervini ★★→★★★ Family estate (7 ha); MERLOT/CAB FR Montagna Magica. Recent vintages seem to have a little more power (and less elegance) than before.

Kastanienbaum, Weingut Luc ★★→★★★ Was Weinbau Ottiger; PINOT N ***Rosenau***.

Lavaux Vd ★★→★★★★ UNESCO World Heritage Site, e of Lausanne, 800 ha, mostly in steep s-facing terraces. Uniquely rich, mineral CHASSELAS. GRANDS CRUS CALAMIN, DÉZALEY, regional and several village AOCS.

Leyvraz, Pierre-Luc Vd ★★★→★★★★ Perfectionist at LAVAUX, now joined by André Bélard; terroir-led ST-SAPHORIN Les Blassinges, age-worthy DÉZALEY.

Litwan, Tom Aar ★★★ Grower at Schinznach, 5 ha, bio: CHARD (Büel, Wanne), single-vyd PINOT N (Auf der Mauer, Chalofe, Rüeget).

Lüthi Weinbau Zür ★★★ Small, perfectionist grower at Stäfa on Lake Zürich: age-worthy PINOT N, MÜLLER-T (labelled RIES x Madeleine Royale).

Maison Carrée, La Neu ★★★ Family estate, est 1827, 10 ha, bio; v. trad winemaking incl old wooden press, esp delicately scented PINOT N.

Malans Gris ★★→★★★★ Top village in GRIS, outstanding PINOT N: DONATSCH, FROMM, Liesch, Studach, WEGELIN. SPÉCIALITÉ is local Completer (Giani Boner).

Maye, Simon & Fils Val ★★★ Raphaël M's SYRAH Vieilles Vignes ages well 11 12 13 15' 16' 17 18' 19 20 22, excellent SPÉCIALITÉS (eg. Païen) too.

Mercier, Denis Val ★★★→★★★★ Meticulous vyd management. Top: FENDANT, DÔLE, SYRAH (93' graceful, fresh in 2025), rare CORNALIN 12 13' 15' 16 17 18' 19 20' 22.

Monachon, Pierre Vd ★★★ Crisp, mineral, v. reliable DÉZALEY Les Côtes Dessus, ST-SAPHORIN Les Manchettes 14 15' 18' 21' 22.

Mondò, Azienda Tic ★★★ Fine producer at Sementina nr Locarno, with 8 ha on 40 parcels. Arguably TIC's best (and most age-worthy) Bondola (local red), and substantial Ronco dei Ciliegi (MERLOT/CAB SAUV).

Mont d'Or, Dom du Val ★★→★★★★ Emblematic VAL estate, schist soils, SCHENK-owned. Nobly-sweet JOHANNISBERG Saint-Martin, v.gd dry wines (RIES Amphytrion).

Montimbert, Dom Vd ★★→★★★ In LAVAUX, precise PINOT GR, refined PINOT N.

Montmollin, Dom de Neu ★★→★★★ Old name in NEU, organic: PINOT N (Vieille Vigne Auvernier La Pierre).

Morcote, Castello di Tic ★★★ Castle ruin and eponymous 14-ha winery; 3rd-generation Gaby Gianini made bio, top Riserva 17 18' 19' 20' 21'.

Neuchâtel ★→★★★ 600 ha around city and lake on calcareous soil. Slightly sparkling CHASSELAS, exquisite PINOT N from local CORTAILLOD clone. Try CH D'AUVERNIER, Dom de Chambleau, Kuntzer, LA MAISON CARRÉE, PORRET, TATASCIORE.

Oeil de perdrix "Partridge's eye": PINOT N rosé, originally from NEU, now elsewhere.

Pircher Zür ★★★→★★★★ Rhine wine, steep slopes: PINOT N Sonnenhalde; RIES due.

Porret Neu ★★→★★★★ Leading family at CORTAILLOD; Burgundian approach to CHARD, PINOT N (Cuvée Elisa).

Provins Val ★→★★★ Switzerland's largest producer, but no longer as large as it used to be: 1000 members, 700 ha, 34 varieties, 100 different wines; owned by Fenaco umbrella co-op. Sound entry-level, gd oak-aged Maître de Chais range. Les Titans series aged at altitude: v. slow development.

Riehen, Weingut Bas ★★→★★★★ Boutique winery; Hanspeter Ziereisen (*see* Germany) and merchants with Jacqueline and Urs Ullrich: CHARD, PINOT N.

Rouvinez Vins Val ★→★★★ VAL giant at Sierre: La Trémaille (w), Le Tourmentin (r). Owns BONVIN, Caves Orsat, Imesch Vins; and makes beer (L'Echappé).

Ruch, Markus Schaff ★★★ Top ultra-rare PINOT N from Hallau (Chölle old vines, Haalde, Buck), Gächlingen (Schlemmweg); 3.5 ha. Amphora MÜLLER-T, Cidre.

Rutishauser, Roman St-G ★★→★★★ Fine family estate ("Am Steinig Tisch") at Thal: aromatic whites (SAUV BL, KERNER), poilshed fruit; dense PINOT N.

St Jodern Kellerei Val ★★→★★★ VISPERTERMINEN co-op: ungrafted old-vines ***Heida Veritas*** 09' 10 15 16 17 18' 21' 22.

St-Saphorin Vd ★→★★★ Neighbour AOC of DÉZALEY, lighter but equally delicate. Try LEYVRAZ, MONACHON.

San Giorgio, Tenuta Tic ★★★ 7 ha, fine Bx blend Arco Tondo, MERLOT Crescendo.

Schaffhausen ★→★★★ A flood of cheap supermarket wines, but also top growers: BAD OSTERFINGEN, Baumann, RUCH, Stamm.

Switzerland's glaciers are retreating: volume of ice has melted 38% since 2000.

Schenk SA Vd ★→★★★ Wine giant with worldwide activities, based in Rolle, founded 1893. Sound wines (esp VD, VAL); substantial exports.

Schwarzenbach, Hermann Zür ★★★ Family estate on Lake Zürich. Age-worthy, full of tension: GEWURZ 76, PINOT N (Klevner) 64 in top form in 2025. Local Räuschling a 3rd of vyd, single-vyd Seehalden 15' 17' 18' 19' 20 21' 22 23', lots of SPÉCIALITÉS.

SWITZERLAND

Sélection Excelsus Val ★★→★★★ Organic family estate, led by Jean-Claude and Renaud Favre. Juniper, black-pepper red 1955 (PINOT N/CORNALIN/SYRAH).

Spécialités / Spezialitäten Minor (quantity) grapes make some of best Swiss wines, eg. GEWURZ, PINOT GR, Räuschling, Completer in German Switzerland; Bondola in TIC; Cornalin, Humagne (Bl/N) or JOHANNISBERG, MARSANNE, SYRAH in VAL.

Sprecher von Bernegg Gris ★★★ Historic estate, only 3 ha; bio. Best: PINOT N Lindenwingert, Vom Pfaffen/Calander. Refined local white Completer too.

Stucky-Hügin Tic ★★★→★★★★ MERLOT-based reds and white Completer/SAUV BL Temenos from steep slopes of Sopraceneri area.

Tatasciore, Jacques Neu ★★★ Powerful (and rare) NEU PINOT N.

Ticino ★→★★★★ Italian-speaking. Taut MERLOT (leading grape since 1948): Agriloro, CASTELLO DI MORCOTE, Chiericati, Delea, GIALDI, Hauser, HUBER, Kopp von der Crone Visini, Moncuchetto, MONDÒ, Monti Pelossi, San Giorgio, STUCKY-HÜGIN, Tamborini, Theilervini, Trapletti, Valsangiacomo, VINATTIERI, ZÜNDEL.

Trécord, Dom de Vd Glorious Rés de la Famille: lemon cream spiked with herbs.

Tscharner, von ★★★ Family estate at Reichenau Castle; tannin-laden PINOT N Gian-Battista, local Completer.

Valais (Wallis) Val Largest wine canton, in dry, sunny upper Rhône V. Best MARSANNE, SYRAH rival French legends. Many exquisite local varieties.

Vaud (Waadt) Vd On shores of Lake Geneva, where CHASSELAS gives most complex terroir expression. Many fine family estates with conservative approach.

Vinattieri Tic ★★→★★★ Large but reliable producer (100 ha) at Ligornetto nr Italian border. Most reds strongly oak-influenced. Flagship Vinattieri (100% MERLOT) has richness, minerality and price of a gd Pomerol (*see* France).

Visperterminen Val ★→★★★ Upper VAL vyds, esp for HEIDA. One of highest vyds in Europe (Riben at 1000m/3281ft+): Chanton, ST JODERN KELLEREI.

Vully, Mont Fri, Vd ★→★★★ AOC on shores of Lake Murten. Insider tip. Fribourg (116 ha), VD (46 ha): Ch de Praz, Chervet, Cru de l'Hôpital, Javet & Javet, Petit Ch.

Wegelin Gris ★★★ Burgundian Frassa CHARD, Bothmarhalde, Weisstorkel PINOT N.

Yvorne Vd ★★→★★★ CHABLAIS village with vyds on detritus of 1584 avalanche: BADOUX, Ch Maison Blanche, Commune d'Yvorne, Dom de l'Ovaille.

Zündel, Christian Tic ★★★→★★★★ Small, bio, elegant: MERLOT/CAB SAUV Orizzonte; single-vyd Merlots Al Ronco, Sass, Villa. Somewhat "wilder" vinifications recently, occasionally funky, animalistic undertones, but still gd fruit.

Zürich Largest wine-growing canton in German Switzerland, 605 ha. Growers incl Bechtel, Besson-Strasser, E Meier, Gehring, Herter, Jet, LÜTHI, PIRCHER, SCHWARZENBACH, Staatskellerei, Zahner.

Zürichsee Dynamic AOC uniting vyds of ZÜR and Schwyz on shores of Lake Zürich.

Zur Linde, Weingut Aar ★★★ Photographer Michel Jaussi renovated listed building in Linn; dense PINOT N.

Warm enough for Syrah

Climate change is particularly noticeable in Switzerland; average annual temperature has risen by 2.9°C (5.2°F) since the start of the industrial age. CHASSELAS appears to be relatively resistant: it doesn't produce extreme sugar levels anyway, and its wines are unlikely to lose their low-alc appeal. PINOT N is more sensitive: in sunny VAL, it's becoming increasingly difficult to avoid cooked flavours. But SYRAH is a rising star here (CAVES DES AMANDIERS Franc de Pied; MAYE Vieilles Vignes). Will these be the Hermitages (*see* France) of the future? Cooler regions of German-speaking Switzerland and of Three Lakes are benefiting from climate change: Pinots are still fresh, berry-scented, but excessive acidity is a thing of the past, and tannins are now ripe, dense.

Austria

Abbreviations used in the text:

Burgen	Burgenland
Carn	Carnuntum
Kamp	Kamptal
Krems	Kremstal
Nied	Niederösterreich
Stei	Steiermark
S Stei	Südsteiermark
Therm	Thermenregion
Trais	Traisental
V Stei	Vulkanland Steiermark
Wach	Wachau
Wag	Wagram
Wein	Weinviertel
W Stei	Weststeiermark

The high quality of Austria's whites is uncontested: mineral, lively and fresh. Reds, more precisely Blaufränkisch, are as good and do not copy international role models, being elegant, profound wines with attractive flow and without overwhelming tannin or alcohol. How is Austrian wine organized? DAC is solidly established now and indicates a complete turnaround in outlook: soils and origin are crucial factors and replace the former "Germanic" system of varieties, alcohol degree and the rule of fruit first and above all. The young generation now taking over wineries focuses on sense of place. The youngsters are ever more committed to quality and to exploring wine horizons. The proportion of organic and biodynamic wine-growing is now 25% of all vineyards; and while Grüner Veltliner still works on all levels, natural and orange wines have overcome their growing pains. Outstanding Pinot Blanc and Chardonnay come from Styria and the Leithaberg DAC. Sparkling, made mainly of Pinot grapes with Austrian-variety participation, is common, most often traditional-method and high quality. It's time for a new wine law. It comes into force in August 2027, and it accepts all the evolution of the past decades. The differences for wine fans are mainly in the designation on the labels.

Recent vintages

2025 Rain when needed, no excess heat, cool summer nights; gd balance; v.gd.
2024 Frost, hail, drought in e, rain, ripe grapes, moderate acidity. Stei v.gd.
2023 Variable: Stei wet, Burgen dry, Nied ideal, all perfect autumn, v.gd quality.
2022 Hot, dry summer, changeable spring/autumn: v. ripe wines, less acidity.
2021 Changeable summer, ideal autumn: balanced, ripe wines, gd acidity.
2020 Some disease pressure, some hail. Balanced and classic.

Achs, Paul Burgen ★★★★ 19' 20 21 22 23' 24 Long experience with dense, spicy BLAUFRÄNKISCH, Paul A's favourite vine. Son Johannes now joined. Excellent PINOT N. Polished CHARD.

Altenburger, Markus Burgen ★★★ 19 20 21' 22' 23' 24 BLAUFRÄNKISCH: mineral Ried Gritschenberg, balanced Spätfüllung. Methode O (sp): fermenting must starts 2nd fermentation. Lean, juicy CHARD Vom Kalk.

Emperor Joseph II (1741–90) decree legalized Heurigen. Thanks, J; great idea.

Alzinger Wach ★★★★ 19' 20 21' 22' 23' 24 Son Leo and wife Katharina continue what father Leo est: precision, finesse. Long-lived RIES, GRÜNER V. Iconic RIED Steinertal equalled in 24 by Ried Loibenberg.

Ambrositsch, Jutta Vienna ★★★ 19' 20 21' 22 23 24 Delicious field blends. BLAUFRÄNKISCH Hetfleisch with WACHTER-WIESLER, pét-nat WELSCHRIESLING with STRAKA. Great HEURIGE in VIENNA: Buschenschank in Residence open c.10 wkds/yr.

Angerhof-Tschida Burgen ★★★★ 20' 21' 22' 23' 24 Hans Tschida in ILLMITZ. Excellent, salty TBA, BA (*see* Germany) from WELSCHRIESLING and aromatic SCHEUREBE, MUSKAT OTTONEL.

Beck, Judith Burgen ★★★ 19 20 21' 22' 23' 24 25 Complex, bio BLAUFRÄNKISCH, PINOT N, ZWEIGELT. Beck Ink Zweigelt/ST-LAURENT, Hunny Bunny Blaufränkisch lighter, Cherry Bomb Zweigelt, v.gd natural Bambule!, field-blend Koreaa.

Braunstein, Birgit Burgen ★★★★ 20' 21' 22 23' 24' 25 Fine-boned CHARD Felsenstein, skin-fermented PINOT BL Brigid, dark-berried BLAUFRÄNKISCH RIED Thenau.

Bründlmayer, Willi Kamp ★★★★ 19 20 21' 22' 23' 24' Organic: GRÜNER V Lamm, RIES, esp Alte Reben, Heiligenstein. Grüner V Käferberg 24. Five styles of SEKT.

Burgenland Region bordering Hungary. Warmer than NIED; (r) BLAUFRÄNKISCH, ZWEIGELT prevalent, (w) CHARD, GRÜNER V, PINOT BL, WELSCHRIESLING. Shallow Neusiedlersee. In SEEWINKEL, ideal botrytis conditions disappearing.

Carnuntum Nied Region e of VIENNA; accomplished fresh reds, esp ZWEIGELT and cuvées. Look for BLAUFRÄNKISCH from Spitzerberg. Try Artner, Auer, Glatzer, Kellerkünstler, Netzl, Taferner, Weiberwirtschaft Wiederstein.

Christ, Rainer Vienna ★★★ 20 21' 22 23 24' 25 Top name from Bisamberg. Chewy PINOT BL Der Vollmondwein. Three different Wiener GEMISCHTER SATZ: Wiesthalen from 85-yr-old vines, skin-fermented Kraut & Rüben. Dried herbs, elegant salinity in PINOT N Kastanienwald (no intervention). Charming HEURIGE.

DAC (Districtus Austriae Controllatus) Provenance- and quality-based appellation system for regional typicity; 18 in all. 13 have hierarchy of Regional, Ort (village), RIED (cru) – CARN, KAMP, KREMS, Leithaberg, Rosalia, S STEI, Therm, Trais, V STEI, WACH, WAG, WIENER GEMISCHTER SATZ, W STEI. Eisenberg has no village category. RUSTER AUSBRUCH is exclusively sweet. Mittelburgenland, Neusiedlersee, WEIN all just Res and Regional.

Diwald, Martin Krems ★★★ 21' 22' 23' 24 25 Organic (1976), upward-moving since Martin took over; refined GRÜNER V, rare Frühroter Veltliner.

Domäne Wachau Wach ★★★★ 21' 22' 23' 24' 25 World-class co-op; 170 ha (of 400) worked organically. Generation change pushed quality to max. GRÜNER V, RIES Achleiten, Kellerberg, Singerriedel a must. All FEDERSPIEL excellent value.

Ebner-Ebenauer Wein ★★★★ 20 21' 22', 23' 24' 25 Driving force in WEIN, esp world-class fizz. Elegance, finesse, depth. Single-vyd GRÜNER V, old-vine PINOT N.

Edlmoser Vienna ★★★★ 20 21' 22 23' 24' 25 Refined, mineral white: RIES, WIENER GEMISCHTER SATZ. Powerful red. Try PINOT BL RIED Himmel at superb HEURIGE.

Engel V Stei ★★★ 20 21 22' 23' 24' 25 Mixed farming turned into a winery. Volcanic soils; SAUV BL v.gd, but PINOT BL Tieschen, PINOT GR Klöch, RIES RIED Klöchberg even better. Firm structure, silky, mineral, slightly smoky.

Federspiel Wach VINEA WACHAU middle category of ripeness, min 11.5%, max 12.5% abv. Understated, food-friendly, age-worthy as SMARAGD; gd value.

Feiler-Artinger Burgen ★★★★ 20' 21' 22 23' 24 25 Intuitive bio maker, complex (w), fine-boned (r), stellar RUSTER AUSBRUCH in historic Baroque house in RUST.

Fischer Weine V Stei ★★★ 21' 22 23' 24' 25 Siblings Claudia, Bernhard, Klaus. Pure wines from mainly volcanic soils. Fine-boned MORILLON RIED Schemming, St Anna (Ortswein). Vibrant, tense RIES Stradenberg.

Frischengruber, Weingärtnerei Wach ★★★ 20 21 22' 23' 24' 25 Hero of s bank of Danube with RIES and GRÜNER V Kreuzberg in refined, cool style.

Fritsch, Weinlaubenhof Wag ★★★★ 20 21 22' 23' 24 25 Fine-tuned in all colours; bio. Sublime RIES Mordthal, juicy ROTER VELTLINER, elegant GRÜNER V both Steinberg and Schlossberg, PINOT N Ruppertsthal (Ortswein).

Fritz, Josef Wag ★★★ 21' 22' 23' 24 25 Leading producer of delicate ROTER VELTLINER, sophisticated spiciness, longevity. Try Rosé and Blanc de Noir (sp).

Fuchs-Steinklammer Vienna ★★★ 21 22 23' 24 25 Vibrant field blends in trad and natural styles. Crisp, fine tangy WIENER GEMISCHTER SATZ Jesuit from v. old vines (r/w); extra-dry Natural Gemischter Satz (rosé); rare (r) Roter Gemischter Satz.

Georgium ★★ 15 19 21 Bio winery in Carinthia, Austria's s-most province. Focus on Pinot varietals (still/sp). Beautifully balanced PINOT N 19. Idyllic hotel.

Gesellmann Burgen ★★★★ 20' 21' 22 23 24 25 Elegance, power in BLAUFRÄNKISCH Hochberg. Fine PINOT N Siglos. Unusual, creamy, fresh Sol CHARD/SAUV BL.

Geyerhof Krems ★★★★ 20 21' 22' 23' 24' 25 Prototype GRÜNER V Steinleithn, RIES. Bio credentials (1988). Experimental Hofstudien, PIWI or different techniques.

Gindl, Michael Wein ★★★ 20' 21' 22' 23 24 25 Barrels from own forest, horses in vyds; bio. Delicate Flora: RIES/SCHEUREBE/YELLOW MUSCAT; creamy, exotic GRÜNER V Buteo; dark-berried, super-dry pét-nat Bubbles (r) Roesler/PINOT N.

Grabenwerkstatt Wach ★★★★ 20' 21' 22' 23' 24' 25 In cool SPITZER GRABEN; bio, low intervention. Elegant RIES Brandstatt, Kalkofen, Trenning; Ries Grosses Werk from selected v. old vines.

Graf Hardegg Wein ★★★ 20 21 22' 23' 24 25 Back to former glory, trad with twist. Notable (sp) VIOGNIER, full Grosse Res (CHARD/PINOT N). RIED Steinbügel.

Grassl, Philipp Carn ★★★★ 20 21' 22 23' 24 25 Regional leader. Remarkable CHARD Höflein, Alte Reben WELSCHRIESLING. Impressive ZWEIGELT Schüttenberg.

Groiss, Ingrid Wein ★★★ 21' 22 23' 24 25 Revives old vyds, specializes in GEMISCHTER SATZ, peppery GRÜNER V. Lovely RIES RES Auf der Henne.

Gross S Stei ★★★★ 20 21' 22 23 24' 25 Father Alois renowned for age-worthy SAUV BL, rich PINOT BL. Sons Johannes, Michael refined style. Michael left 2018 to run Vino Gross (*see* Slovenia). Several famous RIED: Nussberg, Sulz, Perz.

Gsellmann, Andreas Burgen ★★★ 20 21' 22' 23' 24 25 Master of TRAMINER. Blends of unusual varieties; bio. Pét-nat rosé OMG ("Oh My Gsellmann"), salty Zu Tisch (r/w), PINOT BL Másik (amphora), BLAUFRÄNKISCH Gabarinza.

Gut Oggau Burgen ★★★★ 20' 21 22' 23' 24 25 Mouthwatering wines; bio. Mostly blends with a sense of Pannonian place. Strong on PIWIS.

Hareter, Thomas & Claudia Burgen ★★★ 20 21' 22' 23' 24' 25 All bio. Classics express

Outsider wines

The trad Austrian "Weinland" (BURGEN, NIED, VIENNA) and "Steirerland" (STYRIA) are not the whole story. Wine is grown in the other five provinces too, under the denomination "Bergland". Carinthia (125 ha) is known for lakes and winter tourism, Oberösterreich or Upper Austria (91 ha) is between Nied and Salzburg, but Vorarlberg, close to Bodensee in far west (10 ha) has serious ambitions.

variety: PINOT BL, WELSCHRIESLING, BLAUFRÄNKISCH, PINOT N. Lovely Creatures represent best of site. Well-balanced blends. Monovarietal grape juices.

Harkamp S Stei ★★★★ 20' 21' 22' 23' 24' 25 Fascinating, delicate fizz (best: Solera, Zero) and pét-nats. Among top three in Austria, best in STEI.

Heinrich, Gernot & Heike Burgen ★★★★ 20 21' 22 23' 24 25 Made name with BLAUFRÄNKISCH and cuvées; now focus on natural, any colour. Freyheit, Out of the Dark, classic CHARD Leithaberg. Top salty, flinty Yellow TRAMINER Sa Va 23.

You want good value? And a sense of place? Investigate Ortsweine, village wines.

Herrenhof Lamprecht V Stei ★★★ 20 21' 22 23' 24' 25 Complex, mineral field blends. Best: Altsteirischer Mischsatz Schrammelberg from 95-yr-old vines. Adorable FURMINT Vom Sandstein. Try any from Buchertberg.

Heuriger New wine. **Heurige:** inn; growers serve own wines, local food – integral to Austrian culture. Also called *Buschenschank* outside VIENNA.

Hirsch Kamp ★★★★ 20 21' 22' 23' 24' 25 Top RIES of finesse, minerality: pristine Heiligenstein-Rotfels. Complex GRÜNER V (Heiligenstein, Lamm).

Hirtzberger, Franz Wach ★★★★ 20 21' 22 23' 24 25 Elegance replaced opulence. Single-vyd RIES (intense Steinporz 24), GRÜNER V (Honivogl, Singerriedel).

Högl Wach ★★★★ 20' 21' 22 23' 24' 25 Small winery in SPITZER GRABEN, introverted father-and-son team: marvellous, elegant RIES (Brandstatt, Bruck); bold GRÜNER V (RIED Schön, with 57 terraces). Impressive steep terraces behind winery.

Huber, Markus Trais ★★★★ 20' 21' 22 23' 24' 25 Stellar interpretation of TRAIS limestone. Precision, fruit, vibrant minerality: GRÜNER V, RIES RIED Berg 24.

Hugl, Christina Kamp ★★★ 20 21' 22 23' 24' 25 Terroir-driven SEKT and pét-nat; WEIN, KAMP, WACHAU vyds. Three GRÜNER V (sp), from different terroirs.

Jaunegg, Daniel S Stei ★★★ 20 21' 22 23' 24' 25 Intensely mineral PINOT GR Knily, zesty CHARD Muri. Super-complex Yellow MUSCAT Jardin d'Herbes.

Jurtschitsch Kamp ★★★★ 20' 21' 22' 23 24 25 KAMP at its best. RIES: fine-boned, complex Heiligenstein-Rotfels, salty Heiligenstein-Steinwand. GRÜNER V: RIED Käferberg 24 catching up with more famous Lamm. Still experimenting, try blends Mon Blanc, Mon Rouge, Glimmerstein (Grüner V/Ries).

Kamptal Nied DAC; RIES, GRÜNER V; now also CHARD, PINOT BL, PINOT GR. Rounder style, lower hills, minerality, precision (gd sp). Top vyds: Heiligenstein, Käferberg, Lamm, Loiserberg, Seeberg. Try Allram, Aichinger, Arndorfer, Hiedler, Rabl, Steininger (for sp).

Kirchknopf Burgen ★★ 22' 23' 24 25 Michael K works skilfully with Leithaberg terroirs. Focus on BLAUFRÄNKISCH (spicy dark-fruit-juicy Föllikberg) and (w) Pinots. Also intense CHARD Katterstein (schiste), Kalk & Schiefer 23.

KMW Klosterneuburger (viticultural research station) Mostwaage (must weight) – Austrian unit of sugar content of juice in grams sugar/1000g must. 1° KMW = 4.86° Oechsle (*see* Germany). 20° Brix = 83° Oechsle.

Knoll, Emmerich Wach ★★★★ 19' 20' 21' 22 23' 24' Long-lived, esp Vinothekfüllung bottlings. Crystalline pure RIES, GRÜNER V RIED Schütt.

Kögl, Tamara S Stei ★★★ 20 21' 22' 23 24' 25 Gorgeous, mineral wines; great hospitality (idyllic *Buschenschank*), accommodation. Iconic WELSCHRIESLING Alte Reben; bio; all pét-nats, precise CHARD, rich PINOT GR.

Kolfok Burgen ★★★ 20 21' 22' 23' 24' 25 Elegant, mineral. GRÜNER V Vulkan Alte Reben, WELSCHRIESLING Nolens Volens. Adorable herbal FURMINT 23.

Kollwentz Römerhof Burgen ★★★★ 20' 21' 22' 23' 24' 25 Quality fanatic. Iconic power-blend Steinzeiler (r). Complex, mineral CHARD quartet Neusatz, Katterstein, Tatschler, Gloria from different terroirs. Try side by side.

Kopfensteiner Burgen ★★★ 20 21' 22 23' 24' Top Eisenberg name, wines sold with age. Graceful BLAUFRÄNKISCH Eisenberg DAC, RIED Saybritz.

Kracher Burgen ★★★★ 19 20' 21' 22' 23 24 25 Brilliant, complex, botrytized. Library releases of (sw) 10/15/20/25 yrs later. All-encompassing culinary masterpiece incl accommodation. Also project with sommelier Aldo Sohm for dry wines, eg. CHARD St Georg 22 or GRÜNER V Alte Reben 24.

Kremstal DAC. Top for authentic GRÜNER V, RIES. Try Buchegger, Nigl, Philipp Bründlmayer, Thiery-Weber, Vorspannhof Mayer, Zöller.

Lackner Tinnacher S Stei ★★★★ 20 21' 22' 23' 24' 25 Precise, mineral. Old vines; v. low intervention. PINOT BL, RIED Eckberg; SAUV BL, Welles. Ried Steinbach key vyd.

Lesehof Stagård Krems ★★★★ 20 21' 22' 23' 24' 25 Bold, electric RIES from single vyd to experimental Steinzeug; bio. Try Ries Steiner Hund, GRÜNER V Stein (village wine), ravishing entry-level Urban.R and Ries Handwerk.

Lichtenberger González Burgen ★★★ 20 21' 22' 23' 24' 25 Delicious wines from Leithaberg. Some wines renamed for legal reasons. Refined Edel Brunn (formerly Edelgraben), round, balanced GRÜNER V Mira Brunn, Sauspitz.

Löffler Winklhofer Burgen ★★★ 21 22' 23' 24 25 From Niederbayern; stayed because of love for wife and wine. Well-balanced, profound, mineral BLAUFRÄNKISCH: Csaterberg, RIEDS Hannersberg, Szapary.

Loimer, Fred Kamp ★★★★ 20 21' 22' 23' 24' 25 Famed for GRÜNER V, RIES, esp single-vyds Seeberg, Steinmassl; bio; 2nd operation in Gumpoldskirchen, THERM. Experimental Weine mit Achtung, all balanced, defined: Gluegglich Weiss (w). ***Lovely sparkling*** NV, Vintage, Grosse RES Gumpoldskirchen or Langenlois (sp).

Lorenz, Michi S Stei ★★★ 20' 21' 22' 23' 24' 25 Ambassador of SAUSAL's schist. Great aromatic varietals, never loud, but precise, structured: smoky SAUV BL Schist Happens, noble MUSKATELLER Aura M and more.

Macherndl, Erich Wach ★★★ 20' 21' 22' 23 24 25 Organic. Classic, plus skin-fermented, min-sulphur, unfiltered Pulp Fiction.

Malat Krems ★★★★ 20 21' 22' 23' 24' 25 Clean-cut, concentrated still GRÜNER V, RIES, three top sparklers. Pioneer for Winzersekt, today master of mousseux.

Mantlerhof Krems ★★★★ 20 21 22' 23' 24 25 Long-lasting, from loess soils; bio pioneer. Long expertise with ROTER VELTLINER: Reisenthal, Ungut (still/sp). Rare top-class SYLVANER. Spicy RIES Zehetnerin from gravel, sand, loess.

Markowitsch, Gerhard & Johanna Carn ★★★★ 20 21' 22 23' 24' 25 Father and daughter. Powerful but not overpowering Rosenberg (ZWEIGELT/MERLOT/BLAUFRÄNKISCH); convincing, dark-cherried Zweigelt Kirchweingarten. Fresh pét-nats, skin-contact by Johanna solo, labelled JoMa.

Moric Burgen ★★★★ 19' 20 21' 22' 23' 24 25 Focus on diversity of BURGEN terroirs transformed into deservedly famed BLAUFRÄNKISCH. Three top RIEDS: Kircherg, Maissner, Schwemmer. Mentors young Pannonian growers (Austria, Hungary).

Muhr, Dorli Carn ★★★★ 19' 20' 21' 22' 23' 24' 25 Silky, fine, from limestone slopes of Spitzerberg, CARN. Also excellent: Syrah 22. New centre for wine and music.

Muster, Sepp S Stei ★★★ 20 21' 22 23' 24 25 Complex, long-lasting; bio. Salty Graf SAUV BL (old vines), skin-fermented Sauv Bl Gräfin, elegant Sgaminegg (old vines, Sauv Bl/CHARD), Rosé vom Opok blend; Sauv Bl Coprivus by son Elias.

Neumayer Trais ★★★★ 20 21' 22' 23 24 25 Pioneer in Trais. Precise, crystalline GRÜNER V (Zwirch), RIES (Rothenbart). Renowned for Wein vom Stein.

Document, 470 CE, refers to vyds in Wachau. Doesn't say what the vines were, alas.

Neumeister V Stei ★★★★ 20 21' 22' 23' 24' 25 Total art in wine: world-class SAUV BL, Pinots. Sauv Bl ALTE REBEN, MORILLON Moarfeitl, PINOT BL Klausen. Notable PINOT N. Excellent restaurant, hotel.

Niederösterreich (Lower Austria) Region incl over 60% of Austria's vyds. Three climate zones: cooler Danube area in w (KAMP, KREM, TRAIS, WACH, WAG), WEIN (ne) and CARN, THERM (e, s), dry and warm (Pannonian influence).

Climate change in Austria

The gd news: reds, esp BLAUFRÄNKISCH, are riper, and chaptalization is almost obsolete. Less gd news: weather excesses more common now. Long spells of hot days followed by tropical nights. Icewine is rare now: it needs -7°C (19°F) – seldom happens. The SEEWINKEL is in danger of drying out. There are wks or mths without rain, hail in August when berries start ripening, late frosts in early budding yrs, or rain in huge quantities. Luckily there are yrs like 2025, which was beautifully normal but is the exception now, not the rule. Yet alc levels in general tend to go down, even in hot yrs: growers learn to cope with extremes.

Nikolaihof Wach ★★★★ 19' 20 21' 22' 23 24 25 Today run by son Nikolaus Saahs; bio pioneer. Refined, pure, textured GRÜNER V, RIES; look for late-release Vinothek. Try any grape, any vintage. Hotel, restaurant.

Nittnaus, Anita & Hans Burgen ★★★★ 20' 21' 22' 23' 24' 25 Famous Comondor (r) blend; bio pioneers. Precise single-vyd CHARD Bergschmallister, Freudshofer; BLAUFRÄNKISCH Jungenberg, Lange Ohn. New FURMINT Tannenberg. Next generation doing own alternative thing in family winery: Manila.

Ott, Bernhard Wag ★★★★ 20 21' 22' 23' 24' 25 Also vyds in KAMP. Focus on mineral, salty, savoury, long-lived GRÜNER V: Kirchthal, RIED Stein, Rosenberg. Also RIES Kirchthal. Son Moritz makes BLAUFRÄNKISCH in Kamp.

PAX Wach ★★★ 22 23' 24' 25 Light-footed profound GRÜNER V from RIEDS Bachsatz, Hochrain, Kollmitz, Pichl Point. Elegant, complex RIES Biern, Höll.

Pichler, FX Wach ★★★★ 20 21' 22' 23' 24' 25 Legendary estate run by Lucas and Johanna P. Long-lived, fine-boned, intense GRÜNER V, RIES; top WACH sites. Left VINEA WACHAU but adopted Wach DAC.

Pichler, Rudi Wach ★★★★ 20 21' 22' 23' 24' 25 Magnificent RIES from crus Hochrain, Kirchweg; GRÜNER V from Achleiten, Hochrain.

Pichler-Krutzler Wach ★★★★ 20 21' 22' 23' 24' Thrilling RIES Kellerberg, Loibenberg. Outstanding GRÜNER V: der Wand, Pfaffenberg Alte Reben. Organic.

Pittnauer, Gerhard & Brigitte Burgen ★★★★ 20' 21' 22' 23' 24 25 Gracefully ageing BLAUFRÄNKISCH, PINOT N, ST-LAURENT. Serious skin ferments, fresh pét-nats. Perfect Day, Red Pitt, Rosé Dogma... Expect the unexpected.

Prager Wach ★★★★ 20 21' 22' 23' 24' 25 Toni Bodenstein, philosopher-winemaker; son Martin. Family passion RIES: 60% of all vyds. Also GRÜNER V Stockkultur.

Preisinger, Claus Burgen ★★★★ 20' 21' 22' 23' 24' 25 Experimental, bio. Bonsai BLAUFRÄNKISCH; fizzy Puszta Libre (r); Erdeluftgrasundreben. Co-fermented GRÜNER V/apples/quince: Sunny Cide Up 22, FURMINT Attila. Classic PINOT N.

Prieler Burgen ★★★★ 20' 21' 22' 23' 24' 25 Top compelling, age-worthy PINOT BL from different terroirs, Seeberg 24, Leithaberg DAC Alte Reben 23, Haidsatz, Steinweingarten. BLAUFRÄNKISCH needs bottle-age: Goldberg, Marienthal.

Proidl Krems ★★★★ 20 21' 22 23' 24' 25 Reliably brilliant GRÜNER V, RIES (try library releases), both from Ehrenfels vyd. Even better since son Patrick joined.

Reserve (Res) Still: min 13% abv plus longer ageing in winery. SEKT AUSTRIA Res is trad method, min 18 mths on lees, Grosse Res is min 36 mths.

Ried Cru, or single vyd. *See* riedenkarten.at.

Rücker, Elisabeth Wein ★★★ 20' 21' 22' 23' 24' 25 Low intervention, bio. Two-thirds planted 1955–80. Textbook, long, intense GRÜNER V Innere Berge; subtle CHARD Alte Reben; two complex WELSCHRIESLING.

Ruster Ausbruch DAC. Historic botrytized sweet, from Baroque town of Rust, BURGEN. Best: FEILER-ARTINGER, SCHRÖCK, TRIEBAUMER, WENZEL.

Sabathi, Erwin S Stei ★★★★ 20 21' 22' 23' 24' 25 Elegant, profound, age-worthy CHARD, SAUV BL. Best site Pössnitzberg incl subsite Kapelle. Excellent PINOT N.

Sabathi, Hannes S Stei ★★★★ 20 21' 22' 23' 24' 25 Single-vyd SAUV BL Kranachberg; CHARD RIED Graf Woracziczky. Falter Ego: wine from Graz.

Salomon-Undhof Krems ★★★★ 20 21' 22' 23' 24' 25 Consistent, elegant, lean GRÜNER V, RIES (Steiner Kögl 24') single-vyds Pfaffenberg, Wachtberg. Best value: anything called Terrassen, incl village wines.

Sattlerhof S Stei ★★★★ 20' 21' 22' 23' 24' 25 Effortlessly brilliant; bio. Top crus Kranachberg, Sernauberg, monopole Pfarrweingarten. SAUV BL Alter Kranachberg 22'; standout village SAUV BL Gamlitz.

Sausal S Stei Subregion: vyds up to 600m (1969ft). Small enclave, extraordinarily elegant RIES, SAUV BL, also BLAUFRÄNKISCH, even PINOT N.

Schauer S Stei ★★★ 20 21' 22' 23' 24' 25 Schauer bros make light but profound white from schisty SAUSAL: RIES Alte Reben 23, village Kitzeck-Sausal 24, SAUV BL Kitzeck-Sausal, notable PINOT BL.

Schloss Esterházy Burgen ★★★ 20' 21' 22' 23' 24' 25 Serious, organic, balanced, refined; based on Leithaberg, follows Burgundy hierarchy. Central grape BLAUFRÄNKISCH; also PINOT BL, FURMINT, GRÜNER V. Elegant Blaufränkisch (sp).

Schloss Gobelsburg Kamp ★★★★ 20 21' 22' 23' 24 25 Cistercian-founded estate. GRÜNER V with exquisite varietal character, RIES worth ageing. Tradition series, single-vyds Grub, Heiligenstein, Lamm, Renner. Fine fizz. Classic, complex.

Schnabel – Ermihof S Stei ★★★★ 20 21' 22' 23' 24' 25 No-intervention winemaking; unusual varieties in SAUSAL: fine-boned BLAUFRÄNKISCH, elegant PINOT N, crus Hochegg, Koregg, Kreuzegg. Age gracefully.

Schödl Family Wein ★★★ 20 21 22' 23' 24' 25 Siblings Leonhard, Mathias, Viktoria. Went organic to bio to (often) natural; fine-tuned, clean, precise. Reddish Bloody MUSCAT with jasmine florals, spicy Grün Grün Grüner, cool-site GRÜNER V Steinberg, fragrant Blanc des Blancs NV.

Schröck, Heidi Burgen ★★★★ 20 21' 22 23' 24' 25 Doyenne of RUSTER AUSBRUCH, also on dry mission, esp FURMINT. Working with twin sons Georg and Johannes.

Schuster, Rosi Burgen ★★★★ 20 21 22' 23' 24' 25 Purity, elegance. Recent focus on FURMINT, BLAUFRÄNKISCH from different terroirs: RIED Hinkenthal (loam/sandstone) vs Lamer (loam/mica schiste). Ravishing Aus den Dörfern (r/w).

Seewinkel Burgen Region e of Neusiedlersee; several small shallow lakes close to Neusiedler See. Was reliably ideal for botrytis; getting drier with climate change.

Sekt Austria PDO for best sparkling. Entry-level 9 mths; RES 18 mths; Grosse RES 36 mths min on lees. For Res and Grosse Res, trad method mandatory. Most producers exceed min time, esp for Grosse Res.

Smaragd Wach Ripest category of VINEA WACHAU, min 12.5% abv but can exceed 14%; dry, potent, age-worthy. In past, often botrytis-influenced but dry.

Spitzer Graben Wach Cool side valley nr Spitz. Steepest terraces, v. dry, meagre soils, excellent NEUBURGER, RIES. Interesting, off-beaten-track wineries: Johann Donabaum, GRABENWERKSTATT, HÖGL, Martin Muthenthaler, VEYDER-MALBERG.

Stadlmann Therm ★★★★ 20 21' 22' 23' 24' 25 Exemplary, clear-cut ZIERFANDLER/ROTGIPFLER, esp single vyds Mandelhöh, Tagelsteiner. Subtle, poetic PINOT BL.

Steiermark (Styria) Most s region; aromatic, expressive dry white, esp SAUV BL and Pinots. *See* S STEI, V STEI, W STEI.

Fancy wine and music, eg. classic, pop, jazz, rap...? Look for Kultur bei Winzerinnen.

Steinfeder Wach Lightest VINEA WACHAU category for dry wines, max 11.5% abv. Difficult to produce in warming conditions, barely exported.

Stift Göttweig Krems ★★★ 19' 20 21' 22 23 24 Prominent hilltop Benedictine abbey surrounded by vyds; crystalline GRÜNER V Gottschelle, RIES Pfaffenberg.

Straka, Thomas Burgen ★★★ 20' 21' 22' 23' 24' 25 Tasty WELSCHRIESLING. Beautifully spiced BLAUFRÄNKISCH Rechnitz, herbaceous FURMINT Rechnitz.

AUSTRIA

Strehn, Pia Burgen ★★ 20 21' 22 23' 24 25 Passion for BLAUFRÄNKISCH rosé, blends. All dry except Sushi Rosé, inspired by Japanese food; also gd CAB FR.

Südsteiermark DAC. Region close to Slovenian border, famed for elegant, aromatic CHARD (here also called MORILLON), MUSKATELLER, SAUV BL from breathtakingly steep slopes. Try Ewald Zweytick, Landesweingut Silberberg (wine-grower's school), Primus am Grassnitzberg, Warga-Hack.

Tement S Stei ★★★★ 20' 21' 22 23' 24' 25 Subtle, age-worthy, esp MORILLON, SAUV BL (incl from Dom Ciringa, Slovenia). Top sites: Grassnitzberg, Zieregg; v. bio.

Thermenregion DAC (since vintage 2023). Spa region s of VIENNA. Rich, elegant, rare ROTGIPFLER, ZIERFANDLER; historic PINOT N and ST-LAURENT hotspot. Try Alphart, Alphart am Mühlbach, Gebeshuber, Hartl, Reinisch.

Tinhof, Erwin Burgen ★★★ 20 21 22' 23' 24' 25 Below-the-radar Leithaberg estate; bio. Passion for PINOT BL, NEUBURGER: RIED Golden Erd. Also ST-LAURENT Feiersteig, village Eisenstadt.

Triebaumer, Ernst Burgen ★★★★ 20' 21' 22' 23' 24' 25 Iconic RUST producer; bio to core. Try BLAUFRÄNKISCH legend Mariental, also as late release, then the rest.

Tschida, Christian Burgen ★★★★ 20' 21' 22' 23' 24' 25 Cult in natural circles; min intervention without compromise; vyds around Purbach. Notable range Himmel auf Erden, Laissez-faire: elegant, subtle, profound. Uses more RIED names now, but don't expect too much continuity.

Umathum, Josef Burgen ★★★★ 20' 21' 22 23 24 25 Originally famous for reds, ZWEIGELT Hallebühl, ST-LAURENT vom Stein; today legendary in all colours incl PIWI. Worked on propagation of vines suitable for the terroir for yrs: Königlicher Wein MMXXIII. Try BLAUFRÄNKISCH RIED Kirchberg 15 (only gd yrs, 10 yrs after), beautiful Brut Nature (sp).

Velich, Heinz Burgen ★★★★ 20 21 22' 23' 24' 25 Both CHARDS Darscho, Tiglat legends with depth. Less oak now. Try any vintage, the older the better.

Veyder-Malberg Wach ★★★★ 19' 20 21' 22' 23 Terroir fanatic. Precise, even austere. Old vines up to 70 yrs, steep terraces in SPITZER GRABEN and other WACH. Try GRÜNER V, RIES. Also orange Grüner V Alter.Native.

Vienna (Wien) 582 ha of vyds within capital, c.160 wineries. Wine ancient trad, now quality focus; 37% organic. Local field blend enshrined as WIENER GEMISCHTER SATZ DAC. ***Heurigen among vines; visit a must.*** Try AMBROSITSCH, EDLMOSER, Fuhrgassl-Huber, Kroiss, Wieninger am Nussberg. Best crus: Bisamberg, Maurerberg, Nussberg with subsites Preussen, Rosengartl.

Vinea Wachau Wach Quality growers' association. Ripeness scale for WACH (dr w): FEDERSPIEL, SMARAGD, STEINFEDER. Exists parallel to official Wach DAC.

Vitikultur Moser Krems ★★★★ 20' 21' 22 23' 24' 25 Was Sepp M. Family ties with Lenz M; quality completely different. Run by Nikolaus M and daughter Kathi. Early bio adopter. Exemplary GRÜNER V, also RIES, long-lived CHARD. Mineral, salty Blanc des Blancs Extra Brut (spontaneously fermented Chard base).

The return of Furmint

Okay, there's still not a lot of it, but there used to be none. Before that, there was lots. We're talking about FURMINT: it was the most widespread white grape in what is now BURGEN, but it was replaced by GRÜNER V and WELSCHRIESLING. By 2015, Furmint had disappeared. Now there are (wait for it) 35 ha, incl 2 ha in STYRIA (Herrenhof Lamprecht, the vines selected from an old mixed field planting). Dry Furmint from Burgen tastes elegantly of quince, summer flowers, green herbs, with salty minerality and refreshing acidity. Try A&H NITTNAUS, FRANZ WENINGER, KOFOLK, MICHAEL WENZEL, ROSI SCHUSTER and any from Rust.

Vulkanland Steiermark DAC. All Pinots, CHARD, plus SAUV BL, often volcanic soils. Favourites: Frauwallner, Krispel, NeueHeimat (was Goedwinemakers), Ploder-Rosenberg, Scharl, Winkler-Hermaden.

Wachau DAC. Danube region; world reputed, age-worthy GRÜNER V, RIES. VINEA WACHAU classification. Try Johann Donabaum, Muthenthaler, Tegernseerhof. Note newcomers: Bergkirchner, Wabi-Sabi, WEINHAUEREI 378.

95% of all the wineries in Austria are in family hands.

Wachter-Wiesler, Weingut Burgen ★★★ 19 20' 21' 22' 23 24 25 Fine-boned, elegant, silky BLAUFRÄNKISCH with a twist, from iron clay and green schist of Eisenberg DAC. Great ageing potential. Entry-level Handgemenge (r/w/rosé).

Wagram DAC (GRÜNER V, RIES, ROTER VELTLINER); W of VIENNA. Deep loess, spicy Grüner V. Best: FRITSCH, JOSEF FRITZ, Leth, Nimmervoll, OTT.

Weingut Stadt Krems Krems ★★★ 20 21' 22 23' 24 25 Brilliant municipal estate, 31 ha within city limits. GRÜNER V, RIES slightly riper, rounder than WACH, crystalline, expressive at top level; gd single-vyds, value entry-level.

Weinhauerei 378 Wach ★★ 21 22 23' 24' 25 Organic, focus on GRÜNER V, RIES, vyds nr Weissenkirchen, min intervention: finest fruit aromas, mineral, elegant.

Weinrieder Wein ★★★★ 20' 21 22 23 24 25 Was famous for Eiswein, rare now. Instead: fabulous complex RIES, polished GRÜNER V, dry to TBA (*see* Germany).

Weinviertel DAC. GRÜNER V in classic, RES, Grosse RES versions. Region once slaked VIENNA's thirst, now quality counts. Base wine for Viennese Sekt houses like Schlumberger, but also home of excellent fizz: EBNER-EBENAUER, Schödl Family, Sekthaus Madl and ZUSCHMANN-SCHÖFMANN. For still, try Christoph Bauer, Dürnberg, Faber-Köchl, Fidesser, Gruber-Röschitz, Neustifter, Obenaus, Uibl.

Weninger, Franz Burgen ★★★★ 19' 20 21' 22' 23' 24' 25 Expressive, seductive terroir BLAUFRÄNKISCH; single-vyds Hochäcker, Kirchholz. Brilliant FURMINT.

Wenzel, Michael Burgen ★★★★ 20' 21' 22' 23' 24' 25 Excellent natural FURMINT.

Weststeiermark DAC. Super-crisp rosé Schilcher from Blauer Wildbacher grape (r). Different styles: trad rosé, rare sweet, modernist sparkling, natural and orange. Try Jöbstl, Lex Langmann and natural-wines expert Franz Strohmeier.

Wetschka, Magdalena Burgen ★★★ 23' 24' 25 New generation doing own thing: expressive, balanced. Soft NEUBURGER 24 (50-yr-old vines); juicy, vibrant GRÜNER V Altenberg 24 (limestone); creamy, Meyer-lemon CHARD Tannenberg 23, BLAUFRÄNKISCH Jungenberg 23. Big hope for future.

Wiener Gemischter Satz Vienna DAC. Historic (w) field blends. Complex. Fuchs-Steinklammer, Fuhrgassl-Huber, Hajszan-Neumann, Mayer am Pfarrplatz, Peter Uhler. Called Gemischter Satz/Mischsatz elsewhere: *see* GROISS.

Wieninger, Fritz Vienna ★★★★ 20' 21' 22 23' 24 25 Mastermind behind quality renaissance; bio. Exemplary WIENER GEMISCHTER SATZ Nussberg, Rosengartl. Great PINOT N. Also runs experimental winery Hajszan-Neumann (GRÜNER V Steinberg, Wiener Gemischter Satz Weisleiten).

Wohlmuth S Stei ★★★★ 20 21 22' 23' 24' 25 Top SAUSAL producer. Subtle, dazzling CHARD, RIES, SAUV BL, esp from single vyds Edelschuh, Gola, Hochsteinriegl; gd reds. Recultivating Ries in steepest terraces (Dr Wunsch).

Zillinger, Herbert Wein ★★★★ 20 21' 22' 23' 24' 25 Splendid, complex GRÜNER V; bio. Try Kalkvogel, Hirschenreyn, entry-level Neuland. Also WELSCHRIESLING Alte Reben, GEWÜRZ Profund, Toast Hawai 22, Springbreak Rosé.

Zillinger, Johannes Wein ★★★ 20 21' 22' 23 24 25 Bio, min intervention. Velue = varietals; Parcellaire = blends of similar site, character; Revolution = everyday.

Zuschmann-Schöfmann Wein ★★★★ 20 21' 22' 23' 24' 25 Entry-level GRÜNER V SEKT AUSTRIA of exceptional quality. Also RIES Grosse RES Ralessen, Rosé Brut Res. Excellent Pét Nat Why Taille Rosé 24: complex red-berried, fresh, fine.

England

There's a lot of English wine around; what should we drink? Sparkling, obviously: it's what England does superbly. Look here for the really good ones. Still is more mixed, with some wonderful surprises; rosé is a safe bet. Check out too the orange/skin-contact/naturalish side of things: there is some very interesting work being done, and it can be a good way of handling PIWI grapes (*see* Grapes): a boon in an unpredictable climate. I'm beginning to wonder if orange is the English red. Abbreviations: Berkshire (Berks), Buckinghamshire (Bucks), Cornwall (Corn), East/West Sussex (E/W Sx), Essex (Esx), Hampshire (Hants), Herefordshire (Her), Oxfordshire (Oxon), Wiltshire (Wt).

Some vyds welcome, even rely on, local volunteers for picking etc. Pay: good lunch.

All Angels Berks ★★★ Long ageing on lees a feature here, and makes huge difference. Long Aged bottling has even longer, for great depth. No. 36 has softer acidity, softer fizz: v. pretty.

Althorne Estate Esx ★★ Just 6 acres: apple-fresh, sleek fizz; v.gd CHARD/PINOT GR, cleverly oaked CHARD.

Ambriel W Sx ★★ Reliable, appealing sparkling, thoroughly likeable: Blanc de Blancs. Pricey Cloud Ten.

Artelium E Sx ★★ Elegant, mineral, savoury. Try Curator's Cuvée, Blanc de Blancs, Makers Rosé; still PINOTS GR/N.

Balfour Kent ★★ Lots of decent still, incl newish ALBARIÑO. Excellent visitor facilities. Flagship: Balfour Brut Rosé.

Beare Green Surrey Naturalish, unfiltered, taut. Interesting range: steely still CHARD; savoury, light PINOT N.

Beaulieu 58 Hants Delicate GEWURZ; pretty orange. Made by WHARIE EXPERIENCE.

Blackbook ★★ Always something new, interesting. Urban winery in S London, min intervention, small lots: CHARD, PINOT N.

Black Chalk Hants ★★ Sparkling with depth, tension, purity. Back on form.

Bluestone Wt ★★★ Family company, with petting zoo on site. Lovely pure, tense sparkling, v. well made.

Breaky Bottom E Sx ★★★★ Founder Peter Hall died in 2025. Tiny source of wonderful wines: richness, tension; layered flavours. Probably best SEYVAL BL in world.

Bride Valley Dorset New local owners; bottle-age suits it: v.gd 2018 sparkling, gd still CHARD.

Camel Valley Corn ★★ Fruity, appealing wines, v. reliable, esp Special Res Brut, from long-est producer.

Candover Brook Hants ★★★ Classic flavours; gd richness. Made at HAMBLEDON.

Chalkdown Hants Clever name; juicy fizz; pretty, well made, classic. Nice rosé.

Chapel Down Kent Big volumes of acceptable fizz, fresher in past few yrs. ★★ Rich Kit's Coty Coeur de Cuvée.

Coates & Seely Hants ★★★★ As gd as ever. La Perfide (saline, brioche Blanc de Noirs) a star, but all detailed, complex.

Coolhurst W Sx ★★ On the up: fruit, balance, classic flavours. Increasingly gd.

Cottonworth Hants Length, depth gd here. Best: Classic Cuvée.

Danbury Ridge Esx ★★★ In tiny, warm Crouch V: gd still PINOT N. Impressive still CHARD. Solstice (sp) richer, more powerful than most English fizz. New tie-up with Dom Duroché, Burgundy (*see* France): 1st wines 2028.

Denbies Surrey Big focus on tourism, farm shop etc. Wines adequate, could be better. Solaris Orange gd, crunchy, fresh.

Digby Hants, Kent, W Sx ★★★ Arundel tasting room showcases ripe, mineral wines, esp from greensand. Now owns/rents vyds incl Trotton.

Everflyht E Sx Excellent start; fine, salty, tight wines. Much investment. Vines still young, and wines need bottle-age. Late Release has gd depth.

Evremond, Dom Kent ★★★ One sparkling to start; others in pipeline. Taittinger-owned (*see* France), great expertise, depth, grace. Worth a visit.

Exton Park Hants ★★★ Saline, elegant, gd concentration, lots of res wine in blend for richness. NV: RB (Res Blend), graceful, gd depth.

Folc ★★ Rosé, done v. well. Sparkling too. Shows how gd English rosé can be. Pronounced "folk".

Foxford Hants Tiny vyd, gd sp made at BLACK CHALK. Promising, well made.

Grange, The Hants ★★★ Small-scale, classic flavours, lovely balance, elegance. Black from White, White from White, Classic, all gd buys. Lovely magnums.

Gusbourne Kent, W Sx ★★★★ Top quality, grace, concentration, character. Not cheap, but worth it. Late Disgorged evolves beautifully on palate. Deluxe 51°N; single-vyd wines as gd.

Gutter & Stars ★★ Small lots, min intervention. Urban winery in windmill, Cambridge. Visit, taste, experiment, see what you like.

Hambledon Vineyard Hants ★★★ Owned by Berry Bros and Symington Group (*see* Portugal). Lovely Première Cuvée (sp): saline, poised. Lemon-cream Blanc de Blancs. Also v.gd restaurant.

Harrow & Hope Bucks ★★★ Flint breaks harrows, apparently. Wines better every yr: rich Blanc de Noirs; biscuity, pure Brut Res; PINOT N Rosé, delicate red fruit.

Hart of Gold Her ★★ Made at RIDGEVIEW; classic lemon-biscuity fizz. Also vyds in Maury (*see* France): The Dom of the Bee.

Hattingley Valley Hants ★★★ Different vyds blended for balance, elegance, flavour: classic Champagne model, in effect. Distinctive, characterful rosé; Blanc de Blancs, tense, gd depth, savoury.

Henners E Sx ★★ Owned by Boutinot, innovative UK merchant-producer. Sleek Brut, impressive vintage sparkling.

Herbert Hall Kent ★★ Pocket-sized vyd among apple orchards, gd poised sparkling, esp Kirsty's Blanc de Blancs.

Heretics, The Esx Apricot-rich Deluxe Seven CHARD, gd rosés from bought-in fruit. Cool labels, lots of yellow.

Highweald W Sx Evocative name; elegant, complex sparkling, beautifully made; from Sx High Weald clay and greensand.

Hugo, Dom Wt ★★ Characterful, even idiosyncratic; min intervention. Saline, detailed, revelatory Hugo Rosé (sp).

Hundred Hills Oxon ★★★ Beautiful spot in Stonor V, all vintage fizz; lots of investment cleverly done. Preamble low dosage, crunchy, revealing; First Edition richer, tense, long.

Jojo's Oxon Named after dog. Bright, pure Première Cuvée, serious Rosé (sp). Made at LANGHAM.

For ripening grapes in England, chalk = good, clay = good, but climate trumps both.

Langham Wine Estate Dorset ★★★★ Innovative, adventurous, v.gd: started in old farm barns (no insulation, eg.); new winery soon. Indigenous yeasts, lots of character; inspiration was grower Champagnes. Perpetual (solera sp), ravishing. Corallian saline, Culver broader.

Leonardslee W Sx Lots of investment in gd fizz; same owners as Benguela Cove (*see* S Africa); v. promising Creamy Blanc de Blancs, sleek Rosé.

Litmus Project of DENBIES winemaker John Worontschak. Fruit from all over: v.gd still Orange BACCHUS, excellent still ***white Pinot N***, improves for 10 yrs+.

Crouching tiger

Essex's Crouch V is tiny but remarkable. This is where best fruit for still wines comes from: warmer and drier. Simple, really. And it has clay. Grapes largely CHARD, PINOT N; expect tension, depth. Pinot is not burgundian, precisely; lighter, often quite experimental; lots of growers feeling way with and finding out the best oak, best ways of handling it. Chard is more secure, and sparkling is often rich, winey. As well as those listed, try Hollands Crouch V, Marbury Crouch V, Martin's Lane.

Mountfield E Sx Citrus and biscuit: elegant sparkling from greensand and clay; v.gd Classic Cuvée.

Nyetimber W Sx ★★★★ Getting it right across the board. Classic Cuvée has depth; layered Rosé, superb powerful Tillington, complex 1086. Lives up to reputation.

Oastbrook E Sx ★★ Mostly still; CHARD, PINOT N variations; concentration, ripeness.

Pommery England Hants ★★ Layered, elegant. Pommery Champagne's (*see* France) offshoot, and maybe better.

RAD Custom Winery Esx Small quantities from another custom crush: v.gd CHARD, PINOT N, gd-value rosé.

Raimes Hants ★★ Precise, flavoursome fizz. Made at HATTINGLEY V.

Rathfinny E Sx ★★★ Spectacular site; tight, taut, precise fizz, more ageing now. Blanc de Noirs particularly gd. Restaurant, visitor facilities.

Ridgeview E Sx ★★ A little more solid than most contemporary English fizz: focused on weight, breadth. Big range.

Riverview Esx Crouch V ripeness in still CHARD, crunchy PINOT N, plus elegance.

Roebuck W Sx ★★ All sparkling: perfumed, elegant Classic Cuvée; flavoursome, vigorous Rosé de Noirs. Try Rare Expressions and aromatic, complex late-disgorged. Gets better and better.

Sandridge Barton Devon ★★ (Was Sharpham) Still and sparkling, indigenous yeasts, experimental. Try Figgie Daniel Col Fondo, Classic Cuvée Rosé. Also Don't Feed the Ponies range, esp PINOT BL.

Simpsons Kent ★★ Focus on still, though some fizz. Lots of oak on pretty well everything: gd Roman Road CHARD, Chalklands (sp).

Squerryes Kent Lovely depth, classic fizz; rich, poised, lemon shortcake flavours.

Sugrue E Sx ★★★★ Tiny operation, new investment, future looks rosy. Huge character, complexity, depth; pretty well impossible to beat in England. Still CHARD known as Bonkers; now rich, fresh Crouch V PINOT N.

Tidebrook E Sx Still wines, lightish, correct: v.gd balance. Offshoot of Jordan Wine Estate (*see* S Africa).

Vagabond ★★ Urban winery, still wines. Innovative, experimental. Characterful CHARD, pure PINOT N; lovely Night Tripper (w blend).

Westwell Kent ★★★ Try all: innovative, adventurous still; pure, taut, fine Pelegrim fizz. Amphorae, pét-nat, Col Fondo, orange, min intervention.

Weyborne Surrey ★★→★★★ Have some Tennyson with your sparkling. Classic elegance, freshness, liveliness. Structured, toasty Oriana; Blanc de Blancs coming soon; plus rosé. Small vyd, big investment.

Wharie Experience, The Hants ★★ Experimental, min-intervention methods often seem to get best out of grapes like BACCHUS or Ortega: fresh, textured, still.

Winding Wood Berks By Daniel Ham (ex-LANGHAM): delicate fizz, lovely length.

Wiston W Sx ★★★★ Perfect poise; delicate elegance conceals concentration and steely core. Need bottle-age. Wiston Estate Cuvée (sp), a beauty. Doesn't put foot wrong. Also gd Chalk restaurant.

Wyfold Oxon ★★ Nicely elegant wines from Laithwaite-owned vyd. Same family has Windsor Great Park Vyd, from – well, yes.

Scandinavia

The wine scene here is young but dynamic; Denmark and Sweden are home to 1000+ producers (albeit many tiny). With chillier climes (and a copper ban), it is largely disease-resistant hybrids that succeed here. Champagne varieties can also make delicious sparkling, and Frühburgunder (aka Pinot Noir Précoce) makes dazzling light reds; Denmark's Njord planted all available clones; the resulting wines are among the world's most exciting Pinots. Norway's production is tiny.

Denmark

Although tiny, at just 175 ha (but growing), Denmark's vyd landscape is more exciting than ever. Select sites on coastlines and bays of Denmark's islands (mainly Jutland, Zealand, with Bornholm, Funen) planted to hybrids or early-ripening vinifera make possible what one might have considered impossible.

Barfod Vin ★→★★ Regenerative, bio: Solaris, Souvignier Gr, Cabernet Cantor.

Drudgaard ★→★★ Delicious natural wine and cider from Funen.

Garbolund Natural winery; lip-smacking rosé from Regent. Visitor-friendly.

Klitgaard Vin ★→★★ Started in 2005 as a hobby; bio, some of country's most celebrated. Serve sparkling blind to friends.

Njord ★★→★★★★ On sandy hills of W Zealand, Sune Albertsen makes arguably Scandinavia's finest wines. Focus on organic FRÜHBURGUNDER.

Sønderstrand Vin ★→★★ On Jutland's w coast; v.gd organic whites exemplifying potential of hybrids.

Stokkebye Vingård ★★ On Funen, organic, excellent sparkling, Stella (L'ACADIE BL/ Johanniter), Stella Mary (PINOT N).

Vejrhøj Vingård ★→★★ Some of Denmark's most delicious white, sparkling and rosé hybrids. Collaborates with Copenhagen's iconic Fiskebar to create no-sulphur Nøgen (Naked) cuvées for restaurant.

Vexebo Vin ★→★★ Organic natural wines and ciders just n of Copenhagen. Try tasty Solaris.

Weirdloose Overdrive ★→★★ Creative natural wines, ciders, co-ferments; veg farm on ancient grasslands of Særløse Overdrev.

Scandinavia's most northerly vineyards are in Norway, same latitude as S Alaska.

Sweden

Sweden's vyd plantings have overtaken neighbouring Denmark, now sitting at 200 ha+. The North and Baltic Seas – namely the moderating effects from the Kattegat and Øresund straits – make viticulture viable for winemakers in the sw of this otherwise chilly country.

Flädie Mat & Vingård ★ Organic, fruity hybrid wines; try elegantly oaked Midnattssol (Solaris).

Flyinge Vingård ★ Bright, zesty, organic Solaris.

Hällåkra Vingård ★★ Organic, natural Five Generations; orange Cuvée Anna.

Jesper Friberg ★★ On e coast of Skåne, talented winemaker, experience with natural methods. Delightful carbonic Rondo blends.

Kullabergs Vingård ★→★★ From Cape Kullaberg; classy. Try aromatic Lyckeri.

Thora Vingård ★→★★ In Bjäre peninsula; organic Solaris (Pure), also PINOT GR, FRÜHBURGUNDER, PINOT N. Restaurant on-site.

Vingården i Klagshamn ★→★★ Pioneer on w coast of Skåne; precise wines. Try Nordic Light botrytis.

Central & Southeast Europe

More heavily shaded areas are the wine-growing regions.

Abbeviations used in the text:

Bal	Balaton
Cri & Mar	Crişana & Maramureş
Cro Up	Croatian Uplands
Dalm	Dalmatia
Dan P	Danubian Plain
Dob	Dobrogea
Is & Kv	Istria & Kvarner
Mold	Moldovan Hills
Mun	Muntenia & Oltenia Hills
N/S Pann	North/South Pannonia
Pod	Podravje
Pos	Posavje
Prim	Primorje
Sl & CD	Slavonia & Croatian Danube
Thr L	Thracian Lowlands
Tok	Tokaj
Trnsyl	Transylvania
U Hun	Upper Hungary

ALBANIA

This country has a distinctive wine culture with c.6000 ha of wine grapes, 70+ registered producers and an ancient history back to Illyrian times (c.800 BCE). It's making quality progress, helped by a busy tourist industry, but is still catching up with its neighbours. Most vineyards are at altitude (up to 1000m/3281ft), which moderates the warm Mediterranean climate, and a wide range of unique grapes offer distinctive wines. Most important: Shesh i Bardhë (White Shesh), Shesh i Zi (Black Shesh), Debinë e Bardhë, Kallmet (aka KADARKA), Pulës, Serina, Vlosh, VRANAC. Leading producers incl: Arianiti, Alpeta, Çobo, Duka, Enofama, Faba, Kallmeti, Nurellari.

BOSNIA & HERZEGOVINA

The vast majority of the estimated 3000 ha of vineyards are on the hot rocky karst of Herzegovina, with only a handful in the north. There are welcome signs of improvement and cooperation with a new wine law, a Herzegovinian wine route and Ljbubuški producer group, plus some good hotels and restaurants. Local varieties dominate: Žilavka has exciting potential, also renewed focus on sleek Blatina and juicy Trnjak, plus Vranac near Trebinje. Names to watch: Begić, Domano, Knebu, Jungić, Matić, Ostojić, Puntar, Vilinka, Vinarija Čitluk (Teuta only).

Bosnia & Herzegovina waterfalls: 202, more than Italy, France, Germany combined.

Andrija, Podrumi ★→★★ Modern family winery with long trad: Selekcija Žilavka, supple Blatina, gd SYRAH.

Brkić ★→★★ Three generations; bio principles. Žilavka (fresh to orange Mjesečar).

Carska Vina Grgo Vasilj ★★ ***Blatina Premium***, Žilavka and blends (***David***, Sophia).

Imperial Vineyards ★★ Luxury hotel, historic vyds nr Mostar; ***Blatina***, Žilavka v.gd.

Nuić ★→★★ 48 ha on stony karst; son is Austrian-trained. Pioneered red varietal Trnjak (in super-rich style). Also gd: Grk, POŠIP, TOURIGA N, Žilavka.

Škegro Family Winery ★★ Family winery; terraced, high-altitude vyds; Blatina, Trnjak, Žilavka v.gd. Fresh Krš wines; excellent, more complex Carsus.

Tvrdoš Monastery ★★ Wine history from C15, 500,000 visitors/yr, winemaking restarted by monks 1998: VRANAC, Žilavka, impressive long-ageing Grande Res.

Vino Milas ★★ Family winery; age-worthy Blatina Res, v.gd Žilavka Premium.

Vukoje 1982 Podrumi ★→★★ Historic vyd plus restaurant nr Trebinje. Try VRANAC, Žilavka, incl vyd-selection Carsko Vino.

BULGARIA

Indigenous grapes and regional expression are the main focus here. Fine sparkling to pét-nat, orange, fresh whites and increasingly elegant reds. Rebuilding wine culture is also key, especially given the country's multi-millennial wine history back to ancient Thrace. Bulgaria is dotted with fascinating history connected to wine and has nine UNESCO sites.

Madara horseman rock-carving is carrying a glass of wine. Don't drink and ride.

Alexandra Estate Thr L ★★ Experimental small estate, elegant *qvevri*: Beton CHARD, VERMENTINO, RUBIN, dark-pink PINOT GR, orange RIBOLLA GIALLA.

Angel's Estate Thr L ★★ Part of Purcari Wineries Group (*see* Moldova). Stallion, supple red blends; Deneb, v.gd varietals (CAB FR, rosé); great-value Angels range.

Bessa Valley Thr L ★★★ One of 1st true estates, French consultancy. Try Enira, v.gd SYRAH and Enira Res, excellent ***Grande Cuvée***.

Better Half / Dalakov & Sons Thr L ★★ Two brands, small garage winery, limited batches in amphorae, concrete eggs. CHARD, ZINFANDEL, red blends v.gd.

Bononia Dan P ★★ Historic brewery from 1895, turned winery and boutique hotel, close to Danube. Super-precise: DIMIAT, GAMZA, Vrachanski MISKET, estate blends v.gd. Great-value ★★ Gomotartzi.

Borovitsa Dan P ★★ Tiny batches from old vines in nw. Top: age-worthy Dux. Also Canyon Park MRV, Cuvée Bella Rada (RKATSITELI), Great Terroirs (old-vine GAMZAS), Maxxima Res, Sensum.

Boyar, Dom Thr L ★→★★★ Large modern winery, mostly volume commercial production. Labels incl: Bolgaré, Elements, Quantum. Top: single-vyd Solitaire (MERLOT). Separate boutique Korten cellar: Grand Vintage, Natura.

Bratanov Thr L ★★ Low-intervention family estate in SAKAR. Try 3 Blend (r/w); *sur lie* CHARD, single-vyd Tamianka, new SYRAH/VIOGNIER; age-worthy CAB FR, SYRAH.

Burgozone Dan P ★★ Significant family estate close to Danube. Fresh, vibrant: Collection Tamianka, old-vine GAMZA; flagships Eva, Iris Creation.

Clos Bibliothèque Dan P ★★★ New super-premium estate in ne. Expensive but glorious single-vyds: CHARD, PINOT N, SYRAH, even amphora DIMYAT.

Copsa, Ch Thr L ★★ In heart of Rose V, makes one of best MISKET Cherven: ***AXL***. Also gd SAUV BL, improving reds.

Dragomir Thr L ★★→★★★ Big, bold reds, RUBIN star grape (long-lived Pitos, Res). Fruity, unoaked Sarva range. Fab CAB FR Res.

Georgiev / Milkov ★★→★★★ Two top winemakers, old-vine local grapes. Exciting MAVRUD pét-nat, Pink Side of RUBIN, Why Not MISKET, PAMID-based Mixtape.

Haralambievi Dan P ★★ Family winery in n, experiments with PIWIS. Try Kaylashki MISKET in acacia, Royal Rouge CAB FR, RUBIN.

Katarzyna Thr L ★★ Supple, ripe, well made: Flagship Res impresses, also estate MAVRUD, RUBIN, Encore SYRAH.

Logodaj Thr L ★★ STRUMA winery; excellent-value, fine bottle-fermented ***Satin*** from Broadleafed MELNIK. Also Melnik 55 (r/rosé).

Magura Dan P ★★ Ambitiously renovated winery, vyds in nw: v.gd Maiden GAMZA, Oracle MISKET, Celestial Bull RUBIN.

Medi Valley Thr L ★★ Owns vyds at 550m (1804ft) nr Rila Monastery: v.gd red Great Bulgarian, Incanto Black, Excentric MELNIK.

Menada, Dom Thr L ★ Large producer. Tcherga blends, Barrique Point reds.

Midalidare Estate Thr L ★★→★★★ Immaculate boutique winery. Some of country's best ***trad-method sparkling*** (Pas Dosé, Rosé Extra Brut); gd reds.

Minkov Brothers Thr L ★→★★ Large but consistent winery: premium Oak Tree, v.gd Project 7, Le Photographe RIES.

Miroglio, Edoardo Thr L ★★★ Italian/Bulgarian estate. Excellent trad-method fizz. Impressive flagship red Soli Invicto; v.gd Elenovo Res, PINOT N (Res, value Soli).

Odessos Dan P ★★ Garage project, two bros with international experience. Old-vine parcels: RIES, DIMYAT, CAB FR, SYRAH and Claret dark rosé.

Orbelia Thr L ★★ Family winery in STRUMA V; v.gd Via Aristotelis range, also Estate Res, esp MELNIK. Fun pét-nat from Sandanski MISKET.

Rossidi Thr L ★★→★★★ Pioneering winery nr Sliven. Top concrete-egg-fermented CHARD; elegant MAVRUD, ***Rubin***, excellent SYRAH.

Rumelia Thr L ★★ MAVRUD specialist: Merul, Rumelia Res, Erelia blend.

Sakar Dynamic region in se, focus on SYRAH. Joint Birds of Sakar project: each winery has own bird on label, donates to Bulgarian bird protection society.

Salla Estate Dan P ★★ TRY RIES, SAUV BL, TRAMINER, Vrachanski MISKET, CAB FR.

Santa Sarah Thr L ★★→★★★ Quality pioneer, now 40 ha nr Pomorie. Flagship Privat (50-yr-old vines), Bin 60 MAVRUD, single-vyd SYRAH.

Stephan Pirev Wines ★★→★★★ Personal project of respected winemaker. Res du Patron CHARD, superb RIES, CAB SAUV, Eager Top Blend (r).

Struma Valley Thr L Dramatic wine region surrounded by mtns: don't miss the sand pyramids and quaint historic town of Melnik. Focus on local grapes: MELNIK 55, Sandanski MISKET, Shiroka Melnik (aka Broadleafed Melnik). Look

Names to watch

Bulgaria's wine scene is ever-changing, with projects like Bottled Opinions, Wine Hippies and more. Wineries to watch (without own entries): Aya Estate, Bendida (MAVRUD, RUBIN), Ch Avli, Damyanov, Daros, DeVina (***Tessera Dimyat***, Vrachanski MISKET), Dimitrovi, Dragashinov (SYRAH, RIES), Four Friends, Gorun (excellent ***Gamza Res, Cab Fr Res***), Kapatovo, Libera Estate, Lozeto (***Longoza Cab Fr***), Mihovi, Pink Pelican, Rosalea (Rubin Writer's Wine), ROXS, Rupel, Staro Oryahovo (White Story range), Simenta (ALIGOTÉ), Stratsin (VERMENTINO, ***Grenache Bl/ Vermentino***, new PAMID), ***Tipchenitza*** (gd orange Misket, Oak Barrel, Rubin Tochka), Varbovka (GAMZA), Via Verde, Via Vinera (Heritage Mavrud, orange Dimyat), Villa Yustina (Four Seasons Rubin rosé, Monogram), Yalovo (Gamza, Old School Dimyat), Zaara Estate (Dogma).

for: Aya Estate (Aya Melnik Amfora, Disegno PETIT MANSENG), Bottled Opinions, Damianitza (Redark, Volcano), Damyanov (Broadleafed Melnik, Keratsuda Orange), Kapatovo (PETIT VERDOT, GRENACHE/MOURVÈDRE/SHIRAZ), Libera (Hotovo, Melnik 55, Orange Keratsuda), Mihovi (Keratsuda), Rupel (Melnik), Via Verde (Expressions Sandanski Misket, White Blend), Zlaten Rozhen.

Tsarev Brod Dan P ★★ Innovative estate in n. Try Amber CHARD, Evmolpia (r/rosé), rare local Gergana (still/sp), pét-nat RIES, SAUV BL Res. Ries Icewine v.gd.

Villa Melnik Thr L ★★ Family estate, local grapes: MAVRUD, MELNIK. Notable ***Melnik 1300 Jubilee, Family Tree*** under rare varities label; gd Aplauz, value Bergulé.

Vinex Slavyantsi Thr L ★ Fair for Life-certified for supporting local ethnic community. Reliable well-priced varietals, blends, esp Leva brand.

Yamantiev's Thr L ★→★★ Sound, commercial Kaba Gayda, SHIRAZ. Excellent ***Marble Land (r)***, Yamantiev's Grand Res CAB SAUV.

Zagreus Thr L ★★ Organic vyd, MAVRUD in all styles: complex Vinica from semi-dried grapes, Santimenti is fun natural version. Three Generations (r) gd.

Zelanos Thr L ★★ Pristine winery/wines. Try fresh (Red) MISKET, PINOT GR, elegant Z premium wines esp CAB FR, PINOT N, SYRAH.

CROATIA

Croatians are fiercely proud of their wines and increasingly keen to export them beyond the significant seaside-tourism market. Indigenous varieties (Croatia has at least 95) take centre stage, led by Graševina, Malvazija Istarska and Plavac Mali, but with bright futures for once rare, or unregarded, grapes such as Debit, Grk, Pošip, Žuti Plavec, Babić, and many more. Two new PDOs are waiting for approval: for Grk from the sandy soils of Lumbarda, and for Buje on Istria's white soils. Tourists need to watch out and avoid poor-quality, cheap imports.

Ante Sladić Dalm ★★ Next-generation family winery; v.gd local grapes: Lasina, Maraština, Opol, Oya Noya Debit.

Antunović Sl & CD ★★ Mother/son team, at Erdut on Danube. Elegant, age-worthy Tradition GRAŠEVINA, CAB FR.

Arman, Marijan Is & Kv ★★ Family estate for consistent fresh MALVAZIJA and always impressive G Cru from selected plot. Also gd TERAN.

Badel 1862 ★ Largest, oldest producer in Croatia. Best: Korlat Supreme, SYRAH. Owns Benkovac, Duravar, Ivan Dolac.

Benvenuti Is & Kv ★★★ Family winery run by two bros. One of best producers of TERAN, esp Santa Elisabetta, superb San Salvatore MUŠKAT. Try Livio in best yrs (named after late father), consistent classic range (Caldierosso r).

BIBICh Dalm ★★→★★★ Family estate from C15, now with son. Flagship Bas de Bas. Also Superstitious Debit, R6 Lasin/BABIĆ/Plavina blend.

Bire Dalm ★★→★★★ Family estate specializing in rare Grk grape, esp single-vyd ***Defora*** from Lumbarda on Korčula.

Boškinac Dalm ★★→★★★ Top boutique hotel and winery on Pag Island: impressive Cuvée (r). Superb Ocu (rare Gegić w).

Bura Dalm ★★ Artisan winery, organic, wild ferments with next generation at helm. Noted for substantial Rukatac, DINGAČ, PLAVAC MALI.

Cattunar Is & Kv ★★ Hilltop winery notable for MALVAZIJA from ISTRIA's four different soils, plus late-harvest Collina.

Clai Is & Kv ★★ Organic, skin-contact, natural. Try v.gd REFOŠK, serious fizz, MALVAZIJAS Baracija, Sv Jakov.

Coronica Is & Kv ★★→★★★ Pioneer of quality TERAN. Age-worthy benchmark Gran Teran; v.gd Gran MALVAZIJA, fresh DYA version.

Croatian Uplands Međimurje is coolest, vibrant Pušipel (aka FURMINT), expressive SAUV BL: Cmrečnjak, Dvanajščak Kozol, Jakopić, Kocijan, Kopjar, Kos, Lovrec, Preiner, Štampar. Moslavina for mineral Skrlet, also Frankovka (Florijanović, Košutić, Romić). Plešivica for great fizz, Sauv Bl, RIES, orange/amphora: Griffin Ivančić, Jagunić, ***Korak (Sauv Bl, Pinot N, sp)***, ***Šember (sp)***, Šoškić (Haiku), TOMAC.

Dalmatia Sunny rocky coastline and islands, from Zadar to Dubrovnik. Divided into N Dalm, The Hinterland, s-central Dalm. Unique varieties; try Baraka, Birin, Bora, Ego, Katich, Milijas, Miloš, Prgin, Provič, Sikuli, Vislander.

Damjanić Is & Kv ★★→★★★ Smart family winery; v.gd Justina MALVAZIJA, Borgonja (aka BLAUFRÄNKISCH), Clemente (r/w). Revived rare Duranija (w).

Dingač Dalm Croatia's 1st PDO since 1962 for weighty reds from PLAVAC MALI, on steep sea-facing slopes of Pelješac peninsula. Try Benmosche, BURA, Crna Ovca, Kiridžija, Korta Katarina, Madirazza, SAINTS HILLS, Skaramuča, Vinarija Dingač.

Enjingi, Ivan Sl & CD ★★ Legendary natural-wine maker in SLAVONIA. Noted for GRAŠEVINA, long-lived Venje.

Enosophia Sl & CD ★→★★ Ambitious recently renovated cellar in Slavonia. Best: Miraz (v.gd CAB FR, Frankovka), also Trs No. 5 GRAŠEVINA.

Fakin Is & Kv ★★★→★★★★ "Fakin good wines" is winery motto. Exciting: La Prima MALVAZIJA, Il Primo TERAN. Also MALVAZIJA (Monte, Amfora), juicy Teran.

Galić Sl & CD ★★★ Space-age winery: refined CHARD, Crno 9, GRAŠEVINA, PINOT N.

Grabovac Dalm ★★→★★★ Family winery in hinterland of DALM impressing with Kujundzuša, Modro Jezero Ris, Trnjak.

World's first commercial pharmacy opened in Dubrovnik 1317, still open today.

Gracin Dalm ★★→★★★ Professor Leo G pioneered revival of BABIĆ: complex, herby, elegant. Also as sweet PROŠEK and in v.gd Kontra blend made with Kiridžija.

Grgić Dalm ★★ On Pelješac peninsula, founded by late Miljenko "Mike" G of Judgment of Paris fame; trad PLAVAC MALI, typical POŠIP.

Hvar Dalm Island with UNESCO listing for Stari Grad Plain and its vyd *chora* (C4 BCE). Try Carić, Hvar Hills, Marijan, TOMIĆ, ZLATAN OTOK, Svirče co-op.

Iločki Podrumi Sl & CD ★→★★ Large producer, historic C15 cellar, Principovac former royal vyds; gd GRAŠEVINA, TRAMINAC. Try Premium, Principovac, Sofjia.

Istria Adriatic peninsula, more a country within a country, also noted for great olive oil, truffles. Versatile local MALVAZIJA Istarska is main grape and red TERAN. Best (without own entry): Banko Mario, Bastian, Bertoša Robi, Cossetto, Degrassi, ***Deklić***, Dobrovac, Dom Koquelicot, Franković, Bruno Ferenac, Ipša, ***Kadum***, Meneghetti, ***Milan Budinski (Omo)***, Radovan, San Tommaso, Sosich, Trapan, Veralda (organic, v.gd REFOSCO), Vivoda, Zigante.

Kabola Is & Kv ★★→★★★ Immaculate organic estate, wines to match. MALVAZIJA as fizz, young wine, cask-aged Unica and superb Amfora (also a TERAN).

Komarna Dalm Newest wine region, since 2013: all organic, on precipitous slopes by sea. Try Rizman, SAINTS HILLS Sv Roko, Volarević. Watch Deak, Terra Madre too.

Korta Katarina Dalm ★★ US roots; luxury hotel on Pelješac overlooking Korčula; gd POŠIP, weighty PLAVAC MALI (Reuben's Res).

Kozlović Is & Kv ★★★→★★★★ Family winery; pioneer of modern winemaking in ISTRIA, continues to raise standards, joined by daughter. Benchmark entry-point MALVAZIJA, TERAN; v.gd Selekcjia, superb ***Santa Lucia*** vyd.

Krajančić Dalm ★★→★★★ Owner Luka is guru for all styles of POŠIP (Intrada, Macerirani, Statut, Sur Lie), also gd PLAVAC MALI (fruity Sardela).

Krauthaker Sl & CD ★★★ Renowned GRAŠEVINA specialist from Kutjevo (fresh, vyd Mitrovac, sw). Also gd Zelenac (aka ROTGIPFLER).

Kutjevo Cellars Sl & CD ★★ Large cellar from 1232; gd-value, consistent GRAŠEVINA. Also premium De Gotho, lovely Icewine, intriguing archive wines.

Kvarner Is & Kv Bay and islands off ISTRIAN coast. White Žlahtina is main focus, from fizz to PROŠEK (Ivan Katunar, Katunar Winery, Pavlomir, Šipun), and revived Sansigot red (Ivan Katunar, Katunar, Šipun).

Laguna, Vina Is & Kv ★★→★★★ ISTRIA's largest winery at Poreč on *terra rossa*. Vina Laguna for gd-value varietals, premium Festigia range for better vyd selections (MALVAZIJA), new Teran (rosé), gd Blanc de Moi (sp).

Markus Fine Wines ★★★ Ambitious new project, planting on Šolta. Canadian investor. Superb POŠIP: Dan Po Dan, O Tom Potom, Pomalo Maraština (w).

Matošević Is & Kv ★★★ Benchmark, age-worthy MALVAZIJA: Alba, Alba Antiqua, Alba Robinia (in acacia). Grimalda vyd selections v.gd.

Medea Is & Kv ★→★★ Largest of small ISTRIAN wineries. Consistent varietals, excellent top vyd selections: Montiron MALVAZIJA, ***Punta Greca Merlot***.

Pilato Is & Kv ★★ Consistently gd family winery; v.gd MALVAZIJA, esp ★★★ *sur lie*.

Prošek Dalm A trad sweet wine, from sun-dried local grapes on coast (1st mention 1556). Legal battles with Italy, but can't be confused with Prosecco.

Rossi Is & Kv ★★→★★★ Family winery run by three bros; consistent, fresh MALVAZIJA Istarska, excellent ***Templara*** vyd selection.

Saints Hills Dalm, Is & Kv ★★→★★★ Two estates in DALM, ISTRIA. Consultant Michel Rolland (*see* France): Nevina (w), Posh POŠIP, Pape (r), Sv Roko PLAVAC MALI, one of best DINGAČ.

Slavonia / Croatian Danube Heartland of GRAŠEVINA in e of Croatia. Mostly whites, lighter reds (Frankovka, PINOT N). Try Adzić, ***Antunović***, Belje, ENJINGI, ENOSOPHIA, GALIĆ, Jakob, Jakovac, Kast, KRAUTHAKER, KUTJEVO, Royal Hill, Sontacchi, Zlatno Brdo. Slavonia also famous for its oak.

Stina Dalm ★★ Dramatic steep vyds on Brač Island. PLAVAC MALI (Majstor label, top Remek Djelo). Also v.gd POŠIP, Tribidrag, Vugava.

Testament Dalm ★★→★★★ Organic estate in historic area at Šibenik: v.gd POŠIP, BABIĆ, PLAVAC MALI Tribidrag. Fun Dalmatian Dog (r/w). Sister winery, Black Island on Korčula (Merga Victa Pošip).

Tomac Cro Up ★★★ Sparkling specialist, amphora pioneer nr Zagreb, bio: excellent ***Diplomat*** Brut, Marany *qvevri* wines, plus Rockstar RIES.

Tomaz Is & Kv ★★ Family winery pushing boundaries in ISTRIA: complex MALVAZIJA Sesto Senso; impressive Barbarossa TERAN.

Tomić Dalm ★★ Bold wines from leading personality on HVAR; organic Caplar, Illyricum; gd reds (esp Plavac Barrique); PROŠEK Hectorovich (sw).

Zlatan Otok Dalm ★★ Possibly 1st private modern winery on HVAR, vyds also at Makarska, Šibenik. Noted for ripe reds, gd DYA POŠIP.

Zure Dalm ★★★ Specialist in Grk from Lumbarda on Korčula. Try Grk Bartul, ***Reventón sur lie***, Quinta Essentia (sp), new *qvevri* version. Also gd POŠIP Zure.

CZECHIA

Prices of local wines soar, but sales remain stable. Wine tourism is also thriving. According to the Czech Tourism Office, over 65% of Czechs visit wine regions, and half choose accommodation in picturesque press houses in wine-cellar settlements converted to luxury family hotels or B&Bs. Two regions: Bohemia (Boh) and Moravia (Mor).

Baloun Winery Mor ★★★ Radomil B est 1991; specializes in no-nonsense drinkable wines: award-winning GRÜNER V, MERLOT.

Dog in Dock Mor ★★ New winery, restaurant, agriturismo in harbour on Baťa Canal. Modern approach, focus on PINOTS BL/GR, RIES, MERLOT.

Hartman, Jiří Mor ★★ Small producer of burgundian style (r/w) in picturesque Slovácko area. Also v.gd RIES, WELSCHRIESLING, plus a host of PIWIS.

Ilias, Giorgios Mor ★★→★★★ Greek ancestry, est 1998. Remarkable GRÜNER V, burgundian single-vyd cultivars Pod Pálavou, Slunný Vrch, Stará Hora.

Lobkowicz, Bettina Boh ★★→★★★ Swiss-born ex-princess follows up centuries-old winemaking tradition in Mělník: PINOT N Barrique Selection; trad-method Blanc de Noirs Brut, Sekt Bettina Lobkowicz Brut. Also CHARD barrique, PINOTS BL/GR, RIES, TRAMINER, Saphira; v.gd-value entry-level Lady Lobkowicz (r/w/rosé).

Lobkowicz Ch Roudnice Winery Boh ★★ One of oldest wineries (1603); branch of noble family, William and Alexandra L. Award-winning RIES, SYLVANER (Sovice vyd, opoka subsoil); signature PINOT N, ST-LAURENT; new Czech variety Fratava.

Naturvini Mor ★★ Patrik Staško makes aromatic PÁLAVA (TRAMINER X MÜLLER-T), expressive PINOT GR, WELSCHRIESLING from foot of Pálava Hills; 90% bio.

Nepraš & Co Mor ★★★ Architect Radek N makes vibrant Maidenstein PINOT BL, RIES, SAUV BL. Also opulent Gravettien Grande Cuvée CAB SAUV/MERLOT.

Springer, Jaroslav Mor ★★★ Jaroslav S and son Tomáš make outstanding single-vyd Záhřebenské CHARD, PINOT N (flagship label Roučí).

Vican Mor ★★★ Film producer Tomáš V est his Farma Pálava 2015. Accent on WELSCHRIESLING, RIES (Mušlov), PINOT N (Kienberg). Top: Cuvée Jupiter, Karel Roden Edition, Kvevri House range. Also SYLVANER (Kotel), Yellow MUSCADELLE, bone-dry orange TRAMINER (Nesyt).

Wilomenna Boh ★★→★★★ Boutique family winery on volcanic Central-Boh Uplands nw of Prague; CHARD, RIES, SAUV BL. Unusual varieties (Rubinet), blends (Provocateur, Rozmarné Cuvée JM), trad-method Sekt Wilomenna Brut.

Zilvar Boh ★★→★★★ Boutique winery, est 2015, on steep slate slopes overlooking Vltava and Prague zoo. Focus on RIES, PINOT N.

HUNGARY

Today's Hungarian wine stories are all about wine as culture across the country's 22 regions. Lighter, brighter, vibrant styles are proving food-friendly, and the country is becoming a gastronomic destination with multiple Michelin stars. On the downside, producers are fearful of the latest wine "plague" – grapevine yellows (*flavescence dorée*) has already caused widespread destruction and uprooting of vineyards.

Aszú 1st written mention 1571 in deed of inheritance. Supposed to raise dead; didn't.

Aszú Tok Name for extremely shrivelled, noble-rotted berries, and the wine they produce – always picked one by one, with special production method of soaking in fermenting must. Not every yr is an Aszú vintage, but wines consistently among world's best sweet wines thanks to balance of sweetness and vibrant acidity; incredibly long-lived too. Most label as 5-PUTTONYOS (min 120g/l sugar) or sweeter, richer 6-Puttonyos (min 150g/l sugar, often higher).

Balassa Tok ★★★→★★★★ Small family winery with 30 parcels for superb vyd dry FURMINT (Kakas, Nyulászó, Szent Tamás), plus gorgeous Villő ASZÚ, lovely SZAMORODNI. Fruity estate ★★ Furmint gd value, and possibly TOK's only RIES.

Balaton Both shores of Central Europe's largest lake – Hungary's seaside. Volcanic n shore suits Hungarian favourite OLASZRIZLING. New pyramid of quality: community brand Balaton-bor is entry point; Hegy-bor next level up (mtn wine); DŰLŐ for top crus. Also trad varieties return to forefront: FURMINT, KADARKA, KEKFRANKOS, KÉKNYELŰ. Around Badascony and Szent György-hegy: 2HA, Borbély, Buttner, Földi Bálint, GILVESY, Laposa, Nyári, Sabar, Skrabski, Szászi, Szeremley, Ujvári, Villa Sandahl, VILLA TOLNAY. Balatonfüred-Csopak n of lake: Dobosi, FIGULA, Homola, Jasdi, Liszkay, St Donát, organic ZELNA. Balaton Uplands and Zala: Bussay, Káli Kövek, Pálffy. Balatonboglár on s shore (riper): Budjosó, GARAMVÁRI, Ikon, Kislaki, KONYÁRI, bio Kristinus, Légli plus giant TÖRLEY.

Barta Tok ★★★→★★★★ Highest vyd in region, lovely Rákóczi mansion. Superb, elegant wines: Öreg Király FURMINT, HÁRSLEVELŰ, inviting entry-point Egy-Kis Furmint. Gorgeous SZAMORODNI, superb ASZÚ.

Béres Tok ★★→★★★ Owners created popular remedy: Béres drops. Superb rich ASZÚ, gd-value SZAMORODNI, consistent dry wines.

Bikavér ★→★★★ "Bull's Blood". PDO in EGER and SZEKSZÁRD, unique – best are some of Hungary's top reds. Four-variety min: KÉKFRANKOS is base and specified oak-ageing. Szekszárd = min 5% KADARKA: Eszterbauer, HEIMANN, Lajver, Markvart, Schieber, SEBESTYÉN, Szeleshát, TAKLER, Tüske, Vesztergombi, VIDA. Eger: Superior, Grand Superior = restricted yield, longer ageing. Best Egri Bikavér: BOLYKI, Bukolyi Marcell, Csutorás, Egersoul, GÁL TIBOR, Grof Buttler, KOVÁCS NIMRÓD, ST ANDREA, Tóth Ferenc, Thummerer.

Bock, József S Pann ★★→★★★ Bold VILLÁNY Capella, Ermitage, Royal Cuvée, CAB FR.

Bolyki N Hun ★★ Dramatic winery in a quarry in EGER, fun labels: v.gd Bolyki es Bolyki BIKAVÉR Superior, Egri Csillag, Metha Tema HÁRSLEVELŰ.

Danube (Duna) Largest region on Great Plain, lighter wines. Three districts: Csongrád, Hajós-Baja (Koch), Kunság (Frittmann, Font, Gedeon, Szentpéteri); incl PDOs Monor, Soltvadkert.

Degenfeld, Gróf Tok ★★→★★★ Castle hotel, organic vyds. Try Terézia HÁRSLEVELŰ, Zomborka FURMINT, excellent barrel-select ASZÚ, gd fizz.

Demeter, Zoltán Tok ★★★★ Legendary winemaker, nine vyds (all 40 yrs+). Excellent vyd selections. Pioneer of top-notch PEZSGŐ (sp) in TOK. Fine SZAMORODNI: Anett, Eszter; superb ASZÚ. Also runs foundation to promote local culture.

Dereszla, Ch Tok ★★→★★★ Consistent, gd-value dry FURMINT, ASZÚ, reliable PEZSGŐ. Also flor-aged dry SZAMORODNI Experience. Excellent bistro.

Disznókő Tok ★★★★ Dramatic estate; superb, elegant, long-lived sweet, one of v. few to make ASZÚ every yr. Wonderful ***Kapi*** cru in top yrs; v.gd SZAMORODNI (super-complex dr; 1413 sw). Consistent dry FURMINT, Inspiration dry TOK.

Dobogó Tok ★★★ Superb family winery. Benchmark ASZÚ 6-PUTTONYOS, excellent long-lived late-harvest ***Mylitta***; dry, vyd-selection FURMINT Úrágya.

Dűlő Named single vyd or cru. TOK has led way with vyd selections for dry and sweet incl Betsek, Bomboly, Király, Lapis, Mézes-Mály, Nyúlászó, Szent Tamás, Úrágya, Urbán. Dűlő selections also increasing in BAL, EGER, SZEKSZÁRD, VILLÁNY.

Eger N Hun The s-facing slopes of Bükk Mtns. Reds do well here: Egri BIKAVÉR, KÉKFRANKOS, PINOT N, SYRAH. Plus fragrant fresh whites: Egri Csillag (Star of Eger, dr w Carpathian-grape blend). Try Csutorás, Gróf Buttler, Kaló Imre (natural), Marcell Bukolyi, Petrény, Thummerer, Tóth Ferenc.

Essencia / Eszencia Tok Rare, expensive, free-run trickle of syrup from ASZÚ grapes, min 450g/l residual sugar, barely ferments. Reputed to raise the dead.

Etyek-Buda N Pann Rolling limestone hills, increasing emphasis on gd fizz, plus expressive, crisp white (esp SAUV BL), decent PINOT N. Top: ETYEKI KÚRIA, HARASZTHY, Hernyák, Nyakas, Rókusfalvy, TÖRLEY Sparkling Cellar.

Etyeki Kúria N Pann ★★ Top ETYEK-BUDA winery: SAUV BL; refined Red, KÉKFRANKOS, PINOT N. Winemaker Meresz Sandor has personal project; esp gd ***Zenit***.

Figula Bal ★★★ Leading family winery in BAL, v.gd OLASZRIZLING: ***Gella***, Öreghegy, ***Söskut***, Száka. Excellent vyd blends: Köves, Szilénusz. Elegant 2500 ***Kékfrankos***.

Gál Tibor N Hun ★★ Try Egri Csillag, KADARKA, Pajardos BIKAVÉR Grand Superior.

Garamvári Bal ★★ Leading PEZSGŐ specialist: ***Furmint Brut***, Classic Brut NV. Garamvári varietals gd value.

Gere, A S Pann ★★★→★★★★ Standard-setting family winery in VILLÁNY: Attila Cuvée, ***Kopar***, ***Solus Merlot***, ***Ördögárok Villányi Fr*** (CAB FR); varietals (***Fekete-Járdovány***).

Gilvesy Bal ★★ Canadian-Hungarian returned to roots, vyds on Szent-Gyorgy-Hegy volcano: FURMINT, OLASZRIZLING, RIES and blends (try St George) v.gd.

Gizella Tok ★★★★ Simply delicious wines from tiny family estate worked by horse. Wonderful dry HÁRSLEVELŰ, superb SZAMORODNI, gorgeous ASZÚ.

Grand Tokaj Tok ★→★★ Largest winery in TOK. Grand Tokaj label is guided by highly regarded Karoly Áts. Late-harvest Arany Késői is appealing, stylish dry FURMINT Kővágó, v.gd ASZÚ, amphora-aged ESZENCIA.

Haraszthy N Hun ★★ Beautiful ETYEK-BUDA estate for expressive SAUV BL, aromatic fruity Love range, smart PINOT N.

Harry Houdini born Erik Weisz, Budapest, 1874. Escaped to US aged 4.

Heimann S Pann ★★★ Family winery in SZEKSZÁRD: gd VIOGNIER, plush MERLOT, flagship ***Barbár***. Next generation now in charge, increased focus on local grapes, superb vyd selections: KADARKA, KÉKFRANKOS (Bati, Szivem), BIKAVÉR, Piros.

Hétszőlő Tok ★★★ Historic cellar, organic. Elegant Kis-Garai FURMINT, fine ASZÚ.

Heumann S Pann ★★★ German/Swiss-owned estate in VILLÁNY, great Kékfrankos Res, impressive ***Cab Fr La Trinitá***, top Terra Tartaro, delicious rosé, classy SYRAH.

Hilltop Winery N Pann ★★ In Neszmély. Reliable well-made, gd-value varietals; gd Kamocsay Premium range (CHARD, Ihlet Cuvée, PINOT GR).

Holdvölgy Tok ★★→★★★ Super-modern winery in MÁD, TOK's youngest winemaker. Complex, dry Vision, Expression, plus v.gd Eloquence SZAMORODNI.

Juliet Victor Tok ★★★ Ambitious investment by founder of Wizz Air. Excellent vyd FURMINTS, superb rich SZAMORODNI, ASZÚ.

Kikelet ★★★ Tiny family cellar, French winemaker and Hungarian husband. Top: ageable HÁRSLEVELŰ Kassai and elegant FURMINT Tarczal vyd selections.

Királyudvar Tok ★★★ Pioneering private winery in old royal cellars at Tarcal; bio. FURMINT Sec, Henye PEZSGŐ, Cuvée Ilona (late-harvest), flagship Lapis ASZÚ.

Konyári Bal ★★→★★★ Pioneering estate s of lake, son of founder in charge: Loliense (r/w), Szarshegy (w), excellent age-worthy ***Páva***.

Kovács Nimród Winery N Hun ★★→★★★ In heart of EGER. Grand Bleu (KÉKFRANKOS), impressive with age. Also Sky FURMINT, Rhapsody BIKAVÉR, Blues Kékfrankos, 777 PINOT N, NJK.

Kreinbacher Bal ★★→★★★ Standard-setting producer of PEZSGŐ, based in SOMLÓ, always FURMINT in blend; v.gd Classic Brut, superb Prestige Brut. Also gd still: Öreg Tokék, Selection FURMINT, HÁRSLEVELŰ.

Mád Tok Historic village surrounded by top vyds, with protected origin/quality scheme. Leading: Árvay, Áts (family estate of Karoly Áts, also of GRAND TOKAJ), BARTA, Budaházy, Demetervin (Mád FURMINT, Úrágya DŰLŐ), Lenkey (unique, long-aged, complex), Orosz Gabor, Pelle (Szent Tamas Furmint, PEZSGŐ), ROYAL TOKAJI, SZEPSY, Tokaj Classic.

Mád Moser Tok ★★ Project with Austria's Lenz Moser: fruity FURMINT MM5, more serious MM55.

Malatinszky S Pann ★★★ Organic VILLÁNY cellar. Barrel-fermented Maghari impresses, plus long-lived Kúria CAB FR, v.gd Rozé, Serena.

Mátra N Hun ★→★★ Overlooked volcanic region for lively whites, gd rosé, elegant reds. Try Balint, Benedek (PINOT N, KÉKFRANKOS), Centurio (Diós, Liberty), Dubicz, Gábor Karner, NAG (Föld és Ég range), Nyilas (light, fruity w).

Mór N Pann Small region, fiery Ezerjó; CHARD, OLASZRIZLING; ★★ ***Csetvei Winery***.

Oremus Tok ★★★→★★★★ Part of Vega Sicilia (*see* Spain) stable: dry FURMINT Mandolás better than ever. Also fine, elegant SZAMORODNI, ASZÚ.

Pajzos-Tokaj Tok ★★→★★★ Notable French-founded estate. Fruit-driven New Age varietals, T range for estate selections, Selection label from cooler Megyer vyd. Fantastic flor-aged dry SZAMORODNI, excellent ASZÚ.

Pannonhalma N Pann ★★ 800-yr-old abbey, Austrian adviser. Hemina blends v.gd, also SAUV BL, RIES. Consistent, drinkable ***Tricollis (w)***.

Patricius Tok ★★→★★★ Steely, vibrant dry FURMINTS: Sajgo vyd, Profundum. Also PEZSGŐ, appealing Katinka late-harvest; superb long-lived ASZÚ.

Pezsgő Hungarian for sparkling; growing trend. PDO TOK must be bottle-fermented, min 15 mths on lees from 25 vintage.

Puttonyos (Putts) Sweetness indication for TOK ASZÚ, min 120g/l sugar for 5 Puttonyos, 150g/l for 6 Puttonyos. Historically number of 25-kg *puttonyos* or hods of Aszú grapes added to each 136-litre barrel (*gönci*) of base wine. Now more about stylistic balance of sweetness, acidity.

Royal Tokaji Wine Co Tok ★★★→★★★★ MÁD winery leading rebirth of TOK. (Hugh Johnson was co-founder 1990.) Focus on FURMINT only for v.gd ASZÚ, esp excellent 6-PUTTONYOS single vyd. Blue label is benchmark 5-Puttonyos. Look for small parcels of By Appointment, plus consistent Late Harvest and dry.

St Andrea N Hun ★★★★ Leading reinvention of BIKAVÉR as red flagship blend. ***Nagy-Eged-Hegy Grand Superior***, ***Agapé Grand Superior Bikavérs***, some of Hungary's v. best reds, plus single-vyd Hangács, barrel-selection ***Merengő***. Excellent classy FURMINT-based Mária, charming Örökké Egri Csillag (w).

Sauska S Pann, Tok ★★★→★★★★ Returning expat, superb winery in VILLÁNY, new space-age PEZSGŐ cellar in TOK. Champenois consultant Régis Camus guides excellent fizz: Brut NV, ***Rosé Brut***. Reds impress, esp CAB FR, Cuvée 7, Cuvée 5. Consistent dry FURMINT, plus benchmark vyd selections Birsalmás, ***Medve***.

Sebestyén S Pann ★★ Brother-and-sister team in SZEKSZÁRD, gd vyd BIKAVÉR (Görögszó, Ivan-völgy), appealing KADARKA.

Somló Bal Dramatic extinct volcano; mineral white, esp Juhfark (sheep's tail). Small wineries dominate: Kancellar (OLASZRIZLING, FURMINT), ***Kolonics*** (***Juhfark***, ***Hárslevelű***), KREINBACHER, Somlói Apátsági, Somlói Vándor, Spiegelberg, TORNAI.

Sopron N Pann Across lake from Burgenland (*see* Austria). Signature KÉKFRANKOS on old schist rocks; top bio WENINGER; organic Steigler, Taschner, Vincellér.

Szamorodni Tok Name of Polish origin for TOK made from whole bunches, partial botrytis or less shrivelled berries. Gaining popularity: more authentically Tok than late-harvest. *Édes* (sweet) is min 60g/l sugar (usually sweeter), 6 mths' oak-ageing. Try BALASSA, BARTA, Bott, DEMETER ZOLTÁN, Demetervin, GIZELLA, HOLDVÖLGY, JULIET VICTOR, KIKELET, Kvaszinger, Maison aux Pois, OREMUS, Pelle, SZEPSY, TOKAJ-NOBILIS, Zsirai. Dry (*szaraz*) is 24 mths' oak, flor-aged like Sherry: try Breitenbach, CH DERESZLA, DISZNÓKŐ, Hársanyi, ***Pajzos***, ROYAL TOKAJI, ***Tinon***.

Szekszárd S Pann Increasingly supple, refined reds from loess soils, growing focus on vyd selections of elegant BIKAVÉR, KÉKFRANKOS, reviving lighter KADARKA. Try Dúzsi, ESZTERBAUER, HEIMANN, Lajver, Markvárt, SEBESTYÉN, Schieber, Szeleshát, TAKLER, Tüske, VESZTERGOMBI, VIDA.

Szepsy Tok ★★★★ Quality in a different league. Now guided by István Jnr, with focus on complex, parcel-selected dry FURMINT (Percze, Szent Tamás, Úrágya, Urbán), though don't ignore v.gd estate Furmint. Gorgeous sweet SZAMORODNI; superb ASZÚ, incl recent single-vyd releases.

Takler S Pann ★★ Next-generation family estate in SZEKSZÁRD. DŰLŐ focus: Gurovica KÉKFRANKOS, Görögszó CAB SAUV, Szenta. Consistent value ★★ BIKAVÉR Heritage.

Hungarian Béla Barényi original designer of VW Beetle, 5 years before Porsche.

Teleki S Pann ★→★★ Rebranded largest winery in VILLÁNY: Zsigmund T developed grafting to save vines after phylloxera. Try varietals, more serious Kővilla.

Tinon, Samuel Tok ★★★ Frenchman in TOK since 1991. Long-ageing, complex ASZÚ in more trad style, with long maceration, oak-ageing; gd vyd-selected FURMINT. Wonderful, flor-aged dry ***Szamorodni***.

Tokaj / Tokaji Tokaj is the town and region; Tokaji the wine. Recommend (without own entry): Árvay, Áts, Bardon, Basilicus, Bodrog Borműhely, Bott Pince,

Breitenbach, Budaházy, Carpinus, Demetervin, Erzsébet, Espák, Füleky, Harsányi, Karádi-Berger, Kvaszinger, Lenkey, Maison aux Pois, Orosz Gábor, Pelle, Pendits, Péter, Présello, Sanzon, Szarka, Szóló, TR, Zsirai.

Tokaj-Nobilis Tok ★★★ Fine, small organic estate run by Sarolta Bárdos. Excellent dry Barakonyi, Rány FURMINTS, v.gd ASZÚ, Benchmark for Furmint PEZSGŐ.

Törley ★→★★ Reliable, gd-value DYA international and local varieties (labels incl Chapel Hill, St Stephen's Crown, Talisman); György-Villa for better selections. Major fizz producer (esp Gala, Hungaria, Törley labels), v.gd classic-method François, based on history of sparkling back to 1886.

Tornai Bal ★★ Signficant SOMLÓ estate; gd-value ★ entry-level varietals. Excellent, weighty Selection Apátsági FURMINT, Grófi HÁRSLEVELŰ, gd Prime Juhfark.

Tűzkő S Pann ★★ Antinori-owned estate; gd CAB FR, KÉKFRANKOS, MERLOT, TRAMINI.

Vesztergombi ★★→★★★ Family SZEKSZÁRD estate impressing with next generation at helm. Look for Alpha, BIKAVÉR, Kétvölgy KÉKFRANKOS.

Vida S Pann ★★→★★★ Multi-generation family winery in SZEKSZÁRD. Wonderful ***Bonsai (100-yr-old vine) Kadarka***, Hidaspetre KÉKFRANKOS, Petit Bonsai; v.gd Valles Premium BIKAVÉR, Lösz (r).

Villány S Pann Most s region. Serious ripe Bx varieties: top-performing CAB FR, labelled Villányi Franc with rules for premium and super-premium. Juicy KÉKFRANKOS, PORTUGIESER. High quality (with no entry): Bakonyi, Gere Tamás & Zsolt, Günzer Tamás, Hummel, Jackfall, Jammertal, Kiss Gabor, Koch Csaba, Lelovits, Matias, Polgar, Riczu, Ruppert, Streit-Zagonyi, Tiffán, Wassmann (bio).

Villa Tolnay Bal ★★ Swiss-owned organic estate on volcanic basalt slopes for expressive, refined wines. Try FURMINT, GRÜNER V, OLASZRIZLING, RIES.

Vylyan S Pann ★★→★★★ Family estate in VILLÁNY. Fruity Classicus, amphora Variáció. Serious premium KÉKFRANKOS, Montenuovo; appealing rare Csókaszőlő. Top vyd selections: Mandulás CAB FR, flagship Duennium Cuvée.

Weninger N Hun ★★★ Standard-setting bio winery in SOPRON run by Austrian Franz W Jnr. Superb single-vyd ***Steiner Kékfrankos***; try Frettner CAB FR, Rózsa too.

Zelna Bal ★★ Impressive small organic family winery (gd wine bar too). Excellent ★★ OLASZRIZLING (Füred). Also gd: fizz and Bárka, Peregrina reds.

Wines of Kosovo

Western Balkan economy with partial recognition as independent, but crucially not by Serbia. Two wine laws: Kosovo's own and Serbia's. Around 2500 ha under wine grapes, 64% red; 37 wineries. Bodrumi i Vjetër (Old Cellar), Stonecastle dominate; smaller Kosova, Labi Wine, Lakicević, Sefa improving. Vranç (aka VRANAC) most planted red, plus GAMAY, Prokupac; whites led by Smederevka (aka DIMIAT), WELSCHRIESLING.

MALTA

Exciting times for Malta's wines: scientists have discovered ten previously undocumented native Maltese and Gozitan vines that now join Ġellewża and Girgentina, long thought to be the only two native grapes of the islands. The potential of the newcomers remains to be determined, but hope springs eternal: for sure these natives are well adapted to Maltese terroirs. Malta and Gozo boast varied geology, hot/dry climate (irrigation is fundamental), phylloxera-resistance, passionate winemakers and 2000 years of tradition. Ġellewża (rosés and light-bodied reds) and Girgentina (nuanced, high-acid whites; lemon, crisp pear and Granny Smith apple) are lovely, but since the 90s, most island wineries have increasingly planted international grapes (over 20 grow on the islands), leading to a loss of unique, local terroir expressions. Good examples of Maltese Vermentino, Merlot, Sangiovese and Syrah are made from mostly boutique wineries. The 800 hectares are (maybe?) best for reds, especially in the clay-rich soils of the south, but locals prefer whites – and given the heat, can you blame them? Three appellations: DOK Malta, DOK Gozo and IGT Maltese Islands (wines of both). In Malta, try Delicata (Ġellewża Medina, Ġellewża Frizzante), Mar Casar (natural *qvevri* wines), Marsovin (Cassar of Malta traditional fizz), Antinori-owned (*see* Italy) Meridiana (Vermentino Astarte), Zafrana. In Gozo, try Bacchus, Ta'Betta (founded by a couple of Cambridge graduates), Ta'Mena, Tal-Massar.

MONTENEGRO

A country under the radar, home to important grapes like Kratošija (aka Zinfandel/Primitivo), first mentioned in the C15 in the statute of Budva, and inky-dark Vranac, which dominates production with around two-thirds of Montenegro's 2561 ha under vine. Production is mostly in the hands of the giant 13-Jul Plantaže, whose 2310-ha single vyd is one of Europe's largest. Quality is generally good, especially Vranac (Barrique, Pro Corde, Stari Podrum). Small wineries sell mostly at home, and plenty of tourists help drink most wine locally. Try Keković, Lipovac, Patrimonio, Priča, Savina, Sjekloča.

NORTH MACEDONIA

Officially the Republic of North Macedonia. Most vineyards are in the central Vardar River valley, and Vranec [sic] dominates, with 10,800 hectares out of a total 28,000 ha; this is the warmest, driest part of the Balkans, with a continental-meets-Mediterranean climate. There is an increasing emphasis on quality bottled wine and showcasing terroir.

Bovin ★→★★ The 1st private winery of new era. Powerful oaky wines (A'gupka, My Way). Classic collection, fruitier/more drinkable.

Ezimit ★→★★ Large modern winery, beautiful vyds. Well-made, gd-value ★ varietals.

Imako Vino ★→★★ One of largest in N Macedonia, own vyds, competent winemaking. ★ Majestic label, decent value; top Constellation reds v.gd.

Kamnik, Ch ★★→★★★ On hill nr Skopje; 1st proper small estate. Super-rich, repay ageing: v.gd 10 Barrels, Cuvée Prestige, Terroir Grand Res, Spark (sp).

Lazar ★★ Small personal winery; v.gd Erigon reds, also Grashevina Special Edition, appealing Pearl *frizzante* Charmat.

Popov ★→★★ Private estate; try pure Kratošija; gd CARMENÈRE, Dom Vrsnik (w).

Tikveš ★→★★★ Oldest Balkan winery (1885); quality pioneer, winemaker French-trained. Brands: Alexandria, T'ga za Jug. Luda Mara (local grapes). Excellent vyd selections: Babuna, ***Barovo***, Bela Voda. Also Dom Lepovo (CHARD, Grande Res).

Venec ★→★★ Founded 1956; focus now on quality: Koria Temjanika, Kratoshija Single Block, VRANEC Orle, plus selected Disan range.

Small wineries, emerging names

Wine scene here is being shaken up by new names like Dane Hermes, Monteko, Paragon, Wine Cellar Popovi and a new association for small producers (under 30,000 litres). Try Eros, Iliev, Maksimilijan, Old School, Paradžik, Peshkov, Sarika Tomino. Indigenous Stanušina grape (usually rosé) improving, led by small wineries.

ROMANIA

Romania has largest number of growers in the EU (800,000+), and most of its wine stays in Romania. Local grapes Feteascăs Neagră/Regală continue to improve, along with rarities like Alutus, Negru de Drăgășani, Zghihara de Huşi and less usual Aligoté, Syrah. Sparkling is increasingly trendy, plus a smattering of natural and skin-contact styles.

Aramic, Crama Ban ★→★★ Family estate, Italian consultants: FETEASCĂ ALBĂ, Piatra Soarelui SAUV BL, FETEASCĂ NEAGRĂ (oaked and not).

Averești, Domeniile Mold ★★ Large estate, focus on local grapes: Busuioacă and only producer of Zghihară. Try Diamond, Nativus labels.

Avincis Mun ★★→★★★ Historic mansion, dramatic hilltop winery in DRĂGĂȘANI. Only winery for impressive ***Alutus***, v.gd aromatic orange. Benchmark Crâmpoșie Selecționată (still/sp); ***Negru de Drăgășani***; Cuvées André, Grandiflora, Petit.

Balla Géza Cri & Mar ★★→★★★ Family estate, close to Hungary. Top is Stone Wine from vyds up to 400m (1312ft) on Miniș Hills (CAB FR, Cadarca, FETEASCĂ NEAGRĂ, FURMINT). Also Clarus (sp) from Cadarca, ★★ Classic Feketeleányka, ★★ Királyleányka, Kolna Blaufrankisch Selection, Mustoasă.

Banat Dynamic region in w. Try Agape Artă & Natură, CRAMA ARAMIC, CRAMELE RECAȘ, PETRO VASELO, Thesaurus.

Bauer Winery Mun ★★★→★★★★ Top low-intervention winery of Oliver and Raluca B (also at PRINCE ȘTIRBEY). Limited-edition old-vine batches: CAB SAUV, Crâmpoșie, FETEASCĂ NEAGRĂ, Novac (rosé), PETIT VERDOT, SAUVIGNONASSE.

Bogdan, Domeniul Dob ★★ Ambitious bio vyd (Romania's 1st) in DOBROGEA, Stéphane Derenoncourt consults (*see* France). Try Cuvée Experience blends, Patrar and rich super-smart Primordial as tribute to late Philippe Cambié.

Budureasca Mun ★→★★ Modern DEALU MARE estate. Best: Noble 5, Wild FETEASCĂ NEAGRĂ, Origini SHIRAZ, Vine-in-Flames PINOT N, TĂMÂIOASĂ ROMÂNEASCĂ.

Caii de la Letea Dob ★→★★ Brand for VINTRUVIAN's Sarica Niculițel estate inspired by wild horses of Letea. ALIGOTÉ is emblem, also gd FETEASCĂ NEAGRĂ, rosé, multi-vintage Quintessence Res. Co-owns with Crama de Matei (DEALU MARE).

Corcova Roy & Dâmboviceanu Mun ★★ Renovated historic royal cellar, superb vyds. Lady Asquith (w), FETEASCĂ NEAGRĂ, SYRAH, age-worthy Cuvée Racoveanu.

Cotnari, Casa de Vinuri Mold ★★ Next-generation producer in ne using only local varieties. Excellent long-lees-aged fizz from Francușă, GRASĂ de Cotnari. Naiv label for gd modern examples of local grapes: Busuioacă, FETEASCĂS ALBĂ/NEAGRĂ, Grasă. Colocviu for premium whites (Grasă). Vladoianu Fetească Neagră v.gd.

Cotnari Winery Mold ★ Large producer former state winery in Cotnari DOC. Mostly dry and semi-dry whites from local grapes. Aged sweet Collection can impress.

Crișana & Maramureș Cooler region in nw. Look for BALLA GÉZA, Carastelec (v.gd Carassia bottle-fermented sp), Darabont Family (esp Urme), organic NACHBIL.

Dagon Mun ★★→★★★ Small, impressive quality-focused vyd. Best: Clearstone FETEASCĂ ALBĂ, Sandridge old-vine FETEASCĂ NEAGRĂ.

Davino Winery Mun ★★★★ One of Romania's v. best, in DEALU MARE. Focus on blends: age-worthy Dom Ceptura, superb Flamboyant, Revelatio, Rezerva. Valahica (local varieties: Alba, Purpura) v.gd. Entry-level, value ★★ Faurar, Iacob.

Dealu Mare / Dealul Mare Mun Means "Big Hill"; regarded as Romania's Tuscany. Top: AURELIA VIȘINESCU, BUDUREASCA, Crama Mierla Alba, Ceptura, DAGON, DAVINO, DEMATEI, Domeniile Franco-Române, Ferdi, Gramofon, LACERTA, La Migdali, Licorna (Anno 5, Serafim), SERVE, VIILE METAMORFOSIS.

DeMatei, Crama Mun ★★ Notable 92-ha estate in DEALU MARE, part of VINTRUVIAN. Serious reds under Migala, Patima, Prince Matei labels.

Dobrogea Sunny region by Black Sea. Alira (rosé, SAUV BL, MERLOT), BOGDAN, CAII

DE LA LETEA, Dropia (BĂBEASCĂ NEAGRĂ), Gabai, Histria (v.gd Ammos, Nikolaos CAB SAUV, rosé), La Sapata (bio, Băbească Neagră), Rasova (Imperfect, Sur Mer), Vladoi (Alb Cuvée, Anca Maria TĂMÂIOASĂ).

DOC Romanian term for PDO: 40 registered. Sub-categories incl DOC-CMD: harvest at full maturity; DOC-CT: late harvest; DOC-CIB: noble harvest. PGI is *vin cu indicație geografică*, or simply IG.

Domeniile Alexandrion Rhein Mun ★→★★ Winery with 255 ha in DEALU MARE and long history (1892) of Rhein & Cie (sp). Try DAR1892 Alb and Roșu, Hyperion.

Drăgășani Mun OLTENIA plateau and hills. Unique grapes: Crâmpoșie Selecționată, Negru de Drăgășani, Novac. Dynamic wineries: AVINCIS, BAUER, Olterra (part of VINTRUVIAN), PRINCE ȘTIRBEY, Venetic.

Gîrboiu ★→★★ Family estate in one of Europe's most tectonically active areas; names reflect this. Special focus on rare indigenous Șarba, try Tectonic FETEASCĂ NEAGRĂ, Bacanta, top red blend Constantin.

Gramma Mold ★★ Bright, fresh; memorable labels, esp ALIGOTÉ, Cuvée Visan.

Jidvei Trnsyl ★→★★ Romania's largest single vyd, 2500 ha+. Best: Owner's Choice (with Marc Dworkin of Bulgaria's Bessa V), Eiswein, Extra Brut (sp).

LacertA Mun ★★ Estate in DEALU MARE: gd Cuvée IX (r), Cuvée X (w), SHIRAZ.

Liliac Trnsyl ★★★ Impeccable Austrian-owned estate in heart of TRNSYL; *liliac* means bat. Crisp fine whites, elegant reds, v.gd orange CHARD, delicious sweet Nectar, Icewine with Kracher (*see* Austria).

Metamorfosis, Viile Mun ★★ DEALU MARE estate, part of Antinori group (*see* Italy), Italian winemaker. Top: rich, bold Cantvs Primvs, esp MERLOT. Also v.gd: Colțul Pietrei SAUV BL, PINOT N, SYRAH, Via Marchizului Negru de DRĂGĂȘANI. Reliable entry-point Villa Metamorfosis range.

Moldovan Hills Largest ne region. Fresh white, rosé; refined red: AVEREȘTI, GRAMMA, GÎRBOIU, Hermeziu (Busuioacă de Bohotin), Strunga (FETEASCĂS ALBĂ/NEAGRĂ).

Muntenia & Oltenia Hills Major region in s. DOC areas: DEALU MARE, Dealurile Olteniei, DRĂGĂȘANI, Pietroasa, Sâmburești, Stefanești, Vanju Mare.

Nachbil Cri & Mar ★★ Organic producer in Satu Mare. Try almost extinct Grünspitz in amphora, BLAUFRÄNKISCH, fresh juicy MERLOT, v.gd SYRAH Res.

Oltenia Up-and-coming region in overlooked sw: 7Arts, Catleya, CORCOVA, CRAMA OPRIȘOR, Domeniul Coroanei Segarcea, Mosia Galicia Mare, Vinarte (two cellars: Starmina, Bolovanu).

Oprișor, Crama Mun ★★→★★★ Consistent German-owned winery. La Cetate range, v.gd Crama Oprișor CAB SAUV, Jiana Rosé, Rusalca Alba. Top: ***Smerenie*** (r).

Petro Vaselo Ban ★★ Organic vyd in BANAT; fizz focus from Charmat Bendis to serious Kotys; fruity basics, then Melgris, Otarnița, Ovas. Flagship PV range gd.

Prince Știrbey Mun ★★★→★★★★ Pioneering top-quality DRĂGĂȘANI estate (2004), mainly regional grapes. Vibrant dry whites: Crâmpoșie Selecționată, FETEASCĂ REGALĂ, TĂMÂIOASĂ. Impressive local reds (Negru de Drăgășani, Novac), fine fizz.

Recaș, Cramele Ban ★★→★★★ Large, consistent and v. successful; part-British-owned, with long-standing Australian and Spanish winemakers. Leading both export and home market. Multiple labels, incl entry-point Calusari, Paparuda, Schwaben Wein, Wildflower. Mid-range: Implicit, Regno Recaș, Selene, Sole, Solo Quinta. Excellent La Stejari, flagship ***Cuvée Uberland*** (r).

SERVE Mun ★★★★ Romania's 1st private winery, founded by late Count Guy de Poix. Wife and daughter continue vision: v.gd Terra Romana (FETEASCĂ NEAGRĂ). Also Cuvée Clemence (w), Cuvée Sissi rosé. Icons: ***Guy de Poix Fetească Neagră***, standard-setting ***Cuvée Charlotte***.

Tohani Mun ★★ Large winery with S African winemaker; bright fruity Siel label. Initiator of Valahorum project: serious, powerful Apogeum old-vine FETEASCĂ NEAGRĂ, also Mierla Alba, Paolo Mennini.

Transylvania Cool mtn plateau encircled by Carpathians, great wildlife, lots of bears. Crisp whites, lighter, elegant reds. Worth trying (without own entry): Jelna (Navicella r), La Salina (Issa label for gd RIES, PINOT N, SAUV BL), Lechburg.

Villa Vinèa Trnsyl ★★ Stylish wines from cool hilly vyd nr Târnave. Top: Diamant, GEWURZ, FETEASCĂ REGALĂ, RUBIN.

Vintruvian ★→★★★ Multi-winery group, vyds in several regions. DEMATEI (DEALU MARE), CAII DE LA LETEA and Histria (DOBROGEA), Olterra (DRĂGĂȘANI).

Vișinescu, Aurelia Mun ★★ Female-led DEALU MARE estate, Artisan label for local grapes. Top: Anima (3 *Fete Negre*, selected FETEASCĂ NEAGRĂ), flagship Signature.

SERBIA

A progressive wine country, fast catching up on its neighbours, with 20,000 hectares and 500+ wineries. Grapes mix international and revived locals: white Bagrina, Grašac, Morava and red Probus, Prokupac.

Wines from Negotin were famously rich and thick enough to be carried in a cloth.

Aleksandrović ★★→★★★ Pioneering family estate. Top: ***Rodoslov***, Vozd, new ***Aberdar*** CHARD. Also v.gd: Trijumf (w/sp), Prokupac, Regent.

Aleksić ★★ Run by three sisters. Benchmark Tamjanika Žuti Cvet; v.gd Amanet VRANAC, Biser (trad-method sp).

Bikicki ★★ Natural orange wines: Uncensored (TRAMINER), S/O (SAUV BL).

Budimir ★→★★ Grandpa B is legendary figure. Noted for aromatic Tamjanika, long-lived, old-vine Prokupac Boje Lila.

Čokot (aka Radovan) ★★→★★★ Highest winery/vyd in Župa. Prokupac specialist: easier-drinking Experiment, benchmark Radovan.

Deurić ★★ FRUŠKA GORA estate: try Aksiom, La Rem. Specialist in local Probus, Severna Morava. Fizz ***The*** from sparkling sister winery v.gd.

Djoković ★★ Family winery of famous tennis player and his uncle. Refined, precise wines: CHARD, SYRAH so far.

Doja ★★ Modern family winery in s, Prokupac (rescued old clones), flagship Breg.

Erdevik ★★ Serbia's oldest winery (1826), overlooks Danube. Reinvented as quality producer (2015). Controversial labels but v.gd wines: ***Geronimo Grašac***, Ominbus Lector CHARD; plus bold, rich Stifler's Mom SYRAH, Grand Trianon (r blend).

Fruška Gora Dramatic hill and national park close to Danube, birthplace of Serbian wines in Roman times. Dynamic region with many exciting producers (without own entries): Belo Brdo, Chichateau, Đurđić, ***Frug***, Fruškogorski Vinogradi, Kiš, Kovačević, Milanović, Mrdjanin, Trivanović, ***Veritas Cuković***, Verkat, Vinum.

Ivanović ★★→★★★ Father "Gaga" (died in 2021) was key in revival of Prokupac. Now run by son and daughter; v.gd Prokupac, rosé, No. 1/2 (r) , new Grašac.

Matalj ★★→★★★ Pioneering winery in historic Negotin. Great vyd-selection CAB SAUV Kremen Kamen, Zemna; v.gd Bagrina, Bukovski Cuvée.

Matijašević ★★→★★★ Quality-focused; great Sovinoa SAUV BL; v.gd Belina (Smederevka), Čukundeda Prokupac, Tri Doline MERLOT.

Radovanović ★★ The 1st private winery of new era (1990); speciality CAB SAUV Res; gd RIES, oaky CHARD.

Šapat ★★→★★★ Small estate, top restaurant. Super-elegant: Atila label (CHARD, SAUV BL, CAB SAUV), plus pretty Bianca, Šu-Šu rosé, promising bold TEROLDEGO.

Šumadija Hilly volcanic region in geographical centre and start of quality revival. Worth trying (without own entry): Despotika, Jovac, Lastar, Tarpoš, Zmajevac.

TemeT ★★→★★★ Fizz to orange to terroir-select reds: Beli Kamen, Ergo, Tri Morave.

Vinčić ★★★ Tiny boutique winery, 50-yr-old vines on FRUŠKA GORA, fabulous Grašac.

Virtus ★→★★ In Mlava. Flagships MARSELAN, PINOT GR, Prokupac; v.gd Morava.

Vojvodina Autonomous province covering N Serbia, also PGI. Subregions: FRUŠKA

GORA Subotica, S Banat. Try (without own entry): Drasković, Oskar Maurer (natural wines, notable 1880-planted KADARKA), Rjnak, Tonković (Kadarka).

Zvonko Bogdan ★★→★★★ Dramatic estate close to Hungary. Elegant Eclater (sp); v.gd PINOT BL, ***Cuvée No. 1*** (r), ***Merlot***. Icon Campana Albus/Rubimus in top yrs.

SLOVAKIA

European varieties dominate, alongside international staples. Six wine regions: Central Slovakia (C Slo), Eastern Slovakia (E Slo), Lesser Carpathians (L Car), Nitra (Nit), Southern Slovakia (S Slo), Tokaj (Tok).

Belá, Ch S Slo ★★★ Fine Mosel-style RIES by joint Egon Müller (*see* Germany) and Miroslav Petrech venture; Alibernet (ALICANTE BOUSCHET X CAB SAUV), PINOT N.

Dudo, Miroslav L Car ★★★ CAB SAUV; unusual Devín (TRAMINER x Veltliner Rotweiss), Dunaj (MUSCAT Bouschet x Oporto x ST-LAURENT), Muscat Ottonel, popular Naše Cuvée blend (w).

Fedor Malík & Sons L Car ★★★ Family winery, mainly whites. Notable red crosses Hron (Abouriou x Castets, SW France), Rudava (Castets x Tenturier/ALEATICO/Puchljakovskij); blends Hrom (Thunder), Petit Sahral, Sahral N. Modragne fizz.

J&J Ostrožovič Tok ★★★ Pure dry FURMINT, Lipovina (HÁRSLEVELŰ), Yellow MUSCADELLE. Admirable Tok (*see* Hungary) styles from Samorodné (Szamorodni) to Tokajský výber (Aszú) 3–6 Putňový (*puttonyos*). Esencia (Eszencia) yr 2000.

Karpatská Perla L Car ★★→★★★ Laco Šebo specializes in quaffable GRÜNER V (Ingle, Noviny), zesty RIES (single-vyds Kramáre, Suchý Vrch).

Magula L Car ★★★ Family facility with bio principles: GRÜNER V, WELSCHRIESLING. Exquisite Frankovka (BLAUFRÄNKISCH) grown on loess in single-vyd Rosenberg.

Movino C Slo ★★→★★★ Progressive ecological winery; 300 ha in Veľký Krtíš (C Slo). Flagship Sekt Brut Zero St-Laurent Rosé.

Muráni Víno Čajkov Nit ★★→★★★ Doctor Jaromír M est 1993, 15 ha volcanic soils.

Pivnica Brhlovce Nit ★★→★★★ Artisanal production, volcanic wines, troglodyte dwellings, est 2011 by photographer Ján Záborský. Try youthful Pesecká Leánka (FETEASCĂ REGALĂ) Happiness: fruit and hardy earthiness.

Pivnica Orechová E Slo ★★→★★★ Pavol Michálek revitalized former breeding station's vyds with 150 cultivars on volcanic slopes of Vihorlat, overlooking Ukraine. Best site: Hajoš (WELSCHRIESLING, BLAUFRÄNKISCH, top Noble RIES). Also specialities Hrozienko, Bobuľa, Icewine.

SLOVENIA

Not many countries/regions have the terroir and climate to produce wines that can live for a century, but Slovenia is one – shown in rare archive wines, notably Furmint/Šipon; even "lowly" Pinot Bl can live for 50 years here. Add to this a beautiful, forested, hilly landscape, great food and some of Central Europe's best wines, increasingly with a focus on vineyard expressions. Lots of reasons to explore.

Slovenian food festivals: Salt Makers', Cabbage, Chestnut Sunday, Bean Day.

Albiana Pos ★★ Lovely family vyds in DOLENJSKA: try fizz, esp Brut rosé, Brut Natur. Also gd Alto range (LAŠKI RIZLING, Parcele).

Batič Prim ★★ VIPAVA estate; bio; three ranges – Classic, Selekcija, Angel for top selections. Try Marlon for pioneering blend of 20 fungus-resistant grapes.

Bjana Prim ★★★→★★★★ One of country's v. best trad-method PENINA producers in BRDA: Cuvée Prestige Extra Brut. Also v.gd: Blanc de Noirs/Blancs, Rosé Brut.

Brda Prim Top-quality region of hilly terraced vyds. Worth trying (without own entry): Benedetič, Blažič, Bužinel, Dobuje, Domačija Bizjak, Emeran Reya

Organic Winery, Iaquin, Klinec, Kristančič, Medot, Moro, Mulit, Nebó, Ronk, Schumacher Wines, Zalatel, Zanut.

Burja Prim ★★★→★★★★ VIPAVA estate; bio. Overture, Petite Burja (local w). Also v.gd: Burja Bela, Burja N (PINOT N), Burja Reddo; excellent vyd selections in top yrs.

Dolenjska & Bizeljsko Sremič Pos Improving region, moving on from trad sharp red Cviček. Try (without own entry): Dular, Kobal, Jelenič, Martinčič, Mihelin, Pinterič. Local Žametovka/Žametna Crnina proving great for fizz.

Dolfo Prim ★★→★★★ Family winery in BRDA: v.gd Spirito PENINA, consistent fresh, mineral REBULA. Serious Gredič, Res labels.

Dveri-Pax Pod ★★→★★★ Historic Benedictine-owned estate nr Maribor. Bright precise whites; v.gd old-vine selections, esp FURMINT Ilovci, SAUV BL Vajgen, plus age-worthy BLAUFRÄNKISCH, excellent PENINA.

Erzetič Prim ★★ Family winery, organic. Superb Orbis range, aged in five woods.

Ferdinand Prim ★★★→★★★★ Hilltop estate. Superb cross-border ***Sinefinis*** (sp, with Italian Gradis'ciutta), excellent ***Epoca*** (r/w), impressive long-skin-contact Brutus.

Frelih Pos ★★ Mother/daughter team making v.gd SILVANER, MODRA FRANKINJA, PENINA; modern interpretation of trad Cviček.

Frešer Pod ★★ Organic, 7th generation: PINOT N, Markus RIES, LAŠKI RIZLING.

Gašper Prim ★★★ Range by Gašper Čarman with KLET BRDA, v.gd and great value. Try MALVAZIJA, REBULA Selekcija; Bonita, excellent CAB FR, fruity Palamida.

Gross, Vino Pod ★★ Low-intervention terroir wines, steep terraces. Try Colles, Gorca, Iglič, Korže, Maribor Blanc. PENINA FURMINT in some yrs.

Guerila Prim ★★ Pioneering bio estate in VIPAVA: v.gd MALVASIA, Pinela, Zelen; BARBERA, CAB FR; Retro blends.

Herga Pod ★★ Former Kupljen estate reinvented by leading winemaker Mitja H: gd PINOT GR, SAUV BL, MODRA FRANKINJA.

Hiša Joannes Protner Pod ★★ Natura (w), bio. Also gd: RIES, CHARD, PENINA, PINOT N.

Istenič Pos ★★ Top fizz: ***Cuvée Natura***, Gourmet Rosé, Passion, Prestige Extra Brut.

Istria (Slovenska Istra) Slovenian part of the peninsula; mostly MALVAZIJA, REFOŠK. Best: Bordon, Brič, Korenika & Moškon (bio), MonteMoro, Pucer z Vrha, Rodica (organic), SANTOMAS, Steras (Epulon, Saurin Malvazija), VINAKOPER, Zaro.

Jakončič Prim ★★★ Long-est BRDA estate: v.gd Carolina range, Mosaic (sp).

Jermann Prim Silvio J (of Jermann Italy fame) has invested in personal project in BRDA; possibly Slovenia's highest vyd being planted. Watch.

Kabaj Prim ★★★ French-led BRDA estate; complex skin-contact whites, bold reds.

Klet Brda Prim ★★→★★★ Slovenia's largest co-op continues to set quality, environmental standards. Fresh Quercus range v.gd, unoaked Krasno. Bagueri vyd selections excellent, esp REBULA. Impressive De Baguer range incl superb flagship A+ (r/w), single-vyd MERLOT, Rebula. Produces v.gd Schumacher wines.

Klet Krško Pos ★→★★ Reinvented co-op winery. Best: Turn Premium range, older vines (MODRA FRANKINJA, Classic Brut).

Kobal Pod ★★ Low-intervention boutique family winery in Halože. Try: pét-nat, FURMINT, SAUV BL, skin-contact PINOT GR, classic BLAUFRANKISCH.

Kozinc Pos ★★ Improving, thoughtful family estate: v.gd sparklers Nord, Zara, Blanc de Noirs; Selekcija still wines.

Kras Prim Most noted for TERAN PDO made from REFOŠK, also gd MALVASIA, Vitovska. Try Čotar, Colja, Marko Fon, Štoka, Vinakras.

Kristančič Prim ★★ Family estate in BRDA: Cristatus PENINA, excellent Pavó.

Marjan Simčič, Dom Prim ★★★★ Benchmark classic varietal range, v.gd cru selection from older vines, selected plots. Superb single-vyd old-vine Opoka range (wonderful CHARD, Sauv Vert, MERLOT, PINOT N Breg). Superb Numerals Unico M is red flagship; Leonardo (sw) consistently glorious.

Marof Pod ★★→★★★ No-compromise estate. Appealing Goričko range. Grand

Rocking Modra

MODRA FRANKINJA, aka BLAUFRÄNKISCH, may have originated in today's E Slovenia, in Štajerska. Long overlooked, it's now gaining attention for its ability to showcase terroir and offer vibrant, drinkable, food-friendly wines that suit today's trends. Watch.

Vin for vyd selections, incl Bodonci SAUV BL, Kramarovči CHARD, Mačkovci Frankinja. Elegant SP MERLOT.

Movia Prim ★★★→★★★★ Charismatic Aleš Kristančič with son Lan; bio. Top: Veliko range, esp Belo (w), ***Puro Rosé (sp)***. Admired for long-macerated orange Lunar.

Pasji Rep Prim ★★ Next-generation bio VIPAVA estate: local Zelen, Moser bio range.

Penina Name for increasingly popular quality sparkling, Charmat or trad method.

Podravje Largest region, incl ŠTAJERSKA SLOVENJIA and Prekmurje. Best for vibrant, dry whites, esp FURMINT, Laški, SAUV BL; lighter reds.

Posavje Region in se covering DOLENJSKA, Bizeljsko-Sremič, Bela Krajina (Metlika, Prus, Šturm). Emphasis on PENINA, vibrant whites, elegant MODRA FRANKINJA. Izbor (sw) can be excellent: great acidity.

Primorje / Primorska Region in w covering Slovenian BRDA, ISTRIA, KRAS, VIPAVA.

Puklavec Family Wines Pod ★★→★★★ Large family winery, consistent value whites in Puklavec & Friends and Jeruzalem Ormož ranges; v.gd Ena Dva Tri labels, Seven Numbers label. Amazing archive wines (PINOT BL, ŠIPON).

Pullus (Ptujska Klet) Pod ★→★★ Reliable Pullus white label, Black label is step up; gd PENINA. Stunning archive FURMINT from 1927.

Radgonske Gorice Pod ★→★★ Historic sparkling cellar, top-selling Srebrna (silver) PENINA; gd classic-method Selection Brut, Brut Rosé.

Santomas Prim ★★→★★★ Benchmark REFOŠK, organic. Mezzo Forte (r), SYRAH v.gd.

Ščurek Prim ★★★ Family estate in BRDA, five sons; gd entry-point varietal wines. Superb ***Rebula Up***, attractive Stara Brajda (r/w), gd Zero Brut PENINA.

Simčič, Edi Prim ★★★★ Beautiful family winery and standard-setter in BRDA. Top vyd selections: Fojana, Kozana. Some of country's top reds: barrel-selection Kolos, Kozana MERLOT. Also v.gd: classic MALVAZIJA, Triton & Duet Lex, Tokata.

Slapšak, Dom Pos ★★★ Family estate setting new standards for PENINA, with Champenoise winemaker. Excellent Brut Rés, Natur, T.

Štajerska Slovenija Pod Major region in e. Districts: Haloze, Ljutomer-Ormož, Maribor. Vibrant whites, elegant reds, top sweet. Try Dom Ciringa, Doppler, Edvard XXI, Familija, Gaube, Horvat, Jaunik, Kotolenko, Meum, M-Simply Good Wines, Miro, Roka, Sanctum, Steyer, Statera, Valdhuber, Zlati Grič.

Šuklje ★★→★★★ Exemplary family estate; terroir focus in Bela Krajina: Lodoma, Lozice SAUV BL; excellent Vrbanjka MODRA FRANKINJA (new Vrbanjka Selection).

Sutor Prim ★★★→★★★★ Excellent small producer from VIPAVA. Lovely Sutor White, fine CHARD, elegant MERLOT-based red.

Tilia Prim ★★→★★★ Tagline is "House of Pinot". Refined sparkling to juicy estate to top age-worthy. Expressive Sunshine whites, appealing Rubido red blend.

Verus Pod ★★★ Fine, beautifully made, vibrant whites: v.gd FURMINT, PINOT GR, refined RIES, aromatic SAUV BL. Great value too.

Vicomte de Noüe-Marinič, Dom Prim ★★→★★★ Burgundy meets BRDA (J Leflaive connection): CHARD, REBULA, PINOT N, REFOSCO impress from historic cru vyds.

Vinakoper Prim ★★→★★★ Large ISTRIAN winery, local-grape focus. Try Capo d'Istria (new r 1072 label), Capris (notable orange), Rex Fuscus labels.

Vipava Prim Dramatic valley noted for Burja wind in PRIM. Try Benčina, Bizjak, Fedora, Ferjančič, JNK, Koglot, Lepa Vida, Lisjak, Marc, Miška, Mlečnik, Poljšak, Rouna, Saksida, Štokelj, Vina Krapež, Vina Ušaj Ussai, Wipach.

Vipava 1894 Prim ★→★★ Large winery in VIPAVA. Lanthieri range, Terase MALVAZIJA.

Greece

Suddenly, young Greeks see winemaking as a great life opportunity; the influx of talent is amazing (*see* box, p.254). Until recently, wine production was only for the serious, large players. Now it is perfectly possible to start low, with a few barrels and even no vineyards, just for the fun of the game. This is bringing a breath of fresh air to Greek wine in many ways. Styles are lighter, fresher, gluggable. Most wines are sold locally. Abbreviations: Aegean Islands (Aeg), Attica (Att), Central Greece (C Gr), Ionian Islands (Ion), Macedonia (Mac), Peloponnese (Pelop), Thessaloniki (Thess).

Aivalis Pelop ★★★ Tiny NEMEA producer, cult following, esp for "4" and Armakas reds. Full, new-oak style; 2nd generation moving to more nuanced style.

Akrathos Mac ★★→★★★ Rising star just off Mt Athos. Stellar ASSYRTIKO, released with some age, possibly most SANTORINI-like on mainland.

Alpha Estate Mac ★★★ Largest vyd owner in Greece, leading KTIMA in AMYNTEO, now in SANTORINI. Barba Yiannis XINOMAVRO from century-old vines is star for many.

Kydonitsa grape is the new Malagousia, which will be (another) next Assyrtiko.

Amynteo Mac (POP) Captivating XINOMAVRO (r/rosé/sp) from coolest POP, at 600m (1968ft)+ altitude. Many new players kicking in: KARAMOLEGOS, NICO LAZARIDI.

Anhydrous Aeg ★★★ Fine SANTORINI, change of hands recently. Icon is top offering.

Aoton Att ★★ Fine SAVATIANO, offbeat examples. Try bold, full RETSINA.

Argyros Aeg ★★★★ Excellent SANTORINI, largest vyd owner on island; fair prices. Top VINSANTOS (47); Evdemon, Gerontampelo, Monsignori (dreamy ASSYRTIKOS).

Avantis C Gr ★★★ Boutique Rhône ranger in Evia. Top: Agios Chronos (SYRAH/VIOGNIER), Collection Syrah. On rich side but ages beautifully.

Averoff Epir, Mac ★★→★★★ Historic Katogi a popular brand, delivering value. Rossiu di Munte CAB SAUV (firm, reserved) from 1000m (3281ft)+, one of highest vyds in Europe, while Inima range uses fruit across N Greece.

Biblia Chora Mac ★★★ Superb and superbly popular KTIMA. Ovilos (r/w) rivals Bx in style at third of the price. Sister wineries in Pelop (Dyo Ipsi), SANTORINI (Mikra Thira), GOUMENISSA (Mikro Ktima) and NAOUSSA (in the making).

Boutari ★→★★ Historic brand, new owners; volume and value; gd Greek varietals.

Carras, Dom Mac ★★ Historic estate at Halkidiki, recently changed hands, again; Ch Carras most famous label. Work in progress.

Cephalonia Ion Island famous for mineral ROBOLA (w); notable dry, tannic MAVRODAPHNE (r). Excellent growers, complex terroirs; for many next SANTORINI.

Dalamaras Mac ★★★→★★★★ Prodigious producer in NAOUSSA, at top of XINOMAVRO game. Rare, ethereal, dazzlingly complex reds to keep for decades.

Diamantakos Mac ★★→★★★ Solid producer in NAOUSSA: XINOMAVRO, modern yet lean; Preknadi (w) a curiosity grape that has to be tasted.

Dougos C Gr ★★★ Defining RAPSANI. Impeccable reds across price range, esp Old Vines, MAVROTRAGANO and rare Tourtoura.

Douloufakis Crete ★★★ VIDIANO pioneer, but knows LIATIKO as well. Several styles, creamy, expressive, from sparkling to amphora. Try spicy Liatiko Grande Res.

Economou, Ktima Crete ★★★★ One of great artisans of Greece; unicorn status. Recently more oxidative in style, not for faint-hearted. Labyrinthine aromatics.

Gaia Aeg, Pelop ★★★ Exquisite range from NEMEA, SANTORINI. ***Gaia Estate***: solid Nemea, flinty Ammonite Santorini. Lean (r/w) with exemplary tannin profile.

Gavalas Aeg ★★ Low-key producer of SANTORINI, as low-key as someone could be there. Wines reasonably priced, again within context. Solid without too much unneeded fanfare. Enalia is prestige cuvée, a Santorini monolith.

Gentilini Ion ★★★ Historic CEPHALONIA winery. ***Steely Robola***, esp R24, fuller than most. Benchmark dry MAVRODAPHNE Eclipse (r) is v. precise, tannic, imposing.

Gerovassiliou, Ktima Mac ★★★★ Greek wine legend. Practically created MALAGOUSIA genre (smooth, peachy). Lavish Museum (r/w) too gd to spit. BIBLIA CHORA link.

Goumenissa Mac ★★→★★★ (POP) Excellent XINOMAVRO/Negoska (r), a bastion of naturalistas. Try Chatzyvaritis, Ligas, Mikro KTIMA, TATSIS (full-on natural).

Hatzidakis Aeg ★★★ Legend of SANTORINI; 2nd generation now in charge. Louros, Nyhteri, Rambelia, Skytali all impeccable, purer and more precise than ever.

Karamolegos Aeg ★★★ SANTORINI winery, excellent restaurant. Rare Louroi, Pappas, Pyritis: complex, broad-shouldered. Arktos is new venture in AMYNTEO.

Karanika Mac ★★★ Best sparklings in Greece; mainly ASSYRTIKO/XINOMAVRO. Must-buy razor-sharp Cuvée Prestige and Extra Cuvée de Res.

Karydas, Ktima Mac ★★★ Tiny vyd in NAOUSSA, crafting uplifting, light-handed, herbaceous, age-worthy XINOMAVRO. Hidden jewel, crazy value.

Katsaros, Ktima Thess ★★★ Tiny winery on Mt Olympus. KTIMA (r) nods at Bx, ages well. Buttery Stella CHARD is California-like, Valos XINOMAVRO like soft NAOUSSA.

Kechris ★★→★★★ ASSYRTIKO-based The Tear of the Pine, possibly ***world's best Retsina***: full of zing, just a note of pine perfume. Fantastic wine, no kidding.

Kir-Yianni Mac ★★→★★★ NAOUSSA and AMYNTEO originally, now owns SIGALAS in SANTORINI. Huge portfolio, wide range of styles, all juicy, fruit-first.

Kostaki Aeg ★★ Young prodigy Evmorfia K, with Lorenz Immerfall, combine SAMOS MUSCAT and Bavarian approach. Redefining dry whites of Samos.

Ktima "Estate" in Greek; equivalent of Weingut or bodega. Greek producers (and sommeliers around the world) should be using it more often.

Lafazanis Pelop ★★ Large but always reliable. Fresh whites, juicy reds, v.gd value.

Lazaridi, Costa Att, Mac ★★★ KTIMA in Drama and Att. Top: Cava Amethystos CAB FR. After decades of powerful, oaky reds, moving on to less oak and more finesse. Plantings in high Drama promising: try minty MALAGOUSIA.

Lazaridi, Nico Mac ★→★★★ Vast range, v.gd value. Magiko Vouno (r), Bx lookalike.

Lyrarakis Crete ★★★ Extraordinary ***single-vyd versions***; rare Dafni, Melissaki, Plyto. Texture and detail, not flavour acrobatics. Reds light in structure, full-on flavour.

Malvasia Four POPS recreating medieval "Malmsey". Not necessarily MALVASIA, mostly local varieties. POPs are Monemvassia-M in Peloponnese, M of Paros and M Chandakas-Candia, M of Sitia (from Crete). Quite rare.

Manoussakis Crete ★★★ Initially Rhône-inspired (top ROUSSANNE), now focusing on Greek varieties: ASSYRTIKO, MUSCAT of Spinas, VIDIANO, Romeiko (r).

Mantinia Pelop (POP) High-altitude, cool mtn plateau. Almost Germanic whites and, increasingly, Blanc de Gr, from ***Moschofilero***. Excellent fizz next big thing.

Mercouri Pelop ★★ Greece's most beautiful, must-visit KTIMA on W coast. MAVRODAPHNE/REFOSCO, full of herbaceous depth.

12% alc? No problem

The rest of the world might be agonizing over rising alc levels (*see* p.356), but in Greece there's no problem. Greek producers don't have to jump through hoops to reduce alc, because it's already moderate. MOSCHOFILERO, RODITIS, SAVATIANO rarely exceed 12% abv, and the vast majority of indigenous black varieties are fully mature in tannin and flavour at 13.5% or below, despite changing climatic conditions. Only a few specific appellations and/or grapes, most obviously ASSYRTIKO from SANTORINI, regularly go higher.

Young, gifted and Greek

Look out for new, young, experimental: **Abraham Vyds** funky (Mac), **F by Foivos Papastratis** clean (C Gr), **Knack Project** properly knacky (Att), **Mahlin** extracted (Crete), **Manalis** lifted (Aeg), **Milia Riza** Champagne-like (Pelop), **Moropoulos** aromatic bazaar (Pelop), **Myrsini** structured (Paros), **Orfanos** edgy yet correct (Pelop), **Ousyra** powerful (Aeg), **Sant' Or** naturally delicious (Pelop), **Sarris** elegance (CEPHALONIA), **Tsikrikonis** terroir infatuation (Mac), **Zin Ideos** all about purity (Mac).

Mitravelas Pelop ★★→★★★ Producer in NEMEA, making bold reds. If you can have a bottle of Old Vines, why bother with most Super Tuscans?

Monemvassia Winery – Tsimbidi Pelop ★★→★★★ Only producer of POP MALVASIA-Monemvassia (sw). Godfather of Kydonitsa: soft, textured, quince-like whites.

Mylonas Att ★★ Young Stamatis M stubbornly crafts fine SAVATIANO, a grape bad-mouthed by many. A Hunter-SEM lookalike.

Naoussa Mac ★★★→★★★★ (POP) Breathtaking XINOMAVRO: spices, herbs, sun-dried tomato. Best on par in quality, style (not price) with Barolo: DALAMARAS, KARYDAS, KIR-YIANNI, THIMIOPOULOS, many others. Age for 10 yrs++.

Nemea Pelop ★★→★★★ (POP) AGIORGITIKO reds. Try Driopi from TSELEPOS (French-inspired), AIVALIS (New World-style), GAIA (pristine), Ieropoulos (oak), MITRAVELAS (modern), PALYVOS (fruit-focused), PAPAÏOANNOU (classic), SKOURAS (polished). Nemea Lions is a new category: look for extract, ageing potential.

Oeno P ★★★★ New venture of Paris Sigalas, founder of KTIMA SIGALAS. Premier Cru prices, but Grand Cru quality. ASSYRTIKO at its elegant grandest.

Oenops Mac ★★ Top winemaker Nikos Karatzas, put KTIMA PAVLIDIS on map, then started quirky project, sourcing vyds. Refined, low intervention, ultra-focused.

Palyvos Pelop ★★→★★★ KTIMA in NEMEA making big-framed wines with AGIORGITIKO and French varieties, from SYRAH to VIOGNIER. Refreshing Kydonitsa.

Panagiotopoulos Pelop ★★ Reputable producer in Messinia. Specializing in CAB SAUV, v. trad, but ages for a decade or more.

Papagiannakos Att ★★→★★★ Original mouthpiece of SAVATIANO, Vassilis P shows dry-farmed old vines of Att can produce grace, vivacity. Solid fruit, broad texture.

Papaioannou Pelop ★★★ Legend of NEMEA. Top cuvées: Microclima, Palea Klimata (old vines), Terroir. Foursquare, trad reds that keep for ages.

Papargyriou Pelop ★★ Yiannis P refuses mainstream. Big, bold, beautiful wines. Family's Osteria Greca tavern, at winery, is a must-visit; but please take a taxi.

Parparousis Pelop ★★★ Historic producer; some of Greece's most complex, greatest sweet MUSCATS, MAVRODAPHNES. Also Apostagma Oinou Paleothen brandy.

Pavlidis Mac ★★★ KTIMA in Drama. Thema (w) ASSYRTIKO/SAUV BL is hugely popular. Emphasis range more extracted; try Assyrtiko, TEMPRANILLO.

Petrakopoulos Ion ★★★ Capitalizing on diversity of CEPHALONIA'S vyds, Petrakopoulos creates stony, edgy whites and leathery MAVRODAPHNE.

POP Greek equivalent of AOP. Many top wines deserve, but don't have.

Rapsani C Gr XINOMAVRO-based POP on Mt Olympus – the (dr) Nectar the gods feasted on. DOUGOS is leader. Softer than NAOUSSA.

Retsina New-wave Retsinas (GAIA, KECHRIS, natural-style Kamara, 1979 Wines) have freshness, character – impeccable food wine, great alternative to Fino Sherry. If you don't mind oak flavours, why not pine?

Rouvalis Pelop ★★ Original believer in Aigialia, nr Patras – promising area. Plenty of varieties, refined examples. Still, Asprolithi is firm RODITIS at its finest.

Samos Aeg ★★→★★★ (POP) Island famed for benchmark sweet MUSCAT BL. Main producer is co-op; fortified Anthemis and sun-dried Nectar are steals. New producers emerging: KOSTAKI, Nopera, producing mainly dry wines.

Santorini Aeg ★★★→★★★★ Dramatic, windy volcanic island with white (dr/sw) wines to match, from century-old gnarled vines. Luscious VINSANTO, salty, ***bone-dry Assyrtiko***. Even with prices rising given huge tourism/land-grab pressure, cheapest ★★★★ whites around, age 20 yrs. No mediocrity here.

Santo Wines Aeg ★★→★★★ Successful SANTORINI co-op. Kontarades fine, single-vyd, entry-level ASSYRTIKO is a wonderful introduction to the glories of appellation. Lovely veranda next to winery is the place to watch the sunset.

Sclavos Ion ★★★ Brilliant mind studying terroir of CEPHALONIA; bio. Master of MAVRODAPHNE: top Orgion ("orgies"), Sclavos ("slave"). Go figure...

Semeli C Gr, Pelop ★★ Vast range, gd value. Main focus on NEMEA (try rich Grand Res) and MANTINIA (esp perfumed Thea). Same owner as BOUTARIS.

Sigalas Aeg ★★★★ Original winery of Paris S, now in v. able hands of KIR-YIANNI. Kavalieros, Nychteri out of this world; marble-statue-like beauty in full range.

Silva Daskalaki Winery Crete ★★→★★★ Female winemaker based in Heraklion crafts bio LIATIKO, VIDIANO with great sensitivity, depth, richness.

Skouras Pelop ★★★ Ever-evolving KTIMA. Lean, wild-yeast Salto MOSCHOFILERO. Megas Oenos a fine-boned classic. Solera-aged Labyrinth (r), complex Peplo rosé.

Tatsis Mac ★★★ Natural-movement leader in GOUMENISSA. Yes, wines might be cloudy and wild, but also defined and delicious.

Tetramythos Pelop ★★★ From the amazing terroir of Aigialia, a pillar of the natural-wine community. Mavro Kalavritino (r) smells like the surrounding hills on a summer's day, RODITIS (w) crisp, complex.

Theopetra Thess ★★ Tsililis family makes top Tsipouros brandy, but do not miss the wines. Copybook expressions of varieties, full of fruit, dense structures.

Thimiopoulos Mac ★★★★ Superstar in NAOUSSA and RAPSANI (Terra Petra). XINOMAVRO at most delicious best. Single-vyd range is breathtaking, can shame Barolos, esp ultra-focused Kaiafas. Fruit-forward Alma range the big seller.

T-Oinos Aeg ★★★★ From Tinos island, what many consider Greece's finest ASSYRTIKO and MAVROTRAGANO, beyond bold and of epic proportions, with prices to match, esp Rare. Stéphane Derenoncourt (*see* France) a co-owner.

Tour Melas, La C Gr ★★★★ Top-drawer KTIMA in Achinos. Idylle rosé rules the market. Convincingly Médoc-like La Tour Melas and Palies Rizes both top, with eye-popping prices. Amazing B&B.

Troupis Pelop ★★ Redefining MOSCHOFILERO in numerous guises, incl rosé. Hoof & Lur is natural style, but old-style natural, not hipster.

Tselepos Pelop ★★★ Leader in MANTINIA, NEMEA (Driopi, try Res), SANTORINI (Canava Chrysou, try Nyhteri). Not dull; CAB SAUV, MERLOT, velvety masterpieces.

Vassaltis Aeg ★★★ Small establishment in SANTORINI. Quirky Plethora lives where Santorini and Amontillado meet.

Vinsanto Aeg ★★★★ Sun-dried, cask-aged luscious but highly acidic ASSYRTIKO and Aidani (SANTORINI), can age forever; v. low yields. DOA (Drink Oldest Available).

Volcanic Slopes (Pure) Aeg ★★★★ Single-wine winery, tiny, sister project to ARGYROS. Pure, v. fine, crystalline clarity, dazzling structure; v. rare. Keep 20 yrs.

Voyatzis, Ktima Mac ★★ Quiet-genius stuff here, ex-winemaker of BOUTARI. Spicy, herby Tsapournakos, thought to be a rare variety, turns out to be CAB FR.

Robola (Cephalonia) is the new Santorini Assyrtiko: lower alcohol, lower €.

Vriniotis C Gr ★★ At n tip of Evia, Konstantinos V specializes in Vradiano grape (rich, MOURVÈDRE-like). Wild Fermentation ASSYRTIKO is exotic but steely.

Wine Art (Techni Oinou) Mac ★★ Family venture in Drama; fresh, crisp Plano ASSYRTIKO, MALAGOUSIA. Juicy, stylish Techni Oinou entry-level range.

Zafeirakis Thess ★★★ Carrying the LIMNIONA flag with grace. Several versions, all rather burgundian in style. Try Terra Cotta for complexity, Prologue (sp) for lift.

Eastern Mediterranean, North Africa & Eastern Levant

EASTERN MEDITERRANEAN

For a wine-lover or a grower, there are few things more thrilling than finding a long-forgotten ancient indigenous grape variety. We can't yet tell what biblical wine tasted like, but ancient varieties are being rediscovered all the time: identified, preserved and then propagated. And as elsewhere, they may prove well adapted to a warming world.

CYPRUS

Wildfires hit in 2025 after two of the driest yrs on record. Several communities were actually saved by vyds – old, widely spaced bush vines acted as fire breaks. Luckily the vines largely survived too, and analysis shows no smoke taint in the young wines. Solving the water crisis will be a huge challenge for the future, and increased emphasis on drought-adapted local varieties will be part of that.

Cyprus has as many stray cats as people. Oldest pet cat burial: 9500 yrs old.

Aes Ambelis ★→★★ Nr Nicosia. Whites and rosé best: floral/spicy Morokanella, zesty Promara; gd now unfortified COMMANDARIA.

Argyrides Winery ★★→★★★ Stunning 5th-generation winery, one of few female winemaker-owners. Reference ***Maratheftiko***, v.gd VIOGNIER, MERLOT/CAB, MOURVÈDRE.

Commandaria Rich, sweet PDO; sun-dried XYNISTERI and/or MAVRO; mentioned by Hesiod in 800 BCE, may be oldest wine in continuous production. Switch to modern unfortified styles: tiny Evangelou, ***Kyperounda, Tsiakkas, Zambartas.*** More trad fortifieds: St Barnabas (KAMANTERENA), St John (KEO).

Constantinou ★→★★ Family winery. Best: dry reds (SHIRAZ).

Dafermou ★→★★ 30 ha at 600–1200m (1969–3937ft). Emphasis on local grapes: spicy Morokanella, sleek Giannoudi Selection.

Kamanterena (SODAP) ★ Best: Project X. Also trad COMMANDARIA St Barnabas.

K&K Vasilikon ★★ Family winery; consistent XYNISTERI (fresh varietal/single vyd), long-lived Methy (r), floral Vasilissa (w), gd Aeon Maratheftiko.

Kyperounda ★★→★★★ ***Petritis*** remains a benchmark for XYNISTERI; ageable too. Committed to research: next-level exciting Xynisteri Anatoli (East) vyd selection. Entry-level Andessitis (r), super-fruity Alma MARATHEFTIKO. Excellent own-vyd ***Epos*** (w, CHARD, r, CAB SAUV, SYRAH). Modern COMMANDARIA.

Makarounas ★★ Promising young organic winery with experimental approach. Try zesty Vasilissa, fresh Spourtiko, amphora Promara, juicy Yiannoudi.

Mallia Estate ★ Winery part of Keo group; noted for trad-style St John COMMANDARIA.

Tsiakkas ★★→★★★ Organic, v. high vyds, focus on local grapes. Highlights: (w) ***Promara***, XYNISTERI, elegant Exelixis; (r) v.gd Vamvakada (aka MARATHEFTIKO), fruity Porfyros, excellent ***Yiannoudi***, new red flagship Anagennisis blend of local varieties. Fantastic, fruity, modern COMMANDARIA.

Vlassides ★★→★★★ Family winery, quality pioneer. Now emphasis on local varieties, esp excellent Alátes XYNISTERI, ***Óroman*** based on Yiannoudi. Flagship classy Artion (r); entry point is fruit-driven Grifos range.

Vouni Panayia ★ Organic family winery at 1100m (3609ft). Limited batches of local grapes. Try Morokanella, Promara.

Zambartas ★★→★★★ Family winery, Australia-trained winemaker-owner. Try v.gd single-vyd range: Margelina (100-yr vines), XYNISTERI, fab Promara, juicy MARATHEFTIKO, top SHIRAZ/LEFKADA. Superb long-aged Melusine COMMANDARIA.

ISRAEL

Israel makes some rather surprising wines. The Judean Hills are limestone, and relatively cool; Upper Galilee and Golan Heights are also at high altitude; between them, these areas produce the best wines. But there is groundbreaking work in the Negev, where Israel is making the desert bloom with vyds.

5000-year-old Canaanite wine press discovered in Megiddo, Jezreel V.

1848 ★→★★★ ***Orient (r)***, elegant blends (w). Juicy SYRAH, v.gd Argaman, CAB FR.
Abaya ★★ Natural *terroiriste*. Complex to value CARIGNANS; funky COLOMBARD.
Adir ★★→★★★ Entry level, great value: v.gd SHIRAZ, silky Plato.
Agur ★★★ Edgy, well crafted: tone, texture. Entry-level, multi-variety blends. New-style rosé, whites particularly gd. Special Res complex, highly drinkable.
Barkan ★→★★ Giant owned by largest brewery. Beta of interest.
Carmel ★→★★ Historic winery, est by Rothschild (*see* Bordeaux). New premises at Alon Tavor. Big-selling brands Selected, Private Collection.
Castel, Dom du ★★★★ Great consistency at highest level. Pioneer of Judean Hills. Prestige Grand Vin outstanding, ageworthy; C Blanc (CHARD) ages beautifully; Petit Castel underrated; value La Vie (r/w) improving.
Clos de Gat ★★→★★★ Powerful SYRAH, MERLOT. Vibrant, fresh ***Grenache/Syrah***.
Cremisan ★→★★ Palestinian winery. Monastery est 1885, pioneer of local varieties. Other Palestinian wines: **Kassis**, gd vigneron; **Philokalia**, natural, artisan.
Dalton ★→★★★ Fresh ***Majestic Carignan***, mineral CHENIN BL, gd Each SHIRAZ.
Feldstein ★★★ Complex CAB SAUV, Gilgamesh, ***Shemesh*** (r), gd indigenous Dabouki.
Flam ★★★→★★★★ Flam bros offer style, quality. Beautiful Judean Hills vyd on ancient terraces. Elegant, age-worthy Bx blend ***Noble***, classy CAB SAUV. Fruit-forward SYRAH. Classico great value. Fragrant white. New partnership in Bx.
Galil Mountain ★→★★★ Upper Galilee. Bold PETIT VERDOT; gd prestige Yiron.
Golan, Ch ★★→★★★ Geshem v.gd Med blends. Naveh, kosher label.
Gva'ot ★★★ Fruity Bittuni. Complex CAB SAUV/FR, prestige Masada top-notch.
Jascala ★→★★ Israeli-Arab bros. Mt Meron foothills; gd age-worthy MERLOT.
Jezreel Valley ★→★★★ Excellent ***Argaman***, CARIGNAN. Value Alfa. Flagship Icon.
Lahat ★★★ Rhône ranger. Focus on SYRAH, ROUSSANNE. Makes white like red and vice versa. Uses amphorae. Charming ***GSM***; ageable white. New rosé.
Lewinsohn ★★★ Owner MW, creative winemaker. Garage de Papa: elegant CHARD, fragrant rosé, sensual SYRAH blend. Whole Cluster ***Petite Sirah***, fruit-forward.
Libero One to watch. Cherry-berry GRENACHE from Mt Hermon vyd.
Margalit ★★→★★★ Best with Bx varieties. White from CHARD plus local variety.
Mia Luce ★★★ *Garagiste*. Vivid SYRAH, floral ***Marselan***, fragrant Blanc, Noir.
Mika ★★ Steely white blend; crunchy GRENACHE; prestige Outback.
Odem Mountain ★→★★ High elevation in N Golan; gd Volcanic CHARD, CAB SAUV.
Pelter ★★ Popular brand. Light, fragrant SAUV BL. Matar, kosher wine.
Pinto ★→★★ Desert wines. Lean CHARD, CHENIN BL; spicy SHIRAZ.
Psagot ★→★★★ Fast-growing. Peak, succulent Med blend; New Peak (w).
Ramat Negev ★→★★★ Desert pioneer. Bold MALBEC, PETIT VERDOT; flagship Exodus.
Razi'el ★★★ Ben Zaken family (CASTEL). Refined, focused Med blend. Handcrafted trad fizz. Minerally, steely ***Roussanne/Viognier***.
Recanati ★→★★★ Complex CARIGNAN; fragrant COLOMBARD; gd Odem vyd.
Sea Horse ★★→★★★ Idiosyncratic: complex Antoine, age-worthy Elul, alluring Oz.
Shiloh ★★→★★★ Robust CAB S, PETIT VERDOT. Ira v. drinkable, prestige Mosaic.

Shvo ★★★ Non-interventionist, true vigneron. Rare Gershon SAUV BL, super-rustic chewy red, fresh BARBERA, characterful rosé.

Sphera ★★★★ Intense cool-climate White Concept varietals: Unicorn RIES; well-defined, crisp First Page blend. Complex, rare ***White Signature*** (SEM), ageable. Delicate, rare trad-method fizz.

Tabor ★→★★ New Artisanal brand: CHENIN BL, ROUSSANNE, SAUV BL.

Tel ★★→★★★ N Golan vigneron. Best? RIES, GRENACHE, CAB FR.

Teperberg ★→★★ CHENIN BL, SEM v.gd; new DOLCETTO, BARBERA; fruity GSM.

Tulip ★★ Works with adults with special needs; gd SYRAH, SAUV BL; Med-style Maia.

Tura ★→★★ Central Mtns. Full-flavoured Mountain Peak, fleshy MERLOT.

Tzora ★★★★ MW winemaker. Terroir-led, precision winemaking. Beautiful high-altitude Shoresh vyd. Intensity, elegance. Fine, mineral Shoresh Bl; ***Judean Hills (r/w)*** top value. Graceful Misty Hills, tantalizing aroma. New investment in Bx.

UnderDog ★★ Rising star; crisp VERDELHO, chewy Raven (r), quaffable Snunit.

Vitkin ★★★ ABC icebreaker. Quality ***Carignan***, PETITE SIRAH pioneer. Floral PINOT N. Crunchy ***Grenache***, new white GRENACHE. Value entry-level.

Vortman ★★ Passionate vigneron; N Coastal; v.gd COLOMBARD, CARIGNAN.

Yarden – Golan Heights Winery ★★→★★★★ Cutting-edge viticulture, leader in sustainability. Consistency over decades. King of CAB SAUV (all price points). Classic ***sparkling***, delicious HeightsWine.

Yatir ★★★→★★★★ Desert winery, high-elevation forest vyds. Beguiling ***Med blend***, velvet prestige Yatir Forest (r), value Mt Amasa, less-expensive Darom.

LEBANON

Historic diversity is mirrored in winemaking here. International blends and historic Rhone varieties (CARIGNAN, CINSAULT, GRENACHE) now share the spotlight. Innovative winemakers make low-intervention/extended-skin-contact wines often with native Asmi N, Aswad Karesh, Jouzani, Marini, Meksassi, Merwah, Obeideh planted at v. high altitudes. Whites (CHARD, SAUV BL, VIOGNIER) gaining popularity alongside darker, crunchier food-friendly rosés.

Climate change: yields in parts of Bekaa Valley down as much as 60% in 2025.

Coteaux du Liban ★★ Solid, reliable; young, dynamic winemaking couple. RHÔNE blend (r); varietal SAUV BL, Obeideh, VIOGNIER, CINSAULT. Ayn range for UK.

Couvent Rouge ★★★ Remote, high-altitude N Bekaa winery. Easy-drinking (r/w/rosé); posher oaked VIOGNIER, SYRAH, pét-nats (w/rosé), popular in export.

Heritage, Ch Hefty Family Res CAB SAUV/SYRAH; Plaisir du Vin; nine-variety, Cinsault-led blend Nine; SAUV BL, VIOGNIER, MUSCAT Blanc de Blancs. Part of Touma arak dynasty. Charismatic Dargham Touma known locally as Dr D.

Ixsir ★★→★★★ High vyds across Lebanon; stony SYRAH-based blends, floral whites, prestige El (r). Altitudes range, Grande Res Rosé excellent. Cemented Batroun's status as Lebanon's 2nd region. Spanish ex-rugby international winemaker.

Karam Wines ★★★ Family-run; S Lebanon's 1st winery. Extensive range: Meksassi (w), ALBARIÑO; SEM/SAUV BL/VIOGNIER Cloud 9 (owner is ex-pilot), bestseller. Value Maison (r), TOURIGA N; CAB/SYRAH/MERLOT St John more polished.

Kefraya, Ch ★★→★★★★ Innovative; long-serving French winemaker. Les Exceptions varietals; Aswad Karesh (r), SAPERAVI in amphorae; complex ***Comte de M***; oaky Comtesse de M, famous Blanc de Blancs, quaffable Les Breteches (r/w/rosé).

Ksara, Ch ★★★→★★★★ Jesuits est 1857; father of modern Lebanese wine. Icons: Ch and Res du Couvent. More innovative now: old-vine CARIGNAN, Merwah. Consistent, v.gd value. Blanc de Blancs, outstanding CHARD. Sunset "adult" rosé. Superb Cuveé du Printemps (r). Back catalogue to rival CH MUSAR.

Marsyas, Ch ★★★ Syrian Saadeh bros. Flagship CAB/SYRAH, thrilling CHARD/SAUV BL.

Diffusion range B-Qa de Marsyas. Satyr (no-oak Cab, Sauv Bl). Owns complex ★★★ Dom Bargylus, Syria, miracle wines, age-worthy (Bargylus w, Jabal r).

Massaya ★★ Terraces de Baalbeck: refined GSM. Entry-level Les Colombiers v.gd value. Cap Est (r) from E Bekaa vyds. Punchy rosé, elegant white from high-altitude Mt Lebanon. Ramzi Ghosn with high-profile French partners.

Trading Phoenicians introduced wine to the then known world, 1st millennium BCE.

Mersel Perched at altitude in N Lebanon. Natural, pét-nat; reviving ancient Jouzani, Marini; Merwah, Obeideh, often in amphorae; CINSAULT. Winery also incubator for micro-producers: Dar Richi, Heya, Love Letter. Destined for cult status.

Musar, Ch ★★★→★★★★ **02 03 05'** 10 11 12 13 14 15 16 17 18 ***Unique recognizable style.*** Best after 15–20 yrs in bottle. Flagship red still most famous, but trippy Obeideh/Merwah (w) arguably more interesting; ages indefinitely. Second label: Hochar (r) now higher-profile. Musar Jeune, softer, easy-drinking. Winemaker Tarek Sakr, who worked with the late Serge Hochar, ensures house style endures.

Najm, Dom Batroun winery/goat farm run by Hiba N; 6000 bottles of unorthodox, neo-Musar field-blend (GRENACHE/MOURVÈDRE/CAB SAUV); v. little white, rosé.

Oumsiyat, Ch Family-run, Mt Lebanon; no-nonsense, easy-drinking, value Bx/Rhône blends, varietals; also ASSYRTIKO, CINSAULT, Obeidy [sic].

St Thomas, Ch ★→★★★ Now helmed by French-trained winemaker and scion, Joe Touma. Les Gourmets range: white, red (aromatic CINSAULT), rosé. Textured Obaidy [sic]; muscular, high-altitude PINOT N. Vintage Ch wines ageing well.

Sept ★★★ Pioneer *garagiste*, former rugby league player from Batroun. Skin-contact Merwah, Obeideh; min-contact varietals VIOGNIER, GRENACHE, haunting SYRAH.

Tourelles, Dom des ★★→★★★★ Ebullient French-trained Faouzi Issa. Blockbuster SYRAH, gd Marquis des Beys (r/w). Top old-vine CARIGNAN, CINSAULT, Obeideh/Merwah, skin-contact Merwah; top classic range (r/w/rosé). Historic arak Brun.

Wardy, Dom ★★ Varietal pioneer: SAUV BL, VIOGNIER, CINSAULT, Obeideh. Also trad French blends. J-B Soula consults. Ex-orchestra conductor Khalil W winemaker.

TÜRKIYE

The main indigenous varieties are finally familiar, but there is now a whole swathe of new regional varieties being developed by enterprising wineries. Much potential and promise, but old difficulties remain.

Buzbag ★ Main brand since 40s; rustic ÖKÜZGÖZÜ/BOĞAZKERE (Kayra). Improved.

Chamlija ★★★ Aromatic Papaskarasi, expressive CABS SAUV/FR, gd PINOT N.

Doluca ★→★★ Three generations; Villa Doluca gd value, Sarafin noble varieties.

Kalpak ★★→★★★ Deep, rich, full-bodied Bx blends; min intervention.

Kavaklidere ★→★★★ Best: Cotes d'Avanos, ***Pendore***. Also v.gd: Harmonie, ÖKÜZGÖZÜ.

Kayra ★→★★ Plush ***Öküzgözü***, tannic BOĞAZKERE. Fresh NARINCE. Diageo-owned.

Kuzubag ★→★★ Enchanting ***Cal Karasi*** (light r, rosé); versatile NARINCE/CHARD.

Likya ★→★★ Revives lost varieties: vibrant Fersun, gd PINOT N.

Pasaeli ★→★★ Innovative champion of local varieties: cherry-berry Karasakiz.

Sevilen ★→★★ Large winery offering value: SAUV BL, SYRAH best.

Suvla ★→★★ Full-bodied Bx blend Sur; fruity SYRAH backed by oak.

Urla ★★ Big-spend winery. ***Nero d'Avola/Karasi***, concentrated, spicy.

Notable names in North Africa & Eastern Levant

Jordan Zumot (Saint George). **Morocco** Amal, ★★ Baccari (Première de Baccari), Castel Group, ★ Celliers de Meknès (Ch Roslane), La Ferme Rouge, ★→★★ Ouled Thaleb (***Tandem/Syrocco***), ★→★★ Val d'Argan (Orian r), Zouina (Epicuria, Volubila). **Syria** ★★★ ***Bargylus***. **Tunisia** Neferis.

Asia & Black Sea & Caucasus

ASIA

China Myriad wine-grape habitats; of 13 wine provinces, Ningxia, Shandong, Yunnan, Hebei and Xinjiang lead the way. Each is different: coastal (Shandong), foothills (Ningxia), Alpine (Yunnan), extreme (hot/dry – Xinjiang; cold, in ne – Heilongjian, Jilin, Liaoning). Gansu, Hebei, Inner Mongolia, Shanxi, and Shaanxi too. Most famous: CABS SAUV/FR and blends (Yunnan's Xiaoling and LVMH-owned Ao Yun; Lafite-owned Long Dai; Inner Mongolia's LeWei; Ningxia's Legacy Peak and Mulando); Cab Gernischt, now viewed as a Chinese grape (Changyu, Chateau Rongyuanmei, XIGE); MALBEC (Mountain Wave, XIGE); PINOT N (Lansai, Mountain Wave, Silver Heights); RIES (Kanaan, Mulando, Silk Road); SYRAH (Dameiyong, Fei Tswei); CHARD (Ao Yun, Jiabeilan, Mystic Island, Silver Heights), excellent trad-method sparklers (Devo). MARSELAN (GRENACHE x Cab Sauv cross) wines are world's best (Ch HuaHao, Fei Tswei, Longting, Silver Heights); PETIT MANSENG's dry and sweet (Ch Anuo, Ch Nine Peaks, Dom Franco-Chinois, Longting) rival France's SW; SAPERAVI and RKATSITELI thrive in desert-like Xinjiang (Puchang); WELSHRIESLING, mostly abandoned elsewhere, is a cash cow but also surprisingly gd (Li's, Mulando); remarkably gd AGLIANICO, BARBERA, SANGIOVESE (Fei Tswei, Silver Heights; Grace for Aglianico); noteworthy VIDAL Icewines from Heilongjian, Jilin, Liaonining where winters dip v. low; also in Yunnan (must try: Pabala). Chinese-developed hybrids (mostly with cold-resistant *Vitis amurensis*) are turning heads: Beichun (Puchang; also excellent dry and sweet MUSCAT hybrid Roudingxian wines), Beimei (Shengu).

China's most interesting wines: Petit Manseng, Marselan, Cabernet Gernischt.

India Small volumes of fresh whites (CHARD, CHENIN BL, SAUV BL) and rich reds (CAB SAUV, PINOT N, SYRAH) are mostly from Andhra Pradesh, Karnataka, Maharashtra states. Tourist-friendly wineries offer panoramic views and tastings. Largest, best is Sula Vyds in Nashik (Classic dry, late-harvest Chenin Bl, RIES; Dindori Res VIOGNIER; The Source GRENACHE Rosé). Also gd Charosa (TEMPRANILLO), Fratelli (Chenin Bl, M/S Rosé), Grover Zampa (Res: Cab Sauv, Syrah), Vallonne (India's 1st boutique winery, est 2009, also a hotel). For sparkling: Chandon, York.

Japan has grapes that grow nowhere else: Koshu, Muscat Bailey A, Kai Noir.

Japan From Alpine Hokkaido to hilly Yamanashi (most famous, historical area), regional expressions coming to fore. Cool-climate Hokkaido's crisp, fruity KERNER (Chitose Winery) and high-acid, gently bitter Yamasachi red (Tokachi Winery), excellent, ideal with Japan's cuisine. Similarly, Niigata Prefecture's Iwanohara Winery Muscat Bailey A (delicate, fruity red) matches well with soy-sauce glazes (think *yakitori*). Developed in 20s to survive cold, it's a v. popular Japanese grape. Vinifera plantings grown steadily since the 80s (Camel Farm's BLAUFRÄNKISCH), but nothing is more typical than KOSHU, vinifera Chinese hybrid offering delicately citrus, vibrant wines. Best unoaked: Aruga Branca, Ch Mars (orange), Dom Hide (air-dried orange), Haramo, Huggy Wine (sp), Kurambon, L'Orient, Lumiere, Manns Wines, Marquis (oldest winery), Morita Koshu Winery, Sanwa Shurui, Soryu and Suntory's single-vyd Tomi No Oka 21 23'. Further impulse to Japan's fledgling industry is given by foreign investors, like Burgundy's de Montille (*see* France) CHARD, PINOT N Hokkaido project.

BLACK SEA & CAUCASUS

Ukrainian wineries have shown remarkable resilience during the war: domestic situation is uncertain, but exports grow. The Caucasus countries, while clinging to their millennia-old wine heritage, are starting to diverge. Georgia is in search of micro-terroirs; Armenia sees the number of boutique wineries exploding. The wines – made with long skin macerations and vinified in amphorae – find international success among niche drinkers and millennials. Moldova delivers value-driven wines, with an emerging trend of small high-quality production. Some wine curiosities can be found in Uzbekistan and Kazakhstan.

Armenia Shares with Georgia the ancient trad of using amphorae, known here as *karas*. Signature Areni (r); others incl (w) Voskeat, (r) Akhtanak, Karmrahyut. Phylloxera-free vyds at high altitude up to 1800m (5906ft) are common. Vayots Dzor region has most prestige. Now 50+ wineries: try Armenia Wine and Hin Areni, or boutique ArmAs, Frunz, Keush (sp), Noa, Old Bridge, Tushpa, Van Ardi, Voskeni, Voskevaz, Yacoubian-Hobbs, v.gd Zorah. Brandy is also gd.

Georgia Proudly holds *qvevri* as its contribution to world winemaking. Buried into the ground, enormous clay vessels are used for skin-macerated fermentation and ageing (r/w). This has continued unbroken for 8000 yrs: new experiments involve temp control, different sizes and rosé. Ancient methods co-exist with modern production. Of 500 indigenous varieties, around 40 are in commercial use. Ubiquitous white RKATSITELI has prompted the phenomenon of orange/amber wines. Red star SAPERAVI is great in full-bodied, tannic, age-worthy wines. White Chinuri, Kisi, Mtsvane of note. Kakheti region is powerhouse of production. Large producers: Askaneli, Ch Mukhrani, GWS, Khareba, Tbilvino, Telavi Wine Cellar, Teliani V, Vazisubani Estate. Small and medium: Iago's Wine, Jakeli, Lagvinari, Marani, Papari V, Shumi Winery, Tsinandali Estate.

Moldova More vyds than S Africa: wine is central to economy. Backed by long history and fame in tsarist Russia, it now makes approachable wines with value at all price levels. International grapes dominate, but worth seeking local: (w) FETEASCĂS ALBĂ/REGALĂ, Viorica; (r) Codrinschii, FETEASCĂ NEAGRĂ, Rară Neagră. Try unusual red blend Negru de Purcari (CAB SAUV/SAPERAVI/Rară Neagră) and Icewine. Leading producers: Cricova (sp), Mileştii Mici, Purcari Winery, both with great limestone cellars. Also try Asconi, Castel Mimi, Ch Vartely, Et Cetera, Fautor, Gitana, Lion Gri, Radacini, Vinăria Bostavan, Vinăria din Vale.

Russia Due to import restrictions, Russian wine grows by value but not volume. With 100,000+ ha vyds, a quarter are less than 5 yrs old. Natural conditions best in sw by Black Sea and River Kuban. Harsh climate in Don V requires vines to be buried in winter. Reds are better than whites. Indigenous tannic Krasnostop has est itself as signature red grape. Most winemaking is about international grapes, esp CHARD, RIES, CAB SAUV, MERLOT, plus Georgian RKATSITELI. At the time of writing, Russia is under international sanctions.

Ukraine About 150 wineries operate despite war conditions, destroyed vyds and facilities. Stretching from the Black Sea to Carpathian Mtns and Kyiv, winemaking is concentrated in Odesa region, notably Bessarabia. International, Georgian grapes and hybrids are common, local Telti Kuruk (w) and Odesa Black (r) of interest. Russian-invaded Crimea accounts for premium wines, esp Oleg Repin, Uppa Winery. Try Beykush Winery, Big Wines (est during war), Bolgrad, Cotnar, Esse, Guliev Wines, Inkerman, ***Kolonist***, Stoic, Satera, Shabo, Veles, Villa Tinta. Fizz has important heritage: ArtWinery, Novy Svet, Odessavinprom, Zolotaya Balka. Historic fortified styles have niche too: Ch Chizay, Koktebel, Massandra, Solnechnaya Dolina.

United States

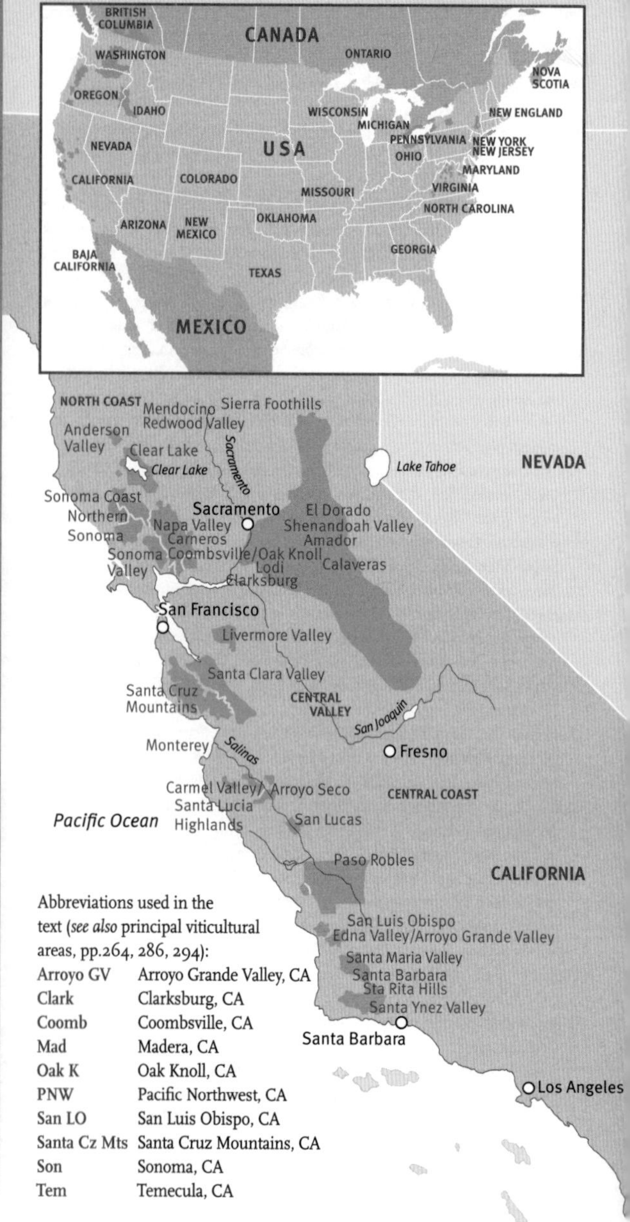

Abbreviations used in the text (*see also* principal viticultural areas, pp.264, 286, 294):

Arroyo GV	Arroyo Grande Valley, CA
Clark	Clarksburg, CA
Coomb	Coombsville, CA
Mad	Madera, CA
Oak K	Oak Knoll, CA
PNW	Pacific Northwest, CA
San LO	San Luis Obispo, CA
Santa Cz Mts	Santa Cruz Mountains, CA
Son	Sonoma, CA
Tem	Temecula, CA

The headwinds affecting wine around the world are felt in the US too – people are drinking less wine, and there is less demand. But winemakers are increasingly sophisticated and always inventive: in some parts of the country, hybrids are becoming fashionable and blends that would be unthinkable in Europe are tried, because – well, why not? There's a huge spread of approaches in the vineyard too: regenerative agriculture is being developed, sometimes tentatively, usually enthusiastically and often expensively – growers want healthier soil that will give greater resilience as the climate changes. What this adds up to is an ever-increasing variety of flavours and styles. Americans have a proper pride in what their home state produces; visitors can have a field day (or many field days) exploring and experimenting.

American Viticultural Areas

With no production rules or trad to protect, AVAs are only loosely comparable to appellations contrôlées. Administered by the US government's TTB, they are instead guides to location – and climate, soil, market – and are a wine-minded alternative to state or county labels. Whether a region within a state or a traits-based overlap such as high-toned Columbia Gorge shared by WA and OR, or NY, PA, OH's cool, water-tempered Lake Erie, there are 277 est AVAs – and a steady queue of applied and pending. Most (154) are in CA, which boasts a wealth of nested AVA subregions, some hyperfocused, like Napa V's Stags Leap District. While an AVA label indicates a min higher standard at the federal level (state and county labels mean min 75% provenance, AVA promises min 85%), some have stricter rules: OR famously demands 100% for state label, 95% for its AVAs. AVA approval standards are rigorous: petitions must show distinguishing features verifiable on US Geological Survey maps and how they affect viticulture inside vs outside the petitioned zone – whose proposed name must be one historically applied to the area. The TTB says AVAs allow "producers to better describe the origin of their wines and... consumers to better identify wines". Some even translate to higher prices.

Arizona (AZ)

Soils vary: Sonoita and Verde V limestone-based; Willcox volcanic-based. Iberian, Med, Bx varieties all do well; MALVASIA leads white. **Arizona Stronghold** ★★★ everyday Provisioner, top Arizona Stronghold. **Bodega Pierce** in Willcox AVA; v.gd. **Caduceus Cellars** ★★★ consistent quality leader, top Nagual del Sensei SAGRANTINO; rotating experimental series. Sibling MERKIN VYDS. **Callaghan Vyds** ★★★ excellent Iberian, Italian, Bx styles; awarded AGLIANICO, La Osa Blanco, Caitlin's PETIT VERDOT/CAB SAUV. **Ch Tumbleweed** ★★ old vyds; single-vyd selections, top Deep Sky Vyd MALBEC. **Cove Mesa Vyd** large range, awarded wines; excellent CHARD, MUSCAT, Deep Sky Vyd MOURVÈDRE; top Bonita Springs MALVASIA (w). **Dos Cabezas WineWorks** emphasis on blends; La Montaña (r), Meskeoli (w). **Javelina Leap Vyd & Winery** Cab Sauv, MERLOT, TEMPRANILLO, Malvasia. **Los Milics** S French, Iberian grapes. **Merkin Vyds** ★★★ Chupacabra range. **Page Springs Cellars** Rhône specialist, Mourvèdre, GRENACHE; Traminette (w). **Pillsbury Wine Company** ★★ owned by film-maker Sam Pillsbury; estate-grown, wild-yeast Rhône varieties; SHIRAZ-based Guns and Kisses (r). **Rune Wines** low-intervention, mainly S French varieties; graphic labels. **Sand-Reckoner** ★★ dry aromatic Malvasia, rich Tempranillo.

California (CA)

It has been an interesting year. The California wine business has endured dire reporting about the economic state of the wine industry, and much of it is fair, as small wineries will remind you of ad nauseam. Small wineries are definitely feeling the pain. At the time of writing, consumption may be bottoming out, trade wars are still pending, much is uncertain and foreign sales are a bust. A reckoning is happening. California wine-growing land is overvalued, and some grapes are going unharvested: there is a surplus of grapes, and vines are being pulled out in some parts of the state. Also, domestic consumption is waning, and disposable income in the US is decreasing as well. There is a new economic reality, and it largely mimics what has been happening in Europe for a while. Even major capital investors are slowing acquisitions. Some good producers, some of them multi-generational who just bang out affordable wines year after year, are doing pretty well. As for climate change, it is real overall, though the effects have been muted in California recently. There were no major fires again this year, again. Remarkably, the Pacific Ocean continues to be California's best friend. In fact, the 2025 growing season was tremendously cool, and CA winemakers are getting really good at making elegant wines in these cool vintages. For all the problems, California wines have never been better than they are right now, which only makes the competition that much more daunting for small producers who can only profit from wines in the $30 and up price range.

Principal viticultural areas

There are well over 100 AVAs in CA. Below are the key players.

Alexander Valley (Alex V) Son. Warm region in upper Son. Best known for gd Zin, Cab Sauv on hillsides.

Amador County (Am Co) Warm Sierra County with wealth of old-vine Zin; Rhône grapes also flourish.

Anderson Valley (And V) Mend. Pacific fog and winds follow Navarro River inland. Superb Pinot N, Chard, sparkling, v.gd Ries, Gewurz, some stellar Syrah.

Atlas Peak E Napa. Exceptional Cab Sauv, Merlot.

Calistoga (Cal) Warmer n end of Napa V. Red-wine territory, esp Cab Sauv.

Carneros (Car) Napa, Son. Cool AVA at n tip of SF Bay; gd Pinot N, Chard; Merlot, Syrah, Cab Sauv on warmer sites, v.gd sparkling.

Coombsville (Coomb) Napa. Cool region nr SF Bay; top Cab Sauv in Bx style.

Diamond Mountain Napa. High-elevation vines, outstanding Cab Sauv.

Dry Creek Valley (Dry CV) Son. Top Zin, gd Sauv Bl; gd hillside Cab Sauv, Zin.

Edna Valley (Edna V) San LO. Cool Pacific winds; v.gd Chard.

El Dorado County (El Dor Co) High-altitude inland area surrounding Placerville. Some real talent emerging with Rhône grapes, Zin, Cab and more.

Happy Canyon Warmer, off-shore area of Santa B hospitable to Bx varieties.

Howell Mountain Napa. Briary Napa Cab Sauv from steep, volcanic hillsides.

Livermore Valley (Liv V) Suburban, gravelly, warm region e of SF, gd potential.

Mendocino County (Mend) Large county n of Son County, incl warm Red V and cool And V.

Mendocino Ridge (Mend Rdg) Emerging region in Mend, dictated by elevation over 365m (1198ft). Cool, above fog, lean soils.

Monterey County (Mont) Big ranches in Salinas V: affordable Chard, Pinot N in cool, windy conditions. Carmel V bit warmer, Arroyo Seco moderate.

Mount Veeder Napa. High mtn vyds for gd Chard, Cab Sauv.

Napa Valley Cab Sauv, Merlot, Cab Fr. Look to sub-AVAs for meaningful terroir-based wines, and mtn areas for most complex, age-worthy.

Oakville (Oak) Napa. Prime Cab Sauv territory on gravelly bench.
Paso Robles (P Rob) San LO. Popular with visitors. Reds: Rhône, Bx varieties.
Pritchard Hill (P Hill) E Napa. Elevated, woodsy, prime terrritory for Cab Sauv.
Red Hills of Lake County (R Hills) N extension of Mayacama range; great Cab Sauv country.
Redwood Valley (Red V) Mend. Warmer inland region; gd Zin, Cab Sauv, Sauv Bl.
Russian River Valley (RRV) Son. Pacific fog lingers; Pinot N, Chard, gd Zin on benchland.
Rutherford (Ruth) Napa. Outstanding Cab Sauv, esp hillside vyds.
Saint Helena (St H) Napa. Lovely balanced Cab Sauv.
Santa Barbara County (Santa B) County n of LA; transverse valleys, several notable subzones, cool and warm.
Santa Lucia Highlands (Santa LH) Mont. Higher elevation, s-facing hillsides, great Pinot N, Syrah, Rhônes.
Santa Maria Valley (Santa MV) Santa B. Coastal cool; gd Pinot N, Chard, Viognier.
Sta Rita Hills (Sta RH) Santa B. Excellent Pinot N.
Santa Ynez (Santa Ynz) Santa B. Rhônes (r/w), Chard, Sauv Bl best bet.
Sierra Foothills (Sierra Fhills) El Dor Co, Am Co, Calaveras County. All improving.
Sonoma Coast (Son Coast) A v. cool climate; edgy Pinot N, Chard, Syrah.
Sonoma Valley (Son V) Note Son V is area within Son County; gd Chard, v.gd Zin, excellent Cab Sauv from Son Mtn sub-AVA.
Spring Mountain Napa. Elevated Cab Sauv, complex soil mixes and exposures.
Stags Leap (Stags L) Napa. Classic red, black-fruited Cab Sauv; v.gd Merlot.
West Sonoma Coast (W Son Coast) Exceptionally cool, marine-influenced parts of Son Coast: Chard, Pinot N, Syrah.

Recent vintages

CA is too diverse for simple summaries. There can certainly be differences between the N, Central and S thirds of the state, but no "bad" vintages in over a decade. Recent relief from drought and autumn fires is welcome indeed.

2025 Long, cool season, mid-Oct rain. Large crop. Some great; jury still out on late-harvested Napa V Cab Sauv.
2024 Classic; v. warm summer, moderate spring/autumn, brisk harvest.
2023 Lower crop, but v. high quality after long, cool season. Late, great harvest.
2022 Spring frosts = smaller crop; state-wide Sept heatwave not ideal, but expect concentration, high quality.
2021 Small crop but high quality; v. impressive wines emerging across board.
2020 Small crop: great whites. Fire issues, but some early picked wines v.gd.
2019 Solid harvest. Minor late losses in Alex V to fires, smoke taint.
2018 Bumper crop of great quality, but smoke issues in Lake County.
2017 Wildfires in Napa, Son after most grapes picked; quality mostly v.gd.

CALIFORNIA

Acorn RRV ★★★ Preserving CA heritage making lively co-fermented field blends from historic Alegria vyd, featuring ZIN plus 17 other mixed black grapes.
Acumen Napa ★★★→★★★★ Pedigreed, hillside Atlas Peak Cabs (mostly) from volcanic terroir; winemaker Phillip Titus (CHAPPELLET). Not cheap, but legit, and age-worthy. I do love ***Mountainside*** SAUV BL, CAB SAUV.
Anaba Car ★★★ Excellent CHARD, PINOT N made by up-and-coming Katy Wilson. Delightful, rich, MOURVÈDRE-driven Rhône-inspired-blend Turbine. Pizza wkds.
Ancien Car ★★★ Visionary Ken Bernards early leader in CAR PINOT N, still making great wines from broader variety of sites. Mostly subscription-driven, but if you have a chance to buy a bottle, don't shy away.
Anthill Farms Son Coast ★★★ Three hard-working WILLIAMS-SELYEM alumni: lively,

ethereal cool-climate PINOT N, SYRAH, old-vine, head-trained CHARD from coastal SON COAST, AND V. Great-value And V Pinot N. Serious up-and-comer.

Aperture Son ★★★→★★★★ Winemaker Jesse Katz has been on steep trajectory for two decades, now controls more land, facilities, finally his own brand. Excellent Bx-inspired reds. Watch.

A Rafanelli Winery Dry CV ★★★→★★★★ Generations of family wisdom shows. Steadily producing superb ZIN-based reds in arguably the ideal terroir for CA Zin.

Arkenstone Howell Mtn ★★★→★★★★ Elevated HOWELL MTN winery at about 450m (1476ft) above sea level, and often above fogline in NAPA V. Home estate planted to Bx varieties (13 acres), tended by estimable winemaker Sam Kaplan: consistently impressive CAB SAUV and more.

Artesa Car ★★★ Gorgeous estate, spectacular architecture, gd wines of all sorts. Founded by Cordoniu family (*see* Spain), but now much more than bubbly.

Au Bon Climat Santa B ★★★ Ever relevant lean, mean, Burgundy-inspired CHARD, PINOT N from visionary Jim Clendenen. Arguably one of most anti-CA-aesthetic wineries ever to come out of CA, but there may be a meeting in middle these days.

Auteur Son V ★★★★ Ken Juhasz's articulate wines can tell stories. Try SON COAST CHARD, notably flinty, reductive burgundian style, hints of lemon, apricot. Constellation of star CHARD, PINOT N vyds up and down the coast, from Ferrington vyd (MEND) to Crown's Gap (Son Coast), all with sense of place. Definitely brand to watch; tasting room in Sonoma.

Aventure, L' P Rob ★★★→★★★★ Shifted from MERLOT-driven Bx blends to more Rhône-style blends in recent yrs. Chloé red blend, named after proprietor Stephan Asseo's daughter, stands out for freshness, vivaciousness. Terrific wines; visitors love relatively new tasting room.

Balletto RRV ★★★ Solid winery; no-nonsense, straightforward, elegant. Fundamental, well grounded and fairly priced. Highly recommended.

Barnett Spring Mtn ★★★→★★★★ Under-radar mtn-top gem managed by David Tate also makes SON V CHARD, PINOT N. Screaming gd wines, towering views, plus 1st-rate NAPA V CAB SAUV – all well worth drive up mtn, but book 1st.

Barra Redwood V ★★★ Most soulful, delicious, sun-kissed CA wines imaginable without an ounce of pretence. Second label: Girasole (organic), source of great values. Honest, pure CA.

Baxter And V ★★★★ Phil B certainly has knack for great PINOT N; he's chosen just the right place to flex his skills. Old World meets New in the MEND woods. All recommended. Start with entry-level AND V Pinot N.

Beaulieu Vineyard (BV) Napa V, Ruth ★★★→★★★★ Iconic Georges de Latour Private Res CAB SAUV is back on fine form; spin-off branded wines are serviceable down the line. Certainly one of crown jewels of RUTH.

Bedrock Wine Co Son V ★★★ Morgan Peterson's label, paean to historic ZIN vyds

Spreading reds

Last year I wrote about climate change with regard to white grapes. Let's look at reds. New grapes are being planted in novel zones. Iberian reds are flourishing in Lodi: GARNACHA, GRACIANO, TEMPRANILLO thanks to Markus BOKISCH and a couple of other growers. ZIN from cool-climate RRV are perhaps more in demand (BEDROCK) – one of few old-time varieties enjoying a deserved comeback. SYRAH has crept to AND V (DREW Valenti vyd), SON COAST (PAX). So far, climate change in CA has been relatively subtle, but sands are shifting: 5 yrs ago I was in a panic over fires; this yr we're coming out of yrs of heavy rain and the coolest summer in 40 yrs. Is this where the shoulder-shrug emoji goes?

and old techniques. Wisdom of ages seen through clear young eyes and claret-style Zins.

Bella Union St H ★★★ NAPA off-shoot of FAR NIENTE now around a decade old; brand named after an old Deadwood brothel/casino, focus on younger generations with requisite Napa CAB plus blends (r/w) at moderately high prices; ST H tasting-room fees bargain for area. It's all about gettin' younger sinners through the saloon doors...

How do you tip on a corkage charge? Start by offering server a glass of your wine.

Benovia Son Coast ★★★ Long-time winemaker Mike Sullivan has been sourcing grapes from coastal vyds for two decades; his experience shows. Super-solid; Tilton Hill PINOT N among best.

Beringer Napa ★★→★★★★ Private Res CAB SAUV, single-vyd Cabs iconic, age-worthy artistically combining mtn and valley fruit; CHARD better than ever. Historic ST H location well worth a visit.

Bevan Cellars N Coast ★★★★ The Bevan path: 1st drink great wines, then learn how to make them. Top wines, select sites in NAPA, SON. Age-worthy Tin Box CAB SAUV (Napa V), Dry Stack SAUV BL (Bennet V, Son) exceptional nectar from oddball Italian clone.

B Kosuge Wines Son ★★★★ Ex-Saintsbury winemaker Byron K devotes himself to subtle, refined PINOT N from N Coast. SON COAST Pinot N, sublime, well priced. Meditative wines coming mostly from CAR, Son Coast.

Blue Farm Son ★★★★ Anne Moller-Racke's next act, piloting PINOT N-driven project in SON, from CAR to Fort Ross-Seaview – 1st-rate farming, 1st-rate wines, a few tasty whites on side.

Bob Cabral Wines RRV ★★★★ Dude is a legend. Williams Selyem alum and music-lover Bob C is slinging wine to his own tune, riffing on RRV, SON COAST CHARD, PINOT N in rare form. Classic rock fans welcome at Backstage Lounge Experience tasting room.

Bogle Central V, Lodi ★★ Solid, under-$15, grocery-store, family-owned brand delivers ever-reliable varietal wines from Lodi, Clark and now more coastal zones, all aged in barriques without oak flavour additives. Respect!

Boisset Collection Napa V, Son ★★★ Ambitious portfolio of sustainably farmed estates and brands assembled by Burgundy-born *boulevardier* Jean-Charles Boisset (*see* France): historic BUENA VISTA, DELOACH, Lyeth, Wattle Creek (SON COUNTY); JCB and Raymond (NAPA V), excellent quality across board.

Bokisch Vineyards Lodi ★★★ Visionary champion of Iberian varieties in warm Lodi: superb ALBARIÑO, GRACIANO; great TEMPRANILLO; flirty Rosado.

Bond Oak ★★★★ Allocated, members-only, oak-based exclusive affair owned by Bill H (HARLAN ESTATE). Excellent CAB SAUV. Recommended if you're looking to spend c.$900–1000 on a bottle. Those determined to re-sell/speculate may be kicked off waiting list (but those rules may relax soon).

Bonny Doon Mont ★★★ You can't not love Randall Grahm, Willy Wonka envisioner of everything plausible. Everything he makes is pretty gd. His art of the presentation is unmatched. Enthusiastically recommend wonderful wines with ridiculous backstories.

Bonterra Mend ★★★ Brand started as spin-off of Fetzer, but now its own thing. For affordable, organic or bio CHARD, SAUV BL, CAB SAUV start here. Great value, farmed with best intentions.

Broc Cellars Mend ★★★ Berkeley-based, crunchy, natty wines mostly from organically farmed vyds (Fox Hill). Some quite austere, but have a following in NorCal. Competently made.

Buena Vista Son V ★★→★★★ Historic winery, est 1857, bedazzled by owner Jean-

Charles BOISSET (DELOACH, Raymond Vyds) with period-costume tours, lights and animatronics straight out of Disneyland. Try The Count's Selection SYRAH.

Burgess Cellars Howell Mtn ★★★ Owned by succession of families since C19; reds always satisfying. Brambly, rich, mildly rustic, pure comfort drink; CAB SAUV, ZIN age remarkably well.

Cade Estate Howell Mtn ★★★→★★★★ In elevated NE NAPA V; some of best CAB SAUV on HOWELL MTN. Refined, structured, sophisticated. Great SAUV BL, too. Part-owned by CA Governor Gavin Newsom and Gordon Getty.

Calera ★★★→★★★★ Mike Waller dutifully continuing vision of Josh Jensen at iconic Burgundy-inspired Central Coast winery. Limestone-driven mtn terroir says it all. Mt Harlan is a one-vyd AVA.

Calling, The ★★★ Celebrity project from sportscaster Jim Nantz. Legit wines by highly qualified James MacPhail: Putnam vyd PINOT N exceptional.

Carneros, Domaine Car ★★★→★★★★ Taittinger (*see* France) outpost, led by women (currently, brilliant Remi Cohen) for decades; one of best Blanc de Blancs fizz in CA, Le Rêve. Other bubblies, PINOT N also superb.

Cattleya RRV ★★★★ Colombian-born Bibiana González Ravé, with mad CV making wine in Europe and US at 1st-tier wineries; now ultra-premium CHARD, PINOT N, SYRAH from N CA top sites, coveted overseas even at high prices; 2nd-tier Alma de Cattleya also resonant, unpretentious, bargain Pinot N; sublime Chard. Don't overlook.

Cedarville Vineyard Sierra Fhills ★★★ Organic estate overseen by winemaker Jonathan Lachs; does everything well: VIOGNIER, GRENACHE, PETITE SIRAH, ZIN, couple of blends. Loyal wine club.

Bota Box brand: inexpensive, sterile, convenient and doesn't require skinning a goat.

Chalk Hill Son V ★★★ Historically important Son winery now owned by wine empire-builder Bill Foley (owns Las Vegas Golden Knights hockey team). His daughter Courtney succeeds a long line of women winemakers here.

Chappellet Napa V ★★★★ Rugged P HILL property; savoury, age-worthy, madrone scrub-laced CAB SAUV. Signature-series Cab Sauv is flat-out killer and beats any NAPA rival for value. Dry CHENIN BL, tangy treat if a bit spendy. Also owns formidable PINOT N, CHARD-themed Sonoma-Loeb brand.

Chimney Rock Stags L ★★★→★★★★ Latina winemaker Elizabeth Vianna elevated Terlato property to next level. Relatively affordable Elevage Bx blend glowing introduction to brand.

Cline Car Stalwart family operation delivers on affordable varietal offerings, with some exotic, old-vine, single-vyd ZIN and Rhône bottles. Eucalypt-inflected Small Berry MOURVÈDRE from Big Break vyd hyper-cool.

Constellation Brands ★→★★★ Publicly traded major wine/beer/spirits company owns famed ROBERT MONDAVI brand, Meiomi, The Prisoner, Woodbridge and many more international brands. Lately re-focusing on beer and cannabis products, but still a big dipper in the wine biz.

Continuum Napa V, St H ★★★★ Tim Mondavi est his bona fides with 2nd-generation, top-tier P HILL estate making impeccable CAB SAUV. Second label: Novicium, from younger vines.

Covenant Napa V ★★★ Professional wine-writer, saxophonist-turned-winemaker Jeff Morgan makes CA's best kosher wines (Hagafen also deserves shout-out), sourced from terrific sites in NAPA V, SON V and beyond.

Crema, La ★★→★★★ Mostly grocery-store CHARD, PINOT N label from JACKSON FAMILY worth noting as relatively high-quality value proposition, but brand becoming a bit scattered, sourcing from CA Central Coast, SON COAST, OR. Wines pretty gd for the money.

Cuvaison Car ★★★ Quiet historic property, great wine yr after yr. Top marks to CHARD, PINOT N from CAR estate; gd CAB SAUV, SYRAH, from MT VEEDER. Single Block bottlings: lovely rosé, slinky, sexy Méthode Béton SAUV BL.

Dalla Valle Oak ★★★★ A 1st-rate hillside estate transitioned to 2nd generation. Maya CAB SAUV, legendary; eponymous Cab Sauv cult wine, Dalle Valle Collina edition *the best* younger-vine, relatively affordable entry to luxury NAPA Cab. Get some.

David Bruce Santa Cz Mts ★★★ Tough place to grow grapes, even a tough place to visit. Rugged mtn PINOT N from cool-climate wilderness. I have a soft spot for people who are this hard.

Davis Bynum RRV ★★★ Acquisition by Rodney Strong proved fruitful for this RRV stalwart. Superb SAUV BL might even outshine fine CHARD, PINOT N.

Delicato Family N Coast ★★→★★★ Powerful wine-growing family, 6000+ acres in Central and N CA. Portfolio from popular, budget Bota Box to Coppola, Gnarly Head, Sofia.

DeLoach Winery Son ★★★ Flamboyant Jean-Charles BOISSET saw gd value in progressive organic, bio-oriented winery making great CHARD, PINOT N. Solid down-to-earth investment, if not his sexiest.

Diamond Creek Napa V ★★★★ Extraordinary longevity of CAB SAUV from iconic sites like Volcanic Hill and Gravelly Meadow makes some of most coveted, collectable wines of NAPA V.

Dominus Estate Napa V ★★★★ Moueix-owned (*see* France). Herzog de Meuron-designed winery is epic, but not open to hoi polloi. Gravelly terroir in cool S NAPA is indisputably great. Second label: Napanook, also great. You can buy the wine, but you can't pet the vines.

Drew Family And V, Mend ★★★→★★★★ Visionary in MEND RDG: minimalist, savage PINOT N from AND V and higher up hills. Look for estate Field Selections Pinot N from Mend Rdg, SYRAH from coastal Valenti vyd. Hunt down.

Dry Creek Vineyard Dry CV ★★★ Standard-bearer on its A-game. Trustworthy, Loire-inspired, grassy FUMÉ BL and other SAUV BL always delicious, CHENIN BL and all reds better than ever. Great stop nr Healdsburg. What's not to love? ZIN/Bx blend Mariner, better than ever.

Duckhorn Vineyards Napa V ★★★→★★★★ Crowd-pleasing, ultra-consistent CAB SAUV, MERLOT, incl legendary Three Palms vyd famed for MERLOT, gd SAUV BL. Second label Decoy hugely successful, excellent value. Owned by private equity firm Butterfly in a 2B deal. Thoughtfully assembled Duckhorn Portfolio also owns CALERA, Goldeneye (AND V), KOSTA BROWNE, Migration brand (N Coast CHARD, PINOT N), SONOMA-CUTRER and Canvasback (WA).

DuMol Son Coast ★★★ Micro-winery evolved into trendy, must-have brand for SON COAST CHARD, PINOT N. Wildrose Pinot N perhaps most notable.

Dunn Howell Mtn ★★★★ Classic HOWELL MTN producer back on form: age-worthy mtn Cabs. Iconic brand back on track; worthy investment.

Emeritus RRV ★★★→★★★★ Emergent estate, three dry-farmed (!) vyds, focused, structured PINOT N under gifted supervision of Dave Lattin. Hallberg Ranch bottlings exquisite, singular, intense, focused.

Etude Car ★★★ Ever-trustworthy brand that always succeeded at making great CAB SAUV, PINOT N under same roof, using same attentive techniques. Now owned by TWE (*see* Australia), but legacy stays true. Pinot N Rosé to die for.

Far Niente Napa V ★★★→★★★★ Pioneer of generous CAB SAUV, CHARD. Hedonism with soul. Dolce: celebrated dessert wine. Also Nickel & Nickel single-vyd Cabs.

Farrell, Gary RRV ★★★ Namesake founder long gone, but wines still terrific despite a few ownership changes, much thanks to winemaker Theresa Heredia, Farrell's hand-picked successor. Basic RRV CHARD beams brightly, Hallberg and Fort Ross single-vyd PINOT N among top offerings.

Flowers Son Coast ★★★→★★★★ Pioneer next to Pacific, now owned by Huneeus Vintners: CHARD, PINOT N remain great illustrations of that climate, elevation.

Follette, La ★★★→★★★★ Titular winemaker no longer involved in brand, but v. talented winemaker Hugh Chappelle is. Seems now to exist under QUIVIRA brand, auspicious bio-label conglomerate owned by Kight family.

Baller or bargain, Anderson V is hands-down best wine-country weekend getaway.

Freeman ★★★ Particularly strong SON COAST CHARD, PINOT N contender; consistently delicious, elegant cool-climate coastal CA. Ken and Akiko F arrived 2001, pioneering drive to cold end of w coast. If you visit, pack a jacket.

Freemark Abbey Napa V ★★★ Classic name claimed by JACKSON FAMILY in 2006, improved. Great-value single-vyd Bosché, Sycamore CAB SAUV bottlings.

Frog's Leap Ruth ★★★ John Williams is pioneer of bio viticulture in CA. He coaxes best out of NAPA V floor with elegant CHARD, refreshing SAUV BL, supple, juicy CAB SAUV, MERLOT and brambly ZIN.

Gallo, E&J ★→★★★ Largest wine company in world, titan in under-$20 sector with dozens of major CA brands (Apothic, Barefoot, Louis Martini). Recent buys: Black Box, Clos du Bois, ROMBAUER, Jayson, RAVENSWOOD. Gallo of Sonoma: excellent, from owned vyds; lately been buying boutique brands (DENNER, MASSICAN).

Gentleman Farmer Napa V ★★★→★★★★ Jeff and Joey offer depth of human hospitality unequalled in NAPA V. Great wine (with Jerome Chéry); they can cook, and will make group bookings feel right at home. Hard to put a price on this kind of warmth. Get there.

Gloria Ferrer Car ★★★ Exceptional CA bubbly. Toast to decades-long team of owners, growers, winemakers that made this Freixenet-owned (*see* Spain) venture extraordinary. All wines v.gd, Vintage Royal Cuvée best.

Green & Red Napa V ★★★ Back-to-the-land hippie winery, founded early 70s by Jay Heminway, still cranks out mouthwatering SAUV BL, some killer ZIN, one custom-blended for Chez Panisse in Berkeley. Hard to argue with.

Gundlach Bundschu Son V ★★★ Terrific wines, welcoming vibe, popular tasting destination, with adventurous cool Huichica Fest music concerts for hipster set. Best: GEWURZ, CAB SAUV, MERLOT.

Hall Napa V ★★★→★★★★ Glitzy ST H winery, great NAPA CAB SAUV, but bewildering variety. Signature offering best, velvety SAUV BL, MERLOT among best in CA. Also owns coastal CHARD, PINOT N brand Walt.

Hanzell ★★★→★★★★ Owned by de Brye family since 1975; est 1953, organic since 2021. Some of best (Sebella CHARD) hail from hillside Moon Mtn District of Son; in general Chards v. notable. Every ingredient on label.

Harlan Estate Napa V ★★★★ Concentrated, robust CAB SAUV from W OAK bench, cult Cab with long waiting list from Meadowood Resort owner Bill H. Resort rebuilding after 2020 fires, but vyds intact. Wines made by Cory Empting.

Harney Lane Lodi ★★★ Family-owned with a century+ of grape-growing under belt. Old-vine ZIN from Home Ranch and Lizzy James vyds the stars, but ALBARIÑO, TEMPRANILLO also impress as Iberian grapes gain momentum in Lodi.

Hartford Family Son Coast ★★★ Winemaker Jeff Stewart is quietly killing it at this JACKSON FAMILY winery, with small batches of CHARD, PINOT N, ZIN from sites up and down N Coast. Taut Seascape Chard, subtle Fog Dance Pinot N (Green V).

HdV Wines Car ★★★ A gem: fine complex CHARD with honed edge; PINOT N from Larry Hyde with Aubert de Villaine of DRC (*see* France); v.gd CAB SAUV, SYRAH.

Hendry Oak K ★★★ Classic, soulful, minimalist wines, est 1939. Note brambly, distinctive CAB SAUV, ZIN (try Block 28) from cool pocket. Never disappointing.

Hobo Son V ★★★ Tough to classify these min-intervention wines. Kenny Likitprakong is skateboarder-turned-winemaker grinding margins of CA wine:

refreshing, expressive from grapes culled from gd sources in Son County, Santa Cz Mts. Pure, fresh fruit with DIY punk attitude. Value tasting in Sta Rosa.

Honig Ruth ★★★ Champion of sustainable viticulture: SAUV BL, CAB SAUV. All-round gd citizens; delicious wines, readily available, deserving of support.

Hope Family P Rob ★★★ Visionary Austin H bangs out some fine Rhône reds from Templeton Gap and CAB SAUV under eponymous label, plus affordable Liberty School varietals, complex Treana brand blends. Experienced, dependable.

House of Brown Napa V ★★★ NAPA's Brown Estate 2nd-generation spin-off; fruit-driven, youthful, naturalish wines. On-point rosé, juicy, chillable blend of CAB SAUV/PINOT N/TEMPRANILLO from Lodi. Timely, youth-oriented, Black-owned label with legit experience and chops. Watch.

Hundred Acre Napa V ★★★★ NAPA V Jayson Woodbridge schooled by some great consultants, forged excellent CAB SAUV brand through many legal battles as civil plaintiff and (petty) criminal defendant. Maybe all publicity is gd publicity. The Diplomat (r blend) resonates. Make love, not war.

Inglenook Oak ★★★ Director Francis Ford Coppola's legendary estate. Rubicon CAB SAUV is flagship proprietary red; v.gd CHARD, MERLOT. Showpiece mansion is spectacular, popular with international visitors.

Jackson Family Wines ★★→★★★★ Visionary, continually expanding privately held company, massive vyd owner in CA and beyond, with remarkable empire of stellar properties. Holdings focus on elevated sites, high-quality terroir. Owns popular Kendall-Jackson brand plus ritzier Brewer-Clifton, Cardinale, Copain, Edmeades, FREEMARK ABBEY, HARTFORD FAMILY, LA CREMA, La Jota, Lokoya, Maggy Hawk, Matanzas Creek, Murphy Goode, Siduri, VÉRITÉ. Jackson Estate series great for N Coast mtn CAB SAUV. Uniformly high quality.

Jordan Alex V ★★★ Showcase estate generates elegant, balanced, Bx-faithful CAB SAUV for devoted following; CHARD, now sourced from RRV, delivers lemony, mouthwatering panache.

Joseph Phelps Vineyards Napa V ★★★★ Insignia Bx blend a CA benchmark luxury wine. NAPA V CAB SAUV and Hyde Vyd SYRAH dazzle. Also Freestone coastal wines.

Keenan Spring Mtn ★★★ Just one of many reliably rocksteady mtn wineries in NAPA V. CAB SAUV age-worthy, but don't sleep on structured MERLOT.

Kistler Vineyards RRV ★★★→★★★★ Style of CHARD, PINOT N adapted over time, wines only improved. Decadent but balanced, nutty Les Noisetiers CHARD from SON V, exceptional.

Kornell, Paula Napa V ★★★→★★★★ This 2nd-gen bubbly specialist brings the party with outstanding CA fizz: 1st-rate Brut and Brut Blanc de Noirs. Seek.

Kosta Browne Son Coast ★★★★ Top-notch, moon-shot PINOT N, CHARD, under The Duckhorn Portfolio umbrella, making world-class wines at world-class prices. Keefer Ranch Pinot insanely gd, and don't sleep on flinty Chards (One Sixteen). They ain't cheap.

Kutch N Coast ★★★→★★★★ Jamie K produces some prime coastal PINOT N. Currently developing a home ranch, he sources from other top sites outside textbook locales. Delivers consistently, like McDougall Ranch Pinot N (vyd at c.305m/1000ft), precise, expressive, special wines.

You never have to try a bourbon barrel-finished white. I took that Bulleit for you.

Lang & Reed Mend, Napa ★★★ If you're interested in CA CAB FR, start here. John Skupny's wines capture perfume, litheness of variety, with NAPA generosity. Also delicious MEND CHENIN BL.

LaZarre P Rob ★★★ Adam L culls fine grapes from warm and cool Central Coast sites like EDNA V, MONT, P ROB. Experience at Hahn paying off in sourcing great grapes. Don't miss Edna V ALBARIÑO.

CALIFORNIA

Leoness Tem ★★→★★★ Favourite in SoCal's Temecula, where weddings and other wine-tourism jaunts seem to drive most traffic. There *is* some gd wine, and gd food while you're at it too. Leoness is an example.

Lewis Grace Winery Sierra Fhills ★★★ Expect a warm welcome and some inspired red wines at this Placerville-area winery in EL DOR CO. One of several in area making terrific wines from BARBERA, PETITE SIRAH. Worth a visit.

Lindquist Family – Verdad Arroyo G, Arroyo Seco ★★★ Rhône ranger Bob L's pivot towards Spain, incl authentic-ish ALBARIÑO, TEMPRANILLO from bio Sawyer Lindquist vyd in nearby EDNA V. *Muy bueno.*

Littorai And V, Son Coast ★★★★ Burgundy-trained maestro Ted Lemon's N Coast CHARD, PINOT N: nervy, coastal, seeking global audience. Small lots, but all sleek, exciting. Thrilling Cerise, Savoy, Wendling Vyd offerings.

Lohr, J P Rob ★★→★★★ Arguably among best value in CA, from CAB SAUV to MERLOT to SYRAH. Everything under $20 is well worth it. Cuvée Pau and Cuvée St E pay homage to Bx. Don't miss seductive, floral Beaujolais-like Wildflower Valdiguié.

Lucia Santa LH ★★★ Access to great vyds and 2nd-generation knowledge has positioned Jeff Pisoni well. Impressive CHARD, PINOT N. Central Coast, SANTA LH brand to watch, Juicy Lucy GAMAY, delicious.

Lynmar RRV ★★★→★★★★ Dazzling CHARD over past 15 yrs. Let's hope they can keep that up, but there may have been some personnel changes.

Macchia Lodi ★★★ One of Lodi's most accomplished winemakers, Tim Holdener vacuums up medals in blind tastings yr after yr. Speciality is balanced old-vine ZIN, but also interesting SANGIOVESE, TEROLDEGO; PETITE SIRAH v.gd.

MacRostie RRV, Son Coast ★★★ Tasting room a post-modern beauty; minimalist screwcapped wines 1st rate. Lovely PINOT N, SYRAH; SON COAST CHARD a delight. Get on the bus.

Martinelli RRV ★★★→★★★★ Long-time winemakers, 5th generation; continues to adapt, pivot, cleverly moving towards cooler climes. Legend Jackass Hill ZIN, named after steepness of vyd. Other wines also rewarding, incl several coastal single-vineyard SYRAHS.

Massican Napa V ★★★ Only whites from ex-Larkmead wiz Dan Petroski. Recently sold to E&J GALLO; Dan stays on for now. Direct wines, some complexity, vivacious Med styles. California Vino Bianco modestly priced but expertly crafted; SAUV BL, fragrant, delightful. Annia (Tocai FRIULANO/RIBOLLA GIALLA/CHARD) creative, well executed.

Masút Mend ★★★★ Underappreciated, elevated Eagle Peak Mendo property, run by Ben and Jake Fetzer, quietly setting own course. Estate PINOT N ethereal. Should inspire others to explore area.

Matthiasson Napa V ★★★ Mostly certified-organic vyd sources in NAPA, making trendy, relatively low-alc CAB SAUV, REFOSCO, VERMENTINO; v. hip.

Mayacamas Mt Veeder ★★★→★★★★ For many yrs, I've wavered over this venerable, stern, rocky estate. Previous iterations could be brutal, coarse, but more polished recent CAB SAUV is civilized, displaying class of mtn Mayacama range terroir. All coming into focus as Mt Veeder warms. Watch.

Zinfandel reloaded

Don't call it a comeback; it's been here for yrs. Respect to LL Cool J, ZIN is one of few grapes seeing increased sales thanks to better-balanced, re-focused, leaner wines. Just look at (or taste): BEDROCK, DRY CREEK VYD (Old Vine), HARNEY LANE (Lizzy James Vyd from Lodi), HOBO, NALLE (DRY CV Classic), Once and Future, RIDGE, Seghesio. TURLEY Zins are also legendary, but they're gonna cost you.

Medlock Ames Son ★★★ Winery on Bell Mtn with reliably delicious, bio, round, mostly Bx-style reds made under respected consultant Jean Hoefliger. Sharp wines, labels, Healdsburg tasting room. Classy.

Melka Napa V, Son V ★★★★ Jewel-box holding of great Napa consultant Philippe M and wife Cherie, comprises hillside properties in CAL (NAPA V) and Knights V (Son). Limited, pricey, coveted. Mostly CAB SAUV, Bx blends, stellar MERLOT.

Michael Mondavi Family Napa V ★★★→★★★★ This Mondavi scion might be best known for his Folio import biz, but he makes great wines too. The M CAB SAUV from ATLAS PEAK is killer. Animo Cab Sauv, SAUV BL also formidable.

Miraflores Sierra Fhills ★★★ Marco Cappelli left NAPA V to set up in Sierra Mtns; vinifies sublime, broad array of fresh, pure, lightly oaked wines from estate and region he rightly believes in.

Mi Sueno Napa V ★★★ Rolando started dishwashing at a NAPA resort, worked his way up at wineries. Lorena's family worked vyds, bought property. Together they make excellent wine, every bit as gd as story.

Montelena, Ch Napa V ★★★ Epic, elevated, historic Mayacamas castle property with sublime grounds so worth a visit. CAB SAUV can be a bit wild, CHARD shocked world at 1978 Judgment of Paris tasting.

Morgan Santa LH ★★★→★★★★ Dan M Lee's organically farmed ranch overdelivers with killer CHARD, PINOT N across board. Double L vyd offerings top charts.

Mount Eden Vineyards Santa Cz Mts ★★★→★★★★ Gorgeous vistas from high vyd, one of CA's 1st boutique wineries, with Burgundian clones dating back to Martin Ray days. Taut, mineral CAB SAUV, PINOT N, stunning CHARD since 1945. Inspired by Burgundy, but pure rugged CA character.

Nalle Dry CV ★★★ Refined craftsmanship-level ZIN, impeccable, elegant claret-style reds. Great family-owned stop nr Healdsburg.

Navarro And V ★★★ Long-time cool-climate N CA outpost reliably delivers fresh, affordable, minimalist, delicious GEWURZ, PINOT N and everything in between. Wine-club subscription you won't regret.

Niner Estate P Rob ★★★ Now managed by Andy N, son of W VA entrepreneur Richard N (est 2001). Some of best-balanced, mosdt drinkable wines in area. In Willow Creek (P ROB CAB SAUV); also in cooler EDNA V (CHARD, PINOT N); craveable.

Obsidian Ridge Lake ★★★ Star of Lake County extension of Mayacamas mtn range. Super CAB SAUV, SYRAH from hillside vyds, volcanic soils scattered with glassy obsidian. Half Mile Cab 1st-rate. Also owns Poseidon brand from CAR.

Opus One Oak ★★★★ Mouton Rothschild family-controlled (*see* Bordeaux) CAB SAUV estate always intended to glamour international markets, and still does. Superb OAK Cab Sauv.

O'Shaughnessy Howell Mtn ★★★★ Outstanding elevated outpost atop HOWELL MTN putting out stellar CAB SAUV that's built to last. Worth seeking out.

Patz & Hall N Coast ★★★★ James Hall one of CA's most thoughtful winemakers; culls fruit from top vyds from Central Coast to MEND. Style is generous, tasteful, super-reliable. Zio Tony ***Chard*** v. special, lemony, electric, opulent.

Paul Hobbs Wines N Coast ★★★→★★★★ Hugely influential winemaker since 90s, working in CA and a lot in S America. Terroir-expressive single-vyd CHARD, CAB SAUV, PINOT N, SYRAH always impressive. Don't sleep on these wines.

Pax Mend, Son ★★★★ Special cold-climate New World SYRAH from coastal and hillside sites since 2000 for fair prices. Fresh TROUSSEAU Gr and GAMAY also available at The Barlow tasting room in Sebastopol, but it's really about cool-climate Syrah done in best possible, crisp way.

Peay Vineyards Son Coast ★★★→★★★★ Standout brand from coldest, elevated zones. Finesse-driven CHARD, PINOT N, SYRAH superb. Second label: Cep, v.gd, esp rosé. Weightless, ethereal wines that reckon international appreciation.

KISS Theory
I am eternally impressed by winemakers who follow the concept Keep It Simple, Stupid: farm organically whenever possible, let the fruit express itself and its place, min oak flavouring, min additives – and don't try to re-invent the wheel. Just make sound, fresh, delicious wine. Some that excel: BALLETTO, BARRA, HENDRY, HOBO, Lolonis, MIRAFLORES, New Clairvaux, PEDRONCELLI, SANDHI, SHANE, SPOTTSWOODE, Vino Nocetto.

Pedroncelli Dry CV ★★★ CA wine at its most exuberant: glowing, unpretentious. Grown on superb terroir, gently made, beautiful without make-up: SAUV BL, CAB SAUV, ZIN all singing in harmony and v. reasonably priced. Unsurprising sales are on upswing; CA wine needs more of this.

Philip Togni Vineyard Spring Mtn ★★★★ No bling, just marvellous, v. collectible Napa Mtn CAB SAUV that goes for decades.

Pride Mountain Napa V, Spring Mtn ★★★→★★★★ Epic Mayacamas mtn-top estate straddles NAPA V/SON V border. Superb, bold CAB SAUV; amazing MERLOT. Tasting appointments required and worth circuitous, steep drive up hill. Call ahead.

Quintessa Ruth ★★★★ Well-conceived, gorgeous, single-wine estate owned by Chilean international wine wizard Augustin Huneeus. That one red Bx blend is special and justifies three-figure price.

Quivira Dry CV ★★★→★★★★ Pete and Terri Kight's bio property, helmed by accomplished winemaker Hugh Chappelle. Estimable SAUV BL and ZIN with integrity and balance.

Radio-Coteau Son Coast ★★★ Notable new-wave PINOT N, serious coastal SYRAH and old-vine, dry-farmed ZIN. Bulletproof CHARD, Zin, but Pinot N steals show. Veg gardens, cider orchard, goats, chickens, honeybees and cats gild the lily.

Ramey Son ★★★→★★★★ Influential David R delivers flinty, reductive burgundy-style whites in his Hyde, Ritchie and RRV CHARD. Reds gd, but his Chards should be *de rigueur* tasting at UC Davis winemaking school.

Ravenswood ★★★ CONSTELLATION-owned, but single-vyd ZIN still from remarkable sites like Bedrock, Old Hill, Teldeschi. "No wimpy wines" motto still applies.

Rhys Santa Cz Mts ★★★→★★★★ Up-and-coming brand, focus on high-elevation CHARD, PINOT N from AND V, Santa Cz Mts, some exciting vyds in its quiver. Wishing tremendous success.

Ridge N Coast, Santa Cz Mts ★★★★ Hi, natty wine kids! Ridge represents decades of natural winemaking with min additives, local oak and 1st-class terroir in Monte Bello CAB SAUV, one of greatest, most age-worthy Cabs in CA. Also a champ of ingredient labelling and transparency. Watch and learn.

Rivers-Marie Napa V ★★★★ Private label of acclaimed vintner and consultant Thomas Rivers Brown (FAR NIENTE, SCHRADER) and partner Genevieve Marie Welsh features superb varietals. Reservations required at Hwy 128 tasting room in CAL. Wicked Herb Lamb CAB SAUV.

Roar ★★★ Santa LH Gary Franscioni's excellent brand driven by SANTA LH grapes from own vyds. Gary's Vyd PINOT N leads pack.

Robert Biale Vineyards Napa V ★★★→★★★★ Multi-generation winery, est 1937. Notable for outstanding Napa PETITE SIRAH, ZIN, esp legendary Black Chicken Zin that makes for a gd story indeed. Read all about it.

Robert Mondavi Winery ★★→★★★ Once iconic, now a corporate concern. Top wines still pretty gd; everything in between mostly okay.

Robledo Family Son V ★★★→★★★★ Along with, and related to, MI SUEÑO, among 1st estate wineries founded by Mexican vyd workers. Luis and his sons came to US in 40s as *braceros* and worked way up from fields. American Dream, now 4th generation. Delicious, rare, claret-style NAPA V TEMPRANILLO.

Rocca Family Napa V ★★★→★★★★ Boutique NAPA winery founded by Drs Mary R and Eric Grigsby in 1999. Sturdy CAB SAUV, culling grapes mostly from COOMB, Yountville with a tasting room in DT Napa. Best known for CAB SAUV: barrel-selection Tesorina perhaps flagship. Notable SON COAST CHARD.

Rodney Strong Vineyards Son ★★★ Strong indeed, across board; 14 vyds producing sinewy coastal CHARD, PINOT N, citrus SAUV BL, super ALEX V CAB SAUV from Alexander's Crown, Rockaway vyds.

Roederer Estate And V ★★★★ Adventurous Champagne Roederer venture brought glamour to AND V fizz. Finesse off charts, esp luxury cuvée L'Ermitage. Also makes Scharffenberger now. Dom Anderson PINOT N also among best of AVA.

Rombauer Napa V ★★★ Buttery CHARD is calling card, but sunny MERLOT, CAB SAUV also deliver juicy roly-poly CA fruit. Now owned by GALLO.

Rosenblum Son Coast ★★★ After Constellation acquired this brilliant ZIN brand, it would have been easy to write off as dull snoozer, but quality remained pretty decent. Jack London Square tasting room in Oakland, lovely for a waterfront glass or two.

Rundquist Amador ★★★ Jeff R roamed around CA for a while, but there's no denying his winemaking chops, esp ZIN. Lately based in Shenandoah V in SIERRA FHILLS, making a long menu of locale-appropriate bottlings.

St Amant Lodi Stuart Spencer has been a visionary leader and booster for Lodi. Started producing Port styles in AM CO in 70s before relocating to Lodi. Still makes some of best fortified reds in state, plus some lovely old-vine ZINS, and stunning VERDELHO from Am Co vyd.

St Jean, Ch Son V ★★★ Solid on all fronts, but consensus flagship for decades has been Cinq Cépages: five Bx varieties. Classic nectarine-rich Robert Young CHARD.

St Supery Ruth ★★★→★★★★ Stalwart, estate-grown certified Napa Green wines from RUTH. Dollarhide Estate SAUV BL is legendary, but some Bx blends that inspired this estate still seem relevant, value. Try Dollarhide Estate CAB SAUV, Elu Bx blend.

Sandhi Sta RH ★★★ Sashi Moorman's visionary SANTA B winery producing Burgundy-inspired low-alc wines with balance, restraint; v. much a "less is more" attitude at play. Appreciated, and not an easy feat at this latitude.

Sandlands Napa V ★★★→★★★★ Tegan Passalacqua rescues ancient, sandy pre-phylloxera vyds from CA; boutique small batches of ultra-premium wine. Lodi Carignane a treat – only a handful of barrels made.

Saxum P Rob ★★★ Famed for opulent, heady Rhône-inspired reds – perhaps a bit too heady for some. James Berry Vyd blend flagship.

Scherrer RRV ★★★ Fred S makes structured Son from CAB SAUV, PINOT N, ZIN, built to last, matured for extra yr or two. Hallberg Ranch Pinot N, finessed Sasha SYRAH standouts.

Schrader Oak ★★★★ Cultish members-only label with wait list. Thomas Rivers Brown-made, incl To Kalon and Beckstoffer To Kalon single-vyd CAB SAUV. You can have a taste, though... Napa tasting room offers 90-min tastings by reservation for $225/person (plus 20% tip, natch).

Cali Cabernet Franc enjoying the spotlight lately. Chinon? Chioui!

Schramsberg Napa V ★★★★ A 2nd-gen CA bubbly specialist not afraid to compete with Champagne, and keeps up well. Memorable tours of historic caves by reservation. Classic Blanc de Blancs.

Sean Minor Son V ★★★ Terrific, family-owned, super-solid wines from purchased grapes in N and Central CA. SON COAST PINOT N for a shade under $30, a pretty gd deal.

Sea Smoke Sta RH ★★★ Cultish, high-end, opulent PINOT N and excellent bubbly made in strictly estate-driven model, with incredible continuity of leadership, talent. Luscious wines, but drink them while they're fresh.

Shafer Vineyards Napa V, Stags L ★★★→★★★★ Solid brand, widely respected. Hillside Select CAB SAUV a lavish CA classic; Relentless SYRAH/PETITE SIRAH blend an artful in-house invention. One Point Five, beautiful Cab Sauv for money.

Shane Son Coast ★★★ Refined wines from KOSTA BROWNE-vet Shane Finley, mostly cool-climate PINOT N, SYRAH (min new oak). Technically perfect, tight, with resonance, without pretence.

Shannon Ridge Lake ★★→★★★ Grand, undulating, high-elevation estate overlooks Clear Lake. Terrific reds and whites, SAUV BL to PETITE SIRAH, esp Res series. Great value. Second label: Vigilance, a big seller.

Shenandoah Vineyards / Sobon Estate Amador ★★★ Green-leaning scientists/engineers got SIERRA FHILLS endeavour going in late 70s, still makes some of best ZIN and more in EL DOR CO. Charging station for your EV while you taste.

Smith-Madrone Napa V ★★★→★★★★ Two Billy Goats Gruff old-school outpost founded by Smith bros in 1971, high atop SPRING MTN, featuring Euro-inspired, balanced CAB SAUV and exotic, trend-eschewing old-vine RIES. Well worth a visit.

Smith-Story And V, Son V ★★★ Always hustling, shared-dream couple makes plucky, v.gd wines and sometimes German RIES from where Eric cut his winemaking teeth. Sometimes the story is everything.

Sobon Estate Amador ★★★ Solid 2nd-generation estate, always excellent BARBERA, ZIN, reasonable prices. There's also a tiny wine museum if you happen to find yourself in SIERRA FHILLS on your way to or from Lake Tahoe. Always worth a minor detour.

Sonoma-Cutrer Vineyards Son ★★★ Big, successful RRV mostly CHARD brand now property of The Duckhorn Portfolio; SON COAST and RRV CHARD still insanely popular with restaurants.

Spottswoode St H ★★★★ Sublime estate always chasing perfection with every sustainable/organic/bio bona fide ever conceived. Estate Cabs thrilling with modest alc. Second wine: Lyndenhurst, superb, value. Zesty, immaculate SAUV BL. Stand and clap.

Staglin Family Vineyard Ruth ★★★★ Refined CAB SAUV from 2nd-generation, family-owned estate on RUTH Benchlands. Always impressive, and a leader, never just another cow in the herd.

Stag's Leap Wine Cellars Stags L ★★★ Founder sold to Ste Michelle Wine Estates (WA), gd to see quality held. Flagship CAB SAUV (top Cask 23, Fay, SLV).

Stags' Leap Winery Stags L ★★★→★★★★ Oft confused with STAG'S LEAP WINE CELLARS, historic estate est by Carl Doumani excels in its own right. Been kicked around like a water-logged football lately, but still a special place to visit. Tasting by appointment, well worth it.

Steven Kent Winery ★★★ SK Mirassou is hands-down best winemaker in LIV V, lately zeroing-in on area's great potential for CAB FR. Best: L'Autre Côte.

Storybook Mountain Napa V ★★★ Dr Jerry Seps's fairytale mountainside estate; some of most stylish, classically proportioned ZIN in CA. Remarkably elegant Eastern Exposures ZIN, CA classic.

Tablas Creek P Rob ★★★→★★★★ When it comes to Rhône and Med varieties, nobody does it better; makes me feel sad for rest. Enlightened regenerative farming begets glorious, well-edited red/white (latter rare in P ROB); CA elite. A wine club worth joining, to be sure.

Terra Valentine Spring Mtn ★★★→★★★★ Talented winemaker Sam Baxter quietly acquired this prime SPRING MTN estate from Wurtele family, continues to make surprisingly fine under-the-radar mtn reds.

Terre Rouge / Easton Sierra Fhills ★★★ Exceptional red producer in AM CO sporting

Rhône and ZIN offerings with equal aplomb. Affordable Tête-à-Tête red blend a steal, Ascent SYRAH reliably special.

Three Sticks Son ★★★→★★★★ Billy "Three Sticks" Price III is major player in SON COAST; interests in Durell and Gap's Crown vyds, GARY FARRELL, KISTLER and other brands. Connected, solid N Coast CHARD, PINOT N done well by N CA native Ryan Prichard.

Tongue Dancer Son V ★★★★ James MacPhail is one of most respected winemakers in Son County. Epic PINOT N (r/rosé), but don't sleep on wonderful Bacigalupi Vyd CHARD. *See* THE CALLING.

Trefethen Family Vineyards Oak K ★★★ Underappreciated winery in cool Oak K deserves more credit: CHARD, delicious dry RIES, elegant CAB SAUV, MERLOT.

Turley Wine Cellars Amador ★★★★ Brilliant CA ZINS from 40+ vyd sites, some ancient vyds, many field-blend fermentations scattered across CA. True CA treasures, Hayne vyd in ST H perhaps most famed of portfolio. Tegan Passalacqua presiding. Zin trending again.

Turnbull Oak ★★★ Outstanding entry-level estate CAB SAUV. Black-label estate Cab also thrilling with gravelly kick, and don't sleep on luscious, tropical SAUV BL.

Vérité Son ★★★★ Luxury Son hillside Mayacamas mtn estate helmed by long-time Jess Jackson *copain* Pierre Seillan and daughter Hélène for five decades now. Age-worthy Bx blends: CAB SAUV-led La Joie, MERLOT-driven La Muse among top. Tastings (book 1st) pricey.

Villa Creek P Rob ★★★→★★★★ Chris Cherry speaks softly but makes some of best Med-inspired wines in Central Coast. Grapes mostly from regenerative/organic/bio MAHA estate vyd; GARNACHA one of best in US. Underappreciated.

Volker Eisele Family Estate Napa V ★★★ Special site tucked way back in Chiles V continues to overdeliver with CAB SAUV and more. Looking for an adventure?

Wente Liv V ★★★ A 4th-generation wine-grower in LIV V; decent wines, but could aim higher. Some of vyd-select pretty gd. Reliable spin-off Murietta's Well (r/w).

Whitehall Lane St H ★★★★ More elegant stop along Hwy 29. Leonardini family farms c.200 acres in NAPA V/SON V; CAB SAUV mainstay, MERLOT delivers value.

Williams-Selyem RRV ★★★ Legendary SON PINOT N since 70s; handcrafted, low intervention, with loyal following. Rochioli vyd (RRV) put N CA PINOT N on map.

Zaca Mesa Santa B ★★★ OG Rhône-variety leader planted SYRAH in 1978, delivering boss wines for five decades. Z (r blend), graceful, affordable. Rhône blends (r/w) exceptional; wines damn gd value.

Colorado (CO)

Cool-climate varieties best. Two AVAs: Grand V more Bx, Rhône varieties; West Elks cooler, more Alsace, Burgundy. Front range of Rocky Mtns has wineries too. **Alfred Eames** ★ historic producer; TEMPRANILLO, SYRAH, PETITE SIRAH all gd. **Bookcliff Vyds** ★★★ oft-awarded, top producer of French grapes: Syrah, CAB SAUV, MALBEC. **Carboy** ★★ four wineries, tasting rooms; mix of CO and CA wines. **Carlson** history of fruit and sweet wines; gd dry GEWURZ. **Colterris** ★★★ top bottlings of Bx-style Cab Sauv, MERLOT; French varieties predominate; signature Coral White Cab Sauv. **Jack Rabbit Hill Farm** ★ only certified-bio winery in state; elegant PINOTS N/M, Alsace whites. **Qutori Wines** ★ Bx varieties; outstanding Merlot. **Sauvage Spectrum** ★★ quality Italian, Bx-style reds; Pet-Nat. **Snowy Peaks** ★★ v. high-altitude; Bx, Rhône (Élevé Blanc w blend) styles. **Stone Cottage Cellars** high-elevation Merlot, Alsace-style specialist, racy Gewurz, PINOT GR. **Stoney Mesa** Bx grapes from Grand V. **Sutcliff Vyds** outlier in frontier area Four Corners, Bx varieties. **The Storm Cellar** focus on high-elevation white, rosé (best). **Veraison Vyds and Winery** estate Dijon Clones Perle Blanche CHARD. **Whitewater Hill** French grapes along with St Vincent (r).

Georgia (GA)

Shares Blue Ridge Mtns foothills with VA, NC; elevation nr 610m (2000ft) beats subtropical climate (gd for se native Muscadine varieties) for vinifera, unusual French/US hybrids. Two AVAs, in hilly n. **Ch Élan** PINOT GR, AGLIANICO, MALBEC, awarded rosé of native Triumph, Noble. **Cloudland** hybrid Lomanto, native Lenoir, PETIT VERDOT. **Crane Creek** hybrid focus, try Enotah (Chardonel fermentation in Hungarian oak), NOIRET. **Engelheim** awarded TRAMINETTE. **Habersham** three lines (**Southern Harvest** for Muscadine). **Sharp Mtn** SANGIOVESE, GEWURZ. **Stonewall Creek** structured Norton. **Three Sisters** AVA line VIDAL Bl, CAB FR. **Tiger Mtn** PETIT MANSENG, TOURIGA N. **Wolf Mtn** top awards for Blanc de Blancs, Claret (CAB SAUV/Malbec). **Yonah Mtn** Estate Marian's Meritage is co-fermented, Merlot-led Bx blend. In s: Muscadine (**Tilford**, bio) and fruit wine (trad blackberry), some v.gd.

Idaho (ID)

If WA sits in CA's shadow, ID is in WA's. It's a tiny region with a mere 65 wineries, 526 ha. There's promise in growing areas and wines, but few bottles make it beyond state borders. It's early days, but SYRAH, VIOGNIER already clear standouts, with lush flavours, vivid acidity.

3100 Cellars Snake RV ★ Only dedicated winery in ID for sparkling.

Cinder Snake RV ★★ Melanie Krause (ex-Ch Ste Michelle, *see* WA) makes velvety SYRAH, stainless VIOGNIER. Valentina standout Bx blend.

Huston Vineyards Snake RV ★ Chicken Dinner RIES blend, surprising delight; MALBEC, pure, varietally correct.

Rivaura ★★ In Lewis-Clark V; reputed consulting winemaker. Watch, esp SYRAH.

Sawtooth Winery Snake RV ★ One of ID's oldest (1987), now Precept-owned (WA). Tasty RIES, SYRAH, TEMPRANILLO.

Ste Chapelle Snake RV ★ ID's founding winery (1975), also largest. Focus on sweet whites, soft reds. Well-priced quaffers.

Maryland (MD)

Mid-Atlantic, emerging e-coast star, 80 wineries, 3 AVAs. Launched post-Prohibition by reporter P Wagner, hybrids fan; focus now on classical styles, pét-nats, meticulous attention to local terroirs; E Shore sandy soils, hills of Garrett and Allegheny mtns, blue-crab-rich Chesapeake Bay checks freezing winters, stifling summers. Reliable ripeners SAUV BL, MERLOT, PETIT VERDOT; also ALBARIÑO, CHARD, CHENIN BL; top hybrids incl VIDAL Bl, Vignoles.

PIWI popular in MD, NJ, PA, VA: Chardonel. And that's enough initials for anyone.

Black Ankle ★★★ Setting MD standards since 2008: spontaneous ferment, dry-farmed, Frederick Co AVA. Serious rosé, incl trad-method fizz. Barrel-fermented CHARD, plus ALBARIÑO, SAUV BL (bottled by clone), MOURVÈDRE. New: Domaine 26, top MD SYRAH, best yrs only. Library wines, unforgettable Bx-style Crumbling Rock, Slate. Owns new Live Edge Vyds, 1st bottles out now.

Old Westminster ★★★ Spontaneous-ferment, cult. Taut, beguiling ALBARIÑO among best in e. Earthy amphora PINOT BL; MALBEC (36 mths French oak); also BLAUFRÄNKISCH, CABS SAUV/FR, PETIT VERDOT, blends. Serious pricey pét-nats. Sister Burnt Hill Farm, small-production CHARD, Malbec, SYRAH, Regent.

Other good estates Big Cork (MALBEC, NEBBIOLO, US-oak SYRAH, Blanc de Blancs), Boordy (1st bonded winery, mid-C20 by P Wagner; prized CAB FR), Bordeleau, Catoctin Breeze, Clyopatra (awarded CAB SAUV), Crow, Elk Run, Linganore (Bx style, ageable; SAPERAVI), Lowe Vyd (BARBERA novello, serious Malbec), Narciso

(Blanc de Blancs, Cab Sauv, VIDAL Bl), Port of Leonardtown (BARBERA Res, aged Chambourcin), Sugarloaf Mtn, The Vyds at Dodon (serious terroir/bio/vintage-minded; Bx varieties, CHARD), Windridge.

Michigan (MI)

Around 200 producers. North and along Lake Michigan "Third Coast" are historic areas, with s and sw on rise. Leelanau and Old Mission Peninsula AVAs since 80s, still top. Sustainability-project collaboration with NY State. Once-popular cherry wines on wane due to climate change. **2Lads** D Cuvée PINOT N flagship, RIES (several). **Black Star** CAB FR, GAMAY, Pinot N (several), trad-method fizz. **Bos Wine** Ries, pét-nat. **Brys Estate** Ries, gd MERLOT, Cab Fr, Pinot N. **Ch Chantal** wide range; non-alc, cherry wine. **Ch Grand Traverse** multiple ranges, v.gd Res Gamay N. **Filkins Vyd** peppery SYRAH. **Left Foot Charly** BLAUFRÄNKISCH. **Lemon Creek** dark-fruit SHIRAZ. **Mari** ★★★ excellent red blends, Troglodyte Bianco. **Mawby** ★★ Blancs de Blancs/de Noirs, rosé (sp); **Modales** Pinot N, Ries, El Suelo (r). **Neu Cellars** skin-contact Ries, VIDAL Bl, fizz. **St Julian** Braganini (Cab Fr). **Verterra** ★ awarded whites; PINOT GR, Merlot Res. **WaterFire** min-intervention GRÜNER V, Gneiss Blanc KERNER/GEWURZ, SIP-certified.

Missouri (MO)

Official state grape Norton (r) one of best US hybrids, along with Vignoles (w) and Chambourcin (r). **Adam Puchta** elegant Dry and heady Res Vignoles (w); awarded Chambourcin. **Augusta Winery** Chambourcin, Chardonel. **Hermannhof** structured Norton can age; Chardonel, Vignoles (w). **Les Bourgeois** Chardonel, Norton. **Noboleis Vyds** juicy Chambourcin, oak-aged VIDAL. **Röbller Vyd** ★★ Le Trompier N (r), Vignoles Res, both can age. **Stone Hill** ★★ complex lauded Norton. **TerraVox** ★★ excellent hybrid and natives; top dry/fortified Norton.

Nevada (NV)

Imported CA grapes, flavoured/fruit wines important here. Pahrump V contains most wineries. **Artesian Cellars** ★ v.gd Battle Born range, NV grapes, vinifera. **Sanders Family Winery** makes "American Sherry", "American Port", etc.

New England

NE Atlantic, six states (*see also* VT) n of NYC sharing hybrids (Cayuga, Petite Pearl, St Croix), vinifera (CHARD, CAB FR, Pinots, RIES) and fruit (esp apples, blueberries), plus mixed wines across cold-climate terrains; three share SE New England AVA, cool Atlantic climate moderated by Gulf Stream. Prolific hybrids creation in C19. **Connecticut** faces North Fork (*see also* NY) across cold-tempering Sound. Three AVAs, small, growing; source of once-everywhere Hartford grape. Hopkins Vyd, Jones Winery (Cab Fr, MUSCAT OTTONEL, Chard), Lake Waramaug (SEYVAL BL, Cab Fr); research station at UConn. **Massachusetts** Martha's Vyd AVA, Concord created here 1849. Many fruit wines, some v.gd; craft cheesemaking. Alfalfa Farm CAB SAUV, awarded blueberry wine; Black Birch Cab Fr (also rosé), VIOGNIER; Glendale Ridge Cab Fr, Corot N, CHENIN BL, VIDAL Bl (orange or pét-nat, blends); Westport Rivers farm, forest, GRÜNER V, RKATSITELI, PINOT N, oak-raised Marquette/Petite Pearl, 36-mth Blanc de Blancs; Willow Spring Léon Millot Res. **Rhode Island** smallest state, ocean, Sound influence. Carolyn's Sakonnet GEWURZ, blends Cab Fr/Chancellor; Diamond Hill synthetics-free farm, barrel-aged Pinot N; Greenvale min-touch family estate; Mulberry Vyds PINOT GR, SYRAH; Newport Gewurz, Bx style; Sakonnet River v.gd Chard, natural-ferment Pinot Gr *ramato* (*see* Grapes), smart-oak

MERLOT; Verde biology-prof-turned-farmer on lake, Cab Fr-led blend Surveyor, awarded St Croix. **Maine** ne-most state, small growers, warming. Bulet, RAS both excellent blueberry fizz; Oyster River natural, orange Chard, Frontenac Gr rosé. **New Hampshire** elevation; many lakes, sandy loam nr coast. Appolo Vyds, hands-off approach, vegan Brianna, Cayuga, Pinot Gr, Cab Fr, CARMENÈRE; Flag Hill Charmat Cayuga fizz, De Chaunac rosé, oak-raised Marechal Foch (r); Hermit Woods serious, quality, dry, no-grapes wines (r) oak-aged wild berries, (w) kiwi, crab apples, donut peaches, green tomatoes, rhubarb (in rosé blends too); NOK Vino St Croix/Sabervois, Marquette field blend, or with L'Acadie Bl; incl 1969 vyd.

New Jersey (NJ)

70 wineries, some among best in e; four AVAs (Hunterdon: proposed 5th). Rutgers University studies say akin to Bx, esp Médoc. Winemakers Co-op: six top wineries share CAB FR to make own Open Source blends. Since 2025, Terroir NJ promotes all quality wines from 100% NJ fruit. Four hardiness zones; growing seasons getting drier, for now. Stretches s–n along Atlantic: Italian varieties in gravelly maritime Outer Coast Plain (incl Cape May); bucolic central NJ, soft hills, focus on agritourism and quality locus; limestone, granite Warren Hills in n for elegant GEWURZ, GRÜNER V, RIES, BLAUFRÄNKISCH, PINOT N, SYRAH. Try also Almathea, Bellview, Cedar Rose, Meadowbrook (ex-UNIONVILLE winemaker; Cab Fr, rosés, PINOTS M/N), Sharrott, White Horse (owns historic Chaddsford winery, PA), Working Dog.

Alba ★★★ Limestone, granite in Warren Hills AVA. One of largest, oldest PINOT N plantings on E Coast. Burgundy aspiration, incl earthy Grand Res; excellent CHARD (oldest vines); gd GEWURZ, RIES (also in aromatic field blend GTR); CAB FR, PINOT GR. Fizz: RIES; Blanc de Blancs, native-ferment base in French oak, soon.

Auburn Road ★★★ Barrel-fermented CHARD Res; Bx style with Chambourcin backbone (Eidolón, US oak), and without (Gaia); PETIT VERDOT, MERLOT, PINOT GR; vermouth; library wines from Giulia (Merlot/Petit Verdot) to Chard.

Beneduce Vineyards ★★★ Family estate with bees, local salumi, gd shop. BLAUFRÄNKISCH, BARBERA, PINOT N (spicy, cool). Intermezzo GEWURZ (dr), RIES. Super Tuscan-inspired Mangione; Chambrusco Chambourcin, Modena style; pét-nats (Blaufränkisch, Gewurz). Acqua Pazza (piquette but Italian, honey-ferment). Soon: DOLCETTO.

Hawk Haven ★★★ Cape May peninsula; glacial, ocean air. Complex, structured CAB SAUV, v.gd CAB FR, MERLOT; dry RIES is Meyer lemon-plush; steely ALBARIÑO; PINOT GR, TEMPRANILLO, barrel-raised SANGIOVESE. Flagship Q, lasting Bx style. Focus on quality fizz could incl US-rare serious Charmat soon.

Mount Salem ★★★ Small, distinguished estate, Austrian varieties (mostly), Burgundy methods. Masterful Matthias (BLAUFRÄNKISCH/ST-LAURENT/ZWEIGELT); barrel-fermented, *sur lie* CHARD, GRÜNER V; BARBERA; CAB FR (Blanc too). Wild ferments. Exploring San Marco hybrid, testing NJ resilience, weather changes.

Unionville ★★★ Three vyds, terroir-serious, 1st plantings 1995. Single-vyd CHARD (French oak-fermented), PINOT N; N Rhône-style VIOGNIER, SYRAH; GRÜNER V, PICPOUL. Savoury CAB FR (also with Chambourcin). Fanciful Hunterdon Mistral Bl (MARSANNE/ROUSSANE/Viognier) and Rouge (Syrah/Counoise/1% Viognier) v.gd, also as 10 yrs+ library wines.

William Heritage ★★★ Outer Coastal Plain AVA. Flagship BDX best-plots red blend. Single-vyd Chambourcin Res; chewy, complex Blanc de Noirs, top Blanc de Blancs; GRENACHE/SYRAH rosé, Provence style; cool maritime Norman's Vyd CABS FR/SAUV, 10 yrs+; single-vyd MERLOT. New: RKATSITELI, SAPERAVI, rosé.

New Mexico (NM)

High-altitude vyds, moderate warm climate. **Black Mesa** ★★ Consistent Bx varieties (r); Abiquiu (w), Traminette/SEYVAL BL. **DH Lescombes Family Vyds** Bx focus; multiple tasting rooms. **Embudo Valley Vyds** eclectic mix. **Gruet** ★★ historic producer of trad-method fizz, now mostly US grapes. **La Chiripada** ★ oldest NM winery; signature CAB SAUV; bright, crisp Kabinett-style RIES (*see* Germany). **Luna Rossa Winery** v.gd range of Italian varieties; Res AGLIANICO, BARBERA, NEBBIOLO. **Noisy Water** ★★ farms historic cool-climate Engle Vyd; large range; awarded Aglianico, Merlot, Res Cab Sauv. **Sheehan Winery** Bx and Italian varieties. **Vivác** ★★ PINOT M shines in French grape line-up.

Top Barbera gaining ground in ne: Three Brothers (Finger L); Beneduce (NJ).

New York (NY)

Almost 500 producers; statewide sustainability via Cornell University. Wide-ranging cool-climate (changes: earlier budding, later frosts, sudden heavy rains, dry spells, early harvest), vinifera experience, 150 yrs of native and French-American hybrids, a culture of experimentation keep US's 3rd-largest producer innovative. Winters are freezing, but lakes, rivers, the ocean, clever viticulture (double trunks, winter hilling-up) moderate. Look for CAB FR, PINOT N, SYRAH, RIES, GEWURZ, BLAUFRÄNKISCH, RKATSITELI, SAPERAVI, notable dry hybrids and natives, top trad fizz, single-site bottles. AVAs total 11, incl Finger Lakes (Finger L), sunlight hours equal Napa's in fewer days; Hudson River Region (Hudson RR), complex soils, microclimates; Lake Erie, cooler spring, warm ripening autumns, lots of Concord; Long Island (Long I), maritime, bio pioneer, some decades-old, own-rooted, in sandy soils, sub-AVA North Fork (N Fork), warmer, for longer than Hamptons; Niagara Escarpment (Niag) on Lake Ontario.

21 Brix ★★ Estate on Lake Erie with 1st-rate CHARD, GEWURZ, GRÜNER V, PINOT GR, SAUV BL, MOSCATO fizz. Aromatic BLAUFRÄNKISCH, oak-raised CAB SAUV, ageable PINOT N, SYRAH, MERLOT. Serious Noiret (r), Icewine (VIDAL BL too).

Anthony Road Finger L ★★★ Seneca Lake; v.gd RIES incl barrel-ferm, trad-method, top natural-ferment Art Series (library too). Vignoles, v. serious, incl Martini-Becraft Selection, worth price. Textbook Finger L PINOT N, CAB FR.

Apollo's Praise Finger L ★★★ Winemakers Kelby Russell (RED NEWT) and Julia Hoyle (HOSMER); famed Lahoma Vyd, Seneca Lake. Cellar-worthy RIES range (The Knoll, cru), CHARD. Also GRÜNER V, dry GEWURZ, Lovejoy (Chard/Grüner V/Ries), SCHEUREBE, GAMAY, CAB FR (Res, classic).

Arrowhead Spring Vineyards ★★★ Never-herbicide estate (est 2006) in Niag limestone. Top PINOT N, Bx blends. Plus CAB FR (Res too), SYRAH (cool-climate acidity), also with MERLOT or VIOGNIER, ageable. Linear CHARD, Viogner, dry RIES.

Bedell Long I ★★★ Pre-eminent estate; Long I-sustainability (LISW) leader. Native yeasts, maritime climate, powerful, saline wines. Top Bx-style Musée (PETIT VERDOT-led). Plus Gallery 21 (CHARD/VIOGNER), Taste Red (MALBEC base), v.gd CAB FR, Malbec. Rare Long I MELON DE BOURGOGNE, VERDEJO. Small Batch label, experiments with varietal rosé, amphora GEWURZ, Austrian-oak PETIT VERDOT.

Boundary Breaks Finger L ★★★ Germanic RIES, ageable, several styles. Medium-dry Ovid Line pleases all; refreshing Icewine. Earthy early-pick GEWURZ; CAB FR, CAB SAUV or MERLOT. The Harmonic, Merlot-led Bx blend.

Channing Daughters Long I ★★★ Known for beachy terroir, experiments, single-vyds. Textured, ageable FRIULANO; cool-maritime LAGREIN; REFOSCO, US-rare RIBOLLA GIALLA. Playful CHARDS, SAUV BL. Single-site floral PETIT VERDOT; SYRAH. Research is CAB SAUV-led, earthy, tart fruit. Local-aromatics vermouth. Watch new

NEW ENGLAND–NEW YORK

Merlot (Sculpture Garden TEROLDEGO/BLAUFRÄNKISCH); best yrs Dorn & Blau. Library blends (r/w).

Damiani Finger L ★★ E Seneca Lake. Fruit from Cayuga, Keuka lakes too. Brut CHARD/PINOTS N/M voted best in NY 2024, Blanc de Noirs. Savoury, linear Chard. Sole e Terra (r); single-vyd GEWURZ, LEMBERGER (best yrs); Little Lotus Flower (w); Vignoles (w); gd CAB FR, Meritage.

NY Finger Lakes Riesling as good as Mosel, Nahe? Who says? German wine hacks.

Dear Native Grapes ★★ Big project: pre-Prohibition native Catawba, Isabella, MN hybrids (Petite Pearl), new US species *Vitis aestivalis*. Try Steuben pét-nat, barrel-aged Delaware (or Catawba). Field blends: Diana (named after C19 creator, MA), Duchess, Empire State, Iona (from specialist Steve Casscles).

Element Winery Finger L ★★★ Smart, exploratory use of terroir/difficult climate. Magical blends (PINOT N/SYRAH/GRENACHE); RIES, Syrah. Library Ries, CAB FR, GAMAY, PINOT N. Young fresh In Our Element; Can't Stop/Won't Stop blend. Colloquial: tiny quantities by plot; trad-method NV Brut. New vines: PETITES ARVINE/MANSENG/VERDOT.

Fjord Hudson RR ★★★ Sustainable; benchmark ALBARIÑO in e. Top: CAB FR (ages; rosé too). Also CHARD, RIES, GAMAY, PINOT N. Ageable MERLOT, also in serious blend with BLAUFRÄNKISH/Cab Fr; field-blend SAPERAVI/Blaufränkish/Cab Fr.

Floral Terranes Long I ★★★ Fruit from N Fork, wild, moody wines. Skin-contact RIES; slow-evolve CAB FR, MERLOT (also co-ferment). Library if you can find: earthy CAB SAUV, ferocious PETIT VERDOT. Ciders, most yrs.

Forge Cellars Finger L ★★★ E Seneca Lake. Single-sites focus: precise RIES (library), 90s-planted CAB FR, PINOT N (Tango Oaks, cool-climate classic; Leidenfrost, lifted power).

Fox Run Finger L ★★★ Range of RIES v.gd; rare Res CAB FR, LEMBERGER; CHARD, CAB SAUV; single-plot MERLOT in best yrs. Retired winemaker Peter Bell mentored many of Finger L's greatest. Café with local ingredients.

Frank, Dr Konstantin Finger L ★★★ Founder of vinifera in Finger L and e, winery on Keuka Lake. Flagship Lena Res. Many RIES. Rare Siberian/N China Amur, rustic elegance. BLAUFRÄNKISCH. Amber RKATSITELI. Old Vines PINOT N (1958 vyd); CAB FR (50 yr+ vines). SAPERAVI, robust (or rosé), sells out. Masterful trad-method.

Glenora Wine Cellars Finger L ★★ Foundational estate on Seneca Lake. Lasting Brut, complex SEYVAL BL pét-nat, RIES, smart Black Diamond Express (r), vinifera-hybrid blend CAB FR to BACO NOIR. Cosy inn, lake view.

Heart & Hands Finger L ★★★ Founded 2010, Cayuga Lake slope for PINOT N (flagship, cellar-worthy Mo Chuisle Res), a little RIES. Also top: ALIGOTÉ (creamy, wild acidity), AUXERROIS, CHARD (meaty 23), PETITE ARVINE, LAGREIN (1st: 24).

Hermann J Wiemer Finger L ★★★ Top US RIES name, incl single-vyd, Res; 1st NY Demeter wine. Top e nursery, supplies neighbours. Experimental Julia vyd incl rare SCHIOPPETTINO, PETITE ARVINE, FURMINT. Fine GEWURZ, CAB FR, PINOT N, superlative fizz (10 yrs+ tirage). Owns Standing Stone: Blanc de Blancs, old-vine Ries, SAPERAVI; also CAB SAUV, Pinot N, testing NEBBIOLO.

Hickory Hollow Finger L ★★★ Seneca Lake. Lauded low-intervention CHARD, RIES (incl 10-yr+ solera), GEWURZ, PINOT BL (Extra Brut too), MERLOT. Winemaker's labels: Chëpìka (Catawba, Delaware pét-nat), Nathan K (library Ries; CAB FR and PINOT N).

Hillick & Hobbs ★★ RIES from Napa winemaker Paul Hobbs (*see* CA). Natural yeast. Flagship Estate, *sur lies* (library, from 21). Single-sites: Klon 90, Lower Terrace, North Ravine.

Hosmer Finger L ★★★ On Cayuga Lake (est 1972); 16 varieties on 67 acres, incl De Chaunac; v.gd RIES; SAUV BL, incl limited releases. Also CHARD, PINOT BL, v.gd CAB FR, 80s PINOT N vines (Blanc de Noirs too); trad-method Cayuga; balanced trad Catawba.

Lakewood Vineyards Finger L ★★★ Finger L knowledge, 3rd generation; gd Res CAB FR; everyday bottle too. Impressive GEWURZ, PINOTS GR/N, multiple RIES.

Lamoreaux Landing ★★★ 50 plots, 1st planted 1977. Single sites: RIES (also prized fizz), MERLOT. Awarded, ageable CAB FR, PINOT N; v.gd Bx blend 76 West; CHARD Res, GEWURZ, GRÜNER V, MOSCATO. Library incl Blanc de Blanc [sic] 16 yrs+.

Macari Long I, North F ★★★ Clifftop estate focused on plot, massal selection, bio. Horses cult CAB FR or PETIT VERDOT blend pét-nat. SAUV BL: grassy Katherine's Field, concrete Lifeforce (also perfumed Cab Fr). Burgundy-method Breakwater CHARD. Excellent Bx blends: Alexandra (CAB SAUV-led), Bergen Road (Merlot-led).

McCall Long I, North F ★★★ Top Long I-terroir PINOT N since 07; gd CAB FR, SAUV BL, CHARD, MERLOT (Res, Bx blends too). On-site Charolais cattle; steaks/burgers in tasting room.

Milea Hudson RR ★★ Rolling, foggy hills; CAB FR passion (Sang's Vyd); solid BLAUFRÄNKISCH. Hudson Valley Heritage: restoration-minded old hybrids (21 Baco N/Marechal Foch/Palmer). Owns Hudson V Projects: goal of top trad-method; PINOT N (r) too.

Millbrook Hudson RR ★★★ Was 1st to grow vinifera in Hudson V: CHARD (Res too), RIES, GAMAY, PINOT N. Single-vyd "Tocai" FRIULANO; complex oak-raised CAB FR Res, classic incl MERLOT.

Osmote North F ★★ Seneca Lake. Try CAB FR (rosé too), v.gd CHARD, RIES, PINOT N. Equal quality focus on hybrids, v.gd pét-nat: Cayuga (w, NY hybrid), Melody (w, NY hybrid), De Chaunac (r, French/US hybrid, still too), Marquette (r, MN hybrid); grass/grapes-fed pigs, bacon soon.

Paumanok Long I ★★★ Complex, cool-climate North F wines; spontaneous ferments, low sulphur. In best yrs, ageable: Assemblage (Bx varieties); Grand Vintage (MERLOT, CAB FR); Minimalist range (CHARD, CHENIN BL, Cabs Fr/SAUV). Tuthills Lane Cab Sauv, Apollo Drive PETIT VERDOT; trad-method Rosé de Pinot (21). Owns Palmer Vyds: Chard, Cab Fr, Merlot (Old Roots), Res (Bx blend); exciting ALBARIÑO, SAUV BL.

Ravines Finger L ★★★ Seneca Lake. Inspired RIES: single-vyd Argetsinger, Falls 16, White Springs. Also SAUV BL, top GEWURZ. Flagship Argetsinger PINOT N; Limestone Springs vyd CAB FR; MERLOT, Bx style. New: GAMAY on Keuka Lake.

Red Newt Finger L ★★★ Renowned RIES, top US quality. Focused on terroirs, incl Seneca Lake crus. Viridescens, Bx style from best sites. Elegant GEWURZ, GRÜNER V, PINOT GR. Single-vyd CAB FR, PINOT N, SYRAH. Bistro, local produce.

Red Tail Ridge Finger L ★★★ Seneca Lake. Wild ferment; super CHARD, RIES; elegant BLAUFRÄNKISCH, CAB FR, DORNFELDER, LAGREIN; v.gd PINOT N (also pét-nat), TEROLDEGO, ZWEIGELT; Blanc de Noirs, pét-nats, Sekt 19, Blanc de Blanc [sic] 19. Perpétuelle Change, takes on NV Champagne, Cuvée No. 4.

Rose Hill Long I ★★★ Was Shinn Estate Vyds; N Fork, bio-minded. Luxury Clarity 19 (CAB SAUV/MERLOT/PETIT VERDOT) awarded NY best 2025; Wild Boar Doe (adds CAB FR, MALBEC to mix); CHARD, GRÜNER V, MERLOT. Owns Croteaux Vyds: SAUV BL, Cab Fr, Merlot rosés.

Bully Hill Vyds museum: uranium-, Depression-era glass. Life before Riedel.

Shaw Vineyard Finger L ★★★ On Seneca Lake, quieter w side, bio-thinking. Focus on Res wines: GEWURZ, PINOT GR, CAB SAUV, MERLOT, PINOT N, RIES (on fine lees or barrel-aged). Orange styles: blends incl Gewurz, Pinot Gr, SAUV BL (gd w too). New: SYRAH.

Sheldrake Point Finger L ★★ Cayuga Lake, w side. Exuberant cool-climate GAMAY; fresh, earthy Meritage; RIES; single-plot PINOT GR, MUSCAT Ottonel; MERLOT, also v.gd rosé, assist to CAB SAUV Res; CAB FR; trad-method fizz. Unwooded CHARD. Experimental Beta bottles: Lambrusco-like Rouge Éclat, Blanc de Cab Fr, bravely acid-driven RIES.

Silver Thread Finger L ★★★ Small-batch cellar blends, bio-minded: CHARD 40-yr+ vines (also Blanc de Blancs); single-vyds (incl 1973-planted Doyle Fournier) RIES (savoury flagship dry, complex semi-dry 24, late-harvest 22); ageable CAB FR-led Bx blend Blackbird; natural-ferment Aravelle/Caguya; off-dry GEWURZ; everyday LEMBERGER/Regent/ZWEIGELT.

Six Eighty Cellars Finger L ★★★ Finger L, experimental vessel range incl Italian clay, concrete, stoneware and French sandstone for various CHARD, GRÜNER V, RIES, PINOT N. *Ramato*-style PINOT GR. Also CHENIN BL, PINOT M.

Sparkling Pointe Long I ★★★ Convincing *fizz*; French winemaker, Champagne grapes. Rich, single-vyd Boisseau Blanc de Blancs (5-yr tirage). Bright, almost fruity, pink Cuvée Cynthia Blanc de Noirs; creamy, floral Topaz Impérial Brut Rosé. Solid Brut (Nature too), Blanc de Blancs. Cuvée Carnaval lets MUSCAT (w), MERLOT (r/rosé) into mix.

Suhru & Lieb Long I ★★★ Showcases NY maritime; union of two top estates for some of Long I's oldest vines, largest PINOT BL plot in US (also 22-mth trad fizz). Mostly varietal: glacial-soil SHIRAZ 10 yrs+, age-worthy CAB FR, MALBEC, PETIT VERDOT, TEROLDEGO Res; rich CHARD, PINOT GR, SAUV BL. Takes La Crescent seriously, rich acidity (sp too). Ember (Bx blend), Estate Meritage (also MERLOT), hold both 10 yrs+; trad-method PINOT BL Brut.

Thirsty Owl Finger L ★★★ Cayuga Lake, w side; RIES and Finger L-rare MALBEC (in blend too), CAB SAUV (also v.gd Icewine). Also PINOTS N/BL, SYRAH (among NY best). French hybrid Chancellor, white Pinot N.

Usonia Finger L ★★ Cayuga Lake. Estate wines: RIES, CAB FR (New Suns), hybrids and sourced (incl SHAW VYD). Responding to climate change with eg. Geneva White #2, skin-contact GRÜNER V; one bio Cab Fr plot.

Wagner Finger L ★★★ Seneca Lake. Deep local knowledge, 5th generation, 50s/60s vyds; 21 varieties incl natives (Delaware, Melody, Aurora). Many single-vyd bottles: Caywood East RIES, aromatic Lone Oak CAB FR (only best yrs), Vignoles (planted 84).

Weis Vineyards Finger L ★★★ Keuka Lake. Winemaker/co-owner from Mosel: dry to sweet RIES (Edel Süss, Winzer Sel 21), TBA-style bottlings (*see* Germany), plus NY hybrid Aravelle. Awarded CHARD, PINOT BL; v.gd GRÜNER V; gd GEWURZ, PINOT N, BLAUFRÄNKISCH, ZWEIGELT (r/rosé).

White blends vs weather in east

With newly chaotic seasons in the e, old trick of blending yr's best ripeners keeps quality whites. **NY** Finger L manages heat/frost, drought/downpours: Heart & Hands Esoterra (CHARD with PETITE ARVINE/ALIGOTÉ/AUXERROIS); Osmote Red Fox (23: FRIULANO/Traminette/Cayuga); Channing Daughters field blend Sylvanus (PINOTS BL/GR/MUSCAT OTTONEL w, orange, or pét-nat). **Piedmont** (between NC, VA) fights humid drought/fierce thunderstorms: Jones Von Drehle Tryst & Twine (23: GROS/PETIT MANSENG/COURBU BL); Linden Wabi Sabi (80s-planted VIDAL BL, 21 incl PETIT MANSENG/SEM/CHARD/VIOGNIER); Blenheim oak-raised Painted White (Chard with ROUSSANNE/Viognier, and/or SAUV BL). Likewise: **MD**'s Old Westminster Trio (varies Chard/ALBARIÑO/RIES); **NJ**'s William Heritage BDX Bl (22 adds Petit Manseng to Bx staples). **VT** hedges bets from start: Iapetus Substrata (co-fermented Louise Swenson/Itasca).

Whitecliff Hudson RR ★★ Vegan, site- and soils-driven, incl Olana (Hudson River School art home) slope for v.gd barrel-aged CAB FR, GAMAY. PINOT N from limestone ridge. Robust RIES, stony CHARD (also fizz). Serious hybrids: Noiret-led red; Traminette, VIDAL BL.

Wölffer Estate Long I ★★★ Premier S Fork estate. Rosé range (set off Hamptons craze): focused, creamy Grandioso top. Limited-release Cellar Series; massal-planted TREBBIANO TOSCANO. Cellar-worthy White Horse range: Christian's Cuvée MERLOT, PINOT N; Bx blend Fatalis Fatum; perfumed Landius Pinot N; rich Antonov SAUV BL; luminous Noblesse Oblige vintage rosé fizz. Winemaker's line: Grapes of Roth, MERLOT (20). Gold Label CAB FR, Classic Red Blend gd value. Leader in 0% abv.

North Carolina (NC)

Seven AVAs, e Atlantic coast to Piedmont foothills (from VA to GA, quality vyds) to Blue Ridge Mtns. Hurdles: humidity, late-season hurricanes, heavy clay; but steady growth of serious inventive producers (storm-ruined **plēb** still shares knowledge), with v.gd CAB FR, PETITS MANSENG/VERDOT, TANNAT. Surry College studies: gd skin-contact ALBARINHO, co-fermented red Trio. In the e: **Cypress Bend** (dr native Muscadine wines); sandy Outer Banks **Sanctuary Vyds** (TEMPRANILLO, SYRAH/Tannat; CHARD/PINOT GR White Pony top value). Hilly central NC: **Jones Von Drehle** (Petit Verdot among best in e, age 20 yrs+; library MERLOT, Chard, steel or oak); **Mountain Books** (incl NC-oak barrels); **Junius Lindsay** (SYRAH from S Rhône vines, 1990); **Parker-Binns**; **Shelton** (est Surry studies, clay-sand Yadkin V AVA, v.gd Tannat, restaurant); **Stony Knoll**. Italy focus in Swan Creek AVA: **Dynamis** (flagship The Mountain Bx blend 19 21 23, oaky CAB SAUV 21 to age, concrete-raised SAUV BL, Blanc de Blancs in 29; restaurant); **Raffaldini** (top *appassimento* skills, new 3-yr cycle for r; v.gd MONTEPULCIANO, incl Grande Riserva blend 22, premium Patrimonio 21, SAGRANTINO, VERMENTINO); **Sotrio** (v.gd FIANO, TEROLDEGO). In the mtns: new steep, tiny Crest of the Blue Ridge AVA: **Burntshirt**; **Euda** (Cabs, v.gd Merlot, Traminette); **Marked Tree** (herbal Cab Fr); **Souther Williams**; **Stone Ashe**. NC Fine Wines lifts wine (and food; NC-style bbq reputed US best) grown in state.

Ohio (OH)

Mid-western state, historic "Wine Belt" fame utilizes Catawba (r). Modern era sees 300+ wineries, five AVAs: rich glacial lake soil, river valleys to Appalachian mtns, and Lake Erie islands. Look for OQW logo on bottles: min 90% OH-grown. **Debonné** (est 70s), largest OH estate, wide range. **Ferrante** Grand River Valley AVA, v.gd Signature Series. **Heineman Winery** vinifera and non-vinifera offerings. **Laurentia** concrete-tank whites. **Markko** Lake Erie CHARD, CAB SAUV, PINOT N, followed NY's Dr Frank to launch Ohioan vinifera in 70s. **M Cellars** RKATSITELI, Bx style. Site-focus **Vermillion Vyds** granite, clay Cabs; sandstone, loam ARNEIS, MALBEC; limestone MOSCATO Giallo, LEMBERGER, Pinot N.

Oklahoma (OK)

One AVA shared with MO and AR: Ozark Mtn. Hybrids most important, Chambourcin top variety. **Bois d'Arc** top Diablo blend, SANGIOVESE using CA grapes; OK, TX versions coming. **C&H Vyd** grower for other wineries making small quantities of quality wines (from winery only). **Clauren Ridge** gd Rhône-style reds and CAB FR. **Pecan Creek Winery** excellent Barrel Res Chambourcin, estate CAB SAUV. **Sabatia** ★★ Steve Sneed crafts some of best wines in OK: top SEYVAL BL (w), Chambourcin (r); v.gd rosé.

Oregon (OR)

Oregon is nipping at Washington State's heels to become the second-largest producer in the US. In 2024, 1076 wineries harvested 129,739 tons of grapes from 19,159 ha of vyd. 58% of the wine produced was Pinot N: OR for Pinot, WA for Cabs/Merlot is the usual mantra. Among other varieties, Pinot Gr, Chard, Syrah,and Cab Sauv have the most land under vine.

Principal viticultural areas

Columbia Gorge (Col G) is split between WA and OR. Experimentation, variety, sustainable viticulture. **Rocks District of Milton-Freewater** (Walla Walla V [Walla]) entirely in OR, producing dense, age-worthy Syrah and sapid Grenache. **Southern Oregon** (S OR) warmest growing region, encompasses much of W OR, s of Will V: s sub-AVA Rogue V (Rog V) incl Applegate (App V); n sub-AVA Umpqua V (Um V) incl Elkton OR and Red Hill Douglas County. Rhône and Spanish varieties best, with some gd Cab Sauv. Quality is spottier than Will V, but future promising. **Willamette Valley** (Will V) sub-AVAs Chehalem Mts (Ch Mtns), Dundee Hills (Dun H), Eola-Amity Hills (E-A Hills), Laurelwood District (LD), Lower Long Tom, McMinnville (McM), Mt Pisgah, Polk County, Ribbon Ridge (Rib R), Tualatin Hills, Van Duzer Corridor (Van DC), Yamhill-Carlton (Y-Car). Pinots Bl/Gr, Ries and Gamay excel; beautiful Chard; Pinot N remains star.

Recent vintages

2025 Mild season, hot August. Projected gd quality with higher alc.
2024 Relatively mild season with long, dry autumn; gd quality.
2023 Warm; heatwave at véraison reduced yield; gd quality.
2022 Cool growing season, small, reduced yield; v.gd bright, fresh wines.
2021 Hot, dry; concentrated, balanced acidities. Outstanding wines.
2020 Wildfires: widespread smoke taint in Will V. S OR less so; Rog V esp gd.
2019 What used to be classic: cool, wet = elegant, restrained. Age-worthy.
2018 Hot, dry; deeply coloured, concentrated, age-worthy; S OR smoke issues.
2017 Bumper crop of excellent quality; Col G smoke issues.

$25 tastings: Björnson, Coleman, Ricochet, Seufert, Stoller, Styring, Tualatin Estate.

Abacela Um V ★★★ Estate est 1995; 1st TEMPRANILLO in US. Fiesta (gd value), Barrel Select, South East Block Res, Paramour quality on up.

Abbott Claim E-A Hills, Y-Car ★★★★ Forward-thinking, organic, dry-farmed. Truffle forest, incredible caves for tasting flinty CHARD, balanced PINOT N. Age-worthy.

Adelsheim Ch Mtns, Rib R ★★ Early producer, David A, responsible for 1st Will V sub-AVAs. Well-distributed, gd-value, classic CHARD, PINOT N, fun sparkling.

Alexana Dun H ★★ Owned by Dr Revana (Revana, Napa; Bodegas Corazón del Sol, Argentina). Fleshy, rich, oaked CHARD, PINOT N.

Analemma Col G ★★★ Gorgeous bio property, 15 estate-grown varieties interplanted with U-Pick red cherries, lavender. GODELLO, MENCÍA, TROUSSEAU, GRENACHE best.

Antica Terra Will V ★★★★ Big textural wines. Rich, spicy CHARD, PINOT N. Deep, fruit-forward rosé. Excellent food, lauded comparative-tasting experiences.

Antiquum Farm Will V ★★★★ Regenerative viticulture using pigs, sheep, poultry. Dry-farmed. Concentrated, complex, expressive PINOTS GR/N.

Archery Summit Dun H, E-A Hills ★★★ Crimson Wine Group-owned. Transitioning to regenerative. Structured, age-worthy PINOT N (Arcus, Summit).

Argyle Will V ★★ Trad-method sparklings with a long history.

Arterberry Maresh Dun H ★★★ One of oldest estates in WILL V, much dry-farmed, own-rooted. Delicate, red-fruit, earthy PINOT N (Maresh Vyd, Old Vines, Weber).

A to Z Wineworks OR ★ Owned by WA's Ste Michelle Wine Estates along with Rex Hill (premium in Will V). Value-priced, soundly made, fruit-forward.

Audeant Will V ★★★★ Andrew Riechers (previously Antica Terra, JK Carriere) crafts toasty CHARD, age-worthy, single-vyd PINOT N.

Beaux Frères Rib R ★★★ Majority-owned by Champagne Henriot (*see* France). Mikey Etzel still in charge of winemaking. Earthy Belles Soeurs PINOT N esp gd.

Bergström Will V ★★★★ Estate fruit (100%) since 2020. One of few WILL V wineries farmed entirely by in-house crew (rather than vyd management). Organic, elegant, powerful. Sigrid CHARD, La Spirale, Le Pre du Col PINOT N.

Bethel Heights E-A Hills ★★★ Old-vine, own-rooted, layered-fruit PINOT N. Delicate CHARD, PINOT BL, rosé.

Big Table Farm Will V ★★★★ Holistic farm with animals, vegetables, wine. Complex, concentrated Elusive Queen CHARD, SYRAH, single-vyd PINOT N.

Brick House Rib R ★★★★ All bio farming; all native ferments. Hands-on, family winemaking team. Excellent Cascadia CHARD, Les Dijonnais PINOT N.

Brooks E-A Hills ★★★ Family estate, bio. Perfumed RIES (dr to sw; up to 20 cuvées: Ara, Bois Joli, Estate), fruity Rastaban PINOT N.

Cameron Dun H, Rib R ★★★★ Opulent yet age-worthy CHARD (Clos Electrique). Structured, age-worthy PINOT N (Arley's Leap). Entry DUN H cuvées gd value. Fun RIB R NEBBIOLO.

Carriere, JK Will V ★★★ St Dolores Estate on Parrett Mtn: one of least recognized, most promising areas in Will V. Exquisitely balanced, nuanced, earthy PINOT N from estate and from purchased fruit; v. age-worthy. Provocateur gd value.

International Pinot Noir Day is 18 August. Raid the piggy bank.

Chehalem Will V ★ Stoller Wine Group-owned. Large-production, soundly made CHARD, PINOT N.

Colene Clemens Ch Mtns ★★ Dry-farmed estate (2006). Classic Will V PINOT N with chewy tannin.

Corollary Wines Will V ★★★ In E-A HILLS, trad-method sparkling with its own estate, fully dedicated (only one in OR).

Cristom E-A Hills ★★★ Wine made by Littorai alum Daniel Estrin (est 1992); organic/bio. Racy, ageable CHARD, PINOT N with firm backbone from lots of whole-cluster inclusion.

Crowley Wines Will V ★★★ Classic, graceful CHARD, PINOT N; gd-value WILL V blends.

De Ponte Cellars Dun H ★★★ Fresh, gd-value MELON DE BOURGOGNE; beautiful, classic PINOT N.

Division Winemaking Co Will V ★→★★ Portland urban winery. Always fun, often affordable: ALIGOTÉ, CHENIN BL, SAUV BL, GAMAY, TROUSSEAU, orange, carbonique PINOT N, NEBBIOLO and more.

Drouhin Oregon, Dom Dun H, E-A Hills ★★★ Drouhin family-owned (*see* France), made by Véronique Boss-D. Restrained Arthur CHARD, v.gd Laurène PINOT N, firm, best aged. Sister label Roserock in E-A HILLS.

Élevée Winegrowers Will V ★★★ Exploration of WILL V sub-AVAs with single-vyd sources. Classic, structured, showcase terroir.

Elk Cove Will V ★★→★★★ Family-owned (1977), 400 acres, dry-farmed, some own-rooted. Single-vyd PINOT N more complex, dark-fruited than entry levels, Clay Court, outstanding Five Mtn, Mt Richmond; v.gd PINOTS BL/GR. Second label: Pike Road, focus on value.

Et Fille Will V ★★★ Family-owned; small WILL V estate plot, six sustainably farmed vyds. Top age-worthy PINOT N (Gabriella, Palmer Creek).

Evening Land E-A Hills ★★★ Label that revolutionized OR CHARD: precise, mineral La Source, Summum. Earthy PINOT N with nuanced oak.

Spotlight on Eola-Amity Hills
Wines from E-A HILLS stand out for their concentration, tension, leaness, with restrained fruit character and minerality. PINOT N has firmer tannins than in other sub-AVAs, CHARD more precise acidity. Why? E-A is mostly planted on Columbia River basalt with shallow topsoil – causing vines to struggle, setting smaller canopies with small-berried bunches. High skin-to-juice ratio results in concentrated flavours and higher tannins. The e and n exposure of E-A captures gentle morning sun rather than hot afternoon sun, creating lean, tense, precise wines.

Evesham Wood Will V ★★★ Bought by Erin Nuccio (Haden Fig). Age-worthy, complex PINOT N made from all dry-farmed vyds (Le Puits Sec).

Eyrie Vineyards, The Dun H ★★★★ Dry-farmed, organic, no-till, min-intervention winemaking. Oldest producer in WILL V (original vines 1965). Elegant, age-worthy, low alc. Incredible library releases; CHARD, Daphne, PINOT GR, Sisters, original South Block PINOT N bottlings textural wonders.

Flâneur Wines Will V ★★★ Excellent-value, entry-level CHARD, PINOT N. More structured Cuvée Constantin, La Belle Promenade.

Goodfellow Will V ★★★ Sources fruit from dry-farmed vyds. Complex, concentrated yet elegant; Durant CHARD, Lewman PINOT GR, Heritage Whistling Ridge PINOT N.

Gran Moraine Will V ★★★ Part of Jackson Family Wines OR (*see* CA), specializing in trad-method sparkling, restrained CHARD, structured PINOT N.

Granville Dun H ★★★ Married 2nd-generation growers Ayla and Jackson Holstein started label 2014. Deeply expressive CHARD, PINOT N.

Hamilton Russell Oregon Will V ★★★ HR investment to complement S African wines (*see* S Africa). Elegant CHARD, restrained, structured PINOT N.

Hundred Suns Will V ★★★ Vibrant, age-worthy PINOT N, own-rooted esp gd. Old Eight Cut bottlings, GAMAY, PINOT M great value.

Illahe Will V ★★ Dry-farmed, worked by horse. Famous 1899 PINOT N made without electricity – carted by horse, destemmed by bicycle destemmer, foot-trodden, transferred to barrel by bicycle pump, transported to Portland via canoe.

Johan Van DC ★★★ Dry-farmed, bio, no-till estate vyd. Unique CHARD, KERNER, PINOTS GR/N, BLAUFRÄNKISCH. Skin-contact wines deeply flavoured, resonant.

Kelley Fox Will V ★★★★ Beautifully energetic, elegant CHARD, GRÜNER V, PINOTS BL/N, also blueberries. Mirabai esp gd value.

King Estate Will V ★★ Now largest bio producer in US. Still family-owned. Appley PINOT GR core of portfolio, a dozen PINOT N, fruity CHARD, GEWURZ, SAUV BL, fizz.

Lavinea Will V ★★★ Owned by EVENING LAND alumni Isabelle Meunier and Greg Ralston. Entire portfolio of lithe, fine-boned PINOT N.

Lemelson Ch Mtns, Dun H, Y-Car ★★★ Family-owned, organic estate growing CHARD, PINOTS GR/N, RIES. Rich, textured wines, often oak-forward.

Limited Addition Will V ★★ Bree Stock MW works with 20 different vines to increase diversity and make affordable, smashable, low-intervention wines. Try CHENIN BL, GRÜNER V, SAUV BL, BLAUFRÄNKISCH, CAB FR, GAMAY, MENCÍA, TROUSSEAU, Cabernet Dorsa at reasonable prices.

Lingua Franca E-A Hills ★★★ Stylish CHARD (Bunker Hill, Estate, Sisters), balanced PINOT N (Mimi's Mind, The Plow). Constellation Brands-owned (*see* CA).

Loop de Loop Col G, Will V ★★★ Organic, dry-farmed, no-till. Bright, fresh CAB FR, ethereal, red-fruited, spicy PINOT N.

Love & Squalor ★★★ Decidedly superior RIES, GAMAY. Great value.

Martin Woods Winery Will V ★★★ Evan M sources from myriad AVAs. Superior whites: CHARD, RIES manage to outperform v.gd reds. One of few producers in OR using OR oak. Koosah, Yamhill V, Pearlstad esp gd.

Morgen Long Will V ★★★ Laser-focused acid, mineral, citrus CHARD, well-integrated oak; v. reductive (smoky) in recent vintages. Best: Seven Springs, X Omni.

Nicolas-Jay Will V ★★★ More Burgundians in OR: Jean-Nicolas Méo of Dom Méo-Camuzet (*see* France) and music entrepreneur Jay Boberg. Bold, structured Momtazi, concentrated Own-Rooted PINOT N.

Patricia Green Cellars Will V ★★★ Excellent, red-fruited, moderate-weight, single-vyd PINOT N. Superb Estate Bonshaw Block, Estate Etzel Block, Mysterious, Notorious. Rare OR SAUV BL.

Perkins Harter E-A Hills ★★★ Fresh, floral, toasty CHARD and lightweight, balanced, wet-earth, cherry-fruit PINOT N from Bracken estate vyd.

Ponzi Lau ★★→★★★ Champagne Bollinger-owned (*see* France). Avellana CHARD, Aurora PINOT N v.gd. Fruit-forward Classico, Tavola Pinot N gd value.

Purple Hands Will V ★★★ Family-owned, dry-farmed, organic estate vyds: ripe, rich yet fresh CHARD, PINOT N.

Résonance Will V ★★★ Jadot's (*see* France) OR project. Découverte CHARD, Estate PINOT N best, most age-worthy. Need vigorous decant when young.

Ribbon Ridge Winery Rib R ★★★ Ridgecrest label gd value, textural: GRÜNER V, RIES, GAMAY, PINOTS GR/N. Aged RIB R Pinot N outstanding, elegant.

Rose & Arrow Will V ★★★ Micro-production; age-worthy PINOT N 18 19 from winemaker Felipe Ramirez and terroir consultant Pedro Parra. Second label: Alit, v.gd value if you subscribe.

Sacred Shore Will V ★★★ Tiny label founded by best friends Andrew Riechers (Audeant) and John Soares to explore Spain's Galician varieties (which they do extremely well). But SANGIOVESE vines that distracted them in 2021 have proven their best work thus far.

Savage Grace Col G ★★★ Regeneration-farmed estate wines and wines from purchased fruit. Meaty SYRAH; opulent CAB SAUV; flavourful GEWURZ, GRÜNER V, SAUV BL, CAB FR, PINOT N.

Sequitur Rib R ★★★ Another project from BEAUX FRÈRES' Etzel family (vyds border): focused, fine CHARD, PINOT N. Labels, names change annually.

Sokol Blosser Will V ★★→★★★ Family-owned, organic, historic producer run by 2nd generation. Estate, Orchard Block PINOT N, structure, length. Evolution early-drinking gd value.

Soter Will V ★★★★ Tony S, CA legend, shines with balanced, age-worthy CHARD, PINOT N, bubbly. Estate-grown Mineral Springs Ranch, all bio, has best portfolio. Planet Oregon for value.

Spearhunter Will V ★★★ Spearfishing couple Victoria Chávez and David DeLaitsch moved to Will V in 2022. Exceptional 1st vintage CHARD, PINOT N 22. Pithy, saline ALBARIÑO 23 just as gd. Best yet to come.

Teutonic Will V ★★→★★★ Laid-back urban winery in Portland; German, Alsace varieties. Some excellent wines sub-$25: GEWURZ/PINOT N; Candy Cap RIES.

Twill Will V ★★★ Dry-farmed, small production: CHARD, PINOT N, SYRAH.

Violin Will V ★★ One-man-show Will Hamilton sources fruit to make sapid CHARD, PINOT N. Entry WILL V cuvées gd value.

Walter Scott E-A Hills ★★★★ Family-owned, focused on vyd sources. Precise, linear, buzz-worthy CHARD. Earthy, balanced PINOT N, well-integrated oak. GAMAY also excellent. Freedom Hill, Sojourner, X-Novo vyds top list. Age-worthy.

Pennsylvania (PA)

Mid-Atlantic, continental climate, humidity; 450 wineries in five AVAs, top wine lists despite restrictive wine-sale laws; 1st commercial vines (Alexander, native) in US, late C18. Now: ALBARIÑO v.gd (esp **Galen Glen**), GRÜNER V, PINOT N, Bx varieties; many Italians (BARBERA to FIANO). Lake Erie-softened nw.

Milder in se: **Va La** cult Avondale field blends (CORVINA, Rondinella), 11 NEBBIOLO clones, funky ageable rosato, Fiano-to-PETIT MANSENG blend; **Vox Vineti** Nebbiolo, sell-out rosé, single-vyd orange SEM/SAUV BL, earthy Bx style (r). Central Lehigh V: **Galen Glen** windy, 305m (1000ft) up, 7th generation; **Stone Cellar** range from oldest vines, Grüner V leader (incl v.gd trad-method), CAB FR; **Stony Run** v.gd Brut, plush Albariño, library Cabs, Chambourcin. Try also **Allegro**, reliable since 70s, Barbera, GAMAY; **Armstrong Vyd** Cab Fr, Sauv Bl; **Chaddsford** Cab Fr; **Fero Vyds** LEMBERGER, celebrated SAPERAVI rosé; **Folino Estate** AGLIANICO, DOLCETTO, Super Tuscan-style MERLOT; **Karamoor** Merlot, Sauv Bl; **Mazza** Lake Erie RIES, TEROLDEGO, Chambourcin rosé; **Penns Woods** Sauv Bl, Pinot N, Chambourcin Res; **Presque Isle** early vinifera PA winery, BLAUFRÄNKISCH, DORNFELDER; **Three Hammers** Grüner V, PINOT GR; **Vynecrest**; **Waltz** Cab Fr; **Wayvine** barrique-aged native Carmine (also rosé; Merlot blend). Philly urban wineries, serious natural style: **Camuna Cellars** PA and coastal NJ grapes, Norton to Blaufränkisch; **Mural City Cellars** Bx-inspired PA Merlot/Cab Fr/PETIT VERDOT with NJ Chambourcin, figgy, citrus Phinato vermouth, barrel-aged range Side Piece; **Pray Tell** PA-grown CHARD, Gamay/Merlot (Gettysburg vyd), Cab Fr rosé. Local sommeliers' favourite: **Nissley** PINOT GR.

PA's Vendemmia Festival sustains Italian-US culture: awards best home winemaking.

Texas (TX)

Texas Hill Country (THC) and Texas High Plains (THP) major AVAs; THC has subregions, THP does not. Other regions outside AVAs incl N TX, nr Dallas, and E TX towards Louisiana. Dell Valley in far W TX tapped to become quality source. Iberian, Rhône and Med varieties do well. Hybrids excel in E TX.

Ab Astris ★★ Textured, refined. Both Estate and Narra TANNAT v.gd. Avignon blend (r), homage to Châteauneuf (*see* France). Estate Souzão excellent.

Adega Vinho ★★★ High-quality specialist in Iberian and Rhône varieties in refreshing style. Estate TEMPRANILLO esp prized; Blends also v.gd.

Becker Vineyards Historic property with lavender fields. Full-bodied, ripe, oaky Bx and Rhône styles; claret and various CAB SAUV bottlings well regarded; Prairie Rôtie is a signature.

Bending Branch Winery ★★★ Big, tannic reds, lesser-known grapes. Recognized for TANNAT in various bottlings. Experimenting with ageing CAB SAUV and PETIT VERDOT in TX white oak. Long-lived Souzão. GRÜNER VELTLINER, PIQUEPOUL v.gd.

Calais ★★★ Frenchman Benjamin Calais crafts traditional Bx-style wines incl awarded THP Narra Vyds Clone 47 Cuvée L'Exposition CAB SAUV.

Christopher, Elisa ★★★ Elisa C makes trad-method sparkling for her own brand and others. Try TREBBIANO or Blanc du Bois.

Duchman Family Winery ★★★★ Benchmark Italian stars here from older vyds: age-worthy, outstanding AGLIANICO; Oswald Vyd MONTEPULCIANO another signature; v.gd SANGIOVESE; crisp, refreshing, textured TREBBIANO, VERMENTINO.

Enoch's Stomp ★ Superb fortifieds from Blanc du Bois and Lenoir in NE TX, outside AVAs. Light Portejas perennial award-winner. Awarded GRENACHE. Also v.gd dry Blanc du Bois in a couple of bottlings.

Fall Creek Vineyards ★ Several ranges from historic winery; Classics: CHENIN BL, SAUV BL. Blends perform well here, incl Meritus signature.

Frio Canyon Vineyard ★ Tim Leach crafts benchmark MOURVÈDRE along with signature FCV Cuvée red blend.

Haak Winery ★★★ Age-worthy vintage Madeira-style Blanc du Bois and Jacquez are classic, world-class. Dry herb-and-citrus Blanc du Bois also v.gd.

Heath Family Brands Owns several brands; try Heath fizz. Owns Kuhlman Cellars (Rhône, Bx r blends) and Invention Vyds (awarded SANGIOVESE).

Hilmy Cellars ★★ Equally regarded red and white. Rhône, Bx reds, plus structured TEMPRANILLO. Perennially awarded Tejas Bl ROUSSANNE/MARSANNE (w); v.gd Doo-Zwa-Zō SAUV BL/SEM.

Kalasi ★ Winery of premier growers Narra Vyds. Estate wines. Three ranges; benchmark is elegant Reincarnated Collection. TEROLDEGO tops.

Kerrville Hills ★★ TANNAT specialist, supple PICPOUL Bl, varietal Souzão, TEROLDEGO.

Lewis Wines ★★★★ Focus on single-vyd Iberian, French varieties, esp leading TEMPRANILLO, outstanding MOURVÈDRE, easy carbonic Estate Tinto Cão, Vinho Verde-style Swim Spot Blanc du Bois.

Llano Estacado ★★ Consistently excellent full-bodied 1836 (r/w); Super Tuscan-style Viviana (r/w) also gd.

Lost Draw Cellars ★★★ Taut sp PINOT M Letkeman Family Vyd; awarded GSM; rosés from CINSAULT, SANGIOVESE. Compare single-vyd or THC/THP bottlings of MOURVÈDRE, SANGIOVESE, TEMPRANILLO.

McPherson Cellars ★★★ Pioneering TX wine family. Restrained, balanced Iberian, Rhônes, plus heritage-vyd SANGIOVESE. Age-worthy ROUSSANNE Res. Crisp PICPOUL Bl. Excellent varietal ALICANTE BOUSCHET, CARIGNAN, CINSAULT. Try Block Selection special bottlings.

Messina Hof Winery ★ Historic producer. Bold, oaky. SAGRANTINO pioneer; CAB FR consistent award-winner. Range of sweet.

Pedernales Cellars ★★★ Rhône, Spanish grapes, structured style. Benchmark VIOGNIER, excellent GSM, age-worthy TEMPRANILLO (plus upcoming Gran Res).

Perissos Vineyard and Winery Italian focus, plus Spanish. Big reds, incl excellent AGLIANICO, TEMPRANILLO, ever-evolving Racker's Blend. Doro Collection of special bottlings each yr.

Robert Clay Vyds ★★★ Allocation only, fewer than 500 cases/yr. Incl estate red blends with extended ageing up to 120 mths.

Signor Vineyards Estate-vyd MALBEC, MOURVÈDRE, SANGIOVESE, TANNAT, all v.gd.

Spicewood Vineyards ★★★★ Sibling winery to RON YATES. Finesse, elegance, vibrancy. Outstanding signature Good Guy field blend (r); El Guey (r), Battle of Toro TOURIGA N/TEMPRANILLO; Louisa Semillon from Dell Valley Vyds.

Valley Mills Vineyards Located in Waco between Dallas and Austin; excellent MOURVÈDRE, v.gd TEMPRANILLO.

Westcave Cellars Winery and brewery; consistent benchmark CAB FR. Awarded Estate TANNAT. Big NEBBIOLO.

"Real Texas wine" is a rallying cry. Try shouting it if you go there.

William Chris Vineyards ★★★★ Terroir-expressive. Multiple ranges. Single-vyd MOURVÈDRE best, v.gd red blends, fresh pét-nat rosé, distinct Jacquez fortified.

Wine for the People ★★ Rae Wilson's reputation began with Dandy Rosé; now excellent range of La Valentía reds, incl CARIGNAN, CINSAULT, GRENACHE, SYRAH.

Yates, Ron ★★★ Single-vyd Friesen among best. Farmhouse Vyds CINSAULT rosé also v.gd. Focus on Rhône, Spanish, Italian varieties.

Vermont (VT)

In ne, by Canada border; 28 producers, many bio-minded. Thought/quality leader of six New England states. With mtns, harsh winters, brief sunny summers, frost, hail, humidity, new flash floods and landslides, daring growers plant vyds, share fruit: hybrids and vinifera in extreme n terroirs. Masterful apple-grape blends. Pioneers **La Garagista** (top r Marquette, skins for w-grapes rosé; Brianna r/w; Frontenac, La Crescent as fizz or raised in local clay; fizzy poiré [some apple] The Beginning of Memory) has many collaborators/ mentees, incl **Iapetus** (weighty L'Acadie Bl; Marquette blends, pét-nats, wild-ferment r; Antecedent rare VT-grown RIES, 24-yr-old vines; Petite Pearl, skin-contact La Crescent). **Chertok** Cayuga, Frontenac N, Noiret, Traminette, aged apple wine too in *qvevri*. **La Montanuela** fizz focus. **Lincoln Peak** nouveau Marquette. **Shelburne Vyds** Marquette Res; owns top Eden cider. **Stella 14** spontaneous-ferment Frontenacs N/Bl. Co-op **Kalchē Wine** social values, gd wine. On Lake Champlain: **Ellison Estate** beguiling St Croix (also blends), Louise Swenson (w); **Isle La Mot** La Crescent (also Louise Swenson blend); **Snow Farm** on family's old dairy farm, VIDAL Bl Icewine, Baco N.

Virginia (VA)

Mid-Atlantic/s-continental climate. Challenges: humidity, spring frost, winter freeze, harvest-time hurricanes, downy mildew, black rot; wide grower knowledge-sharing helps, so do recent rain-free ripening seasons, a little MERLOT in many varietal reds, planting on heights, esp Shenandoah V foothills (least humid of e) and Blue Ridge slopes. Leader in inclusive, collaborative wine culture/making in e. Elegant outcomes statewide in classical (CAB FR, MERLOT, PETIT VERDOT, TANNAT; stars of central and s) and experimental (hardy, rich, high-acid PETIT MANSENG sings in dr or sw; NEBBIOLO; RKATSITELI gaining ground); CAB SAUV, VIOGNIER favoured too. Serious about hybrids (Traminette, Chambourcin, Norton), new VA types being worked out now.

Afton Mtn Vyds ★★★ At 305m (1000ft), est 1978: Bx blends, SANGIOVESE (w), single-site MERLOT, amphora GAMAY, serious rosé, pét-nat (CHARD, GEWURZ, MUSCAT).

Ankida Ridge ★★★ Top, ageable, precise PINOT N: rare, possibly best in VA; rosé, Blanc de Noir too. Steep, ancient-granite slopes up to 590m (1800ft) in Blue Ridge Mtns; CHARD (also Blanc de Blanc); Brut; thoughtful GAMAY (incl nouveau).

Barboursville ★★★ Monticello AVA: rolling hills, cattle, inn, vines forest-/ meadow-buffered. Italian Zonin family-owned. Mainstays PETIT VERDOT, incl flagship blend Octagon since 80s, decades ageable. White Nascent: VIOGNER/ VERMENTINO/FALANGHINA. Monticello-deal CAB FR Res, 99 still energetic. Paxxito is luscious VIDAL/MUSCAT OTTONEL *appassimento*. PINOT M Blanc de Noirs. Italian focus: FIANO Res, plush BARBERA, NEBBIOLO Res age 10 yrs+.

Blenheim ★★ In hilly Charlottesville, elegant wines. Earthy estate ALBARIÑO, GRÜNER V; round ROUSSANNE; pithy RKATSITELI (80s vines); growing GARGANEGA; local-sourced Monticello CAB FR, PETIT VERDOT; Painted White Loire blend, vintage-based labels by founder/musician Dave Matthews. Base of Oenoverse club, an access and wine-education initiative.

Cana Vineyards ★★ Rosé serious; CABS SAUV/FR, MERLOT (also rosés); ALBARIÑO (Res too), PETIT MANSENG. Unité Res (Bx-style r). Also MALBEC, TEMPRANILLO.

Capstone Vineyards ★★ High-altitude, next to LINDEN; CHARD, CHENIN BL, ROUSSANE, cellar-minded CAB FR, MERLOT. Ageable Bx blends estate-bottled since 23.

Cabernet Sauvignon rises in east

In cool-climate e, rising temps turn warmth-loving CAB SAUV ripe/ complex enough for top varietal bottlings: herbal, dense fruit, <14% alc. Among best: NC's **Dynamis**, in best yrs (21); in Finger L, **Dr Frank**'s earthy, old vines (23), **Knapp**'s single-vyd (22); coastal-NJ **Hawk Haven**'s has oak-raised savoury elegance, when made. Best blends (<25% CAB FR, PETIT VERDOT, other local r): VA's **Barboursville** Res, block-based; MD's **Black Ankle** (23, 1st vintage); NY's **Buttonwood Grove**, **Paumanok**.

Cave Ridge ★★ Shenandoah V. Red Silk, vintage-reflecting CAB FR in noteworthy yrs. Fossil Hills Res (CABS FR/SAUV/PETIT VERDOT; library). Oak-raised CHAMBOURCIN.

Early Mountain ★★★ Champions VA winemaking: serious, site-focused bottles, tasting room pours others' too. Made name with lasting rich, earthy Bx-style Eluvium; velvety Rise in best yrs (19 21 22 23 24 soon), incl TANNAT (serious varietal). Glacial Quaker Run site (305m/1000ft), cellar-worthy, acidity-led: aromatic CAB FR 21 22; creamy, citrus CHARD. Elegant, ageable PETIT MANSENG. White blend Intention in best yrs (20). Brut (Chard/PINOT GR co-fermented, 31 mths lees). Top tourist facilities: cottage stays, local-ingredients fine dining.

Vine pest spotted lanternfly dies young on muscadine-only diet; thrives on vinifera.

Glen Manor Vineyards ★★ Historic farm, 5th generation, cellar-blending focus, founder learned from LINDEN. Vines on steep rocky slopes in Blue Ridge Mtns 305m (1000ft) up. Began with SAUV BL, now joined by rich CAB FR from 20-,30-yr-old vines, NEBBIOLO, PETIT VERDOT; lasting PETIT MANSENG.

King Family Vineyards ★★★ Mountain Plains, best lots by yr. Structured whites (CHARD, PETIT MANSENG, VIOGNER); complex reds (Bx style). MERLOT-based Meritage worth waiting for (library); peppery CAB FR; tiny-production *vin de paille*-style Petit Manseng. Experimental Small Batch series (co-fermented PETITS VERDOT/Manseng). SAVAGNIN planted 2020. French winemaker's own Dom Finot, natural yeast, no sulphites: single-vyd Petit Verdot rosé, Cab Fr, TANNAT.

Linden ★★★ Blue Ridge Mtn estate, early believer in site over fruit; classic methods, grapes, structured w and elegant complex Bx-style r, all ageing-minded. Small production, three high-altitude dry-farmed vyds: Hardscrabble, electric pithy CHARD VA benchmark, rich SAUV BL, flagship Red; Avenius, herbal chewy acidity Sauv Bl, Chard, Red; Boisseaux, savoury lasting PETIT VERDOT. Claret is serious daily pour. Library wines; vertical tastes in tasting room. Response to erratic weather: exp vyd incl FIANO, RIBOLLA GIALLA, RONDINELLA, MENCÍA. New: smoky zing Cab Fr 22; hazelnut trees.

Lost Mountain ★★★★ Was RdV: new French owners, same MW winemaker. Named after flagship wine: elegant, powerful CAB SAUV-led Lost Mountain (VA's 1st $100 wine) from granite hillside (complex MERLOT-led Rendezvous is too). New projects: ALBARIÑO, SEM, PETIT MANSENG.

Midland ★★★ Old family farm, limestone soils (400m/1312ft). Sharp, rich no-dosage Rosé Brut, Blanc de Blancs 19. Benchmark CHARD, long spontaneous oak ferment; top, lasting PETIT MANSENG; RIES; peppery, structured BLAUFRÄNKISCH 19 23; structured CAB FR; trad-method co-fermented Chard/Noiret/Chardonel to come. New high plantings incl resistant MERLOT Kanthus. Family's custom-crush Common Wealth is also VA-wine co-op, think tank, tasting room for like-minded producers. Winemaker makes ***Lightwell Survey*** too, bold co-ferments: earthy Cab Fr/Petit Manseng; astounding Ries-assisted Petit Manseng; rosé, three white hybrids.

Pollak ★★ Estate fruit, looks to France for VA understanding, international style: big earthy PETIT VERDOT; hefty ageable Meritage; citrus SAUV BL; creamy CHARD, PINOT GR; lush, spicy VIOGNIER; heftier CABS FR/SAUV, MERLOT, Petit Verdot (20 is single site). NEBBIOLO now planted.

Ramiiisol ★★★ Monticello AVA in Blue Ridge Mtns foothills. No-expense-spared CAB FR (Res, classic), holistic terroir focus incl iron-rich granite gneiss parcels, forest, orchards, top Italian cooperages, bio practices. Complex lasting vintages, 16–20 ethereal, wild site blends; single-vyd trials. MONTEPULCIANO as v.gd rosato inspired by Cerasuolo (*see* Italy).

Rausse, Gabriele / Vino dal Bosco ★★★ Two labels, small quality estate in woods nr Monticello, one of VA's 1st planters, now 2nd generation. NE Italian sensibility,

French tech. Unforgettable single-vyd CAB FR Res (sulphur-free); v.gd GRÜNER V, ROUSSANNE NEBBIOLO, MALBEC (all Res). Blanc de Noirs, *méthode ancestrale* CHASSELAS, PINOT N; amphora-raised US-rare Cabernet Dorsa (also rosé).

Stinson ★★ Small producer in Blue Ridge Mtns. Estate (SAUV BL to PETIT VERDOT) plus sourced VA fruit; v.gd Meritage, acidity-driven ripe fruit; v.gd oak-raised CAB FR, TANNAT (rosé too), MOURVÈDRE (also trad-method Blanc); RKATSITELI.

Veritas ★★★ Solid estate, steep forest vyds, Monticello AVA. Monticello White, CHARD-led blend, 23. Ageable PETIT MANSENG, restrained SAUV BL, aromatic VIOGNIER. Long-macerated Bx-style Monticello Res (dark fruit, leather, acidity), complex PETIT VERDOT, concentrated floral CAB FR (age 10 yrs+), St-Émilion-inspired Claret; Chard (oak or no). Scintilla trad-method (up to 5 yrs on lees). Momentarious range is vintage one-offs (23: intense TANNAT/MALBEC).

Walsh ★★ In VA-wine stronghold Loudoun County. Site-specific SAUV BL, incl Loire-inspired. Terroir-driven VIOGNIER, CHENIN BL, PETIT MANSENG (also late harvest). Paeonia White, Red: single-vyd blends. Single-vyd TANNAT (long maceration, for cellaring), CABS SAUV/FR, MERLOT (granite mtn site). Single-vyd medium-bodied rosés (Cabs Sauv/Fr). New: plot of CAYUGA.

Washington (WA)

WA's signature is consistently high quality, with ripe fruit flavours and plentiful acid/tannin structure across a range of varieties. As the state largely flies below the radar, there's value to be had. Production is often limited, but for those who love the adventure of new wine regions and a treasure hunt, look no further.

Principal viticultural areas

Columbia Valley (Col V) Huge AVA in central and E WA, with a touch in OR. High-quality Cab Sauv, Merlot, Ries, Chard, Syrah. Key sub-divisions incl:

Red Mountain (Red Mtn) Sub-AVA of Col V and Yak V. Hot region known for Cabs and Bx blends.

Walla Walla Valley (Walla) Sub-AVA of Col V with own identity and vines in WA and OR. Home of important boutique brands and prestige labels. Syrah, Cab Sauv and Merlot.

Yakima Valley (Yak V) Sub-AVA of Col V. Focus on Merlot, Syrah, Ries.

Abeja Col V, Walla ★★★ WALLA winery; high-quality COL V CHARD, CAB SAUV. Beekeeper's Blend gd value.

Airfield Yak V ★ All estate wines deliver plump fruit, high quality-to-price wines across entry, Res tiers. Lone Birch value.

Amavi Walla ★★ Estate producer of value-focused WALLA SEM, CAB SAUV, SYRAH.

Andrew Will Col V, HH Hills, Yak V ★★★★ 10' 12' 14' **16** 18 19 Long-time producer explores vyds with a sense of place. Reserved, age-worthy. Sorella flagship.

Avennia Col V, Yak V ★★★ 10 12' 14' 16' 18' 21' 23 Benchmark Woodinville producer has one foot in Old World, one in WA. Focus on old vines. Sestina Bx blend top; Gravura Bx blend v.gd value; Lydian value label.

Baer Col V ★★★ Woodinville Warehouse District stalwart dedicated to luscious Stillwater Creek Vyd red blends that overdeliver. MERLOT-based Ursa standout.

Betz Family Col V ★★★→★★★★ 10 12' 14' 16' 18' 19 21 22 Iconic Woodinville winery mixes ripe fruit with class. Père de Famille CAB SAUV flagship. SUNU label (OR). Recently purchased by Ackley Brands (WA).

Browne Family Col V ★ Brand from wine giant Precept; CAB SAUV highlight.

Cadence Red Mtn ★★★★ 10' 12' 14 16' 17' 19' 21 22 Estate vyd Bx blends taste like nothing else in state; focus on structure, earth, longevity. All standouts that punch well above weight. Coda from declassified barrels exceptional value.

Cairdeas Col V ★★★ Rhône-inspired, through lens of WA. Makes everything from plush, pleasurable red blends to rarely seen varieties. Diffraction value label.

Cayuse Walla ★★★★ 10 11 12' 14 16' 19 21 22 Cult, mailing list-only winery, with yrs-long wait. Emphasis on earthy, savoury, stony style. Stratospheric scores, steep prices on secondary market, but worth it. Sister wineries Hors Categorie, Horsepower, No Girls also top quality. Double Lucky v.gd value.

Charles Smith Col V ★★ Eponymous winemaker spun-off brand that has been passed around, most recently to Ackley Brands (WA) in 2024. Focus remains value RIES, CAB SAUV, MERLOT.

Cimento Red Mtn ★★★★ 21 New cult producer focuses on WALLA estate vyds. Wines transcendent, if you can afford them.

Col Solare Red Mtn ★★★ 10 12' 14 18 19 Antinori-owned (*see* Italy), on RED MTN. Complex CAB SAUV, focus on longevity, balance.

Columbia Col V ★ One of WA's founding wineries, now owned by (WA) Ackley Brands. Value, grocery-store wines.

Columbia Crest Col V ★★ Sister winery to STE MICHELLE, all about quality, value. Well-priced, v.gd Grand Estates label; Res wines cut above, esp CAB SAUV.

Corliss Col V ★★★→★★★★ 08' 10 12' 14 16 18 19 Distinction is extended ageing in barrel/bottle with trophy style. Sister winery Tranche focuses on Blue Mtn fruit. Secret Squirrel value brand.

Côte Bonneville Yak V ★★★ Estate DuBrul Vyd known for class, sophistication, polish. Extended bottle-age before release. ***Train Station*** v.gd value.

DeLille Col V, Red Mtn ★★★ 10' 12' 14' 16 18 19 21 Founding Woodinville winery known for full-bodied, structured style. D2, Four Flags v.gd value. Chaleur Bl often state's best white. Métier entry-level offerings.

Devison Walla ★★★→★★★★ Rapidly rising; attention-getting wines with voice, incl state's best SAUV BL, MALBEC, rosé. Above the Flood outrageously gd Rhône blend.

Dossier Col V ★★★ Joint winery from Seattle businessman and a former NFL player. Focus on sophisticated hedonism.

Doubleback Walla ★★★→★★★★ 10' 12 16 18 21 Classy, elegant WALLA CAB SAUV. Bledsoe Family sister winery. Bledsoe-McDaniels OR PINOT; Walla SYRAH project.

Dunham Walla ★★ Long-time WALLA producer of v.gd CAB SAUV, SYRAH, mixing fruit and barrel. Three-Legged Red, Trutina gd value.

Dusted Valley Walla ★★ Focus on COL V, WALLA, from value Boomtown to high-end single-vyd offerings. Stained Tooth SYRAH consistent standout.

Echolands Walla ★★★ Masters of Wine/Sommelier-backed winery makes fresh lower-alc, food-friendly Bx styles, SYRAH, GRENACHE.

Figgins Walla ★★★★ 08 10 12 14 16 18 21 All wines from single vyd in Upper Mill Creek. Big, structured Bx blends. Patience/decanting required.

Foolhardy Walla ★★★ Swoon-worthy, food-friendly wines show region they're grown. Try CAB SAUV, SAUV BL.

If California and France had a love child, it would be WA wine.

Force Majeure Red Mtn ★★★→★★★★ All-estate winery using RED MTN, WALLA fruit. Big, bold style. Among best in state. Louis Skinner (formerly Betz Family) new winemaker in 25.

Gård Col V ★★★ Expansive estate lineup from Royal Slope, beyond. Focused, flavourful, balanced. All hit high marks.

Goose Ridge Yak V ★★ All-estate producer in Goose Gap appellation, mix of YAK V, RED MTN styles. Standout SAUV BL, MERLOT; g3 wines gd value.

Gorman Col V, Red Mtn ★★★ Outsized wines that focus on hedonism. Try Evil Twin CAB SAUV/SYRAH. Devil You Know/Don't v.gd value. Ashan CHARD project.

Gramercy Walla ★★★ 10 12' 13 16 18 19 Master sommelier-founded winery emphasizes lower-alc/oak, higher-acid, food-friendly wines that "taste like dirt". Speciality earthy SYRAH, herby CAB SAUV. Lower East cheaper label.

Grosgrain Walla ★★ Champion of underdog varieties, eg. sparkling LEMBERGER made in fruit-forward, accessible style.

Don't think evergreen trees; think sagebrush. Columbia Valley is a desert.

H3 Col V ★ Spin-off from COLUMBIA CREST. Value CAB SAUV, MERLOT, Red Blend.

Januik Col V ★★★ 10 12' 18 19 21 23 Consistent quality, 2nd-generation Andrew has eponymous label; value CAB SAUV, Bx varieties; some of WA's best CHARD.

J Bookwalter Winery Col V ★★★ Stylish, hedonistic, old-vine red blends; 2nd generation. Readers v.gd value.

Jett Walla ★★★→★★★★ New top-end project from CA's Jackson Family. Emphasis on site expression, varietal typicity, balance.

Kiona Red Mtn ★★ Estate LEMBERGER v.gd; 3rd-generation winery; 1st to plant on RED MTN, still one of largest growers.

K Vintners Col V, Walla ★★★ Rhône-centric winery focusing on single-vyd SYRAH, Syrah/CAB SAUV blends. Sixto CHARD-focused sister winery. Also CasaSmith.

Latta Col V ★★★ Single-vyd GRENACHE, MALBEC, MOURVÈDRE, SYRAH: vivid, forward fruit. Latta Latta v.gd value. Disruption, Kind Stranger side projects, value.

L'Ecole No. 41 Walla ★★★ One of WALLA's founding wineries now 3rd generation. Superb-value COL V wines, incl MERLOT. Higher-tier Walla offerings. Ferguson flagship Bx blend. CHENIN BL, SEM v.gd value.

Leonetti Walla ★★★★ 08 10' 12' 14 18 19 21 WALLA's founding winery with well-deserved cult status. Steep prices for all-estate, cellar-worthy CAB SAUV, MERLOT, SANGIOVESE; Res Bx-blend flagship.

Liminal Red Mtn ★★★★ 18 21 Cult producer dedicated to high-elevation, intense, supple RED MTN reds, whites that demand attention.

Long Shadows Walla ★★★→★★★★ Founded by former STE MICHELLE head Allen Shoup. Brings globally famous winemakers to WA to make one wine each in classic WA style, mixing New World fruit, Old World structure.

Luke Col V ★★ Producer of lush, well-priced Wahluke reds with that way overdeliver.

Mark Ryan Winery Red Mtn, Yak V ★★★ Woodinville's original warehouse winery; big, bold style with refinement. Dissident v.gd value. Standout Dead Horse CAB SAUV, Long Haul (MERLOT-based). Second label: Board Track Racer, gd value.

Matthews Col V ★★★ New winemaking team has reinvigorated this long-time Woodinville Bx-focused brand, emphasizing hedonism. Sister brands: From the Sky Down, Single Barrel, Tenor.

Northstar Walla ★★★ When MERLOT was WA's guiding star, this producer helped lead way. Decades later, it still does. STE MICHELLE sister winery.

Novelty Hill Col V ★★★ Dedicated to Stillwater Creek Vyd fruit from Royal Slope. Outstanding value across portfolio, esp CHARD, CAB SAUV.

Owen Roe Yak V ★★★ Long-time producer of YAK V CAB SAUV, SYRAH, Bx blends emphasizing restraint.

Pacific Rim Col V ★★ This RIES-centric producer makes dry to sweet and organic. For more depth, single-vyd releases.

Passing Time Col V ★★★→★★★★ Former pro quarterbacks Dan Marino and Damon Huard focus on bold, balanced appellation-specific CAB SAUV. Winemaker Chris Peterson (AVENNIA). Horse Heaven Hills tops. Quickly earning cult status.

Pepper Bridge Walla ★★★ Estate wines, Bx style, from top WALLA sites. Structured, classy. Time in cellar required. SAUV BL v.gd.

Pursued by Bear Col V ★★★ Actor and YAK V native Kyle MacLachlan makes delicious, age-worthy CAB SAUV, SYRAH.

Quilceda Creek Col V ★★★★ 04' 07 10 12' 14' 16' 18' 21 Flagship producer of WA, cult CAB SAUV known for richness, layering, ageing potential. One of most lauded in world. Sold by allocation. Buy if you can find it, and if you can afford to.

Reininger Walla ★★ Long-time producer of tasty WALLA reds. Second label: Helix.

Reynvaan Family Walla ★★★ 10' 11 12' 14 16 18 21 22 All-estate winery with vyds in Rocks District, Blue Mtn foothills. Focus on earthy, savoury style.

Ste Michelle, Ch Col V ★★→★★★ WA's founding winery; gd value (r/w), estate, higher-end Res. World's largest RIES producer, dry and off-dry COL V exceptional value.

Savage Grace Yak V ★★ Producer marches to own drum with eccentric, low-oak, low-alc, low-intervention, single-vyd wines with something to say.

Saviah Walla ★★★ Celebrating 25th yr; soft, plump, refined WALLA estate wines. High quality:value ratio. The Jack label gd value.

Seven Hills Winery Walla ★★★ 10 12' 14 16 18 21 One of WALLA's founding wineries, now owned by CA's Crimson Wine Group. MERLOT v.gd value.

Sleight of Hand Walla ★★★ Winery has upped its game recently. Focus on Bx blends and Rhône styles. Seek Funkadelic SYRAH from Rocks District.

Sparkman Red Mtn, Yak V ★★★ One of Woodinville's original "Grape Killers" known for power, diversity. Ruby Leigh, Stella Mae Bx blends consistent standouts. Evermore top CAB SAUV from old vines.

Spring Valley Walla ★★★ STE MICHELLE property focusing on estate reds with distinctive voice. Uriah MERLOT Bx blend the headliner, showing class.

Syncline Col V ★★★ Columbia Gorge, focus on fresh, pure Rhône styles. Subduction Red v.gd value. Sparkling GRÜNER V insider wine. PICPOUL consistent standout.

Trothe HH Hills ★★★→★★★★ 19 20' 21 22 New producer reaching for brass ring of cult status. Quality is stratospheric. So are prices.

Two Vintners Col V ★★★ Some of WA's best Rhône styles; COL V SYRAH, GRENACHE v.gd value.

Upchurch Red Mtn ★★★ Former DELILLE founder, winemaker Chris U focuses on ripe, structured CAB SAUV from estate site.

Valdemar Walla ★★★ WALLA outpost for Spain's Bodegas Valdemar. Huge investments in vyd, winery.

Valo Col V ★★★ Grower-winemaker Matías Kúsulas focuses on Conner Lee vyd. Classically styled. Massalto, his playground. On way up.

Walla Walla Vintners Walla ★★ Long-time producer: luscious CABS FR/SAUV, MERLOT. Woven Fields gd value.

Walls, The Walla ★★★ Former Pride (Napa) winemaker Sally Johnson Blum now in charge. Opulent RED MTN, WALLA reds.

Waterbrook Walla ★ One of WA's oldest wineries, Precept-owned; focus on value.

Over 100 varieties in WA. Grenache a standout, but minuscule plantings – so far.

WeatherEye Red Mtn ★★★★ New cult micro-producer with eponymous vyd on top, n side of RED MTN. Ripe wines mixing fruit and non-fruit characteristics. Seek.

Woodward Canyon Walla ★★★★ 07 10 12' 14 16 18 21 Founding WALLA producer; 2nd generation. Focus on Bx styles: CHARD among best in state; Old Vines CAB SAUV.

WT Vintners Yak V ★★★ Sommelier-winemaker Jeff Lindsay-Thorsen picks earlier, pulls back oak on single-vyd GRÜNER V, GRENACHE, SYRAH.

Wisconsin (WI)

Specializes in locally grown, cold-hardy hybrids such as Brianna, Frontenac Gr, Marquette. **American Wine Project** dynamic; try Marquette, Brianna, piquette. Historic **Wollersheim Winery** v.gd estate wines.

Mexico

Big bold reds dominate, with exports increasing. High altitudes and cool nights are keys to quality. Over 75% of wines come from maritime-influenced Baja California; subregion Valle de Guadalupe has most wineries. Other states (historic Coahuila; high Zacatecas, Aguascalientes, Guanajuato, Querétaro) making great strides in quality.

Producers moving from Valle de Guadalupe, lacks water. One overworked aquifer.

Adobe Guadalupe ★★★★ Destination winery with an inn. Wines named after archangels; all recommended. Top: Serafiel (CAB/SYRAH). Also v.gd: Jardín Secreto (TEMPRANILLO-led) offers glimpse of signature variety.

Barrigon Reference for natural wines; tiny. Top: Gran Crew SYRAH/TEMPRANILLO.

Bichi ★★ Originally from Sonora but moved to Baja. *Bichi* means "naked" in Sonoran Yaqui dialect. Unique labels, natural, min-intervention, old organic dry-farmed vyds: Pet Mex pét-nat from unknown grape or Listán, alias MISSION.

Bruma Valle de Guadalupe Winery and luxury destination resort in Valle de Guadalupe. Lourdes "Lulu" Martinez Ojeda winemaker, formerly of BODEGAS HENRI LURTON. Top: Ocho Mezcla Res (CAB SAUV/PETITE SIRAH).

Carrodilla, Finca La Organic/bio/sustainable. Estate wines, except Canto de Luna, Ir y Venir. Rich, ripe, luxury-priced. Varietal CHENIN BL, CAB SAUV, TEMPRANILLO.

Casa de Piedra ★★★ Modern; 1st project of prolific Hugo d'Acosta: Vino de Piedra (CAB SAUV/TEMPRANILLO), oaky, structured, age-worthy modern classic Mexican.

Casa Vieja, La Natural yeasts, no sulphur, no oak flavour. Interesting 120 yrs old+, ungrafted Mission (PAÍS), skin-contact PALOMINO. Rosado v.gd.

Corona del Valle Valle de Guadalupe destination. Top: TEMPRANILLO/NEBBIOLO. Also gd varietal CAB SAUV, MALBEC, Tempranillo.

Cuna de Tierra Guanajuato's 1st winery, award-winning architecture. Cuna de Tierra (r), varietal MALBEC, NEBBIOLO, SYRAH v.gd.

Henri Lurton, Bodegas ★★ Lurton family of Bx. Refined yet sturdy CAB SAUV, NEBBIOLO; inky PETITE SYRAH. Vino Naranja (orange). Ex-Bx winemaker.

LA Cetto Italian heritage. Well-known export. High-altitude, juicy, value: Res Privada range (NEBBIOLO, PETITE SIRAH). CHENIN BL largest production.

Lomita, Hacienda La Organic. Award-winning Tinto de la Hacienda (r); Singular (r) from best barrels of each vintage; estate Pagano GRENACHE (60-yr-old vines).

Mina Penelope Estate-grown wines. Winemaker Verónica Santiago at helm, one of growing number of women making wine in Baja. Cutting-edge amber, rosé. Unique, small-production, trad-method AGLIANICO (sp). Signature Julio 14 (r).

Monte Xanic ★★★ High sites; fresh, unoaked CHENIN BL. Top red blends: Calixa, Gran Ricardo. Limited-edition CAB FR, MALBEC. Viña Kristel SAUV BL.

Paralelo ★★ Created by Hugo d'Acosta for terroir exploration. Try difference in Ensamble Colina (hillside vines) and Arenal (old river bed).

San Miguel, Viñedo Largest winery in Guanajuato. Award-winning white (SAUV BL/CHARD/SEM) and SYRAH. Flagship Latiendo (MALBEC/Syrah/MERLOT).

Santo Tomás, Bodegas de Founded 1888; owns most land in Valle de Santo Tomás. Female-led. Flagship old-vine, single-vyd Único.

Tres Valles ★★ Grapes sourced from three subregions: Valle de San Vicente Ferrer, Valle de San Antonio de las Minas, Valle de Guadalupe. Top: Kuwal (r blend). Also gd: MERLOT, SANGIOVESE, TEMPRANILLO.

Vena Cava ★★★ Value, organic/natural. Experimental wines, rotate each yr.

Vinaltura ★ In Querétaro at high altitude: 1829m (6000ft); semi-arid. Try Blanco (French/German varieties), Tinto (PETITE SIRAH/TEMPRANILLO/MERLOT).

Canada

The story at the moment is one of politics and climate. Trade disputes meant boycotts of US wine and higher sales of Canadian: good news for local producers. But short bursts of frigid temperatures in Okanagan Valley, producing 90% of British Columbia's wine, are proving serious: they reduced the 23 crop and destroyed the 24. The long-term viability of some regions is in question. On the other hand, Quebec is warming, and vinifera varieties are making headway. British Columbia and Ontario are producing elegant whites and reds, while racy whites and sparkling from Nova Scotia and Quebec attract attention.

Canada's wine laws

Despite on-going attempts, Canada has no national wine law, and each of the major wine-producing provinces has its own. In Ontario and British Columbia, Vintners Quality Alliance (VQA) wines must be 100% made from grapes grown in the province and satisfy varietal, labelling and other requirements. Quebec's indication géographique protégée (IGP) defines growing areas and conditions, while Nova Scotia's Tidal Bay makes fresh whites from approved varieties.

Ontario

Cool-climate influenced by lakes Ontario and Erie. Key varieties: CHARD, RIES, CAB FR, GAMAY, PINOT N. Three geographical indications: Niagara Peninsula (Niag), most important, has three regional and ten sub-appellations; Prince Edward County (PEC); Lake Erie North Shore (LENS) with one sub-appellation. More and more wineries opening outside appellations.

Once Canada's flagship, Icewine has lost markets. Fewer and fewer makers.

13th Street Winery Niag ★ Quality across portfolio, esp reds. Noteworthy juicy Sandstone GAMAY, textured Res CAB FR.

Bachelder Niag ★★★★ Thomas B understands Niag vyd by vyd; makes superb vyd- and parcel-specific CHARD, GAMAY, PINOT N.

Black Bank Hill Niag ★★ New winery, impressive. Fraternité (w blend); rich CAB FR.

Cave Spring Niag ★★★ Early (80s) winery, RIES specialist. Lovely nervy dry (incl old vines), esp CSV range.

Charmes, Ch des Niag ★★ Long-est early vinifera producer with solid range (r/w/sp), esp CHARD, GAMAY, PINOT N. Notable luscious Gamay N Droit (clone unique to vyd), elegant Equuleus (Bx r blend).

Clos Jordanne Niag ★★★★ Owned by Arterra. Modelled on Burgundy; only CHARD, PINOT N. Try Le Grand Clos.

Cloudsley Cellars Niag ★ Only CHARD, PINOT N, with great success. Try finely focused Parke Vyd Pinot N, luscious Foxcroft Vyd Chard.

Dobbin Estate Niag ★★ New winery, incl vibrant RIES (White Cap), fine CHARD, elegant CAB FR. Stylish Estate PINOT N.

Flat Rock Cellars Niag ★★ Gravity-fed winery with tiers of fine CHARD, RIES (zesty Nadja's Vyd), PINOT N (fresh Gravity).

Henry of Pelham Niag ★★★ Pioneer in Niag. Generous reds, incl Baco N. Fine fizz: vibrant Cuvée Catharine Carte Blanche Blanc de Blancs.

Hidden Bench Niag ★★★★ Superb, esp elegant CHARD (Tête de Cuvée), CAB FR, PINOT N. Try Terroir Caché (r blend).

Leaning Post Niag ★★ Exceptional clone-specific CHARD, single-vyd PINOT N, esp textured Senchuk Vyd.

Malivoire Niag ★★ Founded by SFX director Martin M. Outstanding small-lot CHARD (complex Moira), GAMAY (classic Courtney), PINOT N.

North 42 Degrees Estate Winery LENS ★ In LENS; v. reliable, esp elegant Special Edition PINOT N, brooding Res CAB FR.

Organized Crime Winery, The Niag ★★ Boutique winery, top-notch. Standouts: textured Cuvée Krystyna CHARD, The Download luscious Bx blend (r).

Pearl Morissette Niag ★★★★ Original, pure CHARD, RIES, CAB FR (superb Madeline), PINOT N. Highlights: pungent Irrévérence (aromatic w blend).

Niagara Peninsula is technically an isthmus. "Niagara Isthmus" is harder to say.

Queylus, Dom Niag ★★★ Québec-owned, organic. Fine, focused CHARD, CAB FR, MERLOT, PINOT N. Top: La Grande Rés, Rés du Domaine.

Stanners Vineyard PEC ★★★ *Garagiste* with gorgeous skin-contact Cuivré PINOT GR, elegant Narrow Rows PINOT N. Juicy CHARD too.

Stratus Niag ★★★ Elegant blends, top-tier White Label from micro-sites. Charles Baker, same property, makes bright-acid RIES.

Tawse Niag ★★★ Organic, vyd-specific wines. Try juicy Robyn's Block CHARD, vibrant Limestone Spark! RIES. Partner in Marchand-Tawse (in Burgundy, *see* France). Elegant PINOT N.

Thirty Bench Niag ★★★ Early boutique winery with exciting single-vyd, some old-vine CHARD, RIES, CAB FR, PINOT N. Top: Small Lot series.

Vineland Estates Niag ★★ Founded 1979 by Mosel's Weis family to grow RIES (Elevation St Urban). Many clone-specific, pure (r/w), Res CAB FR.

Westcott Vineyards Niag ★ Small-lot red, white, sparkling. Standouts: elegant Mayfield PINOT N, vivacious Brilliant Blanc de Blancs.

British Columbia (BC)

Cool- and warm-climate regions. Key varieties: MERLOT, PINOT N, PINOT GR, CHARD, CAB SAUV, CAB FR, RIES, SYRAH. Nine GIs incl Okanagan Valley (Ok V), most important by far, with 11 sub-appellations (more due); Similkameen Valley (Sim V); Vancouver Island (Van I) with one sub-appellation. Cold snaps threatening viability.

1 Mill Road Ok V ★★ *Garagiste* making fine, elegant CHARD (East Kelowna Slopes), PINOT N (Black Pine).

50th Parallel Estate Winery Ok V ★★★ Top range: stylish PINOT N; flavourful Estate Blanc de Noir.

Black Hills Winery Ok V ★★★ Full-flavoured (r/w): rich Per Se CAB FR, flagship delicious Nota Bene Bx blend (r).

Blue Grouse Van I ★★ Small, owned by California's Jackson Family; bright, crisp CHARD, PINOT GR, PINOT N (outstanding Res).

Blue Mountain Winery Ok V ★★★★ Stellar reputation: racy fizz, elegant CHARD, PINOT N (graceful Gravel Force Block 14).

CedarCreek Ok V ★★★ Stylish single-vyd CHARD, PINOT N, esp Platinum tier and Aspect Collection.

Garnet Valley Ranch Ok V ★★ Spectacular isolated setting produces zesty trad-method fizz, impressive, focused CHARD, PINOT N.

Little Engine Ok V ★★ Focus on structured CHARD, PINOT N. Try Platinum Tier.

Martin's Lane Winery Ok V ★★★★ Elegant single-vyd PINOT N, RIES from sites throughout Ok V. Stellar Fritzi's Vyd. Some wines for club members only. All sell out quickly.

Maverick Estate Winery Ok V ★ Impressive portfolio: juicy, lively Ella trad-method fizz, rich white from PINOT N, classic SYRAH from bush vines.

Mission Hill Family Estate Ok V ★★★ Spectacular architecture, destination winery. Large portfolio classic styles. Fine top tiers: elegant Oculus (r blend), rich Perpetua CHARD.

Nicol Vineyard Ok V ★★★ Pioneering Naramata Bench winery, specialist in generous structured SYRAH (esp Old Vines), but also fine CAB FR, PINOT N.

Osoyoos Larose Ok V ★★★★ French-owned, planted 1998. Elegant, cellar-worthy Bx reds. Top: Grand Vin. Second Label: Pétales d'Osoyoos.

Peak Cellars Ok V ★★ In cool n; invariably expressive, esp gorgeous Broken Granite GEWURZ, pungent GRÜNER V.

Phantom Creek Ok V ★★★ Destination winery. Fine estate, single-vyd textbook CAB SAUV/FR, SYRAH; whites from Sim V. Top: Kobau Vyd Cuvée (r blend).

Quails' Gate Ok V ★★ Early Ok V (1989), esp fine, layered CHARD, PINOT N. Top: Stewart Family Res.

Roche Wines Ok V ★★★ Founded by couple with Bx roots (Ch Les Carmes Haut-Brion); fabulous Bx blends (Château tier), succulent PINOT N (Vig Len's Cuvée).

Tantalus Ok V ★★ Old-vines (from 70s/80s) CHARD, PINOT N, RIES for gorgeous still and sparkling.

Tightrope Winery Ok V ★ NZ-trained owners, flavourful, balanced BARBERA, SYRAH.

Township 7 Ok V ★ Winery in Ok and Fraser V. Top: impressive Benchmark Series, esp NBO elegant Bx blend (r), juicy PINOT N.

Unsworth Vineyards Van I ★ California's Jackson family-owned. Stylish (r/w/sp): bright Cuvée de l'Île (PINOT N sp), expressive Saison Vyd Pinot N.

Nova Scotia & Québec

Nova Scotia Small cool-climate region of about 20 wineries on Atlantic coast. Hybrids and vinifera, notable for crisp white (Tidal Bay) and bubbly. Benjamin Bridge ★★ top-notch vibrant fizz (trad method/pét-nat): Brut Rés (CHARD, PINOT N), Nova 7 (off-dr from hybrids). Blomidon Estate ★ on Bay of Fundy makes high-acid still (r/w), racy trad-method fizz from hybrids/vinifera (Cuvée L'Acadie Brut Rés). Lightfoot & Wolfville ★ organic/bio; bright, high-acid Annapolis V (RIES, Pinot N, Chard); reliable Terroir Series.

Québec Cold climate, becoming cool in the s thanks to warming temps. Varieties mainly hybrid, with slowly increasing vinifera, esp CHARD, PINOT N, GEWURZ. Many small wineries, some v. promising thanks to growing expertise and site/variety matching. Léon Courville ★ well-made, structured wines from hybrids and vinifera; planted from 90s. Les Bacchantes ★ gd fruit, racy acidity (r/w); note M1 juicy citrus fizz (VIDAL). Les Pervenches ★ small emerging organic producer, crisp Chard, juicy Pinot N. Vignoble Camy ★★ accomplished wines: Pinot N Rés, Chard Hiatella. Vignoble de l'Orpailleur ★ well est; reliable, gd quality, hybrids and vinifera.

Shop till you drop

Go to Canada now, and you'll find buying wine a lot easier: provinces have either closed their retail monopolies (Alberta, Saskatchewan) or allow private sales alongside them. Most recently, in Ontario – the most densely populated province – wine sales are now permitted in grocery and corner stores, private wine stores and gas stations. The movement of wine across provincial borders has also been relaxed, so residents are mostly permitted to order wine directly from wineries in other provinces.

South America

Abbreviations used in the text:

ARGENTINA

Cata	Catamarca
La R	La Rioja
Luján	Luján de Cuyo
Men	Mendoza
Neu	Neuquén
Pat	Patagonia
Río N	Río Negro
Sal	Salta
San J	San Juan
Uco	Uco Valley

CHILE

Aco	Aconcagua
Bío	Bío-Bío
Cach	Cachapoal
Casa	Casablanca
Cho	Choapa
Col	Colchagua
Coq	Coquimbo
Cur	Curicó
Elq	Elqui
Ita	Itata
Ley	Leyda
Lim	Limarí
Mai	Maipo
Mal	Malleco
Mau	Maule
Rap	Rapel
San A	San Antonio

CHILE

Like many wine-producing countries, Chile has had its fair share of challenges in recent years, and land under vine is sadly still on the decline. But that hasn't stopped a healthy dose of innovation or the emergence of new wine regions. The traditional heartlands of the Central Valleys are still suffering a rather brutal hangover from the global economic downturn and local drought, oversupply and dwindling domestic consumption. Yet growers push on, with vineyards appearing in the far reaches of the Atacama Desert in the north, and ever further south into Austral Chile (now home to the world's southernmost vines, though only a few experimental bottles so far). While those extremes make for headline-grabbing tales, most of the real action still lies between Elqui and Bío-Bío – a veritable buffet of climates, soils and ambitious producers. Think meaty coastal Syrah from San Antonio, floral Cinsault from Itata, mineral Chardonnay from Limarí, old-vine Carignan from Maule, and perfumed Cabernet Sauvignon from Maipo. It might not be growing, but Chile certainly isn't slowing down.

Recent vintages

Chile's wine regions are too diverse and varied to generalize, but 22 18 remain most exciting; 25 24 21 v. promising; 23 20 19 17 warmer, riper.

Aconcagua Matriarch of historic Chile, just n of Santiago, a long sweep from the chilly coast to the sun-baked Andes. Rich, powerful reds in centre and foothills; fresher whites, lighter styles closer to Pacific.

Almaule Mau Collective championing "session-worthy" old-vine PAÍS from MAU; the *alma* (soul) of the region in every bottle, or label at least.

Almaviva Mai ★★★★ Classic Puente Alto: structured, age-worthy, complex. Classy Bx blend by Mouton Rothschild (*see* Bordeaux). Second label: Epu.

A Los Viñateros Bravos Ita ★★★ Leo Erazo's soulful revival of ITA's ancient hills on coast. Superb CINSAULT, PAÍS and old-vine whites (often amber).

Altaïr Wines Rap ★★★ SAN PEDRO icon label from CACH; winemaker Gabriel Mustakis; vibrant Bx blend. Second label: Sideral, more approachable young.

Antiyal Mai ★★★→★★★★ National treasure. Alvaro Espinoza, bio pioneer and CARMENÈRE legend, still leads with elegant MAI reds under organic Antiyal label.

Apaltagua Col ★★ Unexciting but dependable range (across Chile), often v.gd value.

Aquitania, Viña Mai, Mal ★★★ Family-run. From rich, age-worthy Cabernets (Lazuli) to crisp southern fizz – proof Chile spans extremes.

Arboleda, Viña Aco ★★ Coastal wines from ERRÁZURIZ, v.gd value. Brisas is juicy blend; CHARD, SAUV BL, PINOT also top.

Baettig, Vinos Mal, Mau ★★★★ Stylish, small-production label. Pristine CHARD, PINOT N; vibrant old-vine CAB SAUV. One of Chile's finest.

Bío-Bío Old vines, indie producers; bubbling with promise, potential. Artisanal, vibrant scene of ancient vines of PAÍS, CINSAULT, emerging RIES, SAUV BL, PINOT N.

Bouchon Mau ★★→★★★ Now under UNDURRAGA stable, but still with own identity under hand of winemaker Christian Sepúlveda. Brilliant old-vine whites (Granito SEM), fresh PAÍS, juicy Med-style blends.

Caliboro Mau ★★★ Javier Rousseau and Count Francesco Marone Cinzano are reviving MAU's deep s with regenerative farming. Bright PAÍS and new life for forgotten Criollas. Historic site, modern energy.

Caliterra Col ★★ The Col outpost of ERRÁZURIZ: juicy MALBEC and Med-style reds.

Calyptra Cach ★★→★★★ Bi-Andean winery with vyds in MEN and CACH (flagship). Youthful unoaked Vivendo, complex Gran (ages); CAB SAUV, oaked SAUV BL v.gd.

Carmen, Viña Casa, Col, Mai ★★★→★★★★ Skip the everyday and go straight to the top: ANA MARÍA CUMSILLE is producing some thrilling stuff. DO range and Delanz pure deliciousness. Flor-aged SEM, linear CHARD (LIM), perfumed CINSAULT (ITA).

Casablanca Casa Chile's coastal cradle of cool-climate wine. From tropical SAUV BL, black-cherry PINOT N to heady SYRAH, there's plenty to taste across the 5000 ha+.

Casa Marín San A ★★★→★★★★ Felipe M now steering this ocean-kissed icon 4 km from sea. Cipreses SAUV BL remains benchmark; RIES, SYRAH strong; Viñedos Lo Abarca range is Felipe's ever-evolving innovation line (GARNACHA, pét-nat).

Casas del Bosque Casa, Mai ★★→★★★ Leading CASA winery offering classics, plus unusual icon for coast… or anywhere, in fact – SYRAH/MALBEC/PINOT N.

Casa Silva Col, S Regions ★★→★★★ Family estate bridging old-school warmth and cool-climate innovation. Luscious CARMENÈRE, chiselled CAB SAUV from Los Lingues; oily SAUV BL and leesy fizz from Osorno lakes.

Clos Apalta Col ★★★★ Seamless CARMENÈRE Bx blend from old vines in Apalta, with 2nd-tier Petit Clos, 3rd Prelude. Andrea Leon is winemaker (of LAPOSTOLLE) and making Clos increasingly bright. New Clos du Lican line incl luscious VIOGNIER.

Clos des Fous Cach, Casa, S Regions ★★→★★★ Radical terroir explorers pushing limits n to s: racy RIES, earthy PINOT N, juicy red blends. Boutique and off-beat.

Concha y Toro Cent V ★→★★★★ Giant and pioneer since 1883; diverse offerings around the country. Don Melchor is top MAI Andes CAB SAUV blend. Amelia is fresh coastal duo of PINOT N, CHARD (LIM). Terruño redefines modern classics. Casillero still delivers bang for buck. *See also* ALMAVIVA, TRIVENTO (Argentina).

Cono Sur Bío, Casa, Col ★★→★★★ Sustainable powerhouse with pedal-powered spirit. Benchmark PINOT N at every level, easy-drinking fruit-driven organic; playful fizz (Centinela) for gd measure. Covers coast to Andes, with base in Col.

Cousiño Macul Mai ★★→★★★ 1856 stalwart still shining. Elegant Cabs (Lota), floral Sauvignon Gr (Isidora) lead; Gota de Luna SAUV BL (MAL) adds crisp new chapter.

Cumsille, Ana María Ita ★★★ Old-vine whisperer making elegant CARIGNAN, CINSAULT, PAÍS, MALBEC, MOSCATEL from s. Deliciously delicate, fresh.

Elqui From pisco pergolas to SYRAH slopes, one of Chile's most scenic frontiers, regions. Fresh coastal whites meet mtn reds under a sky of stars.

Emiliana Bío, Casa, Rap ★★→★★★ Vibrant blends (Coyam, Gê), zesty coastal whites; bio leader under Noelia Orts. Now expanding into LIM with refreshing vision.

Errázuriz Aco ★★→★★★★ Grand classic turned modern benchmark. Emily Faulconer steers with a steady hand from ACO coast to Andes. Top Las Pizarras CHARD (trad-method bubbles also delicious), Kai shows age-worthy side to CARMENÈRE, Don Maximiano timeless. (*See also* CALITERRA, SEÑA, VIÑA ARBOLEDA, VIÑEDO CHADWICK.)

Falernia, Viña Elq ★★ Pioneer still delivering honest pleasure. Meaty SYRAH, crisp PEDRO XIMÉNEZ, sun-dried CARMENÈRE.

Garcés Silva, Viña San A ★★→★★★ Long-time Ley leader, with grapes coveted by top peers. Own CHARD, PINOT N, SYRAH and playful Garden Blend remain standouts, as does solera-style fortified SAUV BL (*see* Spain).

Haras de Pirque Mai ★★→★★★ Antinori's (*see* Italy) Chilean outpost shaped like a horseshoe. Class: sleek CAB SAUV and SYRAH blends galloping ahead of pack.

Henríquez, Roberto Bío ★★★ Artisan of s, min-intervention SEM, CINSAULT, PAÍS bursting with earth, energy. Honest, expressive, utterly drinkable.

Itata Ancient vines, fresh ideas. Region of farmers, not fortunes – yet some of Chile's most exciting wines come from its gnarly CINSAULT, PAÍS and MUSCAT.

Koyle Col, Ita ★★→★★★ Toti Undurraga's bio beacon. Vibrant, juicy; linking Andes and coast in Col, plus old-vine gems from ITA. Cerro Basalto top red.

Laberinto Mau ★★★→★★★★ Rafael Tirado's mtn magic: RIES, SAUV BL, PINOT N and

Grab that fog

Marked as one of the countries most vulnerable to climate change, Chile has put its wine industry on high alert. Prolonged drought and growing water scarcity are reshaping where and how grapes can be grown. Producers are pushing s toward cooler, wetter zones (even Chile Chico), while researchers trial coastal fog-harvesting to tap the camanchaca – the fog that brings moisture to the Atacama Desert. Whether vyd maps shift or fog nets rise, one thing is clear: Chilean viticulture must adapt – fast.

blends all thrillingly mineral. Rare mtn producer in MAU, and proof that Andes can be just as exciting as old vines.

Lapostolle Cach, Casa, Col ★★→★★★ Old vines and new in heart of Apalta. Organic vyd, luxury residence and magnificent winery, where rich, complex Bx-style reds rule. *See also* CLOS APALTA.

Leyda, Viña Col, Mai, San A ★★→★★★ Coastal pioneer that brought water (and life) to Ley. Benchmark CHARD, RIES, SAUV BL, SYRAH. Winemaker Viviana Navarrete reviving PINOT N with increasing purity, elegance. Lot is top line, and top value.

The Andes are young: a mere 120m yrs old. Older than Himalayas, though.

Limarí Dry, saline and stony: a desert cooled by the Humboldt. World-class CHARD, PINOT N thrive, brilliant bubbles too.

Longaví Ita, Mau ★★★ Bouchon family and Christian Sepúlveda's adventure s. Fresh PAÍS, CARIGNAN, CINSAULT, plus CHENIN BL bursting with tension, charm. Old vines, contemporary wines.

Luis Felipe Edwards Cent V ★★ Big, bold, and still family-owned. Vast portfolio across Chile; reliable value but rarely exciting.

Maipo Chile's CAB SAUV cradle: gravel beds, Andes breezes and long heritage. Plush and structured, plus polished Bx-style blends still set the national benchmark, but also gd CARMENÈRE, CAB FR and mtn GRENACHE.

Malleco Tiny s outpost with volcanic soils and big ambition. Superb CHARD, RIES, PINOT N promising; gd bubbles too. Dry-farmed, cool, quietly dazzling.

Martino, De Cach, Casa, Elq, Ita, Mai, Mau ★★★ Champions of purity, place: elegant reds (Cuvée is understated icon), vivid SEM, joyful *tinaja* wines from ITA's oldest vines. Modern Chile in one portfolio.

Matetic Casa, San A ★★★→★★★★ Superb SYRAH (black label a star), crisp whites and PINOT N from granite slopes. GRENACHE now too. Beautiful estate, even better wines; bio coastal master. Hidden gem.

Maule Chile's old-vine heart; dry-farmed bush vines of SEM, CARIGNAN (*see* VIGNO) and PAÍS delivering honest, soulful wines and nuanced CAB SAUV, MALBEC. Innovation rising amid trad.

Montes Casa, Col, Cur, Ley ★★→★★★★ Visionary winery that reshaped Chile's image. Iconic Folly SYRAH, Purple Angel CARMENÈRE; Outer Limits range shows coastal spark. Coast-to-Andes vyds, consistently strong.

MontGras Col, Ley, Mai ★★→★★★ Classic name now reinvigorated. Handcrafted line, bright and expressive. Intriga CAB SAUV (MAI) still highlight.

Montsecano Casa ★★★ PINOT N specialist: ethereal, min intervention. Tiny production; sought after. Also CHARD and limited MALBEC.

Morandé Casa, Mai, Mau ★★→★★★ Ricardo Baettig's steady hand produces smart mix of classics and curiosities. Standouts: Vigno CARIGNAN, LIM SYRAH, Med blends from s, long-aged sparkling.

Neyen Col ★★★ 1890-planted Apalta vines deliver rich, velvety CAB/CARMENÈRE. Silky, refined, age-worthy.

Odfjell Cur, Mai, Mau ★→★★★ Fruit-driven reds; bio pioneer; Bx grapes shine in MAI, Med grapes sing in MAU; v.gd CARIGNAN.

Pedro Parra y Familia Ita ★★→★★★ Terroir guru-turned-winemaker: earthy PAÍS, vertical CINSAULT crus, playful, mineral-tipped blends. Pure granite expression.

Pérez Cruz, Viña Mai ★★→★★★ Alto Maipo specialist known for clean, precise Bx-style blends and bright, juicy GRENACHE. Cot (MALBEC) a tasty outlier.

Pisco Chile's clear, aromatic spirit from MUSCAT-family varieties. Finest drunk neat and chilled; most finds way into classic Pisco Sour or Piscola (Pisco + Coca-Cola).

Polkura Col ★★→★★★ Sven Bruchfeld's hillside SYRAH farm on coast. Rich, warming reds with savoury depth; Syrah consistently gd.

PS García Ita, Mal, Mau ★★→★★★ Felipe G's colourful, personality-filled portfolio – from tropical CHARD to rich CARIGNAN blends (Facundo a standout).

Quebrada de Macul, Viña Mai ★★→★★★ Time-honoured classic from prime slopes of CAB SAUV. Domus Aurea elegant flagship; Viña Peñalolén more relaxed charm.

Rapel Catch-all name covering vast stretches of Col and Cach. Too broad for real meaning; look to specific valleys instead.

Requingua, Viña ★★ Big Central Valley player, steady, gd value (try CARIGNAN).

Reta Lim, Mau ★★★→★★★★ Marcelo Retamal's small, soulful label. Racy yet rich LIM CHARD, fragrant PINOT N; haunting old-vine MAU MALBEC. Tiny but exceptional top crus. New 2nd tier offers gd value.

San Antonio San A Granite, fog, ocean winds define this cool-climate gem. Excellent CHARD, SAUV BL, PINOT N, SYRAH; Ley most celebrated subzone.

San Pedro Cur ★→★★★ Giant producer with strong quality leaps. Top Cabo de Hornos CAB SAUV; 1865 range excellent (ELQ SYRAH esp). Tayu PINOT N supports Mapuche growers. *See also* ALTAÏR, TARAPACÁ; VIÑA LEYDA, LA CELIA in Argentina.

Santa Carolina, Viña Mai ★★→★★★ 1875 stalwart still innovating. Lots of everyday, but top Luis Pereira CAB SAUV a classy throwback, Herencia CARMENÈRE silky.

Santa Rita Mai ★★→★★★★ Big but brimming with gems: historic Casa Real CAB SAUV, vibrant Floresta (racy SAUV BL, peppery CARMENÈRE), top-value Triple C.

Seña Aco ★★★★ Iconic, graceful Bx blend tucked into hills with coastal influence. Poised, sumptuous, age-worthy. Second label: Rocas, offers earlier pleasure.

Sierras de Bellavista Col ★★★ Boutique mtn wines from Andes. Crunchy PINOT N, gloriously waxy RIES.

Tabalí Lim ★★→★★★★ Talinay's coastal limestone-rich slopes give Chile's most precise CHARD, PINOT N. Also laser-bright SAUV BL; savoury, engaging SYRAH. Opulent Roca Madre MALBEC from pioneering vyd in Andes.

Tarapacá, Viña Casa, Ley, Mai ★★ Isla de Maipo staple under SAN PEDRO umbrella. Reliable, full range of classics; predictable but solid.

Torres, Miguel Cur ★★→★★★★ Spain's Torres brings consistency, creativity. Cordillera range a highlight, from Osorno SAUV BL to LIM CHARD; Manso de Velasco CAB SAUV from centenarian vines a national treasure, Escaleras de Empedrado a unique coastal PINOT N in MAU, Los Inquietos MALBEC field blend a vinous gem.

Undurraga Casa, Ley, Lim, Mai ★★→★★★★ Rafael Urrejola drives a terroir-1st revival under superb Terroir Hunter line, from zesty coastal RIES to juicy old-vine GSM. Icons from Pirque and SAN A increasingly compelling, incl top CAB SAUV, PINOT N. Now owns BOUCHON, ever more focused in S.

Valdivieso Cur, San A ★→★★★ Bubble king of Chile, mostly Charmat, brunch fizz. Caballo Loco blends where winemaker Brett Jackson plays with texture, time.

Vascos, Los Rap ★★ Lafite's (*see* France) Chilean home, with structured reds reflective of French philosophy in Chilean terroir. New PINOT N and SEM broaden palette; still plenty of Bx DNA.

Ventisquero, Viña Casa, Col, Mai ★→★★★ Big, ambitious, adventurous. From Atacama's Huasco to Pat's Chile Chico, wines map Chile's extremes. Grey solid; Tara wild; Pangea SYRAH plush.

Veramonte Casa, Col ★★ González Byass-run (*see* Spain) coastal estate in CASA. Straightforward, dependable.

Vigno Mau Collective championing old-vine, dry-farmed CARIGNAN in MAU. Age-worthy, soulful, triumph of New World grower solidarity.

Vik Cach ★★★ Futuristic hillside estate over ridge from Apalta. Powerful, polished red Bx-style blends; playful rosé. Milla Calla fab value. Top wine Stone Vik is in amphorae planted into top of hill.

Villard Casa, Mai ★★→★★★ Strong classics and fun curios under JCV; CASA pioneer. Ramato PINOT GR, cult favourite; PINOT N, SYRAH always solid choices.

Viñedo Chadwick Mai ★★★★ One of Chile's most refined CAB SAUVS, pure Puente Alto pedigree. Polo-field-turned-vyd, now a global benchmark. Emily Faulconer now holding reins of this elegant, single wine.

Viu Manent Casa, Col ★★ Long-est family winery; MALBEC, easy-drinking range.

von Siebenthal, Viña Aco ★★→★★★ Boutique family estate focused on structured, age-worthy reds and lush, perfumed VIOGNIER.

ARGENTINA

Argentina has been a vinous giant for over two centuries and still retains its spot as the seventh-largest wine producer on the planet. Dry, sunny skies and the spine of the Andes make it a winemaker's dream corridor, even if spring frosts, golf-ball-sized hail and a roller-coaster economy keep everyone on their toes. The upside: the country is now making the most refined, focused wines in its history, with freshness and finesse the new watchwords. Malbec still reigns, a fifth of all vines and a universe of styles – from chiselled, floral expressions from Altamira and Gualtallary in the Uco Valley, and old-vine richness from Las Compuertas and Agrelo in Luján, to wild, spicy, high-altitude versions from Jujuy and Salta. A spectrum of lighter reds including floral Garnacha, poised Pinot Noir and juicy Criolla are also finding space. Meanwhile white-wine lovers won't be disappointed by the growing scene of blends, varietal old-vine Semillon and increasingly precise, cool-climate Chardonnay from new southern and altitude extremes.

Achaval Ferrer Men ★★→★★★ Flag-bearer for old-vine MALBEC. Trio of single-vyd classics still the draw; Quimera adds supple, sculpted blends (r/w).

Alandes Men ★★★ Karim Mussi's "anywhere" label, free from borders so long as by the Andes. Paradoux blends shine (zesty SEM/SAUV BL), full-bodied reds close behind. Concrete Tank MALBEC blend charms.

Alpasión Men ★★ Large Las Chacayes estate; polished, modern style. Best: refreshing SAUV BL, aromatic CAB FR.

Alta Vista Men ★→★★★ French-owned, Luján-based, vyds across Argentina: TORRONTÉS consistently v.gd; MALBEC single parcels gd; Atemporal fizz complex.

Altocedro Men ★★→★★★ La Consulta specialist Karim Mussi makes classic, quietly confident reds; TEMPRANILLO a hallmark.

Altos las Hormigas Men ★★★→★★★★ Masters of MALBEC terroir. Jardín de Hormigas (Altamira) among Argentina's finest crus: floral, delicate; SEM, BONARDA, CAB FR.

Anita, Finca La Men ★★ Boutique family estate on Luján's wine route, making warm, plush reds, incl varietal PETIT VERDOT, SYRAH.

Argento Men ★★→★★★ Major organic leader offering fresh, juicy value. Single-vyd CHARD, CAB FR, MALBEC worth seeking out.

Artesano, Viña ★★★→★★★★ Top-notch single-plot CHARD, CAB FR, MALBEC from Uco and Luján. In its debut vintages, but already an icon.

Atamisque Men ★→★★★ Serbal line an Uco bargain; higher tiers deliver refined CHARD, CAB FR and one of best Uco MERLOTS. Charming lodges too.

Bemberg Estate Wines ★★★ Family behind Peñaflor showcasing site-specific, age-worthy wines from across Argentina. Concentrated, serious, built to last.

Pingüino: penguin-shaped jug for serving wine at a traditional Argentine tavern.

Benegas Men ★★→★★★ Historic Luján-Maipú estate, venerable vines. Intense, structured reds; CAB FR pioneer with notable old-vine SANGIOVESE too.

Bianchi, Bodegas Men ★→★★ Expanding strongly in Uco while holding San Rafael roots. Solid, classic style; IV Generación adds modern lift.

Bosca, Luigi Men ★★→★★★ Luján stalwart, renewed focus on DOCs. Finca Las Nobles MALBEC standout; polished, steady hand throughout; Paraíso velvety icon.

Bressia Men ★★→★★★ Walter B's family-run bodega: structured Bx-style blends; youthful Monteagrelo range for lifted varietals. Lagrima CHARD exotically bold.

Cadus Men ★★→★★★ Stylish, premium sibling of NIETO SENETINER. Santiago Mayorga makes bright single-vyd CHARD, sleek Uco reds, joyful Criolla Chica.

Most planted grape: Malbec. Second: Cereza. Don't pretend you've heard of it.

Callia San J ★→★★ Straightforward, fruity everyday wines with broad appeal.

Canale, Bodegas Humberto Río N ★→★★★ Pioneer of Pat, still strong today: crisp old-vine RIES, vibrant PINOT N, plenty of MALBEC too.

Cara Sur San J ★★→★★★ Pancho Bugallo, Seba Zuccardi and wives make high-mtn Criolla Chica, BONARDA, field blends in remote Barreal. Distinctive, pure.

Caro Men ★★→★★★ Catena and Rothschild (*see* Bordeaux) partnership; rich MALBEC/CAB SAUV at top. Amancaya and Aruma easier-drinking siblings.

Casarena Men ★★→★★★ Luján producer highlighting terroir at every tier. Wonderfully spicy CABS SAUV and FR, structured MALBEC, steely SEM.

Catena Zapata, Bodega Men ★★→★★★★ Argentina's modern pioneer. Adrianna vyd in Gualtallary the peak: CHARD (White Bones/Stones), MALBEC (River) of global stature. Nicolas blend (regions and varieties) still worthy icon. Alamos delivers weekday reliability. *See also* CARO, DOM NICO.

Celia, Finca La Men ★★ Uco pioneer (1890), now turning towards more lifted, fragrant styles under Andrea Ferreyra. Great value across range, PINOT N increasingly crunchy.

Chacra Río N ★★★→★★★★ Piero Incisa's Pat jewel. Ethereal PINOT N 1st; now graceful TROUSSEAU too. Thrilling CHARD project with Jean-Marc Roulot (*see* France) combines Bungundy techniques and old-vine wisdom.

Chandon Men ★→★★ Sparkling trailblazer since 50s. Everyday fizz, topped by richer trad-method Baron B. For still, *see* TERRAZAS DE LOS ANDES.

Cheval des Andes Men ★★★★ Cheval Blanc's Argentinian vision (*see* Bordeaux): poised MALBEC/CAB SAUV from old vines in Altamira and Las Compuertas. Now with young Pierre Polbos at helm.

Clos de los Siete Men ★★ Collective estate – Bx families united in Uco – with one group blend plus wineries: CUVELIER, DIAMANDES, MONTEVIEJO, ROLLAND.

Cobos, Viña Men ★★→★★★ Paul Hobbs's project in MEN under hand of Diana Fornasero: silky CHARD; rich, structured CAB SAUV, CAB FR, MALBEC.

Colomé, Bodega Sal ★★→★★★ High-altitude icon, soaring to 3100m (10170ft) in Altura Maxima vyd; brooding MALBEC, age-worthy, intense. Vibrant TORRONTÈS also worth seeking.

Cruzat Men ★★★ Specialist producer of trad-method fizz (w/rosé/orange): Millésime the star.

Cuvelier Los Andes Men ★★→★★★ Organic Uco estate delivering sculpted, structured Bx blends within CLOS DE LOS SIETE.

Decero, Finca Men ★★ Agrelo reds with firmness and concentration. Amano remains flagship.

DiamAndes Men ★★ Malartic Lagravière family's Uco outpost: juicy VIOGNIER, precise CAB SAUV standout. Striking architecture.

Doña Paula Men ★★ SANTA RITA (Chile) sister winery. Lots of everyday classic labels; some fun in sparkling SAUV BL and spicy graphite in Altaluvia CAB FR.

Durigutti Men ★★→★★★★ Pablo and Héctor leading Luján's revival. Las Compuertas superb, fragrant, lively, deeply rooted in place (try 5 Suelos MALBEC, Criolla Chica, white blend).

Enemigo Wines, El Men ★★→★★★★ Adrianna CATENA and Ale Vigil's restless own label: known for CAB FR, but worth hunting rare, flor-aged TORRONTÉS, meaty GARNACHA. Constantly evolving.

Escala Humana Men ★★★ Germán Masera's soulful micro-project highlighting forgotten Uco vines. Excellent SEM (Credo), crunchy CAB SAUV, elegant MALBEC.

Estancia Uspallata Men ★★→★★★ Loftiest vyd in MEN at 2000m (6560ft) nr border with Chile. Floral, finely etched MALBEC, PINOT N from Colo Sejanovich. Now planting whites.

Esteco, El Sal ★★→★★★ Reliable, expressive portfolio, esp peppery CAB SAUV. Expressive Old Vines series: oily TORRONTÉS, floral Criolla.

Etchart Sal ★→★★ Historic presence; gd value TORRONTÉS, MALBEC from Cafayate.

Fabre Montmayou Men, Río N ★★→★★★ Classic Franco-Argentine style; Pat Bx blends shine; elegant MALBEC throughout.

Fin del Mundo, Bodega Del Neu ★→★★ NEUQUEN pioneer offering dependable, rich reds; CAB FR solid.

Flichman, Finca Men ★★ Historic estate (1910), now Sogrape-owned (*see* Portugal). Broad range; refined Dedicado CHARD worth seeking.

Kaikén Men ★★→★★★ MONTES's (Chile) Argentine wing: old-vine MALBEC from Las Compuertas, full-bodied Uco reds. Frankly is new CAB FR icon.

Masi Tupungato Men ★★ Italian accent in Uco: crisp PINOT GR/TORRONTÉS, successful ripasso-style (*see* Italy) MALBEC/CORVINA.

Matervini Men ★★★ Achával and Cipresso explore extremes: mtn vyds, bold reds, long ageing. Mainly MALBEC, but terroirs highlight different expressions.

Mendel Men ★★★ Roberto de la Motta's elegant collection: CHENIN BL, SEM need time; reds timeless, refined. Unus excellent value.

Mendoza Argentina's powerhouse: incredible diversity. From warm e plains to chilly tip of Gualtallary and San Pablo. MALBEC leads; CHARD, CAB FR now major players in quality stakes.

Michelini i Mufatto Men ★★★ Thoughtful, savoury Uco wines, boutique family producer. Striking old-vine whites (CHENIN BL, SEM); lively La Cautiva MALBEC.

Mil Suelos Men ★★→★★★ Colo Sejanovich's soil-driven suite of labels: Buscado Vivo o Muerto, Manos Negras, TeHo, ZaHa. Top CHARD, MARSANNE, CAB FR, MALBEC.

Monteviejo Men ★★→★★★ Part of CLOS DE LOS SIETE; polished Bx blends, refined varietals from Campo de los Andes now under hand of 3rd-generation owner Elise Treiber.

Moras, Finca Las San J ★→★★ Popular SAN J producer: gd-value SYRAH, BONARDA. Pedernal's Sagrado top-tier.

Neuquén Pat Warmest corner of Pat; younger vines, richer reds than RÍO N. Fossils everywhere.

Nico, Domaine Men ★★★ Laura CATENA's PINOT N project with single-plot wines from Gualtallary. Vibrant, focused.

Nieto Senetiner, Bodegas Men ★→★★★ Large, accessible brand, more finesse at top. Benjamin reliable; hunt for single-vyd BONARDA. CADUS, premium sister brand.

Noemia Pat ★★★ Hans Vinding-Diers makes S Argentina's most elegant reds: nuanced MALBEC, refined blends from venerable RÍO N vines.

Seeking value in a land of 220% inflation

Battling runaway inflation (a gobsmacking 220% in 2024, thankfully easing in 2025) and a jittery peso makes export competitiveness a constant challenge. But Argentina's glorious climate still delivers remarkable value. TORRONTÉS, BONARDA and MALBEC offer serious bang for buck under £15. Top-value picks: ALTOS LAS HORMIGAS's Colonia Las Liebres, ARGENTO, SALENTEIN's El Portillo, SUSANA BALBO's Crios.

Norton, Bodega Men ★→★★★ Perdriel classic with Uco vines too. Everyday offerings solid; Lote Negro, single-vyd MALBECS offer more excitement.

Onofri Wines Men ★★→★★★ Mariana O's boutique label: lively GARNACHA, age-worthy white blend, crisp Pedro Giménez, spicy CAB FR.

Otronia Pat ★★★→★★★★ Extreme s latitude (45°S) gives razor-sharp CHARD, racy RIES, textural TORRONTÉS, perfumed MALBEC and thrilling bubbles. One of S America's best.

Passionate Wine Men ★★→★★★ Matías Michelini's boundary-pusher: lean, taut, mineral, with growing polish. Agua de Roca high-altitude SAUV BL star.

Pelleriti, Marcelo Men ★★→★★★ Renowned classical, age-worthy CAB FR, MALBEC.

Peñaflor Men ★→★★★ Giant umbrella group: EL ESTECO, FINCA LAS MORAS, Navarro Correas, Santa Ana, TRAPICHE and highlight, BEMBERG.

Per Se Men ★★★→★★★★ Tiny jewel in Gualtallary's Monasterio. Edy del Pópolo and David Bonomi make solera-aged (*see* Spain) CHARD, tense, chalky CAB FR, MALBEC. Thrilling if you can find it.

Piatelli Sal ★★ Pair of wineries in MEN, Cafayate offering firm reds, aromatic whites, dependable value.

Piedra Negra Men ★★→★★★ François Lurton's Uco hub. Textural SAUVIGNON VERT blends (Corte Friulano) standout, alongside muscular MALBEC (Cot) reds.

Porvenir de Cafayate, El Sal ★★→★★★ Top name in Cafayate: energetic whites, characterful reds, deft orange. Alto Los Cuises MALBEC, n benchmark; MARSANNE/ROUSSANNE, lovely, spicy.

Pulenta Estate Men ★★→★★★ Agrelo base, with Uco vines; CAB FR a signature, Palma Carola (SEM/VIOGNIER/CHARD) a luxurious discovery, lots of gd MALBEC, MERLOT.

Renacer Men ★★ Wide-ranging styles in MEN. Amarone-style (*see* Italy) MALBEC still a talking point.

Riccitelli, Matias Men ★★★→★★★★ Creative powerhouse, electric whites (La Carrera SAUV BL), RÍO N old vines (incl TROUSSEAU), elegant reds.

Riglos Men ★★ Gualtallary stalwart known for firm, structured CABS FR and SAUV, precise reds.

Riojana, La La R ★ Massive co-op with 400+ growers. Best for everyday TORRONTÉS.

Río Negro Río N Old vines and riverside sites in s. Ideal for RIES, SEM, MALBEC, PINOT, heritage TROUSSEAU. Still under threat; worth saving.

Rolland, Bodega Men ★★→★★★ Michel R's (*see* France) Uco baby. Perfumed SAUV BL and dense, plush MALBEC drive house style.

Ruca Malen Men ★★→★★★ Agustina Hanna's revitalized range: lively whites, elegant reds. Particularly strong SEM/SAUV BL, GARNACHA.

Rutini Men ★★→★★★ A trad name, modern mindset now with Juan Pablo Murgia on board. Uco-focused top wines; Antología blends age-worthy.

Salentein, Bodegas Men ★★→★★★ Dutch-owned Uco pioneer in San Pablo. Portillo offers value; single-vyd SAUV BL, MALBEC particularly exciting.

Salta High-altitude drama in Calchaquí valleys. TORRONTÉS exuberant, aromatic; MALBEC, TANNAT powerful, pure.

San Juan Region n of MEN, big volumes, gd value. TORRONTÉS, BONARDA, MALBEC, SYRAH dependable; Pedernal and Calingasta top-quality pockets.

San Pedro de Yacochuya Sal ★★★ Michel ROLLAND and ETCHART: dense, high-altitude MALBEC from vines over a century old.

Santa Julia Men ★★ ZUCCARDI's value brand; natural range. Honest, consistent.

Schroeder, Familia Neu ★★ PINOT N-focused Pat producer; fossils under winery inspire local dinosaur lore.

Sophenia, Finca Men ★★→★★★ Early Gualtallary arrival. Racy SAUV BL, firm Bx blends; ***Antisynthesis Field Blend*** personal favourite.

Susana Balbo Wines Men ★★→★★★★ TORRONTÉS queen, red-wine master, still

Argentina's leading female winemaker. Signature White Blend among country's top whites.

Tapiz Men ★★ Family-run with standout San Pablo estate. Alta CAB FR steals show for value; Notas de Jean Claude MERLOT lush, plush.

Terrazas de los Andes Men ★★→★★★ Classic, polished wines from CHANDON's still arm. Single-vyd MALBECS fresher, higher altitude (up to 1650m/5413ft) than ever.

Tikal / Alma Negra / Animal / Stella Crintina Men ★★→★★★ Ernesto and Joanna CATENA's bio constellation (r/w/orange/sp); diverse, expressive.

Toso, Pascual Men ★★ Maipú stalwart: silky, concentrated old-vine reds.

Trapiche Men ★→★★★ Flagship of PEÑAFLOR. Massive range, but high peaks: Iscay blends. Also coastal Costa y Pampa ALBARIÑO/SAUV BL from Buenos Aires.

Trivento Men ★→★★ CONCHA Y TORO's Argentine arm. Big volumes, reliable fruit; supermarket-hit White MALBEC. Eolo top old-vine Malbec.

Ver Sacrum ★★★ One of Argentina's most distinctive portfolios; Med grapes: GARNACHA, MENCÍA, NEBBIOLO, no MALBEC in sight. Fragrant, free-spirited.

Vines of Mendoza / Winemaker's Village Men ★★ Luxury wine estate and micro-vinification hub in Los Chacayes. Home to boutique producers (Corazón del Sol, Gimenez Riili, SuperUco).

Zorzal Men ★★ Bright, mineral Gualtallary project. Vibrant Eggo range top; SAUV BL, CAB FR, PINOT N all gd.

Zuccardi Men ★★★→★★★★ Sebastian Z's mtn-focused vision: crystalline CHARD, textured SEM, taut, mineral MALBEC. Concrete over oak; place over polish. Finca line is incredibly age-worthy, Concreto fresher appeal today.

BRAZIL

In the contracting world of wine, Brazil is one of the few wine countries still expanding. Brazil is very much on the rise, and so is quality. Rio Grande do Sul remains the heartland, especially for traditional-method fizz, but Campanha on the Uruguayan border is turning out increasingly smart reds (Cabernet Sauvignon, Tannat). High-altitude Santa Catarina gives the best Sauvignon Blanc, while Serra da Mantiqueira's winter-harvest wines (notably Syrah) offer smoky, savoury intrigue not to be found anywhere else in South America. Brazil's wines are hard to measure or find beyond borders, but easy to enjoy while in situ.

Colheita do inverno: winter harvest technique that's all the rage at altitude in Brazil.

Aurora ★ Massive co-op, hundreds of growers, lots of everyday wine, reliable value.

Casa Valduga ★★→★★★ Family estate on Vale dos Vinhedos wine route; excellent fizz and approachable reds.

Cave Geisse ★★★ One of Brazil's trad-method champions. Brut Nature is superb; sparkling orange a fun, left-field bonus.

Era dos Ventos ★★★ Luiz Henrique Zanini's poetic, small-batch project: each bottle comes with a poem instead of a tasting note. Worth trying rare Peverella.

Guaspari ★★→★★★ Spectacular setting in Serra da Mantiqueira; known for winter-harvest SYRAH, with smoky depth, spice.

Guatambu ★★ One of Campanha's most dynamic names. Standout CAB SAUV, TANNAT; sleek, well-balanced reds.

Lidio Carraro ★★ Leading family winery in Rio Grande do Sul; wide range of clean, fruit-led wines, plus unexpectedly tasty NEBBIOLO.

Miolo ★→★★ Big national player; broad, quality-driven. Lote 43 consistently gd.

Pizzato ★→★★★ Among best in Vale dos Vinhedos: SEM, juicy reds, unfiltered fizz.

Salton ★→★★ One of Brazil's most established brands. Huge portfolio, lots of easy Prosecco-style fizz; top cuvée Lucia Canei shows real class.

URUGUAY

Not just Tannat anymore; new investments are breathing life into this thriving small coastal country. Uruguay combines political calm, relative affluence and a remarkably stable economy – a rare oasis on the continent. It's no surprise investors from Brazil and Argentina are increasingly planting vines here, drawn by the relaxed coastal lifestyle, temperate climate and ancient, varied soils that yield distinctive wines. Tannat still reigns by number, but Uruguay shines just as brightly with fresh Albariño, peppery Cabernet Franc and savoury Pinot Noir.

Alto de la Ballena ★→★★★ Family-run pioneer in Maldonado, with spicy CAB FR, savoury SYRAH, deft TANNAT/VIOGNIER. Host of new whites (ALBARIÑO and GODELLO) emerging.

Bouza ★★→★★★ Leading family estate, two wineries, four terroirs, two excellent restaurants. Highlights: ALBARIÑO (family was pioneer), RIES, PINOT N; also classic TANNAT, TEMPRANILLO.

Cerro Chapeu, Bodega ★★→★★★ Rivera estate straddling Brazilian border. Brilliant Castel Pujol Folklore series, incl standout MANSENG N, host of orange, pét-nat.

Cerro del Toro ★★→★★★ Atlantic-facing vyds delivering salty-fresh ALBARIÑO, elegant CHARD, coastal-tinged TANNAT.

Deicas, Familia ★★→★★★★ Santiago D fast becoming one of Uruguay's top talents – from edgy natural Bizarra Extravaganza to refined Cru ALBARIÑO and TANNAT. Extreme Vyds project a must-try; he's the only winemaker to have worked in all of Uruguay's terroirs.

Garzón, Bodega ★★→★★★★ Uruguay's global flagship estate. Slick, consistent, with real excitement at top. Don't miss refined CAB FR; all else reliably strong. Balasto worthy icon, sold on Place de Bx (*see* France).

Pablo Fallabrino Wines ★★ Expect delightful curveballs: orange wines, pét-nats and even a Barolo Chinato-style sweet. Always intriguing, often delicious.

Pisano ★★→★★★ Generational Progreso family crafting age-worthy reds and barrel-aged ALBARIÑO in RPF lines. Bestseller in France is PINOT N.

Progreso, Viña ★★→★★★ Gabriel Pisano's personal label from Canelones: peachy VIOGNIER, lively SANGIOVESE, supple, well-made TANNAT.

Proyecto Nakkal ★★ Uruguay's cool-kid natural collective. Low alc and low intervention, done with precision: crisp pét-nat, juicy amphora reds, even a fresh, featherweight TANNAT.

OTHER SOUTH AMERICAN WINES

Bolivia Although relatively small in size, Bolivia beats most in terms of its altitude, with vines at dizzying heights, sometimes over 2400m (7875ft). Tarija is the heartland, where big, bold, sun-soaked reds (Aranjuez, Kohlberg, Kuhlmann) reign; while the high-altitude Santa Cruz valleys (Vinos 1750) produce fragrant, characterful whites. The gnarly, centuries-old vines of the Cinti Valley (Cepa de Oro, Jardín Oculto) offer a glimpse into S America's viticultural past. These wines aren't polished or predictable, but they're unforgettable. Bodegas Yokitch has impressed recently.

Peru Once the cradle of S America's wine industry, Peru has a rich past that still eclipses its modest present, but a revival is under way. Along the coast, a lively natural-wine scene (Bodega Murga, Mimo) brings texture and personality, while est producers inland (Intipalka, Tacama, Vista Alegre) deliver cleaner, classic styles. Most intriguing of all are the high-altitude mtn vyds of Apu, perched not far from Machu Picchu – a bold, ambitious attempt to reconnect Peru with the wine legacy it helped start centuries ago.

Australia

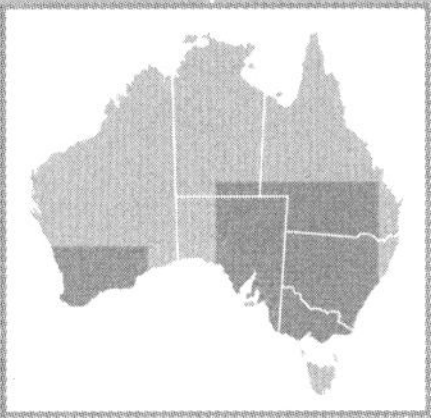

Abbreviations used in the text:

Ad H	Adelaide Hills, SA
Bar V	Barossa Valley, SA
Beech	Beechworth, Vic
Can	Canberra, NSW
Coonw	Coonawarra, SA
Fra R	Frankland River, WA
Gip	Gippsland, Vic
Gra	Grampians, Vic
Gt S	Great Southern, WA
Hea	Heathcote, Vic
Hunt V	Hunter Valley, NSW
Kang I	Kangaroo Island, SA
Lang C	Langhorne Creek, SA
Mac	Macedon, Vic
Marg R	Margaret River, WA
McL V	McLaren Vale, SA
Mor P	Mornington Penninsula, Vic
Tas	Tasmania
Qld	Queensland
Ruth	Rutherglen, Vic

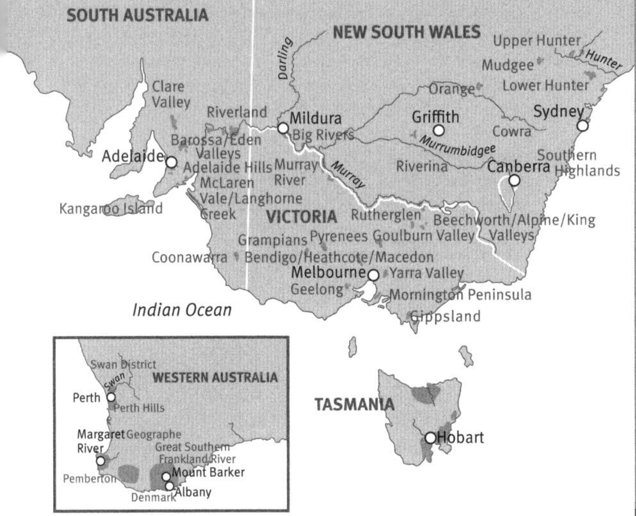

At the end of each year, and on the cusp of harvest, reports about the current state of our vinous landscape come to the fore, including *The Australian Wine Production, Sales and Inventory Report*. In part, this year's report (2025) stated the worsening imbalance between supply and demand comes as global conditions for wine remain tough. Analysis suggests the outlook for wine has deteriorated in the past year, with consumption declining and a forecast to decrease further in the next five years. This should be a wake-up call for large-scale producers and growers alike. Reassess the landscape, including our drinking culture, be more sustainable, and bigger producers should cut their losses and reduce the dross. Yes, there is room for everyday drinks, but there's an excess of ordinary. Let's go up the scale, allowing the premium category to grow and become more competitive. "Strive for excellence and make the best possible wine" should be the mantra. It's why small operators often have the most thrilling drinks to offer; you'll have to pay a bit extra, but it's so worth it. Thankfully, our world-class fine wine range has never been better. Bravo.

Recent vintages

New South Wales (NSW)

2025 Can, superb (r/w) with gd yields; Hunt V variable, Sem the star.
2024 Early vintage, low yields; v.gd Hunt V (r). Frost Can, top made v.gd (r/w).
2023 Cool, wet, disease pressure, low yields, yet Hunt V has excellent Shiraz.
2022 La Niña strikes. Heavy rain, not much heat. Difficult vintage.
2021 Heavy rain, some disease pressure. Whites generally gd, choose wisely.
2020 Hot, fire-affected yr with all manner of challenges.

Victoria (Vic)

2025 Early, warm, dry; lower yields; v.gd to excellent in Beech, Gip, Yarra V.
2024 Unseasonally wet/humid, then heat. Low yields, gd white Mor P, Yarra V.
2023 Challenging, flooding ne. Some fine (r/w). Yields down in Mor P, Yarra V.
2022 Cool, often wet, low yields. High acidity, v.gd whites, esp Yarra V.
2021 Stark contrast to 20. Many calling it season of elegance, balance; gd yields.
2020 Fire-affected in ne and generally challenging. Yields down.

South Australia (SA)

2025 Drought, dry Bar V, McL V; quality Grenache, Shiraz; Coonw excellent.
2024 Dry, some frost, low yields; quality Bar V (r), Clare V Ries.
2023 La Niña in force; wet, cool, lower yields. Clare V v.gd Ries.
2022 Cool, long ripening; v.gd overall. McLaren V solid (r/w).
2021 Said to be nr perfect. Bar V outstanding, Clare V exceptional (r/w).
2020 Hard/tragic yr, but Ries and reds look promising. Seriously low yields.

Western Australia (WA)

2025 Winter/spring rain gd, then dry in Marg R, excellent if moderate yields.
2024 Warm/dry, v. early season, yields down but Marg R, Gt S v.gd (r/w).
2023 Cool spring, mild conditions. Marg R, Gt S v.gd (r/w).
2022 Excellent in Marg R but low yields, esp Chard.
2021 Challenging due to late-season rain but ultimately rewarding.
2020 Early, low-yield, high-concentration yr.

Adelaide Hills SA Stunning cool region in Mt Lofty ranges, up to 650m (2132ft) with two official subregions: Lenswood, Piccadilly V. CHARD, SAUV BL, GRÜNER V; SHIRAZ, PINOT N with superb sparkling. Try ASHTON HILLS, DEVIATION ROAD, Hahndorf Hill, HENSCHKE, JERICHO, SHAW & SMITH, SIDEWOOD ESTATE.

Adelina Clare V ★★★ Family-owned, organic, great vyds; exellent RIES, GRENACHE, MATARO, NEBBIOLO, SHIRAZ.

Agricola Vintners Bar V Star of next-generation BAR V, Callum Powell (son of Dave P, ex-TORBRECK) sourcing excellent fruit from est and/or old vyds, ie. Ashbrook 1864; poised, rich yet refined SHIRAZ.

Alkina Wine Estate Bar V ★★★ Argentinian-owned. No expense spared; est 50s site, now bio; concrete tanks, eggs, *qvevri*, older oak. GRENACHE, SHIRAZ star, v.gd SEM.

Alkoomi Fra R ★★ Large-scale, family-owned; go-to v.gd RIES, regionally expressive CABS SAUV/FR, SHIRAZ.

All Saints Estate Ruth ★★★★ Rating for fortifieds: Museum MUSCAT, MUSCADELLE, average age 100-yrs+ solera. Also table wines.

Alpine Valleys Vic Cool-climate, foothills of Victorian Alps, mostly growers (r/w), esp Italian varieties. Pecorino most recent; top TEMPRANILLO, CHARD. BILLY BUTTON, MAYFORD lead quality, diversity stakes.

Andrew Thomas Hun V ★★ Old-vine SEM; SHIRAZ. A HUN V game-changer, esp with more elegant expressions of SHIRAZ.

Angove's SA ★★→★★★ Family business, founded 1886. Keenly priced range; MCL V site organic, focus on premium and single-vyd GRENACHE, SHIRAZ. Exceptional brandy and Oz finest, St Agnes XXO and XO from its Riverland distillery.

Aravina Estate Marg R ★★ Formerly Amberley Estate; est vyds, v. cool altitude; MARG R's only ARINTO, v.gd GRENACHE, TEMPRANILLO. Classic CHARD, CHENIN BL, CAB SAUV.

Arenberg, d' McL V ★★ Some kooky names (The Cenosilicaphobic Cat SAGRANTINO), yet wines solid, lots of them, incl v.gd GRENACHE, SHIRAZ.

A Rodda Beech ★★ Excellent CHARDS from est vyds; ***Tempranillo*** grown at high altitude can be special.

Ashton Hills Ad H ★★ Distinctive PINOT N 20' **22** 24 from 30-yr-old+ vyds; tiptop CHARD, RIES.

Baileys of Glenrowan NE Vic ★★ Historic property/vyds, organic; excellent Durif, SHIRAZ, fabulous fortified MUSCAT (★★★★), Topaque. Owned by CASELLA.

Balancing Heart Granite Belt, Qld Site bought 2020, renamed Balancing Heart after heart-shaped granite boulder on property; CHARD, SHIRAZ gd, best yet to come, with new plantings of Italian and other varieties.

Ballandean Estate Wines Granite Belt, Qld ★★ Oldest family-owned winery in Qld (1932), cool clime. Old SHIRAZ vines, v.gd fortifieds; Italian varietals steal show.

Balnaves of Coonawarra SA ★★ Family-owned COONW champion. Rich CHARD, flagship Tally CAB SAUV, v.gd spicy SHIRAZ. Joven-style (*see* Spain) Cab gd.

Bannockburn Vic ★★★ (CHARD) 21' **22** 23 24 (PINOT N) 19' 21 **22** 23 Family-owned, pioneers of GEELONG, quality never wavers. Outrageously gd structured Chard, complex Pinot N, RIES, SAUV BL.

Barossa Valley SA Bastion of v. old-vine CAB SAUV, GRENACHE, MOURVÈDRE, SHIRAZ. Expect richness, but new brigade shaking things up. ELDERTON, HENTLEY FARM, JOHN DUVAL, LANGMEIL, PETER LEHMANN, ROCKFORD, RUGGABELLUS, SALTRAM, SAMI-ODI, SEPPELTSFIELD, SPINIFEX, TEUSNER, YALUMBA.

Barry, Jim Clare V ★★★ RIES rules thanks to top vyds and lots of them. LoosenBarry Wolta Wolta a collaboration with Mosel mogul Ernst Loosen (*see* Germany). Reds solid: age-worthy Armagh SHIRAZ. Also Oz's only ASSYRTIKO.

Bass Phillip Gip ★★★→★★★★ (PINOT N) **20'** 21' **22'** 23 24 Tiny amounts of distinctive Pinot N, CHARD equally v.gd, delightful GEWURZ, GAMAY. Burgundian J-M Fourrier (*see* France) leads winemaking.

Battle of Bosworth McL V Organic, gd folk caring for land/wine, top value. SHIRAZ leads many offerings.

Beechworth NE Vic Spectacular rocky region in Victorian High Country; CHARD, SHIRAZ best, impressive NEBBIOLO. Try A RODDA, DOMENICA, FIGHTING GULLY ROAD, GIACONDA, SAVATERRE, SCHMÖLZER & BROWN, SENTIO, SORRENBERG.

Bekkers McL V ★★★ Emmanuelle and Toby B focus on organics; thoughtful winemaker, excellent GRENACHE, SYRAH.

Bellebonne Tas ★★★ Natalie Fryar (ex-Jansz) showcases "pristine fruit power and elegance of Tasmania" with Blanc de Blancs, rosé and more.

Bellwether Coonw ★★ A love of CAB SAUV kept Sue Bell in COONW, turning Glen Roy

1868 shearing shed into boutique winery, cellar door and more. CHARD from TAS v.gd, sources Italian varieties too.

Bendigo Vic Central Vic region with Med climate. Rich reds a speciality; PASSING CLOUDS, SUTTON GRANGE.

Best's Great Western Gra ★★★ Superstar, in best yrs flagship Thomson Family SHIRAZ **17' 19'** 20' 21 22 from 120-yr-old vines; ***v.gd mid-weight reds***; exceptional old-vine PINOT M; excellent RIES. History, great people, worth drive from Melbourne.

Barossa Valley has 80 ha of Ancestor vines, at least 125 years old.

Billy Button Alpine V ★★ Umpteen varieties/styles; alas, small quantities. Italian varietals (rare SCHIOPPETTINO); CHARD, SAPERAVI, SHIRAZ and more. Delicious.

Bindi Mac ★★★★ Outstanding single-block CHARD, PINOT N 20' 21' **22'** 23' 24. Small production, high-density-vyd Block 8 jewel in crown.

Bleasdale Lang C ★★→★★★ Historic winery (1850). Fabulous fortifieds, top CAB SAUV, MALBEC, SHIRAZ, plus gd-value range. Ever reliable.

Bondar McL V ★★ Modern yet thoughtful producer of excellent GRENACHE, SHIRAZ, also Italian varieties; v.gd AD H CHARD.

Bortoli, De Griffith, Yarra V ★→★★★ (Noble SEM) Sauternes style (*see* France) from irrigated region Griffith; YARRA V for cool-climate, quality CHARD, PINOT N, SHIRAZ. Loads of styles, range of prices yet serious player.

Brave New Wine Marg R ★★ Natural wines, loaded with personality; capable of v. high highs, so to speak; CHARD, GEWURZ, SHIRAZ can all be excellent.

Bremerton Lang C ★★ Family-owned/run; stars rich CAB SAUV, MALBEC, SHIRAZ, but CHARD, FIANO and fizz no slouches.

Brokenwood Beech, Hun V ★★★→★★★★ (ILR Res SEM) 11' **13' 14'** 17' 18' 19 (Graveyard SHIRAZ) 17' 18' **19'** 21 22 23 Both HUN V classics. High-quality, gd-value ***Cricket Pitch*** Sem/SAUV BL. Suite of excellent CHARD, SHIRAZ, TEMPRANILLO from BEECH.

Brown Brothers King V, Tas, Yarra V ★→★★ Crowd-pleaser and top producer by volume of Prosecco variety; premium Patricia range, fizz esp excellent. Innocent Bystander (YARRA V), Devil's Corner/Tamar Ridge (TAS) savvy acquisitions.

By Fabiano McL V ★★ S Italian heritage, MCL v-born Fabiano Minchella is a young producer dedicated to reflecting his site via FIANO, PRIMITIVO and more. Gorgeous Italianesque labels. Watch.

Calabria Family Wines Bar V, Riverina ★★→★★★ Family-owned, large-scale, incl excellent BAR V; bought historic MCWILLIAM'S in 2021 (not MOUNT PLEASANT), plus fruit from CAN DISTRICT, TUMBARUMBA. Great wines, all price points incl top.

Campbells Ruth ★★→★★★★ Reds rule, rich and big Durif, SHIRAZ. Unique fortifieds are king: Merchant Prince Rare ***Muscat***, Isabella Rare Topaque.

Canberra District NSW Super-cool climatically and high-end. CLONAKILLA top; also COLLECTOR, LARK HILL, MOUNT MAJURA, NICK O'LEARY, RAVENSWORTH.

Cape Mentelle Marg R ★★ Pioneering producer of region; CHARD promising, SAUV BL/SEM appealing, CAB SAUV often highlight.

Casella Riverina Through Yellow Tail budget range became an empire. Now owns heritage brands BAILEYS OF GLENROWAN, Brand's of Coonawarra, MORRIS and PETER LEHMANN.

Chalmers Hea, Murray D ★→★★ Grower/vine-nursery specialist on Italian varieties, newest add NERELLO MASCALESE. Diverse range: gd FIANO, VERMENTINO.

Chambers Rosewood NE Vic With MORRIS, greatest maker of fortified Topaque (★★★★), ***Muscat***.

Chandon Australia Yarra V ★★→★★★ Cool-climate fizz and table wine. Owned by LVMH. Known in UK as Green Point. NV cuvées in best-ever shape.

Chapel Hill McL V ★★→★★★ Solid performer in MCL V. These days, GRENACHE (esp old vines), SHIRAZ lead show, but CAB SAUV ever a solid back-up.

Charlotte Dalton Wines Ad H ★★ Breath of fresh air. Classic varieties CHARD, SHIRAZ, but also v.gd Lang C FIANO.

Chatto Tas ★★★ Young vyd, yet some v. fine PINOT N. Fragrance, layers of flavours, beautiful tannins, delicious.

Cirillo Wines Bar V Planted 1848, site of world's oldest GRENACHE, SEM, plus ancient SHIRAZ. Lovely wines; Cirillo family brilliant custodians.

Clarendon Hills McL V ★★★ Powerful, rich reds (think GRENACHE, SHIRAZ) yet retain depth, savouriness, freshness. Built for cellaring; always decant.

Clare Valley SA Hilly, pretty region, 142 km n of Adelaide. RIES the star; distinctive CAB SAUV, gumleaf-scented SHIRAZ. Most family-run JIM BARRY, GROSSET, KILIKANOON, MOUNT HORROCKS, PIKES, WENDOUREE (jewel in crown), WINES BY KT.

Clonakilla Can ★★★★ (SHIRAZ/VIOGNIER) 16' **18'** 19' 21' 22' 23 24 Regional legend/superstar. Shiraz/Viognier put on vinous map, but elegant SYRAH often shines brighter. Outstanding RIES, Viognier.

Cobaw Ridge Mac ★★★ Family-owned. Cool-climate, compelling CHARD, SYRAH. Some *qvevri*, amphorae used; bio: super-fine PINOT N, finest LAGREIN in Oz.

Coldstream Hills Yarra V ★★→★★★ Excellent CHARD; PINOT N to drink young, ***Res and single vyd to age***. Part of TWE.

Collector Can ★★→★★★ Alex McKay weaves magic: top CHARD (TUMBARUMBA), fine RIES, Shiraz (CAN), host of delicious Italian varieties.

Coonawarra SA Built upon ancient Terra Rossa soils of limestone, clay, producing unique CAB SAUV, SHIRAZ. Single-vyd wines a feature: WYNNS the shining light. Try also BALNAVES, BELLWETHER, MAJELLA, PENLEY ESTATE, Zema Estate.

Coriole McL V ★★★ (Lloyd Res SHIRAZ) 15' **16'** 18' 19 20 21 from 100-yr-old+ vines. SANGIOVESE pioneer, also FIANO, PIQUEPOUL, NEGROAMARO, NERO D'AVOLA, all v.gd.

Corymbia Marg R, Swan V ★★★ Superstar owner-winemakers. Textural CHENIN BL, elegant CAB SAUV (Marg R); impressive TEMPRANILLO/MALBEC (SWAN V).

Craiglee Sunbury ★★★ (SHIRAZ) 17' 18' **19'** 20' 21 22 Historic farm producing rich CHARD, distinctive, fragrant, peppery Shiraz. One of a kind.

Crawford River Henty ★★★ Outstanding RIES producer. Cool/cold, scintillatingly dry, intense. Highly age-worthy.

Crittenden Estate Mor P ★★→★★★ Focus on v.gd CHARD, PINOTS GR/N; Cri de Coeur Sous Voile SAVAGNIN excellent *vin jaune* style.

Cullen Wines Marg R ★★★★ (CHARD) 20' 21' **22'** 23' 24' (CAB SAUV) 19' 20' 21' **22'** 23' A bio advocate. Kevin John Chard, Diana Madeline and Vanya Cab Sauvs expressing place; long-lived reds.

Dalwhinnie Pyrenees Regional stalwart (est 1973), bought by burgeoning Fogarty Wine Group in 2020; CHARD, CAB SAUV, SHIRAZ, all improving greatly under Julian Langworthy.

Dal Zotto King V ★★ "Prosecco" pioneer, many styles, incl excellent Col Fondo. Italian lineup morphs into fresh, lively or structured, detailed. Legendary patriarch has best name: Otto Dal Zotto.

Wine and fine dine

Several wineries have invested in top restaurants to ensure a gastronomic experience par excellence. Try one of the country's best, TEN MINUTES BY TRACTOR, based in Vic's MOR P, while YARRA V has TARRAWARRA ESTATE, and NSW HUNT V, Margan Restaurant & Winery. Cross states to S Australia, and close to Adelaide's business district is PENFOLDS Magill Estate fine-dining restaurant; BAROSSA V has HENTLEY FARM. In TAS, The Source at MOORILLA holds pole position. To the west in MARG R, VASSE FELIX leads way. While all are classy, in true Aussie style, far from stuffy.

Dappled Yarra V ★★★ Top-flight/value, elegant-but-complex CHARD, PINOT N.

Deep Woods Estate Marg R ★★★★ ALBARIÑO styles/varieties, frisky rosé to succulent SHIRAZ; CHARD, CAB SAUV steal limelight. Star of Fogarty Wine Group juggernaut.

Delamere Tas ★★★ At Pipers Brook vyd, Fran Austin, Shane Holloway make high-end CHARD, PINOT N but also exquisite fizz. Boutique. Unique. Stylish.

Deviation Road Ad H ★★★ Family vyd. Kate Laurie the fizz queen also sources growers' fruit, constantly fine-tuning styles; top Beltana Blanc de Blancs.

Devil's Lair Marg R ★★★ Finely tuned CHARD, complex CAB SAUV (top-tier 9th Chamber), new excellent SYRAH (Fra R). Winemakers give love, but owned and therefore largely hidden/ignored by TWE.

Dirty Three Wines Gip ★★→★★★ Name relates to vyds where Marcus Satchell, aka Mr Gippsland, sources fruit; cracking CHARD, PINOT N (All the Dirts, Magic Dirt, 100% whole-bunch fermented).

Domenica Beech ★★★ Excellent producer with est vyds. Textural MARSANNE. Exuberant, spicy SHIRAZ, but NEBBIOLO shines.

Dormilona Marg R, Swan V Winery in hip industrial area. Josephine Perry's diverse, delicious range, so much personality; eye on sustainability.

Dr Edge Tas ★★★ Smart operator, excellent winemaker, loaded with personality of Peter Dredge. In TAS compelling CHARD, PINOT N; also in Oregon (US).

Eden Valley SA Climatically cooler cousin of neighbour BAR V. Hilly region; RIES, SHIRAZ from HENSCHKE, MAX & ME, PEWSEY VALE, TORZI MATTHEWS and more.

Eisenstone Bar V ★★★ Named after ironstone soils where Stephen Cook seeks out excellent SHIRAZ, often old sites. Small scale, diversity, v.gd wines.

Elanto Mor P Ambitious project: Oz's largest high-density vyd, 10.6 ha with 11,111 vines/ha, only CHARD, PINOT N; 1st vintage 23 v.gd, but 24 outstanding. Watch.

Elderton Bar V ★★★ Family-owned/run. Old vines; opulent CAB SAUV, SHIRAZ built to last. Something for everyone, incl v.gd RIES.

Eldorado Road Beech ★★★ Small, family-owned; old-vine SHIRAZ (1890s); powerful reds (Durif, blends). Arguably Oz's finest NERO D'AVOLA. Distinctive wines.

Eldridge Mor P ★★→★★★ Owned by enthusiasts who appointed ex-GIANT STEPS Steve Flamsteed to help. Expect CHARD, GAMAY, PINOT N to be better than ever.

Entropy Wine Gip ★★→★★★ New name turning heads with thoughtful winemaking, Ryan Ponsfor crafts textural SAUV BL/SEM, expressive PINOT N, peppery SYRAH.

Eperosa Bar V ★★★ Organic off-grid winery, 6th-generation BAR V vigneron. Magnolia (1896 SHIRAZ) and Krondorf (1903 GRENACHE) vyds. Respectful of past with nod to future; flavoursome, detailed wines.

Faber Vineyards Swan V ★★ Guru of WA winemaking, John Griffiths redefines what's possible for SWAN V SHIRAZ. Polished power. Fortifieds always a highlight.

Fighting Gully Road Beech ★★★ Lauded producer, plus fruit from ALPINE V. Outstanding CHARD, AGLIANICO, SANGIOVESE, SYRAH, TEMPRANILLO. New plantings of VERDICCHIO, GRENACHE are v. promising. Oz's only PETITE ARVINE.

Flametree Marg R ★★→★★★ No vyds but sources excellent CHARD, CAB SAUV, esp for SRS (subregional series); v.gd SHIRAZ surprise late entry.

Flowstone Marg R ★★★ Partners/winemaking veterans Stuart Pym and Janice McDonald (ex-HOWARD PARK) bring whimsy, class to diverse range. Top: CHARD, CAB SAUV Queen of the Earth; Moonmilk blends.

Forest Hill Vineyard Gt Southern ★★★ Regional pioneer est 1st commercial vyd 1965; RIES the hero, Block 1 the star; v.gd MALBEC, SHIRAZ, outstanding CAB SAUV.

Frankland Estate Fra R ★★★ RIES royalty 20' 21' 22' 23' 24' 25', outstanding organic vyd, Isolation Ridge (most remote in WA), range of styles. Medium-bodied CABS FR/SAUV, SYRAH, impressive GRÜNER V, MOURVÈDRE.

Freycinet Tas ★★★ Pioneer family winery on TAS e coast; v.gd CHARD, outstanding RIES, fragrant PINOT N, Radenti (sp).

Garagiste Mor P ★★★ Tiny; outstanding CHARD, PINOTS GR/N. Quality from vyd care, run but not owned by winemaker Barnaby Flanders. Impressive.

Geelong Vic Region w of Melbourne, maritime, dry climate. Leaders: BANNOCKBURN, LETHBRIDGE, OAKDENE, PROVENANCE, WINE BY FARR.

Gembrook Hill Yarra V ★★★ Cool site on upper reaches of Yarra River: CHARD par excellence, fine-boned PINOT N. Excellent gin a sideline.

Gentle Folk Ad H ★★ Marine scientists turned vignerons, in natural-wine scene; top CHARD, PINOT N, SYRAH. Viti/regenerative expert Dr Dylan Grigg advises.

Giaconda Beech ★★★★ Put BEECH on vinous map, and internationally. Top: CHARD 18' 19' 21' 22' 23'. Also v.gd: NEBBIOLO, SHIRAZ.

Giant Steps Yarra V ★★★ 19' 20' 21' 22' 23' 24' Top single-vyd CHARD, PINOT N, SHIRAZ. Jackson Family-owned (*see* US).

Glaetzer-Dixon Tas ★★→★★★ Nick G turned SA wine-family history on head by relocating to cool TAS. Euro-style RIES, autumnal PINOT N, Rhôney SHIRAZ.

Goulburn Valley Vic Warm region in mid-Vic taking in Nagambie Lakes. Historic TAHBILK famed for old MARSANNE and big, rich reds. MITCHELTON a drawcard.

Grampians Vic Temperate region in NW Vic; distinct peppery SHIRAZ (and sp), lovely RIES. MOUNT LANGI GHIRAN the beacon.

Granite Belt Qld High-altitude, cool, granitic outpost on Qld/NSW border. Italian/Med varieties stars; CHARD, SHIRAZ. Try BALANCING HEART, BALLANDEAN ESTATE.

Grant Burge Bar V ★★ Smooth red/white from best grapes of large vyd holdings.

Great Southern WA Stunning if remote region at bottom left corner of Oz; Albany, Denmark, Fra R, Mount Barker, Porongurup official subregions; 1st-class RIES, CAB SAUV, SHIRAZ. ***Style, quality, value here.***

7.5m thirsty visitors to Oz wineries p.a. add £25.56bn (A$51.3bn) to economy.

Grosset Clare V ★★→★★★ (RIES) 21' 22' 23' 24' 25' Nervy, acid-driven Ries in youth, many styles incl high-end G110 from one clone, organic site. Appealing FIANO; distinctive ***Gaia*** 18' 19' 21' 22' 23' mainly CAB SAUV.

Gundog Estate Hun V ★ Some v.gd RIES, SEM, SHIRAZ from CAN, HUN V.

Hardys SA ★★ Historic company, but glory days long gone, VINARCHY-owned. CHARD, SHIRAZ can be excellent.

Hatch Bar V, Clare V, McL V Chris Hatcher, chief winemaker at WOLF BLASS for yonks, "retired" in 2023 then created own label. RIES, SHIRAZ mainstays.

Heathcote Vic Central Vic, warm region with 500m-yr-old Cambrian geology; rich, red soils produce distinct SHIRAZ; Italian varieties standouts. JASPER HILL, PAUL OSICKA, TAR & ROSES, Wild Duck Creek.

Helm Can Pioneer of RIES all styles; and yes, even Ries Rosé.

Henschke Eden V ★★★★ (SHIRAZ) 09' 10' 14' 15' 16' 17 18' 19, 20 21 22 (CAB SAUV) 12' 15' 16' 17 18 19 21 Oz wine royalty, 150-yr-old family business; masterpiece is Hill of Grace, site and wine (Shiraz) with v.gd single-vyd Cab Sauv Cyril Henschke. Red blends gd, whites also from AD H, incl GRÜNER V.

Hentley Farm Bar V ★★★ Gutsy SHIRAZ, flavour, tannins, power, for long haul.

Hewitson Bar V ★★→★★★ (***Old Garden Mourvèdre***) 18' 19' 20' 21' 22' Old Garden planted 1853, making it world's oldest MOURVÈDRE; v.gd SHIRAZ, range of prices.

Hickinbotham Clarendon Vineyard McL V ★★★★ Dry-grown SHIRAZ, CAB SAUV planted 1971 (Jackson Family-owned, *see* US); separate business to YANGARRA but same philosophy: organic, respect for land. Excellent suite of wines.

Hoddles Creek Estate Yarra V ★★★ Family-owned/run: outstanding cool-climate CHARD, PINOT N, esp top-tier single blocks. Quality high, value too.

Hoosegg Orange ★★→★★★ Veteran Philip Shaw made Rosemount a roaring success in Southcorp days, now TWE. Eponymous label run by sons, this the nest egg: excellent boutique CHARD, CABS SAUV/FR and more.

Houghton Marg R Brand with VINARCHY, shadow of former self. Fruit from GT S, MARG R, wines made in latter. ★★★★ Jack Mann CAB SAUV; credit to winemaker Courtney Treacher for dedication.

House of Arras Tas ★★★★ Most prestigious fizz house in Oz, all credit to winemaker Ed Carr. Key is magic confluence of tannins, ageing on lees and acidity. EJ Carr Late Disgorged the pinnacle. Bought by Handpicked Wines (2023).

Howard Park WA ★★→★★★ With v.gd RIES from GT S, plus MARG R CHARD, CAB SAUV. Marchard & Burch, family collaboration with Burgundian vigneron Pascal Marchand (*see* France). Value ***MadFish***.

Hugh Hamilton Wines McL V ★★ All-rounder, quirky names: The Larrikin CAB/SHIRAZ, The Mongrel SANGIOVESE; SAPERAVI a speciality, several styles incl powerful Oddball the Great.

Hunter Valley NSW Historic region 250 km n of Sydney. Unique SEM can be steely in youth, elixir with age; mid-weight, earthy SHIRAZ. Try ANDREW THOMAS, BROKENWOOD, MOUNT PLEASANT, SILKMAN, ***Tyrrell's***.

Jacob's Creek Bar V Mostly focused on uninspiring but reliable wines (RIES star).

Jasper Hill Hea ★★ Emily's Paddock SHIRAZ/CAB FR, Georgia's Paddock Shiraz intense. Much-needed vyd work on-going; run by 2nd generation, Emily.

Jericho Ad H, McL V ★★ Careful fruit selection, skilled winemaking, modern, tasty wines: FIANO, GRENACHE, SHIRAZ, TEMPRANILLO.

John Duval Wines Bar V ★★★ John D (ex-PENFOLDS Grange) makes ***delicious Rhôney reds*** of great intensity, character. Son Tim works with dad. Future is bright.

Joshua Cooper Wines Mac ★★★ Son of COBAW RIDGE founders, uber-talented with love of Oz wine history. Site in MAC, sources fruit within and outside region. Outstanding CHARD, PINOT N, teases best from BENDIGO CAB SAUV 1970 plantings.

Juniper Marg R ★★→★★★ With est sites: gluggable Nouveau (r blend), FIANO; single-vyd CHARD, CAB SAUV. Ever reliable; 2nd-tier Higher Plane, drink-now, fun styles.

Kaesler Wines Bar V ★★★ Historic BAR V name, exceptional vyds incl The Old Bastard SHIRAZ (named after gnarly 1893-planted bush vines).

Kalleske Bar V ★★ Old family farm makes captivating single-vyd SHIRAZ; all intensely flavoured; bio/organic.

Katnook Estate Coonw ★→★★ Pricey icons Odyssey, Prodigy SHIRAZ. Big wines in need of restrained love.

Kay Brothers McL V Old-school/trad family winery, wonderful history: 1892 SHIRAZ in top Block 6; v.gd GRENACHE, MATARO, plus fortifieds.

Kerri Greens Mor P ★★ Originally a collaboration: Tom McCarthy (QUEALY) and Lucas Blanck, scion of PAUL BLANCK (*see* France). Now under direction of Lucas and wife Alyce. CHARD and PINOT N stars, no surprise, v.gd RIES.

Club Med McLaren Vale

MCLAREN VALE is Australia's answer to the Med: warm summers, moderate winters. This is a dynamic, sustainable region 40 km s of Adelaide, wedged between Mt Lofty ranges and Gulf St Vincent beaches, both geographies gd for vyd climates. Once noted for rich reds (CAB SAUV, SHIRAZ, plus beautiful GRENACHE), push latterly has been to more appropriate Med varieties, partly to mitigate climate change and partly to reflect changing drinking habits to fresher, more delicious wines. Now Spanish, Italian varieties flourish; credit to Mark Lloyd from CORIOLE, 1st winery to plant SANGIOVESE in 1985 as alternative to Shiraz; he now has FIANO, PIQUEPOUL, MONTEPULCIANO, NERO D'AVOLA and more. Pete Fraser, who died too young (2025), championed Rhône whites BOURBOULENC, CLAIRETTE, GRENACHE BL to complement YANGARRA'S ROUSSANNE.

Kilikanoon Clare V ★★ Top: RIES, SHIRAZ. Luscious, generous, well made.

King Valley Vic Altitude range 155–860m (509–2821ft) has big impact stylistically. Noted for Italian varieties: BROWN BROTHERS, Chrismont, DAL ZOTTO, PIZZINI.

Koerner Ad H, Clare V ★★→★★★ Cool wines, labels showcase best of regions: RIES, CAB SAUV. Host of intrigue via textural VERMENTINO, Mammolo, SANGIOVESE.

Most visited Oz wine region? Hunter V. Aged Semillon and spicy Shiraz the lure.

Kooyong Mor P ★★★ PINOT N, ***excellent Chard*** of detail, structure; PINOT GR of charm. High-quality single vyds.

Lake Breeze Lang C ★★★ Family-owned, salt of the earth: excellent, regionally distinct CAB SAUV, SHIRAZ; few producers do mid-level so consistently well.

Lake's Folly Hun V ★★★ (CHARD) 20' 21' 22' 23' (Cab blend) 18' 19' 20 21 22 Pioneer of HUN V CAB SAUV, part of Fogarty Wine Group. Beacon of quality, character.

Langmeil Bar V ★★ Custodian of some of world's oldest SHIRAZ vines (planted mid-1800s) and other ancient vyds. Big CAB SAUV, GRENACHE, Shiraz. Much loved.

Lark Hill Can Pioneer producer; Chris Carpenter, 2nd-generation winemaker. GRUNER V planted 2005, 1st in Oz. Estate bio; Regional wines from growers.

LAS Vino Marg R ★★★ Nic Peterkin is grandson of Kevin and Diana CULLEN, and son of PIERRO founder Mike. A trailblazer, experimenter, yet fastidious producer of outstanding CHARD, CHENIN BL, CAB SAUV.

Leeuwin Estate Marg R ★★★★ Iconic. Age-worthy Art Series CHARD 18' 19' 20' 21' 22 23. Solid RIES, SAUV BL; v.gd ***Cab Sauv***.

Leo Buring Bar V ★★→★★★ Gets lost in TWE empire, still v.gd. RIES rules; Leonay top label ***ages superbly***.

Lethbridge Vic ★★ Estate wines; bio, v.gd: CHARD, PINOT N, with regional RIES, SHIRAZ. Dabbles in Italian (r/w). Always interesting.

Levantine Hill Estate Yarra V Ambitious, luxury brand; wines thoughtfully crafted by Paul Bridgeman (ex-YARRA YERING). Snazzy restaurant, hotel.

Limestone Coast Zone SA Distinct important region taking in COONW, Mt Benson, Mt Gambier, PADTHAWAY, Robe, WRATTONBULLY.

Living Roots Ad H ★★ Sebastian Hardy and wife Colleen also make wine in Finger Lakes (US). Focus on mid-weight reds: AD H SHIRAZ, MCL V GRENACHE.

Lowboi Denmark ★★ Guy Lyons (FOREST HILL) and wife Nicola bought est site in Porongurup Range. Fine CHARD, RIES and gorgeous GRÜNER V (Forest Hill fruit).

Lowestoft Tas ★★★ Part of expanding Fogarty Wine Group; est vyd nr Hobart, excellent CHARD, PINOT N, terrific fizz.

LS Merchants Marg R ★★→★★★ Motto: gd wine, fun times. Delicious, drink-now blends; also excel in classy, regional CHARD, CAB SAUV, plus Fra R RIES, SHIRAZ.

Macedon and Sunbury Vic Adjacent regions: Macedon high elevation, cool for CHARD, PINOT N; Sunbury, near Melbourne airport, for SHIRAZ. Try BINDI, COBAW RIDGE, CRAIGLEE, JOSHUA COOPER.

Mac Forbes Yarra V ★★★ Savvy Mac Forbes is obsessed with wines of place, ie. single-site CHARD, PINOT N. Also smitten with NEBBIOLO.

McHenry Hohnen Marg R ★★→★★★ More detail, class in past few yrs; winemaker Jacopo Dalli Cani teases out best from CHARD, CAB SAUV, plus surprise, SHIRAZ.

McLaren Vale SA Outstanding, diverse region nr Adelaide. Centre of Italian varieties FIANO, VERMENTINO to NERO D'AVOLA, SANGIOVESE, plus weighty, rich or elegant reds, esp SHIRAZ, but dry-grown, old-bush-vine GRENACHE today's hero. Stars: BEKKERS, BONDAR, CORIOLE, Hither & Yon, OLIVER'S TARANGA VYDS, SC PANNELL, THISTLEDOWN, WIRRA WIRRA, YANGARRA.

McWilliam's SE Aus ★★ Historic producer, owned by CALABRIA FAMILY, quality-focus guaranteed (*see* MOUNT PLEASANT).

Main Ridge Estate Mor P ★★★ Pioneer of region, now owned by Sexton family (not

Phil ex-GIANT STEPS), son James charged with winemaking; respecting history while cementing future. Full, rich CHARD; distinctive PINOT N. Small quantities.

Majella Coonw ★★ Archetypal CAB SAUV, SHIRAZ (also top sp). Value at every level.

Marco Lubiana Wines Tas Thoughtful, clever son of Monique and STEFANO L. Focus on lovely CHARD, PINOT N. All about terroir and its expression.

Margaret River WA Maritime region s of Perth, pristine beaches, bushland. Arguably finest CHARD, CAB SAUV in Oz. Top: CORYMBIA, CULLEN, DEEP WOODS, FLAMETREE, LAS VINO, LEEUWIN, LS MERCHANTS, MOSS WOOD, PIERRO, VASSE FELIX, VOYAGER, WINDOWS ESTATE, WOODLANDS.

Max & Me Bar V ★★→★★★ Phil Lehmann, son of legendary PETER L, with wife Sarah, rich farming life, with est vyds, olive grove. Top: RIES, GRENACHE, SHIRAZ.

Mayford NE Vic ★★★ Tiny, exquisite vyd in hidden valley. Put ALPINE V region on map; CHARD, SHIRAZ and Oz's finest TEMPRANILLO.

Meerea Park Hun V ★★ Age-worthy SEM, SHIRAZ often as single-vyd expressions.

Ministry of Clouds McL V Diversity, difference, refinement define terrific selections: MCL V reds, AD H CHARD, plus cool-altitude PICPOUL, MENCÍA.

Mitchelton Goulburn V ★★ Stalwart RIES, CAB SAUV, SHIRAZ; speciality ***Marsanne***, ROUSSANNE. Fancy new hotel set among fabulous river red gums.

MMAD McL V ★★★★ SHAW & SMITH/TOLPUDDLE make single vyds from Blewitt Springs in separate business: outstanding CHENIN B, GRENACHE, SHIRAZ.

Montalto Mor P ★★→★★★ Focus on single-vyd CHARD, PINOT N highlights best of MORN P. Fab cellar door, restaurant; sculptures dotted through vyd.

Moorilla Estate Tas ★★ Pioneer nr Hobart on Derwent River; CHARD, RIES, PINOT N; v.gd restaurant, extraordinary art gallery (MONA). Also owns nearby Dom A.

Moorooduc Estate Mor P ★★→★★★ Solid performer of region's best varieties: CHARD, PINOTS N/GR.

Mordrelle Wines Ad H, Lang C Argentinian-born, with a degree in viticulture and oenology, Martin Moran calls AD H home, making top fizz, PINOT N, range of exceptional Lang C MALBEC.

Mornington Peninsula Vic SE of Melbourne, maritime climate; v.gd CHARD, PINOTS GR/N. Top: ELANTO, ELDRIDGE, GARAGISTE, KOOYONG, MAIN RIDGE, MONTALTO, MOOROODUC, PARINGA, STONIER, TEN MINUTES BY TRACTOR, YABBY LAKE.

Morris NE Vic ★★★★ In RUTH, 5th-generation David M at helm; CASELLA-owned. Arguably Oz's finest fortifieds, ***Muscats***, Topaques.

Moss Wood Marg R ★★★ Most opulent MARG R reds. Star: CAB SAUV 18' **19'** **20'** 21' 22'. Rich, full CHARD bucks regional trend, gd SEM.

Mount Horrocks Clare V ★★ Racy RIES, SEM, CAB SAUV, SHIRAZ in gd shape. Note NERO D'AVOLA.

Mount Langi Ghiran Gra ★★★★ Peppery, ***Rhône-like Shiraz*** (excellent Langi) 14' **15'** **17'** 18' 19' 21 22. Estate-grown RIES, on special patch of dirt, v.gd.

Mount Majura Can ★★ Leading TEMPRANILLO producer plus other Iberian varieties; CHARD, SHIRAZ gd; excellent RIES.

Mount Mary Yarra V ★★★★ Highly regarded, known for Bx blend Quintet 19' **20'** 21' 22' 23' 24, Triolet (w). Also v.gd: CHARD, PINOT N. Rhône varieties planted by winemaker Sam Middleton, grandson of founder.

Mount Pleasant Hun V ★★★★ Owned by Medich. One of most important names in Oz wine thanks to history, single-vyd SEM (***Lovedale***) and Maurice O'Shea SHIRAZ. Old vyds, great sites, sensational wines.

Mudgee NSW Region nw of Sydney but overshadowed by its more famous cousin, HUNT V. Quality gd; ROBERT STEIN VYD a star, esp RIES.

Mulline Geelong ★★→★★★ Rhymes with divine, so too the wines; collaboration between friends. Fruit from GEELONG, top single-vyd CHARD, PINOT N, SYRAH. Focus on organic, eco business. Winner all round.

Nocturne Marg R ★★★ All about MARG R subregions; limited volumes CHARD, CAB SAUV, v.gd rosé. Side hustle of Julian Langworthy (DEEP WOODS).

Oakdene Geelong Notable fizz, CHARD, PINOT N and more; winery restaurant.

Oakridge Yarra V ★★★★ Leading producer of CHARD, some of best in Oz, plus excellent PINOT N, SHIRAZ, and CAB SAUV. Multiple single-vyd releases.

O'Leary, Nick Can ★★→★★★ Top RIES producer (many styles); TUMBARUMBA CHARD; spicy SHIRAZ; TEMPRANILLO.

O'Leary Walker Clare V ★★ Pure CLARE V RIES, solid CAB SAUV, big, bolshy MCL V SHIRAZ. Value all round.

Oliver's Taranga Vineyards McL V ★★→★★★ Grower (6th generation) supplying top producers (eg. PENFOLDS); GRENACHE, SHIRAZ v.gd. Trailblazer Corrina Wright, 1st family winemaker, esp Italian, Spanish vines: FIANO, MENCÍA highlights.

Onannon Mor P Creative side hustle for friends Will Byron (ex-STONIER), Sam Middleton (MOUNT MARY) and Kaspar Hermann (ROCHFORD): CHARD, PINOT N, different sites/techniques. Super-smart.

Orange NSW Cool-climate, high-elevation region, 600–1000m (1968–3281ft). Best suited to aromatic whites, esp RIES, also CHARD; v.gd fizz, naturally.

Ossa Wines Tas ★★ New, exciting player: CHARD, GRÜNER V, PINOT N, fizz. Watch.

Padthaway SA Rarely mentioned these days, but important region: CHARD, CAB SAUV, SHIRAZ v.gd. Soil salinity on-going issue.

Pannell, SC McL V ★★★★ Trailblazer. Intuitive winemaking, gd vyds. Midas touch with GRENACHE, SHIRAZ, plus AGLIANICO, NEBBIOLO under Protero label. Iberian varieties, esp blends v.gd.

Oldest brand and commercial vyd in Oz: Dalwood Estate (Hunter V), since 1828.

Paringa Estate Mor P ★★ Big, rich PINOT N, SHIRAZ; same with CHARD.

Parker Coonawarra Estate Coonw ★★ In gd yrs age-worthy CAB SAUV of distinction.

Passing Clouds Bendigo ★★ Down-to-earth folk; reliable, robust reds, esp CAB SAUV (often a showstopper), SHIRAZ. Mac CHARD has verve.

Patrick Sullivan Wines Gip ★★★ Smart winemaker obsessed with CHARD. New planting will be highest-density Chard in Oz. Farms other sites (with WILLIAM DOWNIE); Ada River and Bullswamp Chards outstanding, plus PINOT N.

Paul Osicka Wines Hea ★★★ Family-owned/run. Vines back to 50s. Both character/flavour writ large. Small-scale, low-profile, high-impact: CAB SAUV, SHIRAZ.

Pemberton WA Region between MARG R and GT S. Top: distinct PINOT N, fizz. Solid CHARD, RIES, SHIRAZ plus Italian varieties.

Penfolds ★★★★ (Grange) 96' **06'** 08' 10' 14' 17' 18' 19' 20' 21 (CAB SAUV Bin 707) **15'** 18' 19' 21' 22 Oz's most famous (r) brand. So many Bins, so many wines: now incl Bx, Champagne, California, China. Exceptional CHARD Bin A and ***Yattarna*** personally, consistently, two finest in the range; v.gd RIES.

Penley Estate Coonw ★★→★★★ Owned by sisters Ang and Bec Tolley; star winemaker Kate Goodman. Cellar door in MCL V, but CAB SAUV rules; diverse styles, all excellent from experimental Project wines, from whole-bunch Cab Sauv (it works) to high-end, structured Helios.

Petaluma Ad H ★→★★ Croser sparkling can be v.gd; RIES, SHIRAZ (AD H); CAB SAUV (COONW) gd.

Peter Lehmann Wines Bar V ★★ Well priced overall, incl easy RIES. Rich, structured Stonewell SHIRAZ among many others. Part of CASELLA.

Pewsey Vale Eden V ★★ Most recognizable RIES brand and done well. Value with several styles, incl Museum release The Contours grown on beautiful tiered vyd.

Pfeiffer Ruth Historic winery (1885), family-owned, 2nd-generation national treasure Jen P cares for all, plus precious fortifieds: ★★★★ Rare MUSCAT, Topaque (aka MUSCADELLE).

Pierro Marg R ★★★ Now led by 2nd generation, Nik Peterkin. Rich, distinct CHARD 20' 21' 22' 23' 24' (loyal fanbase), gd SEM/SAUV BL, tiptop Bx blend.

Pikes Clare V Excellent winery restaurant, even better RIES, esp flagship The Merle, v.gd CAB SAUV and more.

Pipers Brook Tas ★★ Cool-area pioneer; gd RIES **22 23 24 25**; PINOT N variable; ***restrained Chard and sp*** from Tamar V. Second label: Ninth Island. Owned by Belgian Kreglinger family.

Pizzini King V ★★ Pioneer of Italian varieties: NEBBIOLO, SANGIOVESE (all styles, authentic). Wonderful family.

Place of Changing Winds Mac ★★★ Powerful, rich CHARD, PINOT N, grown on high-density vyds, pushing boundaries. Also Rhône-style SHIRAZ from HEA fruit.

Pooley Tas ★★★→★★★★ Historic, impressive property c.1832 in Coal River V. Some of TAS's – nay, some of Oz's – finest RIES; CHARD, PINOT N. Distinctive wines.

Primo Estate SA ★★ Joe Grilli's many successes: rich MCL V SHIRAZ, tangy COLOMBARD, potent Joseph CAB SAUV/MERLOT, complex NEBBIOLO, Shiraz (sp).

Printhie Orange Super-cool wines in super-cool region. Top fizz, v.gd CHARD.

Provenance Geelong ★★★ Top CHARD from GEELONG and around; SHIRAZ red star.

Pyrenees Vic Central-w of Melbourne; tough, dry if beautiful landscape makes powerful CAB SAUV, SHIRAZ. Typical eucalyptus fragrance.

Quealy Mor P ★★→★★★ PINOT GR-pioneer Tom McCarthy (2nd generation) leads organic estate. Also complex CHARD, FRIULANO (skin-contact), PINOT N.

Ravensworth Can ★★→★★★ Innovative producer, brilliant classic styles (SHIRAZ/VIOGNIER), plus skin-contact whites and Italian varieties, outstanding RIES. Texture focus, no surprise as winemaker Bryan Martin is ex-chef.

Rieslingfreak Clare V, Eden V ★★→★★★ Apt name: John Hughes only makes RIES from CLARE V and EDEN V with winemaker wife Belinda (ex-GRANT BURGE). Gorgeous folk and wines.

Riverina NSW Large-volume irrigated zone centred on Griffith.

Robert Oatley Wines Mudgee ★★→★★★ Three brands: everyday Signature Series, single vyds with Finisterre, best barrels for The Pennant. Fruit from MARG R, GT S, MCL V. Reliable, gd value, can be excellent.

Robert Stein Vineyard Mudgee ★★★ Regional stalwart: young Jacob S carrying torch for brilliant RIES (all styles), plus cool CAB SAUV, SHIRAZ.

Rochford Yarra V ★★→★★★ Main outdoor entertainment venue in YARRA V; complex CHARD, CAB SAUV, PINOT N. Worth a visit.

Battling smoke taint

Australia holds the ignoble title of the world's most fire-prone country. If bushfires don't raze a vyd, the by-product is smoke taint, rendering vintage over before it begins. Smoke hanging around long enough means volatile phenols are absorbed into grapes and plant tissue. Brilliant scientists at the Australian Wine Research Institute (AWRI) discovered those compounds can disappear and reappear later as acrid, bitter smoke or ashy character during winemaking process. Resultant wines are horrible – a waste of time and money to make. At least now, testing can determine volatile and non-volatile compounds, allowing producers to assess risk of any awful flavours developing. AWRI also discovered smoke taint can be absorbed throughout every stage of ripening, starting when berries are hard, green, unripe – it leads the way in smoke-taint research, benefiting every grape-growing country at risk. Next step: working on vyd solution to salvage the vintage.

Rockford Bar V ★★★ Various, old low-yielding vyds; reds best; iconic Basket Press SHIRAZ and noted ***sparkling Black Shiraz***.

Ruggabellus Bar V ★★★ Modern iteration of BAR V, savoury, even lighter-framed. Old oak, wild yeast, whole bunches/stems. Blends of CINSAULT/GRENACHE/MATARO/SHIRAZ. Compelling.

Rutherglen and Glenrowan NE Vic Two regions in warm/hot NE Vic, starring rich reds but fortifieds steal show. Try ALL SAINTS, BAILEYS OF GLENROWAN, CAMPBELLS, MORRIS, SCION.

Salomon Estate S Fleurieu Austrian legend Bert S (*see* Austria): fragrant VIOGNIER, CAB SAUV, SYRAH.

Saltram Bar V ★★ Value Mamre Brook (CAB SAUV, SHIRAZ) and No. 1 Shiraz leaders. Main claim to fame is ubiquitous Pepperjack Shiraz.

Sami-Odi Bar V ★★★ Fraser and Andrea McKinley are BAR V avant-garde. Hand-crafted, tiny quantities, benchmark Shiraz/SYRAH; est sites, uber-cool labels.

Savaterre Beech ★★★ Full-bodied CHARD 19' **21'** 22 23, meaty PINOT N 18' **19'** 21 22; close-planted SAGRANTINO, SHIRAZ.

Schmolzer & Brown Beech ★★ Estate vyd, Thorley, highest in BEECH. Scintillating CHARD, perfumed PINOT N, spicy SYRAH, excellent RIES, NEBBIOLO to watch.

Scion Ruth ★★ Fresh, vibrant approach to region's stalwarts SHIRAZ and Durif.

Scorpo Wines Mor P Top producer, detailed CHARD, PINOTS GR/N, mainstays of region. Skin-contact Pinot Gr reflecting Italian heritage of Paul S.

Sentio Beech ★★★ Chris Catlow picks eyes out of various cool-climate regions incl MAC for compelling CHARD, PINOT N, SHIRAZ.

Seppelt Gra ★★★ Historic in name only, owned by TWE. St Peter's SHIRAZ 18' **19'** 20 21 22. Excellent CHARD, RIES. Lost its way when business gutted; some love now with winemaker Clare Dry. Here's hoping.

Seppeltsfield Bar V ★★★→★★★★ National Trust Heritage Winery owned by Warren Randall. Fortified stocks back to 1878. A must-visit.

Shaw & Smith Ad H ★★★→★★★★ Savvy outfit: complex CHARD; crisp, ***harmonious Sauv Bl***; and, surpassing both, ***Shiraz***. PINOT N v.gd.

Sidewood Estate Ad H ★★ Cidery, winery, snazzy restaurant, cellar door with v.gd wines in tow. Fizz a feature, cool CHARD, SHIRAZ too.

Silkman Hun V ★★★ Star: takes best of region – CHARD, SEM, SHIRAZ – and turns into best wines.

Sinapius Tas Special, high-density site, wonderful CHARD, PINOT N. GRÜNER V, GAMAY too. Drinkability writ large.

Singlefile Denmark Lovely property/cellar door in remote area; sourcing fruit across region incl MARG R; gd value, gd wines.

Sittella Swan V Heady fortifeds, fizz, table wines; vyds in MARG R keep this family-owned business at top of game.

Snake + Herring Marg R Two friends, Tony (Snake) Davis winemaker, Redmond (Herring) Sweeney marketing, make fun wines, sourcing fruit across state: Bizarre Love Triangle PINOT GR; classy CHARD, CAB SAUV.

Sorrenberg Beech ★★★★ No fuss, highest quality; CHARD, SAUV BL/SEM, Oz's finest GAMAY, Bx blend. Ultimate "in the know" winery; legend Barry Morey.

Soumah Yarra V Highlighting best of area with French varieties, plus superb range of Italian varietals from NEBBIOLO, Marzemino to Brachetto.

Southern NSW Zone NSW Cool-climate zone incl CAN, Gundagai, Hilltops, TUMBARUMBA. Racy CHARD, RIES; savoury, spicy SHIRAZ.

Spinifex Bar V ★★★ Reds dominate, attention to detail in winemaking. Spicy GRENACHE, rich MATARO, SHIRAZ. Single vyds of note.

Standish Wine Company, The Bar V ★★★ Dan S quietly goes about his work: distinctive, powerful and oh-so-compelling SHIRAZ. Essence of BAR V.

Stargazer Tas ★★★ Boutique enterprise of Samantha Connew (ex-WIRRA WIRRA). Refined CHARD, RIES, PINOT N; Tupelo, Alsace-style blend.

Stefano Lubiana Wines S Tas ★★★ Beautiful bio vyds on banks of Derwent River. Stamped with quality from fizz to outstanding CHARD, PINOT N; plus Italian, Austrian varieties. Osteria Vista restaurant Italian to core.

Stella Bella Marg R ★★→★★★ Solid performer across range of styles, prices. Top CHARD, CAB SAUV called Luminosa often illuminating.

Stonier Wines Mor P Pioneering CHARD, PINOT N. Re-energized with new owners (2022). Co-owner Julian Grounds (ex-Craggy Range, *see* NZ) winemaker (2024).

Sunbury Vic *See* MACEDON AND SUNBURY.

Sutton Grange Bendigo ★★ Noteworthy SYRAH; Rosé rocks; FIANO, AGLIANICO, SANGIOVESE more than a sideshow.

Swan Valley WA Vines 1st planted 1829, 25 mins n of Perth. Star: CHENIN BL; also SHIRAZ, GRENACHE, fortifieds. Salt-of-the-earth wine folk.

Swinney Fra R ★★★ Grower for decades, now excellent own-label RIES, GRENACHE, SHIRAZ, TEMPRANILLO. Top-tier Farvie; by WA winemaking royalty Rob Mann.

Tahbilk Nagambie ★★ Oldest family-owned winery in Vic, original 1860s estate/cellar door still going strong. Best: old-vine (1927) ***Marsanne*** 12' 13' 15' 16 17 18, 19. Res CAB SAUV, SHIRAZ can be v.gd. Rare 1860 Vines Shiraz.

Tapanappa SA ★★→★★★ WRATTONBULLY collaboration between Brian Croser, Bollinger and J-M Cazes of Pauillac (*see* France). Splendid CHARD, CAB SAUV blend, MERLOT, SHIRAZ. Surprising ***Pinot N*** from Fleurieu Peninsula.

Tar & Roses Hea ★★ Inspired by Med varieties and others. SANGIOVESE, SHIRAZ to NEBBIOLO all gd. Modern success story.

Drink Fiano, savour Sydney rock oysters fresh or grilled with garlic butter. Yum.

TarraWarra Estate Yarra V ★★→★★★ Top Res: CHARD 20' **21' 22'** 23' 24, PINOT N 18' **19** 21 22. Plus Rhône, Italian varieties: BARBERA a delight. Sarah Fagan (ex-DE BORTOLI) joined 2023. Home to TarraWarra Museum of Art.

Tasmania Cold island, hot reputation, with expensive vyd real estate yet envy of mainlanders and strong presence: HOUSE OF ARRAS, TOLDPUDDLE (SHAW & SMITH). Outstanding fizz, CHARD, PINOT GR, RIES, PINOT N.

Ten Minutes by Tractor Mor P ★★→★★★ Top-notch wines, top-notch restaurant. Focus on single-vyd CHARD, PINOT N.

Terre à Terre Ad H ★★★ Xavier Bizot (son of Christian B, Bollinger, *see* France) and wife, Lucy Croser (daughter of Brian C) making mark. Labels incl Down to Earth and Daosa, v.gd fizz; close-planted vyd at WRATTONBULLY.

Teusner Bar V ★★ Old vines, clever winemaking, pure fruit flavours. Leads a BAR V trend towards "more wood, no good".

Thistledown Ad H ★★★★ MWs Giles Cooke and Fergal Tynan champion MCL V old-vine GRENACHE with names to remember: Cunning Plan, Sands of Time, She's Electric. Also BAR V SHIRAZ.

Tolpuddle Tas ★★★★ SHAW & SMITH own this outstanding 1988-planted vyd in Coal River V: CHARD some of best in Oz, PINOT N superb. Demand outstrips supply.

Torbreck Bar V ★★→★★★ Dedicated to (often old-vine) Rhône varieties led by GRENACHE, SHIRAZ. Ultimate expression of rich, sweet, high-alc style.

Torzi Matthews Eden V ★★→★★★ Aromatic, stylish, big-hearted SHIRAZ. Value RIES, SANGIOVESE. Incredible consistency yr-on-yr.

Tumbarumba NSW Cool-climate region tucked into the Australian Alps. Sites at 500–800m (1640–2625ft); CHARD the out-and-out star; v.gd sparkling base.

Turkey Flat Bar V ★★★ Top producer of rich rosé, GRENACHE, SHIRAZ from 150-yr-old vyd. Plus single-vyd wines, kinda old but modern.

TWE (Treasury Wine Estates) Aussie wine behemoth: COLDSTREAM HILLS, DEVIL'S

LAIR, PENFOLDS, SALTRAM, WYNNS COONAWARRA among them. Off-loading brands such as Lindeman's, WOLF BLASS.

Two Hands Bar V ★★★ Big reds, lots of them. They've turned volume down a fraction; glory of fruit seems all the clearer.

Tyrrell's Hun V ★★→★★★★ Family-owned/run, a gem. Benchmark SEM Vat 1 16' **17'** 18' 19' 21 22' 23, plus individual vyd or subregional renditions. ***Vat 47*** 15' **17'** 18' 22 23, Oz's 1st CHARD, continues to defy climatic odds. Outstanding old-vine 4 Acres SHIRAZ, Vat 9 Shiraz.

Utzinger Tas ★★→★★★ Matthias (Swiss) and Lauren (TAS) work picturesque patch of land overlooking Tamar River. In tune with environment, protecting it; lovely RIES, PINOT N, CHARD and more.

Vasse Felix Marg R ★★★→★★★★ Excellent, flinty CHARD: Heytesbury 19' **20'** 21' 22' 23 24. Elegant CAB SAUV: exceptional top-tier Tom Cullity **18'** 19' 20' 21 23. Diversity throughout incl Idée Fixe (sp).

Vickery Clare V Legacy of Oz's greatest RIES master, late John V, lives on. Zeeda Kilm crafting gorgeous "Rizza", also from EDEN V.

Vinarchy Daft name following 2025 merger of Accolade Wines and Pernod Ricard Winemakers. Even dafter mantra "new global leader with a mission to redefine wine". But gd brands/people in mix.

Vino Volta Swan V Cool labels, even cooler wines, albeit mostly from warm clime of SWAN V. Top: old-vine CHENIN BL, GRENACHE. Also focus on Italian varieties.

Vinya Vella Bar V ★★★ Means "old vine" in Catalan: Dylan Grigg has PhD in grapevine age; worked in Spain, international expert in field. Exceptional wines: GRENACHE, some pre-1900 MATARO.

Violetta, La Denmark Quirky names: Das Sakrileg RIES, Fric Frac CAB FR; reflecting quirky personality of winemaker Andrew Hoadley. Don't be fooled: delicious, fascinating wines; fruit from GT S.

Voyager Estate Marg R ★★★ Organic, sustainable; positive changes as winemaker Tim Shand fine-tunes range; CHARD, CAB SAUV take centre stage.

Wanderer, The Yarra V ★★★ Exceptionally fine-boned PINOT N, equally fine CHARD, SAUV BL plus fizz. Excellent gin too, more than a side project.

Wantirna Estate Yarra V ★★★ Family-owned, YARRA V pioneer, led by 2nd-generation winemaker Maryann Egan. Lovely, gentle wines of style, class from CHARD, PINOT N to Bx blends.

Wendouree Clare V ★★★★ DRC of Australia (*see* France). Old vines, commitment to quality, history. Long-lived reds now veering towards more refined, elegant CAB SAUV, MALBEC, MATARO, SHIRAZ. Demand outstrips supply. Respect.

West Cape Howe Mt Barker ★→★★ Ever reliable yet flavoursome: RIES above all else, gd CHARD, reds and more.

William Downie Gip ★★★ Whip-smart farmer, leader of local avant-garde, dedicated solely to PINOT N: single-sites Bull Swamp, Camp Hill organic, minuscule quantities. Always compelling, always thoughtful, cool labels.

Willunga 100 Wines McL V Fabulous collaboration: David Gleave MW (UK importer) and John Ratcliffe. Regionally expressive, site-specific GRENACHE from own vyd plus fruit from v.gd growers, also SHIRAZ.

Windows Estate Marg R ★★★ Bush property with focus on sustainablity. Family-run, all handgrown/made: v.gd CHENIN BL, CHARD, CAB SAUV, SYRAH. Lovely, gentle folk, ethereal wines.

Wine by Farr Geelong ★★★→★★★★ Pioneers of close-planted vyds in dry, windy Moorabool V; est 1994. PINOT N the star of individual blocks labelled Côte Vyd, Farrside, Sangreal, Tout Près. Impressive CHARD, VIOGNIER, SHIRAZ.

Wines by KT Clare V ★★→★★★ Kerri Thompson, aka queen of CLARE V RIES; from pristine, off-dry to textural, wild ferment, plus tiptop reds.

Wirra Wirra McL V ★★→★★★ Renewed and energized; fabulous winemaker Emma Wood (ex-TWE). Wines remain regionally expressive, with freshness, vitality.

Wolf Blass Bar V ★ Not what it was when WB himself led the orchestra. Now churns out big volumes. Another brand being off-loaded by TWE.

Woodlands Marg R ★★★ 40-yr-old+ CAB SAUV among top vyds in Wilyabrup: ★★★★ flagship Cab (name changes each yr, honouring a family or friend). Also younger, v.gd plantings of other Bx-style reds.

Wrattonbully SA Important growing region in LIMESTONE COAST ZONE; profile lifted by activity of Peppertree, TAPANAPPA, TERRE À TERRE.

Wynns Coonawarra Estate Coonw ★★★★ (Michael SHIRAZ) 18' **19'** 20' 21 22 (***John Riddoch*** CAB SAUV) 15' **16' 18'** 19' 20' 21 22 Legendary, yet largest producer in region, excellent vyds. Top: CAB SAUV, Shiraz (Black Label, great value, excellent single-vyds). Decent whites. All long-lived propositions. Quality and detail thanks to long-time winemaker Sue Hodder, who credits her team, as great leaders do.

Xanadu Wines Marg R ★★★→★★★★ 20' **21'** 22 23 24 Outstanding single-vyd Res CHARD, CAB SAUV. Host of different styles, varieties, price points. Winemaker Glenn Goodall one of best, reflected in wines. Should be better known.

Yabby Lake Mor P, Tas ★★→★★★ Focus on CHARD, PINOT N; v.gd PINOT GR, SYRAH. Recently invested in TAS.

Yalumba Bar V, SA ★★★ Oldest family-owned winery in Oz, with eye on quality as much as affordability. Powerhouse of reds: The Caley, benchmark CAB/SHIRAZ. Flies flag for country's finest VIOGNIER, The Virgilius.

Yangarra Estate McL V ★★★★ Exquisite GRENACHE thanks to cherished vyds (incl 1946 old bush vines); bio. Dress-circle producer with respectful winemaking spearheaded by Peter Fraser (died in 2025). *Vale* Pete.

Yarra Valley Vic Cool, high-end region NE of Melbourne. Emphasis on CHARD, PINOT N, SHIRAZ and elegant CAB SAUV. Formidable lineup: COLDSTREAM HILLS, DE BORTOLI, DOM CHANDON, GEMBROOK HILL, GIANT STEPS, HODDLES CREEK, MAC FORBES, MOUNT MARY, OAKRIDGE, ROCHFORD, TARRAWARRA, WANTIRNA, YARRA YERING, YERINGBERG, YERING STATION.

Yarra Yering Yarra V ★★★★ (Dry Reds) 19' **20'** 21' 22' 23 24 High-end, beautiful CAB SAUV (Dry Red No. 1); SHIRAZ (Dry Red No. 2). Detailed PINOT N and CHARD. Winemaker Sarah Crowe, shining light, respectful to site's provenance. Special producer, great history.

Yeringberg Yarra V ★★★★ (MARSANNE/ROUSSANNE) 20' **21'** 22' 23 24 (Bx blend) **19'** 20' 21 22' 23 24 Historic estate (1862) still with founding Swiss family, De Pury, now led by winemaker Sandra. Small quantities, v. high-quality CHARD, Marsanne, Roussanne, CAB SAUV, PINOT N.

Yering Station / Yarrabank Yarra V ★★ Site of Vic's 1st vyd; replanted after 80-yr gap. Solid wines (Res CHARD, PINOT N, SHIRAZ VIOGNIER). Yarrabank (sp), joint venture with Champagne Devaux (*see* France).

Cool Queensland

Known as the Sunshine State, Qld is home to Surfers' Paradise and the Great Barrier Reef, and further s near the NSW border is the cool GRANITE BELT, one of Oz's highest-altitude wine regions, peaking at 1200m (3937ft). Its climate akin to Rhône V, landscape of granite and mostly small, family-run producers. Non-mainstream varieties lead way: ALVARHINO, VERMENTINO, MONTEPULCIANO, NERO D'AVOLA, Tinto Cão and more. Producers created *Strange Bird Wine Guide*, an excellent map with information about diverse alternative offerings and those behind them: BALANCING HEART, BALLANDEAN ESTATE WINES, Golden Grove Estate.

New Zealand

Abbreviations used in the text:

Auck	Auckland
B of P	Bay of Plenty
Cant	Canterbury
Gis	Gisborne
Hawk	Hawke's Bay
Hend	Henderson
Marl	Marlborough
Mart	Martinborough
Nel	Nelson
N/C Ot	North/Central Otago
Nlnd	Northland
Waih	Waiheke Island
Waip	Waipara Valley
Wair	Wairarapa

Abetted by an abundant 2025 vintage, there has been a lot of New Zealand's signature wine style, Marlborough Sauvignon Blanc, around – an oversupply, in fact. This is more of an issue for the large, volume-oriented companies than for smaller wineries that have built respected brands and represent the quality end of the industry. A successful international Pinot Noir conference in Christchurch in 2025, the country's first such event since covid, was a big step in NZ wine's efforts to reconnect with the world. The country's premium producers are confident their best wines are important voices in the global wine conversation. For the wine-lover, there are plenty of Kiwi wines that overdeliver on their price tag. This is particularly so with Sauvignon Blanc, of course, but also Chardonnay, Pinot Noir and some Syrah.

Recent vintages

2025 Gd crop everywhere, but spring frost hit C Ot. Fine quality all over.
2024 Small in quantity, exceptionally high in quality across country.
2023 Rain cancelled some top reds in Hawk/Marl. Dry, mostly warm in s.
2022 Record crop. Marl/Hawk: wet/cold, hit quality. C Ot: clean, ripe Pinot N.

Akarua C Ot ★★★ Most s outpost of Edmond de Rothschild Heritage (France) empire; CHARD, PINOT N (*Akarua* means "two vines" in Māori) grown in Bannockburn. Complex The Siren Pinot N; crowd-pleasing Chard.

Allan Scott Marl ★★ Family-owned/operated. Estate range gd value, fresh, racy (PINOT GR, RIES, SAUV BL). With Steytler family, "Stellenbosch + Marlborough" Sauv Bl, rare, gd-value blend of S Africa/NZ. Delightful winery bistro.

Alpha Domus Hawk ★★→★★★ Owned by NZ-Dutch family (est 1989); organic. Outstanding Bx blends, SYRAH. Richer CHARD, VIOGNIER.

Amisfield C Ot ★★★ Internationally acclaimed. Located nr Queenstown. All estate-grown in Pisa, Cromwell Basin; organic. Quality across range, esp RIES, dark flavoursome PINOT N (RKV Res). Innovative restaurant one of NZ's finest.

Amoise Hawk ★★★ Excellent natural producer, zero-zero, fruit from proven sites. Delightful, mouthwatering CHENIN BL from Two Terraces vyd.

Astrolabe Marl ★★→★★★ Named after explorer D'Urville's flagship. Quality across range: elegant SAUV BL (AWATERE V), statement CHENIN BL from Wrekin Vyd. Winery, cellar door, wine bar in Blenheim.

Ata Rangi Mart ★★★★ Internationally renowned, pioneering PINOT N specialist. Proudly family-owned. Estate Pinot ages well: **13' 14' 15 16' 19'** 20' 21' 22. More recent single vyds: impressive Kotinga Pinot, Masters CHARD, Pinot.

Auckland NZ's largest city (n, warm, humid). Diverse region with history, today 0.7% vyd area (not expanding) but 12% of wineries, almost all small players. Oldest district: W Auckland (incl Henderson, Huapai, Kumeu) clay soils, pioneered by Croatians, CHARD the hero, esp KUMEU RIVER. Newer districts (since 80s): Clevedon, Matakana and WAIH (island known for tourism, weddings, wealthy residents); intense Bx blends and flavoursome SYRAH.

Auntsfield Marl ★★★ Superb sloping site with stories to tell. Historic C19 "hobbit hole" cellar now a museum. Family estate. Textural SAUV BL, savoury PINOT N.

Awatere Valley Marl Sited se of WAIRAU, Awatere is that valley's younger, cooler (literally), wilder sibling. Name means fast-flowing river. Wineries are sparse, but vyd area is greater than HAWK. Loam over alluvial soils, ocean winds and big diurnal temp range. Harvest starts later than Wairau. Awatere SAUV BL typically lean, incisive acidity, greener flavour spectrum. Key component in regional blends of MARL Sauv Bl. Also vibrant PINOT GR, lighter, racier, red-fruit PINOT N.

Babich Hend ★★→★★★ Oldest family-owned winery in NZ (1916); HQ in Henderson, but vyds, winemaking in HAWK, MARL. Largest seller: Marl SAUV BL. Irongate site in GIMBLETT GRAVELS produces single-vyd CHARD, Bx blends of quality, incl flagship red The Patriarch.

Barrowman, Ashleigh Marl ★★★ Exciting new producer uses organic fruit from Wrekin vyd, hands-off winemaking. Delightful High Priestess PINOT N; crisp Queen of Swords CHARD.

Bell Hill Cant ★★★★ Terroir-driven cult label; high-density, organic vyd, limestone soils nr Waikari; CHARD (grace, tension), PINOT N (multi-faceted, energetic).

Bilancia Hawk ★★★→★★★★ Family-owned, jewel in HAWK crown. La Collina SYRAH, one of NZ's finest, grown on slope above GIMBLETT GRAVELS. Vivid, outstanding single-vyd CHARDS. Uvaggio, intriguing white field blend.

Blackenbrook Nel ★★→★★★ Swiss Schwarzenbach (hence Blackenbrook) family-owned; value across range, esp generous MONTEPULCIANO, handsome PINOT N.

Black Estate Cant ★★★→★★★★ Waipara treasure. Sensitive wine-growing on organic, limestone-rich sites. Best: Home Block CHARD, CHENIN BL; Damsteep PINOT N. One of NZ's best winery restaurants, locavore approach.

Blank Canvas Marl ★★★ Quality-focused boutique label. Mostly single vyd, several regions. Recently purchased 9-ha MARL home site. Excellent Reed Vyd CHARD; savoury Escaroth PINOT N.

US owner of Burn Cottage (C Ot) has best name in NZ wine: Marquis Sauvage.

Borthwick Wair ★★ Farming family started growing wine in 90s; 27-ha vyd in Gladstone, mostly SAUV BL, PINOT N.

Brancott Estate Marl ★→★★★ Sold 2024, to VINARCHY. Orignally Montana, Pernod rebranded (2007). Large exports Marl SAUV BL. Quality, value Letter Series range.

Brookfields Hawk ★★→★★★ Boutique, family-owned (1977), guided by old Bay hand Peter Robertson. Reds typically ripe, robust; CAB SAUV often excellent.

Disabling the Abel tale

DNA sleuthing has blown a hole in the origin story of a foundation stone of NZ PINOT N, the Abel clone. Accepted tale had it the clone's original cuttings, found in the luggage of a traveller to AUCK in the 70s, had come from Burgundy's famed La Tâche vyd (*see* France). The material went through quarantine and soon after was planted by WAIR Pinot pioneer ATA RANGI, where it immediately impressed. Now common to every NZ Pinot region, it has also spread to Australia. Recently, Australian researchers punctured some of its mystique by genotyping samples of the clone. Results didn't confirm a Burgundy connection – Abel was placed squarely in a Swiss genetic clonal sub-group.

Burn Cottage C Ot ★★★→★★★★ US-owned with top NZ winemaker Claire Mulholland. Cult label. Basin-shaped, bio site in Pisa, plus vyd in Bannockburn. Ethereal PINOT N; fascinating RIES/GRÜNER V.

Cambridge Road Mart ★★→★★★ Enquiring, innnovative winemaking. Range incl pét-nats, field blends. Latest project: 100-yr-old barrels made from native totara wood to imbue wines with *wairua* (spirit of place).

Canterbury 64 producers, most in relatively warm N CANT district. Best known for savoury PINOT N, increasingly sophisticated CHARD, aromatic RIES; SAUV BL heavily planted, but often minor component in other regions' wines.

Carrick C Ot ★★★ Owned by Cleland family, est player on Bannockburn's Cairnmuir Road. Farmed organically. Fine CHARD, reliably intense PINOT N.

Catalina Sounds Marl ★★→★★★ Australian-owned (est 2005). Top: Sound of White single-vyd, barrel-fermented CHARD, SAUV BL. Also 2nd tier: Crowded House.

Central Otago Most s (and most scenic) region, with as close to a continental climate as NZ gets. Vines grown in Alpine river valleys, most in Cromwell Basin. Collegial wine-growing culture and astute marketing made PINOT N the hero grape, giving region a global reputation – top have depth, structural finesse and are among NZ's best; CHARD on rise, quality/quantity; trad-method fizz.

Chard Farm C Ot ★★→★★★ Pioneering Gibbston winery. Hair-raising home vyd on ledge above bungee gorge. Most vyds now in Cromwell Basin. Top: series of single-vyd PINOT N. Popular second label: Rabbit Ranch.

Chateau Garage Hawk ★★★ Family-owned, boutique, quality focus, small batches from selected sites. Super Tuscan-style (*see* Italy) Lorenzo The Magnificent 24, NZ's most expensive wine.

Church Road Hawk ★★→★★★★ Recently sold by Pernod Ricard to VINARCHY; historic (est 1896). Long-serving, talented-winemaker Chris Scott; strong reputation for quality across multi-tiered range. McDonalds Series, gd value (CHARD, SYRAH). Grand Res Chard and reds superb. Prestige range, featuring Bx blends, named Tom after mid-C20 owner-winemaker Tom McDonald.

Churton Marl ★★★ Gorgeous, elevated, bio-farmed Waihopai V site. Elegant SAUV BL, expressive PINOT N (The Abyss). Innovative Natural State range. Vigneron Sam Weaver a Shropshire (UK) lad.

Clearview Hawk ★★→★★★ A HAWK icon (est 1986). Stony Te Awanga home vyd, plus fruit from other sites. Big local following for diverse CHARD range. Extroverted, powerful Bx blends.

Clos Henri Marl ★★★ Sancerre's own corner of MARL; est by Henri Bourgeois (*see* France); organic. Two compelling expressions of single-vyd SAUV BL: one on stony soils, other on clay. Delightful PINOT N. Cellar door is old converted church.

Cloudy Bay Marl ★★★ NZ brand the whole world knows and loves; LVMH-owned. Despite large volume, SAUV BL maintains prestigious reputation. Pelorus NV, quality trad-method fizz. Premium Te Wahi PINOT N from own vyd in C OT.

Coal Pit C Ot ★★→★★★ Owner Rosie Dunphy's dream realized: quality PINOT N organically grown on elevated Gibbston site. Also SAUV BL. Recent addition: Bannockburn Pinot N.

Collaboration Hawk ★★★ Quality-driven, est by owner-winemaker Julianne Brogden. Fruit from several vyds. Argent CAB SAUV, often fresh, lively. Verdant CHARD, tension, precision.

Constellation New Zealand Auck ★→★★ NZ outpost of global wine titan of same name. Large volume player, mostly MARL SAUV BL under mass-market labels KIM CRAWFORD, SELAKS.

Craggy Range Hawk ★★★→★★★★ Australian Peabody family-owned, HAWK meets Napa (*see* US). Top: Prestige collection. Excellent PINOT N (MART). Glam tourism.

Čuvar Hawk ★★→★★★ Name means "guardian" in Croatian. Fistonich family's post-VILLA MARIA adventure. Excellent-value Iris; smart single-vyd Guardians.

Decibel Hawk ★★→★★★ US-born Daniel Brennan est 2009, former rock-band manager. Testify (MALBEC/SYRAH). Urban cellar door in downtown Hastings.

Deep Down Marl ★★→★★★ Organic, single-vyd, hands-off CHARD, SAUV BL, PINOT N.

Delegat Auck ★★ Publicly listed company (est 1947), stock price often seen as a barometer for fortunes of MARL. Astutely managed, outward-looking. Growth built on successful OYSTER BAY SAUV BL, one of NZ wine's strongest brands.

Delta Marl ★★→★★★ Owned by St Clair; HAWK, MARL wines consistently gd value.

Destiny Bay Waih ★★★★ Meticulous CAB SAUV devotee. Sloping vyd; high-priced/quality Bx blends, French/US oak. Top: Magna Praemia (five-variety blend).

Deutz Auck ★★★ Champagne house lends name to VINARCHY-owned MARL fizz since 1988; gd value, esp Brut NV (min 2 ys on lees), strong local following.

Devotus Mart ★★★ Family-owned, devoted to PINOT N. Small vyd on MART Terrace incl 38-yr-old vines. Three styles made annually.

Dog Point Marl ★★★ Deep roots and respect for terroir. Largest organic vyd in NZ. Elegant whites (Section 94 SAUV BL). Flinty CHARD, harmonious PINOT N.

Domaine-Thomson C Ot ★★→★★★ Small, family-owned, organic. PINOT N vyds in Lowburn and Gevrey-Chambertin (*see* France). Typically dark, muscular style; 2nd-tier Explorer gd value.

Dry River Mart ★★★ Early star performer (est 1979), now owned by neighbouring LUNA ESTATE. Dedicated to top-quality aromatics and PINOT N with depth, structure. Also textural GEWURZ, PINOT GR.

Eaton Wines Marl ★★★ Vastly experienced Mike E and sons craft wines from selected sites. Speciality SAUV BL (bottle-aged 2 yrs before release). Captivating Forte Definition Sauv Bl.

Premium prices nudge upwards

Quality producers in NZ often grumble about prices of their wines. Most feel these are too low. They have looked enviously across the Tasman where the asking price on release of a bottle of Bass Phillip Res PINOT N is over NZ$500. NZ's most expensive Pinots are well below that, and the variety is seen as one where NZ has the edge on Australia – in quality, at least. It's also true that when you compare NZ's best Pinot N and CHARD to burgundies of the same price tag, the Kiwi wines generally outperform their French cousins. We are starting to see pushback. Boutique HAWK producer CH GARAGE produced outstanding SANGIOVESE/CAB SAUV in 2025. Its $695 bottle price made it NZ's priciest-ever wine on release. Soon after, trad-method sparkling specialist Esses released a 14 costing $295 a bottle, the highest price ever for a NZ fizz. There are others. Prices at top end of NZ wine appear to be on move.

Elephant Hill Hawk ★★★ German family-owned. Elegant CHARD, SYRAH and cellar-door architecture. Subregional expressions dubbed Sea, Earth and Stone.

Escarpment Mart ★★★ Founded by original Mr Pinot, Larry McKenna (1998), one of 1st at Te Muna. Now Torbreck-owned (*see* Australia). Organic, classy Kupe PINOT N, plus fascinating old-vine, single-vyd Pinot N from different sites.

Esk Valley Hawk ★★→★★★ Popular domestic brand owned by INDEVIN. Estate wines consistently gd value. Innovative Artisanal Collection: excellent ALBARIÑO, CHENIN BL, GRENACHE, TEMPRANILLO.

NYC bar craze for adding jalapeño to Marlborough Sauvignon Blanc. No comment.

Esses Marl ★★★ Sparkling specialist nr Kaikoura, s of MARL; min 3 yrs on lees. Outstanding Essential Brut NV, plus several distinctive vintage cuvées, incl Grande Dame Syme 14, NZ's most expensive fizz.

Felton Road C Ot ★★★★ Internationally respected label. Long-serving winemaker Blair Walter; English owner Nigel Greening; bio, terroir-driven approach. Multiple expressions of PINOT N, incl nuanced Blocks 3 and 5 from home vyd and extrovert Cornish Point. Classy CHARD, RIES.

Foley Wines Auck NZ arm of US billionaire Bill Foley's empire: MT DIFFICULTY (C OT); Clifford Bay, Dashwood, Goldwater, GROVE MILL, VAVASOUR (MARL); MARTINBOROUGH VYD, TE KAIRANGA (MART).

Folium Marl ★★★ Co-owned/run by Japanese-born Takaki Okada. Organic, dry-farmed, attention to detail. Distinctive SAUV BL. Impressive CHARD, PINOT N.

Forrest Marl ★★→★★★ Early player, est by John and Brigid F (the "Doctors"), now run by daughter Beth. Multi-tiered range from several regions, known for quality, value. Low-alc The Doctors highly successful.

Framingham Marl ★★→★★★ One of NZ's top RIES producers, organic; Sogrape-owned (*see* Portugal). Multiple styles, using some of oldest Ries vines in MARL.

Fromm Marl ★★★ Regional standout. Swiss-owned/managed. Known for sensitive, organic viticulture, wines with detail, depth. Impressive CHARD, PINOT N; elegant SYRAH in gd vintages.

Gibbston Valley C Ot ★★★ Gibbston's 1st winery. Popular wine-tourist stop; alfresco dining, hillside "wine cave". Most vyds in Bendigo. Organic. Exciting range of single-vyd PINOT N (China Terrace, old-vine Glenlee); China Terrace CHARD.

Giesen Cant ★★→★★★ Large player, est by three German bros from Rheinpfalz. Huge producer of MARL SAUV BL. Great success with zero-alc range. Excellent Clayvin CHARD, PINOT N, SYRAH.

Gimblett Gravels Hawk An 800-ha arid former riverbed w of Hastings, since 2001 defined, marketed as HAWK subregion. Stony, low-fertility soils. Each bottle carries "G" branding. Renowned for SYRAH, MERLOT-dominant Bx blends. Top wines are world-class: 13' 14' 15' 18 19' 20' 21'.

Gisborne Once a centre of the NZ industry, today a region in decline; gd sunshine hours, often rainy around harvest; fertile, alluvial soils. CHARD the original star, though most plantings now SAUV BL; ALBARIÑO, GEWURZ can be excellent.

Grasshopper Rock C Ot ★★→★★★ Small Alexandra estate, single-vyd PINOT N focus. Stony, n-facing site, named after rare local grasshopper. Dark-fruited, svelte.

Greenhough Nel ★★★ One of region's best. Best: old-vine Hope Vyd. Also thoughtful CHARD, PINOT BL, RIES, PINOT N. Attractive cellar door.

Greystone Waip ★★★ Great combination of organic farming, limestone-rich slopes, smart winemaking. Delightful CHARD (Erin's Block). Structured PINOT N, SYRAH.

Greywacke Marl ★★★ Label created and owned by legends Kevin (ex-Cloudy Bay) and Kimberley Judd. Flinty CHARD, one of MARL's best. Barrel-fermented Wild SAUV BL. Joyous PINOT N.

Grove Mill Marl ★★ Part of FOLEY WINES. Narrow range from WAIRAU V, gd value.

The Māori way

A new element is added to the growing Māori influence on NZ wine – Hua Parakore, a recently developed verification and validation system akin to organic certification with the added dimension of Māori culture and values. It was created by Te Waka Kai Ora, the National Māori Organics Authority, to facilitate the growing of pure, natural, culturally appropriate food (*kai atura*). Matiti has already attained Hua Parakore-verified status; others are queuing up.

Hāhā Hawk, Marl ★→★★ Created and owned by three families, emphasis on sustainability. Multi-region focus; flavoursome, easy-drinking.

Halcyon Days Hawk ★★→★★★ Thoughtful, natural wines. Zero-zero. Grapes from two organic vyds. Broad, exciting range: pét-nat CHENIN BL, SANGIOVESE.

Hans Herzog Marl ★★★ Labour of love for Swiss couple Hans and Therese H. Low-cropping, organic, attention to detail. Broad quirky varietal range: BLAUFRÄNKISCH, LAGREIN, MONTEPULCIANO. Textural VIOGNIER; impressive Grandezza, NZ's 1st "Super Tuscan" (*see* Italy).

Hawke's Bay Largest North I region. Has history, many attractions for wine tourists. Dry, sunny, diverse soils. Star CHARD (ripe, full), SYRAH (aromatic, elegant). Excellent Bx blends in gd yrs: **19'** 20' **21'** 24. SAUV BL plantings increased recently. *See also* GIMBLETT GRAVELS.

Helio Hawk ★★★ Estate est 2019 as HAWK CHARD specialist. Impressive Haumoana-grown Chard; more single-vyd Chards planned. Fine MART PINOT N, Hawk SYRAH.

Hunter's Marl ★★→★★★ Pioneering, run by region's "first lady of wine", Jane H. Vibrant SAUV BL, gd-value Estate CHARD, funky Offshoot Chard. Successful MiruMiru bubbles programme, esp vintage.

Indevin Marl ★★ NZ-owned behemoth, country's largest grower-producer; 4000 ha across GIS, HAWK, MARL. Major supplier of bulk wine for overseas markets. Controls brands Dulcét, ESK V, Left Field, VIDAL, VILLA MARIA.

Invivo Auck ★★ Synonymous with endorsement of TV star Graham Norton; HQ at old NZ wine research station in Te Kauwhata, s of AUCK. Classic, racy SAUV BL (MARL), plus styles from other regions, countries.

Jackson Estate Marl ★★→★★★ Well-resourced, respected brand owned by NZ-based Benton Wine Group. Top: crisp Stich SAUV BL. Engaging Vintage Widow PINOT N; CHARD improving.

Johanneshof Marl ★★→★★★ Small, German-influenced winery; hillside vyd, cellar door on Picton road. Outstanding GEWURZ, distinctive trad-method sparkling.

Jules Taylor Wines Marl ★★→★★★ Owned-run by MARL-born/bred Jules T. Top: OTQ ("on the quiet"). Strength across range (GRÜNER V, SAUV BL). Organic PINOT N (Wrekin vyd).

Kim Crawford Wines Hawk ★→★★ Owned by CONSTELLATION NZ. Mostly classic, pungent SAUV BL, majority sold in US.

Kumeu River Auck ★★★★ Kiwi CHARD royalty, owned-run by Brajkovich family, originally from Croatia. Several single-vyd expressions (refined Hunting Hill, bold Maté's), both clay sites close to winery. Expansion to HAWK with elevated Rays Road (Chard, PINOT N).

Kusuda Mart ★★★★ Founded and run by Japanese-born Hiro K. Small and meticulously farmed vyd on MART terrace. Ethereal PINOT N one of Mart's best. Also excellent RIES, SYRAH.

Landing, The Nlnd ★★→★★★ Magical, historic coastal site nr Kerikeri; US-based Kiwis Peter and Sue Cooper est 2007. Among region's best CHARD, SYRAH; 1st vintages of SANGIOVESE, TEMPRANILLO show great potential.

Lawson's Dry Hills Marl ★★→★★★ Was leader in screwcap revolution (est 1982). Consistent quality: top old-vine GEWURZ, SAUV BL with depth, gd PINOT N.

Lindauer Auck ★→★★ Lion brewery-owned. Excellent-value trad-method sparkling: Brut NV Blanc de Blancs, Rosé. Once big in UK, now mostly sold in NZ.

Loveblock Marl ★★→★★★ Ex-owners of KIM CRAWFORD, Kim and Erica C, with sustainable, innnovative philosophy. Estate vyd in Awatere V, partly organic. TEE SAUV BL replaces sulphur with tannin extracted from green tea.

Luna Estate Mart ★★→★★★ Locally owned; several sites in and around MART (owns DRY RIVER). Quality across ranges: impressive Eclipse CHARD, PINOT N.

Mahi Marl ★★★ Winery and cellar door under hillside near Renwick. Thoughtful, hands-off winemaking. Expressive, elegant single-vyds: Twin Valleys CHARD, Boundary Farm SAUV BL, Wrekin PINOT N.

Man O' War Auck ★★→★★★ Largest on WAIH, Spencer family-owned, island's largest landowner. Multiple steep, hair-raising island vyds on loam-clay soils. Extroverted styles: Valhalla CHARD, Dreadnought SYRAH. Popular PINOT GR on neighbouring island. New Swiftsure range.

Marisco Marl ★★ Large Waihopai V-based producer. Brands: Leefield Station, The Craft Series, The Kings Series, The Ned. Quality fizz, Diamond Heart.

Marlborough Beating heart of NZ wine, centred on two sheltered river valleys at top of S Island, WAIRAU V and AWATERE V; 1st SAUV BL planted 1975. Diurnal range (hot sunny days, cold nights) one of keys to success. Gravel and silt on valley floors ideal for aromatic whites; clay hillsides in Wairau V suited to CHARD, PINOT N; Sauv Bl dominant. Classic Marl style: intense, crisp, pungent, leafy. More producers making barrel-fermented, less "manufactured" Sauv Bl styles; Chard the big improver: leaner, racier than HAWK. Some of NZ's best GEWURZ, RIES. Pinot N plantings in decline, despite some excellent expressions. Some quality trad-method fizz: watch. Recent SAUV BL oversupply; cause for angst, rethinking.

Martinborough Wair Subregion in S WAIR, NZ's "Burgundian" village, where a PINOT N culture took hold in early 80s. Most wineries nr township on free-draining river terrace. Cold s winds reduce yields; warm dry summers, reliable autumns. Popular destination for Wellington day-trippers. Excellent CHARD, RIES, but best known for savoury-edged, elegantly structured Pinot N.

Martinborough Vineyard Mart ★★★ Helped put MART PINOT N on map in 80s, now owned by US billionaire Bill Foley. Outstanding CHARD, old-vine Home Block Pinot N. Marie-Zelie Pinot N named after pioneer winemaking Frenchwoman.

Matawhero Gis ★★ Legendary in 80s for GEWURZ and idiosyncratic owner Denis Irwin. GISBORNE flagship. Well-made, accessible range. Excellent CHARD Irwin.

Maude C Ot ★★→★★★ Named after nearby Mt Maude. Quality-focused husband-and-wife team. Structured single-vyd PINOT N. Old-vine RIES a highlight.

Misha's Vineyard C Ot ★★→★★★ Estate named after co-owner Misha Wilkinson. Sloping site above Lake Dunstan. Quality across range: Limelight RIES (s/sw), High Note PINOT N.

Mission Hawk ★★★ NZ's oldest winery (est 1851), still owned by Catholic Society of Mary; vyds in MARL, plus HAWK. Top: Huchet, named after NZ's 1st trained winemaker, a Marist brother from Nantes. Estate range gd value.

Moko Hills C Ot ★★★ Passion project of Donald van der Westhuizen. Small single-vyd site in Bendigo producing outstanding CHARD and PINOT N.

Mondillo C Ot ★★→★★★ Boutique Bendigo label est by US expat. Opulent PINOT N; intense, off-dry RIES; honeyed, fresh Nina Late Harvest Ries.

Mount Edward C Ot ★★→★★★ Small organic producer owned/run by old C OT-hand Duncan Forsyth. Gibbston HQ but most vyds in Cromwell Basin. Delightful CHARD, fine single-vyd PINOT N, plus rare, popular GAMAY.

Mount Riley Marl ★★→★★★ Family-owned, named after highest peak of Richmond Range. Dependable quality, gd value (ALBARIÑO). Top: Valley CHARD 17.

Mt Beautiful Cant ★★ Founded by David Teece; large vyd close to highway n of Cheviot. Approachable, attractive wines.

Mt Difficulty C Ot ★★★ Popular brand based in Bannockburn, now owned by US billionaire Bill Foley. Best known for dark, spicy PINOT N, esp estate label, gd-value Roaring Meg (named after a Gold Rush party girl). Popular restaurant perched above vines.

1171 km as the crow flies separate NZ's northernmost winery from its southernmost.

Mud House Waip ★★→★★★ VINARCHY-owned, featuring wines grown in several S Island regions. Strong Waipara Hills brand. Excellent value across range: single-vyds Waipara Hills RIES, C OT PINOT N.

Nautilus Marl ★★→★★★ Strong brand; S Smith & Sons-owned (*see* Yalumba, Australia). Experienced winemaker Clive Jones, 35 MARL vintages. Crisp, flavoursome aromatic whites, quality trad-method fizz (min 3 yrs lees).

Nelson Small region w of MARL, wetter but equally sunny. Two distinct terroirs: rolling Moutere Hills with clay soils (CHARD, PINOT N) and silty Waimea plains (aromatic whites). Delightful Chard, vivid PINOT GR, savoury Pinot N. Large SAUV BL plantings, most of it trucked to Marl for blending.

Neudorf Nel ★★★→★★★★ Finn family-owned, in Upper Moutere on old hippie-commune site. Regional flagship with international reputation; organic. Leader in CHARD: elegant old-vine Home Block Moutere, more extroverted Rosie's Block. Bold Moutere PINOT N, textured ALBARIÑO, PINOT GR.

No. 1 Family Estate Marl ★★★ Founded by Champenois Daniel Le Brun, MARL's trad-method fizz pioneer; 2nd generation. Try Citrus CHARD-based NV (2 yrs on lees), toasty Res Blanc de Blancs (5 yrs+ on lees).

Nobilo Marl ★→★★ Since 2020 owned by E&J Gallo (*see* US). Known for high-volume SAUV BL production: top Icon label grown in AWATERE V.

North Canterbury Dominant CANT subregion, centred on Waipara V. Gravel on flats, richer clay, limestone on e hills; incl wineries on limestone-rich sites to w nr Waikari. The Nor'wester, a hot dry wind, devigorates vines. Best CHARD is taut, thrilling; PINOT N with finesse, structure. Tight-knit culture of quality producers.

Novum Marl ★★★ Small quality producer with deep knowledge of region. Identifies small vyd pockets of top grapes, "sites within sites"; sells most direct. Elegant CHARD, PINOT N.

Oyster Bay Marl ★★ Leading brand of DELEGAT, named after small beach in MARL Sounds. Global success story, esp SAUV BL. Flavoursome, gd value, easy-drinking.

Palliser Mart ★★→★★★ One of region's earliest, largest; CHARD among region's best, top Om Santi. Standout Vintage fizz The Griffin. Pencarrow, gd value; smart quality, value estate range. Popular, attractive cellar door.

Pask Hawk ★★→★★★ Astutely managed; 1st winery on GIMBLETT GRAVELS. Top: Declaration, fine CHARD, SYRAH. Welcoming smart new cellar door.

Passage Rock Waih ★★→★★★ Located e side of WAIH. Award-winning, bold, oak-seasoned styles: SYRAH, Bx blends. Popular restaurant, cellar door.

Pegasus Bay Waip ★★→★★★★ One of Waipara's 1st; arguably finest; Donaldson family-owned/run. Quality across range: flinty CHARD, complex PINOT N; multiple RIES; 2nd tier Main Divide v.gd value. Wonderful garden, cellar door.

Peregrine C Ot ★★→★★★ Wing-shaped Gibbston winery building a delight. Most vyds in Cromwell Basin; organic. Popular, structured PINOT N; approachable whites; 2nd-tier Saddleback range excellent value.

Poppies Mart Former DRY RIVER winemaker Poppy Hammond and viticulturist husband Shayne (est 2012). Well-patronized cellar door where nearly all wine is sold. Moreish rosé a big hit. L'Elu PINOT N one of NZ's most expensive.

Prophet's Rock C Ot ★★★→★★★★ Small Bendigo producer, dedicated to craft; organic. Excellent Alsace-style PINOT GR, RIES; deep PINOT N. Top: Cuvée aux Antipodes (with Burgundy's François Millet).

Puriri Hills Auck ★★★→★★★★ Tiny, publicity-shy estate in Clevedon subregion, dedicated to high-quality MERLOT-dominant Bx blends.

Pyramid Valley Cant ★★★→★★★★ Superb limestone-rich, amphitheatre-like site nr Waikari, est by Mike and Claudia Weersing, now SMITH & SHETH CRU-owned; bio. Excellent CHARD, PINOT N. Other wines from around N CANT.

Quartz Reef C Ot ★★★ Bendigo subregion pioneer; bio, sensitive winemaking. Half made into classy fizz. Stylish CHARD; deep, harmonious PINOT N.

Radburnd Cellars Hawk ★★→★★★ Experienced HAWK winemaker Kate R's personal project. Fruit sourced from around region. Three premium wines: CHARD, MERLOT/CAB SAUV, SYRAH. Also 2nd-tier Penelope.

Rapaura Springs Marl ★★ Perennially reliable SAUV BL; gd-value classic range (CHARD, Sauv Bl, PINOT N). Rohe ("territory") offers subregional expressions.

Rewa, Dom C Ot ★★★ Founded 2010 by NZ-French Fourbet family. Organic vyd in Pisa subregion. Elegant CHARD, lively PINOT GR, characterful PINOT N.

Rippon Vineyard C Ot ★★★★ Pioneering family-owned estate beside Lake Wanaka; NZ's most photographed vyd vista; bio. Compelling RIES (dr). Age-worthy PINOT N of stature, grace: old-vine Tinker's Field, Emma's Block.

Rockburn C Ot ★★→★★★ Experienced producer, based in new winery/cellar door in Cromwell; vyds in Parkburn, Gibbston. Quality across range; popular estate PINOT N.

Rock Ferry Marl ★★★ Family-owned, organic; ten varieties in C OT, MARL vyds (NEBBIOLO, TEMPRANILLO). Seductive C Ot PINOT N. Excellent fizz.

Sacred Hill Hawk ★★→★★★ Now Poulter family-owned, biggest shipper of bananas in NZ (est 1986). Multi-tiered range: easy-drinking orange to Special Selection with acclaimed Riflemans CHARD, Brokenstone MERLOT, Deerstalkers SYRAH.

Saint Clair Marl ★★→★★★ Large, family-owned estate, well known for SAUV BL. Small-parcel Pioneer Block reliably intense, vibrant. Single-vyd PINOT N, dark-fruit charm.

Seifried Estate Nel ★★ Pillar of region, Family-owned/run 50 yrs+. Top: Aotea range (CHARD, PINOT N). Winemaker Collection: delectable GEWURZ, botrytized RIES. NZ's only Wurzer, ZWEIGELT.

Selaks Marl ★→★★ Pioneering Croatian label, supermarket brand of CONSTELLATION NZ. Easy-drinking ranges. Some made with cheaper Australian grapes.

Seresin Marl ★★→★★★ Founded by cinematographer Michael S; organic (2003). Recent downsize, winery and most vyds sold. Thoughtful wines: Marama SAUV BL, complex Res CHARD, Rachel PINOT N; natural Beautiful Chaos.

Sileni Hawk ★★ Large player, now part of NZ-owned Booster Wine Group; HAWK estate vyds in warm Bridge Pa triangle and cooler inland sites. Imposing reds in Grand Res range; Cellar Selection MARL SAUV BL gd value.

Up to 25% of all tourists to NZ visit a winery or vineyard during their stay.

Smith & Sheth Cru Hawk ★★★ Partnership of US billionaire Brian Sheth and Kiwi wine veteran Steve Smith. Single-vyd wines from selected sites: outstanding CHARD, charming Cantera (CABS SAUV/FR/TEMPRANILLO), stylish Omahu SYRAH, lively ALBARIÑO. Exciting visitor presentation at HAWK HQ. *See* PYRAMID V.

Spy Valley Marl ★★→★★★ All that's left of Five Eye satellite dish (which gave Spy V its name) is metal pyramid outside cellar door. Top: Envoy. Quality across range: rich GEWURZ, textural PINOT GR, dependable SAUV BL, approachable PINOT N.

Starborough Family Estates Marl ★★ Jones family-owned; deep farming roots in MARL; vyds in AWATERE V, WAIRAU V. Zesty SAUV BL, PINOT GR, perfumed PINOT N.

Stonecroft Hawk, Marl ★★ Small organic label with history, now Fistonich Family Vyds-owned. Two vyds in GIMBLETT GRAVELS, incl NZ's oldest SYRAH vines. Luscious GEWURZ, harmonioius Syrah; NZ's only ZIN.

Stoneleigh Marl ★★ Now part of VINARCHY. Based on warm, stony Rapaura vyds. Huge-selling flinty, juicy SAUV BL. Sustainability trumpeted, though not organic. Top: Raupara Series, generous, refined, incl gd-value CHARD.

Stonyridge Waih ★★★→★★★★ Small, quality player with loyal following, est 1982 by flamboyant Stephen White. Since 2022 majority-owned by Singaporean company. Best known for five-variety Bx blend Larose (standout 24'), bold Luna Negra MALBEC, dense SYRAH-based Pilgrim. Popular vyd restaurant.

Te Kairanga Mart ★★→★★★ Locally known as TK. FOLEY WINES-owned. Outstanding John Martin PINOT N; estate-range CHARD, RIES, Pinot N gd value. Attractive, spacious new restaurant/cellar door, The Runholder, a regional asset.

Te Mata Hawk ★★★→★★★★ A *taonga* (treasure) of NZ wine, C19 roots, family-owned/run. Collectable MERLOT-dominant Bx blend Coleraine **13' 14' 15' 16 17** 18 19' 20' 21' 22 24'. Lower-priced Awatea Cabs/MERLOT, classy, ditto flinty Cape Crest Sauv Bl, Bullnose SYRAH. Estate range gd-value.

Te Pā Marl ★★→★★★ Owned by Māori family, roots in MARL. Home vyd on Wairau Bar, close to sea. Vibrant PINOT GR, pungent SAUV BL; 2nd-tier Pā Road gd value.

Terra Sancta C Ot ★★★ Bannockburn's 1st vyd; owned by former NZ stock exchange CEO and wife. Several excellent PINOT N: old-vine Jackson's Block, Slapjack Block; gd-value Mysterious Diggings. Special Release First Vines Rosé, expensive but popular.

Te Whare Rā Marl ★★★ Old label (est 1979) revived by quality-focused Jason and Anna Flowerday. Organic, old-vine home vyd. Elegant RIES, deft Toru (GEWURZ/RIES/PINOT GR), outstanding PINOT N from Clayvin Vyd.

Thousand Gods, A Marl ★★★ Bright new natural star. Zero-zero, French experience, bio Churton vyd. Top: exciting Flos PINOT N, ethereal Love Letters rosé.

Tiki Marl ★★ Owned by family with proud Māori heritage. A tiki is a carved figure, often symbolizing fertility. Extensive vyds in MARL, N CANT. Approachable, fruit-forward: N Cant SAUV BL, PINOT N; 2nd-tier Maui.

Tohu Marl, Nel ★★ World's 1st Māori-owned winery; vyds in MARL, NEL; AWATERE V SAUV BL, RIES. Top: Whenua Awa Single-Vyd CHARD, PINOT N. Classy fizz: Rewa Blanc de Blancs, Rosé.

Trinity Hill Hawk ★★→★★★★ Perenially strong performer offering excellent quality/value: CHARD, SYRAH, Bx blend The Gimblett, only NZ Port styles using trad Portuguese grapes. Homage Syrah a NZ classic **14' 15' 16 17 18' 19'** 20' 21'.

Must-visit NZ cellar doors

In every one of the country's wine regions, cellar doors – many with restaurants attached – and other wine attractions abound. Best cellar-door experiences combine personal engagement, authenticity, tasting pleasure and a gd dose of knowledge-sharing. Recommended n–s (for some, appointments will be needed); * indicates a recommended on-site restaurant. Nlnd: THE LANDING. AUCK: KUMEU RIVER. WAIH: Batch Winery*, MAN O' WAR, STONYRIDGE. HAWK: CRAGGY RANGE*, MISSION*, PASK, SMITH & SHETH, TE MATA. WAIR: ATA RANGI, Moy Hall*, PALLISER, Poppies*. MARL: CLOS HENRI, CLOUDY BAY, HUNTER'S, St Clair*, TE WHARE RĀ. Waip: BLACK ESTATE*, PEGASUS BAY. C OT: AMISFIELD*, GIBBSTON VALLEY*, Monte Christo, MT DIFFICULTY*, PEREGRINE, RIPPON VYD.

Two Paddocks C Ot ★★→★★★ Owned by evergreen actor Sir Sam Neill; vyds in Alexandra, Bannockburn; organic. PINOT N mainstay: vivacious main label, resonant single-vyd The Fusilier (Bannockburn), in honour of Neill's father.

Two Rivers Marl ★★→★★★ Co-owned by cricket-loving winemaker Dave Clouston and wife Pip; vyds in WAIRAU V, AWATERE V. Best known for two-valley SAUV BL blend Convergence, Brookby Hill PINOT N, restrained Island of Beauty rosé (dr); 2nd-tier Black Cottage v.gd value.

1903 Wairarapa Pinot N still drinking well. From private cellar – sorry.

Valli C Ot ★★★ Label created by Grant Taylor, Gibbston winemaking legend, now running wine bar in WAITAKI V. Subregional differences in PINOT N highlighted with four versions. Excellent quality; Waitaki V CHARD outstanding.

Vavasour Marl ★★ Was 1st AWATERE V label (est 1986). Long-serving vigneron Stu Marfell's wines epitomize Awatere V style: elegant CHARD; high-wire acidity PINOT GR, SAUV BL; red-fruit PINOT N. Top: complex Papa (mudstone).

Vidal Hawk ★★ INDEVIN-owned (est 1905). Top tiers dropped, leaving standard, Res ranges for supermarkets: gd-value HAWK CHARD, MERLOT/CAB.

Villa Maria Auck ★★→★★★ Still top-selling NZ wine brand in UK, recently acquired by INDEVIN. Entry-level Private Bin; great-value Cellar Selection; Single Vineyard; Res (regional character). Distinguished Icon.

Vinarchy Australian (formerly Accolade); recently bought Pernod Ricard's NZ wine holdings (mainly BRANCOTT ESTATE, CHURCH ROAD, STONELEIGH, DEUTZ brands).

Waiheke Island Sun-kissed isle in Hauraki Gulf where day visits, weddings and lazy holidays comprise key market for local wineries. Pricey wines because (a) they're expensive to make, and (b) wealthy people flock to Waih. Fragrant Bx blends (esp Onetangi district clay soils) and more recently bold SYRAH.

Wairarapa At the base of N Island, similar latitude to MARL. NZ's 7th-largest wine region. Centred around MART, but across large river valley. Driest, coolest region in N Island. Exposed to cold s winds, reducing yields. Farmer William Beetham and his French wife planted 1st PINOT N in 1890s; after long hiatus, grape returned in 80s to great acclaim. Also strong in CHARD, RIES, PINOT GR, SAUV BL.

Wairau Valley Marl Vine-filled flood plain surrounded by sheltering ranges, open to sea (Cloudy Bay) at its e end. Three important side valleys called Southern Vs: Brancott, Omaka, Waihopai; SAUV BL thrives on flat alluvial valley floor, most PINOT N planted on clay-based, n-facing slopes. Recent planting in upper Wairau V. Biggest town Blenheim gateway to 30+ cellar doors.

Waitaki Valley Small, beautiful subregion in N Ot. Limestone the big attraction, but climate marginal. Winemakers still in terroir-discovery mode; CHARD, PINOT GR, PINOT N excellent in top vintages. Potential for bubbles.

Whitehaven Marl ★★→★★★ Part-owned by Gallo (*see* US). Mostly SAUV BL, exported to the US. Pristine whites, stylish PINOT N. Top: Greg (named after winery's co-founder G White).

Wild Irishman C Ot ★★★ Intriguing venture of octogenarian Gibbston founder Alan Brady and another Irishman, Brian Shaw. Several finely crafted PINOT N from different subregions.

Wither Hills Marl ★★ Founded by Marris (now MARISCO) family in 1994. Owned by Lion brewery. Dependable SAUV BL; single-vyds Rarangi RIES and Calrossie PINOT N.

Yealands Marl ★★ Owned by local utility company. Vast vyd (c.1000 ha, NZ's largest) on rolling coastal AWATERE V site, est 2008. Zesty SAUV BL.

Zephyr Marl ★★→★★★ Organic family vyd in lower WAIRAU V. Principled winemaking. Quality across range: expressive CHARD, refreshing GEWURZ.

South Africa

Abbreviations used in the text:

Bre	Breedekloof	Kl K	Klein Karoo
Cdorp	Calitzdorp	Oli R	Olifants River
Cape SC	Cape South Coast	Pie	Piekenierskloof
Ced	Cederberg	Pri	Prieska
Coast	Coastal Region	Rob	Robertson
Const	Constantia	Sim-P	Simonsberg-Paarl
Ela	Elandskloof	Stell	Stellenbosch
Elg	Elgin	Swa	Swartland
Fran	Franschhoek	Tul	Tulbagh
Hem	Hemel-en-Aarde	V Pa	Voor Paardeberg
Rdg/Up/V	Ridge/Upper/Valley	Wlk B	Walker Bay
		Well	Wellington

The eighth-largest producer, with an 880-million-litre output and roughly 4% contribution to quenching the world's thirst for wine, South Africa lies between two oceans at the tip of the continent, on terrain that's mostly dry and viticulturally challenging or outright unsuitable, yet with a ribbon of conducive and often scenic land, chiefly along the coast plus some inland pockets. Almost 95% of wine is grown in the Cape Floral Region, the smallest yet most diverse floral kingdom, with more than 9000 plant species (well over 2000 on iconic Table Mountain alone). Extraordinary variety is reflected too in the almost dizzying array of wine varieties and styles, from Pinotage to pét-nat to *vin de paille*, with detours into bubbly from unheard-of grapes like Irsai Olivér, sweet Muscat aged in bourbon barrels and Sauvignon Blanc raised under a veil of flor. All are made possible by diverse soils and climates, created by wine-growers unfettered by previous generations' conventions. Within this larger picture are sub-genres like old vines, producing wines of graceful intensity; heirloom varieties, made brighter and more alluring by modern vinification techniques; and paler, more savoury and altogether sexier pink wines modelled on Provence.

Plus trends such as low(er) alcohol; a mania for Cabernet Franc; preoccupation with soil vitality and sustainability in general; and, in the cellar, a welcome lighter touch, giving livelier, more appetizing wines with more space left for site and grape to express themselves.

Recent vintages

2025 Rock-star vintage; vibrant, structured, cellar-worthy, with moderate alc.
2024 Variable; let producer track record guide buying/cellaring decisions.
2023 Cool kick-off for whites and early reds, wet 2nd half needed steady nerves.
2022 Smaller crop, but slow ripening built flavour while preserving freshness.
2021 Late but bountiful, gd early rains, cool conditions. Much excitement (r/w).

AA Badenhorst Family Wines Swa ★★→★★★★ With subtle, savoury-edged releases from Med and heritage grapes, accenting site, old vines, wild yeasts et al, prime mover Adi B helped revolutionize SA's wine aesthetic and approach from mid-2000s. New peppery SYRAH joins CHENIN BL, GRENACHE N, pair of CINSAULTS, solo PALOMINO, blends (r/w). Secateurs label remains byword for value.

Alheit Vineyards W Cape ★★★★ Vinous explorers Chris and Suzaan A since 2010s have sought out distinctive, mostly old-vine CHENIN BL and later SEM pockets on Cape coast to vinify (min intervention) alongside profound multi-site Cartology.

Alto Wine Estate Stell ★★★ Red-wine specialist, neighbour and sibling to ERNIE ELS and STELLENZICHT in catalogue of Baron Hans von Staff-Reitzenstein. Industry institution Rouge Bx/SHIRAZ recently celebrated 100 consecutive yrs' bottling.

Angus Paul Wines W Cape ★★★→★★★★ Angus P works gently, thoughtfully in STELL to express uniqueness of the Cape. PINOTAGE and heritage varieties, notably CHENIN BL (Barbary Fictions, Fantamtango). Watch.

Anthonij Rupert Wyne W Cape ★→★★★★ Wide, impressive portfolio honours owner and international businessman Johann R's brother. Some exceptional 3rd-party vyds (in acclaimed Cape of Good Hope collection) but mostly own parcels in DARLING, ELA, FRAN, SWA. Upcyclable Protea range, eye/pocket-pleaser.

Anysbos Bot R ★★★ Heyns family; pure-fruited, aromatic pair of blends, GRENACHE N- and CHENIN BL-led, and recent varietal SYRAH. Winemaker Marelise Niemann also styles her admired Momento label (mostly GRENACHES BL, N) on-site.

Babylonstoren W Cape ★★→★★★ Media tycoon Koos Bekker and wife Karen Roos's bustling wine-and-lifestyle farm nr PAARL with cornucopian cellar-door offering. Plush, long-haul-styled Bx blend Nebukadnesar. Also The Newt (UK).

Bartho Eksteen Estate Wine W Cape ★★★→★★★★ At Eksteen clan's boutique farm in HEM V, CWG-member Bartho and son Pieter Willem make elegant SAUV BL, SYRAH. Also run academy named Wijnskool, with namesake label, for aspiring vintners, hence pedagogy-themed wine names. Pieter and Argentinian wife Sol craft MALBEC and, now, GRENACHE N under Yerden Eksteen banner.

Bartinney Private Cellar Stell ★★→★★★★ Rose and Michael Jordaan's pair of ventures: this boutique winery and panorama on steep STELL slopes of Sim (classic CHARD, CAB SAUV); sweeping Plaisir estate on warmer PAARL side of mtn, hitting stride (Grand Plaisir cedary Bx r and peachy Chard).

Beaumont Family Wines Cape SC ★★→★★★★ Excellent Bot R familial estate with old-time ambience, gnarled vines and handmade, characterful wines: superlative CHENIN BL, one of few solo MOURVÈDRE. Matriarch Jayne B's namesake label: Electrique (was CHARD, now blend with Chenin Bl), PINOT N.

Beck, Graham W Cape ★★→★★★★ Pace-setting CAP CLASSIQUE specialist nr ROB with portfolio that ticks boxes for range of sparkling, water-white to salmon-hued. Delicious, often stellar surprises in experimental Artisan Collection. Welcome emphasis on magnum bottlings.

BEE (Black Economic Empowerment) Initiative aimed at increasing wine-industry ownership and participation by previously disadvantaged groups.

Beeslaar Wines W Cape ★★★★ Masterclass in refined PINOTAGE, mineral CHARD by internationally hailed Abrie B and family. Thrilling trad approach with modern tweaks. Inevitable (given lengthy KANONKOP residency) Bx blend due.

Conventional wine sampling not doing it for you? Try safari tasting at Saxenburg.

Bellingham W Cape ★★→★★★ Enduring DGB brand with v.gd fruit-driven limited releases The Bernard Series and newer The Founders. Latter homage to Pod and Fredagh Podlashuk, who revived FRAN home-farm Belle en Champ, and championed SHIRAZ at the Cape.

Benguela Cove Lagoon Wine Estate Wlk B ★★★ Penny Streeter OBE's cellar, vyds and destination on Bot R lagoon. Top: Catalina SEM, experimental/cellar-door-only bottlings under Vinography flag. Johann Fourie also crafts Penny's UK wines (Leonardslee, Mannings Heath), plus those of Terra Loci, a newer, separate site-focused brand he owns with partners.

Beyerskloof W Cape ★★→★★★★ PINOTAGE champion nr STELL: 11 fruit-forward versions (12, incl spirit for "Port"), soloists, blends and blush. Equally fine CAB SAUV named Eerste Ry for 1st vines planted 1988/9 by co-founder Beyers Truter.

Boekenhoutskloof Winery W Cape ★★★★ Among SA's most important producers, for quality and volume, based in FRAN. Enviable consistency 40 yrs+ under Boekenhoutskloof and Porcupine Ridge labels, later The Wolftrap range and standalone ventures in HEM, SWA (*see* CAP MARITIME, PORSELEINBERG).

Bon Courage Estate W Cape ★→★★★ Bruwer family nr ROB with stylish Brut CAP CLASSIQUE trio, aromatic desserts (MUSCAT, RIES) in broad range.

Boplaas Family Vineyards W Cape ★→★★★ Carel Nel and family at CDORP, known for Port-style and deep-flavoured table wines, Portuguese grapes (r/w).

Boschendal Wines W Cape ★→★★★ Evergreen DGB brand on hospitable C17 estate nr FRAN. Fruit-forward Bx/Rhône (r/w) blends, CHARD, SAUV BL, SHIRAZ and CAP CLASSIQUE in various tiers.

Boschkloof Wines W Cape ★★★★ Acclaimed Reenen Borman in STELL: stellar varietal SYRAH (Boschkloof and blend under Kottabos label). With partners, notable Saga Vyds bottlings, unoaked reds (piquant BRE BARBERA, silky Stell Syrah) labelled Sons of Sugarland; whites (CHENIN BL, blend) branded Patatsfontein after source farm in unsung area Montagu.

Botanica Wines Cit, Stell ★★→★★★ American Ginny Povall on wine/flower-growing home farm nr STELL: succulent CAB FR, newer perfumed ALBARIÑO; draws on old w-coast bush vines for superlative, rich yet refined Mary Delany CHENIN BL.

Bouchard Finlayson Cape SC ★★★→★★★★ Family-owned HEM pioneer, with v. fine expressions of CHARD (unoaked version among SA's best), PINOT N.

Breedekloof Breede River V DISTRICT (c.12,500 ha), trad bulk- and entry-level focus, lately lifted by new generation, often working with heritage vines (CHENIN BL).

Brookdale Estate Paarl ★→★★★ Energized, UK-owned, advised by eminent Duncan SAVAGE. Widely aspired-to, yet still rare, co-planted vyds: awarded Sixteen (w), Twenty Field Blend (r) noted for restraint, vibrancy in warm area.

Bruce Jack Wines W Cape ★★→★★★ From home base nr Napier on S Coast, multitasking Bruce J makes varietals, blends, bubbly from unusual grapes for estate label The Drift. Collaborates with others for namesake international brand and Mary Le Bow (VIOGNIER, r blend), both US oak-scented and Ghost in the Machine, incl skin-ferment version of rare heirloom grape CLAIRETTE BL.

Buitenverwachting W Cape ★★→★★★ Family farm in CONST with lovely trad feel yet modern, forthright wines, exported as Bayten; CHARD, SAUV BL, Bx-style reds, varying mix of Ltd Releases; 1st in area with own-vine CHENIN BL.

Calitzdorp Small DISTRICT in KL K REGION, similar climate to Douro V (*see* Portugal), known for Port-style and latterly unfortified Port-grape wines (r/w).

Cap classique Bottle-fermented sparkling, officially known as "méthode cap classique" but producers urging use of shortened version. Major success: labels have more than doubled the past decade, to well over 400.

Cap Maritime Cape SC ★★★ Classy CHARD, PINOT N specialist in UP HEM owned by BOEKENHOUTSKLOOF, looking to build on enviable track record with bought-in fruit, as own young vyds come on-stream.

Cape Blend Usually red with a significant PINOTAGE component; occasionally a CHENIN BL blend, or simply wine with "Cape character".

Cape Coast Umbrella appellation ("OVERARCHING REGION" in officialese) for COAST (w and central) and CAPE SC regions.

Capensis W Cape ★★★★ Starry venture in STELL owned by US Jackson Family's Barbara Banke. Previously specializing in CHARD, multi-site and single-vyd, now adds equally sophisticated Helderberg CAB SAUV. *See* DALKEITH.

Cape Point Vineyards W Cape ★★★→★★★★ Acclaimed family winery nr tip of CAPE TOWN peninsula. Cellarable flagship Isliedh, previously Bx-style (w), now gets some young-vine SAUV GR without deviating from riveting mineral style.

Cape Rock Wines W Cape ★★→★★★ Willie Brand and son Gavin among OLI R's top boutique growers. Creative varietals, blends (r/w), esp CARIGNAN, VERMENTINO.

Cape South Coast Cool-climate REGION (c.2670 ha) comprising DISTRICTS of Cape Agulhas, ELG, Lower Duivenhoks River, Overberg, Plettenberg Bay, Swellendam, WLK B, plus stand-alone WARDS Herbertsdale, Napier, Stilbaai E. *See also* CAPE COAST.

Cape Town Coast DISTRICT (c.2500 ha) covering namesake city, its peninsula WARDS, CONST and Hout B, plus nearby wards DURBANVILLE and Philadelphia.

Cape West Coast Only subregion; incl DARLING and Lutzville V DISTRICTS, plus Bamboes B and Lamberts B WARDS. *See also* CAPE COAST.

Carinus Family Vineyards Stell, Swa ★★★→★★★★ Blessed with trendiest of addresses, STELL's Polkadraai Hills and SWA, Danie C and distantly related namesake Hugo keep best grapes for standout signature label: mostly CHENIN BL, SYRAH to express site rather than style.

Catherine Marshall Wines W Cape ★★★ Cool-climate (chiefly ELG) specialist Cathy M focused on CHENIN BL, SAUV BL, PINOT N. Satin-textured Ode To Arges SEM.

Cederberg Tiny free-standing WARD in Cederberg Mtns; some of remotest, highest vyds (950–1100m/3117–3609ft), mostly CHENIN BL, SHIRAZ. Main producers: CEDERBERG PRIVATE CELLAR, Driehoek, Kromrivier. New boutique Rugged Rocks.

Cederberg Private Cellar W Cape ★★→★★★★ Nieuwoudt family; among highest (CED) and most s (ELIM) vyds. Chiefly varietals: exceptional Teen die Hoog SHIRAZ. Creamy CAP CLASSIQUE. David N shareholder in Escape Wines in WLK B.

Central Orange River Extensive DISTRICT in N CAPE GU. Hot, dry, irrigated; trad white (most is Sultana for dried/table grapes) and fortified, but major producer ORANGE RIVER CELLARS pushing envelope with eg. SHIRAZ.

Certified Heritage Vineyard *See* OLD VINE PROJECT.

With 880m litres, S Africa makes 3.9% of global wine volume.

Chamonix Wine Farm Fran, Stell ★★→★★★ Norwegian-owned top cellar/vyds overlooking FRAN, bringing in some grapes while redeveloped vyds mature. Age-worthy CHARD, PINOT N, Bx varietals/blends (r/w).

Charles Fox Cap Classique Wines Elg ★★★ Bubbly house founded by 1964 Olympic swimmer and wife Zelda, with eight classic, delicious trad-method Bruts (w/rosé), most vintage-dated, many featuring rarely seen (Pinot) MEUNIER.

Coastal Region Largest REGION; incl ocean-influenced CAPE TOWN, DARLING,

Lutzville V, STELL and SWA DISTRICTS, plus Bamboes B and Lamberts B WARDS. Also incl non-maritime FRAN, PAARL, TUL, WELL districts.

Colmant Cap Classique & Champagne W Cape ★★★→★★★★ Sparkling house at FRAN, founded by Belgian Colmant family, now owned by compatriots Jan and Isabelle Boone. Brut Nature and trio of Brut (w/rosé), all NV and excellent.

Constantia CAPE TOWN WARD, est 1685 on cool Constantiaberg slopes; SA's 1st and most historically famous growing area, still a pace-setter.

Constantia Glen Const ★★★→★★★★ Waibel family-owned model of consistency, quality on upper Constantiaberg. Trio of Bx blends (r/w), solo SAUV BL.

Constantia Uitsig W Cape ★★→★★★ Prime vyds, cellar and multi-faceted cellar door in CONST. Estate and wider-sourced Ex Oppido ranges (mostly w, some sp).

Creation Wines Cape SC ★★★→★★★★ Scenic estate in HEM RDG, part-owned by Martin/Finlayson family, with tourist venue buzzing with inventive projects, and cellar bulging with diverse, bold wines: CHARD, PINOT N; incl versions by 4th-generation Emma and Glenn.

Crystallum W Cape ★★★★ A CHARD, PINOT N specialist, always-impressive single- and multi-site expressions: ELA, HEM, crafted at GABRIËLSKLOOF in Bot R by Peter-Allan Finlayson (brand owner with sibling Andrew, and Albert van Niekerk).

CWG (Cape Winemakers Guild) Independent, invitation-only association of 42 top growers. Stages a benchmarking annual auction of limited premium bottlings, and mentors future stars via Protégé Programme.

Dalkeith Stell, Swa ★★★ Pair of fine, textured CHENIN BL, peppery SYRAH, all single site and named after watering hole in Kgalagadi Transfrontier Park. Siblings to newly expanded CAPENSIS collection in Cape portfolio of US Jackson Family.

Latest wheeze: Delheim Estate pairing wines with fynbos-infused cupcakes.

Darling DISTRICT around this w-coast town. Best vyds in hilly Groenekloof WARD. Most fruit goes into 3rd-party brands, some spectacular.

David & Nadia Swa ★★★★ Quietly arresting sextet of CHENIN BL (single- and multi-site, former incl new bottling named Langland), blends (r/w) and GRENACHE N, mostly from heritage vyds, by Sadie husband and wife on Paardeberg Mtn-side.

David Finlayson Wines W Cape ★★→★★★ Celebrated David F on Edgebaston estate nr STELL. Expressive, fruity (Camino Africana series). Daughter and 4th-generation vintner Daniella recently launched Alpen Glow collection.

De Grendel Wines W Cape ★★★ Sir De Villiers Graaff's Table Mtn-facing venture in DURBANVILLE draws on own and far-flung contracted vyds, notably elevated Ceres Plateau and maritime ELIM. Wines reflect origin with generosity, richness.

De Kleine Wijn Wynand and Anya Grobler on famed ex-Tulbagh Mtn Vyds site: Rhône-style TMV Estate Blend from own vines. Source widely for extensive, playfully named, seriously conceived range: new V Pa GRENACHE N Hoendertande (Hen's Teeth).

De Krans Wines W Cape ★→★★★ Nel family at CDORP. Port styles, fortified MUSCAT. Success with robust unfortified (r/w) from Portuguese grapes.

Delaire Graff Estate W Cape ★★→★★★★ UK-diamond-merchant Laurence Graff's glittering eyrie vyds, winery, venue in STELL's Banhoek V. Consistently superior portfolio: single-vyd Terraced Block Res CHARD, Laurence Graff Res CAB SAUV.

Delheim Wines Coast ★→★★★ Eco-minded Sperling/Thiel family venture high on Sim Mtn nr STELL. PINOTAGE (single-site, rosé), age-worthy Grand Res (Bx-style r). New RIES blend Iconoclast celebrates late patriarch, feisty "Spatz" Sperling.

DeMorgenzon W Cape ★★→★★★★ Music pervades dynamic Appelbaum family's STELL Kloof hillside vyd, catches eponymous morning sun yet has cooler, mostly s aspect. Renowned Res CHENIN BL (occasional vine-selected The Divas), CHARD.

De Trafford Wines Elg, Stell ★★★→★★★★ Family's STELL boutique venture, unabashedly bold wines: Bx-style/SHIRAZ Elevation 393; CHENIN BL (dr/sw), CAB SAUV, SYRAH. *See* SIJNN.

DGB W Cape Long-est producer/wholesaler in WELL/FRAN. Owns/controls high-end brands Avontuur, Backsberg, BELLINGHAM, BOSCHENDAL, Fryer's Cove, Old Road. Also easy-drinking labels, some export only.

Diemersdal Estate W Cape ★→★★★ DURBANVILLE Louw family excelling with site/row/style-specific CHARD, SAUV BL (incl SA's priciest, The Globe, fermented in glass sphere), CAB SAUV, PINOTAGE and among handful of commercial GRÜNER V.

District *See* GU.

Dorrance Wines W Cape ★★→★★★★ French family boutique, cellar in CAPE TOWN city-heritage building. Consistently excellent CHARD, CHENIN BL, SYRAH, PINOT N.

Durbanville Atlantic-cooled WARD on Tygerberg Hills in CAPE TOWN DISTRICT, best known for SAUV BL and whites generally.

Durbanville Hills Dur ★→★★★ Area pioneer, owned by HEINEKEN BEVERAGES, local growers, staff, noted for generous, fruit-focused styling and fair prices. Excellent pinnacle Bx-style blends (r/w), Tangram; ubiquitous entry-level SAUV BL.

Eagles' Nest Const ★★★ Constantiaberg mtn-side winery, lately German-owned, with reliably superior VIOGNIER, MERLOT, SHIRAZ. Also vibrant SAUV BL.

Elandskloof Over Cool-climate WARD, spectacular Alpine setting. Home to Kaaimansgat/Crocodile's Lair vyd (pure-fruited CHARD). Fine SAUV BL, PINOT N.

Elgin Cool-climate DISTRICT recognized for CHARD, SAUV BL, PINOT N. Exciting CHENIN BL, RIES, SYRAH, CAP CLASSIQUE. Mostly family boutiques.

Elim Windswept WARD in most S DISTRICT, Cape Agulhas, producing aromatic white blends, SAUV BL, SYRAH. Grape source for majors and boutiques.

Ernie Els Wines W Cape ★★→★★★★ Star golfer's wine venture nr STELL, centred on CAB SAUV: four cellar-worthy tiers, earlier-ready Big Easy line. Co-owner Baron Hans von Staff-Reitzenstein's portfolio incl nearby eminent ALTO, STELLENZICHT.

Estate wine Grown, made and bottled on "units registered for the production of estate wine". Not a quality designation.

Fairview W Cape ★→★★★★ Back family's caprine-themed wine-and-cheese venture on panoramic PAARL Mtn farm, sourcing on-site and more widely for cornucopia of varietal, blended, single-vyd and fizzy bottlings under Fairview, Goats Do Roam, La Capra, Spice Route and Klein Amoskuil labels. Bustling, multi-faceted cellar-door experience, incl famous goat herd and tower.

FirstCape Vineyards W Cape ★→★★ Huge export venture involving four Breede River V cellars. Mostly entry-level wines in multiple ranges.

Flagstone Winery W Cape ★→★★★ Vinarchy's (*see* NZ) high-end winery at Somerset W, sourcing widely for plush Icon reds (PINOTAGE, Velvet Blend), Bx-style (w), SAUV BL et al. Siblings mid-tier Fish Hoek, entry-level Kumala.

Fleur du Cap W Cape ★→★★★ HEINEKEN BEVERAGES premium label, with opulent headliner Laszlo (Bx r blend) and v.gd Series Privée Unfiltered CHARD, MERLOT.

Foundry, The Piek, Stell, V Pa ★★★→★★★★ Among 1st to focus on the Rhône (r/w) in 2000. Cellar and most of its source vyds in PAARL's V Pa for elegantly crafted single-variety bottlings under Foundry and newer Geographica labels.

Franschhoek Huguenot-founded DISTRICT known for CHARD, SEM, CAB SAUV and CAP CLASSIQUE. Home to some of SA's oldest farms and vines.

Free State Province and GU. Aptly named Mile High Vyds, to date sole producer (under The Bald Ibis label) in viticulturally challenging e highlands. DAVID FINLAYSON winemaker Pieter van der Merwe's small vyd on family farm Sanniesrus nr capital Bloemfontein due.

Gabriëlskloof W Cape ★★→★★★ Lauded range from CWG member and co-owner Peter-Allan Finlayson (and CRYSTALLUM, with brother Andrew) in Gabriëlskloof cellar nr Bot R: CHENIN BL, CAB FR, site/technique-based expressions of SYRAH.

Glenelly Estate Stell ★★★→★★★★ "Retirement" venture in STELL of Bx eminence May-Eliane de Lencquesaing, run by grandson Nicolas Bureau. Glossy flagships Lady May (Bx-style r), Res CHARD and Bx style/SHIRAZ.

Groot Constantia Estate Const ★★★ Magnet attracting 450,000 visitors to beautifully preserved farmstead and SA's longest-producing cellar. Suitably eminent wines, esp MUSCAT DE FRONTIGNAN Grand Constance helping restore CONST dessert to C18 glory.

GU (geographical unit) Largest of the WO demarcations: FREE STATE, KWAZULU-NATAL, LIMPOPO and newer NORTH EAST, plus E, N, W Cape – last three constitute the OVERARCHING GU known as Greater Cape. Other WO appellations (in descending size): overarching region, REGION, subregion, DISTRICT and WARD.

Hamilton Russell Vineyards Hem V ★★★→★★★★ The 1st to succeed with Burgundy grapes in cool s Cape in early 80s at Hermanus: long-lived CHARD, elegant PINOT N. Sibling Southern Right focuses on SAUV BL, PINOTAGE, ditto Ashbourne label, only here Sauv Bl joined by other white grapes. Stand-alone employee brand Tesselaarsdal, made at/by HRV, comprises Chard, Pinot N exclusively.

Hartenberg Estate Coast ★★→★★★ Welcoming, eco-minded family farm nr STELL: CHARD, RIES (dr/s/sw/botrytis), tiers of SHIRAZ/SYRAH, fine Bx-style (r).

Heineken Beverages SA's biggest drinks company, a 2023 merger of Distell, Namibia Breweries and Heineken SA, headquartered in upcountry Sandton. Owns or has interests in many wine brands, spanning styles/quality scales. *See* DURBANVILLE HILLS, FLEUR DU CAP, JC LE ROUX, NEDERBURG WINES.

Hemel-en-Aarde Trio of cool-climate WARDS (Hem V, Up Hem, Hem Rdg) in WLK B DISTRICT, producing outstanding CHARD, SAUV BL, PINOT N.

Flush of success: pink wines now in top five biggest exports.

Iona Vineyards Elg ★★→★★★ Family winery atop cool, breezy ridge nr ocean, co-owned by staff; excels with taut, mineral CHARD, SAUV BL, PINOT N. Also v.gd: Wines of Brocha SYRAH; well-priced lifestyle brand Sophie.

JC le Roux, The House of W Cape ★→★★ In 80s, 1st specialist fizz producer, now HEINEKEN BEVERAGES-owned with welcoming home nr STELL. Huge-selling mostly sweetish carbonated bubbles, some trendily de-alc and/or canned; flagship Scintilla CAP CLASSIQUE can be stellar.

Joostenberg Wines Paarl ★★★ Organic family business with flavoursome CHENIN BL (incl sw botrytis), SYRAH et al. Honours forebears via Myburgh Bros range. Partners with STARK-CONDÉ in revitalized STELL estate Lievland, and in volume, value brand MAN Family Wines.

Jordan Wine Estate W Cape ★★→★★★★ Family venture nr STELL, admired for consistency, quality, value, from entry Chameleon to stellar CWG bottlings. Must-try old-vine Timepiece collection: rare varietal RIES.

Kaapzicht Wine Estate Stell ★★→★★★ Steytler family's charmingly packaged portfolio; boldly fruited (SA's 2nd-oldest) CHENIN BL, age-worthy PINOTAGE.

Kanonkop Estate Coast ★★★→★★★★ "First Growth" status since early 70s; classically styled, long-lived senior wines, Paul Sauer (Bx-style r), CAB SAUV and PINOTAGE (regular and old-vine Black Label). Second label: Kadette. Recently acquired organic STELL neighbour Ladybird Vyds undergoing extensive redevelopment.

Keermont Vineyards Stell ★★★ Wraith family estate; terraced vyds (Cape rarity) in cleft between Helderberg and STELL Mtns. Intense CHENIN BL, SHIRAZ et al by CWG member Alex Starey. Neighbour/grape supplier to A-league DE TRAFFORD.

Keet Wines Stell ★★★★ Having named his debut wine First Verse, applauded owner-winemaker Chris K since 2009 has resisted all temptations to add to single, beautifully crafted, classically inspired, New World-style Bx blend (r).

Ken Forrester Wines W Cape ★→★★★ With French partners, STELL vintner and restaurateur Ken F tireless champion of CHENIN BL (dr/sp/off-dry/botrytis) and Med grapes, lately via creation of 1st SA clone of GRENACHE N from old vines in Pie. Petit range is quintessence of quaffing.

Kershaw Wines W Cape ★★★→★★★★ UK-born MW Richard K's exceptional, refined portfolio headed by Clonal Selection, featuring ELG's standout varieties CHARD, PINOT N, SYRAH. Constituent sites showcased in Deconstructed collection, while GPS and Smuggler's Boot spotlight other prime Cape areas and new techniques respectively.

Klein Constantia Estate Const ★★★★ Iconic mtn-side property; site-specific SAUV BL, non-botrytis MUSCAT DE F Vin de Constance (luscious, cellar-worthy recreation of legendary CONST, now with cellar-door option to have bottle stamped with initials). Sibling STELL winery, Anwilka (r).

Kleine Zalze Wines W Cape ★→★★★★ A STELL star, majority French-owned. Best: Family Res, Vyd Selection. Also lab-range Project Z, Cellar Selection. Standalone BEE venture Visio Vintners uplifts staff.

Klein Karoo REGION (c.1980 ha), mostly semi-arid and known for fortified, esp Port style in CDORP. Revived old vines feature in some premium terroir labels: Le Sueur by ex-DE KRANS winemaker Louis van der Riet.

Krone W Cape ★★★ Made at family-owned Twee Jonge Gezellen estate in TUL. Krone label houses collection of elegant, vintage-dated CAP CLASSIQUE (dr/off-dry), inspired by French grower-Champagne movement. Still-wine range TJG: widely sourced aromatic blends (r/w).

Kruger Family Wines W Cape ★★→★★★ From facilities in Somerset W, Johan K ranges far and wide for his and wife Sophie's extensive portfolio of site-specific wines; CHARD, PINOT N and old vines at core. Much of output is exclusive to Naked Wines (UK, US).

KwaZulu-Natal Province and GU on e coast; not-ideal tropical climate nr ocean; central plateau and, further n, Drakensberg foothills more propitious but no cakewalk. Abingdon Estate, Cathedral Peak, Highgate only producers.

KWV W Cape ★→★★★ Formerly national wine co-op and controlling body; today one of largest producers/exporters, based in PAARL. Dozen labels, headed by serially decorated The Mentors.

La Motte W Cape ★★→★★★ Elegant estate, winery, re-imagined cellar door at FRAN owned by Koegelenberg-Rupert family. Classic varietals, blends. Neighbour-sibling Leopard's Leap emphasizes food side of wine match.

Leeu Passant *See* MULLINEUX.

Le Lude Cap Classique W Cape ★★★→★★★★ Celebrated family-owned sparkling house in FRAN: elegant Agrafe CHARD/PINOT N (1st locally to undergo 2nd ferment under cork). Fine restaurant, guest lodge.

Le Riche Wines Stell ★★★→★★★★ Fine, modern-classic boutique CAB SAUV (varietal and heritage blend with CINSAULT named Richesse) by Christo LR and family. Mineral CHARD (part-clay amphora).

Limpopo Most n province and GU in WO system.

Lowerland Pri ★★★ Meaning "Verdant Land", part of large family agribusiness in N CAPE's Pri WARD. Area's most exciting winery, grapes vinified in PAARL. Gompou PETIT V, named after Kori bustard, said to be partial to acacia tree gum.

Luddite Wlk B On thigh-straining slope overlooking Bot R, Niels, Penny Verburg recently joined by daughter Alice in barnstorming SHIRAZ, CHENIN BL and Saboteur (r/w) blends, latter under suitably unconventional crown caps.

Meerlust Estate Stell ★★★ Myburgh family-owned since 1756; vyds/cellar in S STELL: landscape more undulating, reminiscent of Bx, than mountainous. Cue French-inspired classics led by polished Rubicon (among SA's 1st Bx-style r).

Méthode cap classique *See* CAP CLASSIQUE.

Miles Mossop Wines Coast ★★★→★★★★ STELL member of CWG, many of Miles M's elegant bottlings named after family. Lately wider sourcing, same top quality.

Morgenster Estate Stell ★★★ Historic farm nr Somerset W developed into prime wine-and-olive estate in early 90s by late Italian industrialist Giulio Bertrand; children continue Old World varieties, style, cuisine at on-site restaurant.

Mulderbosch Vineyards W Cape ★→★★★ Reputed US-owned STELL winery and welcoming cellar door with modern, amply fruited CHENIN BL, CAB FR, pair of Bx-style reds. Winemaker Henry Kotzé and family work with rarities: Pilgrim Wines BASTARDO do Castello.

Want to join a wine club? Fuselage Wines' Spittooners, on winelands airfield.

Mullineux & Leeu Passant W Cape ★★★→★★★★ Chris M and US-born wife Andrea transform SWA CHENIN BL, SYRAH, handful of compatible varieties into ambrosial soil-specific varietals, blends, CWG bottlings and *vin de paille*. Leeu Passant portfolio (FRAN), from mostly venerable vines plus some own younger ones, is sublime. Great Heart PINOT N (cool-climate Ceres), owned-made by staff.

Mvemve Raats Stell ★★★★ Mzokhona Mvemve, 1st qualified Black winemaker, and Bruwer Raats (RAATS FAMILY) select barrels for forthright, best-of-vintage Bx red blend named MR de Compostella.

Nederburg Wines W Cape ★→★★★★ One of SA's biggest (2m cases) and best-loved brands, PAARL-based, HEINEKEN BEVERAGES-owned. Top ranges: Two Centuries, Heritage Heroes, Manor House. Many purse-pleasers, wine-list fixtures.

Neil Ellis Wines W Cape ★★→★★★★ Pioneer STELL négociant, majority-owned by VAN LOVEREN. Sources mostly cooler-grown parcels locally and around W CAPE for masterly site expressions.

Newton Johnson Vineyards Cape SC ★★★→★★★★ Family cellar in UP HEM, acclaimed CHARD, PINOT N; SA's 1st commercial ALBARIÑO also superb.

Northern Cape (N Cape) Largest province and GU in WO scheme. Semi-arid to arid, with temp extremes. *See* SUTHERLAND-KAROO.

North West Province, recent GU and neighbour to LIMPOPO, FREE STATE, N CAPE. Continental climate, summer rain; mostly flat grassland with Magaliesberg Mtns in ne; s border is Vaal River.

Oak Valley Estate Cape SC ★★★→★★★★ Extensive family agribusiness in ELG. Tabula Rasa: exceptional, fine-boned, single-clone bottlings of CHARD, PINOT N.

Old Vine Project Pioneering initiative by Rosa Kruger with Johann Rupert (ANTHONIJ RUPERT), to locate, catalogue, preserve SA's old vyds (35 yrs+): 5158 ha. Certified Heritage Vyd seal on bottle shows planting date.

Olifantsberg Family Vineyards Bre ★★→★★★ Restrained CHENIN BL, PINOTAGE, Rhône-style (r/w) from mtn-side venture.

Olifants River REGION on w coast (c.8260 ha). Warm valley floors gd for organics; higher, cooler sites in Citrusdal Mtn DISTRICT and its WARD, Pie, produce some of SA's finest wines.

Opstal Estate W Cape ★→★★★ One of BRE's quality leaders, family-owned, in mtn amphitheatre. Old-vine CHENIN BL, SEM; newer v. fine, floral VERDELHO.

Orange River Cellars N Cape ★→★★★ Vast operation, c.140 grower-owners, 1100-ha vyd on Orange River: Lyra (Res); trad speciality, sweet-fortified MUSCAT.

Overarching GU / region *See* GU.

Paarl DISTRICT (c.13,800 ha) around historic namesake town with WARDS Agter Paarl, Sim-P, V Pa. Diverse styles: Med (r/w), CHENIN BL, CAB SAUV, PINOTAGE.

Paul Clüver Family Wines Elg ★★→★★★ Area pioneer, family-owned/run; elegant CHARD, PINOT N; convincing RIES (wood-touched semi-dry, unoaked botrytis).

Porseleinberg Swa ★★★★ BOEKENHOUTSKLOOF's organic vyds/cellar: one superb SYRAH. Handcrafted, incl front label printed on-site by winemaker.

Raats Family Wines Stell ★★★★ Exquisite CHENIN BL (un/oaked). Melt-in-mouth CAB FR: CWG; recent, partly wooded Vlag ("Flag"). Bruwer R and cousin Gavin Bruwer Slabbert unearth vinous gems at Bruwer Vintners Vine Exploration Co. *See* MVEMVE RAATS.

Radford Dale W Cape ★★→★★★ Dynamic STELL venture (Australian, French, SA, UK shareholders). Radford Dale, Thirst, Vinum, Winery of Good Hope brands, restrainedly New World in style. Organic vyd/cellar in ELG. Strong emphasis on GAMAY N. Viticulturist Edouard Labeye has own namesake GRENACHES BL/N.

Rall Wines Coast ★★★→★★★★ Donovan R has outstanding track record since late 2000s. Initial SWA blends (r/w) joined by Med varietals (r/w), CHENIN BL with same flavoursome understatement. Exciting Callender Peak (w; r/sp soon) from vines (some ungrafted, v. rare) on snowy Ceres Plateau.

Region *See* GU.

Restless River Wines Wlk B ★★★→★★★★ Wessels and Fourie families' small, thoughtfully run vyd/cellar in UP HEM, as successful with area calling cards CHARD, PINOT N as scarcely planted CAB SAUV, all showing cool-climate minerality.

Reyneke Wines W Cape ★★★ Still only bio producer on Polkadraai Hills nr STELL, company-owned but founder-viticulturist Johan R still hugging vines and walking the nature/society-friendly walk. Focus on fruit: pure, elegant CHENIN BL (un/oaked), SAUV BL, CABS SAUV/FR, SYRAH.

Robertson Valley Low-rainfall inland DISTRICT with most WARDS (14); c.12,700 ha; historically gd CAP CLASSIQUE, CHARD, desserts; recently SAUV BL, CAB SAUV, SHIRAZ. Snowballing "Calcrete Project" focuses on unwooded Chard on valley's rare-in-SA limestone soil.

Robertson Winery Rob ★→★★★ Consistency, value throughout extended portfolio. Best: Constitution Rd CHARD, SHIRAZ.

Rogge Cloof ★★★ Gerntholtz family venture; some of SA's remotest, highest vyds (1500m/4921ft) in N CAPE. Perfumed SYRAH, delicate CHARD, labelled De Knolle Fonteyn after original Kanolfontein site; joined by Rogge Cloof site, same varieties plus visitor amenities. Made by KRUGER FAMILY WINES.

Roodekrantz Wines Paarl, Stell, Swa ★★→★★★ Subtly thrilling collection of mostly CHENIN BL from old-vine grapes rescued from big-brand anonymity. Equally satisfying sibling lineup named Fuselage inspired by cellar's location on family owners' private airfield nr WELL.

Rustenberg Wines Stell ★→★★★★ Low-key, high-power Barlow family on Simonsberg Mtn nr STELL; grace of cellar complex, gardens, vyds reflected in always-superb French classics portfolio.

Rust en Vrede Wine Estate W Cape ★→★★★★ Historic STELL farm/winery; powerful, polished reds. Sibling brands owned by Jean Engelbrecht: Afrikaans (trendy CAB SAUV/CINSAULT blend et al); Cirrus (Ceres Plateau-terroir PINOT N); Donkiesbaai (from Pie, v.gd CHENIN BL dr, *vin de paille*); Guardian Peak (fruity, grill-friendly); Stell Res (regional specialities). Last two have tasting venues.

S Africa's vyd: Chenin Bl 18.4%, Sauv Bl 11.8%, Colombard 10.4%, Cab Sauv 10.1%.

Sadie Family Wines Piek, Stell, Swa ★★★★ Iconic portfolio by revered Eben S, now with son Markus. Signature Series: Med blend Columella (r), multi-variety Palladius (w), both Cape benchmarks. Magnificent District Series, pure, detailed, age-worthy, celebrating heritage and site, now also features interplanted vyds (using rare echalas aka *stok-by-paaltjie* trellis) on Rotsvas home-farm.

Sakkie Mouton Family Wines W Cape ★★★→★★★★ Working from Vredendal on w coast, young Izak "Sakkie" M's pared-back, unforgettably named debut CHENIN BL, Revenge of the Crayfish, continues to impress. Dawn of the Salty Tongues SYRAH et al showcase, champion fruit of area (cool, maritime Koekenaap WARD).

Saldanha Wine & Spirit Co, The Swa ★★★→★★★★ Adi BADENHORST jokes that average age of audience for this homage to SA's trad fortified wines (and brandy) is 79.5 yrs. Conceived late 2000s, made on home farm: delicious small lots of Port and Sherry styles etc. Saldanha Bay venue on w coast must-visit.

Saronsberg Cellar W Cape ★★→★★★★ Family estate in TUL. Groaning trophy cabinet for SHIRAZ and Bx/Rhône blends/varietals: rare solo ROUSSANNE, bracing CHARD CAP CLASSIQUE.

Per capita wine consumption keeps dipping: mere 7.23 litres (Portugal: 61.1).

Savage Wines W Cape ★★★→★★★★ CWG member Duncan S ranges far and wide from CAPE TOWN city base. Thrilling, understated, mostly Med varieties and CHENIN BL. Long-time assistant Banele Vakele solo-label Tembela Wines (r/w).

Shannon Vineyards Elg ★★★→★★★★ Grown by siblings James and Stuart Downes, vinified by NEWTON JOHNSON and recently BENGUELA COVE. Elegance, freshness. Top: MERLOT. Also v.gd: SAUV BL, SEM, PINOT N.

Sijnn Mal ★★★→★★★★ Pronounced "Sane", DE TRAFFORD co-owner David T and partners' pioneer maritime venture on stony promontory overlooking Breede R. Distinctive blends and Varietal Series with solo ultra-rare TINTA AMARELA.

Silverthorn Wines Rob ★★★→★★★★ Distinguished collection of CAP CLASSIQUE (w/rosé) crafted in ROB by CWG member John Loubser. All Brut, mostly CHARD, area speciality COLOMBARD, some PINOT N, unusually SHIRAZ. Fascinating The Dog Star (light-alc, still Chard).

Simonsig Family Vineyards W Cape ★→★★★★ Malan family nr STELL admired for unwavering quality; 1st with CAP CLASSIQUE in 70s, original Brut joined by sweeter, equally delicious celebrators. Boundary-pushing Med blends (r/w) The Grapesmith. Stunning Madeira-inspired Rainwater VERDELHO (05 vintage).

Solms-Delta Wine Company W Cape ★→★★★ Ambitious early 2000s wine-growing, land restitution, community-upliftment venture nr FRAN recently revitalized by US national Tommy Hall. Consultant Francois Haasbroek (Blackwater Wine) surpasses previous quality: Amalie GRENACHE BL blend.

Spier W Cape ★→★★★★ Major winery and tourist magnet nr STELL. Flagships: 21 Gables, Creative Block, Frans K Smit (honouring cellarmaster, a CWG member). Expanding organic range (Farmer Angus). Pocket-pleasing Signature (rare ALBARIÑO). All fruit-focused, carefully made, most vegan.

Stark-Condé Wines W Cape ★★★→★★★★ Reputed US-born boutique vintner José C in STELL's postcard Jonkershoek V. Intense, fresh CAB SAUV, SYRAH. Exciting rarities: field blend (w), terraced-vyd (CHENIN BL). Younger brand Kara-Tara showcases sites (some unexpected places) cool enough to grow knockout CHARD, PINOT N.

Steenberg Vineyards W Cape ★★→★★★ GRAHAM BECK's CONST winery, vyds, chic cellar door; glossy SAUV BL/SEM, SAUV BL (still/sp), CAP CLASSIQUE, rare NEBBIOLO.

Stellenbosch Instagrammable university town, demarcated wine DISTRICT (c.11,600 ha) and heart of wine industry (Napa of SA); all tourist facilities and many top estates tucked into mtn valleys and foothills. Heartland of CAB SAUV and powerful reds generally, also major success with CHARD, CHENIN BL, white blends et al.

Stellenbosch Vineyards Stell ★→★★★ French-owned, large-volume winery; impressive, fruit-centred limited releases: savoury CHENIN BL, only bottling of SA-developed white grape Therona (100-vine pocket).

Stellenrust Stell ★→★★★★ Family winery, wide portfolio from trio of own prime STELL sites. Headliner range: magnificent barrel-fermented old-vine CHENIN BL. ArtiSons range pushes envelope: The Albatros CINSAULT (w).

Stellenzicht Wines Coast ★★→★★★ Famous Helderberg Mtn cellar and vyds rejuvenated by Baron Hans von Staff-Reitzenstein, also owner of neighbour

ALTO and long-time partner in nearby ERNIE ELS. Powerful but not blockbusting CHARD and solo/blend CAB SAUV, SYRAH.

Storm Wines Hem Rdg, Hem V, U Hem ★★★→★★★★ Hannes S, CHARD, PINOT N specialist, expresses three HEM wards with precision, sensitivity. Wild Air: Hem V shale-soil SAUV BL.

Super Single Vineyards W Cape ★★★ Boutique vintner Daniël de Waal, on venerable Canettevallei family wine-and-lavender estate in STELL. Mostly single-vyd wines, incl new excellent ROB ALBARIÑO.

Sutherland-Karoo Minuscule high-altitude DISTRICT in viticulturally challenging N CAPE at 1450m (4757ft), not to be confused with separate, distant KL K. Chiefly CHARD, PINOT N, SHIRAZ, nr Sutherland town, known for bitter cold and stargazing. *See* ROGGE CLOOF, KRUGER FAMILY

Swartland COASTAL DISTRICT; profound influence on wine-growing since early 2000s through innovators (SADIE FAMILY); c.11,600 ha mostly shy-bearing, unirrigated bush vines. Concentrated, distinctive, fresh wines.

Testalonga Swa ★★→★★★ Bandit's Kloof, cheeky name of home farm and newer flagship range, signals Craig and Carla Hawkins's steadfast, happy defiance of convention. Natural vinifications, some skin-ferments, heritage varieties (mostly CHENIN BL), rarities (HÁRSLEVELŰ), zany names (Hallelujah Chicken Run VIOGNIER), Mielie (easy-drinkers).

Thelema Mountain Vineyards W Cape ★★→★★★★ STELL pioneer of SA's modern wine revival, still beacon of quality, consistency (touch of hedonism, per Rabelais-inspired brand name). Equally fine Sutherland label (ELG).

Thistle & Weed W Cape ★★★→★★★★ Exceptional, distinctive wines by STELL winemaker Stephanie Wiid and viticulturist Etienne Terblanche. Mostly solo CHENIN BL (one on 32 rootstocks), rarer climate-tolerant varieties like VERDELHO, pair of blends (r/w), new CAP CLASSIQUE. All with Afrikaans names for vyd flora.

Thorne & Daughters Wines W Cape ★★★→★★★★ Bot R vintners John Thorne Seccombe and wife Tasha's wines, some from v. old vines and heirloom grapes, cerebral yet sensual, expressed with marvellous clarity, refinement.

Tokara W Cape ★★→★★★★ Family-owned wine, food, art showpiece on prime Sim Mtn granite overlooking STELL; vyds also in ELG. Bravado derived from site and masterly restraint: mostly French classics (Bx, Burg, Loire), PINOTAGE.

Trizanne Signature Wines Cape SC ★→★★★ Female soloists like Trizanne Barnard still rare. Avid surfer sources from mostly COAST vyds for seriously gd boutique CHARD, SAUV BL (solo/blend), SYRAH. Dawn Patrol brand mostly export.

Tulbagh Inland DISTRICT historically associated with white and CAP CLASSIQUE, latterly also red, esp PINOTAGE, SHIRAZ, some sweet styles.

Uva Mira Mountain Vineyards Stell ★★★ Helderberg Mtn eyrie vyds/cellar owned by Toby Venter. Leashed power in CHARD, SAUV BL, SYRAH et al.

Van Loggerenberg Wines W Cape ★★→★★★★ PAARL/STELL-based Lukas VL, star of light-styled, new-wave scene. Also excellent LOWERLAND, Michaella Wines, most of CARINUS FAMILY VYDS portfolios.

Rambling with your pooch? Rooiberg nr Robertson has dog-friendly garden.

Van Loveren Family Vineyards W Cape ★→★★★ Based in ROB, multiple cellar doors, dynamic VL claims to be Africa's leading family-owned private wine business, producing c.2m cases p.a. Easy-drinking, often sweeter styles, epitomized by Four Cousins labels (named after quartet of Retief men who run it), on-going push into premium markets sees more esteemed Cape names joining clan.

Vergelegen Wines Stell ★★★→★★★★ Resources company Anglo-American's historic mansion, gardens, stylish cellar door at Somerset W. Sheathed power in wines from classic French varieties. Deserved WWF-SA Conservation Champion.

Vilafonté W Cape ★★★ Founded by California's Zelma Long and Phil Freese, and local eminence Mike Ratcliffe. Trio of luxurious STELL red blends.

Villiera Wines W Cape ★★→★★★ Respected STELL winery and eco leader founded by Grier family, lately in French hands. Exceptional quality:value. Famed CAP CLASSIQUE: thrilling flagship CHARD Brut, Pithos.

Vondeling V Pa ★→★★★ UK-owned, sustainability-minded estate nr PAARL. Eclectic yet cohesive, from Bx-style red to probably Cape's top pét-nat. Visit newer off-site venue and tree bar, Vrymansfontein.

Walker Bay Prestigious maritime DISTRICT; top CHARD, SAUV BL, PINOT N, SHIRAZ in Bot R, HEM, Springfontein Rim, Stanford Foothills, Sunday's Glen WARDS.

Ward *See* GU.

Warwick Wine Estate W Cape ★→★★★★ US-owned tourist draw on STELL fringe (famed gourmet picnics newly revamped). Rich yet fresh solo/blends: classic French (standout CAB FR), PINOTAGE.

Waterford Estate W Cape ★→★★★ Jeremy Ord and family's Tuscany-inspired winery nr STELL. Sophisticated myriad-variety flagship The Jem (r). Cellarmaster Mark le Roux's experimental namesake brand. Themed tastings in fountain courtyard.

Waterkloof W Cape ★→★★★ UK wine merchant Paul Boutinot chanced on "hidden amphitheatre of potential" on windy hilltop nr Somerset W in early 00s after 10-year global search for fine-wine terroir. Standout tourist venue, sustainability focus, even on-site celebrity-chef restaurant provides meals for needy local kids.

Wellington Warm-climate DISTRICT bordering PAARL and SWA. Growing reputation for CHENIN BL, CINSAULT, PINOTAGE, SHIRAZ, red blends.

Western Cape (W Cape) Most s province and dominant GU in WO system, with 85% of official appellations, incl new stand-alone DISTRICT Nuveld-Karoo.

Worcester Sibling DISTRICT (c.6370 ha) to ROB and BRE in Breede R basin. Largely bulk for export, but some fine (family) wines and dynamic grower-owned Stettyn Family Vyds.

WO (Wine of Origin) "AOP" but without French restrictions. Certifies vintage, variety, area of origin and, on opt-in basis, sustainable production.

The taste of change

Growing wine in this sunny part of the world means dealing with heat, drought and climate extremes. This means much adaptation is already baked in: staggered harvesting dates to preserve all-important freshness, and careful judging of ripeness levels to avoid jammy flavours. The major challenge for local growers, therefore, is managing the intensity and pace of recent climate change. Tools? Soil regeneration to aid vine and ecosystem health and resilience, leading to more expressive fruit in the bottle; concrete and clay vessels, even glass orbs, in the cellar to capture the taste of the vyd while reducing or eliminating the role of oak. Other items in the toolkit incl rootstock and clone selections, cooler sites and more tolerant, albeit less familiar grape varieties, the latter being perhaps the most visible sign – from a wine-lover's perspective – of climate-prompted change. How will consumers respond to an influx of exotic varieties? In SA, names like ASSYRTIKO and VERMENTINO are already known to many, courtesy of pioneering boutique bottlings whose flavour spectra are not dissimilar to the mainstream. Plus, seasoned palates may recall the taste of FERNÃO PIRES and other strange-sounding grapes that, back in the day, escaped the brandy stills, so they won't be put off by "XINOMAVRO" or "MENCÍA" on a label. Younger drinkers may be attracted by the novelty.

Climate change & flavour

Almost all wine flavours now are the result of climate change. Acidity is lower, tannins are softer, alcohol is higher. Some of this is good for drinkers; some is less so. But it is a fact, and the evidence is there in the glass.

This year's Supplement is not about the whys and wherefores of climate change; it's not about the causes or the wider repercussions. It is about the flavour of wine at the beginning of the second quarter of the 21st century.

On the whole, wine is a lot better balanced than it used to be. Back in Ye Olden Dayes, there was a lot of green-tasting, unripe tannin about; in Ye Not So Olden Dayes there was massive extraction, massive concentration and an abandonment of acidity – not that the perpetrators of such wines described them in those terms.

Now, just when climate change is making it more difficult to achieve, growers want freshness. They want less oak, even less concentration; they aim to make wines we want to drink, rather than wines to admire from a distance. The turnaround, in winery after winery, region after region, has been wonderful to behold. And it means that growers are having to learn to manage some quite unfriendly climate conditions: heat, drought, early budding and the consequent risks from late frost, rain, hail, rot – you name it, it's happening somewhere. What is really hard to have now is a "normal" vintage.

In Europe, the scorching summer of 2003 was the introduction to this new world – and it taught growers a lot. They've learned about managing extremes. The cool vintage of 2024, beset by rain and rot in so many places, would have been a complete write-off 20 years ago. (In some English vineyards, alas, it was.) But such conditions require total vigilance from growers: there are no weekends off in a wet summer, no excuses for picking even a couple of days too late in a hot year.

They also raise questions about whether biodynamic or organic viticulture is always best. What is sustainable in this new world might be a little more complicated.

We'll be looking at these questions, and a few others, in the pages that follow. First: acidity.

Freshness vs acidity

Hotter summers = less acidity. So far, so obvious. But is it a good thing or a bad thing? And why do winemakers now insist on talking about "freshness", rather than acidity, as if they are trying to avoid the subject?

Whether lower acidity is good or bad depends on whether you like it. But freshness is more complicated. It's true that it can sound like a euphemism for low acidity, especially since it can't be measured. Anybody can (and everybody does, especially in warm climates) say their wines are "fresh". Are they just pulling the wool over our eyes?

First, let's think about what acidity is. It's measurable, but it's not just one thing: in wine, it's mostly tartaric or malic. Tartaric tastes riper, malic tastes sharper. Malic acid in grapes tends to be metabolized on the vine in hot climates, while in cooler climates it will be transformed into softer-tasting lactic acid by the malolactic fermentation (*see* A Little Learning) in the cellar. When growers in hot climates add acidity, it's generally tartaric.

Less acidity means softer wines; but if it goes too low, balance goes out of kilter and wine becomes cloying. Can freshness rescue it?

Because freshness can't be measured, it's hard to define. Ask ten different winemakers and you'll get five different answers. It's precision. It's clarity. It's accuracy. It's a feeling of lightness on the palate – the feeling of lightness that comes from just the right level of extraction and ripeness, not the lightness of dilution. It's the opposite of overripeness. Blurred, soupy flavours that lack definition and precision are not fresh. But underripeness is not the same as freshness; underripeness is lack of flavour and thin, tart acidity. Freshness might be most easily described in terms of what it's not, but you know freshness when you taste it – it's a sensation as much as a flavour. Freshness involves salinity (not actual salt; just a sensation of saltiness), precision, length, purity and perhaps a touch of enlivening bitterness on the finish. If you were a cynic, you'd say you can see why winemakers like the term so much. It can mean what they want.

Look at new-wave Garnacha – perhaps from somewhere in Spain like Sierra de Gredos, perhaps from Australia's McLaren Vale. Low acidity, high alcohol. You don't get Grenache/Garnacha ripe at much less than 14.5% abv, and it can happily go to 16%. But these wines are fresh. They're moreish, they're appetizing; they're not like the Garnacha/Grenache of the past, with wearyingly overripe flavours of toffee or raisins.

In Champagne now, the search is no longer for ripeness – it's a search for freshness. Acidity is lower; for a wine that we had always assumed was built on acidity, this should have been a problem. But in fact, great Champagne was always built on ripeness, and ripeness went hand in hand, in that cool, chalky region, with acidity. Champagne may have lower acidity than of yore, but it has enough. Now it is fleshed out with ripeness, and what is needed is freshness – in the form of laser-accurate precision; complex, perfectly defined aromas and flavours that emerge in turn on the palate, driving the wine forward; and a twist of bitterness on the finish to keep us coming back for more. Such wines, because they're riper and have naturally more flesh and alcohol, need less dosage, and the effect of lower dosage (or none) is like the sea receding on a beach to reveal each individual pebble. The wine has to be perfect. There is nothing to hide behind.

There's also nother factor in this new balance, and that is pH. It's not a measure of acidity, though it's often thought of as that, because low pH (up to maybe 3.4) tends to be found in wines with good (ie. quite high) acidity. However, pH is in fact a measure of the concentration of hydrogen ions in a liquid. Malic acid is not very ionized, which is why the malolactic fermentation has little effect on the pH of a wine. Low pH is essential to wine – for stability, for aroma. There is a relationship between pH and acidity, just as there is a relationship between acidity and freshness, but they are best thought of as a threesome.

Wine can thus adapt to one aspect of greater ripeness and turn it to its advantage. What of alcohol? That's what we'll look at next.

Alcohol: how much is too much?

Warmer summers, as well as giving less acidity, lead to grapes with more sugar. That means higher alcohol. So far, so simple. But the fact that alcohol levels for reds around the world are seldom much less than 14% abv now, and often over 15%, is not entirely due to climate change, though that is probably the immediate cause.

Throughout the 1980s and 1990s, and indeed in the chillier decades before, all viticulture was aimed at achieving greater ripeness. Planting, pruning, training and picking dates were all directed towards ripeness – because tannic ripeness (which comes with time, whereas sugar ripeness comes with heat) was hard to achieve in the marginal climates of Europe's greatest wine regions. And not just Europe; even Napa used to make Cabernet with 12.5% abv – and very good it was too.

Ripeness now is easy. But climate change has overtaken us, and those techniques in the vineyard that gave greater ripeness are having to be unwound. Everything now is aimed at slowing ripening, at achieving the long hang-times that give complexity of flavour, without sending sugar levels through the roof.

We have become accustomed to alcohol levels of 14%+, it's true. Wine retailers say that most drinkers aren't very concerned about alcohol and don't base their choices on whether a wine is 13.5% or 15%. But there has to be a limit, surely? Do we want 15% to become the norm, with 16.5% not far off? In the past, sugar was added to ferments to boost the alcohol level in cool climates. Only in poor years like 2024 does this happen much now, although a few producers still do it in Champagne. Many in Napa now pick at a potential alcohol level of around 16% and add water. In Australia's hot Barossa, added water can be 3% of the final blend.

Where wine laws don't allow that, what can be done? Picking earlier is the obvious answer, but whether it is the right one depends on how late they were picking before. In California, the risk of fire later in the season is encouraging earlier picking, and some of those cult Cabs are all the better for it. Some winemakers were just afraid of changing a successful but extreme style and cited their dread of green tannins as the reason; turns out that earlier picking actually gave them better balance.

Most growers in most regions are picking a week or two weeks earlier now, because the grapes are ready. To slow ripening, to get proper flavour development, growers might prune earlier, straight after budding, or leave more leaves on the vine to shade the fruit, or plough at different times, or leave green cover between the rows to cool the soil, or put down straw mulch, which can reduce soil temperatures by 4–5°C (c.7–9°F). There are many tools available to growers. When they replant, they might use different clones – for example, those now used in Chianti Classico are the result of years of research in the 20th century. It might be that clones that wouldn't previously ripen might be better suited to today's climate. Growers might choose to angle the rows differently or bring back into cultivation sites that in the 1970s and 1980s would never ripen. That's the case in Germany's Mosel Valley, where it's much more difficult now to produce the sort of light Riesling needed for fine Kabinett.

It's all change in the cellar too. Indigenous yeasts can give slightly less alcohol for a given sugar level; lab yeasts are often engineered for efficiency in turning sugar to alcohol. If your tannins are a touch unripe, then you must extract them more lightly and treat the skins with extra gentleness. Higher alcohol means more extraction of wood flavours, so larger-format barrels and older wood are in favour; concrete too.

The pattern of growing and making wine is thus changing fast. Balance is the aim: growers want drinkability and elegance, and they want it at a time when the climate is offering the opposite. One result is wines that are ready to drink much earlier. Will they last as long? Let's take a look at that next.

How do wines age now?

The traditional reason for ageing red wines was that great wines when young were unapproachable. Their tannins were hard and aggressive. Drinking young claret could be like chewing bones. Only with time did those tannins soften and the wine emerge into glorious maturity, and thus ageability became a hallmark of quality. If you couldn't age it, it wasn't serious.

It is still true that when the first fruit – the puppy fat – fades, lesser wines will simply die. Only good wines have the wherewithal to emerge from this stage into something more interesting. The difference is that now good wines still have concentration and structure, but they don't have the aggressiveness that made them so charmless in youth. Greater ripeness has combined with precise viticulture and winemaking to give them more grace earlier.

Classic wines still get kudos for ageing for 20 or 30 years, but it shouldn't be the only or even the main criterion of greatness. What counts is what a wine is like at its peak. If that peak comes within ten years, or five years, and it is superb, then it's a superb wine. There's no intrinsic virtue in having to wait. Instead, we should regard it as one of the benefits of our era that a lot of wine does not to need to be locked away while it grows up.

Personal taste plays a big part. Some people like young wines, drunk "on the fruit"; others like the tertiary, savoury flavours of maturity. One Champagne chef de cave recalled sending samples of his 1988 to journalists in Germany, Britain and France. The Germans thought it too old and past it. The British thought it far too young. The French thought it was just right.

Champagne, German Riesling, red Bordeaux, Barolo: there is a long list of wines that can be drunk with pleasure much earlier. Will they also live as long as they used to?

The honest answer is that it's too early to say. The reasons in favour of a long lifespan are that the best vintages of the past were the warmer, riper ones. The 1982 Bordeaux (the first "modern" vintage, if you like) can still be excellent and at their peak – and variability might be partly explained by the speculative nature of the vintage and the amount of travelling around the world that some of those bottles did. The chef de cave of Roederer Champagne maintains that the levels of ripeness he's seeing now are no greater than Champagne was getting around 1900 (known as the early 20th-century warming, c.1890s–1940s), and that it was the 1960s and 1970s (chilly, and with sometimes inferior clones planted) that were the exception. In classic Vintage Port, better selection, more even ripening and, crucially, better and cleaner fortifying spirit mean that a lot of Vintage Port can be enjoyed in infancy. But 20–25 years still seems to be right if you want to age it.

The constituents of wine that enable ageing – acidity, dry extract (think of it loosely as "substance"), tannin in reds – all need to be in balance. Top-heavy wines with too little acidity and too much alcohol simply fall over, which is why those cult Cabs of the Parker era weren't great agers. Too much tannin means a wine will always be chewy. Overripe fruit is always overripe.

For there to be a point to ageing, wine has to be seen to improve in the process. Wine that doesn't change and evolve, that merely survives, plodding its way through the years, is not great wine, no matter how long it clings on; it is boring wine. Predicting precisely how any individual wine will evolve is a good way to be wrong at least 50% of the time. Wine has a way of going up and down – showing well one year, sulking the next. That unpredictability is part of its fascination. For growers, learning to deal with the unpredictability of climate is part of the problem; it's not just a question of warmer summers. We're going to look at that next.

Unpredictability

The cry of every grower now is that there is no such thing as a "normal" vintage anymore. What was a "normal" vintage? One with no more than normal problems. One where flowering goes okay, where there's enough sun and enough water to ripen the grapes, where hail doesn't smash the grapes and drought doesn't shrivel them, and where autumn rains arrive to give the vines a good soaking after the grapes are picked.

Now, it seems, every year brings some sort of extreme: heat, drought, rain, frost, hail, rot, disease. In Santorini, for example, vineyards are in trouble after three years of hail and drought – and this is a place used to tough conditions.

We as consumers, though, want consistency. Yes, we accept vintage variation. "Ah, 2009," we say, as we pull the cork, "such a ripe year." But we don't want too much of it. We don't want to buy wines scarred by rot or underripeness. We want to be able to say, "A tricky year, but you'd never know it." If growers want to sell their wines, they have to overcome unpredictability. How? Rigorous selection, in both vineyard and winery –

poor years might mean much less wine to release, to keep the standard up. Any cluster that is substandard is rejected; any barrel or tank that is less than ideal is demoted.

Viticulture must be quick on its feet. A lot of viticultural decisions have to be made with fingers tightly crossed, because they can't be undone. Growers might prepare for a cool summer by removing leaves, only to face heatwaves. Rain brings mildew and rot, and growers have to be out in the vineyard day after day, spraying between storms, and then spraying again. Take your eye off the ball, and you've lost your crop. And the weather can change in a moment. The weather forecast in France is said to be fairly accurate, but there was the storm in Hermitage in 2023 when the *météo* promised 30mm (1in) rain, and what arrived was 200mm (8in) and landslides.

Preparations for heat might include keeping more shade on clusters, or spraying leaves with kaolin as a sort of sunscreen, or opening the canopy to allow the breeze through. Green cover between rows – for carbon capture, for lower soil temperature, for resistance to erosion – is much more common now. Growers might install drip irrigation; irrigation used to be illegal in Europe for AOP wines, but now it's much more case-by-case, and appellations can get consent to use it.

In the winery, there can be no set recipes. How much skin contact, what temperature of fermentation? Is it a year for steel tanks, concrete vats or oak – and if oak, new or used? What size? And where from? Tight grain or looser? Each answer will have a profound effect on final flavour. Tasting and testing grapes in the vineyard tells you a lot, but you can still be surprised when the grapes come in – perhaps they have less juice than you expected, or more. You have to adapt, fast.

Extremes of weather have always happened; it's just that now they seem to happen all the time, one after another. Advocates of new crossings of vines say that the way to future-proof vineyards against disease and cut the use of chemicals is to plant new PIWI vines, genetically engineered for disease-resistance. We'll look into that more next.

New varieties

How can something called a PIWI be a serious grape? It's an abbreviation, of course. The full name (and it's a brand) is Pilzwiderstandsfähig, which sounds a great deal more serious. They're the result of crossing *Vitis vinifera* vines with disease-resistant American species of *Vitis*, and then crossing with vinifera again, and again, and again.

The programme began in Germany in 1995 and has been adopted by UC Davis in the US with the aim of producing vines resistant to Pierce's disease (a fatal bacterium). Their supporters believe that they're the future. Others do not. Europe has a wealth of old grape varieties, hundreds of which are hardly grown. These are being rediscovered and examined for their resistance to disease or to drought, or their ability to ripen at lower sugar levels and keep acidity.

Torres in Spain has a long-term research programme; so does Producteurs Plaimont in SW France. Numanthia in Toro is looking at the genetic variation in the region's ancient Tempranillo vines. Port producers – Quinta do Crasto, The Fladgate Partnership, Symington Family Estates and others – are preserving and researching their legacies of centenarian vines because of what they can offer for the future. The varieties of the future, they say, will be found in existing vineyards, in vines that simply went out of fashion many years ago because conditions – economic, social, meteorological – changed. But those conditions have changed again.

Some varieties are already being planted where they were never planted before. Touriga Nacional, Marselan, Castets, Arinarnoa, Alvarinho and Liliorila are now permitted in Bordeaux; Cabernet Sauvignon in Germany's Mosel. Others are falling by the wayside – Barocca is a casualty in the Douro because it's too sensitive to heat. But Alicante Bouschet, traditionally despised in the south of France, is now often a respected component of Vintage Port.

There is, however, a lot of noise around PIWIs. They have names like Phoenix, Regent, Rondo, Siegerrebe, Souvignier Gris, Johanniter, Muscaris, Blütenmuskateller, Cabernet Noir, Cabernet Cortis and Floreal. There are many more. The idea is that they taste like vinifera while having the disease-resistance of non-vinifera. Resistance to botrytis and downy and powdery mildew is their selling point in a Europe increasingly prone to extreme weather. They can't dodge fungicide sprays completely – there is the danger of fungi mutating and getting past the vine's defences – but

the need to spray is greatly reduced. So, they're better for the environment and better for the grower's pocket.

They're vigorous and tend to have high yields, so that means plenty of work in the vineyard; but less tractor use means less soil compaction and lower emissions. Environmentally they are clearly good. They're being planted in England, Germany, Czechia, Poland; but also in France and in Italy. Voltis can be planted up to 5% in Champagne, and four varieties with the uncatchy names of F22P9, F22P10, F23P65 and F26P92 have been approved for planting in Italy. Calardis Blanc, Magdeleine Noir des Charentes and Négret de la Canourgue may be planted in France.

Yes, you say, but what do they taste like? Well, I can't honestly say I could recommend any yet. But it takes decades to get to know a new vine, both in the vineyard and in the winery. In time – and we're talking decades – a few might produce great wines. Others will fall by the wayside or be very local successes. They shouldn't be written off just because they're not going to supplant Chardonnay or Cabernet Sauvignon next year.

How much time do they have to succeed? That is the great unknown. Already some regions are benefiting from climate change and others not; we'll look at that next.

Winners & losers

Has wine ever been better than it is today? Everything is ripe, everything is juicy. The fashion for freshness and elegance has taken every region in a thoroughly appetizing direction. There might be a certain uniformity of style in spite of the proliferation of grape varieties and regions, but that is probably inevitable.

Viticulture has improved; winemaking has improved. Precision viticulture, and closer understanding of what goes on during fermentation and ageing, has meant that many more regions of the world can produce wines of international quality. Climate change has often been an ally in this. The classic regions of Europe were all marginal for their particular grape varieties and styles in the past. They've all moved into their comfort zones with climate change.

The marginal regions now are those that were just not viable before: England, most notably. Sparkling-wine regions are generally cooler than still-wine regions, and England is now a good, if small, sparkling-wine producer. The wines we are seeing now could not have been made 20 years ago – and were not. Still wines in England are a more occasional success; the tiny Crouch Valley in Essex produces most of the best.

We are seeing wines now from Scandinavia and Belgium, places that Hugh Johnson, when he launched this book, would not have dreamed of as wine producers. Poland makes wine. Where does that leave the marginal regions of the past? Are they in danger of moving out of their comfort zones to overripeness and too much warmth? In Burgundy, Chablis, most years now, doesn't taste of what used to be thought of as classic Chablis – it now tastes like a slightly steelier version of the Côte d'Or. Pinot Noir from the Côte d'Or can sometimes taste like Pinot from somewhere further south. Every year brings excitable headlines about how Syrah will have to be planted in Volnay – perhaps moving there from the Southern Rhône, which seems to be getting too hot and dry for Syrah. In Châteauneuf, the classic heat-retaining *galet roulé* stones are looking less interesting now than sandy soils.

And yet the most recent few vintages (I am writing this before tasting any 2025s) from the classic regions of Europe have been notable for their freshness. They may have had summers of extraordinary heat and uncomfortable drought, but somehow the wines of Bordeaux, of Burgundy, of Tuscany, of Piedmont, of Rioja and of Germany manage to taste as if they've sailed through without a care in the world. They feel effortlessly elegant. Yes, the style is different; to a new generation of wine drinkers, it can be more appealing.

Ask the growers why, and you get the sense that they're often a bit surprised themselves. They might point to cool nights, or a spot of rain at the right moment, or light extraction in the winery. Clever work in the vineyards clearly helps, and we've already touched on some of the changes they might make (*see* p.360). Small things, but they add up.

The big losers are regions where wildfires are a risk. That, in a dry summer, can mean almost anywhere now: California, Australia, Spain, Portugal, Greece, even Bordeaux. Fires don't spare estates because they're famous. Think of Napa's Newton or Cain estates. Burned.

Smoke taint ruins wines too, even if the flames stay away. Reds are more affected than whites, because the smoke taint is on the skins. And it's not an attractive "fumé" note – it's more like stale ashtrays.

Is the southern hemisphere faring better than the northern? Only up to a point. The proximity of Antarctica might keep the Southern Ocean cold and thus protect New Zealand, or a lot of it, from much warming, but it's melting ice that is keeping it cold, which is less encouraging. And less snow on the Andes means less snow-melt water for irrigation, in wine regions that are utterly dependent on irrigation.

Water, in many regions, is in ever shorter supply. Yet we grow wine in deserts...

Should we grow wine in deserts?

We've looked at some of the ways growers can mitigate climate change; we've looked at some of the winners and losers. But there's an elephant in the room, is there not? Should we be growing wine in places not naturally suited to vines? Should we be growing wine in deserts?

Most of the world's vineyards are not irrigated: the global figure is around 15%. But that's because irrigation is still rare in Europe, though it's coming. In Australia, Chile, Argentina, most of S Africa and much of the US, irrigation is the norm and dry-farming the exception. Below 350mm (14in) rain per annum – some say below 500mm (20in), but it ultimately depends on your soil and when the rain falls – you need irrigation to grow grapes.

Go to Mendoza in Argentina, and you quickly learn what a desert looks like. Mile after mile of sparse scrub and rock – and lush, green vineyards. Without added water there would be no wine industry – and the 1200+ wineries there support an awful lot of people. If wine production there was deemed unsustainable, what of the livelihoods of those people? Sustainability surely applies to people too. The steep terraces of Austria's Wachau, towering over the Danube, are equally dependent on irrigation. The Wachau is a UNESCO World Heritage Site. The vineyards, the landscape, are deemed culturally important. The wines can be among the greatest whites in the world. The image we tend to have, when we think of irrigated vineyards, is of the vast Riverland and Riverina, and Murray-Darling areas of Australia. Harrumph! you might say. Cheap bulk wine. Yes, indeed, in the main. How many of us learned to love wine on the back of it?

Growing wine in deserts is an uncomfortable idea in a world where water is increasingly scarce. (Although vines need a lot less water than data centres.) But deserts tend to be disease-free, or nearly so, whereas non-desert regions can be plagued by mildew, both downy and powdery, and require chemical fungicides. They often get heavily sprayed with pesticides too. In Europe, viticulture accounts for 15% of pesticide use but only covers 3.5% of agricultural land. There's another uncomfortable idea.

If sustainability is the aim, the answer is that every region, every site, needs a different strategy. And that strategy might well not be organic or biodynamic, however seductive those labels might seem. There is as yet no organic or biodynamic solution to Pierce's disease, the blight of many US regions. And grapevine yellows – the name given to a group of fatal diseases spread by insect vectors – can mean a lot of uprooting of dying vines if you want to avoid pesticides.

Take copper sulphate: it's the standard treatment for downy mildew, and it's permitted in organic viticulture when other treatments are not. But it requires repeated applications in wet years, with tractor use adding to soil compaction, and it builds up in the soil. Is a systemic product, which needs perhaps a couple of applications only throughout the summer and breaks down into non-toxic components, really less sustainable than a heavy metal?

And indeed, take irrigation. The days of splashing on water without a care in the world are over. Water in the leaves, trunk and soil is measured constantly: if 0 is a leaf full of water, -0.4 is stress; and at -1 or -2, leaves die and grapes cease to ripen. Water is given only to avoid serious stress. Stress after flowering and at veraison increases tannins – good in reds, not so good in whites. And each variety is different. Some, if stressed, take water from leaves; some take it from grapes.

Take biodiversity: vine monocultures are going out of fashion. Growers are planting fruit trees in vineyards; encouraging wildlife corridors and ground cover; nest boxes for birds are a common sight. More diverse ecosystems are more resilient – some say an increase of just 5% humus in soil means 300% more resilience. More resilience means less use of pesticides. AI can potentially predict the risk of downy mildew so that you spray only when necessary.

Sustainability isn't just about vineyards, however. It carries through into the winery; and that's where we're heading next.

The lightness of being

You can't build a winery these days without thinking of your carbon footprint.

You might have natural cooling by building underground or into a hillside; you will have solar panels; you will have a water-treatment plant; you can capture and re-use carbon dioxide from fermentation. Torres, a leader in sustainability, reduced its carbon emissions by 40% per bottle between 2008 and 2024.

None of this is noticeable to us as consumers, but one thing is very noticeable. Have you ever picked up a bottle and thought it so heavy that pouring it would mean an osteopathy appointment? And I'm not talking about magnums and Jéroboams. An empty standard wine bottle does not need to weigh more than a kilo.

Excessively heavy bottles used to go hand in hand with excessively weighty and over-muscled wine, and what we see now is the tail-end of that fashion. It was a status symbol of a particularly silly sort. But now the need to be sustainable – and to be seen to be sustainable – is having a very good effect, unless you happen to be an osteopath. Termanthia, the Toro red that was a typically overdone 100-pointer in the mid-2000s, has, under LVMH ownership, switched to elegance and swapped its 1.2kg bottle for one weighing 750g. At NZ's Felton Road, they're using 390g bottles; Spain's Torres has gone even further, to 300g. As for status, Château Lafite has never seen the need for heavy bottles: 550g is the norm for this grandest of wines.

There are alternatives to glass, of course: bag-in-box, tins, cardboard and PET, including flat bottles that waste less space in transportation. All are lighter than glass but intended only for drink-now wines; and PET, unlike glass, is not infinitely recyclable. Don't expect Lafite to switch just yet.

This supplement is not about sustainability per se; it's about wine flavour in the shadow of climate change. But growers can't adjust to the new flavours of wine without thinking of sustainability – and that leads them naturally to bottle weights. And for consumers who have to lift the things, that's a very happy thought.

A little learning ...

A few technical words

Winemaking terms inevitably creep into any discussion of wine styles and changing fashions. Here are the ones we use most in the book.

Acidity This is both fixed and volatile. **Fixed** is mostly tartaric, malic and citric, all from the grape, and lactic and succinic, from fermentation. Acidity may be natural or (in warm climates) added. **Volatile (VA)**, or acetic acid, is formed by bacteria in the presence of oxygen. A touch of VA is common and can add complexity. Too much = vinegar. Total acidity is fixed + VA combined.

Alcohol content (mainly ethyl alcohol) This is expressed as per cent (%) by volume of the total liquid. (Also known as "degrees".) Table wines are usually 12.5–14.5%. Controlling alcohol levels is a big challenge of modern viticulture.

Amphora The fermentation vessel of the moment, and the past 7000 years. Throw in grapes, return in 6 months. Risky. *Tinaja* in Spain, *talha* in Portugal.

Barrels Small (225-litre) oak barriques (for fermentation, ageing) are classic, but invisible oak flavours are fashion now. Larger barrels give less oak flavour; used barrels increasingly popular too (same reason). Acacia for whites: subtle aromas.

Bio (biodynamic) Type of viticulture that uses herbal, mineral and ORGANIC preparations in homeopathic quantities, in accordance with the phases of the moon and the movements of the planets. Now mainstream. NB: "bio" in French means organic as well, but in this book it means biodynamic.

Carbonic maceration Whole (red) berries go into closed vat; fermentation starts within each berry. Gives juicy, light style.

Concrete eggs Fermentation vessel; keeps lees moving. Concrete now modish again.

Field blend Different varieties planted together, picked and fermented together. Ultra-trendy, and tastes different too.

Malolactic fermentation This occurs after the alcoholic fermentation and changes tart malic acid into softer lactic acid. Can add complexity to red and white alike. Often avoided in hot climates, where natural acidity is low and precious.

Micro-oxygenation This widely used bubbling technique allows controlled contact with oxygen during maturation. Softens flavours, helps to stabilize wine.

Minerality Tasting term to be used with caution: fine as descriptor of chalky/stony flavours. Should not imply actual minerals from soil in wine.

Natural wines Undefined but start by being ORGANIC or BIO, involve minimal intervention in the winery and minimal SULPHUR or none. At best, wonderful; shouldn't be an excuse for faults. Often made in AMPHORAE or CONCRETE EGGS.

NOLO No- and low-ALCOHOL wine: alcohol removed after fermentation. Growing sector. Never done to improve flavour.

Old vines These give deeper flavours. No legal definition: OIV suggests 35 years minimum. Should be 50+ to be taken seriously.

Orange wines Tannic whites fermented on skins, perhaps in AMPHORAE. Like NATURAL WINES, some good, some not. Excellent with food.

Organic viticulture This prohibits most chemical products in the vineyard; organic wine prohibits added SULPHUR and must be made from organically grown grapes.

Pét-nat (pétillant naturel) Bottled before end of fermentation, which continues in bottle. Slight residual sugar, quite low ALCOHOL. Dead trendy.

pH Not a measure of acidity, but low pH mostly goes with acidity. Wine is normally 2.8–3.8. High pH can be a problem in hot climates. Lower pH gives better colour, helps stop bacterial spoilage and allows more of the SULPHUR to be free and active as a preservative. So, low is good in general.

Residual sugar That which is left after fermentation has ended or been stopped, measured in grams per litre (g/l). A dry wine has almost none.

Sulphur dioxide Added to prevent oxidation and other accidents in winemaking. Some combines with sugars, etc., and is "bound". Only "free" sulphur is effective as a preservative. Trend worldwide is to use less. To use none is brave.